Social Interaction, Social Context, and Language

Essays in Honor of Susan Ervin-Tripp

Susan Moore Ervin-Tripp

Social Interaction, Social Context, and Language

Essays in Honor of Susan Ervin-Tripp

Edited by

Dan Isaac Slobin
University of California at Berkeley

Julie Gerhardt
California Institute of Integral Studies

Amy Kyratzis
University of California at Santa Barbara

Jiansheng Guo
Victoria University of Wellington, New Zealand

LEA **LAWRENCE ERLBAUM ASSOCIATES, PUBLISHERS**
1996   Mahwah, New Jersey

Lawrence Erlbaum Associates, Inc., Publishers
10 Industrial Avenue
Mahwah, New Jersey 07430-2262

Cover photographs by Katya Tripp
Cover design by Gail Silverman

Library of Congress Cataloging-in-Publication Data

   Social interaction, social context, and language: essays in honor of
   Susan Ervin-Tripp/edited by Dan Isaac Slobin . . . [et al.].
         p.cm.
      Includes bibliographical references and indexes.
      ISBN 0-8058-1498-1 (cloth: alk. paper). — ISBN 0-8058-1499-X
   (pbk.: alk. paper)
      1. Ervin-Tripp, Susan M. (Susan Moore), 1927– 2. Sociolinguis-
   tics. 3. Language acquisition. 4. Discourse analysis. I. Slobin, Dan
   Isaac, 1939– . II. Ervin-Tripp, Susan M. (Susan Moore), 1927–
   P40.S5444   1996
   306.4'4—dc20   96-18567
                                                          CIP

Books published by Lawrence Erlbaum Associates are printed on acid-free
paper, and their bindings are chosen for strength and durability.

Printed in the United States of America
10 9 8 7 6 5 4 3 2 1

She opens her mouth with wisdom,
and the teaching of kindness is on her tongue.

— *Proverbs* 31:26

Contents

CONTRIBUTORS

THE EDITORS

We represent several generations of language researchers whose careers have been shaped by knowing Susan Ervin-Tripp. Here we briefly tell our readers who we are in the context of the scholar and teacher whom we celebrate in this festschrift.

Dan Slobin

My interaction with Sue goes back to 1963, before we even met. She had been invited to review psycholinguistics for the *Annual Review of Psychology* and had heard that I — then a graduate student at Harvard — had been reviewing the Soviet literature on psycholinguistics and child language. She wanted to include Soviet work in her review, and asked me to co-author the chapter with her — a flattering invitation that led to continuing collaboration when I moved to Berkeley a year later. I had come fresh from the heady days of early transformational grammar, and Sue introduced me into a group of researchers at Berkeley who were considering language in much broader, and equally exciting frameworks of ethnography, philosophy, and a new field that came to call itself the study of "communicative competence." While this approach fit my natural fascination with crosslinguistic comparison, it took me a long time to learn from Sue (and John Gumperz, Erving Goffman, Dell Hymes, John Searle, and their students) that language could not be studied without attention to the social and interactive contexts in which it is learned and used. In the course of teaching seminars and proseminars with Sue, and following every step of her research over the years, I have become a different kind of psycholinguist. And, in watching her interact with her students and colleagues, I hope to have become a better teacher and member of the academic and larger communities. Over the years, we have worked together to create a functionalist, interactionist, and cross-cultural approach to language. This collection of essays is one of the fruits of that approach.

Julie Gerhardt

I met Susan Ervin-Tripp when I first began graduate school at Berkeley in 1975. The first thing that struck me about Sue's voice was that it was always heard in counterpoint to the voices of others: She was always engaged in a spirited dialectic with other positions — whether it be cognitive universals, indirect speech acts, developmental stage theory, psycholinguistic processing, generative semantics, etc., and she encouraged this attitude in those with whom she worked. Never dogmatic, she continually welcomed the dissenting voice. Throughout the years of friendship and collegiality, we still have the most fun together looking over a transcript or arguing about the value of psychotherapy. Before post-modernism made "difference" fashionable, Sue always welcomed the play of oppositions and dissenting voices — and never lost her own. What I feel most indebted to Sue for was her unstinting encouragement for my interest in the contextual effects on grammatical meaning. Working on her family project in the late seventies gave me the opportunity to begin to examine the relation between language and context, specifically, how grammatical forms come to have particular uses in particular contexts. This experience was indeed quite formative and remains a cornerstone of my work in looking at the relation between language and context in psychotherapy.

Amy Kyratzis

I first met Sue in 1989 when I came to Berkeley's Developmental Psychology Program to do a postdoctoral traineeship with Sue and Dan. I worked with Sue on projects examining the social interactive bases of children's syntactic and conversational development. She taught me a great deal about discourse analysis, the importance of contextual factors in language use, and the role of language in cognitive development and the construction of social identity. It was as a result of that last influence that I became interested in the role of language in gender development and socialization — the focus of my present research. I had come to Berkeley interested in how language and culture shape thought, and Sue gave me insightful ways to think about these issues. She taught me more general lessons as well. First, that scientific inquiry can occur anywhere — from recording a group of children talking together in school to looking at how a graduate student from another culture addresses her professor. Second, that the results of psychological and social research can inform important social issues, such as the linguistic empowerment of women and minorities. And third, that you should always care deeply about your students, colleagues, and important social issues and that by doing so, you also become a better scholar. I left Berkeley a year and a half ago but my collaboration with Sue continues. She has been a profound influence on my life.

Jiansheng Guo

I first met Sue in 1986, as a graduate student coming fresh from China. Sue's seminar on requests was both an intellectual joy and an effective medication for my initial culture shock. The thorough coverage of different approaches, different methodologies, and different cultural settings in that specific area laid a solid foundation for my entire graduate training and had a long lasting effect on my academic directions. Sue never lost an opportunity to make full use of the seminar participants' unique cultural, social, and individual knowledge and insights. A little embarrassed at the beginning, I quickly learned how valuable my own experience and perspectives could be in academic discussions, as well as those of any other person. The most important influence Sue has had on my thinking lies in her appreciation of the importance of the social and interpersonal contexts of language and language learning. She has exerted this influence not only through persistent and convincing theoretical argument, but also, and more importantly, through her sensitivity to the sorts of subtle interactional dynamics that are too often overlooked by researchers. At the same time, Sue provided intensive training in how to convert these interpersonal dynamics into quantifiable categories, providing her students with effective tools for working with large corpora of naturalistic speech data. In her characteristic style of involvement, Sue generously offered me the opportunity to co-author two papers, one on "requests" and one on "face." I was involved in several of her research projects, coding and analyzing data, writing grant proposals, and sharing the joy of successes and the frustration of rejections. I had the honor to have her as the chair of my preliminary examination committee and as a member of my dissertation committee. The social-interactional approach to language acquisition, which is the major theme of my thesis, is chiefly attributable to Sue's influence and training. Her influence now leads me to future "Ervin-Tripp research areas," such as crosscultural pragmatics in natural discourse, social-interactional foundations of grammar in language acquisition, and the interface between the development of certain grammatical components and social-moral development in various languages.

THE AUTHORS

Ayhan Aksu-Koç
Department. of Psychology
Bogazici University
P.K.2, Bebek
Istanbul
Turkey
koc0%trboun.bitnet

Elaine Andersen
Department of Linguistics
University of Southern California
Hedco Neuroscience Building, USC
Los Angeles, CA 90089-2520
elaine@gizmo.usc.edu

Ruth Berman
Department of Linguistics
Tel Aviv University
Ramat Aviv
Israel 69978
rberman@post.tau.ac.il

Roger Brown
Psychology Department
Harvard University
Cambridge, MA 02138.

Michael Bamberg
Department of Psychology
Clark University
Worcester, MA 01610
mbamberg@vax.clarku.edu

Nancy Budwig
Department of Psychology
Clark University
Worcester, MA 01610
nbudwig@vax.clarku.edu

Jenny Cook-Gumperz
Graduate School of Education
University of California, Santa Barbara
Santa Barbara, CA 93106
jenny@edstar.gse.ucsb.edu

Williams Corsaro
Department of Sociology
Indiana University, Bloomington
Bloomington, IN 47405
corsaro@indiana.edu

Judy Dunn
Institute of Psychiatry
De Crespigny Park
Denmark Hill
London SE5 8AF
England
spjwaao@iop.bpmf.ac.uk

Alessandro Duranti
Department of Anthropology
University of California, Los Angeles
Los Angeles, CA 90095-1553
aduranti@ucla.edu

Richard Ely
Department of Psychology
Boston University
64 Cummington Street
Boston, MA 02215
rely@bu.edu

Susan Ervin-Tripp
Department of Psychology
University of California, Berkeley
Berkeley, CA 94720
ervintr1@violet.berkeley.edu

Elanor Escalera
Department of Psychology
University of California, Berkeley,
Berkeley, CA 94720
escalera@cogsci.berkeley.edu

Charles Fillmore
Department of Linguistics
University of California, Berkeley
Berkeley, CA 94720
fillmore@cogsci.berkeley.edu

Lily Wong Fillmore
School of Education
University of California, Berkeley
Berkeley, CA 94720
wongfill@uclink2.berkeley.edu

Julie Gerhardt
California Institute of Integral Studies
765 Ashbury Street
San Francisco, CA 94117
gerhardt@cogsci.berkeley.edu

Jean Berko Gleason
Department of Psychology
Boston University
64 Cummington Street
Boston, MA 02215
gleason@bu.edu

Marjorie Harness Goodwin
Department of Anthropology
University of California, Los Angeles
Los Angeles, CA 90095-1553
mgoodwin@anthro.ucla.edu

Allen Grimshaw
Department of Sociology
Indiana University, Bloomington
Bloomington, IN 47405
grimsha@indiana.edu

John Gumperz
130 East Pueblo
Santa Barbara, CA 93105
gumperz@edstar.gse.ucsb.edu

Jiansheng Guo
Department of Psychology
Victoria University of Wellington
Wellington, P.O. Box 600
New Zealand
guo@kauri.vuw.ac.nz

Leanne Hinton
Department of Linguistics
University of California, Berkeley
Berkeley, CA 94720-2650
hinton@violet.berkeley.edu

Philip Hull
American School of Professional
        Psychology, Hawaii Campus
3465 Waialae Avenue Suite 300
Honolulu, HI 96816
hullp@pixi.com

Dell Hymes
Department of Anthropology
University of Virginia
Charlottesville, VA 22903

Vera John-Steiner
Department of Linguistics
University of New Mexico
Humanities Building 526
Albuquerque, NM 87131-1196
vygotsky@triton.unm.edu

Aylin Küntay
Department of Psychology
University of California, Berkeley
Berkeley, CA 94720
kuntay@cogsci.berkeley.edu

Amy Kyratzis
Graduate School of Education
University of California, Santa Barbara
Santa Barbara, CA 93106
kyratzis@edstar.gse.ucsb.edu

Robin Lakoff
Department of Linguistics
University of California, Berkeley
Berkeley, CA94720
rlakoff@garnet.berkeley.edu

Martin Lampert
Department of Psychology
Holy Names College
Oakland, CA 94619
lampert@cogsci.berkeley.edu

Anny Maes
Eindhovens Psychologisch Instituut
Edenstraat 29
NL-5611 JN Eindhoven
The Netherlands

Douglas Maynard
Department of Sociology
Indiana University, Bloomington
Bloomington, IN 47405
dmaynard@indiana.edu

Laura Nader
Department of Anthropology
University of California, Berkeley
Berkeley, CA 94720

Keiko Nakamura
Department of Psychology
University of California, Berkeley
Berkeley, CA 94720
nakak@cogsci.berkeley.edu

Bhuvana Narasimhan
Program in Applied Linguistics
Boston University
718 Commonwealth Avenue
Boston MA 02215
bhuvana@acs.bu.edu

Ageliki Nicolopoulou
Department of Education &
    Child Study
Smith College
Northampton, MA 01063
anicolop@sophia.smith.edu

Elinor Ochs
Department of TESL/Applied
    Linguistics
University of California, Los Angeles
Los Angeles, CA 90024
ochs@humnet.ucla.ed

Cathy O'Connor
School of Education, SED Bldg. #330
Boston University
605 Commonwealth Avenue
Boston, MA 02215
mco@acs.bu.edu

Maria Pak
Institute of Cognitive Studies
University of California, Berkeley
Berkeley, CA 94720
pak@cogsci.berkeley.edu

Rivka Y. Perlmann
28 York Terrace
Brookline, MA 02146

Ann Peters
Department of Linguistics
University of Hawai'i
1890 East-West Road, Rm 569
Honolulu, HI 96822
ann@hawaii.edu

Gisela Redeker
Letterenfaculteit
Vrije Universiteit Amsterdam,
De Boelelaan 1105
NL-1081 HV Amsterdam
The Netherlands
redeker@let.vu.nl

Judy Reilly
Department of Psychology
San Diego State University
6363 Alvarado Court #221
San Diego, CA 92120-4913
jreilly@ucsvax.sdsu.edu

Lisa Rohleder
Institute for Child Development
University of Minnesota
Minneapolis, MN 55455

Barbara Scales
Harold E. Jones Child Study Center
University of California, Berkeley
2425 Atherton Street
Berkeley, CA 94720

Amy Sheldon
Department of Speech-Communication
    and Graduate Program in Linguis-
    tics
University of Minnesota
460 Folwell Hall
9 Pleasant St. SE
Minneapolis, MN 55455
asheldon@maroon.tc.umn.edu

Bambi Shieffelin
Department of Anthropology
New York University
New York, NY 10003
schfflin@is.nyu.edu

Dan Slobin
Department of Psychology
University of California, Berkeley
Berkeley, CA 94720
slobin@cogsci.berkeley.edu

Richard Sprott
Institute of Cognitive Studies
University of California, Berkeley
Berkeley, CA 94720
sprott@cogsci.berkeley.edu

Charles Stinson
Department of Psychiatry
University of California, San Francisco
401 Parnassus Avenue
San Francisco, CA 94133
stinson@macpsy.ucsf.edu

PART ONE: SUSAN ERVIN-TRIPP

SUSAN ERVIN-TRIPP:
A MIND IN THE WORLD

Susan Ervin-Tripp has shown us the possibility of redefining the life of the intellectual. Rather than allowing her problem domains to be shaped by traditional task definitions, she has — again and again — gone to "the world" to find problems wcrthy of study, and has repeatedly returned to the world to share her gained insights. That is, hers is truly "a mind in the world" — in two senses: a mind that takes inspiration from real-world, consequential human situations and that directs its intellectual activity towards changing those situations. In this brief introduction, we wish to illuminate the striking personal characteristics that reflect this theme.

COMMITMENT TO DIVERSITY

Although born and raised far from both coasts — in Minneapolis — it is hard to think of Sue's life and work without thinking of such places as France, Japan, the Indian reservations of the American Southwest, and, of course, the two coasts of this country. She has enthusiastically explored and studied diverse peoples, languages, social, and cultural settings. In her research methods, too, one thinks of a diversity of approaches: experiments, naturalistic and controlled observations, interviews — using audio recordings of speech, written texts, video recordings of interaction patterns, and a range of stimulus materials over the years. Similarly, looking at the populations Sue has studied, one finds children and adults, natives and immigrants, monolinguals and bilinguals, individuals and groups.

In the academic setting, she has held positions in departments of psychology, rhetoric, and women's studies. Within her home department of psychology she is rare in being an active member of three divisions — developmental, cognitive, and social. And at Berkeley she has placed her research projects in the Institute of Cognitive Studies (formerly the Institute of Human Learning), the Institute of Human Development, and the Language-Behavior Research Laboratory of the Institute of International Studies. This diversity is also reflected in the range of disciplines that Sue has been affiliated with, as committee member and colleague: psychology, linguistics, anthropology, education, sociology, rhetoric, and women's studies.

3

INNOVATIVE

More than once, Sue has played a central role in the definition and establishment of a new area of study: psycholinguistics in the fifties, and in the sixties, the modern study of child language development as well as sociolinguistics. And in all three, she has always directed the attention of Americans to the importance of linguistic and cultural variation.

Equally striking is Sue's repeated innovation in the realms of technology and methodology. She was the first person to realize that computers could be useful in storing and analyzing child language data — and that in the days of punch cards and mountains of printout. And, furthermore, the data that she entered on those punchcards came from tape recordings of child speech in an era that had only known written transcripts taken on the fly. (And, as an interesting reflection of the Zeitgeist, while Sue and Wick Miller were carting "portable" taperecorders to children's homes in California, Roger Brown and Martin Braine were doing the same thing on the East Coast — though they didn't use the computer to help them.) When Sue discovered wireless microphones, she ingeniously sewed them into children's vests, so as to be able to gather natural conversation without the intrusion of cumbersome equipment and observers. Thus, when "portable" video recording equipment came on the market, Sue was ready to study children's behavior in context — the context of interaction between family members in their homes.

In order to deal with such large and complex bodies of data, Sue innovated methods of coding and sorting utterances according to both linguistic and behavioral dimensions. Her procedure was always to begin with naturalistic data, work with teams of students (both undergraduate and graduate) to devise and refine coding schemes, and then move on to more focused studies.

ENGAGEMENT WITH PEOPLE

It is noteworthy that these beginning phases of opening up a new territory always involved students at all levels. (In fact, when Sue was offered an attractive early retirement option recently, she declined it, preferring to stay engaged with students, in both research and teaching.) Sue's way of working with students has always been to treat them as co-investigators in a collaborative quest. Another facet of her involvement with students has been an active concern with their professional development — from their first days at Berkeley on through their individual careers.

Perhaps the "mind in the world" has been most evident with regard to her involvement with problems facing women and ethnic minorities — in the state and nation as well as on the campus. We cannot list the many committees, lobbying efforts, and contributions to public education (and educating the public) that fill every year of Sue's biography. But as an indication of this dedication, this is how she summarized her experience as Ombudsman for the University of California at Berkeley in 1987-89:

> The job of ombudsman is highly rewarding, in particular when we receive
> gratitude for helping to solve a problem that has put someone in jeopardy (e.g.,
> the student who didn't get assurance she was admitted until exam week, the

student whose graduation was blocked in error), or when by proposing a slight change in procedure or the wording of a regulation or instructions we could remedy a chronic problem. We have set aside special time to investigate issues that appear to reveal structural problems. To faculty members, the unseen crises in the lives of the students we teach are especially poignant. We find that the clients who discover us reveal just the tip of profound problems on the campus, such as the burn-out of bureaucrats who then start making rigid automatic decisions, the conflict many students experience between the time demands of jobs and classes, and the heavy financial burdens borne by many students, especially single parents. The Office of the Academic Ombudsmen is both a safety valve and a valuable sensor for campus problems.

In a way, Susan Ervin-Tripp has been an ombudsperson in the intellectual world as well — attempting to reconcile theories, listening to neglected viewpoints, alerting us to structural problems, and seeking solutions. The leitmotif in Sue's opening chapter is CONTEXT. There she talks about the influences of context on the structure and use of language. Here we underline the context of Sue's involvement with the world as determining the directions and impact of her work.

— The Editors

A BRIEF BIOGRAPHY OF
SUSAN ERVIN-TRIPP

Susan Moore Ervin was born in Minneapolis on June 27, 1927. She attended an all-women's high school, then an all-women's college, Vassar College, where she took courses in 11 subjects, among them courses in art history (her major), the social sciences, and several languages. Her undergraduate experiences had already impressed upon her a concern with women's issues, as she noted her good fortune in having had many excellent women professors at a liberal arts college — while those women were not allowed entry at the time to the larger research universities.

After Vassar, Susan Ervin attended the University of Michigan. Her concern with social issues was foreshadowed in her choice of Michigan, where she wanted to work with disciples of Kurt Lewin to use social psychology to try to understand and solve important social problems that were in the forefront of concern in the early postwar years. Disappointed in this quest, but retaining her keen interest in social psychology, she became drawn to the problem of bilingualism by the dramatic personal experience of her bilingual friends, who reported a sense of double identity and dual personality. The issue of the psychological role of bilingualism for individuals became her dissertation topic (Ervin, 1955, Ervin-Tripp, 1964).[1]

Her application to the Social Science Research Council to fund this research brought her to the attention of John Carroll, who in 1951 initiated a move to bring linguistics and psychology together. This connection resulted in two important influences on Ervin's life. First, she was privileged to play a role in the founding of psycholinguistics, taking part (as one of six graduate students) in a workshop sponsored by the SSRC in conjunction with the Linguistic Society of America at Indiana University in the summer of 1953. Ervin made contributions on language learning and bilingualism to the classic report that came out of that summer: *Psycholinguistics: A Survey of Theory and Research Problems* (Osgood & Sebeok, 1954).

The second important result was that John Carroll invited Ervin to work on the Southwest Project on Comparative Psycholinguistics, a wide-ranging attempt to test the Whorf hypothesis by means of comparative research in six language communities: Navajo, Zuni, Hopi, Hopi-Tewa, Spanish, and English. At the outset, then, her formation was cross-disciplinary, cross-cultural, and cross-linguistic (Ervin, Landar, & Horowitz, 1960; Ervin & Landar, 1963). In working with American Indian communities

---

[1] References cited here are listed in the full bibliography following this essay. We have not attempted to refer to each of Susan Ervin-Tripp's many publications here, but have selectively highlighted some as illustrative of the main trends of her intellectual career.

in the Southwest, Ervin was impressed with the coherence that culture confers upon language and its use — a lesson no doubt incorporated into her later influential work on the situated nature of children's as well as adults' language.

After receiving her doctorate in social psychology from Michigan, Ervin was brought into the Harvard School of Education by John Whiting, and one of the courses she taught there was child language. She reports that this experience is what prepared her to be duly impressed by Chomsky's work, *Syntactic Structures*, when it came out in 1957. In the fifties, language was treated as part of social psychology, and linguistics was often housed in departments of anthropology. Added to this, now, was a concern for the structure of language — an issue which Ervin realized had obvious consequences for child language development.

Ervin moved to Berkeley in 1958, where she taught English as a Second Language in the Department of Speech. One of the first things she did after arriving in California was to obtain a grant to study the child's acquisition of the coherent system of rules described by Chomsky. With linguist Wick Miller, she began one of the first modern studies of child speech *in situ*, making use of the new technology of portable tape recorders to record the speech of preschool children in their homes (Ervin & Miller, 1963, 1964). The design followed by Ervin and Miller was innovative in being naturalistic and longitudinal, while at the same time making use of repeated elicitation devices to tap the growing morphological and syntactic competence of a group of five children. And the technological approach was innovative not only in the use of tape recorders, but also in the use of computers — the first attempt ever to store and process child language data electronically. These data formed the beginning of a series of speech archives at Berkeley — archives that Ervin and her students and colleagues have gone back to again and again through the years, as new theoretical questions have arisen.

Several important papers emerged from this study, including "Imitation and Structural Change in Children's Language" (Ervin, 1964), which is widely cited in the child language literature. Here, Ervin documented three stages that children go through in acquiring plural and past tense morphology in English, including the significant intermediate period of overregularization. This problem has remained a central puzzle for psycholinguistics to the present day. On the basis of the longitudinal studies, Ervin — by then Ervin-Tripp — elaborated a process approach to language development, proposing various strategies used by the child (Ervin-Tripp, 1970, 1971, 1972). Also during this period, she began to note syntactic progress in conversational contexts and the role of conversations in supporting that progress, as reflected in a later paper, "From conversation to syntax" (Ervin-Tripp, 1977). She wrote of her early child language work that she began "to see first language development as a series of stages in a changing language acquisition system that selects and alters what it absorbs . . . suddenly I could see that interference was no different from the enduring structure of the monolingual child's own prior language." This insight allowed her two lines of interest, bilingualism and child syntactic development, to converge. "It also brought to the fore the fact that the differences between first and second language acquisition in reality are often just those factors of intent, motive, social milieu, and communicative choice which are left unexamined in first language acquisition as irrelevant to structure." Thus her work during this era left her feeling that social factors remained to be incorporated into the description of systematicity in the child's rule systems.

At the same time that Ervin-Tripp was working on the development of grammar, she also continued her investigations of the role of language and bilingualism in thinking. In the sixties and seventies her studies included the language use of Japanese war brides in California (Ervin-Tripp, 1967) and the second-language acquisition of English-speaking children in French Switzerland (Ervin-Tripp, 1974).

In the course of investigating topics of bilingualism, code-switching, and language and thought, Ervin joined forces with a group of linguists and anthropologists at Berkeley. At that time, a new field was emerging, stimulated by the work of John Gumperz, Dell Hymes, and Erving Goffman, brought together under the rubric of "the ethnography of communication." In 1963 a sociolinguistics committee had been proposed to the Social Science Research Committee, and Ervin was instrumental in the founding of this new field, joining the committee in 1966. In 1967, Ervin wrote a survey paper which became a major foundational document of the field (Ervin-Tripp, 1968). The time was ripe for bringing psycholinguistics and sociolinguistics together in the study of child language development, and Berkeley was the right place for making this approach cross-cultural. Together with Gumperz and Slobin and a group of students in psychology, anthropology, and linguistics, Ervin-Tripp took part in developing *A Field Manual for Cross-Cultural Study of the Acquisition of Communicative Competence* (edited by Slobin, 1967), aimed at studying child language within both linguistic and ethnographic contexts. A group of students went off to field sites around the world, collecting dissertation data guided by the field manual; and in the summer of 1968 a major series of workshops was held at the Institute of Human Learning at Berkeley (directed by Ervin-Tripp, Slobin, Gumperz, and Charles Ferguson, from Stanford) to examine data brought back from the field and chart the further course of this interdisciplinary venture. A number of the students who took part in the 1968 meetings went on to become productive scholars in the several intersecting fields of study.

Of her sociolinguistic work during this period, Ervin-Tripp wrote that "the most important contribution in the new field of sociolinguistics appeared to be the discovery of new strata of structure in language." The social phenomena underlying address terminology and other linguistic contrasts were as orderly and rule governed as the syntactic phenomena that Chomsky had focused on, and Ervin-Tripp's interest in social acts and the communicative situatedness of language led to the discovery and description of new dimensions of sociolinguistic structure and process.

Along with her academic research, women's issues became increasingly important to Ervin-Tripp in the context of the social upheavals that began in the sixties. Moved by some of her own experiences (such as not being allowed to march at graduation at Harvard, being excluded from "The Great Hall" of the Men's Faculty Club at Berkeley), and her concern with the more serious issues of the professional opportunities for women in universities and in society, Ervin-Tripp became an activist for issues affecting her women colleagues and students. She was appointed to a committee to report on the status of women at Berkeley. The findings were disturbing. As a result of the report, which came out in 1970, women in the University became organized and introduced a

Civil Rights Complaint to Kaspar Weinberger, then head of Health, Education, and Welfare in Washington. As a result, an Affirmative Action Coalition was set up at the University, and a coalition was formed in the Academic Senate to deal with issues facing women and ethnic minorities on campus. In the years since then, Ervin-Tripp has remained involved on the state and local levels, working for affirmative action programs and serving for a while as the Academic Senate Ombudsman.

Her research turned more and more to issues of developmental sociolinguistics. When video recording equipment became available, she set out to record family interactions in their homes, now with full contextual support. A new archive was in the making, supported by a new generation of computer technology. Ervin-Tripp's investigation of pragmatics had begun with address terminology, and in the seventies it moved on to another terrain of interpersonal communication: request forms. Requests were interesting to her because of their ambiguity and because of the strong influence of social and situational factors on different forms of requests. In addition to studying patterns of interaction in families, Ervin-Tripp and her students collected spontaneously produced directives, observing people in a range of social settings. It was clear that the role of **context** was becoming a guiding theme in her work. An influential paper that emerged from this work was "Is Sybil there?: The structure of some English requests" (Ervin-Tripp, 1976). Here Ervin-Tripp pointed to the role of language in reflecting and constituting social roles and relationships, analyzing the systematicity of social rules underlying language use.

A central theme in much of the more recent work on requests and social interaction is **control**, as realized in relationships of unequal status, such as families and classrooms. See, for example, "Structures of control" (Ervin-Tripp, 1982) and "Language and power in the family" (Ervin-Tripp, O'Connor, & Rosenberg, 1984).

A major part of Ervin-Tripp's program is based on microanalytic analysis of texts of natural conversation. She has pioneered in creating subtle coding systems, attending to a collection of interacting variables. For example, in analyzing requests, the method takes converging measures of such factors as addressee, cost of request, and linguistic form — in order to arrive at an understanding of the interplay of form and function in the acquisition and use of language. The method is described in a recent paper, "Structured coding for the study of language and social interaction" (Lampert & Ervin-Tripp, 1993).

Most recently, Ervin-Tripp has been concerned with the influence of larger discourse structures on children's acquisition of syntax. This work has examined speech activities such as narratives and arguments, searching for the discourse contexts in which grammatical forms emerge, and tracing their subsequent expansion to serve new functions. Most of her papers from this decade elaborate on these issues, and a number of the chapters in this volume, written by her students and collaborators, carry on these themes.

In addition to the work on children's syntactic and discursive units, Ervin-Tripp's current research deals with the functions of young adults' spontaneous conversational narratives and gender differences in the construction of humorous talk (Ervin-Tripp & Lampert, 1992). Again reflecting her innovative data collection techniques, the database for these studies consists of several hundred spontaneous conversations among young adult friendship groups gathered by her Berkeley undergraduate students. Her concern for the real-life consequences of language and gender has led her to undertake a large-scale study of letters of recommendation, examining the effects of gender — both of letter writer and candidate — on the form and content of letters. As in all of her work, the research is both microanalytic and of social consequence, dealing with language on both the linguistic and social planes.

In 1994 Susan Ervin-Tripp was given the highest honor of the Academic Senate of the University of California at Berkeley. She was chosen to be one of the two annual Faculty Research Lecturers, presenting an overview of her life's work to the campus community. That lecture is the first chapter in this volume. Its title sums up her quest: "Context in Language."

— The Editors

REFERENCES

Osgood, C. E., & Sebeok, T. A. (Eds.). (1965). *Psycholinguistics: A survey of theory and research problems*. Bloomington: Indiana University Press. Original work published in 1954.

Slobin, D. I. (Ed.). (1967). *A field manual for cross-cultural study of the acquisition of communicative competence*. Berkeley: Language-Behavior Research Laboratory / Associated Students of the University of California.

.

BIBLIOGRAPHY OF PUBLICATIONS
BY SUSAN MOORE ERVIN-TRIPP

1948

Ervin, S. M., & Borsook, E. (1948, April). Kaiser Friedrich Art Collection. *Vassar Brew*, **36**, 11-12, 19.

1949

Ervin, S. M. (1949). Mannerist aspects of modern painting. *Vassar Review*, **1**(5), 9-12.

1952

Ervin, S. M., & Bower, R. T. (1952). Translation problems in international surveys. *Public Opinion Quarterly*, **16**, 595-604.

1954

Ervin, S. M. (1954). Information transmission with code translation. *Journal of Personality and Social Psychology*, **58**, 185-192.

Ervin, S. M. & Osgood, C. E. (1954). Second language learning and bilingualism. *Journal of Personality and Social Psychology*, **58**, 139-145.

1955

Ervin, S. M. (1955). *The verbal behavior of bilinguals: The effect of language of report on the Thematic Apperception Test content of adult French bilinguals,* **12**. Ann Arbor: University of Michigan Microfilm Library, p. 571. Microfilm AC-1.

1958

Ervin, S. M. (1958). Review of *Certain language skills in children*, by M. Templin. *Contemporary Psychology*, **3**, 128-129.

Ervin, S. M. (1958). Review of *Intelligence in United States*, by H. Miner. *Psychometrika*, **23**, 388-390.

1960

Ervin, S. M. (1960). Cognitive effects of bilingualism. *Proceedings of the Sixteenth International Congress of Psychology*. Bonn, Germany.

Ervin, S. M., & Foster, G. (1960). The development of meaning in children's descriptive terms. *Journal of Abnormal and Social Psychology*, **60**, 271-275.

Ervin, S. M. (1960). Experimental procedures of children. *Child Development*, **31**, 703-719.

Ervin, S. M., Landar, H. J., & Horowitz, A. E. (1960). Navaho color categories. *Language*, **36**, 368-382.

Ervin, S. M. (1960). Review of *Verbal categories in child language*, by H. Kahane, R. Kahane, and S. Saporta. *Romance Philology*, **14**, 45-48.

Ervin, S. M. (1960). Training and a logical operation by children. *Child Development*, **31**, 555-563.

Ervin, S. M. (1960). Transfer effects of learning a verbal generalization. *Child Development*, **31**, 537-554.

1961

Ervin, S. M. (1961). Changes with age in the verbal determinants of word association. *American Journal of Psychology*, **74**, 361-372.

Ervin, S. M. (1961). Learning and recall in bilinguals. *American Journal of Psychology*, **74**, 446-451.

Ervin, S. M. (1961). Review of *Speech and the development of mental processes in the child*, by A. R. Luria & F. I. Yudovich. *Contemporary Psychology*, **6**, 20.

Ervin, S. M. (1961). Semantic shift in bilingualism. *American Journal of Psychology*, **74**, 233-241.

1962

Ervin, S. M. (1962). The connotations of gender. *Word*, **18**, 249-261.

1963

Ervin, S. M. (1963). Correlates of associative frequency. *Journal of Verbal Learning and Verbal Behavior*, **1**, 422-431.

Ervin, S. M., & Miller, W. (1963). Language development. In H. W Stevenson (Ed.), *Yearbook of the National Society for the Study of Education: Child Psychology*, **62** (1), 108-143. Chicago: University of Chicago Press.

Ervin, S. M., & Landar, H. (1963). Navaho word associations. *American Journal of Psychology*, **76**, 49-57.

Ervin, S. M. (1963). Review of *Psycholinguistics*, ed. by S. Saporta. *American Anthropologist*, **65**, 750-752.

Ervin, S. M. (1963). Review of *Variations in value orientations*, by F. Kluckhohn & F. Strodtbeck. *American Journal of Psychology*, **76**, 342-343.

Ervin, S. M., Sawyer, J., Silver, S., D'Andrea, J., & Aoki, H. (1963). The utility of translation and written symbols during the first thirty hours of language study. *International Review of Applied Linguistics (IRAL)*, **1**, 157-192.

1964

Ervin, S. M. (1964). Abstracts on psycholinguistics. *International Journal of American Linguistics*, **30**, 184-193.

Ervin, S. M. (1964). An analysis of the interaction of language, topic, and listener. *American Anthropologist*, **66** (6, Part 2), 86-102.

Ervin, S. M., & Miller, W. (1964). The development of grammar in child language. *Monographs of the Society for Research in Child Development*, **29** (1, Serial No. 92), 9-34.

Ervin, S. M. (1964). Imitation and structural change in children's language. In E. H. Lenneberg (Ed.), *New directions in the study of language* (pp. 163-189). Cambridge, MA: MIT Press.

Ervin, S. M. (1964). Language and TAT content in bilinguals. *Journal of Abnormal and Social Psychology*, **68**, 500-507.

Ervin, S. M. (1964). Language and thought. In S. Tax (Ed.), *Horizons of anthropology* (pp. 81-91). Chicago: Aldine.

Ervin, S. M. (1964). Review of *Language in the crib*, by R. H. Weir. *International Journal of American Linguistics*, **30**, 420-424.

1966

Ervin-Tripp, S. M. (1966). Discussion. In E. C. Carterette (Ed.), *Speech, language, and communication* (pp. 58-60, 245-246). Los Angeles: University of California Press.

Ervin-Tripp, S. M. (1966). Language development. In L. Hoffman (Ed.), *Review of child development research: Vol. 2* (pp. 55-105). New York: Russell Sage Foundation.

Ervin-Tripp, S. M., & Slobin, D. I. (1966). Psycholinguistics. *Annual Review of Psychology*, **17**, 435-474.

1967

Ervin-Tripp, S. M. (1967). Introduction, phonology, communicative routines, contrastive analysis, informal education, introduction to styles, natural conversation. In D. I. Slobin (Ed.), *A field manual for cross-cultural study of the acquisition of communicative competence.* Berkeley: ASUC Bookstore.

Ervin-Tripp, S. M. (1967). An Issei learns English. *Journal of Social Issues,* **23** (2), 78-90.

Ervin-Tripp, S. M. (1967). Navaho connotative judgments: The metaphor of person description. In D. Hymes & W. E. Bittle (Eds.), *Studies in Southwestern ethnolinguistics* (pp. 91-116). The Hague: Mouton.

Ervin-Tripp, S. M. (1967). On becoming a bilingual. In L. G. Kelly (Ed.), *The description and measurement of bilingualism* (pp. 26-35). Toronto: University of Toronto Press.

1968

Ervin-Tripp, S. M, & Slobin, D. I. (1968). Recenti orientamenti in psicolinguistica. *Rassegna Italiana di Sociologia,* **2,** 382-425.

Ervin-Tripp, S. M. (1968). Language development. *International Encyclopedia of the Social Sciences: Vol. 9* (pp. 9-14). New York: Macmillan & Free Press.

Ervin-Tripp, S. M. (1968). Sociolinguistics. In L. Berkowitz (Ed.), *Advances in experimental social psychology: Vol. 4* (pp. 91-165). New York: Academic Press.

1969

Ervin-Tripp, S. M. (1969). The acquisition of communicative competence by children in different cultures. *Proceedings of the VIIIth International Congress of Anthropological and Ethnological Sciences: Vol. 3* (pp. 406-408). Tokyo: Science Council of Japan.

Ervin-Tripp, S. M. (1969, May). Summer workshops in sociolinguistics: Research on children's acquisition of communicative competence. *Social Science Research Council Items.* **23**(2), 22-26.

1970

Ervin-Tripp, S. M. (1970). Discourse agreement: How children answer questions. In R. Hayes (Ed.), *Cognition and language learning* (pp. 79-107). New York: Wiley.

Ervin-Tripp, S.M. (1970). Structure and process in language acquisition. In J. E. Alatis (Ed.), *Bilingualism and language contact* (Georgetown University Round Table on Languages and Linguistics No. 21, pp. 313-353). Washington, D.C: Georgetown University Press.

Ervin-Tripp, S. M. (1970). Substitution, context, and association. In L. Postman & G. Keppel (Eds.), *Norms of word association* (pp. 383-467). New York: Academic.

1971

Ervin-Tripp, S. M. (1971). Origins of language. In A. Lazerson (Ed.), *Developmental psychology today* (pp. 163-179). Del Mar, CA: CRM Books.

Ervin-Tripp, S. M. (1971). An overview of theories of grammatical development. In D. I. Slobin (Ed.), *The ontogenesis of grammar: Some facts and theories* (pp. 189-212). New York: Academic Press.

Colson, E., Scott, E., Blumer, H., Ervin-Tripp, S. M., & Newman, F. (1971). *Report of the subcommittee on the status of academic women on the Berkeley campus.* Berkeley: Berkeley Division of the Academic Senate, University of California.

Ervin-Tripp, S. M. (1971). Social backgrounds and verbal skills. In R. Huxley, & E. Ingram (Eds.), *Language acquisition: Models and methods* (pp. 29-39). London/New York: Academic.

Ervin-Tripp, S. M. (1971). Social dialects in developmental sociolinguistics. In R. Shuy (Ed.), *Sociolinguistics: A cross-disciplinary perspective* (pp. 35-64). Washington, DC: Center for Applied Linguistics.

1972

Ervin-Tripp, S. M. (1972). Children's sociolinguistic competence and dialect diversity. In I. U. Gordon (Ed.), *The seventy-first yearbook of the National Society for the Study of Education: Early childhood education* (pp. 123-160). Chicago: University of Chicago Press.

Ervin-Tripp, S. M. (1972). Alternation and co-occurrence. In J. J. Gumperz, & D. Hymes (Ed.), *Directions in sociolinguistics: The ethnography of communication* (pp. 218-250). New York: Holt, Rinehart and Winston.

Ervin-Tripp, S. M. (1972). Some strategies for the first two years. In T. Moore (Ed.), *Cognitive development and the acquisition of language* (pp. 261-286). New York: Academic.

1973

Ervin-Tripp, S. M. (1973). *Language acquisition and communicative choice.* Stanford: Stanford University Press.

Ervin-Tripp, S. M. (1973). Reading as second language learning. In M. P. Douglass (Ed.), *Thirty-seventh yearbook of the Claremont Reading Conference: Reading between and beyond the lines* (pp. 12-18). Claremont, CA: Claremont College.

1974

Ervin-Tripp, S. M. (1974). The comprehension and production of requests by children. *Papers and Reports on Child Language Development*, **8**, 188-195.

Ervin-Tripp, S. M. (1974). Is second language learning like the first? *TESOL Quarterly*, **8**, 111-125.

Ervin-Tripp, S. M. (1974). Review of *Language, psychology, and culture*, by W. Lambert. *Language in Society*, **3**, 305-309.

Ervin-Tripp, S. M. (1974). Some bases for early features of production. In J. Mehler (Ed.), *Problèmes actuels en psycholinguistique* (Colloques internationaux du Centre National de la Recherche Sociale, pp. 113-128). Paris: CNRS.

Ervin-Tripp, S. M. (1974). Two decades of Council activity in the rapprochement of linguistics and social science. *Social Science Research Council Items*, **28**(1), 1-4.

1975

Ervin-Tripp, S. M. (1975). *Language development from babbling to sarcasm* (APA Master Lecture Series). Washington, DC: American Psychological Association.

1976

Ervin-Tripp, S. M. (1976). 'What do women sociolinguists want?': Prospects for a research field. *Proceedings of the Conference on the Sociology of Language of American Women* (papers in Southwest English No. 4). San Antonio: New Mexico State University.

Ervin-Tripp, S. M. (1976). Sociolinguistics in the United States. In D. N. Shelev & L. P. Krysin (Eds.), *Sotsial'no-lingvisticheskie issledovaniia* (pp. 188-199). Moscow: Soviet Academy of Sciences.

Ervin-Tripp, S. M. (1976). Is Sybil there?: The structure of some American English directives. *Language in Society*, **5**, 25-66.

Ervin-Tripp, S. M. (1976). Speech acts and social learning. In K. H. Basso & H. Selby (Eds.), *Meaning in anthropology* (pp. 123-153). Albuquerque: University of New Mexico Press.

1977

Ervin-Tripp, S. M. (1977). A psychologist's point of view. In C. E. Snow & C. A. Ferguson (Eds.), *Talking to children: Language input and acquisition* (pp. 335-339). Cambridge, England: Cambridge University Press.

Ervin-Tripp, S. M. (1977). Early discourse: Some questions about questions. In M. M. Lewis & L. A. Rosenblum (Eds.), *Interaction, conversation, and the development of language* (pp. 9-25). New York: Wiley.

Ervin-Tripp, S. M. (1977). From conversation to syntax. *Papers and Reports on Child Language Development*, **13**, 1-21.

Ervin-Tripp, S. M. (1977). Introduction; Wait for me, roller-skate. In C. Mitchell-Kernan & S. M. Ervin-Tripp (Eds.), *Child discourse* (pp. 1-26, 165-188). New York: Academic.

Ervin-Tripp, S. M. (1977). Language and thought. In S. Tax & L. G. Freeman (Eds.), *Horizons of anthropology* (2nd edition, pp. 88-100). Chicago: Aldine.

1978

Ervin-Tripp, S. M. (1978). The onset of grammar. In V. Honsa, & M. J. Hardman-de-Bautista (Eds.), *Papers on linguistics and child language: Ruth Hirsch Weir memorial volume* (pp. 71-91). The Hague: Mouton.

Ervin-Tripp, S. M. (1978). Some features of early child-adult dialogues. *Language in Society*, **7**, 357-373.

Ervin-Tripp, S. M. (1978). 'What do women sociolinguists want?' Prospects for a research field. *International Journal of the Sociology of Language*, **17**, 17-28.

1979

Ervin-Tripp, S. M. (1979). Children's verbal turn-taking. In E. Ochs & B. Schieffelin (Eds.), *Developmental pragmatics* (pp. 391-414). New York: Academic.

Ervin-Tripp, S. M. (1979). Whatever happened to communicative competence?. In B. Kachru (Ed.), *Forum lectures presented at the 1978 Linguistic Institute of the Linguistic Society of America: Linguistics in the seventies, directions and prospects* (pp. 237-257). Champaign: University of Illinois Press.

1980

Ervin-Tripp, S. M. (1980). Speech acts, social meaning, and social learning. In H. Giles, W. P. Robinson, & P. M. Smith (Eds.), *Language: Social psychological perspectives* (pp. 389-396). New York: Pergamon.

1981

Ervin-Tripp, S. M. (1981). From conversation to syntax. *Versus: Quaderni di studi semiotici*, **26/27**, 81-100.

Ervin-Tripp, S. M. (1981). How to make and understand a request. In H. Parret, M. Sbisa, & J. Verschueren (Eds.), *Possibilities and limitations of pragmatics* (pp. 195-209). Amsterdam: John Benjamins.

Ervin-Tripp, S. M. (1981). Social process in first and second language learning. In H. Winitz (Ed.), *Native language and foreign language acquisition* (Annals of the New York Academy of Science: Vol. 379, pp. 33-47). New York: New York Academy of Sciences.

1982

Ervin-Tripp, S. M. (1982). Ask and it shall be given you: Children's requests. In H. Byrnes (Ed.), *Contemporary perceptions of language: Interdisciplinary dimensions* (Georgetown University Roundtable on Languages and Linguistics, pp. 232-245). Washington, DC: Georgetown University Press.

Ervin-Tripp, S. M. (1982). Les effets de l'interaction sociale sur l'acquisition de langage [The effects of social interaction on the acquisition of language]. *Actes du 2me colloque du Groupe de Recherche en Didactique de Langue,* Serie B. Québec: Centre International de Recherche pour le Bilinguisme.

Ervin-Tripp, S. M. (1982). Review of *Women and Language in Literature and Society,* by S. McConnell-Ginet, R. Borker, & N. Furman. *Contemporary Psychology,* **27,** 202-203.

Ervin-Tripp, S. M. (1982). Structures of control. In L. C. Wilkinson (Ed.), *Communicating in the classroom* (pp. 27-47). New York: Academic.

1984

Ervin-Tripp, S. M., O'Connor, M. C., & Rosenberg, J. (1984). Language and power in the family. In M. Schulz & C. Kramerae (Eds.), *Language and power* (pp. 116-135). Belmont, CA: Sage.

Gordon, D. P., & Ervin-Tripp, S. M. (1984). The structure of children's requests. In R. L. Schiefelbusch, & J. Pickar (Eds.), *The acquisition of communicative competence* (pp. 295-322). Baltimore: University Park Press.

Ervin-Tripp, S. M. (1984). The art of conversation: A commentary. Developmental trends in the quality of conversation achieved by small groups of acquainted peers. *Child development monographs,* **49** (2, Serial No. 206), 73-81.

1985

Ervin-Tripp, S. M., & Strage, A. (1985). Parent-child discourse. In T. Van Dijk (Ed.), *Handbook of discourse analysis: Vol. 3* (pp. 67-78). New York: Academic.

Ervin-Tripp, S. M., & Gordon, D. P. (1985). The development of requests. In R. L. Schiefelbusch (Ed.), *Communicative competence: Acquisition and intervention* (pp. 61-95). Beverly Hills, CA: College Hills Press.

1986

Ervin-Tripp, S. M. (1986). Activity types and the structure of talk in second language learning. In J. Fishman (Ed.), *The Fergusonian impact: Papers in honor of the 65th birthday of C.A. Ferguson: Vol.1* (pp. 419-435). Berlin: Mouton de Gruyter.

Ervin-Tripp, S. M. (1986). Activity structure as scaffolding for children's second language learning. In W. Corsaro, J. Cook-Gumperz, & J. Streeck (Eds.), *Children's language and children's worlds* (pp. 327-358). Berlin: Mouton de Gruyter.

1987

Ervin-Tripp, S. M. (1987). About, to and by women. In D. Brouwer & D. de Haan (Eds.), *Women's language, socialization and self-image* (pp. 17-26). Dordrecht (Netherlands) and Providence, RI: Foris.

Ervin-Tripp, S. M. (1987). Cross-cultural and developmental sources of pragmatic generalizations. In J. Verschueren, & M. Bertuccelli-Papi (Eds.), *The pragmatic perspective* (pp. 47-60). Amsterdam: John Benjamins.

Ervin-Tripp, S. M. (1987). Some issues in relating first and second language learning. In H. Blanc, M. Le Douaron, & D. Veronique (Eds.), *S'approprier une langue étrangère...* (pp. 276-282). Paris: Didier Erudition.

Ervin-Tripp, S. M. (1987). Talk that talk. *Contemporary Psychology, 32*, 935-936.

Ervin-Tripp, S. M., Strage, A, Lampert, M., & Bell, N. (1987). Understanding requests. *Linguistics, 25*, 107-143.

1988

Ervin-Tripp, S. M. (1988). Sisters and brothers. In P. G. Zukow (Ed.), *Sibling interactions across cultures: Theoretical and methodological issues* (pp. 182-193). New York: Springer-Verlag.

Ervin-Tripp, S. M. (1988). Request retries. *Lenguas Modernas* (Santiago, Chile), *15*, 25-34.

1989

Ervin-Tripp, S. M. (1989). *Two papers on children's speech acts and syntactic development.* (Berkeley Cognitive Science Report No. 61). Berkeley: Institute of Cognitive Studies, University of California.

1990

Ervin-Tripp, S. M., Guo, J., & Lampert, M. (1990). Politeness and persuasion in children's control acts. *Journal of Pragmatics, 14*, 195-219.

Kyratzis, A., Guo, J., & Ervin-Tripp, S. M. (1990). Pragmatic conventions influencing children's use of causal expressions in natural discourse. *Proceedings of the Sixteenth Annual Meeting of the Berkeley Linguistics Society, 16*, 205-215.

1991

Ervin-Tripp, S. M. (1991). Play in language development. In B. Scales, M. Almy, A. Nicolopoulou, & S. M. Ervin-Tripp (Eds.), *Play and the social context of development in early care and education* (pp. 84-98). New York: Columbia Teachers College.

1992

Ervin-Tripp, S. M., & Lampert, M. (1992). Gender differences in the construction of humorous talk. In K. Hall, M. Buchholtz, & B. Moonwoman (Eds.), *Locating power: Proceedings of the Second Berkeley Women and Language Conference* (pp. 108-117). Berkeley: Berkeley Women and Language Group, University of California.

1993

Ervin-Tripp, S. M. (1993). Conversational discourse. In J. Berko Gleason & N. B. Ratner (Eds.), *Psycholinguistics today* (pp. 237-270). Boston: C. E. Merrill.

Ervin-Tripp, S. M. (1993). La demande dans la famille: Apprendre à être poli et à persuader [Requests in the family: Learning to be polite and to persuade]. *Bulletin de Psychologie, 46*, 51-59.

Lampert, M., & Ervin-Tripp, S. M. (1993). Structured coding for the study of language and social interaction. In J. Edwards, & M. Lampert (Eds.), *Talking data: Transcription and coding methods for language research* (pp. 169-206). Hillsdale, NJ: Lawrence Erlbaum Associates.

1994

Ervin-Tripp, S. M. (1994). Constructing syntax from discourse. In E. V. Clark (Ed.), *Proceedings of the Twenty-Fifth Annual Stanford Child Language Research Forum* (pp. 333-341). Stanford, CA: CSLI.

Ervin-Tripp, S. M. (1994). Impact du cadre interactionnel sur les acquisitions en syntaxe [Impact of the interactional setting on the acquisition of syntax]. *Acquisition et Interaction en Langue Etrangère (AILE)* , **4,** 53-80.

1995

Ervin-Tripp, S. M. (1995). Child psychology and child pragmatics. In J. Verschueren, J.-O. Ostman, & J. Blommaert (Eds.), *Handbook of Pragmatics: Manual* (pp. 227-234). Amsterdam/Philadelphia: John Benjamins.

Ervin-Tripp, S. M., Nakamura, K., & Guo, J. (1995). Shifting face from Asia to Europe. In M. Shibatani & S. Thompson (Eds.), *Essays in semantics and pragmatics* (pp 43-71). Amsterdam: John Benjamins.

Current

Ervin-Tripp, S. M. (this volume). Context in language. In D. I. Slobin, J. Gerhardt, A. Kyratzis & J. Guo (Eds.), *Social interactions, social context, and language: Essays in honor of Susan Ervin-Tripp.* Mahwah, NJ: Lawrence Erlbaum Associates.

Ervin-Tripp, S. M. (in press). The development of sociolinguistics. In C. B. Paulston & G. R. Tucker (Eds.), *The early days of sociolinguistics: Memories and reflections.* Amsterdam: Benjamins.

1 CONTEXT IN LANGUAGE[1]

Susan M. Ervin-Tripp
University of California, Berkeley

Everyone is familiar with contexts in language. We understand that there is hyperbole in introductions but not in mid-career reviews. Yet just how context affects language is not treated in core theories of language. Models for the human capacity for language have focused on the function of description, report, analysis, as if talking about the world — physical description or abstract description — were the main use of language. Language is seen as a map of reality, either the reality outside, an abstract reality, or an imaginary reality. In this view, context gets into language mainly by reference. We talk **about** the context.

A dictionary implies a view of language. A dictionary takes as a definition what is centrally different about the meaning of a word from another. Dictionaries are designed merely to distinguish. But language is not a direct map; multiple meanings, or polysemy, is common in language. Among the common words in the English dictionary, *get* has 72 meanings, and *face* has 23 meanings as a noun and 12 as verb. Language tolerates both polysemy and homonymity heavily because humans are very context-sensitive, unlike a machine translator, which can be tripped up.

EVIDENCE ABOUT CONTEXT IN LANGUAGE

My claim is that context permeates language, that contextual assumptions affect how we understand language, and that contexts of speech have to be better understood to develop realistic theories of language and of language learning. First, let us clarify what we mean by context. Take as an example getting a book from a reserve library counter. We normally remember the setting — the counter — and the activity that occurred — a service request — and we remember that the librarian said the book was checked out. These facts we can report, and we have a focused memory about them. But typically we do not notice, unless they are unusual, the physical layout in detail, who else was present behind the counter or before it, the exact exchange, the librarian's syntax, accent, lan-

---

[1] A version of this chapter was presented as the 1994 Faculty Research Lecture, following Susan Ervin-Tripp's election as Berkeley Faculty Lecturer —· a rare honor. — *Editors.*

guage, address terms, verbatim wording, rate of speaking, or the prosody of the speech. These are aspects of context, in the sense that they are present and backgrounded. If they do not survive in our reported memory of the event, how can we say they are important as context? My next examples illustrate our use of backgrounded, non-focal, incidental information.

Context in humor

One evidence that we notice context is that we make humor about mismatches of speaker characteristics and language and of physical setting and language. Many cartoons are based on a clash between the expectations from the picture, which is the context, and the caption. Normally we process the picture rapidly before we read the caption. For example, we see an organist in a giant cathedral playing the organ. We expect a magnificent piece of music. Then the caption tells us what he is singing while playing: *I love coffee, I love tea, I love the girls and the girls love me,* a two-finger exercise.

We also note discrepancies of style and content in cartoons where occupations are identified. These are funny because certain kinds of talk fit particular work in particular settings. In a cartoon, two women in aprons are cleaning up the debris in a deserted corporate boardroom. One says *The tumult and the shouting cease, the captains and the kings depart.* We saw the image of cleaning women, but we were unprepared for them to quote Kipling. It is not what we expect them to be talking about while cleaning; in addition we may not even expect that memorizing Kipling was part of their education. It is both a situational shock and a social background shock. In other kinds of cartoons, the *New Yorker* has judges talking legalese at home to their wives. The following excerpt of stand-up comedy on a recording is another example of work talk brought home. The asterisks indicate special emphasis on the following word.

(1) Airline attendant and husband at breakfast.
W: I *am preparing a *beverage, but if you'd *rather go *without it I'll *certainly hold it *back for you.
H: *No, *look I can't *stand it any more, do you understand me? I can't *bear it, I'm getting *out, I *quit, I want a *divorce!
W: We-ell, if you *do *feel that *way about it, I'd suggest that you *wait until perhaps *3 PM when I *will be back from shopping at the beautiful *Saks Fifth Avenue.

Nichols & May, 1959

The clash here is at several levels, between setting and occupational talk and between content and style. In addition there is a parody, which wouldn't be funny if we have not been listening to the singsong of stereotypical airline attendants' talk. The features of this style can be said to **index** or call to mind airline attendants as speakers, and airlines as settings, showing us that we have been noticing backgrounded information about style.

Humor is a good test of what people know. The spontaneity of laughter shows that audiences notice these features of speech that index setting and speaker characteristics. The humor in cartoons depends on delicate timing because the caption must catch us just as we have made an inference from the picture about what the people might be saying or how they would be talking.[2]

Context in address

Let me turn now to research on particular speech features that are sensitive to context. The first case is naming, which is familiar to all of us.

(2) Southern white police officer to adult Black male in the 1950s.

O: What's your name, boy?

P: Dr. Poussaint. I'm a physician.

O: What's your first name, boy?

P: Alvin.

"As my heart palpitated, I muttered in profound humiliation. . . . For the moment, my manhood had been ripped from me. . . . No amount of self-love could have salvaged my pride or preserved my integrity. [I felt] self-hate."

Poussaint, New York Times, 1967, p. 53

In working on naming (Ervin-Tripp, 1973, p. 305), I showed schematically in a flow chart of choice points how a northerner in my generation arrived at address terms. Generally such an address choice schema starts with child/adult status of the addressee and with the setting (e.g., *Your Honor* when addressing a judge in court, but not outside the court). This southern policeman was brought up to address adult white males as *sir.*, but the policeman had a selector in his address system for ethnic categorization, which involved calling adult Blacks with the first names, as if they were children.[3] These two understood each other perfectly.

Context in request forms

Requests involve another speech act where many features of context systematically affect choice, but not in such a direct way. The factors affecting requests can include relative status and familiarity with the addressee, cost or difficulty of the request in terms of the addressee's current activity, and physical distance. We noticed that physical distance mattered, because in a study of requests in an office, a staff member speaking to a peer nearby might say *Bring me the file,* but to someone further away *Bring me the file, would you, Rose?* (Ervin-Tripp, 1976).

In some quotes taken from a campus medical laboratory (Ervin-Tripp, 1976), we see a technician who indexed familiarity when he was alone with a doctor he worked with: *Hey, Len, shoot the chart to me willya?* but he shifted to a style which indexed the doctor's higher status when outsiders were present: *Shall I take it now, Doctor?* These shifts reveal sensitivity to contextual information.

We found that one of the major determinants of request mitigation, that is moving to a more polite request, was asking for something outside of role, that is extra, beyond

---

[2] If you show a cartoon on an overhead projector that distorts the size relation of picture to text, it can fail to be funny, showing that the relative processing time for picture and text is crucial to the humor.

[3] There were "respect" variants for older addressees involving kin terms.

normal expectation, as in the example below.

(3) Husband and wife serving stepfather.

[Wife to her husband Ben]

Bring some out, so that Max could have some too. . . .

Geschmacht. Hmm. Oh it's delicious!

Ben could you hand me a napkin please?

Example provided by Harvey Sacks

Here we see the wife can address direct, unmitigated imperatives to her husband in the co-host role since someone else is beneficiary, but she uses a mitigated request when the beneficiary is herself.

Understanding intent

The wife said "Ben could you hand me a napkin?" Why can't Ben just answer "yes" to this question? It is the case that a great many utterances which are treated as requests by listeners could be taken as something else. They look like something else. When I asked a child *Why are you in the garden with your socks on?* I was surprised to hear an explanation rather than to see an exit from the garden or removal of socks, since I heard what I said as a directive. We are surprised when a 10-year-old to whom we say on the phone *Is your Dad there?* says *Yes* and does nothing about it. Below is an example of another misunderstanding.

(4) A misunderstanding between a foreign student and an elderly landlady.

A: Can we move the trash bin over here?

L: Oh, Anna, I didn't know you had a roommate!

This problem arose because of two misunderstandings. One was the *we,* which is used downward by authorities, as in the teacher's *let's take our naps now* or the doctor's *we should check his temperature every couple of hours.* In the context of conventional action, *we* from an authority can mean *you.* Anna used *we* to mitigate a directive, but the landlady heard it as a request for permission. What Anna meant was *could you move the trash bin over here?* or even *could you have the trash bin moved over here?*

Permission requests and directives for the hearer to act, like *can I have some juice,* often look alike. What prevents these apparent ambiguities from causing trouble is that people take contextual expectations, or action trajectories, and social information into account. That is, there are always two interpretive processes. One is understanding the message about action in the current or future time. The other is understanding the social message about status, emotion, or distance in the context of speaking. In most contexts at least one of these aspects is conventional or obvious, so the other can be calculated. Since the context is known before the message is heard, there is little risk of ambiguity. The backgrounded context is thus what makes the other kind of meaning unambiguously interpretable.

Marking social relationship

Naming and requesting appear to be occasions which are not so necessary or unavoidable as to require the indexing of social relationship in every interaction. For instance, we know people who simply avoid naming because they cannot figure out how to position themselves. There are European languages in which reference to a hearer's action or possessions requires choice of familiar or formal, *tu* or *vous* or *usted* or *lei*, *du* or *Sie*. So in awkward situations one does not refer to the addressee in any way. But in Korean and a number of other languages, one cannot talk at all without such social indexing, since every finite verb requires a marker. Even in a comment that it is raining, one must indicate relative social status; these forms are used everywhere, even within the family.

(5) Korean social marking in a church group in the United States[4]

[Eunsun is a 29-year-old-woman in charge of music. Gwangsu is a 33-year-old male economist, president of the church group. Gwangsu is angry at a suggestion of Eunsun and shouts.]

1 Bintae: Please state **-shi** that as a suggestion, and. . . .
2 Gwangsu: <u>No,</u> even after you came to the United States. . . .
3 Chuhee: Let's control our emotions **-ta.**
4 Gwangsu: <u>No</u> you are just . . . The members are expecting only
5 to be receivers and even now,
6 does <u>anyone</u> know everyone's name?
7 That's <u>impossible!</u>
8 Hey, you <u>don't</u> do things like a GAME.
9 <u>Why should we do that?</u>
10 Eunsun: I'm not talking about doing anything like a GAME-**eyyo.**
11 Gwangsu: <u>No!</u> communication is the <u>best means</u> of
12 fellowship-**eyyo.**. [stands up]
13 {[in English] OOOOOKAAYYY? COMMUNICATE!
14 COMMUNICATE!
15 [claps hands, stepping towards each member]
16 ONE! AFTER! ANOTHER!}
17 Chuhee: Please calm down-**shi-eyo.**   Song, 1994

In the Korean part of the text there are two types of marking, the verb suffix *-shi* and the sentence-final markers *-ta* and *-yo*, involving the formality of the situation and the degree of deference to the addressee (See Table 1.1). The *-shi* suffix is the informal polite verb marker. Notice that in lines 4 to 9 Gwangsu does not use any status markers at all. Korean speakers hear this segment as very rude indeed. It's hard to think of what would be comparable, perhaps like shouting "you idiot" at someone. The forms used in the rest of the segment are informal but deferential markers appropriate to speaking about and to people who are not intimates. After it is modeled in 10, Gwangsu uses the appropriate sentence marker in 12. The *-ta* form in 3 is in the first person so it is not deferential, since it concerns the first person. Note that it is not, therefore, a request as in line 17 or in Text 4 above.

---

[4] For ease of reading, the Korean part of the text is given in lower case English, with the markers of status in boldface. Only the upper case segment 14-17 was actually spoken in English.

TABLE 1.1. Korean Speech Levels and Contexts in Sentence-final Markers

Speech level	Context	Declarative	Question	Order/Request
Deferential (jondaetmal)	formal	-pnita	-pnika?	-shipshiyo
	informal	-yo	-ngayo?/ -nayo?/ -uyo?	-sayo
Semi-deferential	formal	-o	-na?	-gae
	informal		-nga?	-shio/-so
Non-deferential (panmal)	formal	-ne	-ni?	-ae
	informal	-ta	-nya?	-ra

So, 1984.

The important fact about Korean is that you must know the addressee's relative age and status to be able to talk to anybody, and you keep reminding people of your age and status by the speech markers you use. You can hear new acquaintances spend five minutes learning when each graduated, what their occupation and company is, and if they are women, whether they are married, and whether they have sons. In order to avoid doing this, sometimes bilinguals switch to English (Howell, 1967).

Code-switching

Gwangsu shifted to English in 13 to 16. English allows him to approach and direct each person but again it takes him away from the distancing markers normal to Korean and makes his colleagues nervous, if we judge the comment in 17.

Code-switching is the most dramatic way of making a shift in context for interpreting speech. Bilinguals frequently do not recall the language of an interactional event. That is, they treat the language, if it was not unusual, as a background feature, using it in interpretation but not storing it as focal information.

Why is the particular language spoken relevant in interpretive outcomes? We all are aware that languages code the physical world differently. A vivid example is the difference between the Navaho and English color system. We tested English and Navaho monolinguals on a range of hue chips controlled for intensity and brightness, and found two points of major difference (Ervin, 1961). The low-brightness mustards were called *hlitso* by almost all the Navahos, who responded quickly, but Anglos were not agreed on naming these hues,[5] only 30% naming them hesitantly a qualified *yellow*, and Anglos call *yellow-green* what is still a good *yellow* for Navahos. The range of hues Anglos call *green*, *blue*, and *purple* are all called *doothlizh* by Navahos, albeit often with nuancing

---

[5] Respondents were asked to name colors, so both the hue name and the time of response when shown a Munsell color ship were recorded. In the "best" or prototypic hues, close to all respondents agree on the name, but at the boundary between two hues, only half give a particular color name.

qualifiers. In English, Navaho speakers still consider *hlitso* to be *yellow*, since there is no good competitor. Navaho dominant-bilinguals had great difficulty in naming chips in the range of *dootlizh* in English; it is unforgettable to hear a Kelly green called *purple* or a purple called *green*. Bilinguals keep the Navaho boundary for green/yellow in English because the categorization of the yellows is less ambiguous in Navaho than in English, but when English insists on dividing up a single Navaho category, and provides no dominant translation for the Navaho name, the amount of experience with the second language predicts sharpness of the new category boundaries.

In addition to physical world category differences, speakers do not have the same ideas about the social world when they shift language. If you require that a particular language be spoken, you can alter message content. In a pilot study as a graduate student in the early fifties, I showed the same picture to Japanese bilinguals, and instructed them to tell stories at one session in Japanese, and in the other, in English. The Japanese bilinguals in the study were American-born Nisei graduate students who had grown up on the West coast until being relocated during World War II. One Thematic Appercep-tion Test picture showed a woman standing in front of a field where a man was plowing. These are the two stories told by the same speaker, revealing difference in family thematic focus. In a later study, involving direct instruction to use a stereotype (Ervin-Tripp, 1967), I was able to show that these story contrasts with language context cannot be simulated easily under instructional set.

(6) *Thematic Apperception Test* picture stories by the same speaker.
[The picture depicts a woman standing in front of a field, with a farmer ploughing]
[in Japanese]
A student is in conflict about being sent to college because her mother is sick and her father has to work very hard to support the student. The father prays for the student's success.
[in English]
A sociology student observes farmers at work and is struck with the difficulties of farm life.

In Japanese, the students tended to talk more about their families, and less about study-ing. I also asked them to complete sentences. The beginning of the sentence is shown in boldface.

(7) Sentence completions by the same speaker on two occasions.
[in Japanese]:
If the work is too hard for me, he says "well, this is merely . . ." and as if whip-ping himself, he works all the harder.
[in English]:
If the work is too hard for me, I'll just quit.
[in Japanese]:
I like to read about sociology.
[in English]:
I like to read comics once in a while because they sort of relax my mind.
[in Japanese]:
My greatest pleasure is to graduate from graduate school.

[in English]:

My greatest pleasure is to lie on the sands of the beach out West.
This was the same speaker, replying on two different occasions in the two languages. Last year one of my Asian-American students studied what is called the "model minority" fallacy. In the difference between the English and Japanese replies, by speakers a generation or more older than our students, we see the dilemma. In one language they are the model minority, in the other, they don't want to be.

The important point for my purposes here is that language choice, whether spontaneous or required, alludes to values and can background interpretation. So even when bilingual speakers cannot recall the language in a segment of talk, we find they use language as contextual information to interpret meaning.

Another context is shared experience or something mentioned earlier in the discourse which sets up expectations for what follows.

(8) Two brothers in a round of earthquake narratives.[6]

a   Art: you know... you know that that nice glass china display case in our
             dining room?
b   Neal: ==in the dining room.
c   Cass: oooooh.
d   Neal: trashed
e   Cass: forget it
f   Neal: absolutely trashed
g   Art: ==whole thing a=bsolutely=
h   Neal: =every single bit of glass and=
i   Neal: =pottery in th-=
j   Art: =   yeah=
k   Olga: ==and crystal?
l   Neal: ==all the crystal trashed
m   Art: ==crystal
n   Neal: ==everything trashed
o   Cass: oooh my *gaaawd

UCB Disclab: QUAKE

Since this story is from a round of stories about the effects of a recent California quake, the previous context sets up preliminary components, so the main event does not need to be mentioned.

CONTEXT IN ACQUISITION

Is this sensitivity to the nonverbal and verbal aspects of context simply a result of adult sophistication, or do we have to consider identifying the details of context sensitivity as

---

[6] In this text, == indicates "latching" or picking up the turn on the beat as if the same speaker were continuing without a pause; = xxx = indicates a segment overlapped with another simultaneous passage.

part of our language learning skill? Context sensitivity was part of our prehuman heritage, and was not relinquished when language developed. A basic condition for language learning is juxtaposition of symbol and event, so learners have to attend to both text and context. They have to make the link to give meaning to the symbols. So let us turn to language learning issues.

Context for purposes of learning can include:
* the physical and social setting,
* the event or activity that occurs in that setting,
* the understood goals and emotions of participants,
* the local topic,
* any speech that is retained, at least the preceding turn, including of course the code used.

Evidence of children's notions of physical context

From the earliest ages, children notice the background contextual information we have been talking about. They pay attention to the physical context of use first, including the people present, as the history below of learning about *from* illustrates. The children begin with the directional, physical orientation, then later the *by means of* use can be seen, which for some children yields *from* answers to *how* questions.

(9) Examples of *from*

2;2 It came from my book-box.
2;3 It come from in the bathroom.
2;5 It came from my toe. [of sock]
2;11 Look at that knocked down tree from the wind.
3;0 I not tired from my games.

Clark, 1993, p. 58.

2;5 A: What do they taste like? (play-doh worms)
    C: Taste from right in here.
       (points in mouth — means they taste bad.)
2;5 A: Where did you get this?
    C: From Daddy.
2.11 C: Because I dropped my rifle on my toe.
       Because I hurt my toe from my rifle.
3;01 A: Ask Chicken Little how do you drink, Harvey.
    C: I drink from a cup.

Miller-Ervin UC Transcripts[7]

Notice that at first *from* means physical directional source. Clark's data give consistently *it came from* or *it come from* (compare *it came off*) even when an adult speaker would have a different wording. That is, the first meaning of *from* is a spatial, directional one. Adults often ask where something comes from or came from. The extension to

---

[7] Coded and computerized transcripts constructed by Wick Miller in the early sixties, now maintained in the disclab account of the cogsci.berkeley.edu computer, accessible by request.

causality is modeled in such adult uses as *He got a bruise from falling down, they're sticky from cooking*, and *you'll get cavities from candy.*

Children notice what is present in the physical context of speech and learn very early in Korean to simply omit noun arguments of the verb in talking about what is present, to presuppose them (Clancy, 1993). Presence in talk as a referent comes to play the same role as physical presence, by age 3. That is the age when English-speaking children have learned to supply pronouns in anaphoric cases where nouns occurred in recent talk (Ervin-Tripp, 1977).

Speech events as context

While turns, or response forming, is one of the earliest kinds of evidence of discourse organization (Ervin-Tripp, 1977), as soon as they play with one another, children begin to form ideas about speech events as organized contexts. Even an 18-month-old may report a phone conversation as *Hi Fine Bye.* So the outlines of speech events are part of the contexts that children come to identify.

(10) Spanish-speaking 5-year-old, with 7 months in English
S: Hello
E: What's you doin?
S: Fine
E: My mommy told me to go to school.
S: Me too.
E: OK, bye. I'll call you back tomorrow.
S: OK, bye.

Ervin-Tripp, 1981

In the above example we see the bare outlines negotiated successfully by a second language learner, including the salutation, correct response to the first move, content acknowledgment, and repetition of farewell.

(11) Spanish-speaking immigrant aged 5, with 5 months in English
S: Hello, come to my house, please.
E: Who are you?
S: Nora
E: Nora, you've got to say, "what are you doing?"
S: What are you doing?
E: Making cookies. What are you doing?
S: Making cookies, too.
E: OK, bye.
S: Bye.

Ervin-Tripp, 1986

In this case something has to be taught, since the child has moved into the content without the correct first move after the greeting. The native speaker makes clear that there is a required first entry after the salutation. In this example we see that the recognizable speech event, a telephone call, has come to have normative components. Children can come to recognize the limited set of appropriate moves at each phase, so each utterance is interpreted according to its place in the event organization.

Although we have seen that adult request forms can be complicated or superficially ambiguous, the contrast between requests and non-requests is evident and important to children. Some children even mark the contrast in their speech, as some languages do. For instance, Budwig (1989) found that some children use a different first-person pronoun for the subject in requests than they do in information statements: *my want that* but *I like that*. *My build tower* represents a desire, and *I see kitty* represents a report, for such a child.

Even more dramatically, Julie Gerhardt (Gee & Savasir, 1986) found that 3-year-olds use the supposed English synonyms *gonna* and *will* very differently. *Will* is the future form for offers, requests, compliance, for agreement, for responding to the other, for questioning desires. *Gonna* is the form for talking about personal goals and intentions (like *I'm gonna be the mommy*), for statements, and for impersonal questions. In short *gonna* is the term for planning, *will* for enacting collaboration with another.

Interpersonal acts as contexts for syntax

Children's requests are a privileged context for certain syntactic advances. The first temporal and causal clauses occur in children's requests and negotiations of future plans.

(12) Speaking to doll
2;3 would you like some juice?
     would you like some more juice, after you eat these?

Ervin-Miller transcripts, UC Disclab

(13) Circus figures doll-play
4;7 M: {[fortis] can I have him because I *like him!}

Kyratzis, 1993

(14) 4-year-old peers
     [John grabs a clown from Carl]
     a clown, guess what I think, cause I have a clown.
     so this is mine, I got an exciting show.

Kyratzis, 1992

(15) Story retelling of 7-year-old girls
     the little *sister *cried, because her brother turned into a *deer.

Kyratzis, 1993

The first causal clauses justify requests. Kyratzis saw many of these in boys' disputes over toys (13, 14). The last example, from a girl's narrative (15) shows the extension of causal clauses from use to justify, which occur in younger children (Kyratzis, Guo, & Ervin-Tripp, 1990), to use for conveying propositional truth relations. Thus grammatical form use is sensitive to the interpersonal functions of language.

Since requests are important to children, and of high frequency, children are sensitive to the form and context variations involved. By 4 they have learned to mark high cost requests to high status persons and strangers differently. They address more polite requests to their fathers than to their mothers, and to owners or at least possessors of toys (Ervin-Tripp, 1982).

The reasons they do this are not clear. Many parents are under the illusion that politeness is learned because it is rewarded. When the likelihood of compliance was high (what we call low-cost requests), politeness actually reduced compliance, according to our data. But the child observes that in cases where compliance is not expected — like asking for something owned or in use — the most effective directives to younger children are aggravated, and the least effective are polite. Loud, angry commands are effective in compelling obedience from younger siblings. And mitigation is less effective to adults than a simple command or request. In conditions where compliance was unlikely (what we call high cost cases), adults complied[8] with 42.6% of plain, unmitigated commands or requests, but only 26.8% of polite requests by children (Ervin-Tripp, Guo, & Lampert, 1990).

The only condition in which there is a payoff for politeness is in talking to older children. Children addressing control acts to peers or older children were successful only 23.8% of the time with neutral direct forms, but 52.6% of the time with polite forms (Ervin-Tripp et al., 1990). The reason for that is clear. Adults are not interested in getting their status rewarded by children, but other children are. Studies in nursery schools also show that subordinate children give more polite requests to dominant children (Wood & Gardner, 1980). Status is up for grabs between children so they pay attention even to symbolic rewards such as being spoken to with respect. Sometimes that is their major focus (Mitchell-Kernan & Kernan, 1977). But we noticed that adults rewarded by compliance neither aggravation nor mitigation in the speech they receive from children.

Understanding directives

If the context of speech is important in establishing how children interpret what is said, what happens when the surface message appears to contradict the context? We did a set of studies in which there were both requests and prohibition events. We created comic books and dialogue, and asked the children to make an outcome. In one story, children were making a mess by spilling food on the living room furniture and rug. When a mother's voice said *are you spilling food*? the children told us the mother wanted the children to stop. In one project, we located American and English children who had lived in Geneva, Switzerland, six to nine months and were in French-medium schools. When we used the food-spilling story with such children in Geneva, and had the mother say, *Eh ben, c'est bien*, the child would still say the mother wanted them to stop. But when for this sample of children we did the story in English, and the mother said *Great, go right ahead, it's good*, children under 7 were baffled. *She's lying, she's tricking*, they say. After 7, they did not expect literal prohibitions any more, even in English, and could interpret the sarcasm.

What this tells us is that language choice provides clues to the interpretation of meaning. Children in Geneva told us they had heard in French this type of sarcastic comment, which is routine in families in continental Europe. They learn early what it

---

[8] We are not sure how adult compliance is altered by videotaping in the home — the conditions under which our data were gathered.

means. English and American children do not hear this type of conversational challenge in their families. When they live in Geneva, they can recognize it in French, however, because it is in the context of French conversations that they hear such talk (Ervin-Tripp, Strage, Lampert, & Bell, 1987).

Code-switching

Children, like adults, switch language to convey new meanings, changing the cultural resources they can draw upon. The belief contexts for their speech have changed along with the language.

(16) Dispute between two Chinese 5-year-olds in American classroom
A: My father, bigger your father.
B: You father big big big big big
A: My father my father like that [reaches high]
B: My father stronger your father!
A: My father like that [wide stretch]
B: Hunhuh, my father stronger, faster.
      [switch to Cantonese]
A: I'm gonna tell your father that you steal things.
B: When did I steal things?
      [A enumerates]
A: When we go outside, I'm gonna hit you.
B: Well, you'll have to run very fast.....
A: ....When you grow up and you steal, your wife isn't going to like you.

Ervin-Tripp, 1981

Now it strikes me that this is an un-American prediction. It would not have been made in English.

Children's subtle observation of the background features of adult speech is never revealed so fully as in their role play. Below are some segments from studies of doll and puppet play in 4- and 5-year olds.

(17) Role playing with dolls
Director: uh now *pretend he doesn't have a broken*arm
Doctor: {[lower pitch] *well, we were *wrong about the broken *arm}

Kyratzis, 1993

(18) Puppet play
Child DOCTOR: uh *well I think ya have a *hernia
Adult PATIENT: what's a *hernia?
Child DOCTOR: it's a *sickness like a *disease..... well **she's dead.

Andersen, 1990

(19) Puppet play
Child FATHER: will my little girl be okay?
Child DOCTOR: yes, she vill. but do you vant to sleep with her all night
                 long? For every day?
Child FATHER: well, yes, I do.   Andersen, 1990

In these scenes, the father and the doctor display their authority with *well* as a marker of being in charge, as well as technical vocabulary. In addition, the voice pitch distinguishes men from women, and sometimes doctors from fathers. The German accent in (19) is another evidence doctors are special.

Andersen found that younger children change the accent and pitch to represent roles. Later they also change vocabulary, speech acts (who gives directives), and the style of directives. The subtlest feature noticed by the children was the coding of status by the little discourse markers at the beginnings of utterances, like these:

(20) Puppet play

Child teacher: *okay *now *well the first thing I would like to ask you
                have you ever been to school, 'kay?
Child teacher: *well now then I think you should
                take out your *papers.

Andersen, 1993

The children noticed that these markers occurred more in high status speakers, and that low status speakers used *uh* more often. The *okay* of teachers is of course stereotypical, but it is precisely these stereotypes that children are busy acquiring from incidental observation of speech features.

Anyone who speaks French knows that there is a high frequency of turn initiators like *eh bon, bien mais. . . .* The French children in playing roles mark status with the choice between these markers, with *bien* more frequent with higher status roles, and *eh* with lower status roles (Andersen, 1993).

CONCLUSIONS

What we have found is that children are sensitive to the social and interactional features of the context very early. These they encode linguistically by their choices of pronouns, person, aspect, modal auxiliaries, pitch, prosody, discourse markers, register, and vocabulary choice. If they are bilingual, they switch language for social purposes, altering rhetorical resources and cultural allusions.

When we look at natural talk we find it filled with indicators of the setting. This situational indexing is learned very much in the same way as word meaning, by a very powerful context-sensitive memory device. Contextual co-occurrences with linguistic features are stored in a frequency calculator, so that the correlated features come to index context, and indeed can be used to change the social interpretation of any malleable features such as situation and status. Economies of form can then occur through multiple meanings (polysemy). That is, if a form changes its interpretation according to context, the storage process must include information about the relevant contextual factors. Since such polysemy is very frequent, the human mind must prefer polysemy and contextual indexing over simple vocabulary expansion.

The language acquisition system cannot discriminate what will go into the dictionary and the grammar from the rest of contextual information. Evidence that there is massive learning of language features beyond those described in current lexicons and grammars suggests that current theories of language acquisition have too narrow a definition of language.

Why have we so systematically kept context out of the language system? There are certain points where it crept in even in the most formalist linguistics. There was no way to deal with such differences as imperative versus interrogative without at least thinking about function (though as we have seen, the relation is complex). Languages like Korean, which index addressee or referent status, force us to find out what status is for the speaker. Robotics designers have been compelled to address those aspects of context at the time of speech that would affect the ability of the machine to carry out commands, that is, aspects of language dealing with contextual physical features such as motion and direction. Such attention is within the paradigm of focused attention and reference mapping. But directions for robots, unlike human directions, do not have to deal with extensive presupposition and allusion. Robots are not polite. They do not run the risks that airline pilots do, of failing to understand directives because of social masking (Linde, 1988).[9]

The omission of context from linguistic accounts has occurred because some linguists have considered contextual structure to be too chaotic, too idiosyncratic, to be characterized systematically. When linguists began to identify variable rules (Labov, 1969), the separation of the variable from the obligatory or categorial was obvious and unavoidable. Variationists have gradually introduced context into their analyses. What we are now beginning to do is use contrasts in linguistic features, including those that are variable, as our guideposts for identifying both the structure of conversation and the structure of context, indeed the immediate social structure for speakers. Linguistic features can tell us what are natural human categories for context. Such an approach can at last systematize the domain of context.

REFERENCES

Andersen, E. (1993, July). *Discourse markers in children's controlled improvisation.* Paper presented at the International Association for the Study of Child Language, Trieste.

Andersen, E. (1990). *Speaking with style: The sociolinguistic skills of children.* London: Routledge.

Budwig, N. (1989). The linguistic marking of agentivity and control in child language. *Journal of Child Language,* **16,** 263-284.

Clancy, P. (1993). Preferred argument structure in Korean acquisition. In E. V. Clark (Ed.), *The proceedings of the 25th annual Stanford Child Language Research Forum* (pp. 307-314). Stanford: CSLI.

---

[9] Linde's study of airplane crashes and airplane simulated cockpit exchanges revealed that important warnings from subordinate personnel might be couched in the language of deference and fatally ignored.

Clark, E. (1993). *The lexicon in acquisition.* Cambridge, England: Cambridge University Press.

Ervin, S. M. (1961). Semantic shift in bilingualism. *American Journal of Psychology,* **74**, 233-241.

Ervin-Tripp, S. M. (1967). An Issei learns English. In J. Macnamara (Ed.), *Problems in bilingualism. Journal of Social Issues,* **23**(2) 78-90.

Ervin-Tripp, S. M. (1973). *Language acquisition and communicative choice.* Stanford, CA: Stanford University Press.

Ervin-Tripp, S. M. (1976). Is Sybil there: Some American English directives. *Language in Society,* **5**, 25-66.

Ervin-Tripp, S. M. (1977). Early discourse: Some questions about questions. In M. M. Lewis, & L. A. Rosenblum (Eds.), *Interaction, conversation, and the development of language.* New York: Wiley.

Ervin-Tripp, S. M. (1981). Social process in first and second language learning. In H. Winitz (Ed.), *Native language and foreign language acquisition (Annals).* New York: New York Academy of Science.

Ervin-Tripp, S. M. (1982). Ask and it shall be given you: Children's requests. In H. Byrnes (Ed.), *Georgetown Roundtable on Languages and Linguistics* (pp. 232-245). Washington, DC: Georgetown University.

Ervin-Tripp, S. M. (1986). Activity structure as scaffolding for children's second language learning. In W. Corsaro, J. Cook-Gumperz, & J. Streeck (Ed.), *Children's language and children's worlds, vol. 1* (pp. 327-358). Berlin: Mouton de Gruyter.

Ervin-Tripp, S. M., Guo, J., & Lampert, M. (1990). Politeness and persuasion in children's control acts. *Journal of Pragmatics,* **14**, 195-219.

Ervin-Tripp, S. M., Strage, A., Lampert, M., & Bell, N. (1987). Understanding requests. *Linguistics,* **25**, 107-143.

Gee (Gerhardt), J., & Savasir, I. (1986). On the use of *will* and *gonna*: Towards a description of activity-types for child language. *Discourse processes,* **8**, 143-176.

Howell, R. W. (1967). *Linguistic choices as an index to social change.* Unpublished doctoral dissertation, University of California, Berkeley.

Kyratzis, A. (1992). Gender differences in the use of persuasive justification in children's pretend play. In K. Hall, M. Buchloltz, & B. Moonwoman (Eds.), *Locating power. Proceedings of the Second Berkeley Women and Language Conference* (vol. 2 pp. 326-337). Berkeley CA: Berkeley Women and Language Group, University of California.

Kyratzis, A., & Ervin-Tripp, S. M. (1993, July). *Discourse markers in child-child interaction.* Paper to International Association for the Study of Child Language, Trieste.

Kyratzis, A., Guo, J., & Ervin-Tripp, S. M. (1990). Pragmatic conventions influencing children's use of causal expressions in natural discourse. *Proceedings of the Sixteenth Annual Meetingof the Berkeley Linguistics Society,* **16**, 205-215.

Labov, W. (1969). Contraction, deletion, and the inherent variability of the English copula. *Language,* **45**, 715-62.

Linde, C. (1988). The quantitative study of communicative success: Politeness and accidents in aviation discourse. *Language and Society,* **17**, 375-399.

Mitchell-Kernan, C., & Kernan, K. (1977). Pragmatics of directive choice among children. In C. Mitchell-Kernan & S. Ervin-Tripp (Eds.), *Child discourse* (pp. 189-208). New York: Academic Press.

Nichols, M., & May, E. (1959). Improvisations: Conversation at breakfast. *Echo Magazine.*

Poussaint, A. F. (1967 August 20). A Negro psychiatrist explains the Negro psyche. *New York Times Magazine,* pp. 52 ff.

So, C. S. (1984). *Jondaetbupaeyungu: Hyunhaeng daewoobupae chaegaewas munjaejum.* Seoul, Korea: Hanshin Munwha.

Song, K. S. (1994, April). Competing ideologies and their impact on gender bias. Paper to Third Berkeley Women and Language Conference, Berkeley, CA.

Wood, B., & Gardner, R. (1980). How children get their way: Directives in communication. *Communication Education,* **29**, 264-272.

PART TWO:
PRAGMATICS AND SOCIOLINGUISTICS

2 THE LANGUAGE OF SOCIAL RELATIONSHIP[1]

Roger Brown
Harvard University

There is a very big idea in psychology and anthropology these days which can be missed because its parts are distributed across authors and fields and there is some shifting of conceptual terms. Nakedly stated, the idea is that the self in Japan, China, Korea, India, Java, Thailand, the East generally, with Japan usually named as the clearest case, is not the same as the self in the West, with the United States usually named as the clearest case. The self in the East is said to be relational, interpersonal, or collective whereas the self in the West is individualistic and autonomous. The self in the West is, furthermore, said by Deborah Tannen (1991) and Carol Gilligan (1986) to be more characteristic of men than of women. Women in the West are said to have a more relational, a more Eastern self. And, what is more, the deflection of the West from its present doomsday course is thought to depend on the moderation of Western male individualism by Eastern-and-female relationism (Geertz, 1975; Gergen & Gergen, 1988; Gilligan, 1982, 1986; Markus & Kitayama, 1991; Marselli, DeVos, & Hsu, 1985; Roland, 1988; Sampson, 1985, 1988, 1989; Shweder & Bourne, 1984; Shweder & LeVine, 1984; Tannen, 1991; Triandis, 1989; Triandis, Bontempo, Villareal, Asai, & Lucca, 1988).

Understandably, no one has cared to step forward as champion of so broad a thesis, so flatly stated. However, Hazel Markus and Shinobu Kitayama in the July, 1991, *Psychological Review* have been bolder and more inclusive than most. Their paper "Culture and the Self" sets forth implications for cognition, emotion, and motivation, together with some persuasive evidence. It is getting a lot of attention.

The self construed as independent is organized as a repertoire of attributes — more or less intelligent, sociable, practical, hard-working, sports-minded and the like; attributes conceptualized with little reference to others. Persons are thought to be inherently separate; connections are means to ends and can always be sundered.

For the self construed as relational, separation is a nightmare. It is imperative to maintain connections. Relations are primary goals in themselves and action is always contingent on the thoughts and feelings of others.

I have no trouble understanding what is meant by an individualistic autonomous self,

---

[1] This paper was given in slightly different form as the Neil Graham Lecture at the University of Toronto, November, 1991.

but my intuitive grasp of what is meant by a relational self is weak. To strengthen it I have been looking at differences in the expression of social relationship between Indo-European languages and Southeast Asian languages, particularly Japanese, Javanese, and Korean.

In any language whenever one person speaks to another, it is necessary before speaking to ask: "Who am I?" "Who is this other person?" "What is this person to me?" For the speaker of English the answer can be as simple as: "My role is that of the speaker, known as *I*; the other person's role is that of the addressee, called *you*." For French, as for all the major European languages, there is one contingency; the speaker is always *je*, but the addressee may be either *tu* or *vous* depending on the relationship between the speaker and the addressee. For Japanese, and some other Asian languages, the contingencies seem endless and there are diverse outcomes on every level of linguistic analysis. Most strangely to us and most interestingly for the theory of the relational self, the speaker cannot even choose a term of self-reference without considering the relation between the self and the addressee.

PRONOUNS OF ADDRESS

Forms of address, especially pronouns of address (Brown & Gilman, 1960), make a good entry point into the language of social relationship. As far as pronouns are concerned, present-day English is the most impoverished case. We have only *you* whether for many persons or for one person. In the past, however, English had *thou* as an alternative to *you* in speaking to one person, a pattern preserved forever in Shakespeare's plays. All the other Indo-European languages (whether Italic, Germanic, Slavic, or Indo-Iranian) have at least two possibilities, the most familiar cases being *tu* and *vous* in French, *du* and *Sie* in German, *tu* and *Lei* in Italian, *tu* and *Usted* in Spanish, *ty* and *vy* in Russian. In all these cases a form originally exclusively plural has been recruited historically to be used also as what is loosely called a polite singular. English added *you* to *thou* in imitation of the French court after the Norman invasion. The European forms can be traced back to Latin *tu* and *vos* and so the abstract symbols T and V are used to stand for no particular phonological realization but rather for pronouns that pattern in ways to be described in whatever language.

T and V are relational forms in the sense that their meanings do not crystallize on the level of either speaker alone or hearer alone. In this respect they are like kinship terms used as vocatives. Just as it is not a property of any person to be addressed by everyone as *mom, dad, son,* or *daughter*, it is not a property of anyone to be always addressed as T or as V. It depends — on the relationship between speaker and hearer. Kinship terms do not serve to relate each person in a community to each other person; for most dyads there is no kin term. Pronouns of address, however, constitute a fully connected language of social relationship. After 30 years of work by many scholars on many languages, it now appears that the same two dimensions universally underlie not only pronouns of address but all address forms, such as, in English, first name, title, and title plus last name. The dimensions are status and closeness or intimacy. The universality of these dimensions in address systems suggests that they are the basic dimensions of social life generally.

Status is the vertical of social life and it is an asymmetrical relation; one member of the dyad is higher and one is lower. The address pattern governed by status is likewise asymmetrical or nonreciprocal. The lesser member, or subordinate, gives V and receives T. On this abstract level the pattern is universal but the calculation of status is culture-specific. In one place or another, in one century or another, every sort of socially significant attribute has entered into the computation of relative status: sex, age, occupation, generation, caste, kinship (V to parent, T to child), lineage (V to nobility, T to peasants), religion (*thou* in Shakespeare's time to Shylock and to all Jews and Turks; *you* to the merchant Antonio and to all Venetians and Christians). The threshold for the expression of status differences, the magnitude of the interval that requires expression, is also culturally specific. It is not claimed that all actual differences of rank must be expressed asymmetrically. In America most of us are on a first-name basis very quickly, if not from the start. In Japan a one-year difference in year of graduation between schoolmates or in year of birth between brothers is expected to be reflected in different address choices for the full life of the relationships.

Intimacy, the term used to designate the range from stranger to close friend, is the horizontal of social life and it is a symmetrical relationship founded on similarity or identity in significant personal attributes that create like-mindedness. The address pattern governed by intimacy is also symmetrical: The two members of the dyad give the same pronoun. The difference is that strangers exchange V whereas intimates exchange T. The personal attributes taken account of in the computation of similarity are culture-specific and have included sex, age, kinship, birthplace, race, dialect, and, in general, just the same attributes that figure in the determination of status. For intimacy it is similarity that counts whereas for status it is relative value. Thresholds for the expression of intimacy are also culture-specific. Professor Roman Jakobson, the great linguist and speaker of many languages, once told me that when he would switch from, say, French to German, with a particular other person, he had to do a quick take on whether the two of them were on a mutual T basis in German as they were in French.

A society in which the asymmetrical status rule is pervasive suggests hierarchical organization whereas the symmetrical intimacy rule suggests pluralistic equality, and so it is not surprising that egalitarian social movements have often included the reform of pronominal address in their revolutionary programs. In France in 1793 the use of *vous* in the singular was condemned as a remnant of feudalism, and mutual *tu*, along with *citoyen* or *citoyenne*, were prescribed for all. In the Russian and Chinese Communist Revolutions it was the local version of mutual T and, of course, *comrade*. The Society of Friends or Quakers, a leveling movement in 17th century England, forbade its members to take off their hats to any, whether high or low, and required them to *thee* and *thou* all men and women without any respect for rich or poor, great or small. It should not be thought that such reforms were painlessly accomplished. Thomas Ellwood, a newly converted Quaker, has written that his father fell upon him with fists for giving him *thou*. Secretaries at the University of Stockholm in very recent years found themselves struck dumb by a new rule requiring them to say T to even the most elderly and eminent of professors.

The efforts to reform pronoun usage and, indeed, usage of all address forms seem implicitly to have assumed some kind of Whorfian position on language and thought. Mutual T should produce or facilitate or perpetuate equality and fraternity. In the event, however, all such reforms have by now failed and the asymmetrical status rule, along with the intimacy rule, is to be found everywhere. No society has ever eliminated status differences; probably they are needed to motivate qualified individuals to fill certain very demanding positions and it seems as though status differences always will find expression — in some linguistic way.

The consistent failure to reform T and V for reasons of ideology might seem to predict failure of the effort, now about 20 years old, to reform another pronoun, English generic *he*, as in "the child he," into something like *he-or-she*, in fairness to women, but in fact this second reform is coming along nicely and will, I think, succeed. Not in any of the ways prescribed or predicted since all of these think of reform as the replacement of one word by another. What is happening instead, I judge from my own writing and the writing of students, is that we have learned to spot the ideological rock downstream and get past it by any one of half a dozen alternatives, including *they* and *he* or *she*, or a slight redirection of course.

The normal rules for the use of T and V create the possibility of expressive uses which break the rule to express emotions or attitudes. There is, for instance, the T of contempt, used to a person entitled to V. In *Twelfth Night*, Sir Toby Belch urges Andrew Aguecheek to send a challenge to Cesario: "Taunt him with the license of ink, if thou thou'st him some thrice, it shall not be amiss." One theory of how English came to lose its *thou* holds that *thou* was so much used to abuse and depreciate that it became impossible to use it *routinely* to people on any status level whatever.

A SOCIOLINGUISTIC UNIVERSAL

There is, finally, a sociolinguistic universal in the use of T and V which tells us something universal about social relationship. Remember, if you will, that T and V are abstract symbols for certain patterns of usage and do not represent any actual words in any language. The universal goes like this: If there is a form, call it "T" or call it "X", that is used symmetrically between equal-status intimates, and if there is a form, call it "V" or call it "Y", that is used symmetrically between equal-status strangers, and if these same two forms, "X" and "Y", are also used asymmetrically between unequals, then it is always the case, in the dyad of unequals, that the intimacy form "X" is used downwards and the stranger form "Y" is used upwards. The logically possible alternative for the asymmetrical pattern, "Y" downwards and "X" upwards is never found. Why should this be so?

There is one additional universal that seems to offer a clue. Relationships between adults normally begin with mutual V. Sometimes, with continued interaction and discoveries of likemindedness, acquaintances advance in intimacy, and mutual T comes to feel right. The question is who will initiate the change or make the suggestion that both change? In German there is even a little ceremony called the *Bruderschaft.* One waits for a mellow occasion, perhaps with a glass of wine, and says: "Why don't we say T to one another?" One says it, but which one? The answer is unequivocal and seems everywhere to be the same. If there is any inequality of status, an advance of intimacy must be initiated by the superordinate: the elder, the nobler, the organizational superior. It was Freud who, after many years, finally suggested to his inner circle: "Why don't we say *du* to one another?"

We think that the invariant norm linking higher status and the extension of intimacy, as when a German professor says *du* and a student *Sie* or an American Professor uses first-name and a student uses title-plus-last-name, can be thought of as the initiation step in a frozen state. While frozen, and it may stay frozen for the life of the dyad, it represents the asymmetrical status pattern. It is not a disagreeable freeze because it looks for all the world as if the superordinate were offering the hand of friendly equality. Subordinates everywhere know, however, that it may not behoove them to grasp that hand right off and reciprocate with first name. Servants in 17th century France, though receiving T from their masters, were never to return it; African Americans in the South in the past, though called by their first names by Whites, were never to return the familiarity; American college students know that it is a delicate judgment when, if ever, to first-name any given professor.

The prescriptive rule that increases of intimacy should be initiated from above governs many kinds of behavior other than forms of address. Among Indian subcastes in Tamilnadu higher subcastes may give gifts of cooked food (a kind of intimacy) to lower subcastes but not vice versa. For American businessmen it is easier for a superior to ask for the loan of a comb from a subordinate than vice versa. There is the famous bridge party in *A Passage to India* when Mr. Turton, the chief British officer in Chandrapore, throws a party for high-ranking Indians — to bridge the gap between Indians and the Raj — but of course Indians were not free to invite him back, and the drama of the novel is propelled by one Dr. Aziz who, wanting to be friends with several English, invites them on an expedition to the Mirabar Caves. Finally, there is the *droit du Seigneur* or *Jus primae noctis* according to which the feudal lord had the privilege of the first night with the bride of any of his vassals. In *The Marriage of Figaro,* it is Count Almaviva's intention of exercising this privilege with Figaro's bride that creates the comic conflict.

Why should there be this particular rule for the development of familiarity between status unequals? It appears to be in direct opposition to social motivation. Status may be assumed to flow between unequals and so the junior member of a dyad of unequals should generally have more to gain from increased closeness than the senior member. Perhaps it is not too strong to say that the junior is always ready whereas the senior is not. Which is just why the rule must oppose the motivation. If juniors freely initiated moves to decrease distance, they might frequently experience rebuffs and that would create strain in the system, possibly even a move to deny status claims. The senior must be the Gatekeeper to minimize conflict.

Most of the work confirming the invariant norm has been done on Indo-European languages. All of these languages have second-person singular and plural pronouns which can be traced back thousands of years to Proto-Indo-European roots, and the use of the plural as a singular of deference in the 4th century seems to have been copied by one royal court from another. It is possible, therefore, that the so-called universal norm is really only an invariant of Indo-European languages and can be fully accounted for by common descent without invoking a general hypothesis about familiar relations between status levels. Japanese, Chinese, and Korean are not Indo-European languages and have no history of common descent. They, therefore, constitute a good test of the universality of the invariant norm.

In all three Asian languages the norm seems, superficially, to fail and always for the same reason. For example, in Japanese, close friends, both male, may exchange a pronoun like *kimi* or *omae* or first names, and strangers may exchange the pronoun *anata* or else last name with the suffix *-san* and, between unequals, it is the case, as the norm predicts, that the intimate forms are used downwards. The problem comes with address upwards to kinfolk of ascending generations or superiors in an occupational hierarchy. The rule is, for Japanese, that no pronoun whatever and no proper name may be used, but only kin terms like *father* or *grandmother* and occupational or professional titles like *Mr. Section Chief, doctor,* or *teacher* (Akimoto, 1990). The forms used upwards between unequals (kin titles or occupational titles) are, in other words, not the same as any of the forms used reciprocally, and so the preconditions for the universal norm are not satisfied and the universality of the invariant norm is not tested in these cases and, in fact, not testable in the usual way. The usual test can only be used when a language uses two forms to express three things: intimacy, distance, and inequality, which is the case for T and V in Indo-European languages but not for the three Asian languages. However, Kroger, Wood, and Kim (1984) have found ways of testing the Asian languages, not for the T and V pattern, but for the hypothesized links among intimacy, distance, and inequality in address forms of any kind, and their results confirm the hypothesized universal. There are confirming results also from other non Indo-European languages, especially Egyptian Arabic and Dravidian Tamil (Levinson, 1982), and so the claimed universality of the invariant norm remains unchallenged.

If I may repeat, the norm is not a direct expression of universal social-psychological motives but a universal control on motives. A control easily lifted for convivial occasions like APA social hours, but when it is in place, as it usually is, it serves to minimize the conflict that familiarity with inequality can cause.

SOCIAL REGISTERS

I have called T and V, titles, and names forms of address, and that they certainly are, but in more careful sociolinguistic use they are called "referent relationals" and distinguished from "addressee relationals." A referent relational, like T or V or a title, in expressing the speaker's relation to some addressee must, at the same time, *refer to* the addressee. An honorific like "your grace," similarly, *refers* to the one it honors. Addressee relationals, properly so called, are another matter. The honorific, or elevated, speech styles, or levels, of Japanese, Javanese, and Korean express respect for the addressee without referring to the addressee. Speech levels or styles are *ways of talking* which reveal the speaker's sense of his relation to the addressee without referring to the addressee; it is something like saying *residence* rather than *home, dine* rather than *eat, steed* rather than *horse*. All languages have referent relationals but only a few have well developed speech levels, and among these few are Japanese, Javanese, and Korean.

Honorific style in Japanese is to be distinguished from polite style and familiar style. Honorific style is the way to talk to people to whom one wishes to express special respect; polite style is usual style. Familiar style is for long-standing intimates, and the student of Japanese-as-a-second-language is sometimes advised that he need not learn to produce it because, as a foreigner, it will never be appropriate for him to use it. In Japanese the styles are distinguished from one another by lexical alternants such as *hito* which is neutral for *man* and *okata* which is honorific, *yaru* which is neutral for *I give* and *kudasuru* which is honorific. The styles are also distinguished by the prefixes *o-* and *go-* and the suffixes *-san* and *-sama* and by the verb ending *-masu* which, in regular ways, create honorific forms. And by much more.

In Javanese, the basic language is called *ngoko*. It is the level first learned in childhood and used throughout life with close friends or those of a lower social order and is said to be the language in which everyone thinks. Among higher levels of respect, the most important is called *krama*. *Krama* provides five-to-six hundred lexical variants for *ngoko* morphemes; for instance, *sega* is *ngoko* for *rice* and *sekul* is the *krama* alternative, *njupuk* means *take* in *ngoko* and the *krama* alternant is *mendhet*. It is difficult to be sure, but Javanese levels of respect seem to be more tightly constructed than Japanese styles in the sense of having stricter co-occurrence rules. Using the *ngoko* word for *take* entails using the *ngoko* word for *rice*. Stylistic combinations that violate rules, mixing words from different levels, would simply be uninterpretable in any social psychological way.

At first one thinks there is nothing in English at all comparable to the speech levels of Southeast Asian languages. However, the late Harry Levin at Cornell in recent years (Levin, Long, & Shaffer, 1981; Levin & Garret, 1990) made a good case for the existence of what he called a "formal register." The formal register in English is characterized by Latinate rather than Germanic words and, for Germanic words, low frequency, and by sentences having a difficult-to-process center-branching syntactic structure. It is, incidentally, interesting that "high style" in all the languages so far studied in this connection is more difficult in a language-processing sense than plain style. It is not learned early nor do all speakers attain the same level of competence. For especially skilled practitioners high style has an exhibitionistic and intimidating function (Smith-Hefner, 1988).

With our ears opened by Levin's research, we begin to notice the many uses of the English formal register. The heroine of Tennessee Williams's play *Summer and Smoke* is Alma Winemiller, a minister's daughter. Alma is Spanish for soul, did you know that, and this Alma is too soulful to win the man she loves and, in the last scene, falls so low as to pick up traveling salesmen. Williams characterizes Alma in part by assigning her a too formal register for every occasion, climaxing on a Fourth-of-July when she says to the young man she loves: "The pyrotechnical display is going to be brilliant but there really ought to be an ordinance forbidding firecrackers." *Pyrotechnical* and *ordinance* are low frequency Latinate words, and Alma's young man says: "Do you know that you have a reputation for putting on airs a little bit . . . you have a rather fancy way of talking . . . pyrotechnical display instead of firework, and that sort of thing."

At the ceremony last year of installation, or should I say investiture or inauguration, for the new president of Harvard, someone said that the first such ceremony had been entirely in Latin and we all chuckled at the vanity of our forebears and dozed as speakers used words like *installation, investiture, inauguration, intellectual, taxing, rewarding, improvisation, affliction, governing*, and *convention*. In fact, the ceremony still is in Latin or, at any rate, it is so Latinate as scarcely to be English at all.

PERSON FORMS IN JAPANESE

The speech levels of Asian languages are distinct strata in ways that formality in English is not, but the existence of these strata is not the most interesting thing for the theory of a relational self. The interesting thing is that in using speech levels, the speaker must be attentive to the self and all that appertains to the self, must distinguish a group to which the self belongs, an ingroup, from all outgroups. The basic principle of Asian politeness is always to humble the self and elevate others. Within the Japanese family, father is both addressed and referred to deferentially as *otoosan* and mother as *okaasan* and elder brother as *oniisan*. Referring to these same persons to an outsider, the speaker must not use the honorific ingroup elevating forms but the humble forms, *chichi* for father, *haha* for mother, and *ani* for elder brother. If, however, the speaker refers to members of the outsider's family, then it is the honorific forms that must be used. When the ingroup is the business firm rather than the family, the same principle applies. An employer will use humbling expressions to refer to members of his own company to an outsider. On the telephone, even a very junior member will refer to department head *Mori* as *buchoo* (department head) or *Mori,* not the more deferential *Mori-san*. The examples I have given happen to be referent honorifics but the same principle applies to the full range of addressee honorifics. For the actions, thoughts, and possessions of the self, honorific forms are never to be used. And, so, to speak politely, it is necessary to have always in mind, the extended self, the self and its close connections, distinguished from others and the connections of others.

I once heard a Japanese linguist begin a lecture by saying: "I am 48 years old." This was her dramatic way of illustrating how much must be known about the other person and one's relation to that person before speaking. Am I, for instance, younger or older? An age difference of 15 years or so can affect the choice of a second-person pronoun in an Indo-European language which may have two or three such pronouns. Japanese has six and any difference of age can determine which of the six, if any at all, can be used. But the psycholinguistic contrast comes nearer the self than second-person pronouns. If I were speaking Japanese, I would not even know how to formulate the question "Am I younger or older?" without "placing" the addressee because there are six first-person pronouns. In view of my relation to the lecturer, and the fact that she is female and I am male, should I refer to myself as *watakushi, watashi, atashi, boku, ore,* or, surely not, *wagahai.*

Probably I would use no first-person pronoun at all. If the lecturer has ever been a student of mine, even if it is now 15 years since she took her degree and even if she has become a very eminent scholar, she will still address me as *sensei* (teacher) and I, in speaking with her, will be entitled to use, and most likely use, *sensei* and not any first-person pronoun to refer to myself.

T and V, I have said, are strictly relational forms in the sense that it is not a property of a person to be always a T or a V, but one or the other, depending on the relation to the speaker. In Japanese, forms of self-reference are also, and in just the same sense, relational. The man who refers to himself as *sensei* to his students calls himself *otoosan* (or father) to his daughter, *oniisan* (or elder brother) to his younger brother, and to a neighbor's son, doing a little fictive kinship calculus, becomes *ojiisan* or uncle. It is as though the self were reconstrued, in each significant relationship, as a term in that relationship.

Dorinne Kondo, a Japanese-American anthropologist, in her book *Crafting Selves* (1990) writes eloquently about the effects of first-person reference in Japanese: "I never felt myself to be an autonomous freely operating individual. As a resident of a neighborhood, as a friend, a co-worker, a teacher, a relative, an acquaintance, a quasi-daughter, I was always defined by my obligations and links to others. I was always caught in webs of relationships . . . where relationships define one and enable one to define others. The epiphanal moment when I realized the lack of importance of any personal self apart from social obligations was perhaps the most eloquent in my experience . . . ."

Takao Suzuki, in his book *Japanese and the Japanese* (1978) draws equally strong conclusions: "Other-oriented self-designation is . . . the assimilation of the self, who is the observer, with the other, who is the observed, with no clear distinction made between the positions of the two. It is frequently pointed out that whereas Western culture is based on the distinction between the observer and the observed, on the opposition of the self versus the other, Japanese culture and sentiment show a strong tendency to overcome this distinction by having the self immerse itself in the other" (p. 145).

BEYOND LANGUAGE

And so we have arrived. The Japanese self is indeed relational in the sense of being thoroughly intertwined with others on the evidence of the structure of the Japanese language. And since the structure of Korean and Javanese are, in the relevant ways, the same, then we may conclude that Javanese and Korean selves are similarly relational. But — the seasoned and often-burnt student of language and thought must hold back. In the past, the evidence of language structure has not proved sufficient to establish psychological conclusions. Differences of color lexicon, strongly suggestive of differences in color perception, have turned out not to be correlated with color perception. Differences in numeral classifiers (between Navajo and English) strongly suggestive of differences in shape categories have turned out not to have such cognitive correlates (Brown, 1986). Differences between Chinese and English in the expression of counterfactual conditionals *irresistibly* suggestive of differences in logical reasoning seem to be associated with just the same universal logic (Au, 1983; Bloom, 1981). The lesson is that language structure can suggest psychological hypotheses, but it is necessary always to test such hypotheses in direct psychological ways. How might that be done with the hypothesis that the Japanese self is relational and the Western self independent and individualistic?

Japanese terms of self-reference and address follow the lines of reciprocal roles: parent-child, teacher-student, elder brother-younger brother, husband and wife. Such roles are inherently relational. The prescription for playing the role of a parent is written in terms of behavior toward children, not only the linguistic behavior of self-reference and address but everything that goes into child-rearing and lifelong concern. And the child's role is similarly defined in terms of what may be expected from parents and what is owed to them. If the Japanese, more than Americans, seem to identify the self with the roles that the self plays, that would be evidence that the Japanese self is more relational than the American self. So, not to put too fine a point on a blunt thought, let both Japanese and Americans be asked to answer the question "Who are you?" some 20 times. If the Japanese more often respond with role terms — an elder brother, a third-year student at Tokyo University, a married woman — that would be evidence of a more relational self. What should be the contrasting American specialty? Nonrelational attributes — the very stuff, as it happens, of all the American instruments that purport to map the self-schema — I am: intelligent, fun-loving, conscientious, and so on and so on.

There is plenty of expert testimony that, for the Japanese, one's social roles are very close to one's self. Lebra writes: "Role commitment among the Japanese can be so strong that . . . the role becomes the core of the individual's self-identity. The incidence of suicide due to an error in role performance demonstrates that role can become identical with self or can come to represent all meaning in life" (1976, p. 85). Observers agree also that what has been called "role perfectionism" (Befu, 1986) and "role narcissism" (De Vos, 1973) is the principal component of self-esteem. The anthropologist Harumi Befu (1986) who created the phrase "role perfectionism" comments: "The Japanese commitment to a role is a commitment to do well against all odds. The implication is also that, no matter how lowly the role might be, it is worthy of a person's utmost efforts" (1986, p. 25). For Ruth Benedict (1946), the name for the same central theme was "taking one's proper station." One of her illustrations is unforgettable. The Japanese have a saying equivalent to our "neither fish nor foul." It is "He is neither elder brother nor younger brother."

There is also linguistic evidence of the centrality to the Japanese self of social role and role perfectionism, evidence in addition to the structure of self-reference and other-reference. There is, for instance, the suffix *-rashii* which may be added to nouns naming categories of human beings but which does not make sense with every such category. We have explored the uses of *-rashii* with native speakers of Japanese and learned that it makes perfect sense to say *onna* (woman) *rashii, otoko* (man) *rashii,* and *otokonoko* (boy) *rashii.* A woman who is *onna rashii* would be sweet, refined, and graceful; a man who is *otoko rashii* would be *majime* (serious), decisive, and strong; a boy who is *-rashii* would be energetic, lively, and sturdy. An elder brother could be *-rashii*, an aunt, a policeman, but not, for instance, a stranger or an acquaintance.

What *-rashii* seems to mean is a model exemplar of a social role, the *real thing* as it were. This is an idea that we can express in English with one or another noun phrase construction. In Japanese, however, the idea has been grammaticized and in two instances lexicalized (*otokorashii, onnarashii*). This is a difference of codability and probably it means something. What it is likely to mean is that perfection in role performance is an idea more salient for the Japanese people than for Americans. As always, however, we cannot be sure without a more direct test.

Stephen Cousins, at the University of Michigan, has, in fact, made a first direct test (1989) by asking Japanese college students, in Tokyo, and American college students, in Ann Arbor, to answer the question "Who am I?" 20 times. Approximately 60% of American answers were psychological attributes whereas only about 20% of Japanese answers were attributes. Approximately 30% of Japanese answers were social roles and only about 10% of American answers. These results, as far as they go, confirm the hypothesis that the Japanese self is more relational than the American. There were, however, no significant differences between men and women of either nationality and so no support for the idea that women are more relational than men.

Several of us at Harvard, myself and Renée Oatway and Satohiro Akimoto, have done a "Who Am I?" study defining relational responses in a way that is closely linked with interpersonal language systems. Our results, obtained from the Japanese women only so far, are very close to those of Stephen Cousins. Japanese women respondents made twice as many relational-self answers as did Americans, and American respondents make four times the attribute answers given by Japanese. The specifics add interest to the general outcomes. Forty-two percent of the Japanese women specified their occupational positions in terms of school and year and 40% specified their family positions in terms of younger and older siblings. Very few American women "placed" themselves in either of these ways. In speaking Japanese, much hinges on these social positions; in speaking English, very little.

The most striking qualitative result to me was the complete absence from the self-characterizations of the Japanese women of what might be called the lexicon of independence; American women described themselves as "autonomous," an "individual," "self-motivated," a "free spirit," an "original," and, of course, an "independent woman." There are Japanese equivalents for all these terms but none, literally none, was ever used.

The "Who am I?" test is a simple way of operationalizing the relational self, but it does not contribute much to one's internal understanding. On that side I have learned the most from Junko Kaji (1993), who is not an anthropologist or a psychoanalyst, but an undergraduate concentrator in psychology at Harvard, and I will close by reading a few passages from her 1992 honors thesis "The Fragmentation of the Japanese-American Self."

"The conflict between my own Japanese and American halves is illustrated . . . by my understanding, or rather my misunderstanding, of two [basic] Japanese terms: *sunao* and *amae*. Since I grew up in a home where my parents and older sister spoke Japanese . . . I was exposed to these terms many times as I was growing up. However, I did not (and still don't) understand the concepts behind the words *sunao* and *amae* as they are understood by the Japanese. I had, I think, the [descriptive sense] of the Japanese words straight. What differed between my understanding and that of the [native]-born Japanese was the evaluative meaning I attached to those words and the concepts they represented.

"*Sunao* . . . refers to . . . a 'gentle sensitive heart' that is responsive to social demands [and] sensitive to social context.' . . . [It is an ideal for the Japanese]. Accordingly, my parents tried to teach me to be *sunao* — to be obedient and filial and to value these traits as the best possible attitudes for a child to take toward his or her parents. Unfortunately, by the time I was old enough to understand that *sunao* was the word to describe this concept, I had already realized that too much compliance with one's parents or with any other authority figure was viewed with suspicion and disdain by my peers. By the time I finished adolescence, during which time my mother would yell at me to be more *sunao* as I went through my acting-out and rebellious phases, I was convinced that *sunao* meant *spineless*. . . . This conflict between *sunao* and autonomy still exists, though I realize now that my parents are the only people in American society who expect *sunao* from me.

". . . *Amae*, the emotion corresponding to 'the sense of, or the accompanying hope for, being lovingly cared for, [that] involve depending on and presuming another's indulgence' . . . appears not to exist as a separately defined emotion in Western cultures . . . . I inferred my own definition of *amae* from the fact that I was always [said to be] *amaeteru* when I was trying to curry favor with my parents by being especially nice. . . . Again, I grasped the behavior involved but formed an incomplete idea of the concept. . . . I believed that if anyone were to notice that I was [using] *amae*, they would [want] to deny me what I was trying to get [by this contemptible means]. I therefore equated *amae* in my own mind with something like being a 'lick-spittle'. . . . I had no idea that *amae* could be a reciprocal emotion in that the person who is being 'buttered up' can more or less agree to be influenced by what still seems to me a rather slimy way to get something for nothing.

"That these interpretations were so inconsistent with what the words actually mean to real Japanese shows how seriously at odds . . . the Japanese and American parts of myself can be."

Someone imaginative may think of a convincing and simple way to test on the individual level for the difference between an autonomous and a relational self, but to my mind it hasn't happened yet.

REFERENCES

Akimoto, S. (1990). Japanese exceptions to the rules of address. Unpublished manuscript.

Au, T. K. (1983). Chinese and English counterfactuals: The Sapir-Whorf hypothesis revisited. *Cognition*, **15**, 153-187.

Befu, H. (1986). The social and cultural background of child development in Japan and the United States. In H. Stevenson, H. Azuma & K. Hakuta (Eds.), *Child development and education in Japan*.

New York: Freeman.

Benedict, R. (1946). *The chrysanthemum and the sword.* Boston, MA: Houghton Mifflin.

Bloom, A. H. (1981). The linguistic shaping of thought: A study in the impact of language on thinking in China and the West. Hillsdale, NJ: Lawrence Erlbaum Associates.

Brown, R. (1986). Linguistic relativity. In S. H. Hulse & B. E. Green, Jr. (Eds.), *One hundred years of psychological research in America: G. Stanley Hall and the Johns Hopkins tradition* (pp. 241-263). Baltimore: The Johns Hopkins University Press.

Brown, R. (1991, August). Language and the relational self. Fourth International Conference on Language and Social Psychology. Santa Barbara, CA.

Brown, R., & Gilman, A. (1960). The pronouns of power and solidarity. In T. A. Sebeok (Ed.), *Style in language* (pp. 253-276). Cambridge: MIT Press and John Wiley and Sons, Inc.

Cousins, S. (1989). Culture and selfhood in Japan and the U.S. *Journal of Personality and Social Psychology, 56,* 124-231.

DeVos, G. A. (1973). *Socialization for achievement: Essays on the cultural psychology of the Japanese.* Berkeley: University of California Press.

Geertz, C. (1975). On the nature of anthropological understanding. *American Scientist, 63,* 47-53.

Gergen, K. H., & Gergen, M. M. (1988). Narrative and the self as relationship. In L. Berkowitz (Ed.), *Advances in Experimental Social Psychology, 21,* 17-56.

Gilligan, C. (1982). *In a different voice: Psychological theory and women's development.* Cambridge, MA: Harvard University Press.

Gilligan, C. (1986). Remapping the moral domain: New images of the self in relationship. In T. C. Heller, M. Sosna, & D. E. Wellbery (Eds.), *Reconstructing individuals: Autonomy, individuality, and self in Western thought* (pp. 237-252). Stanford: Stanford University Press.

Kaji, J. (1993). *Relationships in Japan and the United States: A content analysis of Japanese and American descriptions of social relationships.* Unpublished manuscript. Harvard University.

Kondo, D. K. (1990). *Crafting selves.* Chicago: University of Chicago Press.

Kroger, R. W., Wood, L. A., & Kim, V. (1984). Are the rules of address universal? III Comparison of Chinese, Greek, and Korean usage. *Journal of Cross-Cultural Psychology, 15,* 273-284.

Lebra, T. S. (1976). *Japanese patterns of behavior.* Honolulu: University of Hawaii Press.

Levin, H., & Garrett, P. (1990). Sentence structure and formality. *Language in Society, 19,* 511-520.

Levin, H., Long, S., & Shaffer, C. A. (1981). The formality of the Latinate lexicon in English. *Language and Speech, 42,* 161-171.

Levinson, S. C. (1982). Caste rank and verbal interaction in western Tamilnadu. In D. B. McGilvray (Ed.), *Caste, ideology, and interaction* (pp. 98-203). Cambridge, England: Cambridge University Press.

Markus, H. R., & Kitayama, S. (1991). Culture and the self: Implications for cognition, emotion, and motivation. *Psychological Review, 98,* 224-253.

Marselli, A., DeVos, G., & Hsu, F. (Eds.). (1985). *Culture and self.* London: Tavistock.

Roland, A. (1988). *In search of self in India and Japan: Toward a cross-cultural psychology.* New Jersey: Princeton University Press.

Sampson, E. E. (1985). The decentralization of identity: Toward a revised concept of personal and social order. *American Psychologist, 40,* 1203-1211.

Sampson, E. E. (1988). The debate on individualism: Indigenous psychologies of the individual and their role in personal and societal functioning. *American Psychologist, 43,* 15-22.

Sampson, E. E. (1989). The challenge of social change for psychology: Globalization and psychology's theory of the person. *American Psychologist, 44,* 914-921.

Shweder, R. A., & Bourne, E. T. (1984). Does the concept of the person vary cross-culturally? In R. A. Shweder & R. A. Levine (Eds.), *Culture theory: Essays on mind, self, and emotion* (pp. 158-199). New York: Cambridge University Press.

Shweder, R. A., & LeVine, R. A. (1984). *Culture theory: Essays on mind, self, and emotion.* New York: Cambridge University Press.

Smith-Hefner, N. J. (1988). Women and politenes: The Javanese example. *Language in Society, 17,*

535-554.

Suzuki, T. (1973). *Japanese and the Japanese.* Tokyo: Kodansha.

Tannen, D. (1991). *You just don't understand.* New York: Morrow.

Triandis, H. C. (1989). The self and social behavior in differing cultural contexts. *Psychological Review, 96*, 506-520.

Triandis, H. D., Bontempo, R., Villareal, M. J., Asai, M., & Lucca, N. (1988). Individualism and collectivism: Cross-cultural perspectives on self-ingroup relationships. *Journal of Personality and Social Psychology, 54*, 323-538.

3 THE PRAGMATICS OF CONSTRUCTIONS[1]

Charles J. Fillmore
University of California, Berkeley

I

I have been interested for some time in the kinds of decisions linguists have made in drawing boundaries in and around linguistics, by which I mean both the lines that separate one subfield of linguistics from another, and those that separate linguistics proper from impinging disciplines (Fillmore, 1984). Probably every linguist, while working through some puzzling collection of language phenomena, has had the experience of beginning with the assumption that a given problem will yield to the system of principles that characterize one particular field of linguistics, only to conclude in the end that the explanation really belongs elsewhere. What began looking like a morphology problem turned out to have a phonological solution; what started out as a problem in semantics received a pragmatics solution; or what began as a mystery of syntax proved in the end to be an instance of some semantic generalization. At times, of course, we find that the problem really belongs to cognitive psychology, or ethnography, or logic, rather than to linguistics. The problems that linguists deal with day-to-day don't always have labels on them telling us who owns them.

These surprises are usually not embarrassing, especially in the modern world where integrative results are praised and cross-disciplinary research is encouraged. But in those circles in which disciplinary boundaries are defined in dogmatic or dictatorial ways, one sometimes feels pressure to be sure in advance that the outcome of an inquiry is going to be of the right sort, in the fear that one might not be seen as really working in one's declared field. It's one thing to face the occasional charge that what we are doing isn't really semantics, or isn't really grammar, or isn't really linguistics, but it's awkward to

---

[1] A version of this paper was read at the Kobe, Japan, meeting of the International Pragmatics Association in the summer of 1993.

have our students, and it's dangerous to have our employers, overhear such judgments.[2]

When we read in the Levinson textbook *Pragmatics* the author's lengthy discussion of the problem of defining this field (Levinson, 1983, pp. 7-31), we become aware of two boundary problems: the boundary between pragmatics and sociolinguistics at one edge, and the boundary between pragmatics and grammar (including semantics) at the other. We read that the Anglo-Saxon linguistic world has tended to draw a sharp distinction between pragmatics and sociolinguistics, while much of the rest of the world does not, and we learn that a distinction between pragmatics and grammar is something about which some of the colleagues sometimes dispute quite feelingly. It's this latter boundary, that between pragmatics and grammar, that concerns me here. My goal in this paper is to explore some of the ways in which the study of grammar and the study of pragmatics necessarily overlap, and to suggest that in a grammatical theory that sees pragmatic function as one of the natural dimensions of grammatical description, this "overlap" is not a cause for embarrassment.

On one influential view the main distinction we need to keep in mind is one which separates (a) knowing a language, from (b) putting that knowledge to use in everyday communication. This view yields a *subtractive* view of pragmatics, according to which it is possible to factor out of the full description of linguistic activities those purely symbolic aspects which concern linguistic knowledge independently of notions of use or purpose. A grammar of a language is defined as a repertory of semantically significant primary elements plus a combinatorial mechanism capable of creating and interpreting more complex elements in the understanding that it is the possession of such a repertory and such mechanisms which makes people legitimate speakers and interpreters of their language. The study of what people do with each other, employing these resources, when they speak is something different: this second area is *pragmatics*.

A relevant comparison is with the tools of a culture, on the one hand, and skills that members employ while using those tools, on the other hand. However, telling the difference between linguistic knowledge and the ability to function competently as a member of the community of people who share that knowledge, is not always easy, especially because knowing a language and knowing how to use a language can both involve *conventionality*. The pragmatic conventions can be said to presuppose the grammatical conventions: Descriptions of the resources of the language, on this view, do not, and should not, contain any reference to pragmatic purposes.

This understanding of the distinction is compatible with the view that many usage practices can themselves be institutionalized or conventionalized — as conventions of use rather than conventions of language. Given such a grammar-external view of language use, we find that the study of pragmatics needs to recognize two kinds of pragmatic

---

[2] This little preamble does not mean that I have any objection to scholars wishing to be clear about the assumptions they make on the kinds of phenomena they choose to deal with or the kinds of explanations they are willing to countenance. In any scientific field, if we are to make progress, we will need to formulate our findings on a shared foundation of well established and agreed-upon principles. But I have become convinced that, in the case of language in particular, there are so many layers of explanation for what we observe that we are not yet ready to tolerate exclusivist claims on any of its territories.

inferences, those which involve locally special cultural conventions, and those which involve common sense reasoning. In the latter case, the explanations depend on members being rational and cooperative rather than, say, "trained."

My favorite example of a locally special pragmatic pattern is the Japanese letter-writing convention by which the first part of a personal letter is expected to offer some comment on the current season. The force of this convention is demonstrated by the practice of using the word-sentence *zenryaku*, meaning 'first part omitted', when ignoring the convention for reasons of speed or space.

The kind of pragmatics that involves common-sense inferencing can be illustrated by considering the following (invented) conversation.

(1) Q: Waiter, can you bring me an ashtray?

　　 A: Sir, this is a smoke-free restaurant.

The customer's utterance sounds like a question about the waiter's ability to deliver an ashtray to the customer's table. The waiter's reply is a statement that is not, in the usual information-transmission sense, a proper answer to that question. Our second kind of pragmatics should enable us to explain the nature of this interaction and our ability to interpret it, without appealing to locally specific conventions. Given what is known about the functions of ashtrays, it is rational to assume that the customer's question was an opening move in a sequence of acts that was likely to end in the customer's doing something unpermitted (and loathsome); and the waiter's response can be heard as short-circuiting that process while offering an explanation of why it could not be carried through. The customer did not specifically say that he wished to smoke, and the waiter did not specifically say that the customer was not permitted to smoke.

Let's assume that the reasoning that goes on here is natural, not needing an explanation in terms of specifically linguistic conventions. In agreeing to that we are not necessarily saying that the same communicative purposes could be served, equally naturally, with translations of these sentences in all languages. There could very well be culturally specific conventions for participating in such indirect communications. Our claim of naturalness amounts to saying that in those communities which lack special conversational conventions for covering such a case, it is easy to assume that nobody has to learn anything special to be able to figure out how the two contributions to this conversation fit together, or to be able to participate competently in similar exchanges.[3]

On the view just caricatured, pragmatics includes both conventions governing the use of language and a number of very general principles that do not need to be covered by locally learned conventions. These conventions and principles are distinct from, and presuppose the autonomy of, the grammar of the language in question.

---

[3] I am quite prepared to believe that I am totally wrong about this example, and that there are special dedicated culturally specific conventions which govern this interaction in ways that I am simply too culturally short-sighted to see. I ask the reader merely to assume that there are some cases in which nothing but rationality and cooperation are involved.

II

There is another, nonsubtractive, way of defining pragmatics, based on the idea that linguistic pragmatics concerns itself with any of the ways in which the resources of a language are put to use as tools in human interaction, at any level. On this view, it doesn't matter to what extent our understanding of the ability to perform particular kinds of interactionally relevant linguistic acts requires a prior isolation of what is "purely linguistic." It is possible that some elements of the repertory, some pieces of grammatical or lexical competence, so to speak, exist precisely for the sake of achieving pragmatic goals, much in the way that most tools were created for highly specific uses. The need for at least *some* such connections inheres in the concept of *conventional implicatures*. But while the literature that treats conventional implicatures generally limits itself to individual words like *but*, *therefore*, *even*, or *yet*,[4] the view I am proposing is that pragmatic factors enter fully into the grammar and lexicon of a language.[5]

Linguists mainly concerned with having things come out right when attaching a theory of truth-conditional semantics to a generative grammar need a concept like *conventional implicature* to cover the problem areas. But linguists who emphasize the interactional aspects of language find much more to worry about. When it comes to acknowledging parts of grammar that are inherently pragmatic, even the purest separatists are likely to accept as belonging to such a domain the special category of words known as *pragmatic particles*. These are the little noises, occurring more abundantly in some languages than others, that have such conventional functions as signaling that the speaker is engaged in insisting or pleading, expressing dominance or hostility, marking the boundaries in and around speech events, signaling the difference between foregrounded and backgrounded information, and so on. Of course it was wrong of me to call them "little noises," since that might suggest that they belong in the class of intentional acts that includes hissing and whistling and clearing one's throat. On the contrary, the kinds of words I have in mind typically exhibit canonical phonological structure, they have well-profiled word-class features, they have fixed syntactic distributional properties, and they participate in precise ways in the rules of phrase-formation, etc.; in short, they are necessary to any description of the fundamental workings of the languages in which they occur.

Other sorts of lexico-grammatical entities which have uncontroversial pragmatic aspects can be found in expressive speech, more elaborated in some languages than

---

[4] See Grice (1975, 1978, 1981), Kempson (1975), Karttunen and Peters (1979), and Wilson (1975).

[5] Since the term *conversational implicature* occurs mainly in the context of the residue of problems that are not solvable by the well-behaved parts of grammar and semantics, suggesting in a trivializing way that it concerns that uninteresting corner of language where the regular theory fails, and since from my point of view the phenomena covered by this term fall out as the properties of particular types of grammatical constructions, the theory of construction grammar has no special need for this concept. (The basic ideas of construction grammar can be found in Fillmore and Kay [ms], Kay and Fillmore [ms].)

others; in the wide variety of categories of deixis, including tense; and in the so-called moods, distinguishing statements, questions and commands, from each other, through verbal desinences, syntactic forms, prosodic patterns, etc., again, in ways that can differ broadly from language to language.

My interest here goes beyond these relatively noncontroversial cases. Here my concern is in grammatical constructions which — as I like to say it — are themselves "dedicated" to particular pragmatic purposes. *Far from regarding this involvement of pragmatics in grammatical descriptions as evidence that the general theory of grammar doesn't work for the whole of a language, I wish to regard the pragmatic dimension as an inherent part of every grammatical construction.*[6]

III

For a detailed first illustration of the ways in which pragmatic information needs to be included in the description of a grammatical construction, we can draw from Fillmore, Kay, and O'Connor (1988), a study of the English *let alone* construction. Three varieties of pragmatic information are encoded in sentences built around this construction. First, we find that a *let alone* sentence requires for its interpretation that the hearer be able to call on (or create by accommodation) some background conceptual structure in terms of which certain semantic entailments must operate. Second, the analysis of a *let alone* sentence reveals something about its place in an ongoing discourse. And third, a *let alone* sentence gives information about the quality of its contribution to the on-going discourse, in terms of Gricean relevance and informativity.

Here are three sentences exemplifying the construction I have in mind:[7]

(2) (a) He wasn't wearing a shirt, let alone a necktie.

    (b) I wouldn't give you fifty cents, let alone fifty dollars.

    (c) I didn't get up in time for lunch, let alone breakfast.

Each of these sentences can be seen as somehow posing two propositions: the first of these (the "α" proposition) is completed with the material preceding the phrase *let alone*, the second (the "β" proposition) by substituting what follows *let alone* for the focused constituent in the former part.[8] The semantic segmentation (at this level) of the sentences in (2) are shown in (3).

(3) (a) He wasn't wearing a shirt, let alone a necktie.

        α: he wasn't wearing a shirt

---

[6] The pragmatic dimension may be empty in some cases. That is, there may be some abstract grammatical constructions – very general typological word-order patterns, for example – which are themselves pragmatically neutral.

[7] We note that each of these sentences is negative; while this is the most common context for *let alone*, it is not obligatory. I forego here an attempt to explain the strong preference for negation in such sentences.

[8] It's a *bit* more complicated than this, actually. For details, see Fillmore et al. (1988).

    β: he wasn't wearing a necktie
(b) I wouldn't give you fifty cents, let alone fifty dollars.
    α: I wouldn't give you fifty cents
    β: I wouldn't give you fifty dollars
(c) I didn't get up in time for lunch, let alone breakfast.
    α: I didn't get up in time for lunch
    β: I didn't get up in time for breakfast

The observation of the dual-propositional nature of the interpretation of a *let alone* sentence can be described as semantic, allowing us to think of *let alone* as a kind of coordinating conjunction.[9]

The first pragmatic observation to make is that the interpretation of these sentences depends on the hearer's being able to situate the two propositions in a particular *scalar model*, within which an *entailment* relation can be said to hold between the α proposition and the β proposition. Given the belief structure represented in such a model, wherever one could expect α to be true, one has even more reason to expect β to be true.

In situations in which normal standards of dress are accepted, one does not wear a necktie without wearing a shirt.[10] Given ordinary notions of selfishness and trust, if I am unwilling to give you fifty cents, I would certainly be unwilling to give you fifty dollars. And given the ordinary sleeping and eating patterns of people in my culture and the way in which we linguistically differentiate the meals that we eat during the day, if I woke up in time for breakfast, I was still awake at lunchtime; if I slept through lunch, I was necessarily asleep at the time when I might have been expected to make breakfast.

In all of the cases just given, knowledge of world and culture gives easy access to the assumed scalar model, so we might briefly think that the culturally "normal" scalar positioning of the scenes presented as α and β in these sentences is itself what creates the understanding of a scalar entailment. But now consider sentence (4) and its interpretation.

(4) I wouldn't hire Jones, let alone Smith,
    α: I wouldn't hire Jones
    β: I wouldn't hire Smith

This time, independently of whether the hearer knows anything about either Jones or Smith, or the speaker's feelings about them, the scalar interpretation is clear, and it is the construction itself which creates it: the world in which the speaker would not hire Jones is necessarily a world in which, *a fortiori*, the speaker would not hire Smith.

---

[9] The interpretational asymmetry that goes with the left-to-right order of the two conjuncts is not a matter of conversational implicature, as we will see. Unlike what we find with *and*, in other words, it is not defeasible. With respect to its truth-conditional semantic interpretation as a coordinating conjunction (the "α" and "β" propositions are jointly asserted), *let alone* would figure in "conventional implicatures."

[10] One does indeed occasionally see a bare-chested man wearing a necktie, as a joke, but the judgments we make about such a scene support the scalar implications just suggested. In the world of expected behavior that the interpreter brings to this sentence, a man who is not wearing a shirt is not wearing a necktie.

I repeat that the entailment relationship itself is naturally a semantic notion; but the appeal to the hearer to recognize or construct a scalar model on the basis of which such entailments operate is pragmatic.

A second and different kind of pragmatic observation is that a *let alone* sentence cannot easily be the first contribution to a discourse. There is always what Paul Kay has called a *context proposition* in the air, some proposition whose truth or falsity is at issue, possibly by way of a question which an interlocutor has just asked, possibly in the form of a suggestion in the speaker's own preceding contribution, which in uttering the *let alone* sentence the speaker is reinforcing or contradicting. The β proposition in the interpretation of a *let alone* sentence is always taken as a direct response to such a context proposition. The utterance of a *let alone* sentence, thus, makes a pragmatic demand on the hearer to remember or reconstruct the context proposition.

The following three conversations are intelligible and interpretable, given such an assumption:

(5) Q: What tie was Jimmy wearing at his wedding?
    A: He wasn't even wearing a shirt, let alone a necktie.
(6) Q: Could you give me fifty dollars so I can go to the races?
    A: I wouldn't give you fifty cents, let alone fifty dollars.
(7) Q: Did you make a nice breakfast for the kids today?
    A: I didn't get up in time for lunch, let alone breakfast.

In all of these cases, the context proposition, derivable directly or by presupposition-detection from the preceding speaker's questions (Jimmy wore a necktie at his wedding, you might be willing to give me fifty dollars, you woke up in time for breakfast), was rejected by the β proposition in the *let alone* sentence.

By contrast, the following conversations, in which we pretend that the α part is responding to the interlocutor's question, are pragmatically ill-formed (bearing the prefix ≈):

(8) Q: What color shirt was Jimmy wearing at the wedding?
    A: ≈He wasn't wearing a shirt, let alone a necktie.
(9) Q: How about giving me fifty cents for a cup of coffee?
    A: ≈I wouldn't give you fifty cents, let alone fifty dollars.
(10) Q: What did you have for lunch today?
    A: ≈I didn't get up in time for lunch, let alone breakfast.

The requirement of a context proposition also means that a *let alone* sentence cannot easily begin an interaction. Nobody could make sense of the following first-contributions without working pretty hard to create a context — and that context would have to be one which determined in each case a very precise context proposition:

(11) Have you heard about Harry? He hasn't been married once, let alone twice.
(12) Guess what! You didn't get accepted at Harvard, let alone Yale.

Given all of these observations, what we see is that the β proposition is the relevant response to the context proposition, satisfying a Gricean Relevance (Relation) condition, while the α proposition is a more informative statement, satisfying a Gricean Informativeness (Quantity) condition. In saying that the α proposition "satisfies" an informativeness condition I mean that the speaker regards this news as giving that level of information that the hearer needs for making further inferences. These sentences have the function of responding to a context with a contextually relevant answer while at the same time indicating that an answer that is merely responsive to the context propositions falls short of being fully informative. The α proposition is more informative because, given the scalar model, α entails β. Our third pragmatic observation, then, relates the two parts of the *let alone* structures to judgments about informativeness and relevance. The sentence yields two components, semantically, and assigns to each of them information about the quality of its contribution to the conversation.

The *let alone* construction seemed to us to be a particularly clear case of a pragmatics-rich grammatical construction: It is not possible to derive any of the pragmatic observations in a straightforward way from the kinds of structures conjoined around *let alone,* nor simply from the propositions that can be built from unpacking these conjoined structures, let alone from any independent meanings that a clever semanticist could assign to the individual words *let* and *alone.*

IV

In the case of the *let alone* construction we have what seems to me to be a "clear case." For a number of other candidate constructions, however, the question of the degree to which its pragmatic interpretation involves special conventions, as opposed to general pragmatic principles, could be controversial. Let us briefly explore the pragmatic properties of *negative questions* in English. It would appear that negative yes–no questions express what grammarians have sometimes described as a *negative bias* or *negative orientation.* What does that mean, and how can we find out if it's true? Couldn't we derive the special force of a negative question from what we know about negation and questioning? If so, how would such a derivation proceed? If not, can we speak of a complex construction that is characterized by the combined syntactic-form features of negation and interrogation which has a pragmatic force which is not computable from the meaning of each of its structural components? The whole is greater than the sum of the parts, but how could we go about characterizing the function from those parts to that whole?

It is difficult to pin down the exact effect that negative yes–no questions have, but it has always been clear that there is a sharp affective-cum-interactional difference between, say, two sentences like (13a) and (13b):

(13) (a) Did you like the dessert I made for you?
    (b) Didn't you like the dessert I made for you?

Question (13b) clearly suggests that the speaker is expecting to be disappointed by the answer. On being asked the question in (13b), someone who liked the dessert (or wished to communicate that idea) would have to say something to mitigate the questioner's suspicions, since a simple "Yes, I did" answer would not do. Better would be something like, "Of course I did, it was wonderful." And even such an expression of exuberance would probably be most naturally followed with an explanation for not eating more of it.

In Quirk, Greenbaum, Leech, and Svartvik (1985, pp. 806-809), we read:

Negative questions are always conducive. Negative orientation is found in questions which contain a negative form of one kind or another: Don't you believe me? Have they never invited you home? Aren't you joining us this evening? Has nobody called? Hasn't he told you what to do?

Negative orientation is complicated by an element of surprise or disbelief. The implication is that the speaker had originally hoped for a positive response, but new evidence now suggests that the response will be negative. Thus, Hasn't he told you what to do? means 'Surely he has told you what to do, hasn't he? I would have thought that he had told you.' Here there is a combining of a positive and a negative attitude, which one may distinguish as the OLD EXPECTA-TION (positive) and NEW EXPECTATION (negative). Because the old expectation tends to be identified with the speaker's hopes or wishes, negatively orientated questions often express disappointment or annoyance: Can't you drive straight? ['I'd have thought you'd be able to, but apparently you can't.'] Aren't you ashamed of yourself? ['You ought to be, but it appears that you are not.']

Quirk et al. also recognize that some negative questions are "biased toward positive orientation." It is hard to state precisely what that means, but one can recognize what they had in mind from their examples:

If a negative question has assertive items, it is biased towards positive orienta-tion. Didn't someone call last night? Didn't he recognize you too? Hasn't the boat left already?

With some adjustments necessary for the last examples, it would appear that a grammatical construction that combines negation and interrogation invites certain special interpretation principles, roughly paraphrasable by saying that the speaker would like to hear a positive answer but the context appears to offer some reason to expect a negative answer. Let us consider the possibility that what we have here is best seen as a complex grammatical construction which is a composite of two other constructions, namely that of the yes–no inverted question and that of sentence negation, and that while this construc-tion inherits some of the semantics of each of the other two, it has a package of interpre-tation principles that are, by separate convention, associated with the whole. Would it be upsetting to such a proposal if we found that not all negative questions have such interpretations? The answer, of course, is no. On the contrary, we would be relieved if we found that to be true. Then we could say that there is a negative question construc-tion, which has the pragmatic functions just mentioned, and it coexists in the grammar with the two constructions that give us negative sentences and yes–no questions. Every such sentence could also be formed by combining the two constructions independently, and when that happens we do not get the special pragmatics. This would be particularly satisfying if every negative question could be given both a compositional and a special interpretation.

But suppose that we do not find such differences? Suppose it's simply not possible to separate the special pragmatics we have been talking about from any negative yes–no question. That could mean that within the theory of grammatical constructions we have to devise some theory of blocking, or pre-emption, of the sort often discussed in morphology (see Aronoff, 1976, Scalise, 1984), guaranteeing that a given assembly of constructions cannot be formed, much in the way that certain structurings of morphemes, for an otherwise completely general and productive process, are ruled out.

The alternative is that we simply have to recognize that the special interpretation of negative yes–no questions is derivable from what can be independently known about negation and interrogation. There may be pragmatic dimensions to interrogation and negation, but the pragmatic force of composites of the two is compositional.

An approach to achieving compositionality for negative questions might be suggested based on Talmy Givón's theory of negation, in which he proposes a difference between negation in natural languages and negation in logic, in that a *sentence* with negation, independently of whether it's a statement or a question, "presupposes" (in some sense) that the corresponding non-negative speech act is a part of the discourse context (see Givón, 1979, pp. 103-105; 1984, pp. 321-351; 1989, pp. 156). The task then, is to derive the special interpretation of negative questions compositionally, making it unnecessary to posit a special construction for negative questions.

An interesting consequence of accepting Givón's version of negation is that we would then have to say that there exists in English a very special, somewhat artificial negative construction with "neutral pragmatics" and understood as requiring the sentence that contains it to be false just in case the corresponding sentence without it is true, and vice versa. The phrase "neutral pragmatics" is in quotes because, from one point of view, this particular negative construction is highly specialized pragmatically. Its prototypical use is in providing natural-language pronunciations of certain of the logical propositions that we find in the exercises in logic textbooks. (What could be more context-bound than that?) This turns the "subtractive" view of pragmatics on its head. Now, instead of saying that grammatical negation has the semantics of logical negation and that the pragmatics of negation involves considerations of the occasions when people decide to express propositions negatively, we would instead have to say that the semantics of logical negation, in those rare contexts in which it figures in natural language discourse, is associated with its grammatical form in a very special way.[11]

However suggestive this may be, I don't know of any way of accomplishing this rescue of compositionality for negative questions, since I don't know how to derive the interpretations that have been described for negative questions from the generalizations proposed by Givón. But before we give up on the idea that negative questions can be an argument for pragmatically functioning grammatical constructions, let's consider a new case, that of *requests* being grammatically expressed as negative questions. In English such requests sound quite rude, because of the biases we have just been discussing. Consider the reactions you might have to the questions in (14) and (15):

(14) Won't you give me some (any) more tea?

(15) Can't I have some (any) more tea?

---

[11] A similar reversal can be seen in Knud Lambrecht's treatment of the representation of subjects in colloquial French. Lambrecht proposes a number of syntactic devices for avoiding SVO structures in spoken French, and then isolates the special conditions under which lexical subjects are possible. (Lambrecht, 1987, 1988)

Negative questions of these sorts, used as requests in English, would ordinarily be heard as including a complaint about the waiter's or host's inattentiveness or stinginess. It appears that whatever explanation we might come up with for English negative questions in general would cover the special feelings associated with negative questions used as requests. There is scant reason for claiming special constructional status for the negative-question-requests in English. But not so for Japanese. In this language, by contrast, requests taking the form of negative questions — as in (16) and (17) — are quite standard.

(16) *Otya o moo sukosi kure.mas.en ka?*
    [tea OBJ more a-little give.pol.not QUES]
(17) *Otya o moo sukosi itadak.e.mas.en ka?*
    [tea OBJ more a-little receive.can.pol.not QUES]

These questions ask literally "Won't you give me some more tea?" and "Can't I receive some more tea?" but they are heard as polite — more polite, I am told, than the corresponding affirmative questions.[12]

What are we to make of this? Is this a case of constructional pragmatics or regular pragmatics? Can we find a functional difference in negation itself between Japanese and English? Or could there be slightly different politeness rules distinguishing the two cultures such that the ordinary semantics of the constructions simply operates differently against a background of different politeness conventions? Maybe, for example, the polite character of these sentences in Japanese comes from the idea that by linguistically taking notice of the possibility of the host's unwillingness or inability to provide the tea we are acknowledging the imposition we are making and are revealing that we will have considerable reason to be grateful if our assumption is wrong.

As I said, I don't know what the final solution in these cases is going to be. But in any case, we are dealing with pragmatic questions. The possibility just suggested for examples (14)–(17) is that there are general compositional principles operating in each language, but that, most clearly in the case of requests, these principles interact with different rules of politeness. Another possibility is that in each language negative questions require special interpretations, but these happen to be strongly *motivated* (not *explained*) by facts about culture and politeness. To which we may add the possibility (preferred by me) that in Japanese, a special constructional status is given to negative questions used as requests, questions about the addressee's giving favors, or the speaker's possibility of receiving favors.

---

[12] Negative questions based on an alternative way of forming the negative would convey the rudeness of the English question, as I have learned from Professor Tetsuya Kunihiro (p.c.). Thus *Otya o moo sukosi itadakenai no desu ka?* would be heard as 'Is it the case that I cannot have more tea?' and would be rude.

V

I've looked at two cases in which something pragmatic is going on, one for which a constructional account cannot be avoided (the *let alone* construction), and one for which it is quite difficult to find out just what is going on (the putative negative question constructions). I will now look at another set of phenomena that I suspect belong to the latter type.

In a recently completed Berkeley doctoral dissertation, Seiko Fujii has come up with some insightful things to say about the differences between various types of English and Japanese conditional sentences (Fujii, 1993). One pair of patterns that Fujii considers is the English *even if* construction and the Japanese *te mo* construction. The two are worth comparing, since each is the closest translation of the other, yet the assumption that they "mean" the same thing is wrong, and language learners frequently make mistakes. These are the so-called concessive conditionals. Briefly the difference between the constructions in the two languages seems to be something like this. They communicate the idea that within a particular universe of possibilities identified by the *protasis*, or *antecedent* clause, the speech act performed via the *apodosis*, or *consequent* clause, is universally and unconditionally valid. The Japanese and English versions differ, however, in how they identify that universe of possibilities. In particular, for English the interpreter must call on a scalar model and scalar entailment (familiar from our discussion of the *let alone* construction), but Japanese has a more general means of identifying the universe of situations in which the proposition in the antecedent clause is universally true.

Consider sentence (18)

(18) Even if you paid me a million dollars, I wouldn't marry Louise.

This sentence suggests that the speaker can imagine a range of possible inducements that the addressee might come up with to get the speaker to marry Louise, and within that range, a payment of a million dollars is the extreme case. In speaking of this as "the extreme case" I am not exposing my belief that 1,000,000 is the largest possible number; rather, I am claiming that the construction itself suggests that in the world of possibilities envisioned by the speaker, on this occasion, one million dollars stands for a big enough amount to express the speaker's unconditional refusal to marry the person known as Louise.[13]

In Japanese, the protasis of the corresponding sentences also gives information interpreted as exhausting the possibilities in a given universe, but this is not necessarily done by scalar entailment.

The Japanese expressions can exhaust the possibilities with a universal quantifier, morphologically an interrogative word coexisting with the particle *mo*. (The quasi-trans-

---

[13] A person who follows (18) up with something like "Of course, should you happen to come up with five million, I might be willing to reconsider," from this point of view, should be heard as somehow "switching frames" rather than simply choosing a higher figure within the originally imagined range.

lations in parentheses pretend an equivalence between -*te mo* and *even if.*)
(19) *Dare ni kiite mo, wakaranai.*
    No matter who you ask, you won't know.
    (even if you ask anyone at all you won't find out)
    The possibilities can be exhausted by pairing an affirmative and a negative condition.
(20) *Ame ga hutte mo huranakute mo ikimasu.*
    We'll go whether it rains or not.
    (even if it rains, even if it doesn't rain, we'll go)
    The possibilities can also be shown by listing representative possibilities and allowing
the interpreter to imagine other cases.
(21) *Niwa no kusa o totte ite mo, airon o kakete ite mo, ohuro ni haitte ite mo, anata
no koto bakari kangaeru n desu.*
    Whether I'm weeding the garden, or ironing clothes, or taking a bath, I think only
of you.
    (even if I'm weeding the garden, even if I'm ironing . . .)
    In these last cases, English would have to call on expressions with *whether* or *no
matter*. In a recent sumo tournament in San Jose, California, a member of the troupe
spoke in English to television interviewers explaining the various rituals associated with
the sport, and contributed the information that "Even if we win or lose, we always bow
to our opponent." In ordinary English, of course, it would not make sense to say "even
if we win or lose." Given the meaning of bowing in general English-speaking cultures,
it would only make sense[14] to say "Even if we win, we bow to our opponent."
    Lastly, the protasis can merely set up a situation in which the event identified in the
apodosis could relevantly take place.
(22) *Tanaka-san ni attemo, watasi no koto o iwanaide kudasai.*
    Don't mention me if you happen to meet Tunica.
    (even if you meet Mr. Tunica, don't speak about me)
    Once again, the question we have to ask is, are we dealing with constructional
pragmatics, conventional pragmatics, or regular pragmatics. Seiko Fujii has argued that
while the various properties of the construction in each of the two languages is *motivated*
by its constituents, it still needs to be described in constructionist terms. The "motivation" has a lot to do with the word *even* in the English sentences (see Kay, 1990), and
with the word *mo* in the Japanese case. The "pragmatic" part of it is that the interpreter
is called on to create or recognize the relevant universe of situations within which the
generalization stands as unconditional.

VI

We began with the *let alone* construction, for which a constructional account is unavoid-

---

[14] In western culture the gesture of bowing is seen as symbolic of submission or subservience, so the
occasion of bowing when victorious would be the unexpected extreme case.

able. We continued with two kinds of constructions for which some pragmatic effect could be assigned to certain simple constructions, but it was difficult to determine whether the combination required a separately conventionalized description. In the first of these latter cases we worried, across English and Japanese, about the combination of yes–no questions and ordinary sentence negation; in the second situation we worried about the combination of *even* and *if* in English, and about *te* and *mo* in Japanese: These combinations yielded interpretations that were motivated by the constituent morphemes, but on the question of the interpretation of the whole, the jury remains puzzled.

In this section I give brief mention to several constructions which, though not as richly pragmatic as the English *let alone* construction, nevertheless show evidence of being grammatical patterns dedicated to specific pragmatic purposes.

6.1 The first of these is the family of presentational *there*-constructions treated in Lakoff (1986, pp. 462-581). Sentences of this type are introduced by *here* or *there*, with subject–verb inversion in the case of full NP subjects, in which the main verb is limited to *be, come, go, sit, stand*, and *lie*, with precise constraints on permitted augmentation in the form of secondary predicates, or what Lakoff calls "final phrases." Examples are seen in (23):

(23) (a) Here comes Harry (, all out of breath)
　　 (b) Here I am (, ready to start working)
　　 (c) There he stood (, with his hat in his hand)

For an important class of these sentences, present-tense uses have a deictic presentational function, as in example (24); past-tense uses have a narrative function, reflecting the point of view, with an implicit gaze direction assumed in the narrative, as in (25).

(24) Watch out everybody, here they come!

(25) . . . and there she stood.

Lakoff's discussion of this class of sentences shows them to reflect a complex motivated network of constraints and interpretations the details of which cannot possibly be seen as "falling out from" ordinary principles of generative grammar and compositional semantics.

6.2 There are numerous clearly idiomatic constructions which have special pragmatics. One such example has been discussed by Bolinger (1977, pp. 152-182) under the name "Pseudo-imperative conditional." Examples are:

(26) Show the slightest interest in what he's talking about and he won't let you go.

(27) Criticize him even a little bit and he bursts into tears.

These are disguised conditional sentences in which the first part looks like an imperative clause (except that real imperative clauses do not on their own create negative polarity contexts) and it is oddly conjoined with *and* to the consequent clause. This is not merely a variety of conditional sentence, however, since these sentences have a special interpretation: they are heard, as Bolinger points out (p. 162), as comments, often enough as complaints, about the nature of things, the foibles of life.

6.3 Another is the even more clearly idiomatic construction with the key word *time*, as in the sentences in (28), including (28c) which includes the special pragmatics of negative questions.

(28) (a) It's time you brushed your teeth.

(b) It's high time you thought about getting married.

(c) Isn't it about time we started heading for home?

The special grammatical property of these constructions is the past tense on the embedded clause. Perhaps the most common use of such a construction is in suggesting action. It can also be used in the past tense, in a point-of-view narrative, but in such cases the past-tense form in the embedded sentence is not subject to back-shifting. That is, we do not find, in a narrative (I believe), something like (29):

(29) I was getting impatient. *It was time something had happened.

6.4 Another idiomatic construction with special pragmatics is what Knud Lambrecht (1986) has called the Incredulity construction. It is exemplified by

(30) (a) Harry, get married?

(b) What? Me worry?

With these sentences the speaker is expressing surprise at someone's suggestion that a proposition that could be expressed as NP[nominative] VP[finite] might be true, with the form NP[accusative] VP[uninflected]. Not every sentence has a corresponding incredulity version, since the initial position is topical, and certain subjects cannot be topics.

(31) (a) *It rain?

(b) *There be a problem?

(c) *My foot being pulled?

6.5 One construction is the negative *why* question with head-verb *do*. With this construction one of the keys is the type of verb that accompanies *do*. Compare the following sentences:

(32) (a) Why don't you know your SSN?

(b) Why aren't you the leader?

(c) Why don't you try anything new?

(33) (a) Why don't you learn your SSN?

(b) Why don't you be the leader?

(c) Why don't you try something new?

I would like to claim that in these examples, the sentences in (32) are ordinary negative *why* questions, while those in (33) are instances of a special construction. The ordinary negative *why* questions lend themselves to a particular paraphrase pattern, suggested by the examples in (34):

(34) (a) You don't know your SSN. Why not?

(b) You aren't the leader. Why not?

(c) You don't try anything new. Why not?

The sentences in (33), which exemplify what I consider a separate construction, do not accept such a paraphrase, as shown in (34).

(35) (a) You don't learn your SSN. Why not?

(b) You don't be the leader. Why not?

(c) You don't try something new. Why not?

The difference in the sentences of (32) and (33) is the difference between states and acts, and since our construction is always interpreted as expressing what someone ought to *do*, verbs capable of expressing acts are more appropriate. In the (b) sentences, we know that except for certain imperative contexts, the verb *be* does not welcome *do*-support.

The occurrence of *be* with *do* in (33b) is compatible with the idea that the addressee is being encouraged to take the leadership, to perform an act, and hence the context is directive. For the (c) sentences, the existence of negative polarity in (32c) corresponds to the presupposition that the negative sentence (concerning which an explanation is being sought) is true; the positive polarity form of (33c) is compatible with the notion that the sentence is a call to action.

VII

This chapter has discussed the need for incorporating pragmatic interpretation principles into the description of certain grammatical constructions, and hence has served as an argument in favor of a model of language which does not begin with the assumption that questions of language use and linguistic interaction can only be seriously studied if we first establish a pragmatics-free account of grammar.

Three distinguishable notions of pragmatics emerge from these considerations. First, there is the pragmatics which builds on reasoning about why such-and-such a message was presented on such-and-such a situation. (Mom asks Junior what time it is to make Junior realize that it's time to go to bed.) Second, there is the pragmatics which is based on conventions about what sorts of ideas people can express in given contexts. (One doesn't inquire into a stranger's age as a matter of small talk.) Third, is the pragmatics that belongs in the description of the language's grammatical structures.

The construction grammar principle according to which pragmatic interpretation features are intimate parts of grammatical description does not relieve the analyst of the need to distinguish what is "compositional" and what is "idiomatic." For a structurally complex structure, we need to ask whether its interpretation can be analyzed as a compositional product of its constituent parts, or whether it is an instance of a complex structure with its own status as a separately functioning grammatical construction. The construction grammarian, fortunately, has reason to be pleased however things come out. If a complex structure can be seen as derivable from its component parts, then one can be satisfied that the grammatical structures one already has are sufficient to deal with the newly examined data. On the other hand, if it seems clear that there are special properties attending the whole of a complex construction, one is pleased to be working within a model in which such results are not an embarrassment.

REFERENCES

Aronoff, M. (1976). *Word formation in generative grammar.* Cambridge, MA: MIT Press.
Bolinger, D. (1977). *Meaning and form.* London: Longman.
Cole, P. (Ed.). (1978). *Syntax and semantics 9: Pragmatics.* New York: Academic.

Cole, P. (Ed.). (1981). *Radical pragmatics*. New York: Academic.

Cole, P., & Morgan, J. (Eds.). (1975). *Syntax and semantics 3: Speech acts*. New York: Academic.

Fillmore, C. J. (1986). Varieties of conditional sentences, *ESCOL III* (Eastern States Conference on Linguistics), pp. 163-182.

Fillmore, C. J., & Kay, P. *Construction Grammar Coursebook*. Unpublished manuscript.

Fillmore, C. J., Kay, P., & O'Connor, M. C. (1988). Regularity and idiomaticity in grammatical constructions: The case of let alone. *Language*, **64**, 501-538.

Givón, T. (1979). *On understanding grammar*. New York: Academic.

Givón, T. (1984). *Syntax: A functional-typological introduction, Volume I*. Amsterdam: Benjamins.

Givón, T. (1989). *Mind, code and context: Essays in pragmatics*. Hillsdale, NJ: Lawrence Erlbaum Associates.

Grice, H. P. (1975). Logic and conversation. In P. Cole & J. Morgan (pp. 41-58).

Grice, H. P. (1978). Further notes on logic and conversation. In Cole (pp. 113-128).

Grice, H. P. (1981). Presuppositions and conversational implicature. In Cole (183-198).

Haiman, J., & Thompson, S. (Eds.). (1988). *Clause combining in grammar and discourse*. Amsterdam: Benjamins.

Karttunen, L. & Peters, S. (1979). Conventional implicature in Montague Grammar. In Oh & Dinneen, (pp. 1-56).

Kay, P. (1990). Even. *Linguistics and Philosophy*, **13**, 59-111.

Kay, P., & Fillmore, C. J. *What's X doing Y?* Unpublished manuscript.

Kempson, R. (1975). *Presuppositions and the delimitation of semantics*. Cambridge, England: Cambridge University Press.

Lakoff, G. (1986). *Women, fire and dangerous things: What categories reveal about the mind*. Chicago: University of Chicago Press.

Lambrecht, K. (1986). *Topic, focus and the grammar of spoken French*. Unpublished doctoral dissertation, University of California at Berkeley.

Lambrecht, K. (1987). On the status of SVO sentences in French discourse. In R. Tomlin (Ed.), *Coherence and grounding in discourse* (pp. 217-262). Amsterdam: Benjamins.

Lambrecht, K. (1988). Presentational cleft constructions in spoken French. In J. Haiman & S. Thompson (Eds.), *Clause combining in grammar and discourse*. Amsterdam: Benjamins.

Levinson, S. C. (1983). *Pragmatics*. Cambridge, England: Cambridge University Press.

Oh, C-K., & Dinneen, D. A. (Eds.). (1979). *Syntax and semantics 11: Presuppositions*. New York: Academic.

Quirk, R., Greenbaum, S., Leech, G., & Svartvik, J. (1985). *A comprehensive grammar of the English language*. London: Longman.

Scalise, S. (1984). *Generative Morphology*. Dordrecht: Foris.

Tomlin, R. (Ed.). (1987). *Coherence and grounding in discourse*. Amsterdam: Benjamins.

Wilson, D. (1975). *Presuppositions and non-truth-conditional semantics*. New York: Academic.

4   SHIFTING FRAME[1]

Marjorie Harness Goodwin
University of California, Los Angeles

Within interaction, speech events set up the sequential relevance of appropriate next moves, constraining the realm of appropriate next actions and ways in which those involved are to participate. Any speaker's communicative action is both context-shaped and context- Renewing. As Heritage (1984, p. 242) states,

> A speaker's action is context-shaped in that its contribution to an ongoing sequence of actions cannot adequately be understood except by reference to the context — including, especially, the immediately preceding configuration of actions — in which it participates. . . . Since every "current" action will itself form the immediate context for some "next" action in a sequence, it will inevitably contribute to the framework in terms of which the next action will be understood.

For example, it is expected that participants will answer invitations with acceptances or rejections, summonses with answers, or a ritual insult with a similar move in kind. Listeners to stories are expected to interject displays of attentiveness, displaying their alignment and engrossment in the events being recounted.

While speech events make such proposals about appropriate next moves, participants in fact have available an array of different ways of responding to ongoing talk. They may elect to initiate talk (or activity) which is not proposed by a preceding action or the ongoing activity but instead shift the "frame" (Goffman, 1974) or structure of intelligibility (for example, whether a communication is to be heard as serious or playful). Shifting frame frequently involves a change in stance or "footing" (Goffman, 1981): That is, a "change in the alignment we take up to ourselves and the others present as expressed in the way we manage the production or reception of an utterance" (Goffman, 1981, p. 128). Shifting frame is not done capriciously, rupturing ongoing discourse; it occurs in orderly ways as practical solutions to interactional dilemmas, reshaping the speech event, or constructing distance from the tone of the activity in progress.

---

[1] This paper was presented in the invited session on "Constituting Social Life through Talk: Interweaving Perspectives from Conversation Analysis, Ethnography, and Activity Theory" at the Fourteenth Annual Meeting of the American Association for Applied Linguistics, Seattle, February 29, 1992.

FRAME TRANSFORMATIONS IN ARGUMENT

While Goffman laid out a programmatics for looking at the phenomenon of footing, he did not analyze how shifts in footing are achieved in actual moment-to-moment talk. The intent of this chapter is to demonstrate some of the methodical procedures listeners in conversational interaction make use of in recasting a prior speaker's talk to reshape meaning. Shifting frame may occur on different levels within an utterance, changing the phonology of words (example 1), the utterance's interpretation as a type of speech act (examples 1 and 2), or one's affective stance towards talk being spoken (examples 3 and 4).

One speech activity in which changes in footing occur quite frequently is argument, an event arising with "two or more disputants articulating adversary positions (or "theses") with respect to some topic, including at least an exchange of assertion and counter-assertion with some attendant expansion" (Coulter, 1990, p. 185). Children's disputes in particular provide a perspicuous locale for investigating the phenomenon of changes in footing. Throughout argumentative talk children make creative use of the language provided by their opponents in prior turns, shaping it to their own ends, often with minimal semantic shifts (Labov, 1974). Consider the following argument between 12-year-old African American girls, in which Ruby plays with both the speech act and the phonological structure of Bea's moves. This conversational interaction was collected during an 18 month ethnographic study of African American children in Philadelphia. Data are transcribed according to the Jefferson system described in Sacks, Schegloff, and Jefferson (1974):

(1)   (Ruby is sitting on top of Bea)
   1   Bea: Get off!
   2   Ruby: No. Ain't there's another way?
   3   Bea: Come on, **Ru**by.
   4   Ruby: Come on, Where we **goin**.
   5   Don't say that **ei**ther.
   6   Bea: Come on. // Get off. All y'gotta do-
   7   Ruby: Cuz I gotta answer.
   8   Bea: [Get off.
   9   Ruby: [All ya gotta say **is** (0.2) I mean get-
  10   I mean um- um **Move** please.
  11   and I can't get no rhymes on that one.
  12 Bea: **Move** please.
  13 Ruby: Where the move at.
  14 Bea: I'm tryin to get off rather,
  15 Ruby: **Wa**ther, wh- oh: the weather you want?
  16   The day is sunny and tomorrow's gonna be ra-

This sequence contains a number of playful mishearings that demonstrate ways that participants might transform a prior utterance in a subsequent move. For example, the words "Come on" in line 3 are quite clearly a recycle of the request made in line 1, that Ruby get off Bea. However, when abstracted from a particular context the words could have a range of different meanings. In line 4 Ruby plays with this fact. She first uses a partial repeat format ("Come on"), a turn preface also used in other-initiated repair, to recycle part of Bea's prior utterance. She then treats Bea's prior talk as a request to go somewhere, rather than a request to get off. In line 12 Bea makes a request "Move please" — that has the following format:

[Verb (action requested)]   +   [Please]

A very similar format is used with nouns when asking for objects (for example, "Salt, please" to request salt at the dinner table):

[Noun (object requested)]   +   [Please]

In line 13 Ruby treats the verb in line 12 as a noun by asking, "Where the move at."

In line 15, by systematically varying its phonological structure, Ruby provides a second transformation, changing "rather" into "weather." This is accomplished by utilizing an initial repair-like structure (repeating part of the prior utterance with falling rising intonation; Goodwin, 1983) and effecting phonological changes — first changing the "r" in "rather" to "w" and then changing the "æ" in rather to "ε":

   | ræther

   | wæther

   ↓   wεther

Through this stepwise transformation, Ruby is able to humorously transform Bea's request for her to move into a request for information about the weather. While operating within the parameters of prior speaker's talk, she shows the way in which she can play with both the speech act meaning of the utterance and phonological structure of words within it, to counter her opponent.

FRAME TRANSFORMATIONS DURING STORIES

Playful rendering of talk in which events are transformed from actual to imagined events occur in the midst of storytelling as well. Rather than displaying appropriate enthusiasm for current descriptions or stories through questions (Edelsky, 1981; Goodwin, 1982a, p. 805; 1982b, pp. 89-90; Polanyi, 1979, p. 221; Tannen, 1981, pp. 10-12), exclamations (Goffman, 1981, p. 28; Goodwin & Goodwin, 1992b), or brief comments (Goffman, 1981, p. 29; Goodwin & Goodwin, 1992a; Polanyi, 1979, p. 219; Tannen, 1981, p. 143; Shultz, Florio, & Erikson, 1982, p. 96) participants may open up a complex conversational floor which is simultaneous yet subordinate to the main floor being managed by storyteller and principal addressed recipient(s), through byplay (Goodwin, 1990) — teasing (Drew, 1987), heckling, or playfully dealing with a description or story.

In the following example, which occurs during a family dinner, storyteller is attempting to relate events about experiences which have occurred during the past week.

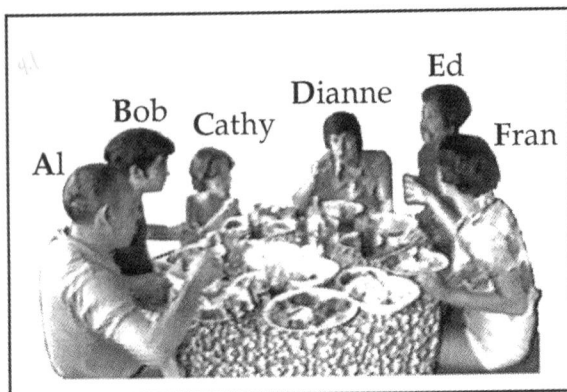

FIG. 4.1.

Fran is describing a table in a mansion belonging to the Christian Coalition group she is a member of which she recently visited. In the midst of this telling participants enter into joking talk about the ongoing speaker's talk, or byplay.

```
(2)   1          Fran:  They have a hu:ge lon::g table in the middle
      2                 that would seat *h I~don't~know
      3                 how~many~people.=//*h And then they have- a
      4     →    Bob:   Hundreds.
      5          Fran:  little    [dining room table at the e:nd.
      6     →    Al:              [(°Hundreds~at~ least.)
      7          Fran:  Which     [is the~size~of ours.
      8     →    Ed:              [°King Arthur:'s. table.
      9          Fran:  *h BY     [their ba:y window.
      10    →    Bob:             [Was it rou:nd?
      11         Fran:  Y'know? Plus they have- *h in all their
      12                bedrooms they have: what~are they
      13                called.= Window seats:?
```

In describing the table, Fran uses a rhetorical device to indicate the table's expansiveness. When she says "*h I~don't~know how~many~people" (spoken rapidly, as indicated by the "~"'s between words) she is indicating the large size of the table, in effect providing an assessment of it, rather than asking help in locating a specific number; as she speaks these words she produces nonvocal appreciative lateral head shakes while her head is directed towards the table. As shown by the "=" (latched talk) sign following her sentence completion she continues quickly on with her talk, not dwelling on the number. Nonetheless this talk is hearable as a perturbation and constitutes one sort of conversational object which regularly engenders entry of recipients in a byplay mode. Bob playfully treats "I don't know how many people" as the initiation of a word search. Providing a candidate solution — "hundreds" — he overlaps her continuing talk (as indicated by the bracket) with a guess at the number and looks toward Ed, signaling his invitation to him to coparticipate in commentary on the talk. Al speaks next in a low voice looking towards his plate; rather than attending to Fran, he builds on and elaborates Bob's guess with "íhundreds~at~least." This theme now gets developed into fanciful versions of the table with Ed's "○King Arthur:'s. table." (produced looking toward Bob with his head in an arched mode — See Fig. 4.2), while Cathy and Dianne gaze towards the speaker, Fran. Bob's subsequent elaboration — "Was it rou:nd?" — is built on the King Arthur theme.

FIG. 4.2.

Differing stances towards Fran's talk are taken up by the women and men at the table. Assessments in stories provide a locus for appreciative commentary; frequently a recipient will provide an assessment (Goodwin & Goodwin, 1992a) concurrently with speaker, showing she is in agreement with the affective stance taken by the speaker. In listening to Fran's story, Cathy and Dianne through gaze and appreciative head shakes display their agreement with the principal storyteller, and willingness to coparticipate in savoring her past experience. By way of contrast, the males present distance themselves from what from their perspective might be considered an overblown assessment by entering a competing participation framework, and dealing with the object under discussion from a humorous point of view.

Fran's original attempt to indicate the expansiveness of the table has been extracted for treatment in ways that are not relevant to the story and becomes a point of departure for an extended playful sequence that occurs simultaneously with the continuation of her description. Indeed another important feature of byplay is its timing with respect to the story proper. Both Al and Ed chain their talk to Bob's commentary rather than Fran's. Specifically, rather than attending to Fran's currently relevant utterances they instead deal with talk of Fran which occurred earlier; time lag in dealing with talk on the floor is frequently a feature of byplay and constitutes one other way in which recipients can selectively operate on a speaker's talk.

In this example of storytelling, as in the previous argumentative sequence, participants selectively operate upon features of a speaker's talk; in accordance with their own interactive projects, recipients provide readings alternative to the speaker's projectable ongoing action. In both instances, participants are roughly status equals. Work situations where there are clear differentiations in status between participants (i.e., boss–employee or employee–customer) and where the institution provides a context within which one is obligated to articulate company policy, provide quite different contexts and constraints for the manipulation of frame.

INTERTEXTUALITY:
SHIFTING FRAME IN A SERVICE ENCOUNTER

Though participants to work situations may not be in a position to create radical frame shifts, they can in various ways restructure alignment or affective stance. In the following examples (drawn from a 3-year ethnographic study, The Workplace Project, analyzing work practices in a mid-sized airport) airline ticket agents frequently distance themselves from the company-related policies they are obliged to articulate, when they come in conflict with the lived experience of passengers they attend (i.e., when passengers must be told they have to find their own means of ground transportation because fog will prevent a plane from flying.)

In the following, an agent, attempting to solicit volunteer status from a customer, encounters resistance from him in agreeing with her proposed plan. He assumes a deadpan face and intermittently looks away. The agent subsequently adopts a new strategy, shifting frame by importing into her talk "traces" of speech from the official airline loudspeaker broadcast genre which is used to solicit volunteers.

"Come-on" speeches typically are presented as offering amazing benefits to those who volunteer to fly on a later flight: for example, vouchers that "can be used against any fare, even discounted ones, to any of our over one hundred eighty worldwide destinations." Here the ticket agent makes use of a similar tactic but instead of foreign air travel offers a cab ride "through the hills of Santa Cruz to Monterey."

(3)   Agent: O:kay, Mr. B at um
                  (if) you're going to Monterey
                  we're offering a (.)
                  two hundred dollar travel voucher
                  and a cab ride, as an alternative, (.)
                  cuz the flight is oversold.=
                  Would you like to ride (.)
                  through the hills of (.)
                  ((smiling voice)) Santa Cruz
                  and up into Montere(hhh)y eh heh
                  [
       Passenger: ((smiling)) heh

Importing talk from another genre into the present can provide a parody or a commentary on the present interaction. In his discussion of intertextuality Bakhtin (1973, p. 156) has proposed that parody and stylization are types of "double-voiced" utterances and as such are intended to be interpreted as the perspective of two speakers. Here the gate agent appropriates the stylized talk of an absent hypothetical agent to make her volunteer solicitation announcement. In analyzing how parody works Morson (1989, p. 65) has proposed that:

> The audience of a double-voiced word is therefore meant to hear both a version of the original utterance as the embodiment of its speaker's point of view (or "semantic position") and the second speaker's evaluation of that utterance from a different point of view.

In the midst of her speech soliciting a volunteer, the gate agent uses a smiling voice intonation to color her description of the option available — taking a cab ride "through the hills of Santa Cruz." In response the passenger reconfigures his alignment, matching the agent's affect by producing a smile and a small laugh. As she continues "up into Montere(hh)y eh heh heh" the agent subsequently produces talk embedded with laugh tokens (Jefferson, 1979); as the passenger begins smiling, the agent, monitoring her recipient (Goodwin, 1980), produces more laugh tokens, thereby creating an affective stance congruent with the passenger's altered humorous orientation. As illustrated in the following two video frame grabs of Fig. 4.3, one before (frame A) and another after (frame B) the frame shift, her talk is effective in reconfiguring the passenger's alignment to the current encounter.

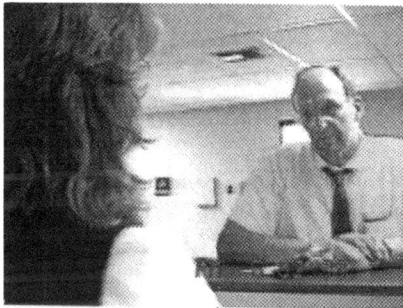

A: Initiating the solicitation   B: Shifting frame
FIG. 4.3.

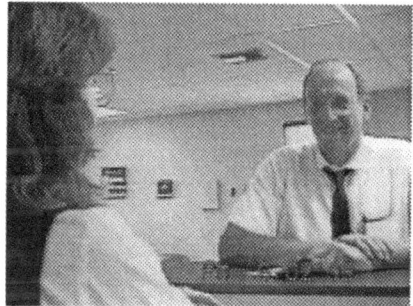

The work of a gate agent entails a skillful management of changing alignments towards the talk she is producing and often makes use of such strategies of "double voicing." In their work, gate agents are often situated within conflicting participation frameworks. While on the one hand they are obligated to articulate the company's policy, on the other they are obliged to present themselves as sympathetic listeners to passenger concerns. By slight shifts in alignment to their talk, agents deal with the conflicting constraints of their jobs. While taking up a humorous stance towards ongoing talk, they distance themselves from the very talk they are producing and step outside of the official gate agent role, if only momentarily, to align themselves with a passenger.

THE USE OF THE BODY IN MODULATING STANCE: RECIPIENT MOVES OF RESISTANCE

Within ongoing interaction participants not only make use of explicit contextualization cues (Gumperz, 1982) such as laughter or parody of a genre in the talk they produce; they might also utilize their bodies to subtly shift alignment towards what is being said. While in the previous example an airline employee displayed her less than full affiliation with the very talk she was producing, in the next example an employee distances herself from the position of her boss through a shift in her body "attunement" (Kendon, 1985).

In the airline one not only experiences a "managed heart" (Hochschild, 1983) but also a managed body. Aspects of one's physical appearance, such as body proportions, hair style, and dress, are all subject to ongoing review by supervisors. In the following, while two ethnographers are filming and asking a gate supervisor about the duties of overseeing employees, an agent approaches. Using the agent as an example of someone who steps outside the bounds of employee rules, the gate supervisor playfully chides her for her hair style. In so doing he touches her body to index points of reference in his speech.

(4) 1 Super: See actually- hair that_s- more than shoulder length is
supposed to be pulled back at the crown.
   2 Agent: It's clipped- by my ears.
          I just got mine cut though.
          I got two and a half inches cut off.
   3 Super: This is a shoulder.
          And this is a hair.
          This is longer than that. so,
          But- It's okay. I'm just telling for their benefit.
   4 Agent: Oh yeah. I'm sure.
          It's probably gonna come down or
          I'm gonna get fired.
   5 Super: Well // we will be-
   6 Agent: Total insubordination.
   7 Super: Well we will be having reviews next month.
          =Remember?
   8 Agent: Thank you Daniel. Are you trying to scare me?
   9 Super: No. Never.
          And your uh:, scarf's hanging out again.
          ⊙Heh heh heh heh

As he says "See actually- hair that's- more than shoulder length is supposed to be pulled back at the crown." (line 1) the supervisor touches the agent's hair.

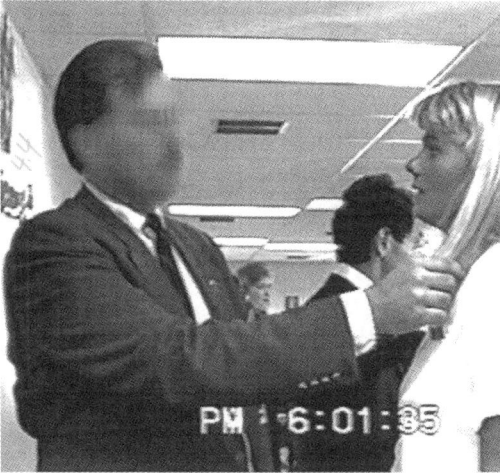

FIG. 4.4.

Ten seconds later after she argues "It's clipped- by my ears. I just got mine **cut** though. I got two and a half inches cut off," he again touches her as he makes reference to a company manual's ruling about hair not being more than shoulder length:

Gate Supervisor: This is a shoulder.
And this is a hair.
This is longer than that. so,

FIG. 4.5.

It is most common to think of transformations in activity frame with respect to ongoing dialogue (Goffman, 1974). In the present example a radical shift in orientation towards the activity in progress occurs with respect to realignment of the recipient's body, a crucial feature for understanding the meaning of human activity (Bourdieu, 1990, pp. 66-79; Foucault, 1984; Merleau-Ponty, 1962, p. 121, pp. 146-147).

In response to the supervisor's touch a second later (during "This is a hair") the gate agent rolls her eyes towards the ceiling and tenses her body, lifting her head, assuming a military-like stance. This gesture lengthens the distance between her hair and her shoulder, making her hair appear shorter; simultaneously she repositions her eyes so that they are not gazing directly at him. Metaphorically, she transforms herself into someone resembling a cadet at attention anticipating an army officer's inspection. In this way she waits out the intrusive gesture, resisting but enduring it, while distancing (Goffman, 1961) herself from the present activity.

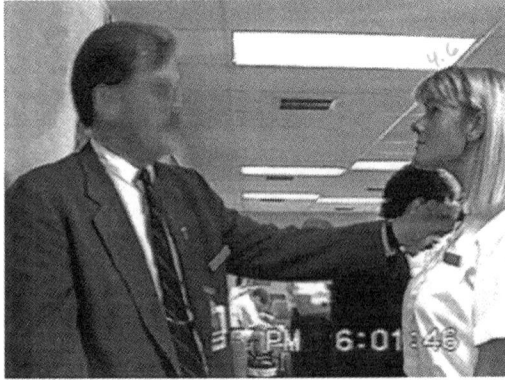

FIG. 4.6.

In order to understand this transaction it is crucial to understand talk as reciprocal embodied action. The talk of the supervisor as well as his nonvocal actions are important in the construction of his chiding action. However, the speaker's action does not stand alone. Its meaning is co-constructed through the response of recipient to it; the activity in progress is distributed across both parties to the interaction. The supervisor's assault, turning the agent's body into an object for public scrutiny, involves a simultaneous re-shifting of her body as she adapts to what he does. In much the same way that cocktail waitresses endure without comment the fondling of their customers (Spradley & Mann, 1975, p. 104), the agent resists making open counters to the supervisor's touch, and continues to hold her hair available for the supervisor's touch.

Later (line 4), as he backs away, she makes an open complaint: "It's probably gonna come down or I'm gonna get fired." This complaint is answered by the supervisor's threat that the airline "will be having reviews next month" (line 7). Acts controlling the appearance of women's bodies, such as supervisors requiring women to wear their hair a specific length or propping quarters against attendants' ears to see that their earrings do not violate a dress-code regulation (Kilborn 1993, p. A7) can result in political activity so forceful it necessitates the President's intervention, as was shown in the November 1993 American Airlines flight attendants' strike.

While most discussion of frame transformations has dealt with speaker categories and verbal interaction (Goffman, 1974), here clearly the transformation of the activity is as much in the eyes and posture of the recipient/beholder as in her talk. Moreover, her transformation of the activity does not occur in a subsequent response position, but rather in the midst of ongoing activity, thus shaping and constituting its meaning as a particular type of event. Thus what the activity comes to be is inherent neither in an abstract set of underlying preconditions defining the speech act nor the speaker's intentions, but rather emerges through the mutual and collaborative framing of the activity in progress by the recipient as well as speaker.

CONCLUSION

Four examples of frame shifts have been presented in this paper. Though the sequencing structure of a speech activity may propose certain forms of next moves and alignments, participants may selectively operate on talk in progress, through phonological shifts (#1), extracting parts for comment in ways subversive to speaker's projected activity (#2), or recasting its meaning through parody and paralinguistic commentary (#3 and #4). Such commentary may occur during ongoing talk, rather than at talk's boundaries, so that the sense of what the activity has come to be is negotiated in its course. Demonstrations of the way in which talk may be crafted for particular interactive ends — whether refusing to go along with a projected argument structure (#1) or story line (#2) or taking up a stance which distances oneself from the talk in progress (#3 and #4) — display some of the optionality available to participants in talk. Rather than buying into the projected type of speech activity under way, participants to talk may "elect to deny the dialogic frame, accept it, or carve out such a format when none is apparent" (Goffman, 1981, p. 52) through specifiable shifts in frame.

REFERENCES

Bakhtin, M. (1973). *Problems of Dostoevsky's poetics.* Ann Arbor: Ardis.

Bourdieu, P. (1990). *The logic of practice.* Cambridge, England: Polity Press.

Coulter, J. (1990). Elementary properties of argument sequences. In G. Psathas (Ed.), *Interaction competence,* (pp. 181-204). Washington, DC: International Institute for Ethnomethodology and Conversation Analysis and University Press of America.

Drew, P. (1987). Po-faced receipts of teases. *Linguistics,* **25,** 219-253.

Edelsky, C. (1981). Who's got the floor? *Language in Society,* **10,** 383-421.

Foucault, M. (1984). Docile bodies. In P. Rabinow (Ed.), *The Foucault reader* (pp. 179-187). New York: Pantheon Books.

Goffman, E. (1961). *Encounters: Two studies in the sociology of interaction.* Indianapolis: Bobbs-Merrill.

Goffman, E. (1974). *Frame analysis: An essay on the organization of experience.* New York: Harper & Row.

Goffman, E. (1981). *Forms of talk.* Philadelphia: University of Pennsylvania Press.

Goodwin, M. H. (1980). Processes of mutual monitoring implicated in the production of description sequences. *Sociological Inquiry,* **50,** 303-317.

Goodwin, M. H. (1982a). 'Instigating': Storytelling as a social process. *American Ethnologist*, **9**, 799-819.

Goodwin, M. H. (1982b). Processes of dispute management among urban black children. *American Ethnologist*, **9**, 76-96.

Goodwin, M. H. (1983). Aggravated correction and disagreement in children's conversations. *Journal of Pragmatics* **7**, 657-677.

Goodwin, M. H. (1990). Byplay: Participant structure and the framing of collaborative collusion. In B. Conein, M. de Fornel, & L. QuÄrÄ (Eds.), *Les formes de la conversation, Volume 2* (pp. 155-180). Paris: CNET.

Goodwin, C., & Goodwin, M. H. (1992a). Assessments and the construction of context. In A. Duranti & C. Goodwin (Eds.), *Rethinking context: Language as an interactive phenomenon* (pp. 147-190). Cambridge, England: Cambridge University Press.

Goodwin, C., & Goodwin, M. H. (1992b). Context, activity and participation. In P. Auer & A. di Luzio (Eds.), *The contextualization of language* (pp. 77-99). Amsterdam: Benjamins.

Gumperz, J. J. (1982). *Discourse strategies.* Cambridge, England: Cambridge University Press.

Heritage, J. (1984). *Garfinkel and ethnomethodology.* Cambridge, England: Polity Press.

Hochschild, A. R. (1983). *The managed heart: Commercialization of human feeling.* Berkeley, CA: University of California Press.

Jefferson, G. (1979). A technique for inviting laughter and its subsequent acceptance/declination. In G. Psathas (Ed.), *Everyday language: Studies in ethnomethodology* (pp. 79-96). New York: Irvington Publishers.

Kendon, A. (1985). Behavioural foundations for the process of frame attunement in face-to-face interaction. In G. P. Ginsburg, M. Brenner, & M. von Cranach (Eds.), *Discovery strategies in the psychology of action*, (pp. 229-253). London: Academic.

Kilborn, P. T. (1992, March 17). Strikers at American Airlines say the objective is respect. *The New York Times*, pp. A1-A7.

Labov, W. (1974). The art of sounding and signifying. In W. W. Gage (Ed.), *Language in its social setting* (pp. 84-116). Washington, DC: Anthropological Society of Washington.

Merleau-Ponty, M. (1962). *The phenomenology of perception.* (C. Smith, Trans.). New York: Humanities Press. (Original work published 1945)

Morson, G. S. (1989). Parody, history and metaparody. In G. S. Morson & C. E. Morson (Eds.), *Rethinking Bakhtin: Extensions and challenges* (pp. 63-103). Evanston, IL: Northwestern University Press.

Polanyi, L. (1979). So what's the point? *Semiotica*, **25**, 208-224.

Sacks, H., Schegloff, E.A., & Jefferson, G. (1974). A simplest systematics for the organization of turn-taking for conversation. *Language*, **50**, 696-735.

Shultz, J. J., Florio, S., & Erickson, F. (1982). Where's the floor?: Aspects of the cultural organization of social relationships in communication at home and in school. In P. Gilmore & A. A. Glatthorn (Eds.), *Children in and out of school: Ethnography and education* (pp. 88-123). Washington, DC: Center for Applied Linguistics.

Spradley, J. P., & Mann, B. J. (1975). *The cocktail waitress: Woman's work in a man's world.* New York: John Wiley and Sons.

Tannen, D. (1981). New York Jewish conversational style. *International Journal of Society and Language,* **30**, 131-149.

5 CODE-SWITCHING OR CODE-MIXING: APPARENT ANOMALIES IN SEMI-FORMAL REGISTERS[1]

Allen Grimshaw
Indiana University, Bloomington

> *"You can't call me honey, you're not the mommy."*
> — A little girl in California (reported by Susan Ervin-Tripp)[2]

INTRODUCTION

The first piece I ever read on the interaction of social dimensions with choice of language variety (or as we now all realize, language production more generally) was Susan Ervin-Tripp's (SET), "An analysis of the interaction of language, topic, and listener," in the now classic special 1964 issue of the *American Anthropologist* edited by Gumperz and Hymes. Within an interview study of native Japanese women who had married American men and come to live in the San Francisco area, SET did an "experiment," seeking to identify how ethnicity of interviewer, language of interview, and topic, influenced code selection and, when code was "fixed" — interference. Many of her reported findings, e.g., that each of the variables just listed affected speech production of those interviewed and that effects were cumulative, are not surprising from the perspective of what we know today — some, such as differences in answers to the same question in different languages, show an influence of language of discourse which is still

---

[1] I am indebted to Doug Maynard for a particularly helpful reading of an earlier version of this paper.

[2] This example is about rules for language use; it certainly doesn't tell us much about code-switching. But of all the stories about language in use told me by Susan Ervin-Tripp it is my favorite — and the most often retold.

startling.[3]

SET's paper along with several of its companion pieces effectively set agendas for much of the work, both descriptive and pragmatic, on code variation, sources, and switching and on such subsidiary or otherwise related issues such as co-occurrence restrictions, hyper- and hypocorrection, and repertoire for the next three decades (see particularly chapters by Albert, Bernstein, Ferguson, Frake, Gumperz, Labov, and, of course, Hymes' introduction in Gumperz & Hymes, 1964). There is absolutely no possibility in this short exploratory paper to review the rich literature on code-switching (and related notions) which has developed in the thirty years since SET published her pioneering article. Any selection of illustrative materials must be in some way arbitrary. In this short comment I'll say something about two of the 1964 pieces and then note very briefly some directions pursued in three pieces of more contemporary research.

As is often the case with pioneering papers, SET had to devote a considerable part of her 1964 article to locating the then new enterprise of sociolinguistics in terms of its principal variables of interest (speech, setting, participants, functions of interactions, forms, and **attitudes** of participants toward each of the other elements), methods of research, and relations to other disciplinary orientations (primarily psycholinguistics in this instance) as well as to presenting her own research and findings. Her research was as specified in her title, i.e., a study of the **interaction** of language, topic, and listener; she reported that each had independent effects and that incongruent combinations (e.g., being required to speak in English on a "Japanese topic" with a Japanese interlocutor) generated difficulties for speakers.

While SET's findings were based on elicitation in an experimental interview design, the results were fully consonant with those reported in Gumperz's (1964) contribution with reference to **situational** switching, i.e., he reported that code (dialect in this case) choice was determined by topic and by social relations among interlocutors. His addition to the theoretical formulation of the phenomena under consideration was his identification of a variety of switching related **not** directly to topic/situation but rather contrastively so, i.e., the marking of talk **metaphorically**.

A substantial proportion of the writing on language variation **in use** in the two decades following the publication of the special issue of the *Anthropologist* was devoted to working out details of the paradigm-setting pieces by SET and by Gumperz. In the

---

[3] SET reports the following sentence completion responses from the same woman in Japanese and English (1964, p. 96):
1. When my wishes conflict with my family,
   (Japanese) *it is a time of great unhappiness.*
   (English) *I do what I want.*
2. I will probably become
   (Japanese) *a housewife.*
   (English) *a teacher.*
3. Real friends should
   (Japanese) *help each other.*
   (English) *be very frank.*

1980s, however, a new literature about meanings of code selection and code variation began to appear in sociolinguistics; I can mention only three exemplars which appear to me to make theoretical claims of quite different scope.

Duranti (1990) is an intriguing study of code-switching between what are known as "good" and "bad" Samoan (with a few short stretches in English) in multiparty talk involving the ethnographer, his stepson, and a Samoan couple. He observes that it is often in situations where visitors are present that those studied may be constrained to resort to more subtle and indirect forms of interaction — whether in engaging in conflict or in, for example, instructing children about appropriate behavior; the verity of this observation is known to all middle class American readers of this note. Duranti also reminds us that in multiparty interaction an utterance putatively directed at one party actually may be directed to another as ally or several others as amused audience, and so on. In the instance of the conversation recorded in Samoa, Duranti argues that code-switching between "good" and "bad" Samoan by the female member of the Samoan couple is employed variously to complain about her husband's drinking, to attempt to shame him for trying to speak English, and to negatively evaluate the child's attempt to speak Samoan. The net theoretical contribution is to underline the importance of multi-functionality of utterances in multiparty interactions where switching takes place.

Beeman's (1986) rich study of Persian stylistic variation in Iran also addresses issues related to the potentialities for multiple meaning in talk — and shows how semantic ambiguities in registerial shift are intendedly exploited in the quest for interactional accomplishment. Early in his book Beeman remarks on the complexities of Iranian interaction (including, as becomes evident as one reads his book, code selection and switching):

> Because a great deal rides on an individual's adeptness at communication, verbal skills and the use of language take on great importance in every person's life. Not surprisingly, too, words are rarely uttered or received idly. A person's verbal performance becomes pregnant with import as the listener, practicing the skills he or she possesses as a communicator, tries to register every nuance of the verbal performance and interpret it successfully. To do otherwise would be less than prudent. (p. 2)

Much of the stylistic variation to which Beeman attends in his study — for example, deletion in final consonant clusters — is linguistically no more complicated than what goes on the contraction mentioned below as a marker of informality in American English: it would appear from Beeman's report to carry very considerably more information (and possibly intention) than we ordinarily assign to contraction (cf., however, Fischer, 1958). Perhaps more careful investigation of both switching between registers and the appearance in one register of tokens of the other, in American English, will reveal that more is going on pragmatically than has been heretofore assumed.

The central assertion of Katriel's (1986) interesting study of *dugri* (talking "straight") in Israeli Sabra culture is that "the speech style is a major vehicle for the projection of the Sabra character" (p. 117). If I do not too grossly misread Katriel, she is saying something to the effect that the way of talking is one which is straightforward and to the point, even when interlocutors' feelings may get bruised; that Sabras make the explicit claim that such honesty and directness was a requirement of the difficult times of early settlement; the implicit claim that they have a right to retain a mode of speech perceived as being less polite because they are veterans of those difficult times; and less clearly, an additional claim that more straightforwardness in public life would benefit contemporary Israel. Katriel cites other ways of talking which are associated with claims about the speaker's self; most of us have made such claims at one time or another in our lives — with varying degrees of intentionality and/or awareness. We may also, of course, make revelations about identities which we would prefer remain unrecognized. Whatever, it may be worth considering some of the examples cited below as projection of identity claims of one sort or another.

AN UNACCOUNTED-FOR EMPIRICAL FINDING

Sociolinguists armed with such notions as repertoire, cooccurrence restrictions, and code-switching, have focused their attention on the motivation, nature, and interactional consequences of variation in language in **use** in social contexts. Both SET (1964) and Gumperz (1964) observed that ways of talking will vary, in talk involving the same interlocutors, when topics change; but also observed that shifts can occur, within topics, when participants change. Gumperz distinguished between "situational" and "metaphorical" shifts, with the former being adjustments to topics, ends, settings, and co-interactant attributes and the latter being marked usages intendedly conveying social information such as solidarity affirmation, social distancing, or status claims, and so on.

Metaphorical switching, in contrast to situational, often occurs within a single utterance, thereby violating co-occurrence restrictions; it is this violation which carries the social information. Co-occurrence restrictions say something like: "If talk is on a certain topic and a certain variety is appropriate for that topic and those interlocutors, then use that variety and continue to do so." If such a rule is violated, Gumperz asserts, the resulting utterance will carry meaning above and beyond that available in its surface form.

A large proportion of the extended utterances in the dissertation defense corpus where I first noticed the phenomenon I look at in this paper included juxtaposed and even alternating elements of formal and of everyday or colloquial style or register. The text is replete with instances where formal expressions such as *in the sense that* or *I shall look for evidence* are found cheek-by-jowl with *y'know* or *yeah* or *okay* and/or phone deletion, or contraction, and so on. Utterances which are consistently spoken in one style, moreover, are responded to by utterances spoken in another. The apparent wholesale violation of co-occurrence restrictions is a consistent feature of talk throughout the defense corpus, finally, found in every segment (though differentially so), between formal equals and between unequals (though not in the same ways at different junctures within the event). The text displays, in short, an apparently unprincipled "mixture" of styles or registers.

It is the modifying **apparently** which is problematic in the last sentence and which has led me to undertake this speculative note. It seems obvious that it cannot be argued that many of the shifts in the ongoing talk can be characterized as "situational." It is quite likely that at least some are "metaphorical"; in my original work on the text (Grimshaw, 1989) I identified several instances in the text where a shift appeared to have been pragmatically determined. I suggest below that there are probably others. It does **not** seem likely, however, that all such shifts or even any substantial proportion of them were pragmatically determined **or even intended** — if they were, the several conversationalists in the defense were all employing such refined subtleties in their moves that no one knew what was going on! Yet, the differences are there. Are they performance errors? Some may be; I doubt that all are. Is style mixture the norm and the interpretive superstructure built on switching phenomena chimerical? I doubt this too; there **are** conversations in which one or another style predominates and where switches do carry import. I found myself wondering, however, whether there might not be some speech events defined as somehow simultaneously formal and informal: formal because of institutional constraints and the importance of the business at hand, informal because of the nature of interpersonal relationships among co-interactants. In the pages below I will introduce another "formally formal" event with different interpersonal relationships; it will be seen that there are still (although many fewer) instances of mixing.

DATA AND SOME DESCRIPTIVE RESULTS

This exploratory paper is based primarily on two data sets. The first, co-occurrence violations which initially stimulated my interest in the topic of this paper, consists of the electronically recorded (and filmed) text of a doctoral dissertation defense, a number of studies of which have already been published (Grimshaw, 1989; Grimshaw, et al., 1994).[4] The defense is about two hours long; variously involves five, four, and three participants; and varies somewhat in degrees of formality in its four major segments (i.e., openings, the defense proper, the in-camera evaluation session, and closings). These materials will be referred to as the MAP data.

The second set of materials consists of audio records (re-recorded from a videotape record) of the original English language production of US participants in a two day meeting of senior US and Soviet military officers (largely retired) who had met to talk about mutually caused threats of nuclear war — and of what might be done to reduce those threats. Variously seven or eight American officers participate in this talk, sometimes reading formal statements, sometimes making responses to Soviet presentations from written notes, sometimes making something approximating spontaneous remarks or rejoinders. Their talk is officially directed to their Soviet counterparts; it is also heard by their fellow American officers, by domestic and foreign members of the media, and by

---

[4] The Multiple Analysis Project (MAP) was an undertaking of the Committee on Sociolinguistics of the Social Science Research Council, in which investigators representing different theoretical and disciplinary perspectives independently studied the same 12-minute segment of a doctoral dissertation defense. The other investigators were Peter Burke, Aaron Cicourel, Jenny Cook-Gumperz, Charles Fillmore, John Gumperz, Michael Halliday, Ruqaiya Hasan, and Lily Wong Fillmore.

an audience consisting primarily of interested citizens of varying degrees of "official-ness." These materials, the focus of projected studies in the Generals and Admirals International Negotiation Project, will be referred to as the GAIN data.

The Search for Co-occurrence "Violations"

My method in this exploratory study was simplicity itself. In the case of the MAP corpus — where I already knew that there were what appeared to be violations — I first reviewed the full transcript and then listened carefully to the audio record. As I read, and then particularly as I listened, I looked/listened for tokens of what appeared to be infor-mal usages; I relied largely on what I suppose are stereotypes. In my initial run through the MAP corpus, for example, I found myself noting such locutions as *you know* (*y'know*), *okay*,[5] *I mean*, contractions (*that's* and *don't* were particularly common), vulgarities (e.g., *crapped on*), blasphemies (e.g., *what the hell*), quantifiers (e.g., *a lot, a little bit, every once in a while*), evaluations (*wow, terrific*), and a variety of informal lexical items (e.g., *gal, stuff, drill* [for procedure], *settle up*) and simply wrote them down — along with the identity of current speaker. All five participants in the defense pro-duced such talk; they produced it in differing quantities and at different junctures in the defense. Summary information on frequently appearing locutions and some examples of inventive informalities are attached as Appendix A.

I do not have a transcript of the complete English language portion of the GAIN corpora; there are short sections for which transcripts have been completed. For this paper I twice listened to the English portions of the GAIN meetings, including straight-forward readings of papers as well as formal rebuttals and more casual questions and answers. I did not tally individual instances of the first varieties of informal production listed about (i.e., *you know* (*y'know*), *okay*, and contractions) but did characterize partici-pants' turns as containing them when they did. I did record instances of informal lexical items and formulaic expressions and particularly of proverbs and folksayings; in both these latter instances speakers often prefaced them with such expressions *as we say* or other kinds of citation. My overall impression is that there are far fewer contractions, *you know* expressions, *okays*, vulgarities, blasphemies, and quantifiers in the GAIN than in the MAP materials — in spite of the former's quite considerably greater length. A listing of some of the informal phrases and expressions which occur in the GAIN text is attached as Appendix B.

Some Examples From the MAP Text

The common text for the MAP consisted of the last few minutes of the in-camera evaluative session (four committee members), a very brief period in which three commit-

---

[5] *Okay* may have become okay; it not infrequently appears embedded — not only in formal talk in English, but also in "simultaneous translation" of the talk of important figures who are not native speakers of English, often in English in their original text. *You know/y'know* is quite different. Academ-ic users of *okay* might use *y'know* in lecturing **to students**. They do not when they **read** lectures to **professional peers** (except in asides?) or **important nonpeer audiences**.

tee members awaited the return of the committee chair and the candidate whom he had gone to seek, and the period immediately after the return of the candidate and her sponsor — a time during which the candidate and the senior male on the committee argued about past gender discrimination in their department. While we had no such outcome in mind when we selected this particular segment of the defense for our study, the greatest bulk of the code-switching in the defense occurs during the shared text and in the period immediately prior (the first part of the in-camera session). There are relatively few instances of code-switching during the main "business" of the defense, i.e., the direct questioning of the candidate.

Two interesting instances do occur during the questioning period: a first when the supervisor undertakes to answer a question about what sorts of women other than the sort studied might have been "radicalized" — and how, the second during an exchange resulting from the candidate's query as to whether there was anything publishable in her dissertation. The two bits of text follow:

(1)   ... there must be women out there *who've* also had experiences and were in some way ready and became radical but I wonder if *they'd* be able to identify *I mean isn't isn't* there also the *kind of thing like it's like grains of sand wearing away you know* it would be very hard to say just which was the thing that really precipitated it *you know* that *ya get crapped on* for a long time and *finally say no more.*

The other, a collaborative production, occurs when the candidate asks about publishing something from her project:

(2)   ... do any of you see anything in here which would lend itself to an article?
1:    *oh my god* (pause)???
2:    you put that in the singular? (laughter)
C: pardon?
2:    you put that in the singular? (laughter)
1:    uh
C: I would hope that I would have *a couple* of answers
3:    I *don't* know *serialize it in some journal* (more laughter)

At least some of the instances in the common text fragment more clearly occur in the context of more formal ongoing talk; the expressions *pushing her on a little bit, write some of this stuff up, a little bit* (a second instance), *get some things done and out, getting things moving,* and a number of contractions occur in the otherwise quite formal evaluation turn of a senior member of the examining committee in the dissertation defense (Grimshaw, 1989, pp. 187 ff.).

Some Examples from the GAIN Text

There is roughly three to four times as much English language text in the GAIN materials as in the defense. The GAIN English-language corpus contains some speeches which had been prepared in advance. It was performed in the presence of representatives (unoffi-cial) of a still formally adversarial power and an audience of over one hundred observers and media representatives, and in front of television cameras of domestic and international news organizations.

There are far fewer instances of informality in the GAIN corpus overall. In particular, there are many fewer contractions and only a very few cases of mild blasphemy. The bulk of instances of lower formality consist of the production of extended expressions (rather than individual tokens) which tend to be distant from one another in the text — rather than clustered. Space constraints prohibit me from citing many exemplars — folk and formulaic expressions and attempts at humor (on formulaic expression in the dissertation defense see Wong Fillmore, 1994; on attempts at humor see Fillmore, 1994) make up the bulk of the instances and a surprising number are in some sort of quoted form. I can give only a few examples:

(3)   ... *to get the load of these things off our back* (reference to weapons systems)

(4)   ... this *goes against the grain* (discussion of reduction of naval force structures)

(5)   ... we're there to *kinda keep the lid on* (responding to complaints about US bases surrounding the USSR)

(6)   ... you know the expression, *"show me, we're from Missouri"* (expressing dubiety re SDI)

(7)   ... we have a saying, a folk saying, in this country ... *"that the pot should be careful when it calls the kettle black"* (in exchange concerning presence of militaries of the two superpowers in countries near the other)

There are no obscenities or true vulgarities in the English-language text of the GAIN corpus. The "strongest" language employed is used in explanation of why military leadership of the USSR (like its American counterpart) didn't want a figure on its military expenditure published (*"it's too damn big"*) **and**, even more mildly, with reference to reduction of arms levels, *"Lord knows*, both sides have reasons to do this."

Summary

The two events from which I have drawn examples of apparent code-mixing are both "formal" in some sense; the actual talk produced in the Generals and Admirals conference appears to be more formal and more consistently so than that of the dissertation defense. In the following section I speculate both about reasons why there is any "mixing" at all and, in the two exemplary instances, why there is so much less in the international negotiation.

SOME SPECULATIONS AND SOME QUESTIONS

Readers will have thought of many features of the speech events which help to make sense out of the presence of and variability of code-mixing in the MAP and GAIN corpora. In this exploratory paper I have space to suggest and briefly comment on only six among many such features, namely: (1) intrinsic formality (including the role and status of written materials in the ongoing), (2) constraints of numbers of participants and of audiences (and of characteristics of the latter), (3) Ends$_1$ and Ends$_2$ (goals and outcomes in Hymes' [1972] SPEAKING heuristic), (4) episode, stages, junctures, and duration of the speech event of interest (and, where appropriate of sub-segments or episodes) and other sequential considerations, (5) topic, both "content" and "staying on or straying off," and (6) what I call the "sociological variables" of interactant relations of power and of affect and of considerations of utility/salience/cost, and so on.[6]

Intrinsic Formality

A feature of the dissertation defense is that a written document was an official focus of attention — and that much of the talk was organized around either notes written at an earlier time or discussion of what would be necessary in order for the candidate to generate an optimally well-done research report. In the case of the GAIN materials, each major segment was initiated by the reading of a "position" statement; written notes were again employed in discussion of that initial statement and of subsequent responses, rebuttals, and so on. I have a hunch that the location of both the GAIN and the MAP corpora in contexts in which past writing was a topic and current writing an aid to ongoing talk had effects on the nature of that talk, specifically its degree of formalness and, in some way, additionally affected the amount of self-monitoring by the American officers.

I suspect that the presence or absence of written material as either a focus or a backdrop to oral production is deeply implicated in the formality of speech. Labov (1972) demonstrated how production of careful and more casual speech was stimulated by, variously, written text, word-pairs, and narrative elicitation; one dimension of formali-ty in "naturally occurring" speech would appear to be linked to written materials. Something like the following may go on with "formality" decreasing from top to bottom of the list:

Levels of oral formality in contexts of written materials:

(1) reading of formal and/or ritualized speech — no contractions or other informalities in written version — none in spoken;

(2) reading of speech "word-for-word" — may or may not have contractions or other informalities in written version, they may or may not be present in spoken presen-tation;

(3) reading of speech prepared for oral presentation "as if speaker were talking" — contractions and possibly other informalities are likely to be written "in" — they will certainly be present in oral presentation;

(4) speaking from notes — highly variable depending upon contexts of situation and other elements of the SPEAKING heuristic. *Ceteris paribus*, however, speech production under such a circumstance is more likely be informal or "mixed."

A substantial portion of the GAIN corpus consists of participants reading prepared

---

[6] While not foregrounded, it will be evident that here as in much of my work I have been influenced in my formulation by Hymes', 1972, SPEAKING heuristic (itself adumbrated in Hymes, 1964, and, as Hymes notes, several earlier formulations).

texts or from notes written in response either to translations of written Russian prepared texts or to "simultaneous translation" of spoken Russian of the various sorts listed. Conversation in a dissertation defense focuses, of course, on a written document (a long one in the instance studied), and several committee participants in the defense employed notes in their questioning. Both events are in some sense formal. It seems likely to me that some of the differences in frequencies of occurrence of tokens of informal register can be attributed to differences in the nature and status of written texts of one sort or another.

A demography of speech registers?

In the course of brooding about the appearance of tokens of informal register in talk that appears, overall, to be more formal, I have found myself pondering the possibility of an inverse relationship between size of audience and the use of informalities in speech (I don't for a moment claim this to be a novel observation). There are obvious exceptions of dramatic performances and some metaphorical switches in speeches to large (including television) audiences at one end of the size range and possibly even dyadic interaction on very "serious" matters at the other. But note, however, the sometimes unanticipated confirmations of the notion as, for example, in the differences in the speech of athletic celebrities in dugouts or on the bench and in front of network television cameras — cliches, yes, but also a generally much more formal register (including, often, a shift to a lower, and presumably more portentous pitch).

Some of the differences in speech production associated with differences in audience size are probably explicable by considerations no more complicated than that people probably increase monitoring because of concerns about impression management (Goffman, 1959). Others presumably have to do with some sort of differences between face-to-face **interaction** and either individual or group presentations **to** or performances **in front of** large live or television audiences in terms of expectations about familiarity. Students of attention maintenance and of rhetorical devices employed to elicit coordinated responses from large live audiences have shown that interaction between speakers and audiences is very different from that in conversations (Atkinson, 1982, 1984; Heritage & Greatbatch, 1986). In addition to rhetorical devices such as three-part lists, contrasts, and position-taking, these students have observed that speakers employ prosodic features such as amplitude, pace, and tempo to manage audience response — it seems reasonable to expect that code-switching and code-mixing might be similarly employed.[7] It may very

---

[7] Heritage and Greatbatch (1986, pp. 43 ff.) refer to the "role of delivery" in making rhetorical devices variably successful — "delivery" includes gaze and gesture as well as prosodic features. Inclusion of metaphorical style or register switching/mixing would seem a likely extension. Indeed, Gumperz and Hernandez-Chavez (1972, p. 98) observe that "code-switching . . . is meaningful in much the same way that lexical choice is meaningful."

Urban (1991), in his very suggestive treatment of style, register, and genre (p. 119) relatedly comments with respect to styles that, "In order for them to have a differentiating capability, they must be recognizably distinct." He subsequently observes that the expressive/pragmatic functions of style may be more important in small rather than larger societies because there may be fewer nonlinguistic signals

well be that there are audience-size effects on switching and mixing which operate independently of other considerations; research is needed to sort out the impacts of such variables as opportunities for live audience response, intra-audience communication, physical arrangements, and so on.

Ends₁ and ends₂: goals and outcomes

While Katriel (1986) and Beeman (1986) both seem to imply conscious choice in the employ of registers, most work on code-switching identifies pragmatic functions/outcomes of such switching but does not address issues of intention in choice. Fillmore (1994) has addressed issues of possible intended outcomes in the use of humor in the dissertation defense, including nonexhaustively, tension management, the reduction of social distance, and, possibly, the expression of solidarity. It seems altogether reasonable to me to suggest that some of these same ends may motivate informal usages in the two data sets I have been discussing in this chapter. This seems particularly to be the case in the GAIN materials, where the speakers often mark their offerings as intended to reduce the likelihood of cross-cultural cross-language communicative nonsuccess by such introductory expressions as, "You know the expression" or "We have a saying, a folk saying" and so on. Drew and Holt (1988) show a close association between the employ of idiomatic expressions and complaint-making in everyday conversation; they do not directly address issues of intent but do characterize some use of idiomatic expressions as oriented toward seeking affiliation. Such an interpretation would seem to be consonant with an interpretation of similar usages in the GAIN materials as directed to tension reduction.

Fillmore (1994) reports that as a nonsociologist he more often than not found it difficult to see what made the sociologist defense participants laugh; apparently the Soviet participants found it difficult to comprehend why their American counterparts' jokes were seen by the Americans as funny and likely to increase solidarity.

If the sorts of outcomes Fillmore identifies are **intended** (Ends₁) by the production of informal expression, awareness of that intentionality will vary for both those who use them in their talk, and their interlocutors. Similarly, it is not easy to discern from the behavioral record whether the officers who produced such informalities in the GAIN text were satisfied with the results (Ends₂) of their efforts. A closer study of the full text might well reveal a monitoring of outcomes — and accommodative behaviors in the subsequent interaction.

It is even more difficult to speculate in a principled manner about possible goals and outcomes of such tokens of informal register as contractions, *okays*, *you knows*, and the like. Some of these may well be performance errors. At the same I think it likely that some of these usages, particularly in the MAP corpus, where there are many more of them, **are** intended to demonstrate that the speaker is not taking himself too seriously or, later in the proceedings, aware that the ongoing is "talk among equals." Again, the

---

(p. 181). Implications of this observation for differences in the MAP and GAIN corpora are not immediately obvious.

questions can be addressed only by close study of the talk in its contexts of text and of situation.

Episode, stages, junctures, duration, and other sequential matters

Just as there are differences between the MAP and GAIN corpora in the appearance, at all, of informality tokens in generally formal speech production, there are also differences over the course of each of the events in occurrences of switching and mixing. These differences may not affect all participants in a same manner; in the defense the faculty committee members used more informal words and phrases in the opening segment than did the candidate, who employed a consistently formal register both in that segment and in the following "defense proper" and began to mix and switch only after she had been told that she had passed the examination and that her dissertation had been accepted. (It might alternatively be argued that defenses are ordinarily divided in pre- and postdecision segments with the latter tending more to the informal but that special features of the defense studied, i.e., a dispute between the candidate and a senior committee member and the reinitiation of "business" by another dampened this shift.) This specific exception notwithstanding, however, we are all familiar with the ways in which more formal events are more often than not bracketed by opening and closing sessions, often oriented to displaying (sometimes spurious) solidarity between parties about to contend — or having just terminated or tabled a dispute. There are such segments in the defense; there are such segments and differences in the Generals and Admirals Conference materials; they are also found in job interviews, real estate closings, parent–teacher interviews, many public lectures, and in a very large variety of events considered important by participants.

There are instances in which such events do not have opening and closing segments in which talk includes informalities. These exceptions are either highly routinized meetings between individuals well known to one another, or occasions in which one or both parties explicitly decline to participate in anything interpretable as expressing solidarity. Instances of the latter sort are often marked by expressions such as, "Let's get down to business" (interestingly, itself a fairly informal expression) or, more abruptly, "Cut the pleasantries" (also informal) often heard in unfriendly divorce negotiations in lawyers offices or from angry faculty complaining to administrators about unfulfilled promises.

With specifiable (and "reportable" in Labov's, 1968, sense) exceptions, it can be anticipated that different amounts of mixing and switching will occur at different stages or segments of events. It also seems likely that the longer talk in a formal register goes on without the appearance of manifestations of informal register, the longer it is likely to continue in the same way (see Vuchinich & Teachman, 1993).

Topic: content, focus, foregrounding, and maintenance

Ervin-Tripp's original paper on this topic showed language choice to be associated with topic and Gumperz showed the same for dialect selection — dozens of studies in the three decades since their pioneering papers appeared have reported similar results. Their studies, however, and most of those that have followed, have attended to code-**switching**, and not to the occasional appearance of a single word or phrase in another variety, i.e., what I have been calling code-**mixing**. In some of his later work on the pragmatics of code-variation Gumperz has shown, for something very much like mixing, the marking of more personal and/or emotional topics or subtopics by use of codes signaling intimacy. Such dimensions of the personal and emotional in the content of topics do not appear in the MAP and GAIN corpora.

While I have not done the necessary systematic examination of the two corpora, I have a strong sense that while there are instances (particularly in the defense) where informal talk is embedded in seriously-taken main topics (evaluation of the candidate, for example), those cases are more unusual than other instances in openings and closings and in "off-topic" talk. Both the off-topic talk itself and the appearance, within that talk, of additional markers of informality may be intended to serve as signals that while the ongoing is serious, that seriousness need not be seen as requiring increased social distance among participants. If this should turn out to be the case it makes the instances of high concentrations of informal tokens in the very serious talk of evaluation, for example, even more intriguing.

The sociological variables

I have (imperialistically, I suppose) used the term sociological variables for relations of affect and of power among interactants and for the "utility" (salience, cost, and so on) of goals; with different labels the same or related dimensions have been shown to constrain behaviors such as address, code selection, and requesting behavior. I have a hunch that the sociological variables influence the appearance at all and amount of informalities in talk in formal register. For example, if informality appears in formal variants it seems likely to me that it will be first **intendedly** introduced (discounting occurrences resulting from performance error) by a participant or participants of higher power. *Ceteris paribus*, I suspect that in contexts of formal talk, informalities are much more likely to appear in situations of mutually shared positive affect than of shared negative affect, with the codicil that when interactants become angry with one another there may be a reduction of monitoring resulting in an increase in otherwise less appropriate informal usages.[8] Life is indeed complex.

---

[8] What is switched in the defense (and in the Generals and Admirals Conference) is not language or even dialect, of course, but register or perhaps style. But just as in bilingualism or bidialectalism there will be social values attached to the varieties — if not status/prestige, then affect/intimacy/social distance and so on. This would seem to raise interesting questions about possible use of code-mixing to include or exclude interlocutors — or to pretend to do so. There are still other considerations, of course. Is it possible that there are speakers who are simply not as competent in a formal variety — or who experience more interference?

CONCLUSION

At the end of the introductory section I made the not very profound suggestion that there are speech events defined as somehow simultaneously formal and informal. I have a hunch that the dissertation defense constitutes such an event, one in which consideration of "official" goals and setting interacts with the character of personal relationships to define the situation as "serious but informal." It may be that the Generals and Admirals Conference is further differentiated as something like "serious and formal — but not unfriendly." If my hunch is correct, mutual selection of a "mixed" variety is itself metaphorical, simultaneously signaling and reinforcing joint acceptance of the situation defined. The frequency and particularities of such varietal mixes can only be determined by looking at other speech events characterized by different ends, degrees of "official-ness," interpersonal relations and, of course, both the kinds of variations in more global pragmatic functions or considerations identified by such investigators as Beeman and Katriel — and a congeries of considerations limned above.

It may well be that to the extent that mixture occurs, the availability of metaphorical marking in Gumperz's sense as an interactional resource will be reduced. The extent to which this may be the case will require much more careful examination of a wider and more systematic range of cases than has been possible in this exploratory paper.

Appendix A
Informal Register in the Map Corpus

You know/Y'know	61	(all participants; range one to 32 instances)
I mean	9	(two participants)
Okay	14	(all participants; two instances apparently quotes)
Yeah/ya/yuh	8	
Contractions:		
don't	19	
I'm/I'll/I'd	14	
that's	7	
it's	7	
you're/you've/you'd	6	
didn't	6	
other	26	(all participants; some doubles; additional instances embedded in longer stretches of informal register)
Quantifiers:		
a little/little bit/little more	4	
lot/lots/awful lot	3	

all/at all	3
couple	2
every once in a while	1

Blasphemies, vulgarities:

hell/what the hell	4	
god/my god/thank god	3	
goddammit	1	
crapped on	1	(male participants only; some used as intensifiers)

Some miscellaneous instances:

stuff (4);	*real hole;*	*slip away from;*	*reamed over;*
shifting gears;	*figure out;*	*what's-her-name;*	*what is the drill?*
gal; boss;	*bounce it back;*	*settle up; terrific;*	*dragging her heels;*
wow;	*you got;*	*you wanta;*	*really work her ...*

Appendix B
A Sampling of Informal Phrases from the Gain Corpus

I'll toss the ball to you ...
okay, okay, thank you ...
something that I had a chance to know a little bit about ...
shouldn't be fiddled with ...
I kind of throw it out of my mind ...
you can't just come in a little bit ...
Japan's really taking it on the head today ...
they have a considerable passel of weapons ...
pretty bloody nutty ...
to just throw it out the window ...
there are some nuts running around ...
here we are with all of this stuff ...
I'll be durned ...
because I'm shifty . . .

REFERENCES

Atkinson, J. M. (1982). Understanding formality: The categorization and production of 'formal' interaction. *British Journal of Sociology, 33*, 86-117.

Atkinson, J. M. (1984). Public speaking and audience response: some techniques for inviting applause. In J. M. Atkinson & J. Heritage (Eds.), *Structures of social action: Studies in conversation analysis,* (pp. 370-409). Cambridge, England: Cambridge University Press.

Beeman, W. O. (1986). *Language, status, and power in Iran.* Bloomington: Indiana University Press.

Drew, P., & Holt, E. (1988). Complainable matters: the use of idiomatic expressions in making complaints. In D. W. Maynard (Guest Ed.), *Language, interaction, and social problems,* Special issue of *Social Problems,* **35**(4), 398-417.

Duranti, A. (1990). Code switching and conflict management in Samoan multiparty interaction. *Pacific Studies,* **14**, 1-30.

Ervin-Tripp, S. (1964). An analysis of the interaction of language, topic, and listener. In J. J. Gumperz & D. Hymes (Eds.), *The ethnography of communication,* Special Publication of *American Anthropologist,* **66**(6, Part 2), 86-102.

Fischer, J. L. (1958). Social influence in the choice of a linguistic variant. *Word,* **14**, 47-56.

Fillmore, C. J. (1994). Humor in academic discourse. In A. D. Grimshaw, et al., *What's going on here? Complementary studies of professional talk* (pp. 271-310). Norwood, NJ: Ablex.

Goffman, E. (1959). *The presentation of self in everyday life.* Garden City: Doubleday.

Grimshaw, A. D. (1989). *Collegial discourse: Professional conversation among peers.* Norwood, NJ: Ablex.

Grimshaw, A. D., et al. (1994). *What's going on here? Complementary studies of professional talk.* Norwood, NJ: Ablex.

Gumperz, J. J. (1964). Linguistic and social interaction in two communities. In J. J. Gumperz & D. Hymes (Eds.), *The ethnography of communication,* Special Publication of *American Anthropologist,* **66**(6, Part 2), 137-153.

Gumperz, J. J., & Hernandez-Chavez, E. (1972). Bilingualism, bidialectalism, and classroom interaction. In C. B. Cazden, V. P. John, & D. Hymes (Eds.), *Functions of language in the classroom* (pp. 84-108). New York: Teachers College Press.

Gumperz, J. J., & Hymes, D. (Eds.). (1964). *The ethnography of communication,* special publication of *American Anthropologist.*

Heritage, J., & Greatbatch, D. (1986). Generating applause: A study of rhetoric and response at party political conferences. *American Journal of Sociology,* **92**, 110-157.

Hymes, D. (1964). Introduction: Toward ethnographies of communication. In J. J. Gumperz & D. Hymes (Eds.), *American Anthropologist,* **66**(6, Part 2), 1-34.

Hymes, D. (1972). Models of the interaction of language and social life. In J. J. Gumperz & D. Hymes (Eds.), *Directions in sociolinguistics: The ethnography of communication* (pp. 35-71). New York: Holt, Rinehart, Winston.

Katriel, T. (1986). *Talking straight: Dugri speech in Israeli Sabra culture.* Cambridge, England: Cambridge University Press.

Labov, W. (1968). *A proposed program for research and training in the study of language in its social and cultural settings.* Unpublished manuscript, Columbia University.

Labov, W. (1972). *Sociolinguistic patterns.* Philadelphia: University of Pennsylvania Press.

Urban, G. (1991). *A discourse-centered approach to culture: Native South American myths and rituals.* Austin: University of Texas Press.

Vuchinich, S., & Teachman, J. (1993). The duration of wars, strikes, riots, and family arguments. *Journal of Conflict Resolution,* **37**, 544-568.

Urban, Greg. (1991). A discourse-centered approach to culture: Native South American myths and rituals. Austin: University of Texas Press.

Wong Fillmore, L. (1994). The role and function of formulaic speech in conversation. In A. D. Grimshaw, et al. (Eds.), *What's going on here? Complementary studies of professional talk* (pp. 230-270). Norwood, NJ: Ablex.

6 ORAL PATTERNS AS A RESOURCE IN CHILDREN'S WRITING: AN ETHNOPOETIC NOTE[1]

Dell Hymes
University of Virginia

This tribute to Susan Ervin-Tripp is essentially a note to a recent book (Himley, 1991). Himley documents one young boy's writing activity. I want to show that what emerges uses patterns of oral narrative. That in itself is not surprising (cf. Dickinson, Wolf, & Stotsky, 1993). One kind of pattern, however, has seldom been taken into account.[2]

Gee (1989, 1991, 1992) comes very close. Stimulated by work in what can be called "ethnopoetics," Gee recognizes that oral narrative is built up of intonational units and lines, and groups of these. He indeed refers in one title to "the line and stanza structure of human thought" (1989, p. 61). The difficulty is that Gee heads straight for meaning, not pausing to consider form.

The elementary unit is an intonational unit. Gee's correct understanding of this is well grounded in work of Wallace Chafe and Michael Halliday (cf. Gee, 1991, pp. 21-22). Others working in ethnopoetics call such a unit a line. Gee calls it an "idea unit"; a line may consist of more than one, and is "something like what would show up as a sentence in writing" (1991, p. 22). Gee knows that narrators have choices when they shape a sequence of words into intonational units, but puts narrative on the page in a way which obscures such choices.

In the work of Virginia Hymes and myself, not all intonational units are equivalent. Some have sentence-like contours, some do not. Those which do are "verses." In a number of Native American languages, several varieties of English, and a few other languages, verses are building blocks of narrative form. In particular, they enter into relations governed by pattern numbers. Narratives are often marked by repetition and parallelism; they also involve succession. (Cf. Hymes, 1991a, 1991b, 1992, 1993, 1994, 1995).

In American English, and a variety of Native American languages, succession is normally of three or five units. The relation holds among verses, among stanzas, among

---

[1] Parts of this chapter are to appear in: Hymes, D. (in press). *Ethnography, linguistics, and narrative inequality: Toward an understanding of voice* (chapter 7). London: Taylor & Francis. Reprinted by permission.

[2] What I can say about oral narrative in English depends on work over the years of Virginia Hymes, who joins me in this tribute. When we were at Berkeley, Virginia for a time assisted Sue (and Wick Miller) in their research on children's acquisition of language.

scenes. This finding has been made so repeatedly as to indicate that Gee's point that stanzas are often four lines long (1991, p. 25) is an artifact.

Space allows a brief example of the difference. Part 1 of the narrative in Gee (1991, p. 17ff) is analyzed as having five stanzas. Each has four Gee lines, except the coda, which has two. In terms of phonological lines (see below):

Strophe	Stanza	Line	Phonological lines
1	1	1	1/2
		2	3
		3	4
		4	5, 6, 7
	2	5	8, 9
		6	10
		7	11, 12
		8	13
2	3	9	14
		10	15, 16
		11	17
		12	18, 19
	4	13	20, 21, 22, 23
		14	24, 25
		15	26
		16	27, 28, 29, 30
Coda	5	17	31, 32
		18	33

Gee is right that these lines are a distinct part, constituted by five groups of lines, of which the first and second pairs go together ("strophes"). But three or five part relations at the larger level lead one to expect them at others. They do appear, if one attends further to succession of lines in terms of verbal parallelism and repetition, and the tendency of narrators to bring units around to the same or a related ending point. Gee's sense of the part, somewhat revised, is confirmed at all levels. (Verses are flush left. Capitalized words have prominent pitch, as in Gee).

[I] [The sea]
Well, when I was LITTLE,
        the MOST EXCITING thing that we used to do is
        there used to be THUNDERSTORMS on the beach that we lived on
And we walked down to MEET the thunderstorms
And we'd turn around and RUN HOME,   5
                running AWAY from the
                        running away from the THUNDERSTORMS.
That was the MOST EXCITING
        one of the MOST EXCITING times we ever had was doing things like
                [that

besides having like when there was HURRICANES OR STORMS out
> [on the ocean.   10

The WAVES
> they would get really BIG

And we'd go down and PLAY in the waves when they got big.

And one summer the waves were ENORMOUS
> they were just about   15
>> they went STRAIGHT UP AND DOWN

So the SURFERS WOULDN'T ENJOY them or anything like that

They'd just go STRAIGHT up and down
> the HUGEST HUGEST things in the world.

Then they would   20
> they would
> they went ALL THE WAY OVER the top of the edge of the road

and went down the road TO OUR STREET

So that's HOW BIG the waves were
> they were HUGE   25

It was SO MUCH FUN just watching them

They made BIG POOLS on the edges of the beach
> that lasted for maybe ABOUT A MONTH   }

The waves were SO SO STRONG

and you'd get SO MUCH OF A CHANGE in the beach that year   }   30

That was when I was REALLY YOUNG
> maybe about 7 YEARS OLD or something

That was uh that was really EXCITING   }

The first three stanzas have the same extent as in Gee, but read differently. In the first stanza each of the three verses has one of three occurrences of "thunderstorm. Each has an initial marker ("Well," "and," "and"). Gee points out the resumptive parallel ("Most exciting") that begins the second stanza, linking the two. Here the first verse seems extended like the first of the first stanza. The second is linked with the third by its ending point ("big"), and the third begins with "And we'd . . . ," like the second and third of the first stanza.

Gee notes that the second pair go together as being about waves (1991, p. 25), and takes the second stanza (fourth in all) as lines 20-30. I perceive line 25 as an ending point parallel to that of the third stanza ("huge"). Moreover, the lines that follow participate in a different pattern, three pairs, with different verbal repetition. The first two pairs (26, 27-8; 29, 30) both begin with emphatic use of *so*. Both end with the beach and a period of time (month, year). The third pair continues that reference to time ("that was when"). Its own paired beginning ("That was . . .") is broken off in its second verse, then repeated to bring the whole round to its beginning ("exciting").

Gee pioneers in exploring levels of discourse on such a foundation. His goal of showing "deeply senseful uses of language" (1991, p. 15) can be aided, I think, by attending to this dimension.

Let me turn now to Himley's exploration of "the particular ways [her son] Matthew has been drawn across time to the semiotic resources of written language" (140). The texts come in chapter 6, after discussions of perspectives on such work. Himley's careful discussion of the texts should be read for an appreciation of all that is going on in them. If these observations lead others to her book, I shall be pleased, especially because the tradition in which she locates it, that of and Patricia Carini, was very important to my colleagues in Reading and Language Arts at the University of Pennsylvania.

Himley herself points out the likely presence of oral patterning in regard to dialogue in connection with the third text (the first of the series of four about the disappearance of the TV):

"After the opening crisis is set up in the opening three lines, the flow of information — that is, the way the text is developed locally — reads like the transcription of a spoken language dialogue. The unit of text, more phonological than graphological, as well as the absence of periods, supports the interpretive possibility that the writer relies on spoken language resources for text generation."[3]

My effort here is to show that the spoken language resources include ethnopoetic patterns (relations). (The written text analyzed in Gee, 1992, p. 146ff), can also be shown to have such a form, one that agrees with the author's periods and capitalization.)

Text I   (1st grade, fall 1980, about age 5 years, 10 months)

Once upon a time there were two little boys.	
Their names were Matt and Matt.	
Their Moms and Daddys were lost.	
They had to spend their own money to buy food	
so they could eat breakfast and lunch and dinner.	5
One day their Moms and Dads came home.	
They asked how they got food.	
[---] "How do you think?	
"With money." }	
[---] "Did you have enough money?" }	10
[---] "Yes, we were almost out." }	
[---] "I'm glad you did not die."	
[---] "We almost did," said Matt Himley. }	

In the original text (141-142) there is no separation between lines. Lines seem condi-

---

[3] She footnotes the work of Michael Halliday at this point, and aptly so. In the third text, the first about the disappearing TV, the dialogic part actually begins, not in the fourth, but in the fifth and sixth written lines with "I/said, 'The TV disappeared./. . . .'"

tioned partly by the space available, and sometimes run over. Punctuation is not used; capitalization occurs, but not always or only in the first word of a sentence. I follow Himley's normalization.

Two temporal expressions "Once upon a time" and "One day" begin parts of the story. Probably the story should be taken as having just those two parts. If so, the first has five elements. The third element is one point of focus (their moms and daddies were lost), the fifth spells out another (they could eat). The second part has three pairs of turns at talk. The initial turn is indirect, the remaining five direct. (Perhaps "One day their Moms and Dads came home" is a separate unit with a single line, but it seems more likely that it and the following line of indirect discourse together are the first of six paired units.) Ms. Himley notes the effective edge in the repeated "almost," and the naming and rhythm of the final line.

Text II (5th grade, May 1985, age 10 years, 5 months)

Matt Himley gave the text (146-147) its title and perhaps its paragraphs:
>   1999
>   "They finally did it," I whispered to myself
>   as I woke up to see the city in crumbles.
>   The bomb must have landed about 80-90 miles away
>   since I was only knocked down and bruised up.
>   I was looking at a huge black cloud to the west   5
>   when my heart stopped. Where was my mom?
>
>   Since the house wasn't damaged very much
>   I went inside to see what I could
>   Then I just remembered
>   that my mom said
>   that she was going to the grocery store.   10
>   I went into the garage to get my bicycle.
>   The wall of the garage must of sheltered it
>   because it was almost exactly like I left it.
>   And then I set out to find my mom.
>
>   When I got to the grocery store   15
>   everyone was up and around.
>   When I saw my mom
>   I was very relieved.
>   She was sitting against the magazine rack,
>   with one eye open and one eye closed.   20
>   We hugged and kissed for a while.
>   And the(n) with our hands around each other
>   we went home.

In some oral traditions words equivalent to "And then" mark verses and larger segments. Matthew here uses the pair to close the second and third parts. Indeed, he shows a fine sense of marking the endings of sections throughout. The first ends with the poignant question, "Where was my mom?"

Three parts are indicated by space in the printed story. Their status as units is shown by consistent internal patterning. The first has three verses, the second five, the third five. Subordinate clauses, introduced by conjunctions, are prominent, and the rhythm appears to make frequent use of pairs of clauses in a unit.

The first stanza marks the second line of pairs of lines, using "as," "since," and "when." (The final line, "Where was my mom?," seems in apposition to the preceding phrase, as if preceded by a colon.)

The second stanza marks its first, second and fifth verses with an initial word: "Since. . . . ," "Then . . . ," "And then. . . . " The third has no marker, but is a pivot, both culmination and onset. The fourth marks its second clause (" . . . because . . . ").

The third stanza is like the second. The first, second and fifth verses are initially marked: "When . . . ," "When . . . ," "And then. . . . " Again the third sentence is straightforward without a marker. So is the fourth. Altogether, a kind of patterning expectable in a tradition that makes use of three and five-part relations: three stanzas, with three, five, and five verses, respectively.

A major contribution of Himley's book is to trace four stages in writing the same story. The writing took place over a three- to four-week period. The first version (153) was written in school.

Text III (2nd grade, fall 1981, age about 6 years, 11 months)

[1] The Day the TV Disappeared
Once upon a time I was playing Atari
    and my TV disappeared.
I didn't know what to do.
I ran to my mom.

I said, "The TV disappeared."
    "What should I do?"
My mom said,
    "Calm down."
    "Should I call the police?"
I said, "Yes!"

The second version (155-156) is not dated, but seems to have followed closely: "Apparently attracted to the imaginative possibilities suggested in the first version, Matthew begins again." (146)

[2]
Once upon a time I was playing Atari,
    and my TV disappeared
I didn't know what to do.

I went upstairs to tell my mom.

She said to calm down.   5
[---] "But what should I do?"   }
[---] "Do you want to call the police?"
[---] "Yes!"   }
[---] "Do you know where the phone is?"
[---] "Of course."   }   10
[---] "Then go."[---]
[---]   "OK."   }
911 I dialed.
        "Hello, please.
        "My TV disappeared," I said.
        "My address is 8201."
        "Please come over."
[---] "We'll be over in a second."   }

Ding dong.
        "Where is the TV?" said the police.
[---] "It was there."   }
[---] "So what happened?"
[---] "I don't know."   }
[---] "Then I don't."
[---] "Well, we can't find it."   }
        The end.

Ms. Himley supplies the quotation marks that distinguish the last two lines as separate turns. That status fits the pervasiveness in these stories of pairs of turns at talk, either three or five. What a distinct source of the last line might be, to be sure, is not certain. One might regard the two last lines as part of the one concluding turn at talk by the police. If so, then the line and signal that start the stanza, "Ding dong," can be counted as the first turn. This indeed is the conclusion reached by Schegloff with regard to the ringing of phones and doorbells counting as a summons. The next thing that happens, indeed, is not an answer to the summons, but a question by one of those who rang the bell. Still, putting the voice of the police in the second position of each of three adjacency pairs maintains the dialogic form. Perhaps the ding dong is taken as implying its correlate, admission to the house, and the police taken as responding to that step. Admitted, they ask. Told, they ask. Told again, they give up. This would fit Himley's (1991, p. 156) observation:

Matthew has invented a kind of paragraph: he indicates an external action (e.g., dialing the phone, the doorbell ringing) and follows that action with the dialogue, or speech act, relevant to that action. These bits of clues about the action and setting seem like nascent exposition, or perhaps even stage directions, as the text does now resemble a script.

Himley noticed this textualizing strategy in the preceding text, and spaced the third version in order to emphasize it.

This third version (157-160) is of such length as to benefit from indications of units and relations at the right margin.

[3]

Once upon a time I was playing Atari   [i] (A)
and my TV disappeared.
I didn't know,
because I went to get something to drink.
I went upstairs to tell my mom.   5

My mom said,   (B)
   "Calm down."
"But I can't," I said.   }
"Then sit down."
"OK, but what should I do?"   }   10
"Do you want to call the police?"
"Yes!"   }
"OK. Do you know where the phone is?"
"Yes, in your room, right?"   }
"Right. Go!"   15
"OK."   }

 911 I called.   (C)
   "Hello. My TV disappeared.
   My address is 8201.
   Please come over."   20
"We will be over in a second."
"OK."

                                                                        [ii] (D)
Ding dong.
   "Where's your TV?"
"It was right there," I said.   25
"So what happened?"
"I don't know,
   I will get my mom."
"OK," said the policeman.

"Mom, the policemen are here."   30 (E)
"I will be down in a second."
"OK."
"Now where's the table?"
"That's what we're trying to find out," said the policeman.

"I went to get something to drink.   35 (F)
    I got a cup and some Pepsi."
"Is anything gone now?"   }
I said, "No, but I might know where everything is going."
"Where?"   }
"There is a robber that has a machine near Ridgeland Park.   40
    Should I call a friend that lives near Ridgeland?"
"OK," said the policeman.   }

383-8377 I dialed.   (G)
   "Hi, Matt.
   Can I come over?"   45
"I will call my mom."
"OK."

771-7044.   (H)
   "Hi, Matt."   50
"Ya?"
"Yes, you can."
"I will be over in a second."
"OK," said Matt.

Ding dong.   55[iii] (I)
"Hi, Matt."   }
"What do you want to do?"
"Well, first I should introduce these people.
  This is Captain Tom from the police station.   (})
  Now this is why he came here.   60
  My TV disappeared
    and Captain Tom might know where it is going."
"Where?" said Matt.   }
"To Ridgeland Park.   }?
  Want to go there?"   65 (J)?
"OK."   }
"Let's go.
  But one thing, I can't play."
"OK."   }
"Well, let's go."   70
"OK."   }

"Captain Tom?"   (K)
"Yes?"
"Can we ride in the cop car?"
"I guess so."   75

"OK."

After they got there,   [iv] (L)
    Matt Himley said, "Where does he live?"
"Right over there."
"OK."   80

"Don't run."
"OK."

"I will go first.
    Get down."
"Yes, sir."   85

"Don't call me sir,
    call me Tom."
"OK, Tom."

"Get down."
"OK."   90

Ding dong.   [v] (M)
"Yes?"

"Hide, Tom.
"My name is Matt.
    His is, too."   }   95

"So what?"
"We have been walking for days.
    Do you mind if we have a bite to eat?"

"No! Get out!"
"Hold it," said Tom.   100
    You're coming with me.   }

    Thanks, Matts and Margaret."

"You're the one that should get thanks."

"Then thanks.
    You can go home now."   105
"OK."   }

[Part II] [i]

"Matt, can you come over now for real?"
"I will ask, . . .
     Yes, I can."

"Then come on!"   110
"OK! What do you want to do?"

"Let's play Space Invaders and kill 'em."
"OK, let's go."

7777 Big score.
Time to go.   115

"Bye, Matt."
"Bye."

Boy, am I sacked.   [ii]
"Matt! Matt!"

"What?"   120
"Time to get up."

"Tough luck.
     "Bye.
     I'm going to school."
"Fine."   125

Lunchtime.   [iii]
"What are we having?"
"Soup."
"Be down in a second.
     Did anything disappear?"   130
"The pot!
The table and the stove,
     the sink, the floor —
     everything (the machine is going crazy).   }
Let's get out of here, let's go.   135
Help! Help!   }
Everything is disappearing.
Let's go to the police office and report it."   }
     the end

Notice the recurrent grouping of signals and turns at talk in groups of three pairs

(23-29, 35-42, 118-125) and five (77-90, 91-106, 107-117). The final sequence of five turns (126-138) has an extravagant three pairs within its fifth turn.

Scene [iii] of Act I is puzzling. The last five lines are a clear stanza, introduced by a change of topic and explicit address (72-76). The three pairs of turns at talk just before (64-71) have coherence, three questions answered with "OK," but do follow directly on what precedes. Perhaps what precedes is a five element stanza (55-63), but it seems more likely that 64-65 is a Janus-faced turn, counting doubly, implicitly at least, so that line 64 completes three pairs with 55-63.

Sometimes the initial group is more complex than others (17-20, 43-47, 48-50, [this might alternatively be three pairs], 77-81).

There is one more written story:

[4]

Once upon a time I was playing Atari
and my TV disappeared
so I told my mom
and my mom called the police
The policeman said   5
    he'd be over in a second.
So he rang the bell
and he came in
and said he might know
    where everything is going.   10
so he caught the robber
and put him in jail
the end.

Himley points out that this is summary, not narrative, and more typical of written language in having exposition, not dialogue (164). Even so, it is shaped as if it were oral. It has five parts. An introduction (1-2) and close (13) enclose three units, each marked with initial *so* (3-5, 6-10, 11-12).

REFERENCES

Dickinson, D., Wolf, M., & Stotsky, S. (1993). The interwoven development of oral and written language. In J. B. Gleason (Ed.), *The development of language* (3rd ed., pp. 369-420). New York: Macmillan.

Gee, J. P. (1989). *Literacy, discourse, and linguistics. Essays by James Paul Gee.* Special issue of *Journal of Education*, **171**, 1.

Gee, J. P. (1991). A linguistic approach to narrative. *Journal of Narrative and Life History*, **1**, 15-40.

Gee, J. P. (1992). *The social mind. Language, ideology, and social practice.* New York: Bergin & Garvey.

Himley, M. (1991). *Shared territory: Understanding children's writing as works.* New York: Oxford University Press.

Hymes, D. (1991a). Is poetics original and functional? *Language and Communication*, **11**(1/2), 49-51.

Hymes, D. (1991b). Ethnopoetics and sociolinguistics: Three stories by African-American children. In I. G. Malcolm (Ed.), *Linguistics in the service of society: Essays to honour Susan Kaldor* (pp. 155-170). Perth, Australia: Institute of Applied Language Studies, Edith Cowan University.

Hymes, D. (1992). Use all there is to use. In B. Swann (Ed.), *On the translation of Native American literatures* (pp. 83-124). Washington, DC: Smithsonian Institution Press.

Hymes, D. (1993). Inequality in language: Taking for granted. In J. Alatis (Ed.), *Forty-third Annual Georgetown University Round Table on Languages and Linguistics* (pp. 23-40). Washington, DC: Georgetown University Press.

Hymes, D. (1994). Ethnopoetics, oral formulaic theory, and editing texts. *Oral Tradition*, **9**, 300-370.

Hymes, D. (1995). Bernstein and poetics. In P. Atkinson, B. Davies & S. Delamont (Eds.), *Discourse and reproduction: Essays in honor of Basil Bernstein* (pp. 1-24). Cresskill, NJ: Hampton Press.

Schegloff, E. A. (1968). Sequencing in conversational openings. *American Anthropologist*, **70**, 1075-1095. Reprinted in J. J. Gumperz, & D. Hymes (Eds.), *Directions in sociolinguistics.* New York: Holt, Rinehart & Winston, 1972; Oxford: Blackwell, 1986.

7 LANGUAGE SOCIALIZATION AND LANGUAGE DIFFERENTIATION IN SMALL SCALE SOCIETIES: THE SHOSHONI AND GUARIJÍO[1]

Wick R. Miller[2]
University of Utah

Child language studies have come of age over the past thirty years or so, a development in which Susan Ervin-Tripp has played a major role. Some of the readers of this volume will know that I was associated with her in an early study, one which influenced some of the work that I have done since that time. Readers whose main interest is in child language may think that I disappeared into the academic woodwork, since I have done little work in this field since our work together in the early 1960s. Most of my research before and after that study has been with American Indian languages. I have developed a particular interest in trying to understand the social and cultural context of language transmission in small scale societies, an interest that was sparked and shaped in important ways by my early association with Susan.

I have had the good fortune to observe language in its social and cultural context for two small scale societies, the Shoshoni in the Great Basin of western United States, and the Guarijío in the mountains of northwestern Mexico. I would like to contrast and compare them with each other, and with the contexts in our own society that we are more familiar with.

SHOSHONI

The Shoshoni were nomadic hunters and gatherers when they came into contact with Euroamericans a century and a half ago. Their territory was sparsely populated: perhaps only ten thousand people stretching over a huge area in what is now southwestern,

---

[1] This paper is based on my Shoshoni and Guarijío field observations, some of which have been published (Miller, 1970, 1971, 1980, 1984, 1986; Silver & Miller, 1993). The discussion of the aboriginal Shoshoni cultural context is also based on Steward, 1938. For a discussion of the problems raised in this paper, see also Hill, 1978.

[2] Our colleague Wick Miller died tragically, in the midst of an active life, on May 9, 1994. We feel fortunate to be able to bring this chapter of his to the light of day, memorializing both his work with Susan Ervin-Tripp and his life's work with native American peoples and languages. — *Editors*

central, and northeastern Nevada, southern Idaho, northern Utah, and southwestern Wyoming. They did not constitute a single political unit. Instead, there were a number of smaller interlocking local social and political groups with variable membership.

The annual subsistence cycle can be described by beginning in the spring. After the snow melted, groups of one or two families would begin foraging in the lower elevations, and in the summer would gradually work their way into the higher valleys. Communal rabbit and antelope hunts took place in the fall, allowing for groups of fifty, one hundred, or sometimes even more to camp together for two or three weeks. Fall was also a time of heightened social activity, with hand games, dances, courting, and visiting among friends and neighbors who had not seen each other for some time. The local groups would divide into smaller groups to prepare for winter. Among most Shoshoni groups, the fall pinenut harvest provided the most important winter food. The winter village consisted of several families, perhaps five or six, usually located near the pinenut groves. Once the snow melted in the lower valleys, the yearly round would begin anew. A given family would try to return to the same places each year, and to spend the winter in the same village with the same families. But sometimes the yearly nomadic round had to change because of local variation in the harvest of plants and in the availability of game. If the pinenut harvest failed in one locality, for example, the families that normally camped together in the same winter village would have to disperse and spend the fall and winter with related families in areas that had a good pinenut crop.

By the late 1800s Euroamerican occupation had disrupted the aboriginal subsistence patterns. Fences and the closing off of many springs no longer allowed the Shoshoni to roam free and follow the traditional seasonal round. In many places in North America, White occupation often led to gathering the indigenous populations together onto a single reservation, with a subsequent leveling of the aboriginal linguistic and cultural diversity. But not so in the Great Basin. Some families drifted to the outskirts of White settlements, with the men seeking jobs as laborers, the women as domestics. Such groupings led to the formation of what have come to be called Indian "colonies," communities that are still found today at the edge of every major Great Basin town. In other cases families attached themselves to local ranches, with the men working as cowboys, the women as domestics. And not a few families made a successful transition from nomadic foraging to settled small-time farming and ranching. Many of these rural settlements are now small reservations. A century and a half of Euroamerican contact has brought about a complete change in the economic patterns, but the settlement patterns show surprising continuity, especially in the western and southern part of their aboriginal range. Scattered across Nevada and Utah are small communities (both colonies and reservations), with populations ranging between fifty and a few hundred. To the north and east in Idaho and Wyoming are three somewhat larger reservations, with populations ranging between one and three thousand. These several communities still preserve much of the original linguistic and cultural diversity.

Shoshoni communities are not, of course, self contained. There is and was considerable visiting between kinfolk and friends. Since most of the communities are small, spouses frequently come from different communities. As economic circumstances change, individuals and families often move between neighboring communities. Such movement can be seen as a continuation of the shifting aboriginal residence patterns brought about by changes in the availability of food plants and game.

I began field work with the Shoshoni in the mid 1960s at Goshute, a community of less than a hundred people that straddles the Utah Nevada border sixty miles south of Wendover. It was, and still is, the most isolated Shoshoni speaking community, and the language is in a better state of preservation there than in any other community. When I began work, there were no paved roads, no electricity, and no phones. Children learned the aboriginal language at home and English when they went to school. While I did not know it at the time, I was observing full transmission of the aboriginal language for the last generation. All of the children born in the mid 1960s and before became complete Shoshoni speakers. Some of the children born in the late 1960s and early 1970s became complete speakers, but not all. Today, a generation later, the children of some families understand Shoshoni, and a few are semispeakers.

During my work at Goshute in the 1960s, I stayed with a family that I will call the Toms (this and following names are pseudonyms.) The father, Kevin Tom, moved to Goshute in 1919 when he was seven years old. He and his family came from a community about a hundred miles to the west, where a different dialect of Shoshoni was spoken. He worked on the Ute reservation during the WPA era. There he found his bride, Molly. Her native language, Ute, is closely related to Shoshoni. She learned Shoshoni so that she could communicate with her parents-in-law. While she was (and still is) fluent in Shoshoni, she still speaks it with a Ute accent; she feels more comfortable now with Shoshoni than with her native Ute. Both Kevin and Molly spoke fluent English, but felt much more comfortable speaking Shoshoni. Kevin's parents lived with Kevin and Molly during their early married life, but they died in the late 1950s, before I had arrived at Goshute. Kevin's father spoke English, but his mother was monolingual. Kevin and Molly had twelve children. When I arrived at Goshute, the youngest was two years old, and just learning Shoshoni. The four oldest were married, two living at Goshute, the other two in another community.

Who did the Tom's children learn Shoshoni from? The parents served as models, and, at least for the older children, their paternal grandparents did also. And the older children served as models for the younger. The Toms lived several miles to the west of the central Goshute settlement area. A couple of families lived within easy walking distance, but none had children. Kevin's younger brother lived a mile or two away with a wife and several children whose age range matched that of the younger Tom children. While there was some interaction between cousins, most of the interaction was between siblings. Some of the neighboring adults would visit occasionally, and one old man would sometimes come on winter evenings to tell stories. We see then that there was some social and linguistic interaction with children and adults outside the family, but most interaction was within the family.

When Kevin's family moved to Goshute, his younger sister, Minnie, was two years old. She married a man from Goshute, and in the 1960s lived in the eastern part of the Reservation, about five miles north of the main community. I came to know her variety of Shoshoni very well because she served as my principal linguistic consultant. Both she and Kevin had made accommodations to the local Goshute dialect, but Minnie had made

more. For example, both used an interdental affricate [tθ], typical of the dialects at
Goshute and to the east, rather than the dental affricate [ts] that was typical of the
dialects to the west (and, I assume, the dialect used by Kevin and Minnie's parents).
Initial [h-], which is dropped in the Goshute dialect, was preserved by both Kevin and
Minnie. At least Minnie preserved it when we did linguistic field work together, but I
noticed she often dropped it when talking to her Goshute husband or to her children.
And, unlike Kevin's children, Minnie's children usually dropped initial [h-].

In conducting a Shoshoni dialect survey, I visited every Shoshoni speaking community in the Great Basin. Part of the dialect schedule included an interview and genealogy
which provided information on the language enculturation context from people born as
early as the 1880s. A rather consistent picture emerges from these genealogies and from
my observations at Goshute. The number of adults involved in language transmission
was rather small, but it was a linguistically variable group. The Shoshoni speaking
household would consist of parents and perhaps one or two other adults: perhaps a
grandparent, perhaps an unmarried or widowed aunt or uncle. There was no stigma
attached to speaking a foreign dialect, but neither was it felt inappropriate to switch
dialects, so that a newcomer might or might not make a full or partial accommodation to
the local variety of Shoshoni. Often one of the child's parents was from a different area,
with the result that the varieties of Shoshoni that a child heard varied almost from house
to house. It was not uncommon for a child to spend a year or two with another family,
for example with a childless aunt and uncle who lived in a different community and
spoke a different variety of Shoshoni. And the peer group played a much smaller role in
language transmission than in most societies. In some cases the peer group was weakly
developed, in other cases nonexistent.

This is the picture of the language socialization context that I observed in the 1960s
and from interviews which can be pushed back to the 1880s. It seems likely to me that
we can assume the same or a similar situation also existed in precontact times: the child
spent most of the spring and summer with his or her own family, and perhaps another
family, the winter in a village with four or five other families, and would be with larger
groupings only a few weeks out of the year. And there is every reason to think that there
was as much dialect variation within and across households as we find in more recent
times.

Variation is found in all aspects. Examples of phonological variation include variation between [ai] and [e], for example /yakai/ or /yake/ 'to cry'. The words that take one
vowel, those that take the other, and those that vary freely between the two vowels vary
from speaker to speaker. Another example involves Proto-Shoshoni /*-ŋŋ/, which
becomes /-nn-/ in some cases, /-nk-/ in others; for example /sínnapin/ or /sínkapin/
'aspen'. And again, there is variation within and across speakers as to which words have
which sequence. Variation between [kwa] and [ko] shows a similar pattern (or rather,
similar lack of pattern); an example is /suikkwakkwa/ or /suikkokko/ 'robin'. I mentioned
the dropping of initial [h-], a feature found from Goshute eastward to the Salt Lake
Valley, and the changing of the dental affricate [ts] to an interdental [tθ], a feature which
is found over a slightly larger area. In certain phonetic environments, Shoshoni has
voiceless vowels, but the rules that specify the environments vary dialectically; in general,

there is greater devoicing as one travels from Nevada to Wyoming. And there are still many other phonological examples, and also similar examples in grammatical, lexical, and semantic variation. But the picture is the same: the features that vary are all little ones, but there are many of them, so that the differences are salient.

If you ask speakers about dialect differences you get two kinds of responses, depending on how you frame the question. If you ask about a given area or given person, you get a generalized response: People from Elko have a different "swing" to the speech; or you can tell that a particular person is from Elko from the way she talks. But if you ask about a particular feature for a particular person you get a precise answer, particularly if that person is well known to individual you ask. And this applies to all aspects of language: phonetic, grammatical, lexical, or semantic. One example will serve for many. In 1992 I recorded, for the first time, the speech of an eighty year old lady named Nancy. I transcribed the recording with the help of Edna, a women in her forties. I discovered that Nancy used a suffix I had never heard before: a plural suffix, /‹míín/, which was used in place of the usual /-niin/, and used only with certain human nouns. Edna pointed out that Nancy's family (not Nancy herself) was from Baker, about eighty miles to the south, and that the suffix was typical of speakers from this area. Edna was able to specify which words the suffix could be used with and went on to say that she never used those words that way herself, but that she was familiar with Nancy's speech because she had spent a lot of time with Nancy when she was a child.

Two facts stand out, one relating to the distribution of the dialect features, the other to the degree of variation. Concerning the first: the dialect variation is gradual, so that there is never a bundle of linguistic isoglosses, or a sharp break between dialects. Dialectologists have noted other places in the world where the variation is gradual, so that this feature is not unique to Shoshoni dialectology. Concerning the second fact: dialectologists have sometimes discussed the extreme diversity found in some parts of Europe, where each village has its own dialect. But Shoshoni dialect variation is even greater: each family has its own dialect. I know of no other group of similar size (about ten thousand) with such extreme variation, but I would predict that if such a group is found, it will be a nomadic foraging group with a low population density. I believe the nature and degree of dialect variation in Shoshoni is a direct result of the type of language socialization.

GUARIJÍO

The Guarijío are corn farmers who live in the canyons and mountains along and near the upper reaches of the Río Mayo in the Mexican states of Chihuahua and Sonora. The territory is approximately fifty kilometers east to west, and sixty-five north to south. They speak two well differentiated dialects, each with about a thousand speakers: the Mountain dialect to the northeast and mostly in Chihuahua, and the River dialect to the southwest and mostly in Sonora. The Mountain Guarijío live in scattered communities that usually number from two to fifteen houses. The River Guarijío live in similar settlements, except for two large ejidos that were formed in the 1970s. Residence at marriage tends to be patrilocal, but the pattern is not rigidly fixed. As horticulturalists, they lead a more settled way of life than foragers, but because most corn fields are abandoned after a few years, new fields must be cleared from time to time; this leads to a semisedentary way of life.

European contact began three and a half centuries ago, contact which changed their way of life through the introduction of new foods (e.g., wheat, peaches), new animals (e.g., goats, chickens, pigs), a new way to fix corn (the tortilla, introduced by the Aztec workers who accompanied the Spaniards), new means of transportation (horse and donkey), new tools (particularly the ax and machete), and a new religion. And the violin and harp are now so much a part of Guarijío ceremonial life that it is difficult to imagine that they have not always been part of Guarijío culture. However, they have remained a small-scale farming society, and until recently communication with the outside world was limited.

Mexicans began moving into the mountains and forming small settlements in the mid-nineteenth century. I have not been able to trace the history of this movement, but many areas were not greatly effected until quite recent times. The whole area is mestizoizing, with the process most advanced where the Mexicans have been the longest and are most numerous.

My first visit was with the Mountain Guarijío for almost a year in 1976. I made several shorter visits over the next ten years, including two three-month visits in which I conducted a dialect survey of both dialects. In 1976, there were no roads or schools, but by my last visit roads had penetrated the southwestern edge, and there were schools and clinics throughout the area.

During my first year I divided my time between three families in two neighboring Guarijío rancherías, Chiltepín (or Kawírere `under the mountain'), and La Barranca (or We?wérere `under the eagles'). There were fifteen families in Chiltepín, in three clusters of adjacent houses, each cluster within fifteen minutes of each other. La Barranca, with nine families, was an hour and a half to the east, over the ridge on the side of a deep canyon. On the ridge between the two communities was La Mesa Seriachi, with seven Guarijío and several Mexican families. In a separate drainage to the southwest of Chiltepín and La Mesa Seriachi, and about half an hour from each was San José, with thirteen families. In the same drainage and about half an hour from San José and Chiltepín was Saucillo with three Guarijío families, several Mexican families, and a store. Across the Río Mayo and a couple of hours north of La Barranca was La Finca with fourteen families; Cuiteco with a single family was between the two. This district of seven rancherías and fifty one families formed the larger social and ceremonial unit known as La Mesa Seriachi community. Most of the men and children spoke limited Spanish, while the women knew many Spanish words but only a few could make connected sentences.

Guarijío children had daily contact with both adults and children of neighboring houses. Two events brought families together from the wider community. One was the cooperative work party, in which several men from the local ranchería, and some from nearby rancherías would spend the morning working at the host's corn field, while the women and children remained at the host's house, preparing for the afternoon meal. The other event was the tuwúri ceremony which attracted families from most of the larger community, and if it was a multiday affair there might be families from beyond the Mesa Seriachi rancherías.

A genealogy will give a fuller picture of the Mountain Guarijío way of life, a genealogy of Martiniano, a Chiltepín man in his mid-thirties. He grew up in both Chiltepín and La Mesa Seriachi. His wife, María, was born and raised in La Finca. They spent the first few years of married life in La Finca before moving to Chiltepín. They have one child, a son born in the mid 1950s. Martiniano has two younger sisters, both born and raised in Chiltepín, but after marriage, they moved to their husbands' rancherías, one in La Finca, and the other to El Barro, a ranchería several hours to the south. Martiniano's father was from Chiltepín, but since he died when he was young, Martiniano did not know him or his family very well. His mother was from La Mesa Seriachi; she had two older brothers, one of whom lived at La Mesa Seriachi, the other at La Barranca. Martiniano's wife has three brothers, all of whom live in La Finca. This genealogy is typical. It displays a net of relations with the greatest density in the immediately neighboring rancherías, and fading out with more distant ones.

There is a little dialect diversity within the Mountain dialect of Guarijío, but not much. For example [s] is palatalized after [i] only in the Mesa Seriachi district. The two communities which are closest to the River Guarijío dialect have /wakasí/ 'cow', while elsewhere Mountain Guarijío has /wagasí/; the lack of voiced stops in this and few other words reflects influence from the River dialect: Voiced stops in the Mountain dialect correspond to voiceless stops in the River dialect. If there is grammatical variation within the Mountain dialect, I have not discovered it. The general lack of dialect differentiation within Mountain Guarijío would seem to be the result of two things: the context for language socialization allows the child to interact with both children and adults of the ranchería on a daily basis, and with those of neighboring rancherías on a frequent basis, and the network of consanguinial and affinal relations is spread out in an even fashion.

Now concerning differences between the Mountain Dialect (MD) and the River Dialect (RD). MD intervocalic /p/ and /k/ are voiced when followed by an unaccented syllable: MD /kehaní/, RD /kepaní/ 'is snowing'. RD drops postvocalic glottal stop when followed by an unaccented syllable: MD /yuʔkuná/, RD /yukuná/ 'is raining'; MD /woʔisí/, RD /woisí/ 'ox'. MD has lost the distinction between the singular and plural second person pronoun, which is maintained in RD, while RD has lost the distinction between singular and plural future tense suffix, which is maintained in MD. Notice that sometimes one, sometimes the other dialect is the innovator. Lexical differences are also found, for example MD /pakó/, RD /akí/ 'river'. There is a 90% match between the dialects on the Swadesh one hundred item basic vocabulary list.

Turning now directly to the River dialect, we find that it contrasts with the Mountain dialect in regard to demographic patterns and the distribution of dialect features. Because of economic and political unrest between 1955 and 1965, the River area has undergone some population movement. Further, there is a noticeable amount of dialect variation, most notably lexical variation, within the River dialect. It is convenient to distinguish a lowland and a highland zone, realizing there is no sharp boundary between the two. With the exception of one ranchería of seventeen households, Bavícora, the highland zone has been depopulated. Since most of the distinctive Highland features are also features typical of the Mountain dialect, this zone can be viewed as a transitional area.

It is instructive to look at three individuals who moved from Bavícora between 1955 and 1965 to Los Bajíos, the most western Guarijío community. Regino and his wife arrived with several small children. Regino was (and still is) a Turelo, or ceremonial singer, and therefore arrived as a highly respected man. When I interviewed him, his wife chided him for giving me Highland vocabulary; he responded by stating proudly that this was his language. Two of the words, *water* and *tortilla*, are high frequency items, so that I was often able to catch them on the fly; I noted that in conversation he sometimes used the highland forms, sometimes the lowland forms, while his wife always used the lowland forms. We can speculate that Regino, arriving as a forty-year-old man, with his status as a respected Turelo already established, felt secure in maintaining many of his Highland vocabulary items.

When I interviewed Rafael in 1984, he was in his late thirties and married to Regino's daughter. He was part of the group of younger politically important men in the community. He was eighteen years old when he arrived from Bavícora and had lost almost all linguistic traces of his Bavícora upbringing. Since his social and political standing was established in Los Bajíos, we can speculate that he felt it advantageous to adopt the speech ways of the locals.

Zanón, Regino's nephew, is exactly the same age as Rafael. He was ten years old when he arrived in Los Bajíos. He can best be described as a simple corn farmer, living in a more isolated area outside the main current of political activity. Even though he arrived as a ten-year-old boy, he still retained several Highland features, though not as many as his uncle. We can speculate that since he, unlike Rafael, has no political ambitions, it did not bother him to retain some of the linguistic features of his Highland heritage.

There is an awareness of the differences between highland and lowland speech. Three words in particular have come to be regarded as shibboleths:

Lowland	Highland
nerói	pa?wí, *water*
takarí	teméi, *tortilla*
tekipáni	inócani, *work*

The three highland words are the same ones used in the Mountain dialect. Speakers seem to be consciously aware only of the vocabulary differences; I never heard anyone mention the phonetic or grammatical differences.

Today there is a sharp linguistic boundary between the Mountain and River dialect, but it is impossible to know if it existed before the depopulation of the highland zone. There is some contact, including intermarriage, between Bavícora and the Mountain community of Guasaremos, communities separated by a few hours of travel. With this exception, there is little contact and little awareness between the two dialect groups. The River people call themselves /warihío/ and the Mountain folk *Tarahumara*, a term not recognized by the Mountain people as referring to them, since *Tarahumara* properly is the term for a related language found further to the east in the high sierras. The Mountain people refer to themselves as /warihó/, and the River folk as /makulái/, a term not generally recognized by the River folk.   Those in the lowland sometimes refer to the transitional community of Bavícora as "half Tarahumara."

SUMMING UP

Among the Shoshoni, the dialectical variation is almost family by family, while among the Guarijío the smallest unit of appreciable variation is a cluster of rancherías of some fifty or so families. Further, there are no sharp boundaries among the Shoshoni dialects, whereas there are two very distinct Guarijío dialects.   To the question: How many dialects are there? one can give an answer for Guarijío, but the question has no meaning for Shoshoni.   For most features of variation in Guarijío, there are usually only two variants, a Mountain and a River variant, even in those cases for which the variants do not respect the exact dialect boundaries.

Why the differences in the two situations? It is impossible to reach firm conclusions based on only one example each, but we can speculate that the differences are linked to the difference in demography and its effect on interaction patterns and the context for language socialization. The Shoshoni child was in contact with a much smaller number of individuals (both children and adults), but there was also much more linguistic variation in that small number.

But these two small scale societies share certain characteristics that are lacking in modern large scale societies. First, there is no standard or prestige dialect. As we saw with the example of Rafael, a speaker of the River dialect of Guarijío, one can be influenced to shift dialects, but in this case it was because it was the dialect of the community, not because it was the prestige dialect. Similar shifts took place in Shoshoni speaking communities.

Even though the enculturating group is larger among the Guarijío than among the Shoshoni, it is still very small when contrasted to modern large scale societies. The two Guarijío dialects, with only about a thousand speakers, are well differentiated and probably would, if it were not for the acculturating setting they are now in, develop into two languages. It is not uncommon to find viable languages in small scale societies of only a thousand speakers, and in aboriginal California there were even some with only five hundred speakers. A viable language of such small size is unthinkable in modern urban societies.

REFERENCES

Hill, J. H. (1978). Language contact systems and human adaptations. *Journal of Anthropological Research,* **34,** 1-26.
Miller, W. R. (1970). Western Shoshoni dialects. In E. Swanson, Jr. (Ed.), *Languages and cultures of Western North America: Essays in honor of Sven S. Liljeblad* (pp. 17-36). Pocatello: Idaho State University Press.

Miller, W. R. (1971). The death of a language: Or, serendipity among the Shoshoni. *Anthropological Linguistics*, **13**, 114-120.

Miller, W. R. (1980). Speaking for two: Respect speech in the Guarijío of northwest Mexico. *Berkeley Linguistics Society*, **6**, 196-206.

Miller, W. R. (1984). Situación sociolingüística de los guarijíos [The sociolinguistic situation of the Guarijíos]. In Lic. Juan Antonio Ruibal Corella (Ed.), *IX Simposio de Historia y Antropología de Sonora* (pp. 113-119). Heromosillo, Sonora: Instituto de Investigaciones Históricas.

Miller, W. R. (1986). The Numic languages. In W. L. d'Azevedo (Ed.), *Handbook of American Indians, Basin Volume, Volume 11* (pp. 98-106). Washington, DC: Smithsonian Institution.

Silver, S., & Miller, W. R. (1993). *American Indian languages in social and cultural context.* Manuscript submitted for publication.

Steward, J. (1938). Basin-Plateau aboriginal sociopolitical groups. *Bureau of American Ethnology Bulletin*, **120**.

PART THREE:
SOCIAL AND INTERACTIVE PROCESSES IN
LANGUAGE ACQUISITION

8 A CROSS-CULTURAL STUDY OF CHILDREN'S REGISTER KNOWLEDGE

Elaine S. Andersen
University of Southern California

INTRODUCTION

In the mid-sixties, Susan Ervin-Tripp, Dan Slobin, and several of their colleagues in Psychology, Anthropology, and Linguistics at the Institute for Human Learning in Berkeley produced a *Field Manual for the Cross-cultural Study of the Acquisition of Communicative Competence* (Slobin, 1967). As stated by Ervin-Tripp in the introduction, the goal of that manual was to provide a set of guidelines for examining both "children's acquisition of linguistic codes and the social rules for the use of such codes." At a time when the focus of developmental psycholinguistics was almost exclusively on discovering universals in the acquisition of grammar (based largely on studies of English), the authors of the manual argued for both (a) the need to expand the notion of competence to include *communicative* as well as grammatical competence, and (b) the importance of looking at cross-cultural variation.

Although the manual has been criticized for not recognizing the importance of an ethnographic approach in cross-cultural research (Schieffelin, 1979), it was extremely successful in setting the stage for whole programs of research over the next two decades. For example, it foreshadowed the impressive cross-linguistic project of Slobin and his colleagues on early grammatical development (e.g., Slobin, 1973, 1982, and the collections of papers in Slobin, 1985a, 1985b); and it lay the foundation for a large body of cross-cultural studies examining language socialization, focusing not only on the nature of Input language ("Babytalk") and the related belief systems of particular cultures (e.g., Broen, 1972; Clancy, 1986; Ochs & Schieffelin, 1984; Schieffelin & Ochs, 1986, 1988; Snow, 1972; Snow & Ferguson, 1977), but also on children's developing sociolinguistic knowledge. Key examples of this latter research are the studies of Ervin-Tripp and colleagues on the acquisition of different speech act types (especially directives) and discourse markers (e.g., Ervin-Tripp, 1977; Ervin-Tripp, O'Connor, & Rosenberg, 1984; Mitchell-Kernan & Kernan, 1977; Sprott, 1992), and the work of Berko Gleason and her colleagues on the acquisition of communicative routines (e.g., Berko Gleason & Weintraub, 1976, 1978; Berko Gleason, Perlmann, & Grief, 1984; Grief & Berko Gleason, 1980). Similarly, the work I will describe below, as well as the larger research program of which it is a part, owes a huge intellectual debt for both its content and its methodology to that field manual and the subsequent work of Ervin-Tripp. Indeed, it was in preparing a presentation for a 1993 symposium on methodology organized by Ervin-Tripp that I convinced myself fully of the value of the method described in this paper; and it was also her suggestion that I participate in a symposium on discourse markers that same year which led me to appreciate the sociolinguistic function of these forms, which constitutes the major focus of this chapter.

THE STUDY OF REGISTER ACQUISITION

The aspect of sociolinguistic development explored in this paper is what most recent work refers to as **register knowledge** (Ellis & Ure, 1969), though the same concept is discussed in the original field manual as "usage patterns," "style variation," or "codes." What it means to acquire register knowledge is captured in a section of the field manual written by a former student of Ervin-Tripp's, Claudia Mitchell(-Kernan), who argued that: "The child's complete enculturation into his speech community necessitates his mastery of the social norms that signal the appropriate use of variants, as well as his proficiency in adapting verbal behavior to relevant social cues" (in Slobin, 1967, p. 159). The nature of these "relevant social cues" was spelled out in greater detail by Ervin-Tripp, when she noted that:

> The more we study speech in natural settings, the more we find systematic variation within every speaker, reflecting who he is addressing, where he is, what the social event may be, the topic of discussion, and the social relations he communicates by speaking. The regularities in these features of speech make them as amenable to analysis as the abstracted rules called grammars. Competence in speaking includes the ability to use appropriate speech for the circumstance and when deviating from the normal to convey what is intended. It would be an incompetent speaker who used baby talk or randomly interspersed sentences in baby talk or in a second language regardless of circumstance. It would be equally incompetent to use formal style in all situations and to all addressees in a society allowing for a broader range of variation.
>
> Ervin-Tripp, 1973, p. 268

The acquisition of register knowledge, then, is the process by which children learn "to use appropriate speech for the circumstance." This involves the coordination of several types of knowledge at once. First, children must have the *linguistic tools* necessary to exhibit the kinds of register variation characteristic of their society — e.g., they must have available different names for the same referent *(potty* vs. *toilet)* and different grammatical forms to express the same speech act ("Close the door" vs. "Would you please close the door?"). Second, they must be aware of those aspects of *discourse participants and setting* that demand register shifts in their society — e.g., do you "simplify" your speech for both children and foreigners, as in many Western societies (Ferguson, 1975), or do you register shift for only one of these groups as in Western Samoa (Shore, 1982). And third, they must know the exact nature of the relationship *between linguistic and social variation:* i.e., which particular linguistic forms cluster together to form the register that is appropriate for a particular social situation. For example, it is not enough to know that in middle-class American society it is appropriate to "simplify" your speech both for very young and for adult foreigners because they are both considered "incompetent" in some way; you must also realize that exaggerated intonation is appropriate to use when speaking to the child, whereas flat intonation is more characteristic of speech addressed to a foreigner.

At the time the Field Manual was produced, there was a general assumption that children first developed grammar and only later acquired sociolinguistic knowledge (see Grimshaw & Holden, 1976; Lakoff, 1975). But researchers began to question this assumption in the mid-70s and early 80s, and presented studies suggesting that even very young children modify their speech to fit the situation of use (e.g., Sachs & Devin, 1976; Shatz & Gelman, 1973). In my own work (Andersen, 1984, 1990), I set out to explore the range of linguistic devices (morphosyntactic, lexical, pragmatic, and phonological) for marking distinct registers that young, middle-class, monolingual English-speaking, American children have available at different stages of acquisition. The data were collected using a method that I have labeled "controlled improvisation." My main concerns in developing this task were to find a procedure that would meet four criteria: a) it should be a task that children would find familiar and comfortable; b) it should neither constrain the children's creativity, nor limit the range of sociolinguistic markers to any preconceived set (since children's categories don't always coincide with adults); c) it should allow for comparison along the same non-linguistic (social) dimensions across children; and d) it should facilitate children's ability to demonstrate their full range of knowledge. After piloting a number of other techniques that were unsuccessful either in terms of keeping the children's limited attention focused on the task, or in producing transcribable recordings, I chose instead to use a number of role-specific puppets for whom the children had to "do the voices," in specific contexts set up by the experimenter. This procedure satisfies the first criterion by taking advantage of the fact, noted by Ervin-Tripp in the 1973 paper cited above, that when preschoolers are involved in pretend play, they often spontaneously adopt consistent speech patterns in accordance with the social categories involved — e.g., mothers, babies, doctors, etc. The use of puppets and predetermined contexts also has the advantage of helping to control the situation (e.g., a child with puppets representing a doctor and a nurse is unlikely to suddenly switch to playing "cowboys and Indians" with them), while at the same time allowing the child freedom to be imaginative and creative within the given limits — thus satisfying criteria b and c. But most importantly, this technique allows children to demonstrate, through role-play, knowledge of appropriateness rules governing language use for roles that are otherwise not available to them; while most adults speak in a variety of roles each day (e.g., the same individual may be both a doctor and a patient, a daughter and a mother, a sister, a wife, a friend), the normal roles available to children in their everyday lives are much more limited.

Although one might question to what degree the language used in role-play reflects actual usage in everyday, spontaneous conversation, this is not necessarily a disadvantage in investigating register knowledge. One might instead argue that an additional strength of this technique is that it allows the elicitation of symbolic form choices stripped of

practical compliance consequences, making more explicit children's abilities to discriminate and express in their language important social relationships.

Using this technique, I recorded the role-play speech of 18 preschool and first-grade
children aged 4 to 7 years, each of whom participated in three sessions with different
pretend settings: a family setting, a medical setting, and a classroom setting. In these
sessions, the children all had the opportunity to "do the voices" for puppets representing
mother, father, spouse, doctor, nurse, teacher, and foreigner, as well as the more natural
(for them) roles of son or daughter, patient, and student.

In the rest of this paper, I will very briefly review some of the major findings of that
earlier study, then present preliminary findings from a current study of sociolinguistic
development in a comparable group of middle-class, monolingual French children. The
major focus of this discussion will be the acquisition of discourse markers as indices of
social relationships.

THE AMERICAN STUDY

General findings

Most generally, the findings demonstrate that there is a wide range of social relationships
that children aged 4 to 7 are able to discriminate and express in their language. The
children in this study displayed their knowledge through choices of content, conversational or discourse strategies, and situationally appropriate grammatical patterns. Over
developmental time, they showed increasing awareness of the topics appropriate for
different contexts and different speaker roles, the linguistic means available for initiating
and maintaining a discourse turn, and the phonological, lexical, and morphosyntactic
markers used to differentiate registers.

Across the different registers examined, some features appear to be used earlier than
others to mark differences in circumstances of language use. In particular, children seem
to first mark roles phonologically, with specific prosodic distinctions. Every child in
every context regularly used appropriate prosodic markings to distinguish roles, most
frequently pitch differences, but also intonation, volume, rate, and voice quality. Thus, in
the family setting, for example, pretend fathers all used deep voices, frequently spoke
louder than any other family member (sometimes yelling), and showed a marked tendency to back and lower vowels in a manner that produces an almost sinister "accent."
Mothers, on the other hand, spoke with higher pitch than fathers, and often used exaggerated intonation, but rarely approached the volume that marked the fathers' utterances.
Other phonological markings were also quite common, especially in baby talk and in
foreigner talk. In the role of baby, for example, there were a number of phonological
substitutions that occurred frequently, including: /θ/ → [d] ("wid de flowers" for "with
the flowers") and /l/ and /r/ → [w] ("aw wedy" for "all ready"). When children attempted to use foreigner talk, the most common modifications were slower tempo and

syllable-timed or syncopated speech (often sounding like a robot); but there were also a number of phonological substitutions, including the use of glottal stops for medial consonants and the use of neutral vowels for some glides *(okay* → [oka]).

The main developmental difference was that the older children maintained these distinctions throughout their role-play, whereas the younger children used them only to contrast voices at role junctures. Overall, in acquiring sociolinguistic skills, there seems to be something particularly salient about phonological modifications that makes them more available for use early on. Indeed, Crystal (1970) has suggested "that the dominant perceptual component of the speech signal is non-segmental, and that some non-segmental patterns are understood and produced prior to anything conventionally syntactic."

After phonological modifications the next aspect of appropriate language use that children seemed to acquire involved choices of both topic and lexicon. All the children, for example, had a general notion of what is discussed in family interaction, and almost all of them knew topics appropriate for the doctor–patient interaction. In the family setting, just as Berko Gleason (1975) found for real fathers, the language of fathers portrayed by these children clearly demarcated the father's role within the family: they talked mainly about going to work, "firing the secretary," having meetings, or building a new "repartment" building. Lexical markings were used consistently across children, though not as prevalent as phonological markings and not always appropriate. Many children appeared to know that special vocabulary should be used (e.g., medical terminology), but were not yet competent to use it; in one such case, the child confused *temperature* and *thermometer* in an exchange where the pretend patient asked "Do I have a temperature?" only to be told by the pretend nurse "I'll get you one." Another example is provided in (1) below:[1]

(1) Sd   Well, I think you have a hernia.
    Ep   What's a hernia?
    Sd   It's a sickness, like a disease.
          ...
          Well, she's dead.

Morphosyntactic markings (principally omissions of copula, articles, and prepositions), though characteristic of registers associated with several of these roles (e. g., baby talk and foreigner talk), were not common in these data, though used occasionally in the role-play of the oldest children. The one analysis of grammatical variation that did reveal a consistent pattern involved the distribution of directive types.

As Ervin-Tripp has stressed, because directives by definition place demands on the addressee, the choice of directive *type* can express a great deal about the social context of discourse, and about the relationship of the interlocutors — e.g., their age, sex, occupation, and familiarity (Ervin-Tripp, 1976; Ervin-Tripp et al., 1984).

Using categories similar to those used by Ervin-Tripp (1976) to demonstrate a

---

[1] In the examples in this paper, *speaker* can be identified by the following code: a capital E represents the experimenter; capital S represents the child; lower case letters represent the role being played: n = nurse, p = patient, d = doctor, m = mother, f = father, t = teacher, and s = student.

systematic social distribution in adult speech, I examined the distribution of six grammatically different directive types across the different pretend roles: *hints* ("Dinner's ready"), *need statements* ("I need food"), *simple imperatives* ("Come to dinner now"), two types of *modified imperatives* (*let's-imperatives* and *you-imperatives* as in "Let's eat dinner" or "You get the milk and I'll bring the roast"), and *requests* (e.g., "Can I have dinner now?").

The findings demonstrated differential usage of directives according to role and role-realization[2], indicating awareness of both the appropriateness of directives in general across the various roles and the social functions of specific types. For example, in the classroom setting the teacher used more directives than either the student or the foreigner, and in the medical setting the doctor used more directives to the nurse than vice versa. While there was no striking difference in frequency of directives across roles in the family setting, there were systematic differences in the frequency of specific directive *types*, with more *need statements* and *requests* in child-to-parent speech but more *simple imperatives* and *hints* in parent speech. Similarly, directive use in the medical setting showed more polite *requests* and *hints* used by nurse to doctor ("Doctor, would you like to look at it?"), but more *simple imperatives* addressed to the nurse ("Oh, okay. Nurse, go get the operating machine. . . . "Lay it (over) her arm." [L. P., 6;7]); in the classroom setting teachers used *simple imperatives, let's imperatives* and *hints*, ("Well, let's pack up for our fieldtrip" [M.S., 5;2]), whereas the students were in large part limited to *need statements* and *requests*.   And in the family setting, children used similar numbers of directives to mother and father, but six times as many of those directed to mother were expressed as *simple imperatives* (e.g., fathers were asked "Would you button me?" while mothers were told "Gimme Daddy's flashlight" [D.P. 5;0]). The data also suggested a developmental sequence with increasing sensitivity to the social meanings of the different types with age, and some strong stereotyping by the middle group of children (see Andersen, 1990, for a more detailed discussion).

Thus, across the sociolinguistic variants I originally set out to examine, the data demonstrate a fairly consistent pattern of acquisition: first, English-speaking children are sensitive quite early (at least by age 4) to the fact that utterances can express a whole range of social information tied to status (age, sex, and occupation) and to familiarity of speaker and addressee; and second, they learn initially to encode this information phonologically, then lexically, and only later morphosyntactically.

Discourse markers

In several of the examples presented in the preceding section, the children's role-play utterances contain a number of what I called at the time "placeholders" or "boundary markers," some lexical (e.g., *well, okay, now, so*) and some nonlexical (e.g., *oh, uh,* and

---

[2] A role-realization takes into account the relationship of the speaker to the addressee, in the sense that Nurse is a role, but nurse-to-doctor is a different role-realization than nurse-to-patient.

um). These forms most frequently occurred at the beginning of turns or utterances, added no semantic content, but seemed to function as indicators of the speaker's intention to take or hold the "floor." Although I had not seen these forms mentioned in any of the descriptions of register markers in the literature, as I pored over the transcripts for the ninth or tenth time looking at other markers, I began to notice a pattern. Analogous to what I have described regarding the distribution of directives and directive types, it turned out not only that these forms were more frequent in some roles than in others, but also that particular types were distributed differently across the roles. While there were overall more of these forms in high status roles (e.g., parent, doctor, teacher), the lexical ones were more likely in these roles, while the non-lexical ones were relatively more frequent in the low status roles (child, patient, foreigner). For example, while the two most common markers in the family context were *well* and *uh*, the pretend child almost never used *well* to the parents, but parents used *well* significantly more frequently, $t(7)$ = 28, $p < .01$. Examples (2) and (3) provide illustrations of the use of lexical markers (*well* and *okay now*) in the speech of husband and father, respectively, while example (4) illustrates both the use of *okay* by the mother and the use of a nonlexical marker (*um*) in the speech of the pretend child to mother:

(2) Em How many guests should we have at the party?
     Sf **Well**, I'm the father, I have to ask you that question.
         Because you're her mother and you take care of her the most.
(3) Sf (to child) **Okay now**, Mother will read you a story.
         I don't have a story. Your mother does.
(4) Em **Okay**, your friends are here.
     Sc No, just a minute, I gotta brush my hair.
         Um, I gotta put a bandage on my eye.

An additional distinction was that parents used *well* twice as often when speaking to child as when speaking to one another, suggesting further that this form has "authoritative" connotations and is more likely to mark utterances directed to someone of lower status. This pattern of use was apparent in the role-play speech of nine of the 18 children; one in the youngest group, three in the middle group, and five in the oldest group, suggesting an increasing awareness of the potential social meanings of these forms with age.

The authority connotation of *well* was even more obvious in the medical and classroom settings. In the medical setting, ten of the children used *well* this way, with the figures of authority, doctor, and nurse, using significantly more than the relatively low authority (in this context) roles of parent and patient, $t(11)$ = 59, $p < .01$. Example (1) in the preceding section is a typical doctor sequence in which two of three doctor utterances commence with *well*.

Data were perhaps most striking in the classroom context, which showed a clear status hierarchy of teacher, then student, then foreigner, with teacher using significantly more *well* than students, $t(7)$ = 28, $p < .01$), and foreigners never using it. What was particularly notable in this setting was that speech as teacher often showed utterance-initial "stacking" of these forms, as in the examples below:

(5) St   **Now then**, there's one thing I have to tell you both.
            And it's also a question.
(6) St   **Okay, well, now**. The first thing I would like to ask you:
            have you ever been to school or is this your first time?

Students never stacked these forms, and when they used *well* at all, it was almost exclusively with the foreigner, or as a boy student talking to a girl, as in example (7):

(7) (boy and girl students on the playground)
     Sb   (I want to) play kickball!
     Eg   Oh, me too? Can I play?
     Sb   **Well**, girls aren't allowed to play.
            (girl kicks ball)
     Sb   **Well**, now you have to get it.
     Sb   **Well**, run around the bases.

A review of the literature at the time this original study was carried out revealed no discussion of these forms as register markers. Further searching did uncover, however, a brief discussion by Sinclair and Coulthard (1975) of the use of what they called "frames" in classroom discourse, along with sample transcripts of teacher–student dialogue in British classrooms which were replete with teacher utterances beginning with *well* or *now*. As summarized by Coulthard (1977, pp. 101-102):

> The boundaries of transactions are marked almost always by frames, realised by four words, *well, right', now, good*. When used to indicate boundaries these words are strongly stressed, uttered with a falling intonation and followed by a short pause. Their normal meaning is suppressed — *now* has no time reference, *right* or *good* no evaluative function — though at other places in the lesson these same items are used normally.

Coulthard goes on to argue that the teacher can use these words this way because "his role involves the choice of topic," at the same time suggesting that it would be anomalous for others to speak this way because "conversationalists do not have this degree of control." Perhaps this is the case if the "conversationalists" are of equal status, but it is striking that even by age 5 some children are using these forms to systematically mark status asymmetry across a variety of situations and roles.

More recently, researchers have begun to systematically explore the functions of an expanded set of such forms, usually referring to them as *discourse markers* (e.g., Fraser, 1990; Redeker, 1990; Schiffrin, 1987; Vincent & Sankoff, 1992). According to Schiffrin, discourse markers (hereafter, DMs) such as *well, then, but*, and *now y'know* are "sequentially dependent elements which bracket units of talk" (Schiffrin, 1987, p. 31). In her model of DMs, she identifies four planes of discourse in which these markers function: "action structures" which coordinate speech acts, "exchange structures" which coordinate turns, "ideational structures" which coordinate propositional content, and "participation framework" which involves the relationships between the interlocutors in any speech event. Thus, these forms serve to create coherence and structure within a discourse, to provide feedback from the listener about whether a prior utterance has been understood or not, to indicate agreement or disagreement, and to signal production problems on the part of the speaker. But they also serve to convey social meanings. When used this way, usually in sentence-initial position, these forms do not carry semantic content and are not grammatically required in the utterance. While the textual uses of these DMs by children have received a fair amount of attention (Sprott, 1992; Jisa, 1984/85, 1987; Berman, Chapter 21), this last function has not been systematically studied. But it is exactly this function which is demonstrated in the consistent use of forms such as *well* and *um* in the role-play speech described here. The data indicate that, at least by age 7, English-speaking children have acquired a fair degree of sophistication in how to use a variety of DMs to mark status and power relationships between speaker and addressee within the participation framework. The next section introduces a cross-cultural perspective to this research, describing comparable data from monolingual French-speaking children.

THE FRENCH STUDY

General findings

The French study was carried out in a middle-class community in Lyon, France.[3] The methodology was basically the same as in the American study, with a few minor modifications (e.g., because the role of nurse is different in this culture, it was not typically included in the doctor session). Also, because there is little discussion of spoken register variation within French linguistics, I decided to collect data from older French children to use as the "model" for the kind of system the younger children would be acquiring. The children in the French study therefore range in age from 4 to 11. In the preliminary analyses presented here, I draw on data from 18 children, six aged 5 to 6, six aged 7 to 8, and six aged 9 to 10.

In general, the French data are remarkably parallel to the English data.[4] For example, some of the earliest markers of role are phonological (e.g., exaggerated intonation and stress patterns in speech as child), and children very early distinguish the activities of father and mother: Fathers talk about being exhausted from working at the computer (*Moi je suis creve a regarder l'ordinateur*; while mothers are tired from doing errands (*Oui alors heu moi tu sais j'ai travaille dur hein . . . Heu je suis alle faire les courses*). In regard to use of directives, the pretend parents produce many imperatives addressed to

[3] This research was made possible by a grant from the Spencer Foundation while the author was a Fulbright Senior Research Fellow. I am grateful to both of these organizations for their support and to the Franco-American Commission in Paris, especially Genevieve Ascher, who was helpful in every respect. A special thanks also to Bridgitte Gros who collected much of the data and provided many insightful comments.

[4] There are also differences (e.g., more formal greetings as the children get older, and earlier use of medical vocabulary) which reflect Franco-American cultural differences; these differences are addressed in Andersen and Dupuy (in preparation).

their children (*Vas te coucher, allez viens*, 'Go to bed, c'mon then'), who in contrast have very few imperatives among the directives they address to their parents. Similarly, the directives that mother and father address to one another are much more frequently indirect forms (father to mother: *Tu peux aller verifier si le petit dort bien?*, 'You can go check that the little one is sound asleep?'). Also reminiscent of the American data, doctors use technical terms (*Celesthamine, plus, heu: Rinanthieu Prometozine et ce sera tout*) and are likely to use the "pseudo-we" in place of first or second person singular (as in *Maintenant **nous** allons te peser*, 'Now **we**'re going to weigh you'), while teachers constantly produce evaluative expressions (*C'est bien, elle est juste*, 'Good, she's right'). The data also demonstrate systematic variation between forms such as *oui* 'yes' and its casual variant *ouais* 'yeh', and indicate that children are sensitive very early to the social distribution of the two forms (familiar *tu* and distant *vous*) of the second person singular pronoun. For example, the teacher portrayed by these children will usually address individual students as *tu,* but will switch to *vous* if angry at the student. But one of the most striking characteristics of the French children's role-play turns out to be their use of discourse markers, which may not be surprising, given the great frequency of these forms in spoken French generally.

Discourse markers

Although the use of DMs was relatively rare among the youngest children in the French study, by the time they were 6 or 7 they not only were using more of them than their American peers, but they were also regularly demonstrating the kind of "stacking" that appeared only occasionally in the American data. And like their American counterparts, they demonstrated systematic variation in their use of particular markers, reflecting the relative status of the participants in the discourse. Thus, for instance, in the family setting, parents are likely to introduce utterances with lexical DMs such as *alors* or *maintenant* (similar to *well* or *now*), while the child is more likely to either not use a DM or use one of lower status, such as the non-lexical *ah* or *euh*, or the lexical *et puis* (literally, *and then*). Example (8) is illustrative; here the mother is negotiating bedtime with her child:

(8) Sm: *T'as fini tes devoirs?*
          'Have you finished your homework?'
     Sc: *Oui.*
          'Yes.'
     Sm: ***Alors** maintenant monte te coucher.*
          'Then go up to bed now.'
     Sc: ***Ah** non, ça non.*
          'Oh no, not that.'
     Sm: *Non mais, qu'est-ce que tu fais là? Tu veux la fessée?*
          'What do you think you're doing? Do you want a spanking?'
     Sc: *Non, non, je veux pas la fessée.*
          'No, no, I don't want a spanking.'

Sm: *Alors tu rentres maintenant te coucher, autrement quand papa il va arriver, je vais lui dire de te donner la fessée.*
'Then go right to bed, otherwise when Dad gets home, I'm going to tell him to give you a spanking.'

Sc: *Et puis je vais dormir et puis il pourra pas me donner la fessée.*
'Then I'm going to sleep and then he can't give me a spanking.'

Sm: *Ben oui d'accord, alors va dormir.*
'Well, yes, alright, then go to sleep.'

As in the American study, the French doctors used high status markers more often than parents, even in the data from the 5-year-olds, as in (9):

(9) Sd: *Alors allonge-toi par terre.*
'Well, lie down on the ground.'

Ep: *Comme ça?*
'Like that?'

Sd: *Ouvres ta bouche. Tu n'as rien. T'as simplement un peu de rouge sur les dents. Tes oreilles, ouvres tes oreilles je veux dire...[...] Ouvres grand tes oreilles. Alors, attends que je mette mes lunettes. Bon, c'est vrai, c'est tout rouge. Il y a un petit peu de sang, je vais aller chercher heu:: les:: pansements. Plutôt l'infirmière va y aller.*
'Open your mouth. You're fine. You just have a little bit of red on your teeth. Your ears, open your ears, I mean . . . open your ears wide. Well, wait until I get my glasses. Well, it's true, it's all red. There's just a little bit of blood, I'm going to look for, uh, the, bandaids. Actually, the nurse will go.'

Although the data from the 5-year-olds contained almost no evidence of "stacking" in the medical session, stacking occurred regularly in the data from the older children, as illustrated in both (10) and (11), where the high status person is a doctor and a dentist (Sden), respectively.

(10) Sd: *Bon alors, j'appuie sur ce bouton là...sur ce bouton là. Bon alors heu, mets-toi comme ça, mets-toi comme ça. Alors, elle s'est fait très, très, très, très, très, très, bobo. Alors il faut lui mettre un bandage.*
'Well, then, I push this button here, this button here. Good, then, um, do like this, do like this. Well, she's got a big, big, big, big, big, big boo-boo. Then, we'll have to put on a bandage.'

Sp: *Aïe.*
'Ouch.'

Sf: *Voilà allez. Alors elle a un petit rhume aussi. Vous pouvez la soigner?*
'There you go. Well, she has a little cold, too. Can you help her get better?'

Sd: *Bon, retourne dans la salle. Bon, ouvre. Est-ce que tu as le nez qui coule?*
'Good, go back in the room. Good, open the door. Do you have a

runny nose?'

Sp: *Heu, oui.*

'Um, yes.'

Sd: *Alors mouche-toi.*

'Well, blow your nose.'

(11) Sden: **Bon alors, maintenant** *tu vas te coucher et rester la bouche ouverte.*

'Good, then, now you're going to bed, and keep your mouth open.'

Sp: *Compris.*

'Understood.'

Assist: *Attendez, je vais appuyer sur le bouchon.*

'Wait, I'm going to push the cover.'

Sden: *C'est bon.* **Alors** *je v. . . , tu restes la bouche ouverte. Sans crier, s'il te plaît.* **Hum bon,** *les ciseaux, shampoing anti-carie. . . poussière . . . ivoire . . . voilà tu as une belle dent en ivoire maintenant. Tu es comme les grandes femmes.*

'That's good. Well, I'm . . . , you keep your mouth open. No screaming, please. Uh, well, the scissors, the anti-cavity shampoo . . . powder . . . ivory . . .there, you have a nice white tooth now. You're like the grown-up ladies.'

In these two examples the doctor and the dentist use *bon* and *alors* either individually or combined to introduce almost every utterance. In contrast, the father uses only *alors* by itself, while the single DM used at all by the child patient is the nonlexical, *heu*.

The differential distribution of lexical and non-lexical DMs was most dramatic in the classroom setting, as was also the case in the American data. Moreover, not only was stacking most frequent in the teacher role, but it was expanded to include up to four markers, as illustrated in example (12) from an 8-year-old and the examples under (13) from 10-year-olds:

(12) St: **Alors** *tu te tais.*

'Well, you shut up.'

Ss: *Moi je travaillais.*

'Me, I worked.'

St: **Bon, alors maintenant** *on va travailler.* **Bon.**

'Good, well now we're going to work. Alright.'

Ss: *Oui.*

'Yes.'

St: **Heu,** *sortez votre livre de:: d'orthographe.* **Bon** *vous prenez le livre à la page 134. Faîtes l'exercice numéro 2. Sortez votre cahier, sortez votre cahier de français.* **Bon, et::** *dans dix minutes je vous dis que c'est fini.*

'Uh, get out your, uh, your spelling books. Good, you turn to page 134. Do exercise number 2. Get out your notebook, get out your French notebook. Good, and in ten minutes I'll tell you your time is up.'

(13)

a)   St: ***Bon, d'accord. allez***, *viens là.* ***Bon, alors là*** *tu vas me faire* ***heu***
*une maison, près de la mer. Il y aura des gens qui seront en train
de se baigner et toi tu fais des gribouillons, ça doit être tout ce que
tu sais faire.*
'Good, alright. Go on, come here. Good, then, now you're going
to make me, uh, a house, near the shore. There will be people
swimming and you, you make scribbles, that must be all that you
know how to do.'

b)   St: ***Hum, bon, alors, maintenant,*** *prenez vos cahiers de francais.*
'Hmmh, well then, now, take out your French notebooks.'

c)   St: ***Heu, bon, alors*** *vous allez faire les multiplications que je vous
dictent. Trois plus, trois fois trois.*
'Uh, well, so you're going to do the multiplications that I tell you.
Three plus, three times three.'

Although the youngest children rarely stacked DMs in the other settings (and never
stacked more than two), as teacher they produced a number of two-term stacks, even
though their teachers were more gentle and friendly than those portrayed by the older
French children. Examples (14) and (15) are representative of the use of stacks among 5-
year-olds:

(14) St: ***Alors maintenant*** *les élèves, allez les élèves asseyez-vous.*
'Well, now students, go on students, sit down.'

Ss: *Ça y est maîtresse.*
'We have, teacher.'

St: ***Bon,*** *j'arrive. C'est bien:: Je vais te mettre . . . ,
je vais te mettre un A.*
'Good, I'm coming. That's good. I'm going to give you,
I'm going to give you an A.'

(15) St: ***Et ben*** *non, tu prends la même feuille que les autres.*
'Oh, well, no, you use the same paper as the others.'

Ss: ***Bon*** *voilà j' ai fini madame.*
'Well, there you go, I've finished, Miss.'

St: *C'est bon. Va le mettre dans ton tiroir.*
'That's good. Go put it in your drawer.'

Ss: *Qu'est-ce que je fais pour reconnaître mon dessin?*
'How will I recognize my picture?'

St: ***Et ben*** *tu marques ton nom!*
'Well, put your name on it!'

Ss: ***Heu,*** *j'arrive pas bien.*
'Um, I'm having trouble.'

St: ***Et ben*** *prends ton étiquette!*
'So, then, take your name tag!'

In all the examples provided above, there is an obvious power asymmetry in the relationship of the interlocutors, based on age or professional competence or some combination of the two.   And the distribution of DMs clearly reflects this asymmetry. One might be tempted to argue that the reason there are more DMs in the speech of high status individuals in these situations is simply that they are the ones who have control of the conversational floor: perhaps, as suggested by Coulthard (1977), DMs simply are attached to utterances that initiate new topics (or serve as coherence and cohesion devices to keep control of the topic).   But this explanation does not adequately account for the data.   The people with greater power or authority in these examples used not only more DMs, but also different types than lower status people.   Overall the data suggest that the higher the status, the greater the proportion of *alors*, *maintenant*, and *bon*, often in combination (as in *et bon alors maintenant*).   When the lower status individual did produce a DM in asymmetrical settings, it was most often a simple nonlexical form such as *heu* or *ah*.   Moreover, the corpus also contains a fair number of dialogues involving equally "low status" speakers interacting with one another, and these dialogues are far from void of lexical DMs.   For instance, the classroom context elicited numerous stretches of child–child discourse, as illustrated by the final example in (16) below:

(16) Ss1: ***Ah bon et puis*** *ça va coller?*
    'Oh, well, and is that going to stick, then?'

    Ss2: ***Ah*** *peut-être ouais. Il faut que j'*essaie, c'est pas sûr **hein**?
    'Uh, maybe, yes. I must try, it's not for sure, eh?'

    Ss1: ***Ouais et ben*** *tu sais ce que j'ai fait moi? Moi (   ) moi j'ai coloré mon ballon, j'ai colorié mon ballon, je lui ai fait des yeux et un nez et une bouche.*
    'Yeh, and uh, you know what I did? Me, ( ) me, I colored my ball, I colored my ball, I gave it eyes and a nose and a mouth.'

    Ss2: *C'est vrai?*
    'Really?'

    Ss1: *Ouais, j'peux t' l'amener c' t' après-m.*
    'Yeh, I can bring it to you this afternoon.'

    Ss2: ***Ouais*** *ce serait bien.*
    'Yeh, that would be fine.'

    Ss1: ***Ouais*** *comme ça on fera un match.*
    'Yeh, that way we can have a game.'

What is interesting about this dialogue is that almost every turn is marked by one or more DMs, but the actual DMs are quite different from those boldfaced in the other examples.   There is no *alors* or *maintenant*; instead there is *ah*, *et ben*, and *et puis* (see also example 8), along with *ouais*, the informal variant of *oui*.   Fig. 8.1 demonstrates this interaction of personal identity and relationship to interlocutor, as evidenced by the use of DMs in the classroom setting.   While the teacher role produces many more DMs (especially lexical ones) than the student role, if the latter is broken down into its realizations of student to teacher versus student to student, it becomes clear that the difference is due entirely to the realization of student to teacher.   The dramatically greater use of lexical DMs when the student interacts with another student may well reflect the fact that the power relationship between the interlocutors is not predetermined.   With this interpretation, one could argue that as they begin to understand how linguistic forms can be manipulated to convey social meaning, children come to use sociolinguistic variables not only to reflect their social identity and their view of the situation at hand, but also to restructure existing social relationships (as has been suggested, for example, in the work of Mitchell-Kernan & Kernan, 1977). Certainly, this is a question worth pursuing in future research.

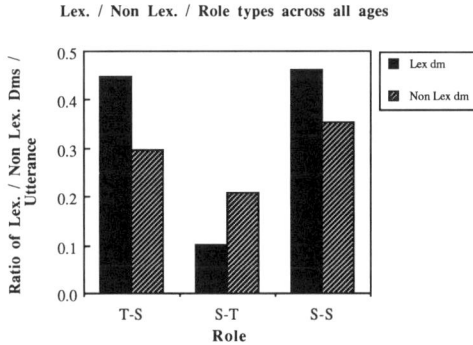

FIG. 8.1. Frequency of DMs (across role-realizations) in French classroom setting

The situation regarding stacking is similar, but not identical. While it is indeed the case that student to student discourse contains many more stacks than student to teacher discourse, the former does not come close to matching the frequency in teacher to student speech. These data are presented in the bar graph in Fig. 8.2.

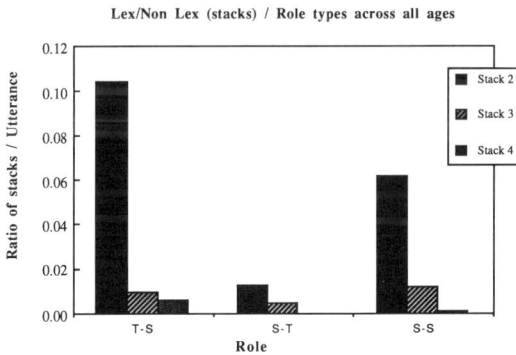

FIG. 8.2. Frequency of stacking (across role-realizations) in French classroom setting

What these data suggest, then, is that the choice of one DM or another carries two types of related social meaning, about the individual speaker as well as about his or her status relative to that of the addressee. The data also indicate that by the time children arrive at school, they are already well aware of even the most subtle sociolinguistic markers, though their skill at using these markers increases over the elementary school years.

CONCLUSIONS

I have attempted to demonstrate in this chapter the value of a particular research methodology ("controlled improvisation") in eliciting evidence from children of an awareness of subtle sociolinguistic rules that would not be revealed in a naturalistic study. The findings from both the American and the French studies demonstrate the success of this technique in eliciting symbolic form choices stripped of practical compliance consequences, revealing the children's abilities to discriminate and express in their language a wide range of social relationships through choices of content, discourse strategies, and situationally appropriate grammatical patterns. I have focused the discussion on the use of discourse markers because the systematic variation revealed in the use of these forms in the children's role-play speech is especially striking, given that researchers are only beginning to understand the social significance of these forms.

In her contribution to this volume, Berman demonstrates how knowledge of the functions of a particular linguistic form (the Hebrew coordinating conjunction *ve*, meaning 'and') develops in children aged 3 to 9, from an initial pregrammatical use to more structure-bound usage, and finally to a more discourse-motivated function — consistent with Ervin-Tripp's notion of local to global development in language acquisition (Ervin-Tripp, 1989). The data on discourse markers presented here appear to present an analogous pattern, in which children acquire a particular form (or set of forms) initially with one function and only gradually learn the other functions that the form can serve. In the case of English, Ervin-Tripp and colleagues have shown functional development (local to global) in the textual uses of discourse markers well before the age of 5 or 6, when English-speaking children are first beginning to show systematic sociolinguistic variation for these forms (e.g., Kyratzis & Ervin-Tripp, 1993; Sprott, 1992). Similarly, in her study of narrative development in French children, Jisa (1984/85, 1987) found consistent functional development of DMs used as sentence connectors between the ages of 3 and 5; e.g., 3-year-olds used *et pis* (their version of *et puis*, literally 'and then') initially as an all purpose connector, then limited its functions as other forms (such as *alors*) were acquired. Again, the French role-play data suggest that the social meanings of these forms develop a bit later. However, to be certain that these age differences are not an artifact of the methodology employed, it would be useful to examine the kinds of naturalistic data used in these textual studies for evidence of social variation. I hope the research reported here will encourage just that sort of investigation.

REFERENCES

Andersen, E. S. (1984). The acquisition of sociolinguistic knowledge: Some evidence from children's verbal role play. *The Western Journal of Speech Communication*, **48**, 125-144.

Andersen, E. S. (1990). *Speaking with style: The sociolinguistic skills of children.* London and New York: Routledge.

Berko Gleason, J. (1975). Fathers and other strangers: Men's speech to young children. In D. P. Dato (Ed.), *Georgetown University Roundtable on Languages and Linguistics* (pp. 289-297). Washington, DC: Georgetown University Press.

Berko Gleason, J., Perlmann, R., & Grief, R. (1984). What's the magic word? *Discourse Processes*, **7**, 493-502.

Berko Gleason, J., & Weintraub, S. (1976). The acquisition of routines in child language. *Language and Society*, **5**, 129-135.

Berko Gleason, J., & Weintraub, S. (1978). Input language and the acquisition of communicative competence. In K. E. Nelson (Ed.), *Children's Language, vol.1.* New York: Gardner.

Broen, P. (1972). The verbal environment of the language-learning child. *Monograph of American Speech and Hearing Association*, 17.

Budwig, N. (1989). The linguistic marking of agentivity and control in child language. *Journal of Child Language*, **16**, 263-284.

Coulthard, M. (1977). *An Introduction to discourse analysis.* London: Longman Group Ltd.

Crystal, D. (1970). Prosodic systems and language acquisition. In P. Leon (Ed.), *Prosodic feature analysis.* Montreal and Paris: Didier.

Clancy, P. (1986). The acquisition of communicative style in Japanese. In B. Schieffelin & E. Ochs (Eds.), *Language socialization across cultures* (pp. 51-78). Cambridge, England: Cambridge University Press.

Ellis, J., & Ure, J. (1969). Language varieties: Register. In R. Meacham (Ed.), *Encyclopedia of linguistics: Information and control* (pp. 251-259). London: Pergamon,

Ervin-Tripp, S. (1973). Children's sociolinguistic competence and dialect diversity. In S. Ervin-Tripp, *Language acquisition and communicative choice: Essays by Susan M. Ervin-Tripp* (pp. 262-301). Stanford: Stanford University Press.

Ervin-Tripp, S. (1976). Is Sybil there? The structure of some American English directives. *Language and Society*, **5**, 25-66.

Ervin-Tripp, S. (1977). Wait for me, Roller Skate. In S. Ervin-Tripp & C. Mitchell-Kernan (Eds.), *Child Discourse.* New York: Academic.

Ervin-Tripp, S. (1989). *Speech acts and syntactic development: Linked or independent?* (Berkeley Cognitive Science Tech. Rep. No. 61). Berkeley, CA: University of California, Institute of Cognitive Studies.

Ervin-Tripp, S., O'Connor, M., & Rosenberg, J. (1984). Language and power in the family. In M. Schulz & C. Kramerae (Eds.), *Language and power*, Belmont, CA: Sage.

Ferguson, C. A. (1975). Toward a characterization of English foreigner talk. *Anthropological Linguistics*, **17**, 1-14.

Fraser, B. (1990). An approach to discourse markers. *Journal of Pragmatics*, **14**, 383-395.

Grief, E. B., & Berko Gleason, J. (1980). Hi, thanks, and goodbye: More routine information. *Language in Society*, **9**, 159-166.

Grimshaw, A. D., & Holden, L. (1976). Post-childhood modifications of linguistic and social competence. *Items*, **30**, 33-42.

Jisa, H. (1984/85). French Preschoolers' use of *et pis* ('and then'). *First Language*, **5**, 169-184.

Jisa, H. (1987). Sentence connectors in French children's monologue performance. *Journal of Pragmatics*, **11**, 607-621.

Kernan, K. (1977). Semantic and expressive elaboration in children's narratives. In S. Ervin-Tripp & C. Mitchell-Kernan (Eds.), *Child discourse.* New York: Academic Press.

Kyratzis, A., & Ervin-Tripp, S. (1993, July). *The development of discourse markers in child-child interaction.* Paper presented at the International Congress on Language Acquisition. Trieste, Italy.

Lakoff, R. (1973). Language and women's place. *Language and Society, 2,* 45-79.

Mitchell-Kernan, C., & Kernan, K. (1977). Pragmatics of directive choice among children. In S. Ervin-Tripp & C. Mitchell-Kernan (Eds.), *Child Discourse.* New York: Academic Press.

Ochs, E., & Schieffelin, B. B. (1984). Language acquisition and socialization: Three developmental stories and their implications. In R. Shweder & R. LeVine (Eds.), *Culture theory: Essays on mind, self and emotion.* New York: Cambridge University Press.

Redeker, G. (1990). Ideational and pragmatic markers of discourse structure. *Journal of Pragmatics, 14,* 367-381.

Sachs, J., & Devin, J. (1976). Young children's use of age appropriate speech styles in social interaction and role playing. *Journal of Child Language, 3,* 81-98.

Schieffelin, B. B. (1979). Getting it together: An ethnographic approach to the study of the development of communicative competence. In E. Ochs, & B. Schieffelin (Eds.), *Developmental pragmatics.* New York: Academic.

Schieffelin, B. B., & Ochs, E. (Eds.). (1986). *Language socialization across cultures.* New York: Cambridge University Press.

Schieffelin, B. B., & Ochs, E. (1988). Language socialization. *Annual Review of Anthropology, 15.*

Schiffrin, D. (1987). *Discourse markers.* Cambridge, England: Cambridge University Press.

Shatz, M., & Gelman, R. (1973). The development of communication skills: Modification in the speech of young children as a function of listener. *Monographs of the Society for Research in Child Development, 38.*

Shore, B. (1982). *Sala'ilua: A Samoan mystery.* New York: Columbia University Press.

Sinclair, J. M., & Coulthard, R. M. (1975). *Towards an analysis of discourse.* London: Oxford University Press.

Slobin, D. I. (Ed.). (1967). *A Field Manual for the Cross-cultural Study of the Acquisition of Communicative Competence.* Unpublished manuscript, University of California, Berkeley.

Slobin, D. I. (1973). Cognitive prerequisites for the acquisition of grammar. In C. A. Ferguson & D. I. Slobin (Eds), *Studies of child language development.* New York: Holt, Rinehart & Winston.

Slobin, D. I. (1982). Universal and particular in the acquisition of language. In E. Wanner & L. Gleitman (Eds.), *Language acquisition: The state of the art.* Cambridge, England: Cambridge University Press.

Slobin, D. I. (Ed.). (1985). *The cross-linguistic study of language acquisition: Vol. 1. The data.* Hillsdale, NJ: Lawrence Erlbaum Associates.

Snow, C. E. (1972). Mothers' speech to children learning language. *Child Development, 43,* 549-565.

Snow, C. E., & Ferguson, C. A. (Eds.). (1977). *Talking to children: Language input and acquisition.* New York: Cambridge University Press.

Sprott, R. A. (1992). Children's use of discourse markers in disputes: Form-function relations and discourse in child language. *Discourse Processes, 15,* 423-439.

Vincent, D., & Sankoff, D. (1992). Punctors: A pragmatic variable. *Language Variation and Change, 4,* 205-216.

9 WHAT INFLUENCES CHILDREN'S PATTERNING OF FORMS AND FUNCTIONS IN EARLY CHILD LANGUAGE?

Nancy Budwig[1]
Clark University

Over the past years, there has been a growing number of studies demonstrating that children's acquisition of various aspects of linguistic structure are related to aspects of the interactional and discursive contexts (see Berman & Slobin, 1994; Budwig, 1993, 1995; Ervin-Tripp, 1977, 1989, 1993; Slobin, 1985). Children of a variety of age groups, acquiring different sorts of languages, have been noted to link the use of particular linguistic forms with clusters of semantic, pragmatic, and discursive notions. In this chapter, I attempt to go beyond the claim that children link particular linguistic devices with specific semantic and pragmatic notions, and examine the question of the *basis* for such linkages. Although there have been many illustrations that grammar and discourse are linked in important ways in children's early linguistic productions, there has been little attention to the study of the sources of such systematizations.

Elsewhere (see Budwig, 1993, 1995) I have argued that until fairly recently the issue of sources of form–function pairings has received little empirical investigation within functionalist approaches to child language. I have noted that a gradual shift in empirical studies has involved moving from a discussion of how the domain of language ought to be defined towards a trend to chart out various courses of development en route to adult-like usage (see Budwig, 1993). Many functionalists seem to hold some more or less implicit assumptions that what the children are doing with particular forms is "child-like." The children's use is said to be special or "deviate" from the target language they are acquiring, to the extent that adult speakers are assumed to use forms in a more decontextual way (see for instance, Bamberg, Budwig, & Kaplan, 1991; Bloom, 1991; Tomasello, 1992). Other functionalists have implicitly or explicitly assumed that what children are doing is very much like what adults are doing with forms (see for instance

[1] Portions of this paper were first presented at the American Association for Applied Linguistics, Seattle, Washington, 1992. Angela Wiley and Heather Quick played a central role in coding and analyzing some of the material reviewed in this chapter. In addition, I would like to thank the volume editors for helpful commentary on an earlier draft of this manuscript.

Van Valin, 1991). At least at some general level there seems to be the assumption that all speakers of a language — whether children or adults — will link particular forms with semantic and pragmatic functions.

While such assumptions have guided much functionalist research, few studies have examined caregivers' and children's patterning of forms and functions in an interactive way. When caregivers' language patterns are discussed, researchers have focused on assumptions about how a given language functions based on typological studies of adult discourse. Little has been said about the relationship between such assumptions and the patterns found in speech addressed to young children (see also Miller & Hoogstra, 1992). Most functionalist analyses in fact have focused exclusively on children's linguistic patterning. Thus, we have little empirical research on the relationship between the form-function patterns in children's speech and those patterns found in the discourse of those around them.

In this chapter, I will discuss a series of studies which has examined children's special use of personal pronouns in the earliest phases of acquiring English as a first language. Of particular interest here will be what such studies can tell us about the sources of children's early systematization of first-person pronominal forms with specific functions. In so doing, I will provide something of a personal narrative about the transitions in my own thinking as I have attempted to make sense of some puzzling uses of personal pronouns by six young children acquiring English as a first language. In my review I am interested in highlighting the relationship between the implicit and explicit assumptions guiding the analyses rather than highlighting the specific findings themselves. I take transitions in my own reflections on the relationship between the role of the child and the role of input to be symptomatic of the way functionalist approaches to child language in general have made implicit assumptions about causal relations between the children's and adults' linking of forms and functions. After reviewing the logic behind these three studies and the ways in which findings from each led me to revise my thinking, I will point out the limitations of the sort of framework I have adopted and suggest some alternative ways I have begun to answer these questions.

METHOD

The data I will review in this chapter stem from a longitudinal study I conducted with six white middle-class families in Northern California in the mid 1980s. The children, ranging between 20 and 32 months of age at the onset of the study, all attended a daycare center associated with a large research university. Two girls and four boys were studied. I video- and audio-taped the children's language development for a four-month period. Half of the children in the study were just beginning to combine words at the start of the study; their mean length of utterance (MLU) ranged between 1.72 and 2.82. The other three children were producing utterances with an MLU of over three morphemes per utterance (range = 3.22 – 3.91).

The six children were videotaped twice a month in the daycare setting. In each session they were either involved in dyadic play with a peer or their caregiver. The play sessions included three activities that were introduced by the researcher: play with wooden blocks, play with manipulative toys, and looking through a photo-book which included pictures of the children and their peers engaged in activities at the daycare center. During the duration of the study I acted as a regular participant at the daycare center the children attended.

STUDY I:
THE CHILDREN'S USE OF SELF-REFERENCE FORMS

The question of focus in the first study concerned the development of the six children's use of self-reference forms. Based on pilot work I had conducted, I hypothesized that children who used personal pronouns in ways that deviated from the target language would nevertheless employ these forms in a systematic way. Specifically, I predicted that the children would use personal pronominal forms and their own name to contrastively mark various perspectives on a cluster of semantic and pragmatic notions having to do with agency and control.

Preliminary Analyses

A preliminary set of analyses led me to divide the children into two groups: ego-anchored children and nonego-anchored children. This distinction was based on three kinds of preliminary analyses: (1) an examination of the mean length of utterance, (2) the distribution of reference to self and others in subject position, and (3) the range and distribution of self-reference forms used by the children. The three ego-anchored children (Megan, Grice, and Jeffrey) could be characterized as follows: (1) their MLUs were below 3.0; (2) they primarily referred to self in subject position (i.e., 75% of more of their references to persons in subject position were references to self); and (3) these three children regularly relied on multiple forms of self-reference, often in subject position in ways that deviated from adult usage (i.e., *My open that*, *Me jump*). In contrast, the nonego-anchored children (Eric, Keith, and Thomas) (1) had MLUs over 3.0; (2) more equally distributed their references to self and other; and (3) used a range of self-reference forms, but primarily relied on the single form *I* and used self-reference forms in conventional ways.

Functional Analyses

The central question of the original study of these six children's use of self-reference forms focused on the basis upon which the various children employed such forms. In particular, I was interested in the question of whether the ego-anchored children systematically made use of these forms to mark various perspectives on the self's relation to what Slobin (1985) has referred to as the "manipulative activity scene":

> . . . the experiential gestalt of a basic causal event in which an agent carries out
> a physical and perceptible change of state in a patient by means of direct body
> contact or with an instrument under the agent's control. (p. 1175)

I was not only interested in whether the children gave specific linguistic treatment to something like the manipulative activity scene, but also, following DeLancey (1984), I was curious as to whether children might mark deviations from the prototype of agency outlined above, with a related set of forms. In addition, borrowing from Ervin-Tripp's (1981) notion of control moves, I suspected that the children might integrate their budding notions about the power of language to bring about change into their prototypical agency scene. In short, I suspected that at a time before the children regularly referred to others, they temporarily borrowed the first person forms to mark various perspectives on their own subjectivity in ongoing discourse.

Ego-anchored children's usage

In examining the children's distribution of forms according to an array of semantic and pragmatic factors relating to agentivity and control, it was found that the three ego-anchored children did distinguish the use of the various self-reference forms based on a functional contrast. For instance, *I* was found in clauses with stative verbs in which self was viewed as "experiencer" in assertions about the world. In contrast, *my* was found in the context of utterances in which the child acted as prototypical agent, often by attempting to use language to bring about change. Examining the distribution of *I* and *my* in terms of semantic agency, we find that 71% of all uses coded high in semantic agency by the ego-anchored children involved the use of *my*. In contrast, 69% of the uses coded for low agency linked up with the use of *I*.

The following example illustrate this contrast:
(1) Megan (M) and Mom (MM) are playing with manipulative toys.

    a M: **I** want that one. (lifting container)
    b MM: Oh you want that one, okay.
    c M: (tries to open container then says:) **My** open that.
    d MM: What?
    e M: **My** open that Mommy. (giving container to MM)
    f MM: Wanna open that?
    g M: Yeah. (MM opens container)

In this play example, the 20-month-old child, Megan, makes use of two different self-reference forms. The form *I* is used in line (1a) as she expresses her desire to play with a clear container which contains a nut inside. The mother's utterance in line (1b) and her lack of action support the conclusion that the mother had also contextualized the child's statement as an assertion of desire, in contrast to a request for the mother's assistance. Note though, that as Megan recognizes that she is unable to open the container on her own to get the nut out, she gives the container to her mother. What is interesting is the shift in the way she indexes herself in this utterance, switching in lines (1c) and (1e) to the more dynamic form *my*.

A comparative analysis of the ego-anchored children's use of *I* and *my* in subject position revealed a cluster of interrelated semantic and pragmatic features linked up with the children's use of forms. As has been reported elsewhere in detail, distributional differences were found at the individual coding levels of semantic meaning and pragmatic function, and in the combined distributional analyses (see Budwig, 1989, 1990, 1995). For instance, comparing the use of *I* and *my* in subject position by the ego-anchored children we find that 100% of these instances coded as high in semantic agentivity and pragmatic control co-occurred with the use of *my*. In contrast, 82% of these usages that were coded as ranking low in both semantic agency and pragmatic control involved the use of *I*. That is, only 18% of the uses of *my* ranked low on both dimensions, while none of the uses of *I* ranked high on both dimensions.

In summary, the functional analyses of the ego-anchored children's use of self-reference forms were guided by the question of whether these children might be systematically employing various self-reference forms to take various perspectives on themselves with regard to degree of semantic agentivity and pragmatic control. Based on a series of distributional analyses which examined form, meaning, and function I concluded that there was evidence that the ego-anchored children's use of various self-reference forms (i.e., *I*, *my*, *me*, *'own name'*) was indeed linked to the issues of agentivity and control (see Budwig, 1989, 1990, in press for further discussion).

Nonego-anchored children's usage

In my original interpretation of the nonego-anchored children's use of self-reference forms I suggested that for these three children the use of *I* is not solely linked to the notions of agentivity and control (see Budwig, 1989). For instance, in contrast to the ego-anchored children who contrastively employed self-reference forms for the high and low ends of the semantic and pragmatic agentivity and control scales, the nonego-anchored children tended to rely on a single form in all instances. As I have illustrated in greater detail elsewhere, the nonego-anchored children did not distinguish the use of *I* and *my* based on degree of agentivity and control. As was the case with the ego-anchored children, *I* was the preferred form (94%) for the low end of the agentivity and pragmatic control scale. But in addition, *I* was also the preferred form at the high end of the scale, accounting for 86% of all usage of *I* and *my*. Thus the nonego-anchored children relied on the form *I* at both ends of the semantic agentivity and pragmatic control scale. Thus, the conclusion was drawn that the nonego-anchored children's use of self-reference forms differed from the ego-anchored children, not only to the extent that they tended to rely on a single form (*I*), but also that they used this form multifunctionally (Budwig, 1989).

Discussion

The question then can be raised: On what basis did the ego-anchored children come to employ the forms as they did? Furthermore, if one wants to claim that the ego-anchored systems represent a temporary developmental phase en route to the more adult-like systems, a second question can be raised regarding what motivates the children to give up their child-like linkages of form and function. In earlier writings, the answers I provided to these questions relied heavily on a constructivist perspective towards language development. Following Slobin (1985), I claimed that the children were linking specific linguistic forms with salient conceptual units and communicative goals. At a time before children regularly referred to others, the ego-anchored children temporarily "borrowed" first person pronominal forms to mark notions related to agentivity and control (see Budwig, 1986, 1989, 1995, for further discussion of this position).

In summary, Study I is characteristic of many of the implicit assumptions discussed with regard to functionalist approaches to child language. Like previous work within this tradition, the study's emphasis is on the nature of the form-function pairings and the course of development, rather than an empirical examination of sources of such pairings.

STUDY II: EGO-ANCHORED CHILDREN'S CAREGIVERS' SELF-REFERENCE FORMS

As I became more interested in the factors motivating the ego-anchored children's special patterning of pronominal forms and semantic and pragmatic functions, it seemed important to examine the input children received when interacting with their caregivers. In Study I, children's production data were examined from monthly play sessions when the ego-anchored children interacted with their caregivers, as well as monthly sessions in which the children interacted with their peers. For the purposes of Study II, all utterances made by the mothers of the three ego-anchored children were analyzed. The aim at the outset was to show that the caregiver's use of first person pronominal forms was multifunctional.

Basing expectations on what we know about the "target language" the predictions seemed straightforward. That is, it seemed obvious that the children's caregivers would not regularly employ various self-reference forms in subject position in ways similar to the children (i.e., *My want that*, *Me jump*) and rather would rely on the single form *I* when referring to themselves. Furthermore, it was expected, based on what is known about English, that the ego-anchored children's caregivers would use *I* in multifunctional ways. Thus we expected caregiver's use of *I* to be employed with both state verbs and action verbs. In addition, it seemed clear that this form would function pragmatically both in assertions about states in the world, as well as in more dynamic contexts in which language was being used to bring about change. In short, the general expectation was that the ego-anchored children's caregivers' use of the pronominal form *I* would look distinct from that of their children, who restricted its use to a particular cluster of semantic and pragmatic notions.

Preliminary Analyses

An analysis similar to that undertaken for the ego-anchored children was carried out with Angela Wiley (see Budwig & Wiley, 1995). At the level of form analysis, we found the caregivers relied on one form of self-reference in subject position, namely the use of *I*. Although we expected they might use alternative forms such as *mommy* or their own name, this turned out to be the case in less than 3% of all instances. Thus, while the ego-anchored children used multiple forms of self-reference in subject position, their caregivers primarily relied on the form *I*.

Functional Analyses

The analyses of the function of the ego-anchored children's mothers' use of *I* revealed some unexpected findings. As expected, all three of the mothers did use *I* with a variety of semantic verb types and such usage was found in utterances with varied pragmatic functions. It was the distributional regularities of such usage, though, that were surprising. At the semantic level of analysis, we found that all three caregivers tended to employ *I* with mental state verbs (i.e., *I like your little teapot, I think we need to leave that there*). That is, 59% of all utterances with a self-reference form uttered by the caregiver included a state verb. What was unexpected was less frequent usage of *I* with action verbs. Only 41% of all caregiver usage of *I* linked up with action verbs.

An analysis of the pragmatic function of the caregivers' use of *I* also revealed a tendency to restrict the usage of *I* to utterances which functioned as assertions. 61% of all of these caregivers' uses of *I* functioned as non-control acts. That is, the caregiver's rarely indexed themselves in control acts which attempted to bring about change. Only 20% of the caregivers' usage of a self-reference form linked up with attempts to bring about change. These tended to take the form of requests to the child for the caregiver to act in certain ways, for instance asking *Can I pour the tea?* or *May I use your block?*. What is interesting about these permission requests is that although they are coded as control acts they nevertheless act to mitigate the caregiver's agency. Compared to other sorts of control acts the caregivers might have used (e.g., commands), the children might construe these as actually ranking low in agentivity and control.

Discussion

The findings from the functional analyses did not match our assumptions about the target language. These findings are important in that they suggest that *both* the children and their caregivers restricted the use of *I* to a similar semantic and pragmatic cluster in which self was viewed as nonagentive and noncontrolling. This is not to imply that this finding can be generalized to all adult discourse. It suggests, though, that the original interpretation of the data stemming from our analysis of the ego-anchored children's use of self-reference forms may have overemphasized the extent to which the children actually constructed such patterns based on salient independently constructed conceptual units. On the one hand, the caregivers' usage may indirectly guide children's constructions such that they may determine which conceptual contrasts are made salient; on the other hand, it seems equally plausible that children are simply following dominant patterns provided in the input they hear.

STUDY III: NONEGO-ANCHORED CHILDREN'S CAREGIVERS' SELF-REFERENCE FORMS

Study II has revealed some similarities in the semantic and pragmatic functions of the form *I* in the ego-anchored children's and caregivers' speech. This leads us back to a consideration of the nonego-anchored children's use of self-reference forms. It was noted above, in the review of Study I, that in contrast to the ego-anchored children's reliance on multiple self-reference forms, a second group of children — namely the nonego-anchored children — primarily relied on one self-reference form in subject position. In order to evaluate the relationship between form and function in caregiver and child speech, it seems necessary to also examine the input that the nonego-anchored children received. Given that the nonego-anchored children were noted to use the self-reference form *I* in a multifunctional way, we can question whether this pattern is also reflected in their caregivers' speech. The third study, undertaken with Heather Quick, examined the distribution of self-reference forms and their functions in the speech of the three nonego-anchored children's caregivers (see Quick, 1991).

Preliminary Analyses

All instances of the nonego-anchored children's caregivers' references to self were targeted and coded according to form used. All three of the mothers of nonego-anchored children also primarily relied on the single self-reference form *I* in subject position. Like the caregivers of the ego-anchored children these mothers made use of alternative forms (such as *mommy*) less than 3% of the time. We can turn now to an examination of the function of the nonego-anchored children's caregivers' use of *I*.

Functional Analyses

All uses of *I* uttered by these caregivers were coded in terms of the same semantic and pragmatic function codes employed in Studies I and II. At the semantic level of analysis it was found that the majority of the mothers' uses of *I* occurred with state verbs (58% of all usage). In contrast, *I* linked up with action verbs only 43% of the time. This finding almost exactly replicates the distribution reported for the caregivers of the ego-anchored children.

At the pragmatic level of analysis, the caregivers of the nonego-anchored children almost exclusively made use of utterances that were not control acts (79%). This finding points to the same general trend as that reported for the caregivers of the ego-anchored children. The main difference is that these caregivers were even *more* likely to link the use of *I* with noncontrol acts.

Discussion

In conclusion, we find that both groups of mothers, namely the mothers of the ego-anchored and nonego-anchored children, revealed a fairly similar distributional pattern. Both groups of mothers relied on a single self-reference form, and this form primarily was used in the context of utterances with state verbs which did not function as control acts.

GENERAL DISCUSSION

The above three studies have been presented in order to better understand how children come to relate form and function in the early phases of acquiring the English pronominal system. These studies, when considered together, present some puzzling findings. Study I seems to show some "child-like" ways of organizing pronominal forms around semantic and pragmatic functions in early child language. Study II, though, highlights the importance of checking the *actual* form–function patterns of caregivers interacting with the child, because some of the children's seemingly "special" uses of pronominal forms can also be found in their caregivers' speech patterns. The findings from Study II suggest that children may make more use of the available input concerning form–function relationships in pronominal input they receive.

Accounting for Differences in the Ego-anchored and Nonego-anchored Children's Systems

Even if one were to suggest that the ego-anchored children make more use of the dominant patterns in caregiver input than originally claimed, this nevertheless leaves the question of what leads children to give up the ego-anchored systems and organize forms and functions in the way described for the nonego-anchored children. Put differently, given that the caregivers' form-function patterns were noted to be quite similar for both the ego-anchored and nonego-anchored children (compare studies II and III), why do their children's patterning of forms and function differ?

A possible answer to this question can be found in Karmiloff-Smith's (1979) model of the development from unifunctional to plurifunctional systems. According to Karmiloff-Smith, early on, after a phase of using forms in unanalyzed ways, children use forms unifunctionally. The selection of which function the child gives a specific form depends on characteristics of the input received. In the early phase of unifunctional usage, Karmiloff-Smith claims children identify the form with the most consistent functional pattern found in the input. At this point in time children may develop slightly ungrammatical usages to link up with less dominant functions. After going through a phase of unifunctional usage, children are said to consolidate the various functions within one plurifunctional marker. At this time the ungrammatical usage fades.

Relating Karmiloff-Smith's position to the transition from ego-anchored to nonego-anchored functioning, we might want to suggest that early on, the ego-anchored children attend to the most consistent pattern in caregiver input, here for instance, the caregiver's linking of *I* with mental state verbs in non-control acts. For the time being the ego-anchored children "borrow" related forms (e.g., *my*, *me*) to mark other less-consistently used functions associated with the caregivers' usage of *I*. After the ego-anchored phase of using distinct and often ungrammatical ways to mark each function, the children develop nonego-anchored systems which involve the plurifunctional use of *I*.

Accounting for the Caregivers' Form-Function Patterns

While the above framework provides one way to make sense of the transition from ego-anchored to nonego-anchored functioning, it does not help us to understand why the caregivers use *I* in the way that they do. What is it that leads all the caregivers in this study to primarily use *I* with mental state verbs in the context of utterances that do not function to bring about change? Searching to answer this question has pointed up another possible way to account for the differences in the ego-anchored and nonego-anchored systems.

In viewing the videotapes it becomes clear that the caregivers rarely talk about their own actions as independent, volitional, and goal-directed. This might be related to the caregivers' beliefs concerning the importance of fostering their 2-year-old children's sense of autonomy (see Lin, 1993; Wiley & Budwig, 1994, for further discussion). Most often, the caregivers focus on evaluative comments about their children's action sequences. Interestingly, when the caregivers do talk about their own actions, they tend to refer to these actions with the pronouns *you* or *we*. That is, the caregivers often talk *as if* the action was being carried out by the child alone, or the caregivers construe their own actions as joint ones. For instance, the caregivers often arranged the building blocks into "towers" and accompanied such actions by saying *I like your little tower*, *Wow, you built a nice tower*, or *We're making a nice tower aren't we*. In these instances the adults are often working on their own along side their children.

One possible interpretation of the caregivers' input is that the caregivers might be downplaying their own agency and accentuating that of their child. These caregivers not only seem to structure their talk in such a way that their own agency is not in focus, but also the caregivers organize the environment in ways that encourage the child to act as an independent agent, and they prompt the child to talk about themselves. What this suggests is that the caregivers' use of pronominal forms is part of the way they are indexing social relationships with their child. Such usages are also part of their beliefs about their children's role as communicative partners, as developing selves, and their own role in their children's development.

This account of form–function patterns in the caregivers' discourse shifts focus from an approach that looks fairly locally at the tallying of forms and functions in particular activity contexts, towards such issues as the impact of the speakers' belief systems and attitudes on the organization of form-function patterns in ongoing discourse. Relating this account to the patterns found in the children's systematizations one could argue that the change from the ego-anchored to nonego-anchored systems can be tied to developmental changes in the children's beliefs about themselves, their communicative partners, and their goals of conversational interchanges. For instance, over time the children may come to recognize the need to be vague or indirect about requesting and the functional utility of their system may be called into question.

According to this latter account, linguistic devices function to transmit cultural patterns of being. Linguistic forms, for children and adults alike, act as contextual cues (Gumperz, 1982) which provide information about beliefs, values, and attitudes of members of social groups. This account highlights the interrelationship between socio-cultural processes and language usage (see Berko Gleason, Ely, Perlman, & Narasimhan Chapter 13, this volume; Cook-Gumperz, 1986; Miller & Hoogstra, 1992; Schieffelin & Ochs, 1986; among others).

Avenues of Future Research

In the introduction to this chapter, I noted that researchers examining the relationship between linguistic forms and functions in child language have begun to move beyond detailed descriptions of children's form–function systems en route to adult-like systems, towards an understanding of the mechanisms that lead children to organize and reorganize linguistic systems as they do. While I believe this shift is central, important revisions are necessary in order to make progress on this issue.

A review of my own work over the last decade is symptomatic of two dominant ways of approaching the issue of sources of children's early form–function patterning to date. On the one hand, we have assumed that children systematically link linguistic forms to previously developed and salient conceptual packages, and on the other, there has been the assumption that children are influenced by structural regularities of the target language.

The joint implications of these two approaches are that either children across language groups can be assumed to construct similar child grammars (see for instance Slobin's 1985 discussion of Basic Child Grammar) or children acquiring the same language can be assumed to construct similar form-function pairings given their close attention to typological regularities in the input. My attempts to work with both of these assumptions, as described above, have been problematic. I now turn to discuss some necessary changes in focus if we are going to better understand what motivates the organization and reorganization of children's systems of forms and functions in early child language.

One assumption that has always been central to functionalist approaches to child language is the belief in the need to study situated talk. While we have emphasized the importance of collecting data about what children actually say in natural speech contexts, my sense is that we have not adequately done this with regard to the discourse children hear around them in their everyday interactions. In order to better understand the relationship between form–function patterning in caregiver and child discourse, it will be essential to not only conduct crosslinguistic studies in which children are presented with distinct typological clusters, but also to make use of *within-language* variation.

Recent work in the area of language socialization has emphasized that even when children grow up in environments in which the same language is spoken, the input they receive may nevertheless be quite distinct (see for instance, Dunn & Brown, 1991; Heath, 1983; Miller, 1982; Shatz, 1991). This has led me to begin collecting data from groups of speakers who speak the same language, but for whom it seems likely that children might be receiving distinct input regarding the indexing of self and other in ongoing discourse.

Within this framework, Lin (1993) has examined the creation of child as conversational partner in two groups of middle-class caregivers and their toddlers. This research has shown the extent to which these caregivers construct distinct participant roles for their children. We are just beginning to examine whether these same caregivers also provide children with different form-function patterns in their discourse about self and other. Pilot work suggests that one group of English-speaking caregivers that we have studied is less likely to restrict their use of self-reference forms to utterances ranking low in agentivity and control thereby providing different input patterns for their children than that reported in Studies II and III above. Such work provides a "natural experiment" for studying the impact of input even when language typology is held constant.

In suggesting a need to address input in an alternative way, I nevertheless should point out that such a stance should be integrated into previous approaches, rather than to their exclusion. I am convinced by the mounting evidence that children are actively involved in the construction of language. For instance, although adults have been noted to use particular linguistic devices globally, children do not passively make use of such functions. Crosslinguistic studies have highlighted the extent to which children reinterpret such forms in more local ways (Bamberg, 1987; Berman & Slobin, 1994; Kyratzis & Ervin-Tripp, 1993). And my own work reviewed above has highlighted ways in which children's use *does* differ from that of adult speakers of a given language.

Likewise, acquisition work that has examined children's form–function patterning with special attention to typological contrasts has highlighted that children can and do adopt form–function patterns found in the input they hear. For instance, a series of studies have shown ways in which Korean and American children are willing to distinctly make use of spatial prepositions, with each group of children looking like adult speakers from the start (for instance Bowerman, 1985; Choi & Bowerman, 1991).

The central revision, though, that I am suggesting is one of carefully attending to the *actual* form–function patterns available to children in the speech around them. Only with such information in hand will we begin to piece together the complex array of factors that influence children to construct language as they do.

REFERENCES

Bamberg, M. (1987). *The acquisition of narratives: Learning to use language.* Berlin: Mouton de Gruyter.

Bamberg, M., Budwig, N., & Kaplan, B. (1991). A developmental approach to language acquisition: Two case studies. *First Language, 11,* 121-141.

Berman, R., & Slobin, D. I. (1994). *Different ways of relating events in narratives: A crosslinguistic developmental study.* Hillsdale, NJ: Lawrence Erlbaum Associates.

Bloom, L. (1991). *Language development from two to three.* Cambridge, England: Cambridge University Press.

Bowerman, M. (1985). What shapes children's grammars? In D. I. Slobin (Ed.), *The crosslinguistic study of language acquisition: Vol. 2: Theoretical issues* (pp. 1257-1319). Hillsdale, NJ: Lawrence Erlbaum Associates.

Budwig, N. (1986). *Agentivity and control in early child language.* Unpublished doctoral dissertation, University of California, Berkeley.

Budwig, N. (1989). The linguistic marking of agentivity and control in child language. *Journal of Child Language, 16,* 263-284.

Budwig, N. (1990). A functional approach to the acquisition of personal pronouns. In G. Conti-Ramsden & C. Snow (Eds.), *Children's language: Vol. 7* (pp. 121-145). Hillsdale, NJ: Lawrence Erlbaum Associates.

Budwig, N. (1993). Perspectives on the grammar-discourse connection in child language: 25 years at the Stanford Child Language Research Forum. In E. V. Clark (Ed.), *The proceedings of the twenty-fifth annual Child Language Research Forum* (pp. 207-306). Stanford, CA: Center for the Study of Language and Information.

Budwig, N. (1995). *A developmental-functionalist approach to child language.* Hillsdale, NJ: Lawrence Erlbaum Associates.

Budwig, N., & Wiley, A. (1995). *Maternal input and children's special use of pronominal forms.* Manuscript, submitted for publication.

Choi, S., & Bowerman, M. (1991). Learning to express motion events in English and Korean: The influence of language-specific lexicalization patterns. *Cognition,* **41**, 83-121.

Cook-Gumperz, J. (1986). Caught in the web of words: Some considerations on language socialization and language acquisition. In J. Cook-Gumperz, W. Corsaro, & J. Streeck (Eds.), *Children's worlds and children's language* (pp. 37-64). Berlin: Mouton de Gruyter.

DeLancey, S. (1984). Notes on agentivity and causation. *Studies in Language,* **8**, 181-213.

Dunn, J., & Brown, J. (1991). Becoming American or English? Talking about the social world in England and the United States. In M. Bornstein (Ed.), *Cultural approaches to parenting* (pp. 155-172). Hillsdale, NJ: Lawrence Erlbaum Associates.

Ervin-Tripp, S. (1977). From conversation to syntax. *Papers and Reports on Child Language Development,* **13**, 1-21.

Ervin-Tripp, S. (1981). How to make and understand a request. In H. Parret, M. Sbisa, & J. Verschueren (Eds.), *Possibilities and limitations of pragmatics* (pp. 195-210). Amsterdam: John Benjamins.

Ervin-Tripp, S. (1989). *Speech acts and syntactic development: Linked or independent?* (Berkeley Cognitive Science Report, 61). Institute of Cognitive Studies, Berkeley, CA: University of California.

Ervin-Tripp, S. (1993). Constructing syntax from discourse. In E. V. Clark (Ed.), *Proceedings of the twenty-fifth annual Child Language Research Forum* (pp. 333-341). Stanford, CA: Center for the Study of Language and Information.

Gumperz, J. (1982). *Discourse strategies.* Cambridge, England: Cambridge University Press.

Heath, S. (1983). *Ways with words: Language, life and work in communities and classrooms.* Cambridge: Cambridge University Press.

Karmiloff-Smith, A. (1979). *A functional approach to child language.* Cambridge: Cambridge University Press.

Kyratzis, A. & Ervin-Tripp, S. (1993, July). *The development of discourse markers in child-child interaction.* Paper presented at the Sixth International Congress for the Study of Child Language, Trieste, Italy.

Lin, A. (1993). *The child as conversational partner: The creation of participation roles as cultural activity.* Unpublished doctoral dissertation, Worcester, MA: Clark University.

Miller, P. (1982). *Amy, Wendy, and Beth: Learning language in South Baltimore.* Austin: University of Texas Press.

Miller, P., & Hoogstra, L. (1992). Language as tool in the socialization and appreciation of cultural meanings. In T. Schwartz, G. White, & C. Lutz (Eds.), *New directions in psychological anthropology* (pp. 83-101). Cambridge: Cambridge University Press.

Quick, H. (1991). *Maternal input and children's use of self-reference forms: A functional approach.* Unpublished manuscript, Clark University, Department of Psychology. Worcester, MA.

Schieffelin, B., & Ochs, E. (1986). Language socialization. *Annual Review of Anthropology,* **15**, 163-246.

Shatz, M. (1991). Using cross-cultural research to inform us about the role of language development: Comparisons of Japanese, Korean, and English, and of German, American English, and British English. In M. Bornstein (Ed.), *Cultural approaches to parenting* (pp. 139-153). Hillsdale, NJ: Lawrence Erlbaum Associates.

Slobin, D. I. (1985). Crosslinguistic evidence for the Language-Making Capacity. In D. I. Slobin (Ed.), *The crosslinguistic study of language acquisition: Vol. 2: Theoretical issues* (pp. 1157-1256). Hillsdale, NJ: Lawrence Erlbaum Associates.

Tomasello, M. (1992). *First verbs: A case study of early grammatical development.* Cambridge, England: Cambridge University Press.

Van Valin, R. (1991). Functionalist linguistic theory and language acquisition. *First Language,* **11**, 7-40.

Wiley, A., & Budwig, N. (1994). Parental language and the child's self development: An examination of two American sub-cultural groups. *Infancia y Aprendizaje, Proceedings of the I Conference for Socio-cultural Research*, **3**, 83-90.

10 FORMAT TYING IN DISCUSSION AND ARGUMENTATION AMONG ITALIAN AND AMERICAN CHILDREN

William A. Corsaro
Douglas W. Maynard
Indiana University, Bloomington

Nearly twenty years ago I[1] arrived in Berkeley ready to undertake what was one of the very first ethnographies of preschool children. Fresh from the completion of my dissertation which relied heavily on videotaped records of primarily adult–child interaction, I was eager to use this new technology to videotape naturally occurring peer interaction and discourse in a nursery school. I had been told that videotape equipment would be available for my use in the postdoctoral research. What I found out was that there was indeed equipment available — an early model, reel-to-reel Sony video tape recorder. The video recorder and separate camera were large, bulky, and very cumbersome to operate. Worse, nearly fatal, was the restriction that any recordings made on the machine could only be played back on the same model. Given that this model was already becoming an antique, I realized immediately that I had a big problem.

I was in a new place. I knew few people. I was doing unorthodox research involving videotape recording. I was not sure how to go about dealing with the problem. So I moped around for a week. I stewed. Then things got better.

I met Jenny Gumperz who became a great friend and collaborator. I still today pursue theoretical ideas regarding children's language and socialization that had their origins in my first conversations with Jenny. Second, Jenny came up with the solution for my problems with the equipment: Sue Ervin-Tripp. Jenny told me Sue had just received a grant to study children's discourse which included funds for videotape equipment. However, Sue had always relied on audio recording in the past and was not sure about exactly what video equipment she needed or how to go about using it.

I was somewhat in awe of Sue back in 1974. She was one of the very first scholars to develop theoretical ideas and carry out empirical research on children's development of communicative competence. Sue was very open and gracious in our first meeting. I learned about her ongoing research and shared with her my knowledge and experience regarding videotaping naturally occurring adult–child and peer interaction. We worked

---

[1] In this section of the paper the first person pronoun refers to the first author (Corsaro).

out an exchange. I could use the videotape equipment she would obtain through her grant for my research in a Berkeley child development center and Sue would get my assistance in the collection of videotape data of adult–child and peer discourse in a home setting.

I benefited greatly from the exchange which was very unbalanced in my direction. First, I not only solved my difficult equipment problems, I also profited from the two month wait for the camera and video recorder to arrive. During this period I reconsidered my plans for videotaping and developed a data collection strategy that embedded the audiovisual recording in traditional ethnography (Corsaro, 1982). I spent the next several months carefully entering into the nursery school setting, gaining the confidence of the children and teachers, engaging in participant observations, and isolating patterns in early field notes. These initial accomplishments paved the way for successful videotaping of key activities and events later in the school term.

Second, I learned a great deal from my interactions with Jenny and Sue, and put into practice a number of their ideas about studying child language. Of all the ideas and wisdom I took from these exchanges two stand out: the value of patient, careful, micro analysis of naturally occurring speech; and the crucial importance of a comparative analytic framework. Sue Ervin-Tripp's ground-breaking studies on the structure and use of directives and requests by adults and children (Ervin-Tripp, 1976, 1977, 1982; Ervin-Tripp, Strage, Lampert, & Bell, 1987) are classic examples of the value of comparative, micro analysis. Her early work on children's language from a comparative perspective drew the attention of those in socio- and psycholinguistics who at first saw little value in children's speech and discourse. As Sue illustrated so well in her research, "work on children's discourse pushes back to the earliest stages of interaction" and can enable us "to find through comparative studies those facets of human interaction which are fundamental and universal" (Ervin-Tripp, 1977, p. 23).

FORMAT TYING IN CHILDREN'S DISPUTES

A number of recent studies of children's disputes have demonstrated how children explore, recognize, and exploit the power of language to organize and produce shared activities (see Corsaro & Rizzo, 1988, 1990; Goodwin, 1990; Maynard, 1985a, 1985b). In particular, Goodwin has called attention to the importance of children's awareness and use of the surface structure of their talk in organizing their activities.

In developing her ideas, Goodwin (1990) introduced the notion of "format tying." According to Goodwin, format tying generally involves participants' strategic use of phonological, syntactic, and semantic surface structure features of prior turns at talk (Goodwin, 1990, p. 177; see also Goodwin & Goodwin, 1987). Goodwin contrasts such strategic use of surface structure for conversational sequencing and organization with the position of Labov and Fanshel who argue that "sequencing rules do not appear to be related to words, sentences, and other linguistic forms, but rather from the connections between abstract actions such as requests, compliments, challenges, and defenses" (1977, p. 25). While Labov and Fanshel search for the underlying discourse goals or intentions in explaining conversational organization, Goodwin points to the power of speakers strategic use of surface structure elements in organizing speech activities in her development of the concept of format tying.

Goodwin presents and analyzes numerous types of format tying in her work with American Black children. Consider the following example from Goodwin (1990, p. 177).

```
(1)  Billy, who has been teasing Martha about her hair, has just laughed.
     M:   I don't know what you laughin' at.
     B:   I know what I'm laughin' at. Your head.
```

In her analysis of this example Goodwin points to the importance of the first phrase in Billy's response. This sentence is tied to Martha's previous sentence through its repeating of many of the exact words. However, two strategic changes ("you laughin'" to "I'm laughin'" and the deletion of the negation of the first sentence) brings about a systematic transformation of Martha's sentence in such a way that her own words are used against her. In this case, Billy uses format tying as a preface to his reply to Martha, "your head." It is clear that the partial repetition and transformation of Martha's prior sentence intensifies Billy's counter.

Goodwin found in her work that the children explored, "in an almost musical way," the structure of the utterances they were producing in the strategic back-and-forth of debates and oppositional discourse. In this Chapter we are interested in further exploring format tying from a comparative perspective by examining the oppositional talk of Italian nursery school children and American nursery school and first grade children. We do not have space to examine fully all instances of argumentation or debate in our extensive data base. Therefore, we will focus on children's use of format tying in what we see as representative examples of debate and argumentation in our comparative data. We see these examples as representative of debates and argumentation in our data in terms of the length and complexity of the debates, the number and type of participants (in terms of gender and age), and the topic or focus of the dispute or argumentation in each of the three groups.

ETHNOGRAPHIC CONTEXT
AND DATA COLLECTION PROCEDURES

The data for this study were collected at four sites. The Italian research was conducted over a four year period in a *scuola materna* in Bologna, Italy (see Corsaro & Emiliani, 1992, for details about the Italian preschool system). The *scuola materna* studied was staffed by five teachers, and 35 children attended for approximately 7 hours (9:30 until 5:30; some children returned home at 1:00) each weekday. The most intensive period of research in this school was in 1983 to 1984 when Corsaro accomplished field entry and acceptance into the children's peer culture, engaged in participant observation, collected extensive field notes, and recorded numerous episodes of peer interaction on audio or videotape. He videotaped additional episodes during a six-week return to the school a year later, and also returned for another two months (May through June, 1986) to check on transcriptions and initial data analysis with the teachers and children still at the school. Because children entered the school when they were 3 years old and moved on to first grade when they were 6, some of the children were present during all three observational periods, while others were present for only one or two of the periods. Finally, Corsaro collected some additional audiovisual data of peer interaction, attended several teacher-parent conferences and conducted in-depth interviews of the teachers over a period of several months in 1989.

The U.S. sites included a Head Start center, a private developmental learning center, and a first grade classroom in three different Midwestern cities. At the first two sites, Corsaro began his research in the early fall of 1989 and continued to visit the centers once or twice a week throughout the school year. During this time, he observed and participated in the children's activities, kept detailed field notes, and did a small amount of audiotaping. With the help of research assistants, he videotaped a sample of the children's activities during the final month of the study, in the late spring of 1990. He also conducted interviews of the teachers in the two centers and several mothers of children in the Head Start center.

Each of the classrooms (one which met in the morning, the other in the afternoon) Corsaro studied in the Head Start center was staffed by a head teacher and an assistant, and met for approximately 3½ hours Monday through Thursday. Although attendance varied greatly, there were normally from 12 to 16 four-to five-year-old children on any give day in each of the classrooms. Head Start is a federally sponsored "compensatory" preschool education program. Parents must meet income or "special need" (i.e., physical or behavioral handicaps) eligibility criteria in order to enroll their children in this free program. The children attending this center reflected the population of its inner city location in that the overwhelming majority of the children were black[2]. In fact, in the two classrooms studied, only one child was not (this exception was an Hispanic child). Likewise, very nearly all of the employees at this Head Start Center (i.e., teachers, bus-drivers, cooks, janitors, and administrators) were also Black (see Corsaro, 1994, for more detail).

The private developmental learning center, that we call University Preschool, has a reputation for being among the best child care facilities in the small university city in which it is located. In line with its reputation, the cost of enrolling a child in this center is quite high, and the great majority of the children come from middle- and upper-middle class families. Although most of the children are white, there are a small number of blacks and Asians. Corsaro collected data in two classrooms: one group of 3½- to 4-year-olds and another group of older 4½- to 5-year-olds, each of whom had one head teacher and one assistant teacher. Most of the children attended for the entire day (from 8:00 a.m to 6:00 p.m., Monday through Friday). On an average day, there were any-where between 12 and 20 children in attendance in either group (see Corsaro, 1994).

The first-grade children were Caucasian, native speakers of English, from middle class families, who were videotaped during participation in reading groups composed of

---

[2] Throughout this article, we use "Black" rather than African American when referring to the Head Start children, teachers, and parents. We recognize that there is controversy over this issue. However, our choice of terminology reflects the children's, parents', and teachers' own usage and their self-identification at the time the data were collected.

four to six children. The principal official group activities were reading (silently or aloud), completing worksheets, and drawing pictures related to the reading material. Fifty-four children (23 male and 31 female) from eight groups in three classrooms of one elementary school in a medium-sized Midwestern city were subjects in the study. The original data collection was done by Louise Cherry Wilkinson, as part of a study concerned with classroom communication processes (e.g., Wilkinson & Calculator, 1982). Professor Wilkinson made videotapes of the reading groups available to Maynard, who selected disagreements and arguments from the tapes for a study of children's disputes.

"*I LUPI NON ESISTONO*": FORMAT TYING IN A *SCUOLA MATERNA*

Format tying is a common feature in debates or what Italians call *discussione* in the *scuola materna* (Corsaro & Rizzo, 1988, 1990). Consider, for example, the following dispute sequence.

(2) While drawing with a group of children at a worktable, one girl, Sara, claims that wolves (bad or werewolves) do not exist. Several other children (Giovanna, Luigi, and Franco) challenge Sara.[3]

1. S: *I lupi non esistono*
        'Wolves do not exist.'
2. Ga: *Si, esistono i lupi.*
        'Yes, wolves exist.'
3. S: *Non esistono — solo gli ossi.*
        'They don't exist — only their bones.'
4. F: *Non è vero, esistono i lupi.*
        'It's not true, wolves exist.'
5. L: *Si.*
6. F: *Ma, non esistono solo sulle montagne.*
        'But, they do not exist only in the mountains.'
        ((Giovanni, Gi, who had been painting nearby, now enters the scene. He stands near Stella and Franco and with paintbrush in hand says:))
7. Gi: *È vero, esistono!*
        'It's true, they exist!'
8. S: *Te non c'entri.* ((Waves away Giovanni with her hand))
        'You're not in this.'
9. F: *Te non c'entri. Perché-* ((Pokes his finger at Sara's chest))
        'You're not in this. Because — '
10. S: *Te —* ((Pokes her finger at Franco's chest))
        'You're — '
11. F: *Tu dici che non'centro. Esistono i lupi!* ((Pushes Sara's hand away and again pokes his finger at her chest))
        'You say I am not in this. Wolves exist!'
12. S: *No, non è vero.*
        'No, it's not true.'
13. Gi: *Neanche i fantasmi.*

---

[3] In the transcripts the following notational devices are used: — marks self-interruption and interruption by others; ( ) notes probable transcription when words are enclosed in parentheses, and blank parentheses denote unintelligible speech; (( )) notes nonverbal behavior; [ ] marks overlapping speech when placed at the beginning and end of overlapping speech; ::: denotes elongated pronunciation; and italics mark stressed words or speech.

'Not even ghosts.'
14. Le: È vero.
'It's true.'
15. Lo: I fantasmi —
'Ghosts — '
16. Le: Yah! Non esistono.
'Yah! They don't exist.'
17. S: No. No. Quelli, no.
'No. No. Those, don't.'
18. Le: Si. Si. Si, esistono i fantasmi. [Però esistono —]
'Yes. Yes. Yes, ghosts exist. But they exist — '
19. N: [Sono nel bosco.] Sono
nel bosco.
'They are in woods. They are in the woods.'
20. Le: Eh, non è vero.
'Eh, it's not true.'
21. N: Si.
22. Le: I fantasmi esistono sotto il mare, nelle case — nelle
case —
'Ghosts exist under the sea, in houses — in houses — '
23. Lo: No, no.
24. Ia: Nelle ca — nelle case abbandonate.
'In hou — in abandoned houses.'
25. Le: È vero, sottomarine.
'It's true, underwater houses.'

The episode from which this sequence is drawn is transcribed and analyzed in much more detail in Corsaro and Rizzo (1990). Here we focus on format tying, which in this sequence primarily involves the children's strategic use of repetition (both of words and actions) to organize their participation in the *discussione*. The general point of contention, the existence of bad wolves, is established in the first exchange between Sara and Giovanna. Since number and person is marked in verb endings in Italian the subject (in this case "wolves" or the personal pronoun "they") does not need to be expressed. Therefore, one could minimally participate in this debate by repeating the word "*esistono*" or its negation, "*non esistono*." We see that repetition of "*esistono*" does in fact occur in turns 3 to 7 except for Lorenzo's simple marker of agreement with Franco in turn 5. However, in every instance the children embellish and expand their repetitions in interesting ways.

One type of embellishment is the nonobligatory expression of the subject ("*i lupi*") for emphasis (see lines 2, 4, and 11). These turns are even more stylized because of the children's placement of the subject after the verb ("*esistono i lupi*," literally "they exist, the wolves") to magnify or doubly stress their position. In addition to the non-obligatory expression and strategic placement of the subject, the children also employ various prefaces or what Goodwin (1983) has referred to as predisagreements (see turns 2, 4, 6, 7). In many instances these particular phrases could stand alone as markers of disagreement. However, here they can be seen as predisagreements because they signal and stress the more fully expressed disagreement that follows — the embellished production of "*esistono*."

Format tying is also important in the children's embedding of a second point of contention, Stella's attempt to exclude Giovanni from the discussion (lines 8-11). Giovanni's entry into the debate is interesting because he was originally painting in another area of the school. Upon hearing the discussion he enters the scene, paint brush in hand to voice his opinion. Third party entry of this type was common in the *scuola materna*, but it very seldom occurred in peer disputes in our American data. This sequence is also interesting because format tying is accomplished both verbally and through gesture.

Sara (line 8) tries to exclude Giovanni, waving him away with her hand and admonishing: *"Te non c'entri"* ("You're not in this"). Coming to Giovanni's defense, Franco challenges Sara's action as inappropriate by throwing her own phrase back at her (9). Franco embellishes his position by appropriating Sara's earlier use of gesture, here poking at Sara's chest to stress his point. In this way Franco contests Sara's attempt to be the boss. Sara attempts to interrupt Franco (10) and although she does not finish her phrase, she is successful in returning Franco's poke.

In line 11, Franco nicely brings closure to this subdispute over rights of exclusion by embedding it in the more general debate about wolves. Format tying is again the key. Franco begins by pushing Sara's hand away and again poking her in the chest saying: *"Tu dici che non'centro."* This phrase is a partial repetition and interesting transformation of turns 8 and 9 which in essence means "who are you to say I'm not in this." Franco then goes out to end his turn by repeating the earlier refrain, *"Esistono i lupi,"* tying the *discussione* back to the original point of contention. Although Sara's response at 12 is ambiguous (is it untrue that she does not have the right to exclude others or is it untrue that wolves exist?), the debate continues with further discussion about the existence of supernatural figures as Giovanni, now an active participant, maintains that ghosts do not exist (13). This introduction of ghosts leads to debate about where they live, if indeed they do exist. The children rely on format tying (mainly repetition and expansion of prior talk) to propose that ghosts live in the woods, in abandoned houses, and eventually in abandoned houses under the sea (lines 14-25).

Participation in *discussione* is highly valued in the peer culture of Italian children (Corsaro, 1988; Corsaro & Rizzo, 1988, 1990). Example 2 aptly captures many of the features of the Italian children's skillful use of format tying in *discussione*. It also demonstrates how the children's careful attention to and playful use of the surface structure not only organizes and structures their discussions, but also emotionally intensifies their participation as the children passionately take stances and defend their positions in lively debate.

"JESUS IS BIGGER THAN EVERYBODY": FORMAT TYING IN A HEAD START CENTER

We do not have space to describe adequately the rich variety of speech activities that the Head Start children displayed in peer interaction. Here we want to focus on a particular aspect of the children's language styles, oppositional or competitive talk, that was related to friendship processes in the peer culture. Like the somewhat older inner-city Black children studied by Goodwin (1990), the Head Start children constructed social identities, cultivated friendships, and both maintained and transformed the social order of the peer culture through opposition and confrontation. Peer interaction and play routines were peppered with oppositional talk such as: "Why you following me like that for?", "What you think you're doing boy?" and "Get that block out the way!" These were rarely taken as offensive. The children seldom reacted negatively to oppositional talk or complained to teachers, instead they normally responded in kind and serious verbal or physical disputes were rare. In fact, oppositional talk and teasing were valued in the peer culture (much like the Italian children's *discussione* as part of the verbal enrichment of everyday play routines). Particularly clever oppositions or retorts were often marked as such with appreciative laughter and comments like "good one" or "you sure told her" by the audience and, at times, even the target child.

In addition to producing stylized oppositional talk in brief exchanges and disputes, the Head Start children also engaged in extended debates. These debates were in some ways like the *discussioni* of the Italian children in that they often involved conflict resulting from one or more children's opposing the stated beliefs or opinions of another child. For the Italian children, however, there was a clear enjoyment of their display of knowledge about the world and the activity of debate itself, while the Head Start children seemed more interested in competing with and trying to "win out" over their peers. For example, the Head Start children would frequently turn many types of play into contests. After sitting down at a work table with puzzles, one child would typically challenge the others to a race, and the winner would yell out: "I beat you'all!" This proclamation would often lead to further debates about the difficulty of particular puzzles or cheating by not fully separating all the pieces (see Corsaro, 1994).

However, even as these extensive disputes continued pre-existing competitive relations among the participants, they also revealed much about the children's knowledge of the world and also served as arenas for displaying self, building group solidarity, and testing emerging friendships. Consider the following example.

(3) Several children are seated at a table eating lunch: Roger (R), Jerome (J), Darren (D), Andre (A), Ryan (Ry), Alysha (Al), Denise (De), and Zena (Z). All of the children are between the ages of 4 and 5. The researcher, Bill (B), is also seated at the table. A teacher (T) sits nearby at a serving table and addresses the children from time to time.

1. R-J: I saw somebody on Hard Copy who had a bullet through the back of his head.
2. J-R: I'm getting — I'm getting hard copy in the back of my head.
3. R-J: You can't get that word in the back of your head.
4. J-R: Ok, (   ) in the back of my head.
5. R-J: Can't get that word either.
6. J-R: Yeah, I can.
7. R-J: Un-uh. (   ).
8. J-R: (   ).
9. R-J: (   ).
10. J-R: It comes on every night.
11. R-J: We watch that channel and it don't come on our T.V. We got eighty channels. And we got that channel, but when we watch that channel that don't even come on... What channel it come on?
12. J-R: HBO.
13. R-J: We watch HBO.
14. J-R: It comes on cable.
15. R-J: We have cable.
16. Z: We got cable too. For real.
17. Ry: We do too.
18. D: We do too.
19. J-D: [Don't (   ) Darren.]
20. R: [I got the biggest cable.] I got the biggest cable.
21. J: I got the little — ((holding his hands close together)).

```
22.  T:   I thought all cable was the same.
23.  B:   ((Laughs)) So did I.
24.  J:   (They ain't either.)  My cable's this big. ((holds one hand under
          the table and the other above his head))
25.  Z:   Un-Uh.
26.  R:   My cables 'bout this big   [holds hands about a foot apart].
27.  Al:  [(Jesus is) bigger than everybody.]
28.  D:   [My — My cable's like this        ] big. ((holds one hand about
          two feet above the table))
29.  Ry:  ((also holds one hand up way above the table))
30.  Z:   Marvin Johnson's head is a bigger (than anybody's) ((referring to
          a child at the other table))
31.  J:   I'm bigger than (Jesus).
32.  Al:  Nah uh. [Jesus            ] is bigger than everybody.
33.  T:           [You'all got to stop.]
34.  J:   My cousin's bigger than Jesus. ((again holds his hands apart))
          [My cousin's bigger than Jesus. My cousin's is that big. Yeah.]
35.  R-T: [Ms. Smith. Can I eat my desert now?                           ]
36.  T-R: Have you tasted everything on that plate?
37.  R-T: Yes
38.  T-R: Go for it
39.  Al:  But he don't do — this..((reaches as far up as she can))  He's
          this big.
40.  J:   My cousin's this [big.   ]  ((reaches up))
41.  T-A:                  [Alysha,] get through so you can drink your milk
          today.
42.  A:   He's this big. ((holds hand far above table))
43.  J-A:  Who?  Who?
44.  A-J:  Jesus.
45.  J-A: I'm this big — I'm this big. ((indicates very small))  I'm this
          little. ((holds his hands to the sides of his head and then
          brings them forward showing how little he is))
46.  A:   (    ) ((also holds his hands to show something very small))
```

The first 15 lines involve competitive talk between Roger and Jerome. The boys had a history of trying to outdo one another in their displays of knowledge of media events. In many ways, their shared knowledge of the media, desire to display that knowledge, and enjoyment of competitive talk was the main basis of their friendship. Unfortunately, some of the boys' speech in these opening lines is inaudible because the researcher (Corsaro), who was wearing a cordless microphone, was talking with another child, Denise and his voice is, therefore, evident on the tape as it overlaps that of Jerome and Roger.

In any case the competition begins in line 2 as Jerome claims he is getting: "hard copy in the back of my head." Jerome employs format tying by taking up on Roger's reference to the show, *Hard Copy*, and repeating the phrase "back of his head," replacing the personal pronoun "his" with "my." Simultaneously, Jerome seems to be tying this talk about the show to a hair style that was valued at the time among Black male children at the Head Start center and throughout the country; having various words or slogans carved in the hair on the back of their heads. Also using the phrase, "back of your head," Roger (line 3) challenges Jerome, saying he can not get the word "hard copy" in the back of his head. Jerome seems to agree with Roger at line 4, but then goes on to propose a different word (which was inaudible) to be carved in the back of his head. Roger again disagrees (line 5) and we then have a simple assertion–denial sequence in lines 6 and 7.

Although lines 8 and 9 are inaudible, from the talk which follows it seems that Jerome has responded to Roger's introduction of *Hard Copy* by referring to a TV show that he likes to watch. At line 10 Jerome notes that it (the probable show) "comes on every night." At line 11 Roger incorporates the phrase "*come on,*" embellishing it in a variety of ways to deny Jerome's assertion. He starts out by arguing that he and his family watch the channel the disputed program comes on and it "*don't come on*" our TV. His claim of 80 channels is an exaggeration (the local cable company offers about 40 channels), but it does magnify his denial of Jerome's claim. Roger then goes on to repeat his main argument again, claiming that they got that channel but when they watch it Jerome's show "*don't even come on.*" Roger finishes his turn by challenging Jerome with the question: "What channel it *come on?*"

Having already claimed that his family has 80 channels, Roger's question can be seen as a way of setting up Jerome. If Jerome answers the question, whatever channel he names enables Roger to again assert that his family has the channel and, thusly, to contradict Jerome by asserting that Jerome's show does not appear on it. Jerome falls into the trap, naming a channel (HBO) which Roger dismisses as incorrect because his family has HBO as well. Jerome is eventually able to escape Roger's interrogation because his mention of cable moves the competitive talk from a dyadic to a group discussion.

Several children (Zena, Ryan, and Darren) now enter the debate, claiming that they have cable TV in their homes (lines 16-18). We see this more general group discussion as competitive bragging, because having cable TV would be a luxury among the families of the Head Start children. In our interviews with mothers it was clear that although they wanted to have things like cable TV and VCRs for their children, many could not afford them. For the families that did have them, the children were reminded of the expense and the families made heavy use of the costly service. In fact, in the dispute some of the children's claims may not have been true. Zena and her mother and siblings, for example, were living in a homeless shelter at the time this sequence was recorded. The shelter may have provided cable TV, but Zena's family could not afford it. This may be why Zena underscores her claim with the phrase "for real" (line 16).

The talk about cable TV then leads Roger to claim that he has the biggest cable (line 20), prompting the teacher and researcher to remark that cables are all the same size. Jerome denies the adults' contention (line 24) and the talk about the size of cable continues as the children challenge each other by repeating both phrases and gestures (lines 24-26; 28-29). Alysha now speaks for the first time, building on the comparative talk about size to argue that "Jesus is bigger than everybody" (line 27). We know from interviews with the teachers and Alysha's mother that Alysha often attends church services with her mother and grandmother. Here, Alysha is using her acquired knowledge about Jesus and religious beliefs (i.e., that Jesus is all-knowing and powerful) to participate in the valued activity of competitive talk in the peer culture.

Alysha's first mention of Jesus overlaps with Ryan's turn at line 29. Zena then attempts to transform the talk about size by teasing a child, Marvin, at another table, noting that his head is bigger than anybody's (line 30). Marvin either did not hear Zena or did not have a chance to respond as Jerome challenges Alysha by claiming, "I'm bigger than Jesus" (line 31). This challenge ratifies Alysha's entry bid and Alysha immediately repeats her earlier assertion that Jesus is bigger than everybody (line 32).

Jerome counters by bringing up his cousin, who would be a very big boy, indeed, if he were as large as Jerome's gestures indicated (line 34). Of course, never having seen Jerome's cousin, none of the participants could fully dismiss Jerome's claim. However, Alysha is wisely doubtful, arguing that the cousin cannot reach up as high as Jesus is tall (line 39).

At this point the teacher demands that Alysha, a picky eater, make progress on her lunch and, thus, draws her away from the discussion. However, Andre, now speaking for the first time, takes up Alysha's position, asserting that Jesus is indeed the biggest (lines 42-46). This general discussion ended soon thereafter when the teacher told the children to begin to clean up their places and get ready to brush their teeth.

This sequence is representative of the types of competitive peer talk that occur routinely at the Head Start center. Participation in such competitive talk builds a general peer group identity and, at the same time, provides the children with opportunities to pursue more personal agendas. Format tying is central to participation in competitive talk. The children seem to follow a general strategy: Listen carefully to the surface structure of what is said, repeat elements of it, and propose permutations in line with personal experiences and interests.

Roger and Jerome initiate this sequence of competitive talk with one of their many debates about media events. In this dispute the boys introduce the topic of cable TV, providing several of the other children the opportunity to claim that they have cable TV in their homes. Other children continue to monitor the talk, waiting for the opportunity to use their personal experiences to extend or transform the debate. For example, neither Alysha or Andre claim they have cable TV. In fact, we know from interviews with Alysha's mother that they do not have cable TV and that the family faces very challenging economic circumstances. Alysha has 11 closely-spaced siblings and her father has worked periodically at a religious radio station. Thus when the comparative talk about size of cables arises, Alysha deftly introduces her religious beliefs to the debate, noting that Jesus is bigger than everybody. Finally, when the teacher limits Alysha participation by telling her to finish her lunch, Andre, in tag team fashion, enters the debate in Alysha's stead.

Overall, careful attention to surface structure and format tying serves the children well. The talk moves from a debate between two close friends about a violent television show and contemporary hair styles to a multi-party discussion about cable television, the size of cable, and finally talk about religions beliefs and spirituality. All of these topics are relevant to the children' lives in the local peer and school cultures and in their communities. The example impressively demonstrates the power of this type of competitive talk for the organization and constitution of culture among these children.

"DID TOO, DID NOT": FORMAT TYING IN UNIVERSITY PRESCHOOL AND A FIRST GRADE CLASSROOM

Among the middle and upper class children in University Preschool and in the first grade classroom that we studied, most disputes or debates stemmed from disagreements over the possession of materials or over the nature of ongoing activities. Also, as was the case in the Italian *scuola materna* and the American Head Start center, friendship processes were often embedded in conflictive and competitive talk. However, unlike the complex, unpredictable (in terms of content and direction), and highly stylized debates of the Italian and Head Start children, those of the preschool and first grade children were often predictable, linear, and based on extensions of a simple inversion format. The following sequence from a longer disagreement among first grade children coloring in workbooks is typical of debates among the American middle class children.

```
(4)   Two girls (A and B) are working at a worktable with several other
      children
1.    B:  A ((A's last name)).  Shame on you! This is my crayon, right here.
2.    A:  It is not.
3.    B:  It is.
4.    A.  It is not.
5.    B:  It is too.
6.    A:  It is not.
7.    B:  Yes it is, yes it is, yes it is.
```

These assertion–denial exchanges are often repeated several times until someone gives in or the children wear themselves down. In some instances, the back and forth becomes ritualistic with the participants more interested in insulting and/or teasing each other than in settling a disagreement. Consider Example 5.

```
(5)   C, D and JN in first grade classroom filling in workbooks.  D leans
      over and JN and takes C's eraser.
1.    JN:  Oh.
2.    D:   You're a pig, know why?
3.    JN:  Why?
4.    D:   You're hogging everything.  ((D pushes JN's arm))
5.    JN:  I am not.
6.    D:   Yes you are.
7.    C:   Hey ((Wants eraser back))
8.    D:   I'm using it.
9.    C:   I know, I'm waiting for you.
```

Here D sets up JN with the question at 2 and the predictable assertion–denial sequence (4-6) involves playful teasing. On other occasions what begins as teasing can become more serious. Consider Example 6 from University Preschool.

```
(6)   Adam, Peggy, Mark, Sally, and Researcher are at a work table in Uni-
      versity Preschool.  They have been drawing pictures and talking for
      around 30 minutes.  There had been earlier talk about going to the
      principal's office when they are in first grade.
1.    P:   ((Writing on her paper))  This is going to say: "You got to go to
           the principal's."
2.    M:   This is going to say: "You got to go to the Peggy's." ((teasing
           voice))
3.    P:   Do — on't.
4.    M:   And you're the Peggy's.
5.    P:   ((Pokes at M)) Uh.
6.    A:   Uh. ((Directed At Peggy))
7.    M:   The Peggys are toughest.
8.    A:   Yeah, the Peggys are — are — uh —
9     M:   The Peggys — No, they're real tough.
10.   A:   Yeah, the Peggys are stinkers.  ((Laughs))
11.   P:   Ah — Uhh!
12.   A:   I wasn't talking about you, [Peggy.        ]
13.   P:                              [Yes you were!]
14.   A:   I was not.
15.   P:   Was too.
16.   A:   I was not.  I was talking about another Peggy!
17.   P:   You were talking about me.  I know it.
18.   A:   I wa::s not.  ((Seems to be blowing out the words under his breath
```

```
        as he leans toward P))
19. P:  Was too.
20. A:  ((Crosses his arms and looks at researcher)) I was not!
21. Re: He was talking about another Peggy.
22. M:  Peggy ((Last Name of Another Child named Peggy in the School))
23. P:  Well, Peggy ((Last Name)) is not here.
```

Mark begins the dispute in line 2, repeating the last part of Peggy's previous turn substituting "Peggy's" for "Principal's." Given his tone of voice and the nonsensical "the Peggy's," Mark appears to be using format tying to tease Peggy. Peggy's negative responses at lines 3 and 5 are produced in a mocking whine, and her poke at line 5 is clearly playful. After Mark notes that "the Peggys are toughest," Adam enters the debate (line 7-8). His is quickly cut off by Mark who again stresses that "the Peggys are real tough" (line 9). It is difficult to interpret Mark's turns at line 7 and 9. His switch to the plural (Peggys) in line 9 is an ambiguous extension of his earlier use of format tying with the preservation of the possessive (Peggy's). Also his labeling of Peggy, a girl, as tough could be seen as positive or negative. However, Adam's characterization of the Peggys as "stinkers" (line 10) invokes a strongly disapproving response from Peggy (line 11). Adam immediately backs off at line 12, using the ambiguity of the referent (the Peggys) to claim he was not talking about this Peggy in particular. Peggy rejects the disclaimer and we then see the familiar assertion denial sequence in lines 13 to 16. Adam is then more specific, indicating he is "talking about another Peggy" (line 16). Another, more heated, assertion–denial sequence follows leading the researcher to support Adam's earlier claim. Mark then comes to Adam's defense by specifying the last name of the other Peggy in the school (line 22). Peggy rejects this proposition, noting that the particular child is not around. Adam then left the table briefly and the dispute ended.

Example 6 is more complex than Examples 4 and 5 for several reasons. First, there are two children who collaborate to playfully tease another. Second, when the dispute becomes serious, the children attempt to justify their assertions and denials. Third the boys collaboratively shift from offensive teasing to defensive denial of serious intent. The end result is a complex structure in which simple assertion–denial exchanges ("did too–did not") are embedded in the children's attempts to provide evidence for their positions. Despite this more complex structure, the central device of the dispute remains relatively simple: one participant asserts or challenges something in the character or behavior of the other, who denies it. The dispute eventuates in relatively abstract utterance types (e.g., "was not," "was too") with a predictable linear trajectory.

It is not that children in the white, middle class schoolrooms are incapable of more complex argumentation (Maynard, 1985a, 1986). Even their enhanced disputatious assertions and denials, however, seem attenuated in comparison with episodes among the Italian and the Head Start children. While the Italian and Head Start children's disputes may begin with or contain simple (and often dyadic) denial–assertion initial oppositions, these oppositions are often transformed into multi-party debates with intricately constructed and substantively rich topics. The disputes of the white middle class, on the other hand, may involved embellishment or extension, but they were seldom complex multi-party debates. Consider the following, one of the most embellished disputes among the middle class children:

```
(7) Alice, Harold, Kay, and Barb are sitting at a square table, on person
    to a side. At one point, Alice asks Harold, who is sitting on her
```

right, "Can I use your eraser, I don't have any left." He first refuses the request, but after she says, "please," he says "that's better"
and hands it to her. Alice starts using the eraser on her workbooks
and continues for 25 seconds of steady rubbing before the following
talk occurs. Alice goes on rubbing throughout the episode except as
noted in line 2. Kay is across from Harold, gazing at Alice's work.
Barb is on the right of Harold and remains concentrated on her work-
book throughout the episode.

```
1.   H:   Don't take up my whole eraser please
2.   A:   ((stops erasing)) [I will        ] ((continues erasing))
3.   K:                     [eh heh        ] eh heh .hhh
4.   H:   No you won't
5.   A:   No I [won't ]
6.   H:        [Cause ] if you do I'll tackle you (when we) play football
          ((smiles briefly, flicks tongue))
7.   A:   I'll play football (over) you
8.   K:   uh huh heh .hhh
9.   H:   I'll tackle you and you'll fall down
10.  K:   No you won't I'll tackle you
11.  A:   And I'll throw you over the fence
12.  K:   eh heh [heh heh heh heh]
13.  A:          [heh heh        ]
14.  A:   .hhh I'll throw you over the whole school
15.  H:   Who cares I'll pick up both of you and throw- throw you guys over
          (your) head into a pile of jam
16.  A:   Puhhhh heh heh heh heh .hhhhh
17.  H    land in the jam
                     (2.5 seconds silence)
18.       ((Harold reaches and grabs eraser, pulling it from Alice, who
          holds onto it))
19.  H:   Don't take up my whole e[raser           ]
20.  A:                           [hahh! heh heh    ] heh
21.  H:   take up my whole eraser ((pulls eraser from Alice))
22.  A:   Okay
23.  H:   Eeyou!
```

This episode is transcribed and analyzed in much more detail, especially with regard to
the smiling of the involved children, in Maynard (1985b). While semantically, the
episode contains all the elements of a serious dispute, the smiling, laughter, game
imagery, and so on, transform or "key" (Goffman, 1974) the children's argumentative
utterances into aspects of a teasing and playful activity.

Our interest here is in features of utterances, particularly those that are related to
format tying. Initially, the dispute is of the typical assertion-denial form. Notice how,
when Harold (line 1) opposes Alice's erasing activity with an admonishing request, which
is mitigated by a politeness form ("please") and smiling, Alice rejects his request (line 2)
by avowing to continue. This is followed by a contradiction (line 4) and then Alice (line
5) verbally backing down but continuing to erase. However, Harold (line 6) overlaps her
"backing down" utterance with an extension of his previous (line 4) turn that is a fanciful
and mild threat. It is framed as a future possibility that would occur within the legitimiz-
ing context of a game. Alice counterthreats (line 7), preserving the reference to "football." This is the first in a series of format-tied threats. A second one is between Harold
and Kay about tackling (lines 9-10), and a third series is comprised of Alice's proposal
to throw Harold over the "fence" (line 11) and the "whole school" (line 14), followed by
Harold's suggestion of throwing Alice and Kay "into a pile of jam" (line 15). Harold's
humorous threat occasions Alice's explosion into laughter (line 16), and he then produces
a rerun version of the punchline to his threat (line 17). Following this, Harold reaches
for and takes the eraser, while once more admonishing Alice (lines 18, 19, 21, 23), who

initially resists (line 18) and then verbally assents to this action (line 22).

While there is a kind of embellishment of the assertion–denial structure here, then, it is also, as we said, attenuated. Furthermore, the three instances of format tying are preceded and followed by the assertion–denial form and are relatively brief in total duration. There is also an instrumental character to the episode; Harold wants and eventually retrieves his eraser, and the mitigated and teasing threats, although sparking some appreciative laughter, seem to be subordinated to his purposeful actions. Additionally, rather than occasioning a variety of related threats or rivalries, the format-tying is monotopical. Relatedly, while it can be argued that tackling and football derive from the children's experience with the larger culture, the threats are entirely fanciful and probably do not derive from their own concrete experiences with the game. Finally, the episode is filled with smiling, laughter, and joking, which indicate a different type of discourse than *discussione* in the Italian context and the competitive claims in the Head Start data.

CONCLUSION

Goodwin has found that aggravated disagreements are activities that children work to achieve in their own right (1983, p. 675). We have argued here and elsewhere (Corsaro & Rizzo, 1990) that this tendency to display rather than put off the expression of opposition can be seen as an important feature of peer culture. Format tying is particularly important in this regard because it can be used to aggravate disputes and to display individual knowledge and skills within disputes. As a result, format tying is essential for making disputes mutually shareable events in the course of their production.

In this comparative analysis we have found that the nature or style of format tying and the resulting trajectories of disputes varied across the groups of children that we studied. For the Italian children much of their use of format tying involved the repetition and stylized embellishment of prior talk. In this way the highly valued activity of *discussione* is collaboratively produced with individual participants pursuing personal positions and agendas. These collaborations resulted in highly stylized debates with diverse, unpredictable and complex trajectories. Finally, although *discussioni* were complex, rational, and orderly, they were always pursued with passion. *Discussione* involves serious (but enjoyable) debate and not playful teasing. Nevertheless, style is as important as substance, and the Italian children relish making points and counterpoints with enthusiasm and zeal.

As we have noted elsewhere (Corsaro, 1994) peer interaction and friendship processes in the American Head Start center were often competitive and oppositional. The debates of the Head Start children, like the *discussioni* of the Italian children, often emerge when one child opposes the stated beliefs or opinions of another. However, once underway what begins as dyadic opposition is often transformed into a multi-party debate involving substantively rich topics which are intricately constructed and extended. In essence, in such disputes the Head Start children **compete individually to collaborate collectively**, transforming individual oppositions into mutually shareable events. Consider Example 3 involving the Head Start children. The episode begins as a specific competition between Roger and Jerome about particular television programs they receive on cable. However, the entry of other children expands the debate to the size of the cable, who has cable, and whether or not someone can be as big as Jesus. Although almost all of the children's turns at talk can be competitive at a surface level sense, there is general collaboration in support of the right of any child to expand the general competitive talk in ways that enable participation and the addressing of personal interests or concerns (e.g., Alysha's interest in Jesus, Zena's watching cable TV at a homeless shelter, and the size of Jerome's cousin). In this way the children compete individually while collectively collaborating to extend the overall scope of the original dispute. This same pattern can be seen in Example 2 from the Italian data where two children start out debating the existence of "bad wolves" with others joining in and taking sides on that specific issue. However, once in the debate the children do not simply compete through a serious of assertion–denial sequences, rather they move the debate to a wider set of issues includ-ing: who has the right to enter a dispute, who has the right to exclude such entry, a consideration of whether ghosts exist, and where ghosts live if they do indeed exist.

Finally, both the *discussioni* of the Italian children and the disputes of the Head Start children are often lively and passionate. In many ways this very passion is a signal of the collective nature and collaboration of such multi-party debates. However, it is the raw edge to some of the children's exchanges which make what is cooperative to the children often seem threatening and disturbing to American middle class sensibilities.

The disputes of the American middle class children in our data were more individual-ized and less complex in structure and content than those of the Italian or Head Start children. The disputes of the American middle class children frequently originated from dyadic oppositions, but they were seldom transformed into complex multi-party debates. Collaboration, when it occurred, normally involved other children joining the attack on or coming to the defense of the target of an opposition (Maynard, 1985a, 1986). Both dyadic and multi-party disputes frequently involved simple assertion-denial exchanges which, at times, were extended over several turns. These disputes were normally limited to one topic which was often abstract or fanciful rather than substantive. In contrast to the dispute strategies of the Head Start children, the American middle class children seemed *to cooperate to compete*. That is, the children would stake out their positions regarding the focal point of the dispute, take sides, and push the opposition sometimes through the almost relentless recycling of the same assertion–denial sequences as we saw in Examples 4 and 6. Finally, the disputes of the American middle class children often involved playful teasing that sometimes escalated into more serious threats and counter-threats which were emotionally charged and tense rather than impassioned.

As Ervin-Tripp (1977) noted nearly 20 years ago the value of comparative research is that it reminds us of the complexity of children's language and their sociolinguistic development. In this report we have documented similarities and differences among Italian and American children's production of a particular speech activity — dispute or argumentation. In particular, we documented the importance of format tying in the children's disputes, noting that it was both more frequent and elaborate in the disputes of the Italian nursery school children and the American Head Start children than in those of the American middle class nursery school and first grade children. However, we can not easily generalize these results to other speech activities or genres. In fact, in other of our research (Corsaro, 1985) it was clear that American middle class nursery school children frequently relied on format tying to produce highly complex fantasy play. In short, there is always a need for more comparative work for needed theory building on children's language. Appreciating the value of such comparative work and knowing the best directions from which to pursue it owes much to the legacy of Sue Ervin-Tripp.

REFERENCES

Corsaro, W. A. (1982). Something old and something new: The importance of prior ethnography in the collection and analysis of audiovisual data. *Sociological Methods and Research*, **11**, 145-166.

Corsaro, W. A. (1985). *Friendship and peer culture in the early years*. Norwood, NJ: Ablex.

Corsaro, W. A. (1988). Routines in the peer culture of American and Italian nursery school children. *Sociology of Education*, **61**, 1-14.

Corsaro, W. A. (1994). Discussion, debate, and friendship processes: Peer discourse in U.K. and Italian nursery schools. *Sociology of Education*, **67**, 1-26.

Corsaro, W. A., & Emiliani, F. (1992). Child care, early education, and children's peer cultures in Italy. In M. Lamb, K. Sternberg, P, Hwang, & A. Broberg (Eds.), *Child care in context: Cross cultural perspectives* (pp. 90-113). Hillsdale, NJ: Lawrence Erlbaum Associates.

Corsaro, W. A., & Rizzo, T. A. (1988). *Discussione* and friendship: Socialization processes in the peer culture of Italian nursery school children. *American Sociological Review*, **53**, 879-894.

Corsaro, W. A., & Rizzo, T. A. (1990). Disputes in the peer culture of American and Italian nursery school children. In A. Grimshaw (Ed.), *Conflict talk* (pp. 21-66). New York: Cambridge University Press.

Ervin-Tripp, S. (1976). Is Sybil there?: The structure of some American English directives. *Language in Society*, **5**, 25-66.

Ervin-Tripp, S. (1977). Wait for me, roller skate! In S. Ervin-Tripp & C. Mitchell-Kernan (Eds.), *Child discourse* (pp. 165-188). New York: Academic.

Ervin-Tripp, S. (1982). Ask and It shall be given to you: Children's requests. In H. Byrnes (Ed.), *Contemporary perceptions of language* (pp. 232-245). Washington, DC: Georgetown University Press.

Ervin-Tripp, S., Strage, A., Lampert, M., & Bell, N. (1987). Understanding requests. *Linguistics*, **25**, 107-143.

Goffman, E. (1974). *Frame analysis*. New York: Harper & Row.

Goodwin, M. H. (1983). Aggravated correction and disagreement in children's conversations. *Journal of Pragmatics*, **7**, 657-677.

Goodwin, M. H. (1990). *He-said-she-said: Talk as social organization among black children*. Bloomington, IN: Indiana University Press.

Goodwin, M. H., & Goodwin, C. (1987). Children's arguing. In S. Phillips, S. Steele, & C. Tanz (Eds.), *Language, gender, and sex in comparative perspective* (pp. 200-248). Cambridge, England: Cambridge University Press.

Labov, W., & Fanshel, D. (1977). *Therapeutic discourse: Psychotherapy as conversation*. New York: Academic.

Maynard, D. W. (1985a). On the functions of social conflict among children. *American Sociological Review*, **50**, 207-223.

Maynard, D. W. (1985b). How children start arguments. *Language in Society,* **14**, 1-29.

Maynard, D. W. (1986). Offering and soliciting collaboration in multi-party disputes among children (and other humans). *Human Studies,* **9**, 261-285.

Wilkinson, L. C., & Calculator, S. (1982). Requests and responses in peer-directed reading groups. *American Educational Research Journal,* **19**, 107-22.

11 USE AND ACQUISITION OF GENITIVE CONSTRUCTIONS IN SAMOAN

Alessandro Duranti
Elinor Ochs[1]
University of California, Los Angeles

INTRODUCTION

The analysis presented here considers ways in which adult and child speakers of Samoan use genitive constructions in their social interactions to encode a variety of semantic roles. We will consider in particular displayed preferences for encoding would-be agents as genitive constituents. In other research, we have noted that while Samoan speakers can express agency through ergative-marked noun phrases, these constructions are used infrequently in spoken discourse (Duranti, 1981, 1994; Duranti & Ochs, 1990; Ochs, 1982, 1988). Generally, ergative constructions are used to mark responsibility, either to praise or to blame (Duranti, 1990). In the present discussion, we indicate how genitive constructions are useful alternatives to either expressing agency explicitly (through ergative casemarked NPs) or not at all (leaving the interlocutor to infer the agent from background knowledge or other means.)

How perceived scenes and perspectives are mapped onto grammar has been a central concern within psycholinguistics. Developmental psycholinguists have been particularly interested in children's understanding and linguistic articulation of transitive scenes — what Slobin (1985) calls "manipulative activity scenes" — in which an agent performing some action affects some object. The concern of the present study is to extend our understanding of manipulative activity scenes and grammar beyond the articulation of major sentential constituents, more specifically to attend to ways in which children and

---

[1] In 1972, one of the authors, Elinor Ochs, then a graduate student writing a dissertation on Malagasy oratory and a mother of 2-year-old twins, wrote to Professor Susan Ervin-Tripp about the enterprise of documenting the conversational competence of very young children. Ervin-Tripp had participated in crafting an interdisciplinary framework to interface anthropology and developmental psychology and pioneered research on the developing sociolinguistic skills of children in the first few years of their lives. Fortunately for Ochs, Ervin-Tripp wrote back, providing the initial scaffolding of what has become a lifetime professional focus on ways in which the language of children and other novices is constitutive of their membership in particular communities.

adults grammaticalize manipulative activity scenes and perspectives within genitive constructions. Genitives have been primarily associated with the encoding of locative relationships such as possessor or goal (Clark, 1978; Lyons, 1967, 1977). In languages such as Samoan, however, the genitive construction encodes a wide range of semantic roles including human agents and actors. The fact that genitives, often called "possessives," do not simply or exclusively express relations of ownership has been noted by a number of scholars working on a variety of languages (see Clark, 1978; Lyons, 1967, 1977; Parisi & Castelfranchi, 1974; Bugenhagen, 1986).[2] Further, the link between genitives and agency has been reported in the acquisition literature (Budwig, 1985) and in typological studies of ergative languages, which note that in several languages, e.g., Eskimo (Woodbury, 1977), Mayan (Craig, 1977), and Kaluli (Schieffelin, 1985), the genitive and ergative marker are the same. In Samoan the genitive marker and the ergative marker are *not* the same. Nonetheless there is a strong semantic link between the two. Our Samoan data represent what is to our knowledge both the most varied and the most recurrent use of genitive constructions for semantic roles other than possession. In this paper, we will first provide a brief description of the uses of genitive constructions by Samoan adults; then we will compare the adult data with the patterns produced by four young children. We suggest that in Samoan, a major locus of grammatical development lies not so much in the increased production of the three major sentential constituents (verb, subject, object) as in the internal complexity of the constituents themselves.

DATA COLLECTION

The research on which this analysis is based was carried out in a traditional village in Western Samoa, on the island of Upolu, over a total period of about 16 months (for ethnographic and methodological details, see Ochs, 1988). The collection of children's speech in 1978-1979 was carried out by E. Ochs and M. Platt. The longitudinal study focused on six children from six different households, ranging from 19 to 35 months at the onset of the study (Ochs, 1985). A total of 128 hours of audio and 20 hours of video recording of these children were collected and transcribed in the field. During the same period, A. Duranti collected more than 50 hours of adult speech from a variety of speech activities, including informal conversation and formal speechmaking (Duranti, 1981). About half of this corpus was transcribed in situ. Additional field work on language acquisition and grammatical variation across contexts was conducted by A. Duranti and E. Ochs in 1981 (March-May) and in 1988 (August).

---

[2] Lyons (1977, p. 474) writes: "It can be argued that so-called possessive expressions are to be regarded as a subclass of locatives (as they very obviously are in terms of their grammatical structure, in certain languages)." This "localistic" view places the emphasis on a different dimension from what we have been noticing in our Samoan data, where location is only one of the possible semantic relations expressed by genitive constructions and not necessarily the most frequent or salient one.

A PREFERENCE FOR TWO CONSTITUENTS

Our previous research on Samoan language acquisition indicated that preferences in the expression of major sentential constituents and in the use of ergative case marking differ little in adult and child language use. Both Samoan children and adults display a strong preference for verb-initial utterances that contain only two major constituents: a verb or verb complex (VC) and a nominal argument.[3]

(1)   VC + Nominal Argument

We call this preference the "Two Constituent Bias" (Duranti & Ochs, 1983, 1990; Ochs, 1988). The tendency to express two constituents is illustrated in examples (2) and (3). Example (2) is from a letter. Example (3) is an excerpt from a conversation in which two chiefs and an orator (F.) are discussing different people's ability to perform traditional speechmaking. The VC constituent and the NP (or PP) which follows are separated by brackets:[4]

(2) (Ma2, letter)

50   *Malae [fai] [i le toeaina]*
     Malae say to ART old man
     'Malae, tell the old man'

51   *[e malie] [lona loto]*
     TA agree   his   soul
     (lit. 'his soul agrees')
     'I am sorry'

---

[3] The term "verb complex," often found in grammatical studies of Bantu and other language families, has been extended to the analysis of Polynesian languages by Seiter (1982). The VC contains a number of syntactico-semantic markers in addition to the verb stem, including tense aspect markers, auxiliary verbs, adverbial particles, deictic particles, and clitic pronouns.

[4] Note on transcription and data sources: All the examples with a source (e.g., "Pastor & Deacon") are either taken from transcripts of audio-recorded spontaneous interaction or from personal letters written to or received from family members abroad (e.g., "Ma1"). The rest of the examples have been elicited from native speakers. We have tried to use Samoan orthography as consistently as possible with two exceptions: (i) for the spoken data, we have transcribed each long vowel with two identical vowels rather than with a macron on a vowel; (ii) the written material (viz. letters) has been left in the original written version, which often leaves out glottal stops and long vowels (we should also mention that glottal stop deletion is quite common in everyday speech). The letter *g* stands for a velar nasal and the inverted apostrophe (') for a glottal stop. The large amount of "bad speech" (viz. no *t*s or *n*s) in our examples is quite characteristic of our spoken corpus and is *not* a function of formality as erroneously portrayed by Milner (1966) and Cook (1988, on this topic, see Duranti, 1981; Duranti & Ochs, 1986; Ochs, 1985, 1988).

Abbreviations: AFF = affect particle; ART = article; Cia = verbal suffix; DX = deictic particle; EMP = emphasis particle; INT = intensifier, sometimes with reflexive function; Prep = preposition; pro = clitic pronoun; PST = past; TA = tense/aspect marker.

52 *[e   le   o avatua   ai] [ana mea*
    TA NEG TA give+DX+Cia pro his thing
    '(that) the things'
53 *[ia   sa   tusi mai ai]*
    that PST write DX pro
    'that he wrote to me about'
54 *[e avatu]]*
    TA give+DX
    'to send are not included'
55 *ona [ua tuai mai] [le tusi]*
    bec. TA late DX   ART letter
    'because the letter was late'
56 *ae [ua lafo atu]   [le   pusa]*
    but TA send DX   ART box
    'but the box has been sent'
57 *ne'i te'i   fo'i   [ua oso] [lona ita]*
    otherwise EMP   TA jump   his angry
    'otherwise he will get angry'

In example (2), line 50 has a VC and a PP, and the rest of the main clauses (in lines 51, 52-4, 55, and 56) are all VC + NP — with 53, a relative clause, and 54, an infinitival clause, being part of a complex NP whose head noun, *ana mea* 'his things' is in line 52. In (3) below, except for the interrogative *â?* 'what?' in 505, all lines have two constituents (see lines 500, 501, 503, 506, 509, 511).

(3) (Watch)

500 F; *[e feololo â]   [le   lâuga   a si   koiga].*
        TA not bad EMP   ART speech of AFF   old man
        'The poor old man's speech is not bad.'
501 T; *laga   [lelei] [Pua].*
        because good   Pua
        'Because Pua is good.'
502   (1.0)
503   *'a   [e pau â   le mea]   ['o   le   u'umi].*
        but TA only EMP the thing   Pred ART long
        'but the only thing is the length.'
504   (0.6)
505 F; *-hh   â?*
        '-hh what?'
506 T; *[pau le mea]   ['o   le   u'umi].*
        only ART thing   Pred ART long
        'The only thing is the length.'
507 F; (CL)
508   (2.0)

509 T; *'a   [e   lelei   kele] [Pua].*
  but TA good   very   Pua
  'but Pua is very good.'
510   (0.5)
511 F; *[pu'upu'u] [le   lâuga   a   le   kamaloa o   Pua].*
  short   ART speech of ART man   Pred Pua
  (lit. 'the man Pua's speech (was) short')
  'the man Pua gave a short speech.'

The analysis carried out in Ochs (1982) of the frequency of the two constituent pattern in transitive constructions in adult and children's speech indicates that 1) all three major constituents appear in less than 25% of adult transitive utterances, and 2) in children's speech, there is no developmental trend towards expression of all three constituents. Younger children encode more constituents than older children, and taping sessions across eight months display highly variable encoding patterns.

In both adult and children's speech, the NP expressed in two constituent clauses tends to be an absolutive NP, either Subjects of intransitive verbs or Objects of transitive verbs. This tendency has also been referred to as "the preferred argument structure" by Du Bois (1987). Across a large number of languages, speakers display a preference for encoding absolutive arguments over agents as major sentential constituents. This means that (1) could be more accurately represented as (4):

(4)   VC + Absolutive NP

These observations led Du Bois to suggest that in all languages, speaker-hearers tend to avoid expressing agents as full lexical NPs. Speaker-hearers typically identify agents from referents expressed in prior discourse as absolutive constituents. Our examination of Samoan speech and writing, however, suggest that this presumption requires further thought. In Samoan, agent participants may be expressed through genitive constructions within the absolutive NP. If we take a strictly syntactico-semantic definition, viz. Agents to be Subjects of transitive clauses, then our data largely confirm Du Bois' findings. On the other hand, if we widen our notion of Agent to include potential or factual agents in described, evoked, or presupposed events, regardless of the grammatical role of the phrase in which they are linguistically expressed, our data show different results.

ABSOLUTIVE AS A COMPLEX NP

In Samoan, in a significant number of cases, the "Absolutive NP" of a two constituent utterance is in fact a complex NP that includes both an Affected Object (or Undergoer) as a Head Noun and an Agent or some other semantic role(s) in the Modifier. The

Modifier is typically a genitive phrase, which is marked by the preposition *o* or *a*.[5] The syntax of these constructions is schematically represented in (5) (the angled brackets indicate an "either or" condition in the case of coreferentiality of Pro and NP):

(5) Verb Complex + [Art <Gen Pro> Head Noun <Gen NP>]
                    NP

While genitive constructions in Samoan often express a relation of "possession," they express a wide range of other participant roles as well. Thus, in (6), the genitive phrase *a Eki* 'Eki's' refers to the person who prepared the food. Given that Eki is the young untitled male of the family, it would be inappropriate, in a Samoan cultural context, to define the food he cooked for others as "belonging" to him. We consider this an example of genitive construction used to express an Agent participant:

AGENT:

(6) (Pastor & Deacon)
D; *fai le   umu kalo a Eki ma lu'au*
     do ART oven taro of Eki and palusami
     (lit. 'make Eki's oven taro and palusami')
     'Eki made baked taro and palusami'
     e   fa'akali mai ai.
     TA wait   DX pro
     'to welcome (them) with it.'

The widespread use of the genitive construction to express Agent roles that would be expressed as Subjects in nominative-accusative languages, is further illustrated by examples (7) and (8). In (7), for instance, the full NP which one would typically expect to be in the "controller" position for reflexivization (*le kagaka* 'the person') appears instead as part of the Absolutive NP, with the accompanying intensifier *ia* giving the reflexive interpretation:

(7) (Pesio 2;3)
I; *e usu â   le   pese a le   kagaka ia.*
     TA sing EMP ART song of ART person INT
     (lit. 'do sing the very person's song')
     'A person should sing his own song.'

In (8) the NP expressing the Agent of the verb *aumai* 'bring, give' is again part of the genitive modifier within the Absolutive NP:

(8) (Watch)
F; *'e aumai   le   maga'o o le   kagaka.*
     TA give+DX ART want   of ART person
     (lit. 'give (us) the person's wish')

---

[5] The use of one marker over the other is determined by a number of semantic, pragmatic, and idiosyncratic factors pertaining to the relation between the referent of the genitive phrase and the referent of the head noun. The distinction between *a* and *o* in Polynesian languages is generally characterized as that between alienable/inalienable, controlled/noncontrolled, or dominant/subordinate possession (cf. Biggs, 1969; Chapin, 1978; Chung, 1973; Comrie & Thompson, 1985; Wilson, 1976).

'each person gave (us) his request.'

Furthermore, when a relative clause is a transitive clause, the Agent participant often appears as the genitive modifier of the head noun rather than as an overt Agent NP within the relative clause. An example is provided in lines 52-53 in (2) above.

Examples (9) through (12) show other kinds of semantic roles expressed through genitive phrases:

GOAL:

(9) (Watch)

A; *fai mai avaku le fagu susu <u>a le kama.</u>*
 say DX give+DX ART bottle milk of ART boy
 'said "give the milk bottle to the boy"')

BENEFACTIVE/GOAL:

(10) (Watch)

P; *e lee faia gi <u>a lâkou</u> kupe a lafoga.*
 TA NOT do+Cia any of them money of offer
 (lit. 'not made their money of offer')
 '(we) didn't give them any money for the fund-raising'

ACTOR:

(11) (Pesio 2;3)

I; *vala'au Kaepii lale sau*
 call Taepii there come
 'call out for Taepii over there to come'

 *fai le **kou** sa'asa'a.*
 do ART your dance
 '(so that) you (pl.) do a sa'asa'a (dance)'

LOCATIVE:

(12) (Pesio 2;10)

I; *kâ   ô le pasi [o] Falevao.*[6]
 we-DU goPl ART bus of Falevao
 'we'll go with Falevao village bus.'

Table 11.1 shows the distribution of different semantic roles in genitive phrases in adult speech. As shown in Table 11.1, along with Possessor and Social Relationship, Agent is one of the most common types of semantic roles expressed through genitive phrases. This finding opens up a whole series of questions about the definition and distribution of not only Agents but Actors, Experiencers, and other semantic roles in a language like Samoan. Rather than the putatively "natural" or "universal" tendency for human participants to appear as Subjects, a tendency codified as "subjectivization" in Case Grammar (Fillmore, 1968, 1977; see also Kuno, 1973) and "genitive ascention" in Relational Grammar (Kimenyi, 1980), Samoan seems to favor "genitivization," that is, the embedding of a potentially major participant NP role within another NP, typically the NP

---

[6] In this example, the genitive marker *o* is absent, but it would be present in a careful speech version of the same utterance.

that contains the Affected Object, as a genitive modifier. This would be a kind of "detransitivization" (Mosel, 1985; Ochs, 1982).

TABLE 11.1. Semantic Roles in Genitive Constructions* (Adult)

Context:	Semantic Roles** Encoded:								
	POSS	BEN	GL/LC	AG	ACT	EXP	PART	PNT	REL
Informal Women's Speech	.19	.14	.06	.16	.16	.06	.04	.01	.16
	(27)	(20)	(9)	(22)	(23)	(8)	(6)	(2)	(22)
Informal Men's Speech	.21	.12	.16	.19	.08	.06	.10	--	.23
	(7)	(10)	(13)	(16)	(7)	(5)	(8)	(0)	(19)
Total	.20	.13	.10	.17	.13	.06	.06	.01	.23
	(44)	(30)	(22)	(38)	(30)	(13)	(14)	(2)	(51)

*   Each genitive construction may encode more than one semantic role. Percentages were calculated with respect to total number of semantic roles encoded in the corpus of genitive NPs.

** POSS = possessor, BEN = benefactive, GL/LC = goal/locative, AG = agent, ACT = actor, EXP = experiencer, PART = body part or other part/whole relation, PNT = patient, REL = social relationship.

However, this transformational view is misleading for a number of reasons. It implies that complex NPs containing genitive Agents can always be paraphrased as canonical transitive clauses. In many cases, however, there are more or less subtle semantico-pragmatic differences between the version with the genitive Agent and the one with the agent expressed as an NP marked by the ergative particle. The use of an Absolutive NP with a genitive Agent focuses on the Object or result of an action and may imply the Agent to be not necessarily responsible for the creation or pursuit of the Object, whereas the ergative NP with a canonical verb highlights the human participant (Agent) as a willful and responsible actor whose actions may directly affect an object. This is illustrated in (13a-b):

(13a) (Pastor & Deacon)

D; *koiki   maua le   <u>mâkou</u>   fâ   kâlâ*
   almost got   ART our   four dollar
   (lit. 'almost got our four dollars')
   'we almost got four dollars'

(13b)

   koiki maua le   fâ   kâlâ   <u>e   mâkou</u>
   almost got   ART four dollar ERG we
   'we almost got the four dollars (we were actively looking for, as if they had been hidden from us)'

These two examples also show that the change from genitive to ergative involves not only a difference in the way in which the human participant's role is presented, but also a change in the identifiability of the Patient: the Object is more identifiable in (13b) — with the ergative NP — than in (13a) — with the genitive phrase (Timberlake, 1975); this property of utterances with ergative agents matches Hopper and Thompson's (1980) characterization of transitivity.

Furthermore, the genitive phrase may encode more than one role for the same human participant, (viz. Agent and Benefactive), whereas the ergative NP encodes only one role (viz. Agent). Example (14a), for instance, implies that the Youth Association (*autalavou*) is involved in the practice and is also the beneficiary of the event (viz., thanks to the money that will be raised during the feast). (14b) instead implies that the Youth Association does the practice and the practice only:

(14a) (letter "Ma1")
41 *e   fai fa'afiafiaga a le   autalavou   a K. ma L.*
TA do rehearsal of ART youth assoc. of K. and L.
'K.'s and L.'s youth association has been doing the rehearsal'
(lit. 'do rehearsal of the Youth Association of K. and L.')
42 *e sue   ai   tupe*
TA search pro money
'to raise money (with it)'
43 *e fai   ai   le   latou falesa fou.*
TA do pro ART their church new
'to make (with it) their new church.'
(14b)
e   fai fa'afiafiaga e   le   autalavou   a K. ma L.
TA do rehearsal   ERG ART youth assoc. of K. and L.
'K.'s and L.'s youth association has been doing the rehearsal'

In general, an ergative NP implies that the Agent participant is involved in the action described by the verb in a more restricted sense than is implied by the genitive NP.

In contrast to languages like English, where Subjects of transitive verbs can express a wide range of semantic roles (Keenan, 1984), in Samoan, ergative NPs cover a restricted set of roles, viz., typically human initiators of actions (Cook, 1988). Furthermore, from the point of view of language use, the use of ergative NPs seems associated in Samoan discourse with a stance that assumes or assigns accountability to the participant role (Duranti, 1990; Ochs, 1982). When the genitive phrase, as opposed to the ergative phrase, is used to refer to the putative agent, the description of the event seems to focus on the *product or result of the action* of the verb (if the verb is a potentially transitive verb) rather than on the party who is responsible for the process. For this reason, genitive phrases seem to cover cases that in other languages might be expressed by passives or stative-like clauses where the Patient or underlying Object acquires the syntactic role of Subject.

THE ACQUISITION OF GENITIVE CONSTRUCTIONS

Investigation of the internal structure of the frequently used Absolutive NP opens up a series of new questions concerning acquisition: Is complexity of the Absolutive NP something that unifies both adult and child language? Or is it here that adults' and children's speech differs? Can we hence say that the locus of grammatical development in Samoan may lie primarily **within the NP** rather than in clause structure? From our preliminary investigation, we are leaning toward a positive answer to these questions. In contrast to acquisition of clause structure, the acquisition of genitive construction shows a clear progression towards a broader range of semantic roles encoded and more complex head nouns.

Semantic Roles

Let us consider first the distribution of semantic roles, especially agent roles, in children's genitive constructions. Table 11.2 indicates the acquisition patterns of four children: Kalavini (at 19, 21, 23, and 25 months), Iakopo (at 25 and 32 months), Pesio (at 27 and 34 months) and Niulala (at 35 and 42 months).

TABLE 11.2.   Semantic Roles in Genitive Constructions (Children)

Child/Age	Semantic Roles Encoded:								
Kalavini	POSS	BEN	GL/LC	AG	ACT	EXP	PART	PNT	REL
1;07	-	-	-	-	-	-	-	-	-
1;09	-	-	-	-	-	-	-	-	-
1;11	1.0 (1)	-	-	-	-	-	-	-	-
2;01	.24 (10)	.63 (26)	.10 (4)	-	-	-	-	.02 (1)	-
Total	.26 (11)	.62 (26)	.10 (4)	(0)	(0)	(0)	(0)	.02 (1)	(0)
Iakopo	POSS	BEN	GL/LC	AG	ACT	EXP	PART	PNT	REL
2;01	-	.67 (2)	-	-	-	-	.33 (1)	-	-
2;08	.33 (17)	.39 (20)	-	.02 (1)	.008 (4)	.06 (3)	.12 (6)	-	-
Total	.31 (17)	.41 (22)	(0)	.02 (1)	.07 (4)	.06 (3)	.13 (7)	(0)	(0)

TABLE 11.2.   Semantic Roles in Genitive Constructions (Children)

Child/Age	Semantic Roles Encoded:								
Pesio	POSS	BEN	GL/LC	AG	ACT	EXP	PART	PNT	REL
2;3	.34 (11)	.31 (10)	.09 (3)	.03 (1)	--	--	.03 (1)	.13 (4)	.06 (2)
2;10	.65 (129)	.12 (24)	.07 (13)	.04 (8)	.01 (3)	.02 (4)	.05 (10)	.03 (5)	.01 (2)
Total	.61 (140)	.15 (34)	.07 (16)	.04 (9)	.01 (3)	.02 (4)	.05 (11)	.04 (9)	.02 (4)
Niulala	POSS	BEN	GL/LC	AG	ACT	EXP	PART	PNT	REL
2;11	.21 (20)	.43 (42)	.16 (15)	.02 (2)	.05 (5)	-	.10 (10)	.02 (2)	.01 (1)
3;06	.30 (14)	.22 (10)	.02 (1)	.09 (4)	.02 (1)	.04 (2)	.30 (14)	-	-
Total	.24 (34)	.36 (52)	.11 (16)	.04 (6)	.04 (6)	.01 (2)	.17 (24)	.01 (2)	.01 (1)
Grand Total	.43 (202)	.29 (134)	.08 (36)	.03 (16)	.03 (13)	.02 (9)	.09 (42)	.02 (12)	.01 (5)

Table 11.2 suggests that at an early point in acquisition, children use genitives primarily to express possessor and benefactor roles and rarely express agency. The youngest child, Kalavini, does not encode genitive agents at all. The next youngest child, Iakopo also does not encode genitive agents in the earliest recording session and produces only one seven months later, accounting for 2% of that corpus. Genitive agents account for somewhat more of Pesio's and Niulala's genitive constructions, with the last session of Niulala at 3 years 6 months showing the greatest proportion at 9% (4). These data suggest a developmental pattern towards increased use of genitive NPs to encode Agent roles. If we consider the children's corpus as a whole, we can see that the distribution of genitive Agents in children's genitive constructions differs greatly from adult language patterns. Genitive agents characterize 3% of children's genitive constructions in comparison with 16% of adult genitive constructions.

Examples of children's use of genitive constructions to express agency are presented in (15) through (17) below:

AGENT:

(15) (Pesio, 2;10, speaking to researcher (Elinor))

P: *Egoa!/*
      'Elinor!'
E: Uhm?

P: *kusi:::* -*si::* ***lou*** *aka?/*
      write   -te   your picture
      (lit. 'draw -aw your picture?')
      'Are **you** drawing the picture?'
(16) (Niulala, 2;11)
N: *masae le   (ofu)vae (o) Fineaso*
      ripped the pants   (of) Fineaso
      'Fineaso ripped his pants'
AGENT/BENEFACTIVE
(17) (Pesio, 2;10)
P: *sa fai   mâkou   mea'ai*
      TA make our(excl) food
      'We made food for ourselves.'

Nominalized Head Nouns

Genitive constructions of children and adults differ as well in terms of complexity of the head noun. As seen in Table 11.3, in adult genitive constructions where the modifier is an agent, actor, or experiencer, the head noun is often a nominalization. As seen in Table 11.4, in children's genitive constructions, nominalizations are both rare and relatively late to be productively acquired.

TABLE 11.3. Nominalized Head Nouns in Genitive Constructions (Adults)

Informal Women's Speech	Informal Men's Speech	Total
.13	.07	.11
(18)	(6)	(24)

TABLE 11.4. Nominalized Head Nouns in Genitive Constructions (Children)

Kalavini		Iakopo		Pesio		Niulala	
Age	Nom.	Age	Nom.	Age	Nom.	Age	Nom.
1;07	-	2;01	-	2;03	-	2;11	.01 (1)
1;09	-	2;08	-	2;10	.01 (2)	3;06	.10 (4)
1;11	-						
2;01	-						

Tables 11.3 and 11.4 indicate that whereas 11% of adult genitive constructions contain nominalizations, nominalized head nouns are absent or rare before children reach 3½

years. To some extent this developmental pattern is linked to the late emergence of agents, actors, and experiencers as genitive modifiers in children's speech. An example of children's use of genitive constructions with nominalized head nouns is provided in (18):

(18) (Niulala. 3;6)
N;   *koeafe o'u fasiga oe*
    never   my hitting you
    'I never hit you'
    faiaku â   koeafe o'u fasiga   oe
    say   EMP never   my hitting you
    'I'm telling you "I never hit you"'

CONCLUSIONS

The Samoan interactions analyzed here suggest that while Samoan adults and children both favor a clausal strategy of highlighting the affected object in a manipulative activity scene, Samoan children have difficulty exploiting the grammar of genitive noun phrases to encode Agent roles as well. This pattern implies that children's two-constituent utterances differ from those produced by adults. Adults more commonly express agency by means of genitive modifiers in two-constituent utterances (VC + Absolutive NP). In children's utterances, when an Agent is not encoded as Subject of a transitive clause, it is rarely encoded as a genitive modifier.[7] In interpreting children's speech, then, hearers must resort to one of the pragmatic strategies suggested by Du Bois (1987), namely, locating Agent participants in previously mentioned as absolutive NPs (or in the immediate setting). In contrast, interpreters of adult speech may locate the agent participant inside the absolutive NP itself.

For all acquirers, the morpho-syntax of noun phrases is an important dimension of linguistic competence. In Samoan, however, and perhaps in other languages with a two-constituent bias, genitive constructions, nominalizations, and other types of complex noun phrases lace even the most informal of conversations. In all kinds of Samoan talk, the absolutive NP in a two-constituent utterance is often heavy, loaded with information concerning human participants and the actions, states, and locations that bind them. Speakers regularly produce such verb-initial utterances as "Look at the stretching of that one" (*va'ai le fa'ake'e'ku'u a lele*), "Exceptional is the anger of the girl" (*'ese fa'ali'i o lea kegikiki*), "Look at the actions of Sio" (*va'ai le fai'iga o Sio*), "Do you know about our going to New Zealand?" (*'e ke iloa 'oe le mâ ôga i Giusila?*). That such constructions are used so often and with such a variety of meanings suggests that the internal

---

[7]   For the expression of agency through Subject constituents in children's discourse, see Ochs (1982, 1988). For adult data, see Duranti (1994), Duranti and Ochs (1990), and Ochs (1982).

structure of the noun phrase is a particularly central domain of grammatical and conversational competence for Samoan children to acquire.

REFERENCES

Biggs, B. (1969). *Let's Learn Maori.* Wellington, N.Z.: Read.

Bugenhagen, R. D. (1986). Possession in Mangap-Mbula: Its syntax and semantics. *Oceanic Linguistics XXV,* 124-166.

Budwig, N. (1985). I, me, my and 'name': Children's early systematizations of forms meanings and functions in talk about the self. *Papers and Reports on Child Language Development,* **24,** Stanford, CA: Stanford University, Department of Linguistics.

Chapin, P. G. (1978). Easter Island: A characteristic VSO language. In W. P. Lehmann (Eds.), *Syntactic typology: Studies in the phenomenology of language* (pp. 139-168). Austin: University of Texas Press.

Chung, S. (1973). The syntax of nominalizations in Polynesian. *Oceanic Linguistics, 12,* 641-686.

Clark, E. V. (1978). Locationals: existential, locative, and possessive constructions. In J. H. Greenberg (Ed.), *Universals of human language, Vol. 4, Syntax* (pp. 85-126). Stanford, CA: Stanford University Press.

Comrie, B., & Thompson, S. A. (1985). Lexical nominalization. In T. Shopen (Ed.), *Language typology and syntactic description III: Grammatical categories and the lexicon* (pp. 349-398). Cambridge, England: Cambridge University Press.

Cook, K. W. (1988). *A cognitive analysis of grammatical relations, case, and transitivity in Samoa*n. Unpublished doctoral dissertation, University of California, San Diego.

Craig, C. G. (1977). *The structure of Jacaltec.* Austin: University of Texas Press.

Du Bois, J. (1987). The discourse basis of ergativity. *Language, 63,* 805-855.

Duranti, A. (1981). *The Samoan FONO: A sociolinguistic study.* Pacific Linguistics, Series B, Vol. 80. Canberra: The Australian National University, Department of Linguistics, R. S. Pac. S., .

Duranti, A. (1990). Politics and grammar: Agency in Samoan political discourse. *American Ethnologist, 17,* 646-666.

Duranti, A. (1994). *From grammar to politics: Linguistic anthropology in a Western Samoan village.* Berkeley and Los Angeles: University of California Press.

Duranti, A., & Ochs, E. (1983, July). *Word order in Samoan discourse: A conspiracy toward a two-constituent pattern.* Lecture presented at the Linguistics Institute, University of California, Los Angeles.

Duranti, A., & Ochs, E. (1986). Literacy instruction in a Samoan village. In B. B. Schieffelin & P. Gilmore (Eds.), *The acquisition of literacy: Ethnographic perspectives.* Norwood, NJ: Ablex.

Duranti, A., & Ochs, E. (1990). Genitive constructions and agency in Samoan discourse. *Studies in Language 14,* 1-23.

Fillmore, C. J. (1968). The case for case. In E. Bach & E. T. Harms (Eds.), *Universals of linguistic theory* (pp. 1-88). New York: Holt.

Fillmore, C. J. (1977). The case for case reopened. In P. Cole & J. M. Sadock (Eds.), *Syntax and semantics,Vol.8: Grammatical relations* (pp. 59-81). New York: Academic Press.

Hopper, P., & Thompson, S.A. (1980). Transitivity in grammar and discourse. *Language, 56,* 251-300.

Keenan, E. L. (1984). Semantic correlates of the ergative/absolutive distinction. *Linguistics, 22,* 197-223.

Kimenyi, A. (1980). *A relational grammar of Kinyarwanda.* Berkeley: University of California Press.

Kuno, S. (1973). *The structure of the Japanese language.* Cambridge, MA: M.I.T. Press.

Lyons, J. (1967). A note on possessive, existential, and locative sentences. *Foundations of Language,* **3,** 390-396.

Lyons, J. (1977). *Semantics, Vol. 2.* Cambridge, England: Cambridge University Press.

Milner, G. B. (1966). Samoan dictionary: Samoan-English English-Samoan. London: Oxford University Press.

Mosel, U. (1985). *Ergativity in Samoan.* Arbeiten des Kölner Universalien - Projekts, Nr. 61, Cologne.

Ochs, E. (1982). Ergativity and word order in Samoan child language. *Language, 58,* 646-671.

Ochs, E. (1985). Variation and error: A sociolinguistic approach to language acquisition in Samoa. In D. I. Slobin (Ed.), *The crosslinguistic study of language acquisition, Volume I: The data* (pp. 783-838). Hillsdale, NJ: Lawrence Erlbaum Associates.

Ochs, E. (1988). *Culture and language development: Language acquisition and language socialization in a Samoan village.* Cambridge, England: Cambridge University Press.

Parisi, D., & Castelfranchi, C. (1974). Un 'di': Analisi di una preposizione italiana [A 'di': Analysis of an Italian preposition]. In *Fenomeni morfologici e sintattici nell'italiano contemporaneo. Atti del Sesto Congresso Internazionale di Studi.* Rome: Bulzoni.

Schieffelin, B. B. (1985). The acquisition of Kaluli. In D. I. Slobin (Ed.), *The crosslinguistic study of language acquisition, Vol. 1: The data* (pp. 525-594). Hillsdale, NJ: Lawrence Erlbaum Associates.

Seiter, W. (1982). *Studies in Niuean syntax.* New York: Garland.

Slobin, D. I. (1985). Crosslinguistic evidence for the Language-Making Capacity. In D. I. Slobin (Ed.), *The crosslinguistic study of language acquisition, Vol. 2: Theoretical issues* (pp. 1157-1256). Hillsdale, NJ: Lawrence Erlbaum Associates.

Timberlake, A. (1975). Hierarchies in the genitive of negation. *Slavic and Eastern European Journal, 19,* 123-138.

Wilson, W. H. (1976). The o/a distinction in Hawaiian possessives. *Oceanic Linguistics, 15,* 39-50.

Woodbury, A. C. (1977). Greenlandic Eskimo, ergativity, and relational grammar. In P. Cole & J. M. Sadock (Eds.), *Syntax and semantics, Vol. 8: Grammatical relations* (pp. 307-336). New York: Academic.

12 ARGUING WITH SIBLINGS, FRIENDS, AND MOTHERS: DEVELOPMENTS IN RELATIONSHIPS AND UNDERSTANDING[1]

Judy Dunn
University of London

Susan Ervin-Tripp's extraordinary sensitivity to the differences in children's discourse in varying social situations has not only taught us key lessons about children's developing language (Ervin-Tripp, 1987), about their understanding of power relations, and about the structure of control and deference within the family (Ervin-Tripp, Guo, & Lampert, 1990; Ervin-Tripp, O'Connor, & Rosenberg, 1984). Her arguments for the importance of focusing on children's talk in a variety of discourse contexts also have far-reaching lessons for those interested in the development of relationships and the links between social understanding and emotional experience. In this chapter I take the example of young children's arguments in conflict with their mothers, siblings, and friends, over the course of their fourth year, as an illustration of what we can learn from studying children's talk in different close relationships (Dunn, 1992). Conflict talk is an especially useful forum for investigating children's social understanding: Their knowledge of social rules can, for example, be revealed in their excuses and justifications, and their grasp of the other person's desires, expectations, and beliefs in their attempts to conciliate and negotiate. The lessons to be learned concern a range of developmental issues, centering on a core question: What are the connections between children's developing understanding of others and their social relationships with those others?

The wealth of current research on children's developing understanding of others' minds and emotions (e.g., Frye & Moore, 1991; Perner, 1991; Wellman, 1990) has shown that there are major developmental changes between the ages of 3 and 5 years in children's grasp of others' inner states. It is paradoxical that with all the interest in

---

[1] The research described was supported by grants from NICHD (HD 23158), and by the Medical Research Council of Great Britain.

children's "theories of mind," there has been very little examination of the significance of their growing understanding of other people for children's real-life relationships. Yet what we understand of others' inner states must profoundly influence the kind of close relationships we have. With a consideration of how children manage conflict through talk with other family members and friends we can begin to explore the connections between children's close relationships and their understanding of others' emotions and mental states. Such an exploration also leads to the questioning of some current assumptions about relationships and children's development — assumptions for instance about the role of mother-child relationships in sociocognitive development, about the connections between relationships and differences in social understanding, and about the relations between children's emotional state and their reasoning.

REASONING IN CONFLICT

Consider the following exchanges, drawn from a longitudinal study of children recorded at home in Pennsylvania (Dunn, Brown, Slomkowski, Tesla, & Youngblade, 1991):
Example 1:
(Sarah, aged 47 months and Kay, her friend, are playing princesses, and both want to wear a particular crown. Sarah to Kay)
"I should have the crown. Because it matches my dress. It looks ugly on you!"

Sarah's attempts to argue for the crown are — for a child not yet 4 years old — quite subtle. The matter of whether you look pretty or ugly loomed large for many of the girls we studied by the time they reached 4 and 5 years, and it was a topic that recurred frequently in their conversation. The issue of *matching* clothes mattered too. The exchange suggests that Sarah's grasp of what will carry weight with her companion is quite subtle. She used these powers to get her own way in the dispute — successfully.

Now consider two other exchanges. First a parallel incident in which Kerry, another 47-month-old, is also in conflict with a friend over who should have a prized crown.
Example 2:
(Kerry to her friend)
"I know — we'll **both** be queens, because we both want to. Two queens in this palace, and you'll have the crown first, then it'll be my turn — O.K.?"
Example 3:
(Sarah again, this time as a 33-month-old in conflict with her older sister Lynn about who should have a desired toy. Sarah to sibling)
"Belt up, Lynn, and give it me!"
In this conflict with her sister, Sarah offers no justification, and no compromise or recognition of her sister's desires.

These three exchanges raise a number of different developmental issues. The first concerns the developmental course of children's reasoning in argument and its relation to the quality of their close relationships. Consider the differences between Sarah's comments to her sibling as a 33-month-old, with no reasoning offered (Example 3), and as a 47-month-old arguing with her friend (Example 1). Do the differences reflect a developmental change? As children become more able to appreciate the perspectives, intentions, and thoughts of others, does the likelihood that they'll offer reasoning in disputes with family members change? Does the extent of conflict in their close relationships decrease? Do their relationships with others become more harmonious, in consequence?

Sarah's comments, in the first example, remind us that socially skilled behavior is by no means always applied in the interest of harmonious social relations (Smith & Boulton, 1990). During the second and third year, for instance, children increasingly use their understanding of excuses and social rules to shift blame and responsibility for transgressions to their siblings, and get them into trouble, and to draw attention to their siblings' misdeeds (Dunn, 1988). The issue of the **purpose** for which a sophisticated argument is used needs to be considered separately from the issue of whether a child uses a relatively sophisticated argument, or simply insists on her wants without providing a justification (as in Example 3 above, the case of Sarah in conflict with her sister). Sophisticated reasoning can be applied towards quite different ends: It can be used too in a non-conciliatory way to gain one's own ends (Sarah), or it can be used in a conciliatory manner for compromise or negotiation (Kerry). Some have argued that as children leave behind the "terrible twos" they become more likely to compromise and to be compliant (Kopp, 1987). Does this trend continue over their fourth year? Or do children use their new powers of recognizing others' needs and feelings towards achieving their own ends — as in the example of Sarah arguing with Kay?

A second set of questions raised by the examples of Sarah and Kerry concerns the differences in children's discourse in conflict with different partners. How does the particular relationship between child and partner affect the way that the child argues? Are there systematic differences among children's arguments with their siblings, their friends, and their mothers, for instance? If so, do these differences reflect differences in the power relations, or the affective quality of the relationship? While children's friendships are characterized by commitment and affection, their sibling relationships are more ambivalent and hostile (Buhrmester, 1992). Is this difference reflected in their propensity to negotiate and take account of the other child's needs? Are children in general more likely to marshal their powers of reasoning and negotiation when in conflict with their friends than when in disputes with their siblings? Did Kerry's negotiation reflect the quality of her affectionate friendship with her companion — in contrast to the more competitive relationship between Sarah and Kay?

A related set of questions concerns the pattern of developmental influences on children's conflict strategies and arguments. The central issue concerns the potential developmental influence of family relationships. Are there links across relationships in styles of handling disputes? For instance, are children who reason frequently with their mothers more likely to do so in later months with their friends than children who have not had the experience of handling conflicting interests and goals in this way within the family? What is the relative developmental significance of the experience of arguing with your mother, as compared with arguing with your sibling?

Finally, there is the issue of how the emotional context of a dispute is related to the reasoning children bring to bear in the conflict. Some studies indicate that children use more justification in conflict and more sophisticated language in situations when they are expressing negative affect (Dunn, 1988; Eisenberg, 1992). Other research indicates that in situations of heightened emotions children behave in a less mature way (see, for instance, Bloom & Beckwith, 1989). Studying discourse in disputes which vary in emotional intensity offers an opportunity to examine a key but intractable issue in psychology — the relation of emotion and cognition.

THE STUDY

We examined each of these sets of questions with data from the observations of 50 secondborn children observed at home with their mothers and older siblings at 33, 40, and 47 months (Dunn et al., 1991), and with a close friend at 47 months. The children's understanding of others' feelings, and their grasp of the relation of others' beliefs to their behavior was also assessed in standard assessments at 40 months, and the children were then followed up through kindergarten and first grade. The families, recruited from sequential births in a community hospital in central Pennsylvania, included a wide range of socioeconomic and educational backgrounds (for details see Dunn et al., 1991). During the unstructured family observations the family conversations were taperecorded and a narrative record of the people present, affect expressed and details of conflict incidents and play was kept by the observer. The procedures for gathering data on the children's interactions with their friends were based on Gottman's (1983) study: The children were taperecorded while they played alone with their friend in a room at home. In this chapter the findings that relate to the general questions raised are simply summarized (for further details see Dunn & Brown, 1993; Slomkowski & Dunn, 1992; Tesla & Dunn, 1992). We focus here on the conflict discourse between the children and their mothers, siblings, and friends at 33 and 47 months, and on their success on the sociocognitive tests at 40 months.

DEVELOPMENTAL CHANGE IN ARGUMENTS
IN CONFLICT WITH MOTHER AND SIBLING

The first set of questions concerned the developmental changes in children's arguments in disputes with family members. Of special interest was the growth of children's ability to take account of others' wishes in conflict, and the issue of first, whether there would be an increase in the proportion of conflicts in which children reasoned with their antagonists over the period between 33 and 47 months, and second, whether children would use their growing powers of reasoning in the interests of harmony and conciliation or in their own immediate interests.

Conflict episodes were frequent in these families — paralleling in frequency the disputes reported in other studies of families with several young children (e.g., Dunn & Munn, 1985, 1987). A unilateral definition of conflict was used (see Hay, 1984), with the episode beginning with the first oppositional verbal turn. The coding was restricted to those conflicts directly involving the focal child, and was based on the verbal interactions. Disputes between our 33-month-olds and their mothers, for example, occurred on average 11 times an hour, while conflicts between the siblings averaged 9 an hour. Conflicts did not become more or less frequent over the next 14 months, however, there was indeed an increase in the proportion of such conflicts in which the children reasoned over the children's fourth year. For instance with their mothers, the children reasoned in an average of 36% of their conflicts at 33 months, and this proportion rose to 45% of mother–child conflicts at 47 months.

This increase in reasoning during conflicts was not, however, associated with an increase in taking the antagonist's point of view into account for conciliatory purposes. We distinguished two types of reasoned argument in disputes. First, OTHER-ORIENTED or CONCILIATORY ARGUMENT (see also Kruger, 1992) included those conversational turns in which the speaker took account of the other's needs and desires in attempts to conciliate or negotiate — as in Example 2 above, where Kerry offered a compromise. This category also included bargaining, in which the speaker attempts to trade-off with the conflict partner: "I'll give you He-Man, if you give me two Shredders," and conciliation, in which the speaker "gives in" to the conflict partner, giving a reason for doing so: "Okay, I guess since I went first last time, you can go first this time."

The second category was SELF-ORIENTED ARGUMENT, in which the reasons offered were used explicitly and solely in the service of the speaker's own interest — as in Example 1. This category included references to social rules: "I should go first 'cause I'm the guest. Guests get to go first"; it also included references to the speaker's own needs or emotional state: "Be quiet, I have a headache" (a common maternal comment!), or status: "I'm older so I get to go first." A third category of conflict management included conversational turns in which no REASON or JUSTIFICATION was offered, and the speaker failed to justify or provide reasons or excuses. Examples included simple refusal: "No!" and prohibitions: "Stop that!"

The longitudinal analyses showed — perhaps sadly, for family harmony — that there was no increase in other-oriented argument for conciliation over the 14 months. Instead there was an increase in children's reasoned argument towards achieving their own immediate goals. Children were in fact **less** likely to argue for conciliation at 47 than at 33 months in disputes that had begun with their own oppositional moves (see Fig. 12.1). It seems that as the children became more sophisticated in understanding other people they applied their skills of reasoning in defense of their own self-interest, rather than towards resolving the conflict in ways that took account of the other's interests, and thus increasing the harmony of their close relationships.

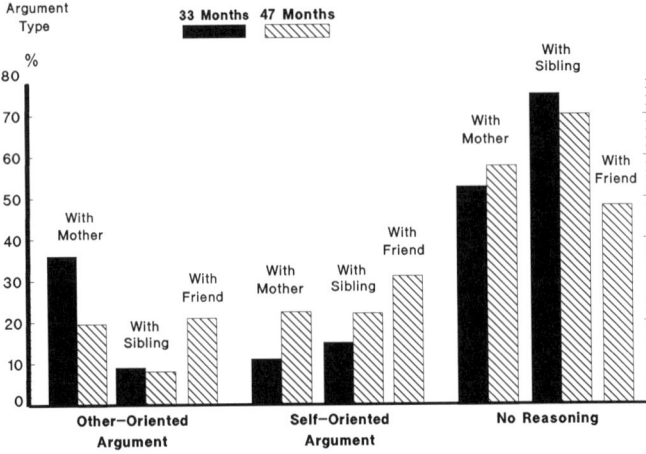

FIG. 12.1.

Proportion of argument types in conflict episodes in dyadic relationships

There were parallel changes in the behavior of mothers and older siblings towards the target children over the same 14-month period. In disputes with the children in which the mothers and siblings had made the first oppositional move, the proportion of episodes in which they used other-oriented argument actually decreased, while the proportion in which they used no reasoning at all but simply insisted without justification increased. And mothers were much more likely to use reasoning in their own interests at 47 months than they had been at 33 months: the proportion of mothers' self-oriented reasoning more than doubled in child-initiated conflicts, for instance, rising from an average 15% at 33 months to 32% at 47 months. We could interpret this parallel between children's and mothers' increased use of self-oriented argument in a number of different ways. It could be that mothers' expectations that their children were able to conform and behave more "acceptably" rose as the children grew up and that this led to their mothers' increasing arguments in support of their own position. That is, mothers may have assumed that older children's desires do not have to be compromised with, or conformed to, as much as those of younger children because they are better able to understand what is expected of them. It could also be that the children's increasing use of reasoned argument for their own position itself influenced their mothers to respond in a similar way. Either way, it appears that both mothers and siblings made fewer allowances for the children by the time that they were 47 months, and were less inclined to compromise and offer conciliation to the children as they showed themselves to be more independent and capable of arguing for their own ends. It is interesting to note that the changes in siblings' use of argument were less closely linked to those of the children than were those of their mothers. The closer parallels between developments in child and parent behavior as opposed to sibling behavior have been noted in a study of child–parent and child–sibling play (Stevenson, Leavitt, Thompson, & Roach, 1988).

DIFFERENCES IN ARGUMENTS
WITH DIFFERENT PARTNERS

This comparison of parents and siblings brings us to the second set of issues raised by the initial three examples, which concerned the differences in children's discourse in their conflicts with different partners. First, a notable developmental change in the pattern of children's interactions with their mothers and siblings should be noted. Between 33 and 47 months, the time that children spent with their mothers dropped markedly, as did the amount of conversation between mother and child. For example the average number of mothers' conversation turns to their children dropped from 98 to 66 per hour between the 33 month and 47 month observations, while the number of child-to-mother turns dropped from 82 to 52 per hour over this period. In contrast the conversational turns between child and sibling increased greatly, from an average of 44 to 70 per hour for the child-to-sibling turns, and from 52 to 75 sibling-to-child turns per hour. The prominence of siblings — rather than mothers — as the chief conversational partners for these secondborn children from the end of their fourth year onwards has shown up strikingly in a variety of different domains, for instance in discourse concerning inner states (Brown & Dunn, 1992) and in pretend play.

There were, moreover, systematic differences in the pattern of children's conflict talk with their different interlocutors. In conflict with close friends, for instance, children were significantly more likely to use reasoning that took account of the other's point of view or feelings than they were in conflict with their siblings (Fig. 12.1). This pattern could reflect the greater equality of power between the two children in the friend dyad as compared with the sibling–child or mother–child dyad. It could also reflect the affective quality of the exchange: Children may care more about managing to maintain continuous equable communication with their friends than they do with the family members (especially their siblings). Children's relationships with their siblings do not have to be "worked at" to ensure their continuation. Friends in contrast may lose interest in each other, drift apart, quarrel, and their relationship can break up if the individuals don't have a commitment to maintaining it. The issue of how the emotional context relates to children's use of argument we consider later. First, we focus on the question of how individual differences in conflict discourse between child and parent, child and sibling, and child and friend are related.

This is a question of considerable developmental interest. It has been widely assumed that it is within the mother–child relationship that children develop not only emotional security and expressiveness, but expectations concerning others' interactive behavior, styles of interaction and sociocognitive abilities more generally, and that experiences with parents are of special importance in relation to children's peer interactions later (e.g., Parke & Ladd, 1992). If the interactions between mother and child form some kind of prototype for children's handling of conflict we might then expect correlations not only between the style of children's argument in conflict with their mothers and that with their siblings and friends, but also between their mothers' conflict style and the children's later conflict talk. On the other hand, if conflict exchanges are viewed as an aspect of particular dyadic relationships — which may differ in dynamics, in structure and emotional quality — then we might predict **differences** in a child's style of arguing in conflict across his or her different relationships.

The findings of the Pennsylvania study clearly supported the second prediction. There were marked individual differences between the children in their propensity to argue with their siblings and friends, and there was evidence for reciprocity **within** dyads in argument style. There were, for example, at the 33 month observations significant correlations between the use of other-oriented argument by mother-to-child and child-to-mother $r(50) = .46$, $p < .05$, and by sibling-to-child and child-to-sibling $r(50) = .37$, $p < .05$ (see Slomkowski & Dunn, 1992, for further details). But there was little evidence for carryover between the children's argument style with their mothers, their siblings, and their friends. Of particular interest is the finding that the use of other-oriented argument in children's conflict with their friends was not correlated with the use of other-oriented argument in conflicts between child and sibling, or between child and mother, nor were there links between children's argument use in dispute with mother and with sibling.

Children's use of argument, these results show, was specific to each relationship. Some children who took their siblings' viewpoints into consideration in their sibling conflicts simply repeated their protests and unreasoned accusations when in conflict with their mothers; others who negotiated and compromised within conflicts with their mothers simply yelled and protested without argument in their disputes with their siblings.

RELATIONS BETWEEN ARGUMENT USE
AND PERSPECTIVE-TAKING TEST PERFORMANCE

The lack of association between children's use of argument with their mothers and their siblings brings us to the issue of whether children's, mothers', or siblings' use of other-oriented argument in conflict bears any relation to differences in the development of children's ability to understand others' emotions and "other minds" as conventionally assessed in tasks by psychologists. In the Pennsylvania study we included such assessments when the children were 40 months (Dunn et al., 1991). The examination of over-time correlations between measures of family discourse when the children were 33 months and their performance on the tests 7 months later showed there were indeed longitudinal links between child-sibling discourse during conflict and the later assessments. Children who used more other-oriented and self-oriented arguments with their siblings, and who less frequently disputed without any reasoned argument did better on both tests of emotion-understanding and "other minds" tasks (Slomkowski & Dunn, 1992). The emotion understanding tasks involved scenarios played out with puppets in which a variety of emotions were engendered, and the child was asked to identify these. The "other minds" tasks were standard tests of children's understanding of the relation between the beliefs held by someone (which the child knew to be mistaken) and their subsequent action (Bartsch & Wellman, 1989). These assessments were also enacted with puppet scenarios.

In contrast to these connections with the sibling interactions, there were no significant links between children's conflict discourse with their mothers and the later measures of socio-cognitive understanding. And it is particularly notable that there was no link between the mothers' own discourse style and the children's later understanding.

What can we conclude from these correlations? Clearly no causal inferences can be made concerning child-sibling conflict. It could be that the individual children who were high scorers on the social cognition tasks were more likely to use reasoned argument in their disputes with their siblings **because** of their greater understanding, not as a consequence of their conflict experiences with their siblings. But although we cannot draw conclusions about causal influence it is worth emphasizing that the connections differed for the different relationships (sibling–child versus mother–child), and that it was the sibling–child relationship which showed the over time associations. Here we see that the results fit well with the Piagetian idea that child–child interaction may have particular significance for the development of social understanding. And other findings from the study support such a notion: individual differences in the tests of children's ability to understand "other minds" and emotions were also found to be related to the extent of cooperative interactions observed between the children and their older siblings seven months earlier (Dunn et al., 1991).

EMOTIONAL CONTEXT AND ARGUMENT IN CONFLICT

The final set of questions that we examine concerns the possible links between children's emotional state and their use of argument. Some studies of social conflict show that when children's goals are frustrated, and their interests touched most closely, their arguments are especially mature (Eisenberg, 1992; Stein & Miller, 1991).

We examined the proportion of children's conflict turns engaged in when angry or upset that fell into each of the three argument categories, and then compared these proportions with the children's use of each argument category in conflict episodes when they did not express negative affect. The results showed that at 33 months, when the children were **not** upset they engaged in a larger proportion of other-oriented, conciliatory argument with both mothers and siblings than they did in conflict episodes in which they were upset (mean proportion of other-oriented argument when not upset = .19, mean proportion when upset = .06, $z = 1.97$, $p < .05$; see Tesla & Dunn, 1992). By 47 months children used reasoned argument equally often in conflict episodes with siblings when they were and were not upset; in conflict with their mothers, they were more likely to use unreasoned protest when upset than when not upset.

For this particular sample, then, it seems that when the children were angry or distressed as 33-month-olds they were less able to draw on their developing sociocognitive skills and employ reasoned argument — whether in their own interests or to resolve the dispute through conciliation. It is interesting to note that mothers, in contrast, engaged in more conciliation and negotiation when their children were showing signs of anger or distress than when they were affectively neutral. However, the children's state of emotional upset did not affect the way that siblings argued in conflict. Here, again, mothers appear to be more responsive than siblings to the children's behavior and state during conflict.

It is interesting to compare these findings with the evidence from another domain — the children's discourse concerning the causes and consequences of inner states. Here, in contrast to the conflict management results, our analyses showed that at 33 months children were more likely to engage in causal discourse about feelings when they were expressing negative or neutral affect than when they were expressing positive affect (Dunn & Brown, 1993) — that is, the results parallel those of Eisenberg (1992) and Stein and Miller (1991). However by 47 months their causal talk about inner states was most likely to take place when they were emotionally neutral — not upset or happy and excited. One possibility suggested by these results is that the significance of children's emotional state for their engagement in causal thought concerning inner states changes over time as their own powers of reflective thought increase. As their metacognitive abilities develop over the fourth year, they engage more frequently in causal discourse when they are not aroused emotionally; at earlier time points it is when they are emotionally engaged that they participate in this relatively sophisticated talk about inner states. However the findings on conflict discourse and on other domains — such as the children's use of humor and their engagement in pretend play — suggest an important caveat to the generalizations we can make from the talk about inner states.

This is that the significance of children's affective state appears to differ for different domains of sociocognitive development. Thus engagement in joint pretend play, which involves the cognitive demands of sharing of an imaginary world, is less frequent when children are emotionally upset. We found that children who were frequently expressing negative affect engaged in less role enactment in pretend play than other children in this sample. The same point can be made with a consideration of children's engagement in shared humor. Children made different jokes to their mothers and siblings in both the Pennsylvania study and in a study of English children in their second and third years (Dunn, 1988): With their siblings their jokes often focused on the forbidden, the disgusting, or the scatological, whereas with their mothers their jokes were less often on these topics. This differentiation shows us that already in their third year children are aware what **different** others will find funny — quite sophisticated understanding for such young children. And this engagement in shared humor was, unsurprisingly, rarely shown when the children were angry or distressed. The general point here is that we should appreciate the different — and separate — domains of social understanding in which children are becoming increasingly sophisticated during their preschool years, and not think in terms of "social understanding" as an undifferentiated whole.

CONCLUSIONS

In their daily life at home, children continually face conflicts with the goals, actions, and wishes of others. A close look at how they talk and act in these encounters — the apparently trivial exchanges of family life — can teach us much about their relationships and their understanding of their social world. Recall Ervin-Tripp's (1987) trenchant comments on the value of examining **both** the social situation and the syntax that children use, for understanding the development of language and its use:

My advice to those who study syntax is to get a video camera and look at what is going on. And my advice to students of discourse is to see what morphological and syntactic clues children are using to mark the larger structures of their discourse.

She goes on to argue for the inclusion of a wide variety of discourse contexts, which "allows phenomena to appear which are otherwise masked or absent." The argument of this chapter is in some respects a parallel one. What children are trying to do in their conversations in conflict with their various relatives and friends can be enormously illuminating both for those interested in social relationships and for those studying sociocognitive development — and especially for our understanding of the links between these domains. The lessons from our examination of children's discourse in conflict can be summarized in the following points:

1. Over the course of children's fourth year, the likelihood that they would bring reasoned argument to bear in their conflicts increased markedly.

2. The increased use of argument was employed not to negotiate or conciliate and thus to resolve conflicts more frequently, but to advance the children's own self-interest.

3. Individual differences in children's style of handling conflict were marked, and while there was some reciprocity within dyads in argument style, there was no evidence for connections across family and friend relationships in children's management of conflict. Children's use of argument in conflict was specific to each relationship.

More generally, the new social understanding that children demonstrate in their close relationships over the fourth year is not expressed uniformly across their relationships; rather than regarding social understanding as a "within-child" characteristic or trait we should acknowledge that how children use their social understanding depends on the nature of the particular relationship.

4. The evidence suggests that it is misleading to view mother–child conflict interactions as prototypical in relation to individual differences in the children's later argument style in conflict with close friends, or as related in any simple way to their social understanding as assessed in formal tasks. Indeed, several lines of evidence highlight the connections between children's interactions with their siblings — rather than mothers — and their later social understanding.

5. The significance of children's emotional state for the cognitive maturity they show varies across domains of social behavior. The findings raise the possibility that as children's powers of reflective thought and their metacognitive abilities develop, the significance of their current affective state for such reflection decreases.

To make progress in understanding these and other developmental patterns in children's social relationships we need to study children in situations that are of emotional significance to them, within their own social world. Students of social relationships and social understanding have much to learn from studies of children's discourse in different relationships — as Susan Ervin-Tripp has so clearly shown us.

REFERENCES

Bartsch, K., & Wellman, H. (1989). Young children's attribution of action to beliefs and desires. *Child Development*, **60**, 946-964.

Bloom, L., & Beckwith, R. (1989). Talking with feeling. *Cognition and Emotion*, **3**, 313-342.

Brown, J., & Dunn, J. (1992). Talk to your mother or sibling: Developmental changes in early family conversations about feelings. *Child Development*, **63**, 336-349.

Buhrmester, D. (1992). The developmental course of sibling and peer relationships. In F. Boer & J. Dunn (Eds.), *Children's sibling relationships: Developmental and clinical issues* (pp. 19-40). Hillsdale, NJ: Lawrence Erlbaum Associates.

Dunn, J. (1988). *The beginnings of social understanding*. Cambridge, MA: Harvard University Press.

Dunn, J. (1992). Lessons from the study of children's conversations. *Merrill-Palmer Quarterly*, **38**, 139-149.

Dunn, J., & Brown, J. (1993). Early conversations about causality — Content, pragmatics and developmental change. *British Journal of Developmental Psychology*, **11**, 107-123.

Dunn, J., Brown, J., Slomkowski, C., Tesla, C., & Youngblade, L. (1991). Young children's understanding of other people's feelings and beliefs: Individual differences and their antecedents. *Child Development*, **62**, 1352-1366.

Dunn, J., & Munn, P. (1985). Becoming a family member: Family conflict and the development of social understanding in the second year. *Child Development*, **56**, 764-774.

Dunn, J., & Munn, P. (1987). The development of justification in disputes. *Developmental Psychology*, **23**, 791-798.

Eisenberg, A. R. (1992). Conflicts between mothers and their young children. *Merrill-Palmer Quarterly*, **38**, 21-43.

Ervin-Tripp, S. M. (1987, October). Speech acts and syntactic development: Linked or independent? Keynote address to the Boston Child Language Conference.

Ervin-Tripp, S. M., Guo, J., & Lampert, M. (1990). Politeness and persuasion in children's control acts. *Journal of Pragmatics*, **14**, 307-332.

Ervin-Tripp, S. M., O'Connor, M. C., & Rosenberg, J. (1984). Language and power in the family. In M. Schulz, C. Kramerae, & W. M. O'Barr (Eds.), *Language and power* (pp. 116-135). Newbury, CA: Sage Publications.

Frye, D., & Moore, C. (1991). *Children's theories of mind*. Hillsdale, NJ: Lawrence Erlbaum Associates.

Gottman, J. M. (1983). How children become friends. *Monographs of the Society for Research in Child Development*, **48** (Serial No. 201).

Hay, D. (1984). Social conflict in early childhood. In G. Whitehurst (Ed.), *Annals of child development* (Vol. 1, pp. 1-44). Greenwich, CT: JAI Press.

Kopp, C. B. (1987). The growth of self-regulation: Caregivers and children. In N. Eisenberg (Ed.), *New directions in developmental psychology* (pp. 34-50). New York: Wiley.

Kruger, A. C. (1992). The effect of peer and adult-child transactive discussion on moral reasoning. *Merrill-Palmer Quarterly*, **38**, 191-211.

Parke, R. D., & Ladd, G. W. (1992). *Family-peer relationships: Modes of linkage*. Hillsdale, NJ: Lawrence Erlbaum Associates.

Perner, J. (1991). *Understanding the representational mind*. Cambridge, England: Cambridge University Press.

Slomkowski, C. L., & Dunn, J. (1992). Arguments and relationships within the family: Differences in young children's disputes with mother and sibling. *Developmental Psychology*, **28**, 919-924.

Smith, P. K., & Boulton, M. (1990). Rough-and-tumble play, aggression and dominance: Perception and behaviour in children's encounters. *Human Development, 33,* 271-282.

Stein, N. L., & Miller, C. A. (1991). The process of thinking and reasoning in argumentative contexts: Evaluation of evidence and the resolution of conflict. In R. Glaser (Ed.), *Advances in instructional psychology* (pp. 284-334). Hillsdale, NJ: Lawrence Erlbaum Associates.

Stevenson, M., Leavitt, L., Thompson, R., & Roach, M. (1988). A social relations model analysis of parent and child play. *Developmental Psychology, 24,* 101-108.

Tesla, C., & Dunn, J. (1992). Getting along or getting your way: The development of children's argument in conflict with mother and sibling. *Social Development, 1,* 107-121.

Wellman, H. M. (1990). *The child's theory of mind.* Cambridge, MA: Bradford Books.

13 PATTERNS OF PROHIBITION IN PARENT-CHILD DISCOURSE

Jean Berko Gleason, Richard Ely,
Rivka Y. Perlmann, and Bhuvana Narasimhan
Boston University

Very young children have remarkable linguistic abilities that enable them to acquire language under the varying conditions that exist in all the different societies of the world. This is obvious, since there are no cultures in which children fail to acquire language. At the same time, at least in the societies we know, children develop language in the course of conversations with those around them, in conversational context, and not simply by first observing adult speech to other adults and then deriving the rules.

In this chapter we will explore some early developmental, gender, and contextual differences in the language that parents address to their young daughters and sons in the course of everyday interactions, and we will consider the role such differences may have in children's linguistic socialization. By LINGUISTIC SOCIALIZATION we mean two things: in the narrow sense, how children are socialized to use language appropriately, and in the broader sense, how children are socialized through language to conform with our society's construction of their roles and behavior (Gleason, 1988).

Child-directed speech produced by adults in a given community has been shown by many investigators to be characterized by numerous shared features, which are related to the speakers' need to communicate with a language learner: Speaking to an infant, for instance, requires modifying that speech so that an infant can process it — this can include, among a long list of other special features, speaking with exaggerated intonation and high pitch, using simple and repetitive sentences, and speaking relatively slowly. Not every society uses the same set of features (Snow, Perlmann, & Nathan, 1987), but every society we know has a special register for speaking to infants and children. As children grow older, the specialized input they receive also changes in complexity and focus: Adults and children calibrate their language and other behaviors in response to subtle cues from one another.

All speakers in a community do not speak in exactly the same way to all children, even to children of the same age or stage of development. There is individual stylistic variation on the part of the adult (Perlmann, 1984), as well as role related variation — that is, mothers, for instance, and fathers speak in ways that distinguish their roles (Gleason, 1975); and variation may occur in speech to children based on characteristics of the child — for example on the child's gender. Most early studies on input language to children found few differences in parents' speech to little boys or to little girls (Snow & Ferguson, 1977); this is certainly true of the major grammatical features — every child hears a representative sample of the basic grammatical structures of the language.

In the past few years, however, as attention has shifted from grammar to other features of language, differences in speech to boys and girls have begun to emerge. Early differences in input language to boys and to girls may underlie later linguistic — and even behavioral — differences that are observed in men and women. For example, women's speech has more emotional content than men's speech (Lakoff, 1975; Tannen, 1990). The origin of this difference may be related at least in part to the differential treatment of female and male infants: Dunn, Bretherton, and Munn (1987) reported a greater use of inner state words to infant girls than to boys. Thus, these differences in the speech of adults may be related to the greater emphasis on feelings in speech to infant girls.

In some of our earlier work (Gleason, 1975), we also found that parents of boys addressed them in a more imperative fashion and used more jocular, tough, and demeaning names with them, such as *tiger, wiseguy*, and *nutcake*. Cherry (1975) found that teachers of preschool children asked more questions of girls and gave more directives to boys. And Warren-Leubecker (now Warren; 1982) and we (Gleason, Perlmann, Ely, & Evans, 1993) found that mothers of girls used more diminutives such as *doggie* and *blankie* than mothers of boys. Such variation may contribute to children's differential gender role socialization, including ultimately their linguistic style.

PROHIBITIVES

One important aspect of socialization through language is the pervasive use of language to mediate the child's ongoing activity. Prior to the child's acquisition of language, both parents and children appear to be attuned to certain prosodic aspects of language. Mothers use variations in pitch to praise and prohibit behaviors when speaking to infants as young as two months of age, and infants are responsive to these paralinguistic features (Fernald, 1984). As children's language development unfolds, parents control their behavior with explicit linguistic directives such as prohibitives (e.g., *no, don't*; Ely & Gleason, in press).

This study examines variation in parents' use of the lexicon related to prohibition when speaking to their daughters or sons in several settings. The style a parent uses, whether mitigated or demanding, reflects the parent's conception of the child; for instance, even the parents of newborns apparently believe that infant boys are relatively tougher and bouncier and that infant girls are weaker and more sensitive (Rubin, Provenzano, & Luria, 1974). If this view of the child is revealed in the parents' speech, we might expect speech to boys to be in some sense "tougher." Both anecdotal evidence and our own earlier work (e.g., Gleason, 1975) has indicated that parents are more abrupt and imperative with preschool boys than with girls; the present study extends this work by examining parents' use of explicit prohibitives in speech to a large number of young children.

SUBJECTS AND METHODS

As data for this study, we examined transcripts of conversations between parents and children in several settings. All transcripts were computerized and came from the Child Language Data Exchange System (CHILDES; MacWhinney & Snow, 1990). For purposes of this analysis we divided them into two groups: samples containing children of infant/toddler age and corpora of preschool age children.

Infants and toddlers

New England Sample

This corpus consists of semistructured play sessions between 34 mothers and their young children at two points in time: when the children were 14 months old and when they were 20 months old. Sixteen of the children were boys, and 18 were girls. The play sessions were held in a laboratory setting, and each lasted for about 20 to 25 minutes, during which time the mother and child were given a standard set of activities to perform, for example, ball play, peekaboo, drawing with crayons, and reading a book.

Rondal Corpus

This sample (Rondal, 1978) consists of 21 toddlers, 7 girls and 14 boys, seen in two sessions, a week apart. Children's ages ranged from 20 to 32 months. The children were engaged in free play sessions at home with their mothers, each session lasting about a half hour. All families were middle class, and homes contained very similar toys.

Warren-Leubecker Corpus

These data (Warren-Luebecker, 1982) were collected in the homes of 20 children, 10

boys and 10 girls. There was a younger group of children, aged 18 to 37 months, analyzed here, and an older group, aged 54 to 74 months. The older group was analyzed
along with the preschool group in the next section. Parents were middle class. Fathers
and mothers were recorded playing with their children in sessions lasting 15 minutes to
half an hour. Each parent played separately with the child, using toys present in the
home.

Preschoolers

Gleason Corpus

These data are drawn from family dinners in the homes of 22 children, ranging in
age from 27 to 61 months, and there were equal numbers of boys and girls. Mothers and
fathers were present at these meals, and each family was seen once. Dinners lasted about
a half hour in these middle class homes. The children were also seen in semistructured
laboratory play sessions of about a half hour each, once with mothers and once with
fathers.

Warren-Leubecker Corpus

The data analyzed here were from the older group, aged 54 to 74 months, described
above. Fathers and mothers played with their children in separate sessions lasting 15
minutes to half an hour, using the child's own toys.

The characteristics of each sample can be seen in Table 13.1.

TABLE 13.1.   Characteristics of the samples

Corpus	Age Group	N	Setting	Age in Months	Children's MLU*
New England	14 months	34	lab play	14.0	1.152
	20 months	34	lab play	20.0	1.326
Rondal	Younger	9	home play	23.2	1.428
	Older	12	home play	28.8	2.480
Gleason		24	lab play	42.3	3.311
		22	dinner	42.3	3.693
Warren-Leubecker	Younger	10	home play	26.5	2.305
	Older	10	home play	64.7	3.905

*Note: MLU = mean length of utterance.

ANALYSES

Prohibitives

For purposes of analysis the transcript of each session was coded for the presence of prohibitives (e.g., the way the parents couched their intent to tell the children not to engage in an activity). To identify the prohibitives, we first used one of the Child Language Analysis programs (CLAN; MacWhinney & Snow, 1990) called FREQ to generate frequency lists of the entire lexicon used by the parents. We then selected the likely candidates for words used as prohibitives — words like *don't, not, can't*, and *stop*. Next, we used another computer program (KWAL) to bring up parents' use of these words in context. Specific uses of these words, when used as prohibitions, were examined for each group of parents.

Forms of prohibitive

For the largest corpus, the New England Sample, a further set of more detailed analyses were undertaken.

Direct prohibitives.   Once the prohibitives were identified, each prohibitive utterance was coded for whether it was direct or mitigated The direct prohibitives consisted of *no*'s and *don't*'s uttered without any modifications or adjustments that would soften, or mitigate, the prohibition:

    Mother: "Don't touch!"
    Father: "No, no, no!"

Mitigated prohibitives.   Mitigated prohibitives consisted of utterances that expressed a prohibition, but in a mitigated or softened fashion. For example, they might include a term of endearment or a semantic softener:

    Mother: "Don't touch, honey!"
    Mother: "You can't touch, though."

Sometimes the prohibitive was couched in a manner that was instructive or explanatory in some fashion:

    Mother: "We don't stand on desks."
    Mother: "Don't pick it up cause it might break."

Clustered prohibitives.   Each prohibitive was also coded for whether it stood alone or was clustered, for example, whether it was preceded or followed by another prohibitive utterance.

RESULTS

Prohibitives are a common feature of parent–child discourse. They appear to be more frequent in the speech of parents of infants and toddlers than in the speech of parents of preschoolers. Around the second birthday (20 to 24 months), gender differences appear, with mothers directing more prohibitives to toddler boys than to toddler girls. There are also contextual factors that influence the frequency with which parents use prohibitives.

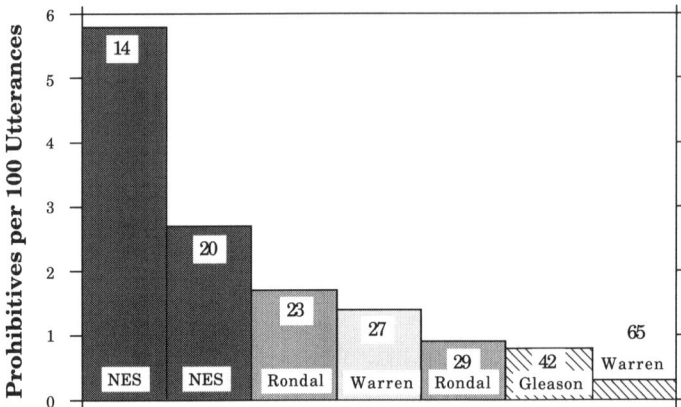

Note. Figures at top of columns are ages in months

FIG. 13.1. Prohibitives to children in play sessions.

Developmental patterns

In the laboratory play sessions with their infants, mothers addressed more than twice as many prohibitives to their children when they were 14 months old than when they were 20 months old (New England sample). At 14 months, children heard 5.8 prohibitives per 100 utterances; at 20 months they heard 2.7 prohibitives per 100 utterances. In play sessions with mothers at home (Rondal corpus), mothers of young toddlers (20-26 months) directed prohibitives to their children at a rate of 1.7 per 100 utterances; older toddlers (27-32 months) heard slightly fewer, 1.4 per 100 utterances. Preschoolers (27-61 months) drawn from the Gleason corpus in laboratory play sessions (but not dinners) with their mothers and fathers heard even fewer prohibitives, 0.7 and 0.9 per 100 utterances, respectively. The oldest subjects examined (M_{age} = 65 months), the older 10 children drawn from the Warren-Leubecker corpus, heard the fewest number of prohibitives, 0.3 from mothers and 0.6 from fathers per 100 utterances. Thus, in the context of a play session with either parent directives containing lexically marked prohibitions (e.g., *no, don't*) decline markedly as children's age increases. Fig. 13.1 shows the standardized average number of prohibitives children heard per 100 utterances in the play sessions that were analyzed.

Since the children in the New England sample were seen twice, at 14 and 20 months, we were able to examine possible developmental changes in the actual **form** of prohibitives mothers direct to their infants. As might be expected, mothers speaking to 14-month-olds used more direct prohibitives (69% direct versus 31% mitigated), whereas by 20 months the mothers produced about equal numbers of direct and mitigated prohibitives (53% versus 47%).

Gender differences

Detailed analysis of the prohibitives directed to infants and toddlers in both the New England sample and the Rondal corpus revealed some clear gender differences: In the New England sample, although there were no differences in the number of prohibitives directed to boys and to girls when the children were 14 months old, six months later, at 20 months, mothers were directing twice as many prohibitives to boys (3.8 per 100 utterances) as to girls (1.8 per 100 utterances), $p < .05$. At 20 months, boys heard more prohibitives than girls in both the mitigated and direct categories; but there were no gender differences in the *proportions* of mitigated and direct prohibitives heard by each group. Thus, 20-month-old girls did not hear a higher proportion of mitigated prohibitives than 20 month old boys, but they heard fewer prohibitives overall.

In the same sample, we also looked at the use of what we called CLUSTERED PROHIBI- TIVES: prohibitives embedded in a series of prohibitive utterances. At 20 months, boys heard nearly three times as many clustered prohibitives as girls: 14.7% to boys versus only 5.3% to girls, a significant difference, $p < .05$.

Similar gender differences were found in the small sample of mothers of young toddlers (age range 20-26 months) drawn from the Rondal Corpus. Here, more than twice as many prohibitives were directed to boys (2.4 per 100 utterances) as to girls (1.0 per 100 utterances), $p < .06$. Thus, very young boys hear many more prohibitives than girls, and they are more likely to hear them repeatedly. These gender differences can be seen in Fig. 13.2.

By preschool age, however, gender differences in the frequency of prohibitives were no longer apparent (Table 13.2). In both the Gleason and Warren-Leubecker corpora, the standardized number of prohibitives parents directed to boys and girls were not signifi- cantly different. In addition, there were no statistically significant differences between the frequency with which mothers and fathers directed prohibitives to their preschool children, either in play sessions or at dinner (Gleason corpus).

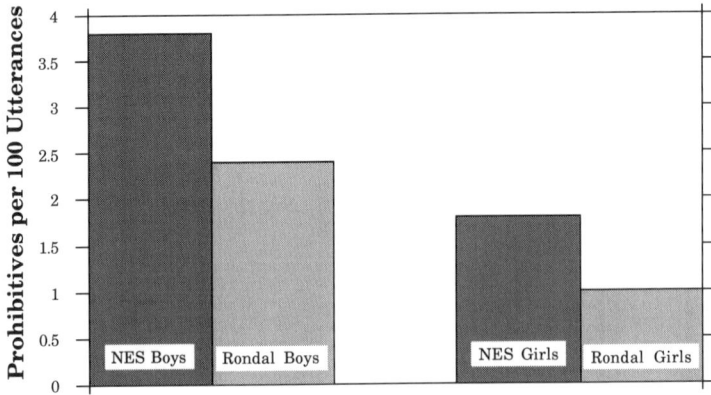

FIG. 13.2.   Gender differences in prohibitives to toddlers.

TABLE 13.2.   **Prohibitives per 100 utterances to preschoolers**

Corpus	N	Age (months)	Mothers		Fathers	
			Girls	Boys	Girls	Boys
Rondal - Older (older children)	12	28.8 (1.6)[1]	1.9	1.2	-	-
Gleason - Lab	12	51.2 (6.5)	0.6	0.8	0.8	1.1
Gleason - Dinner[2]	11	52.0 (6.1)	3.0	2.7	2.1	2.5
Warren-Leubecker (older children)	10	64.7 (8.2)	0.2	0.3	0.4	0.7

[1]   Standard deviations in parentheses.
[2]   Dinner transcripts from one family were unavailable.

Context

As noted earlier, the context or setting appears to influence the degree to which parents use prohibitives to guide their children's behavior. The developmental trends and the gender differences reported above were based on discourse drawn from dyadic (parent-child) play sessions, either at home or in the laboratory. Contextual differences were also examined in one of the samples (Gleason corpus); here we analyzed transcripts of family dinner time conversations and compared them with transcripts derived from the laboratory play sessions. The number of prohibitives used by mothers and fathers at dinner greatly exceeded the number of prohibitives they used in the laboratory, $p < .0001$. For mothers, the standardized mean number of prohibitives was nearly five times as high at dinner as in the laboratory: 2.9 versus 0.6, respectively; for fathers, the means were more than twice as high at dinner as in the laboratory, 2.3 versus 0.9, respectively. Contextual differences in the frequency of prohibitives can be seen in Fig. 13.3.

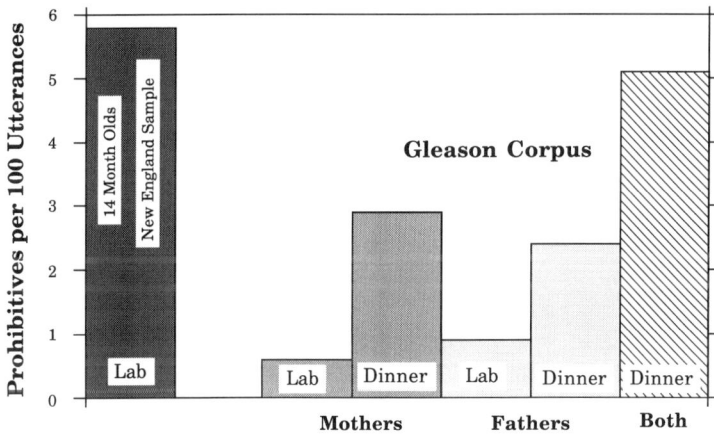

FIG. 13.3. Contextual differences in prohibitives to preschoolers.

It should also be noted that at dinner with their parents children hear prohibitives from both their fathers and mothers; when we combine the mothers' and fathers' prohibitives in these family dinners, the standardized rate is 5.1, a frequency comparable to that directed to the 14-month-olds in the play sessions (New England sample). Thus, lexically marked prohibitives are far more common in the dinner time discourse of parents of preschoolers than in dyadic (parent–child) play sessions in the laboratory.

CONCLUSION

In our data, there are clear developmental, gender, and contextual differences. In comparable play settings, infants and toddlers hear more direct prohibitives than preschool age children. Although there are no gender differences in the frequency of mothers' prohibitives to their 14-month-olds, by the time they are 20 months old, little boys hear many more, significantly more, prohibitives than little girls. This result is accentuated by the finding that boys tend to hear more repeated, or clustered prohibitives than girls.

One possibility, of course, is that the boys are engaged in more behaviors that elicit prohibition by their mother and need stronger language to be stopped. These children were all in the same situation, however, and there is no evidence in the observational notes in the transcripts that the boys were behaviorally different from the girls. Another interpretation of our findings is that mothers of boys and mothers of girls may make different assumptions about their children: For instance mothers of daughters may regard them as sensitive and easily dissuaded, and mothers of sons may think of them as impetuous and determined. Some of our own earlier research showed that daughters hear more diminutives, and are called by more loving pet names by both mothers and fathers. Boys hear more imperatives and are often addressed in a rougher manner. Here we have shown that they are told "*NO!*" much more frequently than girls, and these differences are well established by the time the children are 20 months old.

Even before 20 months, when differences in the frequency of prohibitives becomes significant, at 14 months and thereafter, we have some additional evidence that boys in these samples are treated in a tougher and more jocular manner, just as our own and others' previous research has shown. As we have noted earlier, mothers speaking to their infant sons, are more likely to call them by names that are not endearments (to put it mildly), and to invoke rather tough images in their speech to boys, and this seems to be a rather pervasive feature of speech to boys at all levels of our society. For instance, one of our colleagues who has recently had fraternal twins, one a girl and the other a boy, reports that even though she is familiar with our work on differences in speech to boys and girls, and has herself engaged in research on gender typing, she recently found herself calling her three month old infant son both *Champ* and *Tiger*! In the transcripts we have analyzed here, there are numerous examples of parents' use of such terms to their sons, but not to their daughters. To a 14-month-old boy:

Mother: "Don't put it in the trash! No, not over there, pal."

In speech to their sons, parents in our samples called them various jocular names such as *wise guy* and *pal*. Speech to the girls did not include such names. Thus, there are clear and consistent differences in the ways that parents speak to girls and boys.

This early linguistic socialization provides a model for children to use when speaking to boys and girls themselves, thus perpetuating this variation in the register that characterizes child directed speech. The parental style also sends children a message about how to construe their roles as males and females: Males must be told *"No!"* repeatedly and often, but females can be turned aside with a gentle word. If girls from early infancy are spoken to in a more indirect way, we can surmise that they learn to pay close attention to the speaker and become sensitive to subtle interpersonal cues in order to understand that statements like "We don't want to do that, sweetie" mean "Stop that!"; it is also likely that the stronger forms of prohibition ultimately have a negative effect on girls, since they are a departure from their usual experience. The language experience of girls may thus contribute to the kind of interpersonal sensitivity and vulnerability that are often thought of as innate female traits. By the same token, if young males routinely hear strong prohibitions and jocular names, they may come to expect directness and a level of "tough talk" from others. Here again, the linguistic socialization of males may contribute to their perceived characteristics.

We have also shown that lexically marked prohibitives are far more common in the dinner time discourse of parents of preschoolers than in dyadic (parent–child) play sessions. Thus, it is important when describing parent–child discourse to take account of the context. In the free play sessions, the frequency of parental prohibitions is highest in sessions with younger children and lowest with the older children. In general, the prohibitions to the young children have to do with behavioral socialization—for instance with preventing them from putting the crayons in their mouths; at the older ages the children were well comported in their play, and parents were easygoing and good natured in taking their leads from the children. This changes dramatically at the dinner table, where another type of socialization is undertaken with preschoolers, in this case socialization to behave politely at dinner: to refrain from talking with a full mouth, to use one's napkin, and so on. In this context the frequency of prohibitives, especially if we combine mothers' and fathers' speech to reflect the actual experience of the children, is almost as high as it is to 14-month-olds in the play sessions, the children who heard the highest frequency of prohibitives. In the intense socializing context of the family dinner, preschoolers hear as many prohibitives as they did when they were infants in other contexts. Considering these statistics, we should not be surprised if the family dinner is not a particularly enjoyable experience for either children or parents. Gender differences have been well established at earlier ages, and here at dinner the emphasis is on socialization of a more general nature, for girls and boys alike.

Gender differences are not immediately apparent to the casual observer of discourse between parents and children, and it is not always easy to determine the contextual variables that might account for the frequency of some features. In this chapter we have tried to show how the examination of just one feature of discourse, the use of prohibitives, may account for part of children's linguistic socialization in the broadest sense of the term.

REFERENCES

Cherry, L. (1975). The preschool teacher-child dyad: Sex differences in verbal interaction. *Child Development,* **46**, 532-535.

Dunn, J., Bretherton, I., & Munn, P. (1987). Conversations about feeling states between mothers and their young children. *Developmental Psychology,* **23**, 132-139.

Ely, R., & Gleason, J. Berko (in press). Socialization across contexts. In B. MacWhinney & P. Fletcher (Eds.), *Handbook of child language.* London: Blackwell.

Fernald, A. (1984). The perceptual and affective salience of mothers' speech to infants. In L. Feagans, C. Garvey & R. Golinkoff (Eds.), *The origins and growth of communication.* Norwood, NJ: Ablex.

Gleason, J. Berko (1975). Fathers and other strangers: Men's speech to young children. In D. Dato (Ed.), *Developmental psycholinguistics: Theory and application.* Washington, DC: Georgetown University Press.

Gleason, J. Berko. (1988). Language and socialization. In F. S. Kessel (Ed.), *The development of language and language researchers: Essays in honor of Roger Brown.* Hillsdale, NJ: Lawrence Erlbaum Associates.

Gleason, J. Berko, Perlmann, R.Y., Ely, R., & Evans, D. (1993). Aspects of babytalk: Parents' use of diminutives in speech to infants and children. In J. L. Sokolov & C. E. Snow (Eds.), *Handbook of research in language development using CHILDES.* Hillsdale, NJ: Lawrence Erlbaum Associates.

Lakoff, R. (1975). *Language and woman's place.* NY: Harper and Row.

MacWhinney, B., & Snow, C. (1990). The Child Language Data Exchange System: An update. *Journal of Child Language,* **17**, 547-472.

Perlmann, R. Y. (1984). *Variations in socialization styles: Family talk at the dinner table.* Unpublished doctoral dissertation, Boston University.

Rondal, J. (1978). Maternal speech to normal and Down's syndrome children matched for mean length of utterance. In C. E. Meyers (Ed.), *Quality of life in severely and profoundly mentally retarded people: Research foundations for improvement.* Washington D.C.: American Association on Mental Deficiency.

Rubin, J. Z., Provenzano, F. J., & Luria, Z. (1974). In the eye of the beholder. *American Journal of Orthopsychiatry,* **44**, 512-519.

Snow C. E., & Ferguson, C. A. (Eds.). (1977). *Talking to children: Language input and acquisition.* Cambridge, England: Cambridge University Press.

Snow, C. E., Perlmann, R. Y., & Nathan, D. (1987). Why routines are different: Toward a multiple-factors model of the relation between input and language acquisition. In K. E. Nelson & A. Van Kleek (Eds.), *Children's Language, Vol. 6*. Hillsdale, NJ: Lawrence Erlbaum Associates.

Tannen, D.   (1990).   *You just don't understand: Women and men in   conversation.*   New York: Ballantine.

Warren-Leubecker, A. (1982). *Sex differences in speech to children.*   Unpublished master's thesis, Georgia Institute of Technology.

14 REGULATING HOUSEHOLD TALK[1]

Laura Nader
University of California, Berkeley

In 1984 Susan Ervin-Tripp and her collaborators published an article called "Language and Power in the Family." This paper was based on research among four middle-class Berkeley, California families and concentrated on forms of requesting, or how children make requests of their primary caretaker. It was a paper about deference, demeanor, and mothering. The findings were intriguing and raised many questions about the relative distribution of power at least in four U. S. nuclear families. Dr. Ervin-Tripp and colleagues asserted that the children internalized gender rankings by using less polite forms to their mothers, and more mitigating expressions with their fathers. Specifically they found:

> The mothers in our sample were an important exception to the pattern of power and esteem correlating with age. In their role as care givers, they received non-deferent orders, suggesting that the children expected compliance and believed their desires to be justification . . . Though based on a small sample, these findings suggest many areas of family interaction that provide the training ground for later patterns of social behavior. In many respects, the structure of power and deference in adult life is prefigured in the families. (Ervin-Tripp, O'Connor, & Rosenberg, 1984, p. 135)

The paper stimulated many heated conversations about the significance of relative positions of mothers and their children in societies characterized by male dogma. Anthropologists who had completed long research stays in cultures as far from each other as Saudi Arabia and Mexico indicated to me that there was more variability in male dogma and how children spoke to their mothers as a result of same than we had previously thought. Somehow the results from the Ervin-Tripp et al. paper seemed counterintuitive because of the ranking accorded family members. From my work in Mexico and Lebanon it seemed "right" to expect father dominance to be followed by mother dominance with last place falling to children.

Discussions over the findings in "Language and Power in the Family" inspired me to write a paper titled "The Subordination of Women in Comparative Perspective" (1987)

[1] I am grateful to my students in Anthropology 3 class of 1985 for allowing me to study and utilize their Household Papers, to A. Khachadoorian for help in coding the data and discussing with me the significance of what was in the materials, and to T. Milleron, R. Milleron, and P. Dohlinow for perceptive critiques.

in which I noted that different structures of male domination were bound to result in different forms of female subordination which would be reflected in patterns of talk. Furthermore, the U.S. practices of motherhood where male dominance prevails had served to isolate women and to weaken their position in the family and society, as reflected in Ervin-Tripp's observations about Berkeley women receiving nondeferent orders from their young children.

Sociolinguists often describe marginal systems within languages such as hesitation forms, or politeness forms, but would it not be equally valuable to examine household talk more holistically? It would be useful to know by a look at regulation, at what channels and shapes household talk. The questions are two-fold: Can we make statements about household talk that are generally applicable to other group situations while at the same time articulating the nature of particular varieties of household talk?

In the present chapter I deal in a preliminary way with the question of who or what regulates talk in families or households. If the findings from the four Berkeley families study are widely applicable, then we might find patterns of regulating talk amongst American families that support assumptions of order underlying language and culture. Under such conditions the status of women in these settings would be shaped by household talk, what Ervin-Tripp refers to as "the training ground for later patterns of social behavior." But if there was greater variability in household talk than indicated by the study of four Berkeley families then we need to reconsider the significance of different "training grounds" and their relative frequencies. We also need to ponder the assumption that these household settings may regulate the performance of members in verbal expression and communication beyond household units; they might be retained as family-specific behavior especially if such verbal behaviors are in contradiction with the greater culture, in which individuals are contextualized in politics and economics, gender, ethnicity, class, race and other parts of life.

APPROACHING HOUSEHOLD TALK

Anyone who has contemplated studying talk or conversation knows access to households is a major problem for research in American society. So too is sampling a large number of households. Recognition of these and other methodological difficulties encouraged me to work with written materials produced for another purpose. For many years freshman students in my introductory class in sociocultural anthropology have written brief descriptions about specified aspects of their households as they remembered them from their senior year of high school. By assignment, they wrote two pages a week on such topics as household history, kinship and the household, division of labor in the household, household food patterns, and in addition to other topics they were to write on household talk patterns. The directions for household talk patterns were variations on the following paragraph:

> Just as cultures vary in the amount of talk and in the manner and place in which talk takes place, so do households. Where in your household does the greatest amount of talk take place? Where is silence expected? Is talk inter-generation-

al? What is talk like at the dinner table, e.g., what do you talk about, what is the place of humor, loud talk, etc. Were you taught of talk, e.g., how to handle intimidation by verbal retort? Or how to intimidate by verbal retort? Was there use of proverb or storytelling?

Partly I wanted to alert them to yet another aspect of culture that helped characterize their households; partly I was responding to the current lack of data on household talk patterns. Scholars in anthropology and other disciplines traditionally have not included data on language content when studying households. While data on social organization is included, as well as demographics, or ideology, or belief systems, language is most always missing, especially where it might have been expected as in the works of anthropologists writing on kinship in other cultures. For example, in a recent compilation of essays *Households — Comparative and Historical Studies of the Domestic Group* (Netting, Wilk, & Arnould, 1984), there is no mention at all of language, talk, or conversations in households and it does not matter whether the people studied are from other cultures or from our own. The authors in *Households* were concerned with types, forms, morphology and the like, not with talk or conversation.[2]

In contrast, popular authors like Bombeck give foremost place to language. Bombeck's (1987) description of the American family in *Family — the Ties that Bind. . . . and Gag!* is about talk, its absence, miscommunication or the astute observation that family members do not speak the same language (even though they would be classified as monolingual). While she is an author known for wit and humor, those who have lived in an American family know that her work is humorous partly because of its truth value. "There is simply less time to talk" is the way therapists, psychologists, and linguists may have put it. Bombeck may not be exaggerating when she notes after a family reunion:

The floodgates of the past opened and once again we slipped into the comfortable role of a family . . . One by one, stories were resurrected of the fun times we had shared. We must have sat there for five or ten minutes. (1987, p. 10)

Yet, her descriptions of one on one verbal exchanges standing outside the bathroom, in the garage or elsewhere indicate that talk is an integrated phenomenon, ubiquitously found in the household. Researchers may, as Ervin-Tripp does, look at request patterns, but if researchers **could** take a holistic view to understanding household talk we would have to include such items in our ethnography of communications (see Gumperz & Hymes, 1972) as:

I collared my son and said, "About the snake."

"Mom," he said, "there is no need to hyperventilate. It's just for a couple of days. Besides I thought mothers were supposed to be there for their children."

"You show me a boy who brings a snake home to his mother and I'll show

---

[2] Some anthropologists such as Bateson and his colleagues (1956) who worked on "double bind" theory certainly utilized family conversation in research on schizophrenia as did others interested in mental health problems. Linguists such as Ochs and colleagues have been studying discourse processes in American families. See for example Ochs, Smith, and Taylor (1989), and of related interest is the work of Schieffelin (1990) on children.

you an orphan."
His siblings joined in.   (Bombeck, 1987, p. 23)
or
We all froze like a tableau.
"Well, excuse me. I didn't realize there was someone still in this room"
. . . "It's your father . . . the 'Prince of Darkness' . . . making a point . . ."
His sermons on saving money and energy fell on deaf ears.   (Ibid, p. 29).

There is an effect of such humorous writings on household talk along with television shows like "The Brady Bunch," or "The Cosby Show," or "Leave it to Beaver." The portrayal of household conversation is always lively dinner-talk, friendly fireside chats, and meaningful exchanges of advice. Real households are different than entertainment, but many families may measure themselves against such portrayals.

Maybe only family members can study who or what regulates household talk or conversation — author-mothers like Bombeck, anthropologists, or students of anthropology who study their own families. As one student put it, "The home is like another world, one which outsiders will never witness as their very presence alters the scene and causes a different act to be performed."

LOOKING IN ON HOUSEHOLDS

What follows is a preliminary look at a sampling of student descriptions. I examined over 200 descriptions looking for styles, patterns and clues as to the ways in which household conversation is regulated in American households. These descriptions are constructed memory, what young students said they remembered about household talk patterns. While self-reporting is limited in scope, the descriptions nevertheless contained material useful to give overview and to encourage thinking about more holistic approaches to studies of household talk in order to redress the imbalance in the literature on households.

It was interesting that so many students thought their household had a unique style of talk, and prefaced their remarks by assertions of uniqueness. Some would start by noting that "unlike most American families there was not much conversation in our home." Some described household members as unique: the talkers, the listeners, the reticent, or the taciturn. Yet, a review of all their descriptions yielded characteristics shared with other households by virtue of similar cultural experiences.

The following excerpts were selected to illustrate the varied combinations of components that "regulate" talk, and to point out **difference**. Many of the writers indicate that demographics and life cycle changes such as divorce, death, or long working hours, or children leaving the household are reflected in household talk. Ethnicity, father-dominance, time, recipient bilingualism, limited biculturalism, and mediation are part of the household conversation descriptions. The first two excerpts are about talkative households.

Statements such as "we are a vocal family" are often followed by descriptions of talk as omnipresent.

1. Talking is an ongoing activity in our household . . . this is a household of chatter . . . I believe that our house is a particularly noisy one because we are Greek . . . where there is a congregation of people, there is conversation . . . there are times when silence is expected. My father normally goes to bed about nine . . . so calls are not expected after this time . . .

2. My family follows no set rules or guidelines concerning speech and conversation . . . has no guidelines for content of conversation at a given location or time. Serious, humorous, trivial, and all other categories of speech could take place anywhere and at anytime. Some dinners would be laughing, joking affairs, while some would be sullen and low-spirited.

Whether the household was perceived as talkative or lacking in conversation, there was often explanation. Keeping in mind that such explanation is often stereotypic and oversimplified, it is nevertheless useful to notice such perceptions as native categories. The size of the family (the more people, the more talk; or we talk a lot despite the small size of our family), ethnicity ("We're Greek, Irish, Hungarian," etc.), the absence of rules ("My family talks and jokes a lot everywhere. There are no real rules . . ."), the ubiquitous humor, family joking, and the association of talk with food all were often cited as significant.

Households of limited bilingualism exemplify the functional consequences of parents and children not sharing a common language. Children speak to each other in English, parents to each other in Tagalog, or Chinese, and to the children in English or "Chinglish." The children often speak not at all to monolingual non-English speaking relatives or "make it short" when they do. There is a good deal of anguish in describing lack of intergenerational conversation: "They only speak Chinese . . . they're just left out of our conversation." One report noted that when it was necessary they spoke. "Can you do the laundry tonight?" Parents ask questions such as "Did you call the insurance company yet?" The same person reported, "Sometimes there is no talk at all at the table because we don't have anything to ask them and they don't have anything to ask us about."

3. Lack of conversation is not uncommon in our present household of four . . . since dinnertime is one of the only times we are all together, it is where most conversations take place ... it does not consist of the general light conversations . . . I believe it is due to a feeling of discomfort between the children and the parents due to a linguistical gap in communication . . . Although it may seem odd, the younger of the children do not speak a lot to the parents because, since their knowledge of the English language has far surpassed their usage of the Chinese language, they find it difficult to speak to the parents of whose knowledge of the first two languages are the complete reverse of the children's. Thus, even simple conversations take a lot of effort for the two groups and often they end in frustration if one cannot communicate one's ideas to the other . . . There are very few private conversations in the household . . . probably due to the fact that it is easier to say something in public since one may attain the aid of a bystander in translating.

The following excerpt is about lack of conversation, thought to be somehow deviant or idiosyncratic under certain conditions, completely understandable by others. There is frequent reference to "my father doesn't like a lot of talking, so when he is around, the rest of the family doesn't talk too much," or "no real conversations between more than two people really occur," or "since we never formally eat together, it follows that no conversation takes place in the dining room except in passing." Others compare American with European eating patterns, pointing out that the Europeans have more time to talk because of the midday family meal.

> 4. At the breakfast table, conversation is limited by the fact that family members tend to eat independently. My father enjoys listening to the radio and reading the morning paper as he eats; he speaks very little with my mother, who also reads the paper . . . Like breakfast, conversation at lunch is limited by the fact that family members do not often eat as a single unit . . . [but when they do] there is not much conversation . . . although there is no awkward silence either. Conversation is limited to comments about the food and other trivial matters. One reason for the "shallowness" . . . could be that we are all fast eaters with the exception of my father. We tend to concentrate on eating, and perhaps we treat conversation as a distraction . . . The greatest amount of conversation takes place while watching television, and the least during dinner and on long automobile rides.

Limited talk or conversation seems to accompany formality about when and where one can talk, to whom, but again purely structural reasons are given: "My parents are workaholics (working from 8 a.m. to 8 p.m.) so they are absent from the household around eating times." In the same vein children of immigrants whose parents are pursuing the "American dream," (and **many** descriptions reported on the impact of pursuit of the American dream) and children of mother-child households say that occasions for talk are rare: "My mother was working 14 hours a day, 5 days a week, two jobs plus a third one on Saturday . . . There was not much conversation in our home." Reports from such households indicate that conversation in such homes are dyadic rather than group. Such households do not organize what some describe as "family meetings" or "town meetings," events which seem to result from a focus on the family as a **group** rather than a set of dyadic constructs, as in the following example.

> 5. Talking while we were eating dinner was an exception, because we had so much to catch up on . . . In contrast to when we were eating dinner, talking while watching T. V. was "illegal" in my household . . . While driving on long trips, we usually have nothing better to do than talk and listen to music . . . Silence is never expected in the living room. We get loud in the car and quiet when we work.

Sometimes reports of "rules" governing talk were not justified. They were "just there" — as for example the family that did not allow singing at the table, although there was no explanation for why there was such a rule. The following excerpt is indicative of a context both structured and strained.

> 6. The dinner table is where the talk is most structured according to social role. My father can talk to all and ask questions, and will not be interrupted. My brother and I can talk back and forth across the table, but if we get out of hand my parents will interrupt . . . I was usually silent. Since I did not enjoy my

father's company I would answer his questions as quickly as possible . . . My mother did most of the talking . . . My father, always wanting to be in control, would often give orders. [Talk] was usually strained if my father was present. Many of the statements from bi-cultural descriptions refer to "family hierarchy" and "power structure" as relevant to the place and content of speech: "We tend to hold back a lot because we are intimidated by my father. My father, being the authority figure, tends to dominate all conversations." The following is an example of cultural etiquette about children being quiet.

7. In our household, there were many unspoken rules dealing with saying the right words at the right time. This was because my parents were strict, and also because they were brought up in India where there is a closely followed etiquette on speaking to others . . . Dinnertime was the one time during the day that the family sat down together, but it was not where most conversations took place . . . chatty little children are always told to talk less and eat more at dinner, and so it is a virtue to be able to finish the meal quickly and quietly . . . Most real family conversation on weekdays took place after dinner . . . in the living room. Just as my brother, sister and I were more talkative when my parents were out, we were also more quiet when they were there. In Indian society, being quiet is associated with being good-natured and thoughtful. This is why a quiet person is more likely to be publicly praised than a talkative one, although the latter may be more amusing. . . . We had a lot of respect and order in our family, but at times, it was at the expense of much-needed communication.

Although some people do not see lack of conversation as indicative of weak family ties, others most certainly see the absence of talk as somehow not "normal," a lack.

8. Conversation is one thing that my family lacks . . . This is mainly due to the formal type of household . . . I must be very careful in addressing my mother or my stepfather because I am the youngest one in the family and I have to use the appropriate level of Indonesian language. Also I must choose the appropriate topics . . . I am not supposed to talk to my mother or my father about my relationships with friends.   The most appropriate topic on which I converse . . . is my study, but there is not much I can tell them; as a result, I do not talk very much at home.

9. Most of my family get-together is held in the living room where my father takes over a spotlight, talking to us about politics and other repetitious subjects . . . My father holds the highest rank in the family . . . Manner in which my father talks is very commanding, and most of his talk is about schools and politics as to which school's the best or how Korea'll reunify someday . . . As dull as our family seems to be, there are times when the whole family burst into a big laughter . . . My mom's usually responsible for this brief moment of family joy. She'd make us laugh by trying to speak in English . . . There's a time . . . when my family does not talk at all. That's at dinner time . . . "When you're eating, you shouldn't talk" my pa would say . . . My father's discipline is that one must retain the taciturn, patient, and quiet characteristics . . . One

time when my brothers and I broke into a loud talk in the livingroom, which is next to my parent's room, we got into big trouble. My father scorned us for nearly twenty minutes, lecturing to us about etiquette . . . When I have my family . . . I'll make sure that . . . my house will be full of laughter and happy, loud family.

Talk that was regulated by cultural etiquette, if that is what is operating in the above three examples, may be distinguished from what some called "family specific" patterns, as in talk characterized by an implicit control style. The following excerpt is an example of indirect control in nonbicultural households.

10. The amount of time spent talking in my household is quite substantial . . . The dinner table . . . is where the most discussion is likely to take place . . . When I get home from school, my mother and I have several hours to ourselves and we have lots of opportunity for discussion . . . One time . . . when talking is really restricted is as soon as my father walks in the door from work. My mother and I know that we must take care not to hassle him before he has time to change and come down for dinner . . . I just know it is a definite time to keep my mouth shut . . . After dinner my parents are both willing to talk and I enjoy it very much . . . In general, we have a lot of communication in my household.

One report described a "father's intolerance for disagreement, which he interpreted as defiance, and for loud talk which he considered disrespectful." The same person noted that the amount and nature of conversation were limited not only by his father's intolerance but also by the "omnipresent television set." Many referred to the father's role as explicitly regulative.

11. [Conversation] rules were set down primarily by my father. Although talking and joking were frequent elements of the household . . . he could determine when and how it was going to stop . . . the moment Dad walked in from work, Mom would instinctively run over to her radio and shut it off. Conversations would stop . . . We were expected and trained to abide by his silence rules . . . Yet, by dinner time, he had unwound and conversation began to flow . . . At the dinner table, we still talked largely about his work . . . Occasions where silence reigned . . . when he wanted to sleep . . . when he was doing something important to him . . . There was a time when we could freely talk . . . at the table on Sunday nights . . . A little gossip and some happy stories . . . sometimes he would break out into some old German songs.

There was a sizable number of examples of household talk regulated by an ethic of harmony. One description listed the rules: no interrupting, no yelling, no arguing, no using examples from the past, which might impede harmony construction. Others said their mother liked peaceful mealtime talk and if discussion turned with an argument it would be continued elsewhere. One made the distinction between "safe" conversations — dinner table talk about sports, music, or local events, or "war" conversations — emotional and heated verbal exchange about economics, politics, or in-laws, events that generated what one person called "conversation evasion."

12. Conversation would be intentionally directed by my parents towards light

subjects and daily events. Any unsettling controversy or family quarrels were discouraged while at the meal. Normal meal-time conversation would include anything from our school situation to Soviet politics, as long as it did not blemish the harmony of the gathering.

Others often spoke of lightheartedness:

13. Since we usually eat two to three meals a day in the kitchen, it is the room of most talk . . . the conversations there are generally lighthearted and concern the events of the day or near future. Because everyone feels most comfortable speaking at dinnertime, however, the conversations can get very emotional, making the kitchen table the primary place of humor and loud talk. . . . Silence is expected for reasons of common courtesy and religious respect. Common courtesy may mean moving the phone when your conversation is bothering someone. . . . Religious respect refers to the Roman Catholic tradition of saying "grace" before eating a meal. . . . The type of conversation often depends on the individual speaking as well. . . .

It appears that households with least explicit regulation are more uninhibited in talk. Some spoke of yelling as a way of communicating and commented on visitors who were not accustomed to yelling being uncomfortable until they realized that yelling was customary. A daughter spoke of her relationship to her mother with whom disagreements were easily and loudly verbalized. Her stepfather was hesitant to verbalize conflict: "Where conflict arose we spoke different languages-one Jewish, the other Irish." In a similar vein loud is considered fun conversation.

14. In my household, conversation takes place in a variety of forms and found throughout most of the house. Loud talk, which is the most interesting and fun form of conversation, generally takes place in the kitchen or the family room. Rules on when and how to speak (i.e. loud or soft) are not specifically drawn or enforced . . . they are accepted as "common sense" guidelines. For instance, when someone is watching television or listening to the radio, people are expected to keep their voices at a low . . . The only strictly kept rule . . . concerning speaking is the fine of one dollar for someone who tells another member of the family to "shut-up. . . ." One of the most interesting situations for conversations . . . is on the Sabbath . . . During the prayers and blessings over the wine and bread, silence is expected and talk is considered rude. After the blessings . . . talk resumes on a loud and expressive scale . . . involves politics, weekly activities, school, work . . . Israeli and American politics.

While the following excerpt is from a household with a strong value on "speaking up," another student reported that being democratic was fine in theory but outside the house democratic impulses had to be tempered: "What was 'free speech' to my parents was 'smarting off' to my grandmother. What was 'expressing myself' to my family was 'talking dirty' to my teachers." The answer he concluded was "communicative adaptability," an indication that household settings may not regulate communication beyond household units.

15. Most of the conversations take place in the living room and at the dinner table. My parents usually lead the conversations, but it is always acceptable for

the children as well as myself, to interject our own ideas and feelings. . . . This freedom of expression within our household has made each one of us relatively uninhibited . . . Often . . . this does as much harm as good . . . we are forever getting into trouble at school for expressing opinions that are either stated at the wrong time or are inappropriate to a classroom situation . . . My father always said, "Will you just say what you want to say?"

Gender-specific talk seemed to cut across ethnicities and religious differences. Let me illustrate by series of statements:

16. The men in my family usually talk about business and sports whereas the women talk about cooking and soap operas. None of these topics really interests the opposite sex. It is difficult for me to picture my sister speaking about Wall Street as it is to hear my father talk about general hospital . . . the reason why the women are silent at dinner is because my brother, father, and myself are discussing something. (male)

17. Talk with my mother is rather colloquial and familiar, while with my father it is more formal. (male)

18. If someone asked my father a question in the living room while he was reading . . . that someone might never get an answer. My mother was pretty much accessible at all times. In fact she loved to talk with us . . . my father would talk about the news, science, or politics; my mother liked talking about what was happening in our lives. This difference does not mean that my mother does not know about politics . . . she does . . . (female)

19. Phone calls are a real good example of the difference in the patterns of conversation used . . . when my dad talks . . . he'd ask how school is, say I sound fine and ask if I want to speak to my mother. Mom on the other hand, will talk to me up to half an hour on twenty different subjects . . . Although I do horse around with my dad, I seem to joke with my mom a lot more and she jokes back also. She also accepts the swearing more than my dad. (male)

20. My mother's appearance in the house unified our small separate conversations . . . When my father spoke we also listened out of respect but his words did not have the group impact that my mother's words did because he was not viewed as the discipliner and usually did not have important household affecting news to tell us. (male)

These excerpts basically corroborate the assertions that each household has its unique profile, in the sense that households have their own gestalt. In some households talk is not allowed at dinner, in another it is. In some, T. V. is a time for silence, in others a time for talk. Mostly humor is reported as ubiquitous where talk occurs, and mostly the young think loud is fun. In some families only the father can dominate; in others it is free and relatively uninhibited expression. Frustration may occur because of limited bilingualism or biculturalism, and learning the rules of talk is not always easy. In some households the rules are unspoken, in others explicit. A degree of variation not reported in sociolinguistic studies of the family.

Beyond all this variation, is there anything that is characteristic of all of these households, are there common dynamics that shape, channel or filter household talk? For all the uniqueness there is something about the profiles that reflected class position, whether the household could afford a kitchen, a dining area, a living room, bedrooms, television, a child that went to college.

HOUSEHOLD TALK:
QUANTITATIVE ANALYSIS AND ROUTINIZED PATTERNS

Coding household talk does not yield the "feel" for a holistic perspective on who regulates talk, but in the hopes of discovering something about the dynamics of language and power in the family, I developed a code and with the help of a research assistant set about looking for patterns and corelational phenomenon for categories covered topics such as where the majority of talk took place, when, what rules governed household dinner talk, and what tone the majority of talk had, such as loud, soft, funny, serious. Other divisions included power, tension and humor, many of which were deemed important enough to have been frequently mentioned. It had been a long time since I had tried such an approach, and I was surprised by my own revulsion at reducing what were basically autobiographical statements about a unitary to numbers reducing the unit to parts. Nevertheless, and revulsion to one side, the exercise stimulated some insight as to the dynamics of household talk, or its absence, some of which is reported in what follows.

From the point of view of young people household talk is primarily regulated by adults, particularly by the father, by work outside the family, by common language, or not regulated at all. None of the statements indicated that talk was regulated by the power of children. This is interesting because so many descriptions of the American family see family interaction as child-centered.

While around half of the students observed the role of the dominant father, few spoke of the dominant mother. Those that did referred to the amount of talking as "fill in" or to her influence on the style and content of meal talk that was "pleasant and not argumentative." About a third of the households were described as neither mother or father dictated, rather egalitarian or mutually respectful.

Avoidance habits were as common as argumentative ones. Families who prefer to avoid spending a good deal of time in each others company do not waste time in small-talk or storytelling but use their limited contact to do "business" — that is address family issues and keep up to date on issues that require decision-making. Many of the statements spoke of the presence of humor in family talk and it is a toss up whether such humor (hostile, light, and spontaneous) should be taken at facevalue or seen also as avoidance and as many said, tension reducing. The same might be said of patter talk. Confrontative patterns were part of the father-dominated households, as well as the more boisterous and egalitarian households. Very few students connected the style of talk (whether confrontative or avoiding) to their talk outside of the household except to say confrontatious, argumentative, and debating styles got them in trouble in school settings, at least before college.

One does not leave this body of data with a sense of dynamic processes that are creative or imaginative. Rather the word *gestalt* is more appropriate, because family talk falls into a patterned form, maybe even a rigid form and stays that way until demographics or any special life cycle event change. Small talk, rap talk, even humor talk or sermon talk is not creative in the sense of ongoing exchange. Perhaps most families are prone to routinized talk. Perhaps that routinization is what cements their family as a culture. The reports are sometimes specific about this as in the following example:

> When we eat dinner together we talk.
> My mother says, "Son, how was your day?"
> I say, "Okay." Sometimes I elaborate.
> Then my father says, "How was work today, dear?"
> "Long and tiring," my mother replies.
> He says, "Oh."
> I say, "How was your day, Dad?"
> "The usual. Boring and tedious."
> That's about it.
> After dinner my father reads and drinks a cup of coffee.
> He sometimes quizzes me about school and my grades.
> "How are you holding up in school, son?"
> "Well enough."
> "Getting good grades?"
> "Yeah."
> If I had to draw any conclusions I would say that my family doesn't communicate much by talking.

Another notes:

> Eating at the dinner table and discussing the events of our day every evening is sort of like a ritual. It is a ritual in the sense that it is a repeated act every night in which the members of my family exchange their daily experience as part of our "family togetherness" . . . my father has a huge beer belly, so we usually make jokes about him being fat. My brother has a really close shaved hair cut so we usually call him "big head" or "rock head" . . . My mother often flies off the handle when she is mad so we call her 'mean Susie', and the Tasmanian Devil . . . there are never any hard feelings . . .

Their descriptions of formulaics are humorous because of their caricatured quality:

> Mom would usually start by rambling off things that happened at work, either positive or derogatory. Next would come Dad's classic line he's been saying every night since any of us kids can remember. "How was your day at school?" This was addressed to each of us and often we'd retort with, 'How come you always ask that?' And the expected reply comes, 'Because I'm interested in what you kids do.' From here the conversation would start and gain speed . . .

Descriptions of gestalt or formed patterns are certainly in the data but patterns do not describe everything found in a data set, especially talk in household were to be tracked through the life cycle of households, which it usually is not in our set. Order as well as the lack of order is likely to be the underlying reality of most households. Households in constant flux resemble chaos more than gestalt when viewed comparatively. Order and lack of order are both intrinsic features of and determinants of household conversation. If there is structure in what I will call nongestalt households, its prime feature is loose structure. In other words both order and lack of order are found in this sample reminding us that while the group may be most important for many households, the household is also made up of individuals whose unique trajectories generate the dynamic potential in the gestalt.

CONCLUDING REMARKS

At the start of this research my expectation for finding patterns in the regulation of household talk from self-reporting was optimistic. After all, culture is patterned, and language is even more patterned. My comment that the variations reported were unexpected revealed an implicit bias for order, but it was not strong enough to sustain me. While thinking about the data I read a series of papers published by Ochs and her colleagues (1989, 1992a, 1992b) as part of their research on discourse processes in American families. If I had read the work prior to the present analysis of several hundred descriptions about household talk I might have nodded in assent at their findings.

For example, in their first paper "Mother's Role in the Everyday Reconstruction of 'Father Knows Best'," Ochs and Taylor analyze the dinnertime narratives of seven two-parent families who reside in Southern California with their young children (5 years and older). "All seven families are 'English-speaking, European-American, and earned over $40,000 a year.'" The families were videotaped and audiotaped twice. The 100 narratives (reports and stories) comprised their data base. In their conclusion they suggest that the "Father Knows Best" gender ideology was in considerable evidence; the authors point to the degree to which women as wives and mothers contribute to this patriarchal style through their dinnertime narratives.

A second paper, "Family Narrative as Political Activity," uses what appears to be the same data base to conclude something about "how the family is constructed as a political institution through conversational interaction." Both papers are driven by pattern analysis, written in an almost scientific manner with attentiveness to precision through the use of technical language, not necessarily a sign of precision. Both papers indicate that the authors have concluded something about family narratives in seven families that is more widely generalizable than my experience suggests they should be. Perhaps the discrepancy between the present data and theirs are caused by a difference in method rather than over-patternizing on their part, something that can be checked in future studies.

Having concluded my preliminary examination of more than 200 descriptions of household talk, themselves part of a series of descriptions about other aspects of the household, I thought about the degree of order that was implied in the Ochs et al. papers on discourse and their generalizability. I was trying to deal with was an extraordinary amount of variation. The macropolitical life of the family can be talked about or avoided as a topic of family talk exactly because of the effect on the family, as for example in the firing of a parent by a company (not spoken about at dinnertime), or because of the conflict between an egalitarian home, and sexist, racist features of the society at large.

In other words my sampling made me question the significance and generalizability from both sets of materials. I might say the data humbled me, and the experience generated a critical perspective on the kind of discourse analysis carried out by Ochs and colleagues albeit based on video and audio taped materials rather than self-reporting. I kept thinking I was possibly missing something. At the same time my experience argued there was something wrong. The Ochs material was too ordered, and mine not ordered enough, and that fact could not be explained by the difference in what we were looking at — in her case discourse arranged for taping, in mine what was being reported about the regulation of talk in household.[3] The rereading of Friedrich's 1986 book relieved my anxieties. In his work, *The Language Parallax*, Friedrich refers to the "rage for order" serving to silence the reality of lack of order:

> Firm faith in a mechanistic order in language and culture has often been com-
> bined with the principle of "fruitfulness" (or heuristic value) to mislead linguists
> into both exaggerating order in the phenomenon being studied and generalizing
> it. This emerges in the statements by leading theorists that language, in this
> ordered sense, is ubiquitous, all-pervasive,and universally operative: a sort of

---

[3] How would the following fit into contemporary discourse analysis:
"In terms of conversation, the one thing I ever wanted from my family was complete silence in the morning. They, of course, had difference conversation requirements, which included lots of noise and useless chatter in the morning.

My ideal would be to rise in the morning, go through the cleansing process, dress, eat breakfast, read the paper — all in complete silence to allow me crucial contemplative time — a chance to organize my thoughts for the day, to think of something funny to say to that certain girl or an explanation for my lack of homework. Each morning I hoped for this, but it never happened.

My father is the only one in the family like me. His answer to this daily problem would be to get up, shave, dress, and quickly leave. No shower, no breakfast and almost no talk — he was usually out the door in less than ten minutes after rising. But best of all he had a solitary forty-five minute commute. I really envied him.

All I could do was try and block my mother, brother and sister out and answer their pointedly useless questions as shortly and with as little enthusiasm as possible. This did much to curtail my brother and sister — unless they were in especially feisty or cruel moods — but this method did nothing to stop my mother who is always incredibly and falsely happy in the morning. She thought it would make us feel more cared for or help do better in school or something. Anyways, her attitude was to pester me repeatedly with questions and cheerfulness until I left for school.

Both my parents worked full time so it was not until dinner that the family gathered again completely. When we were younger our parents directed the conversation in a way that entertained us, at the same time they enforced proper table manners. I remember these times with fondness and a certain longing. They were always humorous and innocent.

By the time I was through high school they had changed completely. I don't know if we realized our parents were boring, if we had too many other things on our minds, or if the conversation became just too forced. My mother made a strong effort not just to teach us proper table manners, but to teach us interesting and intellectual conversation. My brother and sister began to miss meals frequently, they accredited this to school and friend activities, things beyond their control, but it was an actual desire to avoid the dinner table.

I always stayed at home for dinner. Perhaps, I felt guilty for my attitude in the morning or perhaps I felt more responsibility to my parents. Anyway, I always ate with them. However, I came to say less and less, until I got so that I was silent for the entire meal. It was of great relief to leave for college."

projection onto the entirety of experience of a linguistic order from which no one is ever free — a claim which is of course partly, but only partly true. (p. 138)

Perhaps the most general of the research problems that are raised would be to show empirically that many of the orders that have been posited are actually false reductions or false expansions, or that the data that were . . . overordered, were/are in fact significantly chaotic (p. 149).

Friedrich's observations on a more "open linguistics" are applicable to the question in this paper about who or what regulates talk in households. What Friedrich calls the paradox of order and the lack of order forced me to think carefully about what could be coded, forced the rethinking about the usual analysis using ideal informant. What remains is to use sets of methodological approaches to understanding such that one kind of insight (as in discourse analysis) does not block out other equally valuable finding (as in ethnographic self-reporting) by dogmatic adherence to single methods of analysis which may be more amenable to expression in percentages, charts, and the likes. Even controlling for two-parent families, monolinguality, sex of the informant, and income did not yield patterns in terms of where the most talk happened, where we found silence, and the meaning of any such findings. Indeed, if the students had recorded actual dinnertime discourse their analysis of same might have contradicted their own descriptions which included a wider scope. Questions can be answered in different ways. The approach used in this paper reveals far more variability than earlier papers suggest. The key methodological point would indicate that the ethnographic self-reporting method may reveal a kind of data not found in the discourse analytical approach, data which complicates the possibilities for answering two of the questions the study raised earlier — is father-dominance of household talk prevalent? and is household talk the training ground for later patterns of social behavior? The answers to such difficult questions must lie in what Gumperz and Hymes (1972) called *ethnography of communication*, referring to the idea in ethnography that a plethora of methods used simultaneously are the most likely to yield answers.

REFERENCES

Bateson, G., Jackson, D., Haley, J., & Weakland, J. (1956). Toward a theory of schizophrenia. *Behavioral Science*, 1, 251-264.

Bombeck, E. (1987). *Family — The ties that bind. . . . And Gag!* New York: McGraw Hill Book.

Ervin-Tripp, S., O'Connor, M. O., & Rosenberg, J. (1984). Language and power in the family. In C. Kramarae, M. Schultz, & W. M. O'Barr (Eds.), *Language and power* (pp. 116-135). New York: Sage.

Friedrich, P. (1986). *The language parallax: Linguistic relativism and poetic indeterminacy.* Austin: University of Texas Press.

Gumperz, J., & Hymes, D. (Eds.) (1972). *Directions in sociolinguistics: The ethnography of communication.* New York: Holt, Rinehart and Winston.

Nader, L. (1987). The subordination of women in comparative perspective. In A. S. Barnes (Ed.), *Urban Anthropology*, 15, 377-397.

Netting, R., Wilk, R. R., & Arnould E. J. (1984). *Households: Comparative and historical studies of the domestic press.* Berkeley: University of California Press.

Ochs, E., Smith, R., & Taylor, C. (1989). Detective stories at dinnertime: Problem-solving through co-narration. *Cultural Dynamics*, 2, 238-257.

Ochs, E., & Taylor, C. (1992a). Family narrative as political activity. *Discourse and Society*, 3, 301-334.

Ochs, E., & Taylor, C. (1992b). Mother's role in the everyday reconstruction of "Father knows best." In K. Hall, M. Bucholtz & B. Moonwomon (Eds.), *Proceedings of the Berkeley Women and Language Conference, vol. 2* (pp. 447-462). Berkeley, CA: University of California at Berkeley.

Schieffelin, B. (1990). *The give and take of everyday life: Language socialization of Kaluli children.* Cambridge: Cambridge University Press.

15 THE USE OF POLITE LANGUAGE BY JAPANESE PRESCHOOL CHILDREN[1]

Keiko Nakamura
University of California, Berkeley

Japanese is a language particularly rich in grammaticalized features in the social/relational domain. Any study of polite language in Japanese would reveal enormous differences in usage according to various factors, such as gender, age, dialect, educational background, context (e.g., topic of conversation, formality of setting), and degree of familiarity. Politeness can be both nonverbal and verbal. Nonverbal politeness includes bowing, physical distance, and posture. Verbal politeness in Japanese involves two dimensions, namely: (1) formality, which reflects the psychological and/or social distance between participants, and (2) honorific and humble language, which indicates respect and deference. The system of polite language in Japanese applies not only to pronouns (as in Indo-European languages), but also to verbs, adjectives, nouns, and conventional expressions. Furthermore, politeness is also marked by paralinguistic features such as intonation, as well as conversational strategies such as indirectness.

Speakers of a given language must have more than mere linguistic competence. To use language effectively, they must undergo language socialization and develop communicative competence (Hymes, 1972). All languages have pragmatic rules, and politeness is an integral part of pragmatic competence. A speaker with a fluent command of a variety of politeness styles is capable of communicating effectively in a wide range of social roles. For the nonnative speaker, it is often these pragmatic subtleties that prove to be more difficult than the use of complicated vocabulary and grammatical constructions.

In order to comprehend and produce polite language, children must first learn the linguistic forms of politeness, and second, they must understand the pragmatic rules that govern each socio-interactional context (Ervin-Tripp, 1977). Children's appropriate use of polite language is dependent upon their language acquisition, cognitive development, and social experience. The data presented here are from a study of polite speech used by Japanese preschoolers. The children, ages 3 to 5, were able to use a wide range of polite language in pragmatically appropriate ways. Research on children's acquisition of

---

[1] This research was supported by a Fulbright award from the Japan-United States Educational Commission, and doctoral dissertation grants from the National Science Foundation and the Woodrow Wilson National Fellowship Foundation. The original idea for this paper came from a seminar on politeness given by Susan Ervin-Tripp in the Spring of 1989.

235

Japanese, a language with an extremely elaborate politeness system, can help better our understanding of children's pragmatic development and communicative competence.

THE ACQUISITION OF POLITE LANGUAGE BY ENGLISH-SPEAKING CHILDREN

Social routines are usually the earliest form of polite speech used by children. Children rapidly learn to recognize specific social contexts and produce ritualized expressions such as *hi, thank you,* and *please.* Unlike other aspects of language, such as syntax and semantics, parents often directly instruct their children in the use of social routines, as well as polite language (e.g., Grief & Gleason, 1980).

Children initially use language as a tool for interacting within the immediate home environment, but gradually must use it to deal with a vast number of different individuals and situations. Over the years, children become more skillful at modifying the form and/or content of their speech to fit the situational context. Early research (e.g., Piaget, 1926; Lakoff, 1973) claimed that young children were insensitive to listener and contextual variations, and could not alter their speech in socially appropriate ways until they reached age 7 to 10. Using experimental tasks, some researchers have claimed that children do not fully master polite register until age 7 to 9, although they can produce and understand polite sentences at about age 5 to 6 (e.g., Axia & Baroni, 1985).

Relying on naturalistic observations and role-playing tasks, recent research has illustrated that even young children are capable of comprehending and making politeness-related adjustments in their speech. Much of this research has focused on requests. Children both produce and comprehend a wide range of request forms by the time they are 4 to 5 years of age (e.g., Bruner, Roy, & Ratner, 1982; Ervin-Tripp, 1977). With age, there is an increased proportion of indirect directives (e.g., Ervin-Tripp, 1982; Ervin-Tripp, O'Connor, & Rosenberg, 1984). Furthermore, children become better at making sophisticated judgments about the "niceness" and appropriateness of requests, based on factors such as syntactic directness, semantic markers and tone (e.g., Bates, 1976; Becker, 1986). These results show that even before they begin formal schooling, children have fairly sophisticated knowledge of the rules governing appropriate language use.

POLITENESS AND HONORIFICS IN JAPANESE

Most descriptions of Japanese *keigo* 'polite language' divide *keigo* into three general categories: *sonkeigo,* 'honorific/respectful language', *kenjoogo* 'humble language', and *teineigo* 'formal language'. In addition, many grammarians have advocated the use of a fourth category, namely *bikago* 'beautification honorifics'. These four categories combine to form an extremely complicated system (refer to Bunkacho, 1974, and Martin, 1975, for a full description of the *keigo* system).

Many factors are involved in the use of *keigo.* Neustupny (1978) and Niyekawa

(1991) claimed that polite language is determined by factors such as status (e.g., rank/position, age, and sex) and group orientation. Mizutani and Mizutani (1983) asserted that current use of honorific and polite language serves to mark social and psychological distance. Oishi (1983) claimed that polite language is not only indicative of respect, but also suggests good upbringing and cultural refinement. He listed respect, formality, distance, demeanor (beautification), and sarcasm as the five functions of *keigo*. It appears that *keigo* is moving away from its initial purpose of indicating respect to one's superiors, and is gradually becoming more of an indicator of psychological and/or social distance and a mark of good breeding.

Sonkeigo 'respectful/exalted language'

Sonkeigo 'subject honorifics' are used to show respect when one is describing another's actions (if you are addressing or talking about a person whose social status is higher than yours). For example, the question, *Sensei wa meshiagarimasu ka?,* could mean 'will you (the teacher) eat (this)?' or 'will he/she (the teacher) eat (this)?' *Sonkeigo* raises the referent's status by increasing the vertical distance between the speaker and the referent (usually an out-group member such as the speaker's superior). Verbs that are used frequently tend to have honorific lexical substitutes. For example, in the case of the verb *suru* 'to do' (neutral form), *nasaru* is the honorific form. For verbs that do not have lexical substitutes, honorific forms are produced grammatically, either: (1) by adding *o-* and *-ni naru* to the verb stem (e.g., *kaku* 'to write' -> *o-kaki ni naru*) or (2) by attaching the passive suffix *-are* to the consonant-ending root of a verb, or *-rare* to the vowel-ending root of a verb (e.g., *kaku* 'to write'-> *kakareru*). As for nominal referents, one can add honorific suffixes such as *-san* or *-sama* to last names, first names, and kinship terms (e.g., *Yamada-san*). Most individuals who have titles are addressed by their titles (e.g., *shachoo* for the president of a company).

Many nouns can take honorific prefixes such as *o-, go-,* and *on-* to refer to actions and objects belonging to people the speaker respects (e.g., *go-kekkon* 'marriage', *o-namae* 'name'). A small number of adjectives and adverbs also may take the *go-* or *o-* prefix, either to express respect for the addressee, or as refinement. For example, the prefix *o* can be added to the adjectival stem as in *o-genki desu* 'he/she is well'. There are also special honorific terms that are used to refer to someone else's family (e.g., *go-ryooshin* 'parents').

Kenjoogo 'humble/deferent language'

Unlike *sonkeigo,* a humble form increases the vertical distance between the speaker and the referent by lowering the speaker's status. Humble forms (object honorifics) are used to depict actions of the speaker/ in-group member in relation to the referent. Verbs that are used often tend to have humble lexical substitutes. For example, *moosu* is the humble form of the verbs *iu* 'to say'. As in the case of *sonkeigo,* humble forms are produced grammatically for verbs that do not have lexical substitutes, by adding *o-* and *-suru* to the verb stem (e.g., *kaku* 'to write' -> *o-kaki suru*). In the sentence *kaban o o-mochi shimasu* 'I will carry your bag', the speaker elevates the referent by referring humbly to his own actions.

The first person pronoun has a humble form, *watakushi*. Several nouns can take humble prefixes, but these are not common, due to morphological constraints. There are also special humble nouns that are used to refer to one's own family (e.g., *haha* 'mother'). Adults who use incorrect forms to refer to their own family members when speaking to out-group members are considered poorly educated.

Teineigo 'addressee honorifics'

Teineigo describes language that is formal and polite, as opposed to language that is informal and casual. It is used in order to show consideration to others, and to show "respect" to the addressee (Bunkacho, 1986). Formality involves a dimension separate from honorific/humble language. For example, it is possible to be informal, and yet show respect to the referent. If one were to ask *ashita sensei irrasharu?* 'Is the professor going tomorrow?' to a friend, one would use the honorific predicate *irrasharu* to describe the action of the referent, although the predicate itself is in informal form since it is being used in a casual context. Use of *teineigo* depends on the situational context. Even among close friends, *teineigo* is used in certain formal settings (e.g., during weddings and funerals).

Use of *teineigo* has generally been explained in terms of 'formality', as determined by factors such as the in-group/out-group relationships of the interlocutors, the social setting involved, and the nature of the information being given. In particular, factors such as social position, power, age, sex, and in-group/out-groupness seem to play key roles in determining the use of formal as opposed to informal language (e.g., Ide, 1982; Martin, 1964; Mizutani & Mizutani, 1987). Ikuta (1983) claimed that speech level shifts between formal and informal language are determined by distance, which is social, attitudinal or cohesional.

Formal predicates are usually marked with *desu/-masu* endings, or with derivative endings such as *deshita/-mashita* 'PAST', *-masen* 'NEGATIVE', *-mashita* 'PAST NEGATIVE', and *-mashoo* 'VOLITIONAL'. There is also an ultra-polite form, *gozaimasu*. *Desu/-masu* style sentences are considered to be formal, while those without the ending are informal *-da* style sentences. The *desu/-masu* form could be used in a conversation with one's superior, or perhaps in a formal setting, such as a public speech. The informal *-da* style would be used in a more informal setting, such as in a conversation with one's friends.

There are also personal pronouns with varying degrees of politeness. For example, for first person pronouns, both men and women can use *watakushi* to be formal. However, in casual contexts, women may use *atashi*, while men use terms such as *boku* and *ore*. It is often difficult to tell whether adjustments to polite language are motivated by a desire to sound more respectful, formal, or refined.

Informal language is generally used reciprocally among family members, social equals, and peers, promoting casualness and intimacy, while formal language is used among nonintimates. Recently children have begun to use the informal style even to speak to elder members of the family. In contemporary Japanese families, intimacy often weighs more heavily than hierarchy in determining style choice. However, in other contexts, such as school, hierarchy still remains important. Children continue to use the -da style to classmates, but usually use the *desu/-masu* style to upperclassmen and non-family members.

Bikago 'beautification honorifics'

Unlike other forms of *keigo, bikago* are not used to express respect for the addressee or referent. They are used to "refine" one's language. Many of these forms are now used as the standard form (e.g., *o-kane* 'money', *o-cha* 'tea'). Women, in particular, frequently use honorific prefixes for refinement (e.g., *o-hashi* 'chopsticks', *o-sushi* 'sushi').

Finally, along with the four categories described above, there are a large number of greetings and polite expressions that involve gratitude, apology, self-blame and humility (Martin, 1964). For example, there are polite expressions such as *arigatoo* 'thank you', and greetings such as *ah gozaimasu* 'good morning'. There are also many formulaic expressions, such as *itadakimasu* 'I will receive it', which is said at the beginning of a meal, and *itte mairimasu* 'I will go and come back', which is said when leaving the house. Some of these expressions consist of humble/honorific forms, while others do not.

LITERATURE ON THE ACQUISITION OF POLITE LANGUAGE IN JAPANESE

Although many Japanese researchers acknowledge the need for research on the topic of pragmatic competence, few such studies exist. In general, researchers believe that children do not have productive use of different registers until they receive direct instruction during elementary school. They also assume that children seldom use polite speech because they do not encounter contexts in which they need to use them. For example, Mizutani and Mizutani (1987) claimed that young children can only use plain -da forms, and that polite language is usually acquired around the age of 6, after the start of elementary school. Once in school, children continue to use informal forms with their classmates while gradually learning the usage of polite forms toward older persons and unfamiliar people. However, it is important to note that in reaching this conclusion, researchers have relied mainly on spontaneous production data (Clancy, 1985).

Many educators feel that *keigo* instruction should begin by teaching greetings and polite expressions. According to Bunkacho (1986), a 1984 study showed that kindergarten children used greetings and proper expressions in approximately 85% of appropriate contexts (e.g., when leaving the house, before meals). Researchers such as Clancy (1986) report that Japanese mothers seemed to take every opportunity to teach these formulas to their children and that they expected earlier mastery of such social routines than American mothers.

Bunkacho (1986) reported that the earliest forms of polite language used by children were *teineigo*, referent honorifics (e.g., adding the suffix *-san* to names, using titles to refer to people) and polite expressions/greetings. As one might expect, children often use beautification honorifics, which are frequently used by women in child-directed speech

(Murata, 1983). Clancy (1986) referred to studies in which children as young as 2;1 used formal *-masu* forms during role-play. By age 3, children not only created make-believe contexts for using polite speech, but could respond appropriately to the level of politeness used by their addressees.

Furthermore, sensitivity to context in selection of different polite forms also appears to emerge early. A sociolinguistic analysis of person references by Japanese and American children by Ide (1979) showed that Japanese preschoolers used a greater variety of personal referential forms than American children, and that use of these first and second person pronouns varied according to context.

According to Okuda's 1979 study, acquisition of honorific and humble forms occurs extremely late. Only 5.7% of first graders, 8.9% of third graders, and 20.4% of sixth graders used honorific forms in a telephone dialogue between a mother and a doctor. Okuda explained that late acquisition of honorific and humble forms is probably due to the morphological, semantic, and social complexities involved in their usage. Similarly, Mackie's (1983) study of Japanese children's politeness strategies, reported that young children control politeness strategies like hedging (e.g., sounding hesitant when making requests and demands), long before they master subject and object honorifics. First and second graders in Mackie's study used no referent honorifics and were only able to use addressee honorifics (*teineigo*). Honorific and humble language is generally believed to be acquired relatively late except for some nonproductive forms (i.e., in greetings and polite expressions). One possible explanation for this is the fact that the use of humble and honorific language depends on complex relationships contrasts (e.g., in-group/out-group) while use of *teineigo* depends on situational contrasts which may be easier for children to comprehend.

Japanese children must learn to function in an extremely hierarchical society by varying their language appropriately according to social context. Although they may not use certain linguistic forms spontaneously, they will most likely be able to use a large repertoire of polite forms appropriately in role-play contexts, which allow children to use forms that may not often appear in everyday interaction by presenting a wide variety of hierarchical relationships.

METHOD

This study is part of a project to examine the acquisition and development of language that reflects pragmatic and social knowledge in young Japanese children. The data illustrate how pragmatic factors play a crucial role in the selection of syntactic and lexical forms even in preschool children.

Subjects

A total of 18 children (three girls and three boys in each age group: 3-, 4-, and 5-year-olds) were observed in their homes once a month for one year. The children were recruited from middle-class families living in the Tokyo area.

Procedure

During each two-hour visit, the children were audiotaped and videotaped in a variety of contexts.   Research on English-speaking children has shown that there are strong socioecological constraints on children's use of language and has pointed to the need for researchers to collect data across different contexts (Cook-Gumperz & Corsaro, 1977). Efforts were made to observe the same group of children across a wide range of activities (e.g., role-play, object construction, phone conversations) with different interactants (e.g., parents, peers, siblings, familiar and unfamiliar adults).

In particular, a variety of role-play contexts were used (e.g., store clerk–customer, doctor–patient, mother–baby, father–child, teacher-student).   Such contexts were chosen to present a wide range of hierarchical power relationships.   Ervin-Tripp (1973) discovered that when preschool children role-play they can often consistently use appropriate speech patterns that match the social roles involved.   For example, Andersen (1990) found that children often used more polite language when playing the role of a mother in a family setting.

Unstructured, free play sessions with mothers, siblings and peers were also recorded and questionnaires targeting issues pertaining to children's use of language in different contexts and language socialization were administered to the parents.   All sessions were audiotaped, videotaped, and then transcribed.

RESULTS AND DISCUSSION

It is clear that even preschool children are aware of sociolinguistic differences which vary according to context and require usage of different linguistic forms.   Every one of the children in the study was able to comprehend and produce a wide range of polite language across a variety of contexts.   Nonverbal politeness such as bowing routines seem to emerge even earlier.   Even 1-year-old children were able to bow at appropriate times, such as when greeting people.

Greetings and Polite Expressions

Preschoolers quickly master formal expressions such as *ah-gozaimasu* 'good morning' and *sayonara* 'goodbye'.   Most kindergartens place a strong emphasis on greetings such as *konnichi wa* 'hello' and polite expressions such as *arigatoo-gozaimasu* 'thank you'. Many teachers have their classes recite them in unison at specific times during the day. At some kindergartens, children are asked to repeat their greetings over and over until they are able to say them properly.

Generally though, young children are able to spontaneously produce a wide range of greetings and polite expressions in their daily interactions.   For example, upon opening the front door for a friend, Nobu (3;6) says:

Hai doozo . . . irrashai.
yes   please   welcome
'Yes, please (come in)...welcome.'

Pretending to offer a customer some ice cream, Maki (3;10) says:

Aisukuriimu doozo.
ice cream   please
'Please (have some) ice cream.'

On the phone, Toshi (3;7) says properly:

Toshi-chan desu . . . konnichi wa
              COP:POL[2] today   TOP
'This is Toshi-chan . . . hello.'

While playing store, Nobu (3;8) says *arigatoo gozaimashita* 'thank you very much' after a friend buys a basketful of groceries. These examples show that children are able to use many greetings and polite expressions appropriately, without prompting.

Sonkeigo 'Honorifics' and *Kenjoogo* 'Humble Language'

The few examples of honorific and humble language used by the children were in formulaic, ritualized expressions, such as *itadakimasu* 'I will humbly receive this' (stated before meals) or *itte-mairimasu* 'I will humbly go and come back' (stated when one leaves the house). There were no other examples of honorific or humble predicates. As Clancy (1985) proposed, it seems extremely likely that children initially may associate certain polite forms with a specific context (e.g., ritualized social routines). Gradually they develop an understanding of the relevant interpersonal factors, generalizing such forms to a wide variety of contexts, with increasing productivity and appropriateness.

Most mothers were referred to as *okaasan*, and fathers were referred to as *otoosan*. Children were also able to address people with the honorific suffix *-san*. Few other examples of referent honorifics were observed. Several children were able to use honorific prefixes, but not consistently. In addition, there were no examples of humble nouns (e.g., *chichi* for father, or *haha* for mother).

Teineigo 'Addressee Honorifics'

As Clancy (1986) reported, *teineigo* is fairly well established by age 3. All the children in this study showed mastery of *desu/-masu* forms and the ability to use them in appropriate contexts. For example, Eri (5;2) pretending to be a store clerk packing items into a customer's basket, tells her customer:

moo   ippai desu . . . moo   hairikire-masen.
already full COP:POL already fit   NEG:POL
'It's already full . . . . nothing else will fit.'

---

[2]   CONT = continuative; COP = copula; DO = direct object; EMPH = emphatic;
EP = extended predicate; NEG = negative; POL = polite; PRT = particle; Q = question;
QUOT = quotative; SUBJ = subject; TOP = topic; VOL = volitional.

Koji (3;7) pretending to be a cooking instructor, says:

    *hai. . . . nasu   supagechii o   tsukuri -**mashoo**. . . . san-jikan   yaki**masu**.*
    yes . . . eggplant spaghetti   ACC make   VOL:POL   three hours cook:POL
    'Yes . . . let's make some eggplant spaghetti . . . (we'll) cook it for 3 hours.'

Children are also able to adjust their level of speech to that of the addressee and the context. While pretending to be interviewed on television by the experimenter, Toshi (3;7) uses *teineigo* consistently over many turns:

    EXP: *ichiban suki na   omocha wa   nan   desu   ka?*
                most   like PRT toy   TOP what COP:POL Q
                'What is (your) favorite toy?'
    Toshi: *kyuukyuusha **desu**.*
                ambulance   COP:POL
                '(My) ambulance.'
    EXP: *ookiku nattara nani ni nari - tai   desu   ka?*
                big   become what to become want COP:POL Q
                'What do you want to become when (you) grow up?'
    Toshi: *patokaa   **desu**.*
                police car   COP:POL
                'A police car.'

Occasions in which children code switch between different levels of politeness for different purposes are another excellent source of data. Some of the children used polite forms to address the experimenter during the first 2 to 3 visits, but eventually switched to more casual forms. For example, during the first and second visits, Toshi (3;6) uses *teineigo* to ask the experimenter:

    *kore nan **desu**   ka?*
    this   what COP:POL Q
    ''What is this?'

By the third visit, he switches to informal forms, as in the following example:

    kore   nani?
    this   what
    'What is this?'

Obviously familiarity is a key factor in determining *keigo* usage. Phone conversations are also a rich source of data regarding appropriate use of formal and informal language. In most cases formal and polite language is used until the social status of the caller is identified. Initially, children, not knowing who is calling, use polite *desu/-masu* forms but quickly switch to informal language upon finding out who is on the phone. Research on English-speaking children has shown that in making requests, children are sensitive to factors such as age and likelihood of compliance (Gordon & Ervin-Tripp, 1984; James, 1978). In future research, it will be interesting to pinpoint which contextual factors Japanese children are sensitive to when using *keigo*.

    Children also code switch between different politeness levels depending on the group orientation and status of the addressee. Maki (3;10), pretending to be a waitress, uses polite language when she addresses her customers, but then quickly switches to casual language when she talks to the cook.

Maki (to customer):   *okawari   iri - **masu** ka?*
                              another helping   need POL   Q
                              'Would you like another helping?'
Maki (to cook):   *okawari   iru - tte.*
                              another helping   need QUOT
                              '(She) said (she wants) another helping.'

In this case, the customer is clearly an out-group person who requires formal language, while the cook is an in-group person with whom Maki can be informal.

Similarly, it is relatively easy to tell when children are assuming a role and when children are speaking in their own voice. In this example, Toshi (3;7) switches between his role as a chef, talking to customers, and his own identity as an older brother:

Toshi (to customer):   *ryoori   mo   yatte-**masu**   yo.*
                              cooking also do POL   EMPH
                              'I also cook.'

[At this point, Toshi's 1-year-old brother puts a plastic knife in his mouth]

Toshi (to brother):   *dame   . . .   hoochoo   abunai   kara   dame!*
                              no good . . . knife   dangerous so   no good
                              'No! The knife's dangerous so don't do that!'

As one might expect, children's use of polite language is not always consistent. For instance, Nobu (3;6) assuming the role of a doctor, switches between different registers:

[checking his patient, his baby brother]

Nobu: *hen   **da** . . . guwai   ga   warui-n   **da** .*
         strange   COP   condition SUBJ bad   EP COP
         'It's strange. . . . he's sick.'
Mother: *guwai   ga   warui-n   da.*
         condition SUBJ bad   EP COP
         'He's sick'
Nobu: *hai . . . moo   owari **desu**   yo.*
         yes . . . already end   COP:POL EMPH
         'Yes, (the examination's) over now.'

In the beginning of the conversation, the child uses the casual *-da* style, but eventually switches to the more formal *desu* style. Younger children seem to have more difficulty is maintaining a consistent level of politeness. With age, children become more skillful at using the appropriate form consistently.

Beautification Honorifics

Children use many of these forms in both polite and casual language. Upon counting the play money in his wallet, Toshi (3;8) says *konna okkii **o-kane** motta koto nai ne* 'I've never had so much **money** before!'. The children also used words such as *o-sakana* 'fish', *o-uchi* 'house', *o-sara* 'plate', *o-ryoori* 'cooking', *o-shigoto* 'work', and *o-hashi* 'chopsticks'. In general, girls used more of these forms than boys. This pattern mirrors adult usage. Excessive use of these forms by women, especially mothers and preschool teachers (e.g., *o-ekaki* 'drawing', *o-kutsu* 'shoes') has recently been the target of much public criticism (Bunkacho, 1974). Some women, in their effort to sound refined and polite, overuse beautification honorifics, using incorrect forms.

Requests

Children only used polite request forms when they assumed the role of another person and when they were addressing unfamiliar adults. For example, Nobu (3;6), playing the role of doctor, uses many requests in the *-te kudasai* form, which is considered to be more polite than requests in the gerund form (*-te*). He consistently asks the patient:

    *hai   onaka   dashi-**te-kudasai***
    yes   stomach open CONT give
    'Please show me your stomach.'
    jitto shi-   te-   kudasai
    still do. . . . . CONT   give
    'Please stay still.'

However, when addressing his mother, he uses a direct informal request:

    kore yon- de
    this read CONT
    'Read this (for me).'

According to the Bunkacho (1974), requests using the form *o* + verb stem + *kudasaru* are considered to be more polite than the common form *o* + verb gerund + *kudasaru*. Some of the older girls were able to use this form. Eri (5;2), pretending to be a store clerk, asks a customer to sign a credit card receipt by saying *kore ni namae o o-kaki-kudasai* 'Please sign your name here'.

It is clear that children are sensitive to the social context. For example, while all the children used *teineigo* in role-play contexts, few of them used *teineigo* and other forms of polite language (e.g., polite requests) during lego construction. Furthermore, children were able to make other types of language adjustments to make their speech more polite. During polite speech, they used fewer sentence fragments, contracted forms and colloquial sentence particles.

With increasing age, children gain greater control over polite speech and are able to switch between formal and informal speech spontaneously in contextually appropriate social situations. However, it is also important to note that there are individual differences in children's use of polite speech. For example, although 17 of the 18 children used some form of polite language during doctor–patient role-play contexts, one girl (5;4) used no polite language at all.

Although the preschool children were generally able to use many different forms of polite language they did not use any honorific or humble forms. Clancy (1986) stated that late acquisition of honorific and humble forms is caused by the lexical, morphological, semantic, and social complexities of the system. Furthermore, unlike *desu/-masu* forms referent honorifics rarely appear in mother's speech. One of the main reasons for the late acquisition of honorific and humble forms is the fact that they involve complex relationship contrasts as opposed to the situational contrasts which underlie the usage of *teineigo*. Indeed, it is difficult for the average preschooler to use honorific and humble forms due to limited experience and a simple network of social relationships. Fukui (1985) reported children's difficulty in acquiring honorific and humble forms resulted from their inability to comprehend the in-group/out-group concept in particular.

Furthermore, questionnaires administered to the mothers in the study revealed attitudes that underlie their children's acquisition of polite language. While 100% of the mothers felt that their children were able to use greetings and polite expressions, only 66% felt that their children would be able to speak politely if necessary. Interviews with the mothers revealed that most of them felt that it was unnecessary for their children to use *sonkeigo* and *kenjoogo* as long as they could use *teineigo* appropriately.

Language Socialization

How do Japanese children learn to use *keigo* appropriately? Iijima (1974) reported that there were three distinct stages of acquiring *keigo*: (1) through modeling in the home and preschool, (2) through instruction in the school system, and (3) through correction in society. Japanese parents use a variety of language socialization methods (e.g., modeling, direct instruction, verbal routines) to help young children acquire and use appropriate linguistic forms. Clancy's data (1985) of Japanese mothers' speech to 2-year-olds clearly illustrates situations in which mothers use -*masu* forms to their children or prompt their children to use such forms (e.g., when reading storybooks to their children or, imitating or quoting authority figures such as doctors). Clancy also noted that mothers used a formal style when they were correcting their children's behavior. This sudden switch to the formal register serves a distancing function, making the mood more formal.

Guidelines issued by the Ministry of Education advise instructors to teach various aspects of *keigo* usage throughout primary school (e.g., learn basic greetings in first grade, learn to use *teineigo* in third grade). Despite such guidelines, Morioka, Miyaji, Teramura, and Kawabata (1981) noted that in reality, children are rarely corrected or encouraged to use *keigo* at school. Teaching such a complicated system is not an easy task, especially since it is impossible for schools to prepare students for all conceivable situations.

Unlike other aspects of language, *keigo* cannot be learned through rote learning (Bunkacho, 1974). Ideally children should be able to acquire it naturally by observing their parents' use of language. In fact, many books recommend parents and teachers to use *keigo* frequently in the child's immediate environment so that children are exposed from an early age (e.g., Murata, 1983; Okubo, 1993). However, with the recent increase in the number of nuclear families and the concomitant decrease in the number of siblings and the increasingly intimate nature of the parent–child relationship (as opposed to more traditional hierarchical relationships), children have fewer opportunities to practice *keigo* in the home and to observe contexts in which *keigo* is used. Indeed, Matsumori (1981) reported that Japanese mothers insisted that their children use polite forms when addressing others, but not when speaking to the mothers themselves. For example, one mother instructs her child to speak politely on the phone:

Child: *Toshi-chan **desu*** . . . *konnichi   wa*
                    COP:POL   today   TOP
          'This is Toshi-chan . . . hello.'
Mother: *Doozo ki   -te-   kudasai-tte.*
          please   come CONT   give   QUOT
          'Say "please come over".'
Child: *Doozo **ki-   te   kudasai.***
          please   come CONT   give
          'Please come over.'

Furthermore, preschool also is an inconsistent source of instruction. On the one hand, greetings and polite expressions are practiced rigorously. However, after children start preschool, mothers frequently complain about the sudden increase in slang and colloquialisms resulting from their children's exposure to peer culture. Finally, the democratization of the teacher–student relationship has led to teacher–student friendships that decrease the formality of the relationship and consequently the need to use keigo forms.

Attitudes Regarding Polite Language

Politeness standards have changed drastically over the last century. Terms and forms in postwar Japan have been simplified and a greater degree of equality in language usage between men and women, and between different social classes has emerged. This aspect of change and variation in Japanese *keigo* seems to be of major concern to Japanese sociolinguists, who frequently write about the "corruption" and "erosion" of the Japanese language (e.g., Sibata, 1985). While many people are criticized for impolite speech, others, such as department store employees, are often criticized for being excessively polite (e.g., overusing *desu/ -masu* forms, beautification honorifics, and honorific/ humble forms). Niyekawa (1991) claimed that the nature of *keigo* is changing by becoming more addressee-oriented and less used for third-person referents. Opinion polls have revealed that more young people are having difficulty using *keigo*, and that many people feel the system should be simplified (e.g., NHK, 1980; Oishi, 1983).

Directions for Future Research

In general, Japanese women tend to use more formal and polite language than men (e.g., Ogino, Misono & Fukushima, 1985). For example, women use a larger number of nouns with honorific prefixes (e.g., *o-tomodachi* 'friend', *o-benkyoo* 'study'), many of which fall into the category of beautification honorifics. The Japanese girls in our study used politer forms of requests and more beautification honorifics than the boys. A detailed analysis of the sex-based differences in the use of polite language by Japanese children may reveal interesting differences.

Another direction for future research is a functional analysis of children's use of polite language. According to Brown and Levinson (1978, p. 66), politeness can be defined in terms of *face*, "the public self-image that every member wants to claim for himself." People are motivated to be polite by respecting two basic human needs: (1) the need not to be imposed on (negative face) and (2) the need to be liked and approved by others (positive face). There is considerable debate concerning the functional purpose underlying the use of politeness forms across languages (e.g., Matsumoto, 1988; Ide, 1982), and an examination of Japanese children's use of polite language may provide invaluable insight into this issue.

CONCLUSION

It is not the grammatical structure that makes polite language so elusive in Japanese, but rather, the socio-interactional relations which underlie the whole system. There is no given "standard" of polite speech. Politeness levels vary greatly from person to person, as well as according to factors such as situation, gender, dialect, and age. In order to become a competent language user, a child must acquire many registers and learn when and how to use them. Such communicative competence facilitates social interaction. Children who lack this flexibility are at risk. Although Japan has become less hierarchical and more democratic, sociolinguistic errors involving inappropriate use of *keigo* tend to trigger an instantaneous negative reaction in the listener.

Even preschoolers clearly have a fundamental understanding of the appropriateness of polite forms used to indicate particular roles and situations. They are able to use a variety of greetings/polite expressions, as well as referent, addressee and beautification honorifics. They receive much prompting and guidance from their parents and teachers. With increasing age, aided by better grammatical skills and more sophisticated cognitive abilities, as well as a wider range of social experiences, they gradually expand their repertoire of pragmatic skills and acquire communicative competence.

REFERENCES

Andersen, E. S. (1990). *Speaking with style: The sociolinguistic skills of children.* London: Routledge.

Axia, G., & Baroni, M. R. (1985). Linguistic politeness at different age levels. *Child Development, 56,* 918-927.

Bates, E. (1976). *Language and context: The acquisition of pragmatics.* New York: Academic.

Becker, J. (1986). Bossy and nice requests: Children's production and interpretation. *Merrill-Palmer Quarterly, 32,* 393-413.

Brown, P., & Levinson, S. (1987). *Politeness: Some universals of language usage.* New York: Cambridge University Press.

Bruner, J., Roy, C., & Ratner, N. (1982). The beginnings of request. In K. Nelson (Ed.), *Children's language, Vol. 3* (pp. 91-138). New York: Gardner Press.

Bunkacho. (1974). *Kotoba Shiriizu 1: Keigo* [Language series 1: Honorific Language]. Tokyo: Ministry of Finance.

Bunkacho. (1986). *Kotoba Shiriizu 24: Zoku-keigo* [Language series 24: Honorific Language, Part 2]. Tokyo: Ministry of Finance.

Clancy, P. M. (1985). The acquisition of Japanese. In D. I. Slobin (Ed.), *The crosslinguistic study of language acquisition, Vol. 1: The data,* (pp. 373-534). Hillsdale, NJ: Lawrence Erlbaum Associates.

Clancy, P. M. (1986). The acquisition of communicative style in Japanese. In D. Schieffelin & E. Ochs (Eds.), *Language socialization across cultures* (pp. 213-250). New York: Cambridge University Press.

Cook-Gumperz, J., & Corsaro, W. (1977). Social-ecological constraints on children's communicative strategies. *Sociology of Education, 52*, 15-79.

Ervin-Tripp, S. (1973). Children's sociolinguistic competence and dialect diversity. In A. Dil (Ed.), *Language acquisition and communicative choice* (pp. 262-301). Stanford: Stanford University Press.

Ervin-Tripp, S. (1977). Wait for me, roller skate. In S. Ervin-Tripp & C. Mitchell-Kernan (Eds.), *Child discourse,* (pp.165-188). New York: Academic.

Ervin-Tripp, S. (1982). Ask and it shall be given unto you: Children's requests. In H. Byrnes (Ed.), *Georgetown University Roundtable on Languages and Linguistics. Contemporary perceptions of language: Interdisciplinary dimensions* (pp. 235-245.) Washington, DC: Georgetown University Press.

Ervin-Tripp, S., O'Connor, M., & Rosenberg, J. (1984). Language and power in the family. In M. Schulz & C. Kramerae (Eds.), *Language and power* (pp. 116-135). Belmont, CA: Sage.

Fukui, Y. (Ed.) (1985). *Hito to hito no kakawari no hattatsu shinrigaku* [Developmental psychology from the perspective of interpersonal relations]. Tokyo: Fukumura Shuppan.

Gordon, D., & Ervin-Tripp, S. (1984). The structure of children's requests. In R. E. Schiefelbusch & A. Pickar (Eds.), *The acquisition of communicative competence* (pp. 296-321). Baltimore, MD: University Park Press.

Grief, E. B., & Gleason, J. B. (1980). Hi, thanks, and goodbye: More routine information. *Language in Society, 9*, 159-166.

Hymes, D. (1972). On communicative competence. In J. B. Pride & J. Holmes (Eds.), *Sociolinguistics: Selected readings* (pp. 269-293). Baltimore: Penguin.

Ide, S. (1979). Person references of Japanese and American children. *Language Sciences, 1*, 273-293.

Ide, S. (1982). Japanese sociolinguistics: Politeness and women's language. *Lingua, 57*, 357-385.

Iijima, T. (1974). Keigo o doo shidoo suru ka [How to teach *keigo* (honorific language)]. In Bunkacho (Ed.), *Kotoba Shiriizu 1: Keigo.* Tokyo: Ministry of Finance.

Ikuta, S. (1983). Speech level shift and conversational strategy in Japanese discourse. *Language Sciences, 5*, 37-53.

James, S. (1978). Effect of listener age and situation on the politeness of children's directives. *Journal of Psycholinguistic Research, 7*, 307-317.

Lakoff, R. (1973). The logic of politeness or minding your P's and Q's. *Papers from the Ninth Regional Meeting of the Chicago Linguistic Society* (pp. 292-305). Chicago: Chicago Linguistic Society.

Mackie, V. C. (1983). Japanese children and politeness. *Papers of the Japanese Studies Center, 6.* Melbourne.

Martin, S. E. (1964). Speech levels in Japan and Korea. In D. Hymes (Ed.), *Language in Culture and Society* (pp. 407-415). New York: Harper & Row.

Martin, S. E. (1975). *A reference grammar of Japanese.* New Haven: Yale University Press.

Matsumori, A. (1981). Hahaoya no kodomo e no gengo ni yoru koodoo kisei-yookyuu hyoogen no nichibei hikaku [Behavior regulation by mothers through child-directed speech: A comparison of requests in Japan and the United States]. In F. C. Peng (Ed.), *Gengo shuutoku no shoosoo* [Aspects of Language Acquisition] (pp. 320-339). Hiroshima: Bunka Hyooron.

Matsumoto, Y. (1988). Reexamination of the universality of face: Politeness phenomena in Japanese. *Journal of Pragmatics, 12*, 403-426.

Mizutani, O., & Mizutani, N. (1983). *Nihongo notes.* Tokyo: Japan Times.

Mizutani, O., & Mizutani, N. (1987). *How to be polite in Japanese.* Tokyo: Japan Times.

Morioka, K., Miyaji, Y., Teramura, H., & Kawabata, Y. (1981). *Nihongogaku 9: Keigo-shi* [The Study of Japanese 9: The history of honorific language]. Tokyo: Meiji Shoin.

Murata, K. (1983). *Kodomo no kotoba to kyooiku* [Children's language and education]. Tokyo: Kanebo Shobo.

Neustupny, J. V. (1978). *Poststructural approaches to language.* Tokyo: Tokyo University Press.

NHK (Nihon Hoosoo Kyookai [Japan Broadcasting Corporation]). (1980). *Nihonjin to hanashi kotoba.* Tokyo: Meisendo.

Niyekawa, A. (1991). *Minimal essential politeness: A guide to the Japanese honorific language.* Tokyo: Kodansha.

Ogino, T., Misono, Y., & Fukushima, C. (1985). Diversity of honorific usage in Tokyo: A sociolinguistic approach based on a field survey. *International Journal of the Sociology of Language, 55,* 23-39.

Oishi, H. (1983). *Gendai keigo kenkyuu* [Current research on honorific language]. Tokyo: Chikuma Shobo.

Okubo, A. (1993). *Nyuuyooji no kotoba no sekai* [The world of children's language]. Tokyo: Ootsuki Shoten.

Okuda, A. (1979). *Kodomo to taiguu hyogen* [Children and referential expressions]. Unpublished master's thesis, Tsukuba University.

Piaget, J. (1926). *The language and thought of the child.* London: Routledge.

Sibata, T. (1985). Sociolinguistic surveys in Japan: approaches and problems. *International Journal of the Sociology of Language,* **55**, 79-88.

16 THE MICROGENESIS OF COMPETENCE: METHODOLOGY IN LANGUAGE SOCIALIZATION

Bambi B. Schieffelin
New York University

Elinor Ochs
University of California, Los Angeles

1. INTRODUCTION

The discussion that follows centers on the enterprise of conducting language socialization research. We consider practical and theoretical issues and tools that enhance description and analysis of communicative practices and their socialization within culturally organized speech communities. Our discussion outlines five goals of language socialization research. In so doing, we suggest a framework for comparative research on language socialization across communities.

A turning point in the history of research on the cultural organization of children's talk was a symposium on child discourse organized by Susan Ervin-Tripp and Claudia Mitchell-Kernan at the 1974 Meetings of the American Anthropological Association. Both authors of this paper participated, one as presenter (Ochs) and the other as a member of the audience (Schieffelin). The session stimulated at least two important outcomes: one, an enduring collaborative partnership between the co-authors of this chapter; and two, the volume, *Child Discourse* (Ervin-Tripp & Mitchell-Kernan, 1977), which was the first comprehensive appraisal of the complexity of children's discourse across speech communities and genres. This volume inspired a number of research projects that formed the basis for a second collection, *Developmental Pragmatics* (Ochs & Schieffelin, 1979). In the last fifteen years developmental pragmatics has become an important theoretical domain of inquiry, examining children's developing competence in the use of language within and across socially organized contexts. Ervin-Tripp's studies of children's competence in performance of speech acts, conversational turn-taking, and verbal activities more broadly (Ervin-Tripp, 1976, 1977, 1978, 1979, 1982) have been a model for many of us engaged in research on children's pragmatic competence (cf., Andersen, 1990; Clancy, 1986; Garvey, 1984; Iwamura, 1980; Keenan & Schieffelin,

1976; McTear, 1985; Ochs & Schieffelin, 1983; Schieffelin, 1981, among others).

Research on language socialization extends the program of study on children's pragmatic competence by situating children as novice members of a community, who, through interaction with more expert members, become competent participants of that community (Cook-Gumperz, 1977; Heath, 1982; Ochs & Schieffelin, 1984; Schieffelin & Ochs, 1986a, 1986b). Like developmental pragmatic research, studies of language socialization examine children's skill to use language; however, the emphasis is on relating children's knowledge and performance to the social and cultural structures, processes, activities, understandings and ideologies that give meaning and identity to a community (Crago, 1988; Goodwin, 1990; Heath, 1983; Kulick, 1992; Ochs, 1988; Schieffelin, 1990; Scollon, 1982; Watson-Gegeo & Gegeo, 1986).

Language socialization has as its goal understanding how persons are socialized to become competent members of social groups and the role of language in this process. The study of language socialization, therefore, concerns two major facets of socialization: socialization through the use of language and socialization to use language (Ochs, 1986; Schieffelin & Ochs, 1986). The notion of language socialization is premised on two assumptions about the nature of language, culture, and socialization. First, the process of acquiring language is deeply affected by the process of becoming a competent member of a society, and second, the process of becoming a competent member of society is realized to a large extent through language, by acquiring knowledge of its functions, social distribution, and interpretations in and across socially defined situations. This is largely achieved through participation in exchanges of language in particular social situations. From this perspective, language is seen as a source for children to acquire the ways and world views of their culture (Ochs & Schieffelin, 1984; Ochs, 1988; Schieffelin, 1990; Schieffelin & Ochs, 1986a).

Research on language socialization focuses on the language use of novices and members in and across culturally meaningful social activities. The emphasis is on understanding the mundane, everyday, and routine. Language socialization has as a goal linking microanalytic accounts of children's discourse to more general ethnographic accounts of cultural beliefs and practices of families, social groups, and communities into which children are being socialized. The relation between language behavior and cultural ideologies is not explicit or obvious, but must be constructed from a range of ethnographic data, including recorded and transcribed social interactions, interviews, and participant observations. The linking of micro interactional and linguistic structures to social, cultural, and historical processes is what distinguishes language socialization from both language acquisition and developmental pragmatics and what places it within the domain of anthropological inquiry (Schieffelin & Ochs, 1986).

2. GOALS OF LANGUAGE SOCIALIZATION RESEARCH

In the discussion that follows we will detail five goals of language socialization research and methodological tools for achieving those goals.

2.1. The organization of communicative practices

A basic goal of language socialization research is to articulate the organization of recurrent *communicative practices* of novice and expert members. These members routinely use a range of vocal and nonvocal semiotic modalities to convey and interpret messages including grammatical, lexical, discursive, and gestural structures.

To analyze the linguistic organization of speech activities language socialization researchers prefer not to use idealized accounts of talk or reports of ideological stances, nor do they rely on spot observations or randomly taken language samples without contextual notes. Instead, they examine in detail video/audiotaped naturally occurring social interaction organized as coherent practices or activities related to each other over time and across situations (Bourdieu, 1977, 1991; Leontyev, 1981). Electronically recording and analyzing both the details and cultural framing of such naturalistic data distinguishes language socialization research from other socialization research based on handrecorded field notes of observations.

Video and audio taperecording with contextual notetaking allows the researcher to capture a continuous lengthy behavioral record of interactions involving young children and those with whom they regularly interact, including peers and more mature members. Continuous recording of interaction enables analyses of how novices become competent in recognizing shifts from one type of communicative context to another. A continuous detailed record provides a basis for establishing the extent to which children and other novices utilize diverse linguistic and nonlinguistic structures to signal and interpret shifts in communicative act, activity, identity, affect, and knowledge of interlocutors (Goodwin, 1990; Ochs, 1979a; Schieffelin, 1979; Watson-Gegeo & Gegeo, 1986). Such a record allows the researcher to illuminate not only how novices are socialized to develop communicative skills within a single language but also how they are socialized to draw on **multiple** codes to constitute shifts in communicative acts, activities, identities, affects and other facets of the situation in linguistically heterogeneous speech communities (Kulick, 1992; Schieffelin, 1994; Zentella, in press). A continuous audio and video record also allows analysts to explore how novice interlocutors are socialized to use immediate and more distant interactional history to make sense of attitudes and ideas conveyed through talk and action.

If we want to understand ordinary, unremarkable, taken-for-granted everyday events from the perspectives of the participants, attention to the details of talk, including pauses and overlaps, unintelligible utterances, is critical (Atkinson & Heritage, 1984; Sachs, Schegloff & Jefferson, 1974). These details provide critical information about stances, actions, activities, and social identities of interlocutors as well as the cultural patterning of conversation and other discourse genres in diverse speech communities. We should not be fooled into thinking that ambiguity and indeterminacy disappear because we have captured interaction through electronic recording and detailed transcriptions. Ambiguity and indeterminacy are important social and communicative resources, necessary in conversation and social life, and the best we can do is identify them as such when they occur. As Goffman (1976) reminds us, the laconicity of talk, what is not said, is central to interpretation and social conduct. We need to incorporate speakers' interpretations into our own linguistic and ethnographic accounts, including local theories of interpretation and intentionality (Duranti, 1993a, 1993b). Native speakers do not rely on the spoken record alone — neither should we.

An annotated transcript is an important theoretical and methodological component of language socialization research, and the first step in its creation is the integration of contextual notes with transcription of speech and nonvocal conduct (Ochs, 1979b; Schieffelin, 1990). Preparation of an annotated transcript, however, is neither a simple nor a mechanical data collecting task, but is in itself a deeply ethnographic process. Annotation and translation require on-going discussions with native speakers about the cultural significance of the recorded events, culturally recognized types of speech activities, and named discourse strategies, all of which contribute to the interpretation of conduct and speech (Goodwin, 1990).

Both participants in those events, for exammple, caregivers and older siblings and other members of the community are often excellent assistants in the transcription and annotation process in that they can identify speakers in multiparty talk, specify the history and ownership of objects involved, and convey their own interpretations and evaluations of the event itself. Relistening with them provides a context for their opinions about the speech and conduct of novices and others, which in turn, are valuable sources for constructing analyses of local interpretive procedures and linguistic ideologies (Miller, Potts, Fung, Hoogstra, & Mintz, 1990).

In Schieffelin's field research on language socialization of Kaluli children, meta-commentaries by members of the community who did not participate in the recorded interactions were especially critical in learning how features such as prosody, voice quality, affect-marked affixes and expressives and formulaic expressions convey affect and stance (Schieffelin, 1990). In Kaluli, requests for assistance, food, and other objects are usually in one of two modalities: an assertive, demanding modality or one based on appeal where the speaker hopes to get what is wanted by making the addressee "feel sorry" and comply. In Kaluli request sequences based on appeal, these metacommentaries revealed that children must demonstrate particular verbal competence to achieve the desired responses. They must select the appropriate set of linguistic resources, including expressive words to elicit compassion, vocatives to frame the request within a particular relationship based on sharing, morphemes to mark affect such as intimacy and to intensify each repeated request, affect-marked pronouns to elicit pity, particular syntactic constructions to put the agent in focus in addition to the use of a whining voice, which Kaluli call *geseab*. Transcripts of situated speech plus elicited commentary on them thus provide important sources for examining and interpreting linguistic details of the interactions between experts and novices, including how they are organized to achieve particular social ends.

2.2. The Context of Situation

A second goal in language socialization research is to examine the context of situation (Malinowski, 1978) relevant to talk and nonvocal conduct. In coming to understand the context of situation as constructed by novice and expert members, the researcher asks questions such as: When do different utterance types and actions of novices and experts occur? How are these utterances and actions organized with respect to one another? How do novice and expert members use these structures to form coherent sequences, practices, acts, and/or activities (Crago, 1988; Duranti & Ochs, 1986; Ervin-Tripp, 1979; Heath, 1983; Michaels & Cazden, 1986; Miller et al., 1990)? What are the preferred and dispreferred, routine and unusual, participant roles in interactions involving novice and expert members (Goffman, 1979; Jacoby & Gonzales, 1991; Lave & Wenger, 1991; Philips 1983)? How is attention to the situation socialized (Ochs, 1979a; Rogoff, 1990)?

Features of the context of situation interact in nonrandom, that is, culturally coherent ways. Indeed, such syntagmatic relations are a crucial component of what novice members must come to master to successfully participate in social life (Ervin-Tripp, 1972). When particular contextual features routinely co-occur to create recognizable situations, the signaling of one contextual feature through language or other means may invoke other contextual features that usually accompany it. For example, in Kaluli communities, children must come to understand that when they use a particular type of vocative (*ade*), they not only signal a particular named relationship (siblingship), they also invoke a type of affect (sympathy) and social act (a request based on appeal). Requests for food are more frequently made by males to females, less often the reverse. This is consistent with Kaluli gender appropriate behaviors which vary according to recipient, activities, and developmental time, and language encodes these relevant factors. All Kaluli children are socialized to use these forms to invoke these situational features (Schieffelin, 1990).

2.3. The Context of Culture

A third goal of language socialization is to situate the socialization and emergence of communicative practices within the context of culture. A defining perspective of language socialization research is the pursuit of cultural underpinnings that give meaning to the communicative interactions between expert and novice members within and across contexts of situation. While researchers theorize about culture within different theoretical frameworks, we take culture to include "bodies of knowledge, structures of understanding, conceptions of the world, and collective representations [which are] extrinsic to any individual and contain more information that any individual could know or learn" (Ochs & Schieffelin, 1984, p. 284). The analysis of how communicative practices of experts and novices are organized by and organize cultural knowledges, understandings, beliefs, and feelings is what distinguishes language socialization approaches from developmental pragmatics.

For example, a developmental pragmatic analysis of Kaluli children's communicative skills might focus the extent to which Kaluli children are able to use the range of appropriate linguistic forms to perform the act of requesting (Schieffelin, 1990, pp. 183-201). A language socialization analysis, on the other hand, embeds that analysis in a larger discussion of how the acquisition of these practices is also part of a broader socialization into Kaluli about notions exchange and social relationships. From a Kaluli perspective, social relationships are fundamentally constituted through giving and sharing, a primary

social relationships are fundamentally constituted through giving and sharing, a primary means of conveying sentiment and affection. A primary means for accomplishing these sharing activities is through the use of appropriate request forms. Competence underlying sharing is indexed and socialized in everyday talk to children, and children's own ways of speaking express fundamental cultural concerns about reciprocity and social relationships. Sharing, accomplished through requests and responses, is linked to other social practices and symbolic forms such as exchange systems, gender roles, sibling relationships, rituals and myths. In Kaluli society, as in many others in Papua New Guinea, sharing, reciprocity, and exchange more generally organize and give meaning to social life.

Our approach to language socialization is similar to the anthropological perspectives of Bateson (1972), Gluckman (1958), and Turner (1967) — exploring a culturally focal event and its relation to other events and cultural meaning systems. However, language socialization research tends to focus on everyday, informal, even routine events and draws out connections between these ordinary events and the socialization of social and cultural skills. Such mundane events are significant in that they provide a basic, recurrent grounding for the socialization of cultural meanings.

2.4. The Context of Human Development

A fourth goal of language socialization research is to contribute to an understanding of connections between human development and culture, including relation between language acquisition and the socialization of cognitive and social competence. In other words, we are interested in how human development is situated in a cultural matrix.

One way of addressing the interface between culture and human development is to investigate developmental constraints on children and other novice's participation in particular communicative practices. For example, a discussion of Kaluli children's participation in culturally salient activities of sharing objects (reciprocity and exchange) could, and perhaps should, consider cognitive and biological processes that help organize children's performance and recognition of requests and other forms of conduct that are integral to these activities. Thus in examining the acquisition of requests based on appeal, we observe that Kaluli children's speech evidences formal elaboration over developmental time that reflects these cognitive and biological factors (Schieffelin, 1990, pp. 128-135, 183-201).

On the other hand, language socialization research suggests that, in certain communities, cultural preferences facilitate the use of certain grammatically more complex forms earlier in the developmental cycle than less complex comparable forms (Ochs & Schieffelin, 1995). For example, while there is an acquisition trend among Kaluli children towards increased complexity **within** the category of requests based on appeal, there is another acquisition trend in which Kaluli children acquire the category of requests based on appeal before the grammatically less complex category of assertive requests. Requests in both modalities can be accomplished by single words, either imperative verbs or indirect pronouns. Young children's assertive requests, however, are usually single word utterances while requests based on appeal are multiword utterances constructed with vocatives, expressives, direct and/or indirect pronouns and imperative verbs that are marked with emphatic particles (Schieffelin, 1990, pp. 187-198). While surprising from a developmental psycholinguistic perspective, this developmental progression is entirely compatible with Kaluli notions that children "naturally" beg, but must be explicitly socialized to request assertively using a different set of linguistic resources (Schieffelin, 1990, pp. 132-135). Similarly, young Samoan children produce the semantically more complex deictic verb *give/bring* related to begging before the simpler deictic verb *come* related to requests of change of location of addressee. This developmental progression can be explained, in part, by the cultural appropriateness of children's begging for food, but the inappropriateness of their directing others to come to them (Platt, 1986). Thus there are indications that socially appropriate demeanors guide the acquisition of particular linguistic forms. Children are not only immature speakers, but also social beings participating in socially ordered interactions.

2.5. Universals and Particulars

For some time now an important goal of language socialization research has been to articulate a model that reconciles what is particular and what is universal about the communicative practices of novices and of experts (Ochs, 1986, 1988, 1990, 1992; Ochs & Schieffelin, 1984, 1989, 1995; Schieffelin & Ochs, 1986a). The feeling of the authors is that anthropologists have been miscast as seekers of the exotic and the unique, and revelers in the exception to the rule. In our loosely articulated language socialization paradigm, universal and cultural are not logical oppositions but rather potentially compatible qualities of practices; the same communicative practice may be both universal and cultural at once. If we examine ordinary verbal practices that constitute daily interaction, we find that the vast majority of these practices are cultural universals. Further, we find that these practices also have a similar linguistic form. For example, the cultural practices of asking questions, requesting, and clarifying unintelligible utterances or expressing affect or epistemic stance are both universal in appearance and realized through common linguistic structures (Besnier, 1990; Levinson, 1983; Ochs, 1982, in press; Ochs & Schieffelin, 1989). These observations lead us to posit certain universal relations between utterance form and utterance function and certain universal outcomes of language socialization. In many respects, children everywhere have been socialized to use language in similar ways. Such similarities provide us with a basis for accounting for how indeed people from vastly different speech communities manage some level of communication.

What then is culturally particular? In our view, while a particular communicative practice may occasionally vary in form across social groups, cultural variation lies primarily in the features of the situation and cultural contexts which that practice invokes. In terms of the immediate context of situation, the same practice may differ cross-culturally in the extent to which it is **preferred** or **expected** given certain social identities and settings. In one community, the practice may be unmarked for certain identities and settings, that is, expected and preferred; in another, its occurrence is unusual and inappropriate for comparable identities and settings.

The same communicative practice in different communities may also differ in its **duration** across interactional time. A practice may recurrently endure over twenty turns of member–novice interaction in one community and in another, the practice typically occupies less than five turns. Such differences in duration certainly characterize the practice of elicited imitation across societies. While widespread in appearance, elicited imitation pervades the interactions of Kaluli (Schieffelin, 1990), Kwara'ae (Watson-Gegeo & Gegeo, 1986), Basotho (Demuth, 1986), and Samoan (Ochs, 1988) caregivers and children far more than in caregiver–child interactions among the American white middle class (Gleason & Weintraub, 1976; Gleason, Perlmann, & Greif, 1984; Golinkoff 1983).

The net result of these differences in preference and duration is that communicative practices universal in appearance and form have different cultural significance across speech communities. From another point of view, the net result is that universal communicative practices have different social meanings in the hands of different groups of language users. In terms of cultural universals and particulars of language socialization, children everywhere are being socialized through language use to interpret and generate locally relevant social meanings. Children come to associate certain practices with certain situational and other contextual conditions and develop a sense of what is preferred and expected (Ochs & Schieffelin, 1984). It is in this realm of social meaning that cross-cultural communication flounders as interlocutors violate one another's expectations concerning conversational practices and fail to comprehend the social contexts indexed by one another's practices (Gumperz, 1982; Ochs, 1990, 1992). It is also this realm of social meaning that is so easily lost on audiences to language socialization research. Audiences tend to focus on the formal and functional universals of a socialization practice without grasping its situational scope and cultural significance.

Language socialization research has begun to capture some of these universal and cultural facets of communicative practices. For example, the authors (Ochs, 1982, 1988, 1991, 1992; Ochs & Schieffelin, 1984) have posited a set of universal responses to unintelligibility under two conditions: The first is where one interlocutor perceives the utterance of *another* to be unintelligible (addressee-rooted unintelligibility). The second is where an interlocutor perceives his or her *own* utterance to be unintelligible to another (speaker-rooted unintelligibility). In the case of addressee-rooted unintelligibility, the coauthors propose that interlocutors everywhere employ the following four conversational strategies in responding to another's unintelligibility:

1) ignore unintelligibility;
2) display nonunderstanding;
3) verbally guess at what another might be saying;
4) negatively sanction addresee's unintelligibility
   (e.g., by teasing or shaming).

Similarly, in cases in which interlocutors perceive their own utterances to be unintelligible to others (speaker-rooted unintelligibility), they universally set in motion any of the following cultural strategies:

1) ignore unintelligibility;
2) repeat own utterance;
3) reformulate own utterance by simplifying, expanding, or otherwise paraphrasing it;

4)   negatively sanction addressee's nonunderstanding of speaker's utterance.

We have pointed out that while universal, these practices differ in the extent to which they are employed and the contexts in which they are employed in different speech communities.   Thus in American White middle class communities, verbally guessing is a highly preferred response to addressee-rooted unintelligibility (Schegloff, Jefferson, & Sacks, 1977), whereas in Kaluli (Schieffelin, 1990) and Samoan (Ochs, 1988) communities, verbal guessing is rare, particularly where the unintelligible utterance is produced by a young child.   Kaluli and Samoans tend to ignore, display nonunderstanding and tease or shame the producer of unintelligible utterances.   In both communities, these practice preferences are tied to local notions of thinking and knowing.   For both Kaluli and Samoan interlocutors, there is a strong dispreference for guessing what another is thinking, that is, making explicit another's unexpressed intentions and feelings.   Kaluli claim that one person cannot know what another person thinks or feels, which results in their extreme reluctance to explicitly verbalize or guess what another speakers means and wants (Schieffelin, 1990, pp. 72-73).

Additionally, in Samoan communities, tolerance for and accommodation to unintelligibility is hierarchically distributed in that unintelligibility among high ranking persons is tolerated and accommodated to by low ranking persons far more than the reverse.   In this sense each time American, Kaluli, and Samoan children produce unintelligible utterances and are exposed to the unintelligible utterances of others, they are provided with opportunities for learning universal ways of responding to unintelligibility, yet at the same time, variation in these responses across contexts provide opportunities for socializing local ideologies and social orders.

Similarly, in American White middle class speech communities, speakers very often grammatically simplify their utterances if they perceive that their utterances are not intelligible, particularly when talking to a young child (Cross, 1977; Ferguson, 1977, 1982; Newport, Gleitman, & Gleitman, 1977).   In Kaluli and Samoan communities, however, speakers rarely grammatically simplify under these circumstances, particularly when talking to a young child.   Kaluli and Samoan speakers typically assist the process of comprehension by repeating or paraphrase a difficult utterance without necessarily grammatically simplifying it.   These preferences in turn are tied to local ideology and social order.   Kaluli dispreference for grammatical simplification is tied to a local theory of language acquisition in which children are thought to need to hear complex language to become competent interlocutors (Schieffelin, 1990).   In Samoan communities, grammatical simplification is a form of psychological and social accommodation appropriate in speaking to high ranking addressees (Ochs, 1988).   One finds grammatical simplification in talk to high ranking foreigners but not in talk to young children.

As the social and cultural contexts of grammatical simplification vary across communities, so does the social meaning of this practice in these communities.   In one community (Samoan), the use of grammatical simplification indexes only that the speaker is talking with a foreigner.   In another community (mainstream white middle class American), grammatical simplification can index that one is talking either to a foreigner, a young child, an elderly person, or a pet.   It is in this sense that a single practice has both cultural and universal structure. While speakers the world over struggle to achieve intelligibility, they do so in culturally arranged ways.

3. CONCLUSION

Language socialization research is committed to articulating interfaces between language, mind, and society by exploring the role of language in human development and socialization. Our perspective pushes research on children's pragmatic competence beyond the bounds of children's capacity to perform particular actions and participate in particular activities towards an integrated cultural account of children as members of communities with histories, values, ways of understanding the world and organizing their identities and interactions. This includes culturally-specific theories and practices surrounding child development. While language socialization is centrally engaged in the close analysis of perfectly ordinary recurrent language practices involving language and cultural apprentices, the field is more broadly dedicated to situating and visualizing the specific linguistic and interactional structures that constitute such practices in terms of culturally universal and particular processes and meanings.

REFERENCES

Andersen, E. (1990). *Speaking with style: The sociolinguistic skills of children*. London: Routledge.

Atkinson, J. M., & Heritage, J. (Eds.) (1984). *Structures of social action*. Cambridge, England: Cambridge University Press.

Bateson, G. (1972). *Steps to an ecology of mind*. New York: Ballantine.

Besnier, N. (1990). Language and affect. *Annual Review of Anthropology,* **19**, 419-451.

Boggs, S., & Watson-Gegeo, K. (1978). Interweaving routines: Strategies for encompassing a social situation. *Language in Society, 7*, 375-392.

Bourdieu, P. (1977). *Outline of a theory of practice*. Cambridge, England: Cambridge University Press.

Bourdieu, P. (1991). *Language and symbolic power*. Cambridge, MA: Harvard University Press.

Clancy, P. (1986). The acquisition of communicative style in Japanese. In B. B. Schieffelin & E. Ochs (Eds.), *Language socialization across cultures* (pp. 213-250). Cambridge, England: Cambridge University Press.

Cook-Gumperz, J. (1977). Situated instructions: Language socialization of school age children. In S. Ervin-Tripp & C. Mitchell-Kernan (Eds.), *Child discourse* (pp. 103-121). New York: Academic Press.

Crago, M. (1988). *Cultural context in communicative interaction of Inuit children*. Unpublished doctoral dissertation, McGill University, Montreal, Quebec.

Cross, T. (1977). Mothers' speech adjustment. In C. Snow & C. Ferguson (Eds.), *Talking to children: Language input and acquisition* (pp. 151-188). Cambridge, England: Cambridge University Press.

Demuth, K. (1986). Prompting routines in the language socialization of Basotho children. In B. B. Schieffelin & E. Ochs (Eds.), *Language socialization across cultures* (pp. 51-79). Cambridge, England: Cambridge University Press.

Duranti, A., & Ochs, E. (1986). Literacy instruction in a Samoan village. In B. B. Schieffelin & P. Gilmore (Eds.), *The acquisition of literacy: Ethnographic perspectives* (pp. 213-232). Norwood, NJ: Ablex.

Duranti, A. (1993a). Intentionality and truth: An ethnographic critique. *Cultural Anthropology*, **8**, 214-245.

Duranti, A. (1993b). Intentions, self and responsibility: An essay in Samoan ethnopragmatics. In J. H. Hill & J. T. Irvine (Eds.), *Responsibility and evidence in oral discourse* (pp. 24-47). Cambridge, England: Cambridge University Press.

Ervin-Tripp, S. (1972). On sociolinguistic rules: Alternation and co-occurrence. In J. Gumperz & D. Hymes (Eds.), *Directions in sociolinguistics: The ethnography of communication* (pp. 213- 250). New York: Holt, Rinehart and Winston.

Ervin-Tripp, S. (1976). Is Sybil there? The structure of American directives. *Language in Society*, **5**, 25-66.

Ervin-Tripp, S. (1977). Wait for me, Roller Skate! In S. Ervin-Tripp & C. Mitchell-Kernan (Eds.), *Child discourse* (pp. 165-188). New York: Academic.

Ervin-Tripp, S., & Mitchell-Kernan, C. (Eds.) (1977). *Child discourse*. New York: Academic Press.

Ervin-Tripp, S. (1978). Some features of early child-adult dialogues. *Language in Society*, **7**, 357-373.

Ervin-Tripp, S. (1979). Children's verbal turn-taking. In E. Ochs & B. B. Schieffelin (Eds.), *Developmental pragmatics* (pp. 391-414). New York: Academic Press.

Ervin-Tripp, S. (1982). Ask and it shall be given you: Children's requests. In H. Byrnes (Ed.), *Georgetown University round table on languages and linguistics 1982* (pp. 235-245). Washington DC: Georgetown University Press.

Ferguson, C. (1977). Babytalk as a simplified register. In C. Snow & C. Ferguson (Eds.), *Talking to children: Language input and acquisition* (pp. 209-235). Cambridge, England: Cambridge University Press.

Ferguson, C. (1982). Simplified registers and linguistic theory. In L. Obler & L. Menn (Eds.), *Exceptional language and linguistics* (pp. 49-66). New York: Academic.

Garvey, C. (1984). *Children's talk*. Cambridge, MA: Harvard University Press.

Gleason, J. B., & Weintraub, S. (1976). The acquisition of routines in child language. *Language in Society*, **5**, 129-136.

Gleason, J. B., Perlmann, R., & Greif, E. (1984). "What's the magic word?". *Discourse Processes*, **7**, 493-502.

Gluckman, M. (1958). Analysis of a social situation in modern Zululand. Rhodes-Livingstone Paper no. 28, Reprinted from *Bantu Studies* (1940).

Goffman, E. (1976). Replies and responses. *Language in Society*, **5**, 257-313.

Goffman, E. (1979). Footing. *Semiotica*, **25**, 1-29.

Golinkoff, R. (1983). The pre-verbal negotiation of failed messages. In R. Golinkoff (Ed.), *The transition from prelinguistic to linguistic communication*(pp. 57-78). Hillsdale, NJ: Lawrence Erlbaum Associates.

Goodwin, M. (1990). *He-said-she-said: Talk as social organization among Black children*. Bloomington: Indiana University Press.

Gumperz, J. J. (1982). *Discourse strategies*. Cambridge, England: Cambridge University Press.

Heath, S. (1982). What no bedtime story means. *Language in Society*, **11**, 49-77.

Heath, S. (1983). *Ways with words*. New York: Cambridge University Press.

Iwamura, S. (1980). *The verbal games of preschool children*. New York: St. Martin's Press.

Jacoby, S., & Gonzalez, P. (1991). The constitution of expert-novice in scientific discourse. *Issues in Applied Linguistics*, **2**, 149-181.

Keenan, E. O., & Schieffelin, B. B. (1976). Topic as a discourse notion. In C. Li (Ed.), *Subject and topic* (pp. 335-384). New York: Academic.

Kulick, D. (1992). *Language shift and cultural reproduction: Socialization, self and syncretism in a Papua New Guinea village*. Cambridge, England: Cambridge University Press.

Lave, J., & Wenger, E. (1991). *Situated learning: Legitimate and peripheral participation*. New York: Cambridge University Press.

Leontyev, A. N. (1981). *Problems in the development of mind*. Moscow: Progress Publishers.

Levinson, S. (1983). *Pragmatics*. Cambridge, England: Cambridge University Press.

Malinowski, B. (1978). *Coral gardens and their magic: The language of magic and gardening.* New York: Dover.

McTear, M. (1985). *Children's conversations.* Oxford: Basil Blackwell.

Michaels, S., & Cazden, C. (1986). Teacher-child collaboration as oral preparation for literacy. In B. B. Schieffelin & P. Gilmore (Eds.), *The acquisition of literacy: Ethnographic perspectives* (pp. 132-154). Norwood, NJ: Ablex.

Miller, P. J., Potts, R., Fung, H., Hoogstra, L. & Mintz, J. (1990). Narrative practices and the social construction of self and childhood. *American Ethnologist, 17,* 292-311.

Newport, E., Gleitman, H. & Gleitman, L. (1977). Mother, I'd rather do it myself: Some effects and noneffects of maternal speech style. In C. Snow & C. Ferguson (Eds.), *Talking to children: Language input and acquisition* (pp. 109-149). Cambridge, England: Cambridge University Press.

Ochs, E. (in press). Linguistic resources for socializing humanity. In J. J. Gumperz & S. Levinson (Eds.), *Linguistic relativity.* Cambridge University Press.

Ochs, E. (1979a). Introduction: What child language can contribute to pragmatics. In E. Ochs & B. B. Schieffelin (Eds.), *Developmental pragmatics* (pp 1-17). New York: Academic Press.

Ochs, E. (1979b). Transcription as theory. In E. Ochs & B. B. Schieffelin (Eds.), *Developmental pragmatics* (pp. 43-72). New York: Academic Press.

Ochs, E., & Schieffelin, B. B. (Eds.). (1979). *Developmental pragmatics.* New York: Academic Press.

Ochs, E. (1982). Talking to children in Western Samoan. *Language in Society, 11,* 77-104.

Ochs, E., & Schieffelin, B. B. (1983). *Acquiring conversational competence.* London: Routledge & Kegan Paul.

Ochs, E. & Schieffelin, B. B. (1984). Language acquisition and socialization: Three developmental stories and their implications. In R. Shweder & R. Levine (Eds.), *Culture theory: Essays in mind, self and emotion* (pp. 276-320). New York: Cambridge University Press.

Ochs, E. (1986). Introduction. In B. B. Schieffelin & E. Ochs (Eds.), *Language socialization across cultures* (pp. 1-13). New York: Cambridge University Press.

Ochs, E. (1988). *Culture and language development.* Cambridge, England: Cambridge University Press.

Ochs, E. & Schieffelin, B. B. (1989). Language has a heart. *Text, 9,* 7-25.

Ochs, E. (1990). Indexicality and socialization. In J. W. Stigler, R. Shweder, & G. Herdt (Eds.), *Cultural psychology* (pp. 287-308). Cambridge, England: Cambridge University Press.

Ochs, E. (1991). Misunderstanding children. In N. Coupland, H. Giles, & J. M. Wiemann (Eds.), *"Miscommunication" and problematic talk* (pp. 44-60). Newbury Park: Sage.

Ochs, E. (1992). Indexing gender. In A. Duranti & C. Goodwin (Eds.), *Rethinking context: Language as an interactive phenomenon* (pp. 335-358). Cambridge, England: Cambridge University Press.

Ochs, E. & Schieffelin, B. B. (1995). The impact of language socialization on grammatical development. In P. Fletcher & B. MacWhinney (Eds.), *Handbook of child language* (pp. 73- 94). Oxford: Basil Blackwell.

Philips, S. (1983). *The invisible culture: Communication in classroom and community on the Warm Springs Indian reservation.* New York: Longman.

Platt, M. (1986). Social norms and lexical acquisition: A study of deictic verbs in Samoan child language. In B. B. Schieffelin & E. Ochs (Eds.), *Language socialization across cultures* (pp. 127-152). New York: Cambridge University Press.

Rogoff, B. (1990). *Apprenticeship in thinking.* New York: Cambridge University Press.

Sachs, H., Schegloff, E., & Jefferson, G. (1974). A simplest systematics for the organization of turn-taking in conversation. *Language, 50,* 696-735.

Schegloff, E., Jefferson, G., & Sacks, H. (1977). The preference for self-correction in the organization of repair in conversation. *Language, 53,* 361-382.

Schieffelin, B. B. (1979). Getting it together: An ethnographic approach to the study of the development of communicative competence. In E. Ochs & B. B. Schieffelin (Eds.), *Developmental pragmatics* (pp. 73-108). New York: Academic Press.

Schieffelin, B. B. (1981). Sociolinguistic analysis of a relationship. *Discourse Processes, 4,* 189-196.

Schieffelin, B. B. (1990). *The give and take of everyday life: Language socialization of Kaluli children.* New York: Cambridge University Press.

Schieffelin, B. B. (1994). Codeswitching and language socialization: Some probable relationships. In J. F. Duchan, L. E. Hewitt & R. M. Sonnenmeier (Eds.), *Pragmatics: From theory to practice* (pp. 20-42). Englewood Cliffs, NJ: Prentice Hall.

Schieffelin, B. B., & Ochs, E. (1986a). Language socialization. *Annual Review of Anthropology, 15*, 163-191.

Schieffelin, B. B., & Ochs, E. (Eds.). (1986b). *Language socialization across cultures.* New York: Cambridge.

Scollon, S. (1982). *Reality set, socialization and linguistic convergence.* Unpublished doctoral dissertation, University of Hawaii.

Turner, V. (1967). *The forest of symbols: Aspects of Ndembu ritual.* Ithaca: Cornell University Press.

Watson-Gegeo, K., & Gegeo, D. (1986). Calling out and repeating routines in Kwara'ae children's language socialization. In B. B. Schieffelin & E. Ochs (Eds.), *Language socialization across cultures* (pp. 17-50). New York: Cambridge University Press.

Zentella, A. C. (in press). *Growing up bilingual in el Barrio.* Cambridge, MA: Basil Blackwell.

17 LISTENING TO A TURKISH MOTHER: SOME PUZZLES FOR ACQUISITION[1]

Aylin Küntay
University of California, Berkeley

Dan I. Slobin
University of California, Berkeley

Most studies of child-directed speech (CDS), or "input," have used English data. However, detailed studies of several other languages have begun to raise new questions, at all levels of linguistic analysis.[2] In the present chapter we examine the speech of one Turkish mother, in natural settings, speaking to a child in the one-word period. Using these data, we seek to systematically explore several characteristic linguistic devices of Turkish in the light of some current claims about input and children's strategies for dealing with it. We attend, particularly, to the "puzzles" presented to a child by a language with flexible word order, complex nominal and verbal morphology, and a high rate of nominal ellipsis. These factors are relevant to current debates about the roles of nouns and verbs in early acquisition, with regard to both lexical and morphological acquisition. More broadly, we attempt to characterize the structure of CDS in a language that is different in important ways from the other types of languages that have been described in the input literature.

Our data come from one mother, speaking to her daughter over the course of seven

---

[1] This study was carried out with support of a National Science Foundation Grant (BNS-8812854) to the second author, using facilities provided by the Institute of Cognitive Studies and the Institute of Human Development of the University of California at Berkeley.

[2] See for example, a review chapter by Peters (1996) on the influence of phonology and prosody on the acquisition of grammatical morphology across different types of languages; a review chapter by Lieven (1994) on crosslinguistic and crosscultural aspects of CDS; and studies of individual languages: Ziesler and Demuth (1995) on the role of prosody, register, and frequency in Sesotho CDS; Fernald and Morikawa (1993) on syntactic and discourse factors in Japanese CDS; Choi and Gopnik (in press) on the roles of nouns and verbs in Korean and English CDS; Tardif (1993, 1994) on similar issues in Mandarin CDS; Camaioni and Longobardi (1994) on discourse factors in Italian CDS; and Ochs and Schieffelin (1984) on the role of a number of sociolinguistic variables in American, Samoan, and Kaluli CDS. For an early crosslinguistic study of the nature of talk to children see Slobin (1975). For a current state-of-the-art overview, see Gallaway and Richards' (1994) edited volume, *Input and Interaction in Language Acquisition.*

months, during the age period of 1;8 to 2;3. We have given the child the pseudonym Gül. Mother and child were videotaped at home, in routine interactions, such as dressing, bathing, and mealtime. The child was a slow developer in Turkish, perhaps because she was being raised in a bilingual household, with an English-speaking father. The parents each spoke their native language to the child. Both parents were college-educated professionals. Recordings were made in the United States and Turkey. During the period under study, the child remained at the one-word stage, with a limited vocabulary in both languages. It is our impression, on the basis of informal observation of many Turkish families, that this mother's child-directed speech was in no way out of the ordinary; we will therefore cite child language data from other studies to suggest the consequences of this type of input.

The database consists of 3,167 maternal utterances, transcribed from the videotapes and grammatically coded.[3] In this paper we consider aspects of the use of nouns and verbs, word order, and rhetorical devices in the mother's speech, considering their significance for language acquisition.

Turkish is a canonically subject-object-verb (SOV) language, but all six possible orders of these three elements are both grammatical and freely occurring in discourse. More generally, there is a broad variety of word-order patterns in both spoken and written Turkish, signaling such discourse notions as topic and focus, given and new information, and the like (Erguvanlı, 1984). Verbs are richly inflected, marking person, number, tense, aspect, modality, voice, negation, and interrogation. As a consequence, many clauses consist of a single verb and its affixes, often accompanied by pragmatic particles. Examples such as the following are frequent in our data of mother's speech to a toddler:

(1) *Götür-mi-yecek-mi-sin?*
    take-NEG-FUT-Q-2SG
    'Won't you take (it)?'

(2) *Koy-du-m   tamam.*
    put-PAST-1SG alright
    'I put (it) alright.'

(3) *Yık-an-dı.*
    wash-PASSIVE-PAST
    'It has been washed.'

Nouns and pronouns are inflected for number, case, and possession, resulting in as many as three grammatical morphemes following a stem, e.g.:

(4) *El-ler-in-i   ver.*
    hand-PL-POSS.2SG-ACC give
    'Give (me) your hands.'

As is evident in these examples, morphological structures are agglutinative; that is, affixes are added to an initial stem, each bearing an additional meaning component. The morphological system is completely regular and transparent, and is quickly acquired by children younger than 2. Indeed, the first productive morphology is attested at the

---

[3] Transcriptions were made by the first author, who is a native speaker of Turkish.

one-word stage, with regard to both noun and verb suffixes (Aksu-Koç & Slobin, 1985).

THE SHIFTING TEXTURE OF INPUT: VARIATION SETS

It is typical of parental speech to a small child that the same content is repeated and rephrased in successive utterances. This is, of course, a natural consequence of the difficulty of securing a toddler's attention and compliance. Consider, first, an English example. A father is trying to prompt the memory of a child of 2;3 (Slobin, unpublished data):

(5) Who did we see when we went out shopping today?
     Who did we see?
     Who did we see in the store?
     Who did we see today?
     When we went out shopping, who did we see?

The basic question, *Who did we see?*, is repeated four times in first position, and then in second position. The first time, the question is accompanied by both a locational and a temporal setting: *shopping* and *today*. Both of these situating frames are then dropped, and afterwards reintroduced one after another: *in the store*, followed by *today*. In addition, there is lexical and phrasal substitution: *went out shopping* and *in the store*. Finally, there is a reordering.

We will refer to a series of adult utterances of this sort as a **variation set**. Underlying a variation set there is a **constant intention** — in this case, prompting the child to recall a particular event. Variation sets are characterized by three types of phenomena: (1) lexical substitution and rephrasing, (2) addition and deletion of specific reference, and (3) reordering. All three phenomena are present in the English example. In Turkish, however, there are richer possibilities for ellipsis and reordering, as well as a much broader range of morphological variation. As a result, the Turkish language learner is presented with complexly textured variation sets.

The majority of repetitions in our data are variation sets; there are 65 exact repetitions of multiword utterances in the entire corpus, compared with 220 variation sets — that is, partial repetitions of maternal utterances, with changes in lexical items, grammatical morphology, and/or word order, maintaining a constant communicative intent. There is a total of 667 utterances in variation sets; that is, about 21% of the mother's child-directed utterances are in variation sets. The average variation set is three utterances long, with a range from two to twenty-five utterances in length. (However, except for a few outliers, six seems to be the typical upper bound of variation sets.)[4]

---

[4] Each author coded the entire corpus for variation sets. The small number of disagreements were resolved by discussion. Variation sets are defined as stretches of discourse in which the mother repeats a constant communicative intent in varying form, excluding question–answer sequences in which the mother provides both the question and the answer.

NOUNS AND VERBS

Nouns and verbs have been treated rather differently in the acquisition literature. With regard to nouns, there has been a concern with the "constraints" or "principles" that may aid the child in determining the meaning of the lexical item (for a recent review, see Golinkoff, Mervis, & Hirsh-Pasek, 1994). With regard to verbs, theorists have been concerned with how children use syntactic frames to help in identifying verb meanings (reviewed by Gleitman, 1990) and with how they acquire verb argument structure — that is, learning the types of nominal arguments that are expressed with various types of verbs (e.g., Pinker, 1989; Tomasello, 1992).

A prerequisite to all of these issues, however, is the child's ability to differentiate nouns from verbs (Maratsos & Chalkley, 1980). An examination of variation sets in the input provides some clues as to how this problem might be solved in Turkish, due to the fact that nouns and verbs have different patterns of occurrence in the sequences of utterances in a set.

The core of a variation set — the constant intention — almost always consists of a verb, with optionally expressed arguments. There are only five variation sets without a verb (or implicit verb, since the copula is a zero form). By contrast, there are 44 sets without a noun (that is, 20% of all sets). Nominal and verbal categories also differ with regard to utterance position, morphological diversity, and substitution patterns. Together, this complex of factors should play a role in drawing the child's attention to the existence of two different lexical classes. (To be sure, these facts exist in isolated utterances as well. However, the variation set may play a special role, in that the same lexical items are presented within a short time frame, with regard to the same situation.)

We have a fair amount of acquisition data pointing to early acquisition of these major lexical classes. Although the child in the present study was not yet speaking, beyond a few single words, data on other Turkish children between the ages of 15 and 24 months give ample evidence that both nouns and verbs are represented in early vocabularies, and that children at the one-word stage have productive control of grammatical morphemes that are differentially applied to the two word classes (Aksu-Koç & Slobin, 1985; Ekmekçi, 1979). That is, both nouns and verbs receive several different types of inflections from very early on in Turkish child speech. Here we will consider patterns in the input that could help the child to distinguish nouns from verbs on distributional bases. Of course, semantic factors play a role as well; but we shall leave these aside, as Turkish does not seem to differ from other languages in this regard.

Word Order

As we have noted, a salient fact about Turkish speech is variability in word order. Slobin (1982) reported that adult speech to 2- and 3-year-olds uses five of the six possible orders of subject, verb, and object (omitting VOS), and that these five word orders are used by preschool children as well. Table 17.1 (from Slobin, 1982, p. 152) gives representative statistics, using the speech of two female research assistants interacting with fourteen 2- and 3-year-old Turkish children.

Table 17.1.
Percentage Occurrence of Utterance Types in Natural Conversation[1]

	Children (N = 14) (Age 2;2 – 3;8)	Adult speech to children
SOV	46	48
OSV	7	8
SVO	17	25
OVS	20	13
VSO	10	6
VOS	0	0

[1] The figures represent only utterances in which both subject and object were present, either as nouns or pronouns.

These patterns hold for each individual child in the sample, as well. In a larger sample, reported in Slobin and Talay (1986), VOS orders occur, typically with postposed subject pronoun (e.g., *Korkuttum onu ben* 'scared him I' [= I scared him]). Slobin (1982, p. 152) also reported that, in a sample of 500 adult utterances to a child of age 3;2, the first noun in the sentence was the subject only 47 percent of the time. That is, over half of the sentences addressed to the child had a case-inflected noun at the beginning. In a study of comprehension, Slobin and Bever (1982) found that all six orders could be comprehended by children as young as 2;0 in an acting-out task. That is, case inflections are used as a reliable cue to agent-patient relations, in preference to word-order patterns.

Our data show similar flexibility in word order in child-directed speech. Fully 25% of the variation sets that maintain the same lexical items have a change in word order. As a consequence of this flexibility, there is no fixed position for the verb. It is not in a privileged, utterance-final position, as is typical of other verb-final languages discussed in the literature (that is, Japanese and Korean).[5] If we examine all of the sets that have an explicit verb maintained across utterances, we find that in 37% of the cases the verb changes position from one utterance to the next. The following is a simple example:

---

[5] Aslin (1993), in a study of English and Turkish CDS, considers noun-final sentences to be "ungrammatical" in Turkish. This is a misunderstanding of the role of word order in Turkish. Each word-order pattern is grammatical, and each has pragmatic constraints on its felicitous use. Aslin's example of a "clear instance" of an "ungrammatical sentence" (p. 310) is not only grammatical, but is typical in a variation set aimed at getting a child to point to a body part: *Göster kız-ım yüz-ün-ü* 'show daughter-POSS.1SG face-POSS.2SG-ACC' [=My daughter, show (me) your face]. The final placement of the noun is not an indication "that mothers have tacit knowledge of some global strategies which may facilitate word-learning in young infants" (p. 311), but is simply the normal use of a word-order pattern in discourse context. A parallel example is given in example (6).

(6) **Ver** *el-ler-in-i.*
   give hand-PL-POSS.2SG-ACC
   'Give (me) your hands.'
   El-ler-in-i   ***ver**-ir-mi-sin?*
   hand-PL-POSS.2SG-ACC **give**-AOR-Q-2SG
   'Will you give (me) your hands?'
   El-ler-in-i   ***ver**.*
   hand-PL-POSS.2SG-ACC **give**
   'Give (me) your hands.'

Even in sequences in which word order does not change, patterns of addition and deletion of lexical items often function to change the utterance position of a verb. In the following variation set there are two verbs: *dök* 'pour' is the second word in the first utterance, is utterance-final in the third and fifth utterances, and in the sixth utterance the previously elided object noun, *su* 'water', takes over final position. The second verb, *götür* 'take', is utterance-final in the fourth line, but "retreats" deeper into the utterance as additional material is added:

(7) *Git* ***dök**-elim*   *artık bu su-yu.*
   go   **pour**-OPT.1SG just   this water-ACC
   'Let's just go and pour this water.'
   Git.
   go
   Nere-ye ***dök**?*
   where-DAT **pour**
   'Where (should we) pour it?'
   Banyo-ya ***götür**?*
   bath-DAT   **take**
   'Take (it) to the bath(tub)?'
   Banyo-ya ***götür** **dök**.*
   bath-DAT   **take**   **pour**
   'Take (it) to the bath(tub) (and) pour.'
   Kalk   banyo-ya ***götür** **dök** su-yu.*
   get.up bath-DAT take   pour water-ACC
   'Get up (and) take (it) to the bath(tub) (and) pour the water.'

Note, also, that the object noun, *su* 'water' disappears in the middle utterances and returns at the end of the sequence. Both times it is in utterance-final position — the backgrounded slot for old or given information.

Another way to approach word-order factors is to ask if nouns and verbs, overall, tend to occur in distinct utterance positions. There are actually two sorts of questions that can be posed: (1) If nouns and verbs tend to occur in different utterance positions, this can serve as a positional cue to differentiate the two classes. (2) If a particular lexical class predominates in a salient position (i.e., initial or final), that class may be more salient for the learner.

Comparable data have been presented for English by Goldfield (1993) and for Mandarin by Tardif (1994). In English CDS, nouns appear much more frequently than verbs in final position. Verbs tend to appear somewhat more frequently than nouns in initial position, but the predominant position for verbs in English is utterance medial. In Mandarin CDS, verbs are the most frequent lexical class in initial position, and in final position they are more than three times as frequent as nouns. Tardif argues that verbs are more perceptually salient than nouns in Mandarin, because they are the most frequent lexical classes to appear in both initial and final positions. By contrast, Goldfield argues that nouns are more salient than verbs in English, because they predominate in final position, while verbs tend to be in less salient medial positions.

Turkish presents yet another pattern. Table 17.2 presents the proportions of nouns, verbs, and other part-of-speech categories in initial and final positions in utterances of two or more words (excluding vocatives and discourse particles).[6]

TABLE 17.2.
Proportions of Lexical Classes in Initial and Final Utterance Positions

	Verbs	Nouns	Other
Initial	33	35	32
Final	56	25	19

To begin with, it is striking that a fairly large proportion of utterances have neither a noun nor a verb in the salient initial and final positions. These two major classes occur 68% of the time in beginnings and 81% of the time in endings. When we look at beginnings, we find that no part of speech predominates. And although verbs predominate in final position, 44% of endings are not verbs, thus reinforcing previous studies that have demonstrated that Turkish is not a strongly verb-final language. The distributional differences between nouns and verbs do not seem to be sufficient to make verbs more salient than nouns. At best, these patterns may provide the learner with a weak cue that there is some difference between the two classes, but morphological cues are far more salient than positional cues.

Morphological Form: Verbs

It is thus evident that fixed utterance position cannot guide the child to the identification of verbs in Turkish, although the language is described in the textbooks as canonically verb-final. It is also evident that invariant form cannot be used to identify a verb. In the preceding two examples, we see morphological variation in verb form: *ver / verirmisin*, *dök / dökelim*. Overall, in 35% of the cases of verb repetition within a variation set,

---

[6] The "other" categories in Table 17.2 are pronouns, adjectives, adverbs, postpositions, and question words. Utterances also begin and end with vocatives (the child's name or pet name) and various discourse markers (*please*, emphatics, etc.). We have assumed that the child can "edit these out" as not part of the message-bearing utterance, and we have done the same in Table 17.2. However, we have also done a complete count of the utterance positions of lexical items, excluding utterances that begin or end with vocatives or discourse markers. The distributional patterns of nouns and verbs is virtually identical (within 1-3 percentage points) for both types of counts.

there is a change in form of the verb. What remains constant, though, is the consistent pattern of suffixation. The verb stem is always in word-initial position; furthermore, it can stand alone as an imperative. The verb is also a reliably constant member of a variation set: In 81% of the sets with an overt verb, the verb is repeated in more than one utterance. To summarize: Most sets have repeated verbs. Although verbs change position about one-third of the time, and change form about one-third of the time, the core semantic element is always in first position in the word.

Ellipsis and Substitution: Nouns

Nouns present a somewhat different pattern of distribution. They are repeated less frequently: 53% of the time, in comparison with 81% of the time for verbs. This is primarily due to patterns of ellipsis: once a nominal argument appears, as either a full noun or a pronoun, it is replaced by zero — that is, it is no longer acoustically present in the utterance. In addition, transitive verbs can appear without their object noun in Turkish. In many instances, the object is evident in context, and it is sufficient for the mother to simply say things like *koy* 'put', *götür* 'bring', *ver* 'give', without using a noun at all. Furthermore, there is more frequent lexical substitution for nouns than verbs, as discussed later, with regard to lexical acquisition principles. However, when a noun **is** repeated, it tends to reappear in the same morphological form, as in the cases of *el-ler-in-i* 'hand-PL-POSS.2SG-ACC' in example (6) and *su-yu* 'water-ACC in example (7). Repeated nouns change form 23% of the time, in comparison with 35% for verbs. Like verbs, the noun stem is always in word-initial position, and can stand alone as the citation form or sentence subject. But, as discussed later, bare nouns are much less frequent in this corpus than bare verbs. To summarize: nouns are more likely than verbs to come and go within a variation set, but, when they are repeated, they tend to preserve the same grammatical form across utterances.

Discourse Factors

These patterns take on more meaning when considered from the point of view of discourse. Our videos deal with everyday activities, such as bathing and dressing. There is little need to label objects in such interactions: They are physically present and familiar, and are the focus of ongoing activity. What is at issue is the activity itself, and the mother is at pains to engage the child in joint or directed action, repeating verbs with various modal nuances in an attempt to keep the practical action progressing. The naturalistic setting of our data differs considerably from both laboratory studies of the meanings of new object labels and from mother's checklists of new vocabulary. Both of these techniques focus on noun learning. By contrast, routine activities of the sort sampled here focus on the **actions** involving objects, rather than the objects themselves. As Nelson, Hampson, and Shaw (1993) have pointed out, "non-object words referencing locations, actions and events . . . are used in distinctive pragmatic and grammatical contexts." The context of action focus tends toward a verb-dominant pattern, as shown by differences between the numbers of verbs and nouns in the data. Goldfield (1993) has found similar patterns in English. She compared frequencies of nouns and verbs in maternal speech during two play situations, one with toys and one without. In the toy play situation there were more nouns — both types and tokens; in the non toy play situation there were more verb types and tokens.

In our situation, which was generally both non-toy and non-play, there are more **types** of nouns, but more **tokens** of verbs. Table 17.3 presents a summary.

TABLE 17.3.
Verbs and Nouns: Types and Tokens

	Verbs	Nouns
Types	153	319
Tokens	2,518	1,859
Token/Type Ratio	16.5	5.8

The mother uses 153 different verbs, as opposed to 319 different nouns; however, these verbs are used 2,518 times, in contrast to 1,859 occurrences of the nouns. Expressed in terms of token-type ratios, the ratio for verbs is 16.5, while the ratio for nouns is 5.8. That is, verbs have less lexical diversity than nouns, but individual verbs tend to be used more frequently than individual nouns, overall. This is, in itself, unsurprising. Any similar corpus will have fewer, but more frequently repeated verbs than nouns. However, given the discourse patterns of Turkish, we propose that verbs are **more stable** and **central** elements of variation sets. Nouns, on the other hand, are ephemeral linguistic elements which move in and out of verbal frames. In addition, when we consider one-word utterances within variation sets, we find that 63% of them are verbs, whereas only 27% are nouns. (The remaining one-word utterances are pronouns, adjectives, and question words.) Thus the behavior of the two word classes in variation sets, along with the patterns of ellipsis and null-pronoun use, make verbs the more reliable lexical items in the input. We suggest that these patterns may facilitate the development of verbs. In a similar vein, Hoff-Ginsberg (1990) reports that although the number of mothers' verb phrases per utterance did not predict verb development in children, self-repetitions and expansion — which repeat some constituents while changing others — did predict verb development. This is probably due to the pivotal role of verbs in variation sets.

Morphological Form: Verbs and Nouns Compared

Verbs and nouns also differ with regard to the inflectional forms in which they occur in maternal speech. Both parts of speech can occur in their root form: nouns in the nominative or citation form, verbs in the imperative. The most frequent nouns, however, do not appear in this zero-marked form, but rather in casemarked forms, as the examples of 'hands' and 'water', cited earlier. This is because, in the context of everyday activities, objects tend to be acted on rather than named or described. Some of the most frequent nouns never occur in the citation form at all — nouns such as body parts, items of clothing, and names of locations.

Verbs, by contrast, are more likely to occur in their root form, because that is the form of the imperative. This is the predominant version of most of the frequent non-mental verbs, that is, verbs that can be used as imperatives, such as *koy* 'put', *gel* 'come', *dur* 'stop', *al* 'take', *ver* 'give'.

Both nouns and verbs, of course, occur in a range of inflectional forms. The diversity can be quite staggering from an English point of view. A graphic illustration can be seen in the following two examples, where we present the range of forms of a high frequency verb, *koy* 'put' and a high frequency noun, *el* 'hand'.

(8) *Number of occurrences of forms of* koy *'put'*:

  53 *koy* [=put]
  20 *koy-ma* 'put-NEG' [=don't put]
  18 *koy-alım* 'put-OPT.1PL [=let's put]
   5 *koy-acağ-ım* 'put-FUT-1SG' [=I'll put]
   4 *koy-acağ-ız* 'put-FUT-1PL' [=we'll put]
   4 *koy-acak-sın* 'put-FUT-2SG' [=you'll put]
   2 *koy-uca-n* 'put-FUT-2SG' [=you'll put (*contracted*)]
   2 *koy-ma-n-ı* 'put-NOML-POSS.2SG-ACC' [=your putting]
   2 *koy-mak* 'put-INF' [=to put]
   2 *koy-ma-dan* 'put-NOML-ABL' [=before/without putting]
   2 *koy-du-m* 'put-PAST-1SG [=I put (past)]
   2 *koy-du-n* 'put-PAST-2SG [=you put (past)]
   2 *koy-du-k* 'put-PAST-1PL [=we put (past)]
   2 *koy-ar-mı-sın* 'put-AOR-Q-2SG' [=will you put?]
   1 *koy-uyor-uz* 'put-PRES-1SG' [=we're putting]
   1 *koy-muş-lar* 'put-PAST.EVID-PL [=they apparently put (past)]
   1 *koy-ayım* 'put-OPT.1SG' [=should I put]
   1 *koy-alım-mı* 'put-OPT.1PL-Q' [=should we put?]

  Total = 126

(9) *Number of occurrences of forms of* el *'hand'*:

12	*el-ler-in-i* 'hand-PL-POSS.2SG-ACC'	[=your hands (ACC)]
11	*el-in-i* 'hand-POSS.2SG-ACC'	[=your hand (ACC)]
7	*el-in-le* 'hand-POSS.2SG-INST'	[=with your hand]
4	*el-ler-i* 'hand-PL-ACC'	[=hands (ACC)]
4	*el-in* 'hand-POSS.2SG'	[=your hand]
3	*el-ler-in* 'hand-PL-POSS.2SG'	[=your hands]
2	*el-ler-in-le* 'hand-PL-POSS.2SG-INST'	[=with your hands]
2	*el-in-e* 'hand-POSS.2SG-DAT'	[=to your hand]
2	*el-in-de* 'hand-POSS.2SG-LOC'	[=in your hand]
2	*el-imiz-i* 'hand-POSS.1PL-ACC'	[=our hand (ACC)]
1	*el-ler-im-i* 'hand-PL-POSS.1SG-ACC'	[=my hands (ACC)]
1	*el-ler* 'hand-PL'	[=hands]
1	*el-in-in* 'hand-POSS.2SG-GEN'	[=of your hand]
1	*el-in-de-yken* 'hand-POSS.2SG-LOC-CONVERB'	[=while in your hand]
1	*el-in-de-ki-ni* 'hand-POSS.2SG-LOC-REL-ACC'	[=the one in your hand (ACC)]

1 *el-im-den* 'hand-POSS.1SG-ABL'   [=from my hand]
1 *el* 'hand'

Total = 57

With regard to inflectional diversity, verbs differ from nouns in two important ways: (1) There is a greater diversity of available verb inflections, because so many different types of notions are marked on the verb in Turkish, while nouns can only be marked for number, case, and possession. The average verb type occurs with 16.95 different combinations of suffixes, while the average noun occurs with 7.65. (2) The suffixes that apply to verbs and nouns, by and large, come from two different sets, with the salient exception of the plural, which applies to both (e.g. *gel-di-ler* 'come-PAST-PL [=they came], *el-ler* 'hand-PL [=hands]).

There are extensive child language data with regard to these factors in Slobin's (1982) cross-sectional study of 39 children between the ages of 2;0 and 4;8. With regard to diversity of inflectional forms, we have calculated mean inflectional length of verbs and nouns in these data. At all age groups, and for each child, verbs exceed nouns in the number of morphemes added to the root, as shown in Table 17.4.

TABLE 17.4. Mean Morpheme Lengths
of Verbs and Nouns in Child Speech and Child-Directed Speech

	Children (N = 39) (Age 2;0 – 4;8)	Mother (this study)
Verbs	2.60	2.18
Nouns	1.67	1.96

Overall, the average mean length in morphemes is 2.60 for verbs and 1.67 for nouns. This compares with adult averages of 2.18 and 1.96 in our maternal speech corpus. (Our CDS sample has a lower average verb length than the child sample due to the frequent use of imperatives, which consist of a bare verb stem. This form is infrequent in the child speech samples, drawn from child–adult interaction.) Furthermore, these child data are consistent with the second factor distinguishing nouns from verbs, in that the appropriate morphemes are added to each lexical class. Thus, the patterns we find in our maternal speech data are matched by patterns in a large sample of Turkish children. And, clearly, there is no evidence of a "noun advantage" at any point in the available data: early speech at the one-word stage, speech in the 2 to 5 age range, and maternal speech.

Verbs in Variation Sets

Returning to the maternal speech data, it is informative to track the successive occurrences of a verb through a variation set. An individual verb can change position, suffixes, and accompanying nouns from utterance to utterance. Consider the following extended sequence, in which the mother is trying to elicit action from the child:

(10) **Çıkart-tı-m** benimkinin çekirdeğini. [removes pit from fruit]
     '**I.removed** the pit from mine.'
     Sen de mi **çıkart-ıcan**? [child nods]
     '**Will.you.remove** too?'
     Çıkart bakim. [child removes pit]
     '**Remove** (it), let's see.'
     Immh! Aferin yavrum! Sen de çekirdeğini **çıkart-tın**.
     'Mm-hm. Good for you! **You.removed** your pit too.'
     İkimiz de çekirdeğini **çıkart-tık**.
     'Both of us **we.removed** the pit.'

Several important features can be noted in this variation set. If you listen to it, even without knowing Turkish, the verb stands out as an acoustic unit. It is a sort of acoustic gestalt which achieves saliency as it stands out against a shifting background. The root, too, begins to stand out, against an array of different suffixes. This seems to be a figure-ground phenomenon in auditory speech perception.

In terms of discovering the verb's argument structure, however, another kind of strategy is required. Lila Gleitman (1990; Landau & Gleitman, 1985) has insightfully argued that the syntactic frame in which a verb occurs provides the learner with information about its argument structure. This is her "syntactic bootstrapping" hypothesis: The child can learn much about the meaning of a verb by observing the set of syntactic frames in which it occurs. In a language like Turkish, with its high rate of null elements and ellipsis, we propose that syntactic bootstrapping must attempt to "reconstruct" the full argument structure of a verb by comparing a series of utterances, such as those in the variation set in (11). This set has the following sequence of frames for the verb çıkart:

(11) VERB   NOUN-OBJECT
     PRONOUN-SUBJECT   VERB
     VERB
     PRONOUN-SUBJECT   NOUN-OBJECT   VERB
     PRONOUN-SUBJECT   NOUN-OBJECT   VERB

The last two utterances give the full argument structure of the verb. The child could be led astray, however, by trying to determine the argument structure for each individual utterance. Rather, it is the **set** that provides the fuller definition. In other instances, some argument may remain implicit across an entire set, as in the following series of utterances during block play:

(12) Bi sen bi ben koy-alım.
     one you one I put-OPTATIVE
     'Let's each of us put.'
     Ağız-ın-a koy-ma güzel-im.
     'Don't put in your mouth, sweetheart.'
     Üzer-in-e koy.
     'Put on top.'
     Yerine- yere koy- halının üzerine.
     'Put in place- on top of the rug.'

Halının üzerine koy güzelim.
    'On top of the rug put, sweetheart.'
In this series, the object — block — is never mentioned, and the full locative goal
argument — 'on top of the rug' — with location noun and postposition, does not occur
in each utterance. In fact, the first utterance has neither patient-object nor goal, while it
is the only one in the series that has subject pronouns. Thus, in order to extract the full
argument frame for 'put' — AGENT, PATIENT, LOCATION — it is necessary to collapse across
the variation set and extract the relevant elements.
    Recall, also, that 79% of maternal speech in this sample does **not** occur in variation
sets. This gives us a more realistic picture of the task facing a child learner of this type
of language. It must be necessary to store information across a range of separate utterances — not only in order to discover the range of subcategorization frames for an
individual verb, as Gleitman has proposed, but also to assemble any particular subcategorization frame, since the full frame may not be explicitly expressed in any individual
utterance.
    Patterns of suffixation may also serve as cues to the learner that there are semantic
subclasses of verbs. It appears that some verbs appear to be "specialized" with regard to
the suffixal patterns which they exhibit. For example, *koy* 'put' is often followed by the
negation marker, since babies are notorious in placing objects in locations where they
don't belong. The verbs *al* 'take', *ver* 'give', *gel* 'come', and *git* 'go' often occur with
the connective suffix *-Ip*, followed by another verb, because these verbs function in serial
directives, such as:
(13) *Gid-ip alır-mı-sın bi mendil bana.*
       go-CONNECTIVE get-Q-2SG one kerchief to.me
       'Can you go get me a kerchief?'
(14) *Gül-cüm mavi peçeteyi al-ıp yüzünü silermisin?*
       Gül-DIM blue handkerchief take-CONNECTIVE your.face can.you.wipe
       'Gülcüm, can you take the blue handkerchief and wipe your face?'
The verb *iste* 'want' is used with the conditional in a sort of mitigating function for
directives, such as:
(15) *Öbür pabucunu giyelim istersen Gülcüm.*
       'Let's put on the other shoe if.you.want, Gülcüm.'
    Such patterns might, at first, be learned verb-by-verb, as Tomasello (1992) has
suggested in characterizing a "Verb Island" hypothesis. That is, each verb is "an island
onto itself" with regard to its inflections and argument structure. The next step, however,
might be an examination of the verbs that can occur with a given suffix. For example,
the verbs that can be suffixed by the connective *-Ip* describe a preparatory movement or
action to that described in the following main verb. At first, these may constitute a
small, closed set for the child, all having to do with moving to act and causing objects to
move in the process: 'go', 'come', 'give', 'take', 'get', 'bring'. These verbs, when
suffixed by *-Ip*, are followed by a consequent action. The pattern of VERB-*ip* VERB may
orient the child, at first, to the sequence of 'orienting act, consequent act', and later
generalize to other verbs. In the process, of course, the syntactic function of the suffix
is also acquired. This is, to be sure, pure speculation at this point — but speculation

stimulated by the observation of cooccurrence patterns in child-directed speech.

Nouns and Verbs Again

To summarize: Nouns and verbs differ not only semantically, but with regard to their privileges of occurrence in individual utterances and sequences of utterances. Neither word class has a fixed utterance position. Each has a distinctive set of suffixed inflections. Verbs are more likely to change position and form across utterances, whereas nouns are more likely to be elided or replaced, but maintaining form when repeated.

LEXICAL ACQUISITION PRINCIPLES

Learning Noun Meanings

In recent years there have been numerous proposals for principles or constraints that may aid the child in lexical acquisition. Much attention has been paid to difficulties that the child may have in determining the referential range of a lexical item, particularly a noun. Here we wish to focus on one sort of problem: differentiating the meanings of two nouns that are used to refer to the same type of object in child-directed speech. Markman (1989, 1990, 1991) provides the child with a **Mutual Exclusivity Assumption**: "children constrain word meanings by assuming at first that words are mutually exclusive — that each object will have one and only one label" (Markman, 1990). Thus, for example, if a child knows the referent of *mittens* and is offered a new hand-covering called *glove*, she will not assume that *mitten* and *glove* both mean 'hand-covering', but rather will look for a new meaning for *glove*. Golinkoff, et al. (1994) provide a different explanation for such situations. They propose the **Novel Name – Nameless Category Principle** (N3C): "Novel terms map to previously unnamed objects" (p. 143). That is, a child using mutual exclusivity thinks: "*Glove* can't mean the same thing as *mitten*, because my mitten already has a name, so *glove* must mean something else"; whereas the child using N3C thinks: "I know what *mitten* means, so *glove* must be the name of this new kind of object."   Note that, in both scenarios, the child must be able to notice a difference between the two referent objects.   This is a basic factor in most of the research and theorizing on strategies for acquiring the meanings of object names.

Both of these proposals can be treated as part of a broader principle, the **Principle of Contrast** proposed by Eve Clark (1987, 1988, 1990, 1993): "Speakers take every difference in form to mark a difference in meaning" (1993, p. 64).   Clark argues that languages have no true synonyms; even words that have the same reference differ in sense, reflecting different registers (e.g., *teach* vs. *instruct*), dialects (e.g., *truck* vs. *lorry*), or various pragmatic nuances, such as "emotive coloring" (e.g., *dog* vs. *mutt*).

Equipped with any or all of these principles, the child will not use *mitten* and *glove* interchangeably, and will seek to discover some difference in the references or contexts of use of the two nouns. Our data suggest, however, that this may not always be possible.   This mother — and probably parents in general — substitutes nouns referring to the same object, in the same communicative situation, with the intent of securing the child's attention or compliance. Consider, for example, the following variation set, with two terms for 'shoe', *pabuç* and *ayakkabı*. In the adult language these two terms are not synonyms. *Pabuç*, originally from Persian, simply means 'shoe'. *Ayakkabı* is transparently Turkish in origin: *ayak* 'foot' plus a form of the root *kapa*, referring to covering or closing — thus, 'foot-cover'. *Ayakkabı* can refer to a boot as well as a shoe, and it also serves as the generic term for footwear. Thus the two words clearly adhere to Clark's Principle of Contrast. But do they in the following variation set, in which the mother is unsuccessfully urging the child to remove her shoes?

(16) **Pabuç**-*lar-ın-ı çıkarırmısın lütfen?*
    'Will you take off your shoes (*pabuç*) please?'
    Gülcüm **pabuç**-*lar-ın-ı çıkar.*
    'Gülcüm, take off your shoes (*pabuç*).'
    Yavrucum **pabuç**-*lar-ın-ı çıkarırmısın?*
    'My pet, will you take off your shoes (*pabuç*)?'
    Çıkarırmısın **ayakkabı**-*lar-ın-ı?*
    'Will you take off your shoes (*ayakkabı*)?'

Here there is no difference in register, in referential scope, in taxonomic level, or in emotive coloring. Rather, the lexical substitution marks the mother's frustration in achieving her communicative intent.

In a recent experimental study with 2-year-olds, Mervis, Golinkoff, and Bertrand (1994) have demonstrated that, in certain circumstances, children will accept two names for the same object. They conclude: "A novel term heard in the presence of only objects for which the child already has a name will most likely be interpreted as a second basic-level name for the category to which the object(s) belongs" (p. 1175). However, they are vague about the factors that might guide the child to such an interpretation, rather than, for example, a decision that the second term is a subordinate or superordinate of the first. And they have nothing to say about the child's possible search for such pragmatic factors as "emotive coloring," although children clearly hear a variety of diminutives, augmentatives, pejoratives, and affectionate terms for the identical objects. Yet this is a start. They propose that 2-year-olds are capable of searching for cues of communicative intent, and will treat two terms as labels for the same object if, in their terms, "the input is relatively neutral" (p. 1174).

We believe that it is possible to go further, by allowing the child to make more subtle use of communicative cues than simply identifying a context as "relatively neutral." In the variation set we have been considering, the child knows that she is not involved in a "naming game," but rather in a negotiation about removing the objects on her feet. Lois Bloom, in a recent paper with Tinker and Margulis (Bloom, Tinker, & Margulis, 1993) has proposed a **Principle of Relevance**, inspired by the work of Sperber and Wilson (1986). Bloom et al. propose (p. 447):

> In the successful language-learning scenario, a language tutor shares a child's focus of attention and the word the child hears has relevance because its target is already part of what the child has in mind. . . . [T]he representations one

already has in mind from the discourse context narrow the possible meanings one might set up on hearing a sentence.

We would add to this principle, the child's awareness of the sort of activity type in which she is engaged and the sort of speech act used by the mother. As Susan Ervin-Tripp has pointed out (1986, p. 420):

[A]ctivity conditions in which interaction is occurring set up the context for language acquisition. The relevant features include shared goals, pertinent objects and actions, and presuppositions which underlie what is easily understood in talk, and what must, on the other hand, be made explicit. . . .

In the "shoe-removal" scene, the mother is trying to instill a shared goal, directing the child's action to the pertinent objects, the shoes. What is at issue is not what the objects are called, but what is to be done with them — that is, the activity type. This should be evident to the child on the basis of the mother's requesting/demanding speech act. Many years ago, when "input" or "child-directed speech" was still called "baby talk," Ervin-Tripp pointed out the importance of a speech-act analysis (1980, p. 394):

It now appears that many of the structural peculiarities of baby talk are a result of the different interactional goals of adults interacting with children. Control acts reflect adult managerial and protective roles, naming reflects teaching, confirmation checks and repetition reflect concerns with intelligibility.

We suggest that Bloom's Principle of Relevance can only function in contexts of joint attention to **activity type** and **speech act**. A variation set that consists of a repeated control act is a cue to the child that the Principle of Contrast need not apply. This is signaled in our example by the constant verb-stem çıkar 'remove' across utterances, with grammatical inflections indicating directive speech acts — the yes–no question, which is an indirect speech act, and the bare stem, which is the imperative. In the naming game, by contrast, these inflections would be replaced by declarative forms. In that context, pabuç and ayakkabı may indeed have different senses, but in the context of a control act directed at the objects on the child's feet, the lexical variation is not relevant. Thus, to expand on Mervis et al. (1994), we suggest that children do not only accept multiple names for the same object in "relatively neutral" contexts. They are more adept social beings than that. They are able to assess the relevance of lexical choice to the inferred communicative goals of the speaker.

Lexical Substitutions Not Limited to Nouns

Gathercole (1989), in a critique of the Principle of Contrast, introduces Gricean conversational principles to guide the child in determining the speaker's communicative intent. Her cases, however, are all based on the assumption that speakers do, indeed, use contrasting forms to carry out contrasting conversational purposes. She would not expect to find many examples such as pabuç and ayakkabı. In fact, she states directly (p. 699): "The probability that any two forms will be heard in exactly the same set of contexts is, if not nil, near nil." However, in our variation set data there are numerous examples of substitutions of lexical items, and within a range of part-of-speech categories. The following are typical examples:

(17) *Verb substitution*:
   Şapka!
   'Hat!'
   Tak *kafana şapkayı.*
   'Put (**tak**) the hat on your head.'
   Bak şapka.
   'Look, hat.'
   Koy *kafana şapkayi'.*
   'Put (**koy**) the hat on your head.'
(18) *Adjective Substitution*:
   Güzel-mi erik?
   'Is the plum nice?'
   Tatlı-mı?
   'Is (it) sweet?
(19) *Postposition Substitution:*
   *Ayaklarını koyma masanın **üzerine**.*
   'Don't put your feet on.top.of (**üzerine**) the table.'
   *Ayaklarını masanın **üstüne** koyma.*
   'Don't put your feet on.top.of (**üstüne**) the table.'
(20) *Vocative Substitution:*
   *Gel benim **sevgilim**.*
   'Come my love.'
   *Gel benim **yavrum**.*
   'Come my pet.'

In some cases, the words that are substituted have different overall distributions, as is true of 'nice' and 'sweet', for example. But, in the context of this variation set, they are equivalent: they both refer to a positive evaluation of the taste of the plum, and the child should not be led to try to differentiate their meanings, recognizing that they are being substituted within a variation set. In other cases, the words seem to be true synonyms. The two locative postpositions, *üstüne* and *üzerine* seem to have identical distributions as locative terms, though the latter may have temporal extensions not available to the former. Yet, in locative contexts, the child would be led astray to search for contrasts. And, finally, in probably all cases of CDS, caretakers use a wide range of pet names for the child, all occurring in identical vocative contexts. Gül was not only called *sevgilim* 'my love' and *yavrum* 'my pet', but was also frequently called *canım* 'my soul', *güzelim* 'my pretty one', *maymunum* 'my monkey', and more. Furthermore, these terms also occur with diminutive suffixes, with no change in affective or interactive meaning: *yavrucum, canikom, Gülcüm*, and the like. In sum, synonymity is not such a rare phenomenon — especially when we consider such "functional synonyms" as those that co-occur in variation sets.

THE CAPACITY TO INFER

As has been frequently pointed out, a linguistic message does not fully determine an interpretation. Rather, by providing particular lexical items in a particular grammatical frame in a particular context, the speaker "nudges" the listener towards a preferred interpretation. Child-directed speech is no different, as we have seen, for example, in patterns of ellipsis. However, the mother's assumption of Gül's capacity to infer is more pervasive than simply the assumption that an elided noun can be filled in from context. A similar phenomenon occurs repeatedly in constructions which we characterize as "verb ellipsis." These occur in serial verb constructions using nonfinite forms that are designated as "gerunds" or "converbs" (Slobin, 1995). In some instances, the mother uses a construction with both a nonfinite and a main verb, such as:

(21) *Otur-arak   iç.*
      sit-GERUND drink-IMP
      'Drink sitting.'

The gerund *oturarak* 'sitting' describes the manner in which the action designated by the main verb is to be carried out. However, most often the child is simply presented with a gerund, and must infer the elided main verb. The following example is typical:

(22) [Gül refuses to sit while eating.]
      Otur-arak.
      sit-GERUND
      '(Eat) sitting.'

In such communications, the focus is on the manner in which the action is to be carried out. In some situations, the action itself is not so much elided as simply not at issue — perhaps not even easily lexicalizable. In the following example, the mother wants Gül "to do something to her arm" in a particular manner:

(23) [Gül bites mother on arm; mother objects and wants to be kissed]
      Isır-arak değil, öp-erek.
      bite-GERUND not, kiss-GERUND
      'Don't (act on my arm) bitingly, (but rather) kissingly.'

Another frequent elided verb construction uses a negative form, focusing an implicit imperative on the manner of action. Here are two examples, one with an explicit verb and one with an implied verb:

(24) *Gel, denize kenarına gidelim, çamura bas-madan.*
      'Come, let's go to the sea shore, **without.stepping.in** the trash.'

(25) *Bağır-madan.*
      'Without-shouting.'
      [=Whatever you're doing, do it **without shouting**.]

Again, we are faced with a learning task in which the child must successfully infer the mother's communicative intent in order to correctly assign meaning to linguistic form. These nonfinite forms are not used for description of actions, and they are not morphologically imperatives. In order to be interpreted, they must be understood as control acts directed at the manner in which an action — named or unnamed — is to be performed (or not performed).

COMPLEXITY: SCOPE OF INTERROGATION

As a final "puzzle for acquisition," we present data on the mother's use of the yes–no question suffix *-mI*. This suffix is affixed to the verb for general polar questions, and is affixed to any particular lexical element that is the focus of specific interrogation. Its scope is thus determined by position with regard to the preceding content word. Lexically, however, it is always treated as part of that word, since it matches the final syllable of the word in vowel harmony. (That is, it occurs in the forms *-mı, -mi, -mu,* and *-mü,* depending on the preceding vowel.) The suffix occurs in the following range of contexts in our data:

(26a) **Verb**:
Aç-tı-n-**mı**?
open-PAST-2SG-Q
'Did you open (it)?'

(26b) **Adjective**:
Güzel-**mi**?
pretty-Q
'Is (it) pretty?'

(26c) **Noun**:
Kabuk-**mu** ist-iyor-sun?
peel-Q want-PRES-2SG
'Is it the peel that you want?'

(26d) **Pronoun**:
Ban-a-**mı** telefon?
PRO.1SG-DAT-Q telephone
'Is the telephone for **me**?'

(26e) **Adverb:**
Bur-da-da-**mı** bubu var?
here-LOC-FOCUS-Q sore exist
'Is it here that there's a sore?'

A further level of complexity occurs with regard to verbs in which the person/number marker is a form of the copula. This occurs in present progressive and future forms, among others. In such verbs, the question particle precedes the person-marker. For example:

(27) İst-iyor-**mu**-sun?
want-PRES-Q-2SG
'Do you want?'

(28) Yut-abil-ecek-**mi**-sin?
swallow-ABILITY-FUTURE-Q-2SG
'Will you be able to swallow?'

If the mother is making any attempt to simplify the input for the sake of the learner, we might expect her to limit the use of the yes–no particle to verbs, and perhaps only to verbs in which it appears in final position. However, all of these types of forms appear freely and abundantly in the data, as do nonfinite verb forms and long strings of agglutinative affixes wherever applicable, as in adult-directed speech. At all identifiable points of morphological complexity, we see no evidence of simplification or avoidance of complex forms in child-directed speech. (And, on the basis of our cross-sectional developmental data, comparable morphological complexity is to be found in pre-school-age speech.)

CONCLUSIONS

In conclusion, this detailed analysis of some aspects of Turkish CDS makes it clear that each language presents the learner with a particular set of multiply-intersecting problem spaces. Part of acquiring a language lies in determining the relevant cues to each of those spaces. In Turkish, the child must learn to track lexical items across varying utterance positions, with different associated collections of agglutinated morphemes, moving in and out of patterns of ellipsis. This mother did not seem at pains to simplify these tasks for the child. If anything, we would propose that the entire set of cues is necessary for the child to be able to solve the problem. That is, without being exposed to this range of variety, it would probably take much longer to identify the relevant dimensions of lexical, morphological, and syntactic variation in the language.

Because so many factors interact, we would urge caution in generalizing from one language to another. For example, Turkish, Korean, and Japanese are all verb-final languages with a great deal of nominal ellipsis. Yet Turkish differs in several important respects — particularly with regard to its extensive and obligatory system of agglutinative morphology and its considerable use of post-verbal elements in discourse.

Finally, we underline the importance of studying the acquisition of linguistic forms in the context of their use in communicative situations. The child is working at understanding the structure of interpersonal action as part and parcel of the task of deciphering and organizing linguistic structure. It would be strange, indeed, to equip the child with subtle means for detecting lexical, morphological, and syntactic structures, while leaving her with only the most primitive equipment for learning to become an interactive member of human society. Every linguistic structure that we have explored in CDS takes its meaning in definable communicative contexts. We believe that the child is at least as good at defining those contexts as we are.

In conclusion, of course, we will not be able to tell the full story until we have detailed data on both CDS and the speech of the child, gathered longitudinally, across children and languages. We are only at the beginning of understanding the roles of individual differences and individual languages in the process of language development.

REFERENCES

Aksu-Koç, A. A., & Slobin, D. I. (1985). The acquisition of Turkish. In D. I. Slobin (Ed.), *The crosslinguistic study of language acquisition. Vol. 1: The data* (pp. 839-878). Hillsdale, NJ: Lawrence Erlbaum Associates.

Aslin, R. N. (1993). Segmentation of fluent speech into words: Learning models and the role of maternal input. In B. de Boysson-Bardies, et al. (Eds.), *Developmental neurocognition: Speech and face processing in the first year of life* (pp. 303-315). Dordrecht/Boston: Kluwer.

Bloom, L., Tinker, E., & Margulis, C. (1993). The words children learn: Evidence against a noun bias in early vocabularies. *Cognitive Development, 8*, 431-450.

Camaioni, L., & Longobardi, E. (1994, June). A longitudinal examination of the relationships between input and child language acquisition. Paper presented at First Lisbon Meeting on Child Language with Special Reference to Romance Languages, Lisbon.

Choi, S., & Gopnik, A. (in press). Early acquisition of verbs in Korean: A cross-linguistic study. *Journal of Child Language.*

Clark, E. V. (1987). The principle of contrast: A constraint on language acquisition. In B. MacWhinney (Ed.), *Mechanisms of language acquisition* (pp. 1-33). Hillsdale, NJ: Lawrence Erlbaum Associates.

Clark, E. V. (1988). On the logic of contrast. *Journal of Child Language, 15*, 317-335.

Clark, E. V. (1990). The pragmatics of contrast. *Journal of Child Language, 17*, 417-431.

Clark, E. V. (1993). *The lexicon in acquisition.* Cambridge, England: Cambridge University Press.

Ekmekçi, Ö. F. (1979). *Acquisition of Turkish: A longitudinal study on the early language development of a Turkish child.* Unpublished doctoral dissertation, University of Texas, Austin.

Erguvanlı, E. E. (1984). *The function of word order in Turkish grammar.* Berkeley: University of California Press.

Ervin-Tripp, S. (1980). Speech acts, social meaning and social learning. In H. Giles (Ed.), *Language: Social psychological perspectives* (pp. 389-396). Oxford and New York: Pergamon Press.

Ervin-Tripp, S. M. (1986). Activity types and the structure of talk in second language learning. In J. A. Fishman, et al. (Eds.), *The Fergusonian impact; Vol. 1: From phonology to society* (pp. 419-435). Berlin, New York, Amsterdam: Mouton de Gruyter.

Fernald, A., & Morikawa, H. (1993). Common themes and cultural variations in Japanese and American mothers' speech to infants. *Child Development, 64*, 637-656.

Gallaway, C., & Richards, B. J. (Eds.). (1994). *Input and interaction in language acquisition.* Cambridge: Cambridge University Press.

Gathercole, V. C. (1989). Contrast: A semantic constraint? *Journal of Child Language, 16*, 685-702.

Gleitman, L. (1990). The structural sources of verb meanings. *Language Acquisition, 1*, 3-55.

Golinkoff, R. M., Mervis, C. B., & Hirsh-Pasek, K. (1994). Early object labels: The case for a developmental lexical principles framework. *Journal of Child Language, 21*, 125-155.

Goldfield, B. A. (1993). Noun bias in maternal speech to one-year-olds. *Journal of Child Language, 20*, 85-99.

Hoff-Ginsberg, E. (1990). Maternal speech and the child's development of syntax: A further look. *Journal of Child Language, 17*, 85-99.

Landau, B., & Gleitman, L. (1985). *Language and experience: Evidence from the blind child.* Cambridge, MA: Harvard University Press.

Lieven, E. V. M. (1994). Crosslinguistic and crosscultural aspects of language addressed to children. In C. Gallaway & B. J. Richards (Eds.), *Input and interaction in language acquisition* (pp. 56-73). Cambridge, England: Cambridge University Press.

Maratsos, M., & Chalkley, M. A. (1980). The internal language of children's syntax: The ontogenesis and representation of syntactic categories. In K. E. Nelson (Ed.), *Children's language, Vol. 2.* New York: Gardner Press.

Markman, E. (1989). *Categorization and naming in children: Problems of induction.* Cambridge, MA: MIT Press, Bradford Books.

Markman, E. (1990). Constraints children place on word meanings. *Cognitive Science*, **14**, 57-77.

Markman, E. (1991). The whole object, taxonomic, and mutual exclusivity assumptions as initial constraints on word meanings. In J. P. Byrnes & S. A. Gelman (Eds.), *Perspectives on language and cognition: Interrelations in development*. Cambridge, England: Cambridge University Press.

Mervis, C. B., & Golinkoff, R. M., & Bertrand, J. (1994). Two-year-olds readily learn multiple labels for the same basic-level category. *Child Development*, **65**, 1163-1177.

Nelson, K., Hampson, J., & Shaw, L. K. (1993). Nouns in early lexicons: Evidence, explanations and implications. *Journal of Child Language*, **20**, 61-84.

Ochs, E., & Schieffelin, B. B. (1984). Language acquisition and socialization: Three developmental studies and their implications. In R. Shweder & R. LeVine (Eds.), *Culture theory: Essays on mind, self, and emotion* (pp. 276-320). Cambridge, England: Cambridge University Press.

Peters, A. (1996). Language typology, prosody, and the acquisition of grammatical morphemes. In D. I. Slobin (Ed.), *The crosslinguistic study of language acquisition, Vol. 4*. Hillsdale, NJ: Lawrence Erlbaum Associates.

Pinker, S. (1989). *Learnability and cognition: The acquisition of argument structure*. Cambridge, MA: MIT Press.

Slobin, D. I. (1972-73). Crosslinguistic study of the acquisition of English, Italian, Serbo-Croatian, and Turkish. Unpublished raw data.

Slobin, D. I. (1975). On the nature of talk to children. In E. H. Lenneberg & E. Lenneberg (Eds), *Foundations of language development: A multidisciplinary approach, Vol. 1* (pp. 283-297). New York: Academic Press.

Slobin, D. I. (1982). Universal and particular in the acquisition of language. In E. Wanner & L. R. Gleitman (Eds.), *Language acquisition: The state of the art* (pp. 128-172). Cambridge, England: Cambridge University Press.

Slobin, D. I. (1995). Converbs in Turkish child language: The grammaticalization of event coherence. In M. Haspelmath & E. König (Eds.), *Converbs in cross-linguistic perspective: Structure and meaning of adverbial verb forms — adverbial participles, gerunds* (pp. 349-371). Berlin, New York: Mouton de Gruyter.

Slobin, D. I., & Bever, T. G. (1982). Children use canonical sentence schemas: A crosslinguistic study of word order and inflections. *Cognition*, **12**, 229-265.

Slobin, D. I., & Talay, A. (1986). Development of pragmatic uses of subject pronouns in Turkish child language. In Aksu Koç, A., & Erguvanlı Taylan, E. (Eds.), *Proceedings of the Turkish Linguistics Conference: August 9-10, 1984* (pp. 207-228). Istanbul: Boğaziçi University Press.

Sperber, D., & Wilson, D. (1986). *Relevance: Communication and cognition*. Cambridge, MA: Harvard University Press.

Tardif, T. (1993). *Adult-to-child speech and language acquisition in Mandarin Chinese*. Unpublished doctoral dissertation. Yale University.

Tardif, T. (1994, April). Nouns are not always learned before verbs, but why? Evidence from Mandarin Chinese. Poster presented at Stanford Child Language Research Forum, Stanford University.

Tomasello, M. (1992). *First verbs: A case study of early grammatical development*. Cambridge, England: Cambridge University Press.

Ziesler, Y. L., & Demuth, K. (1995). Noun class prefixes in Sesotho child-directed speech. In E. Clark (Ed.), *Proceedings of the 26th Annual Child Language Research Forum* (pp. 137-146). Stanford, CA: CSLI.

18 LITTLE WORDS, BIG DEAL: THE DEVELOPMENT OF DISCOURSE AND SYNTAX IN CHILD LANGUAGE

Maria Pak
Richard Sprott
Elena Escalera
University of California, Berkeley

INTRODUCTION

Why should people pay attention to little words when exploring language acquisition? By "little words," we mean particles or morphemes which don't seem to have a central role in syntax or even have clear semantic content. What can these little words, like *okay, yeah, right, and, well,* and *but* tell us about the way in which children acquire their first language?

In this chapter we wish to illustrate an ongoing exploration into the connections between discourse and syntax which has been directly influenced and inspired by Susan Ervin-Tripp. Her life's work in examining both discourse and syntactic acquisition have set the stage and defined some of the theoretical questions which face the next generation of language acquisition explorers.

DISCOURSE AND SYNTAX

The answer to our question of "Why little words?" is found in the connection between syntax and discourse. Traditionally, theories of language, and linguistic structure in particular, have assumed an atomistic approach to discourse, with the belief that discourse is nothing but the building up of sets of syntactic and semantic entities which are primarily characterized by "sentences." In essence, all of linguistic structure can be character-ized at the sentence level; structures at a higher level than the sentence are not central and most assuredly derivative, if there is any structure at all. The same goes for func-tions as well as structures. The linguistic functions of particular morphemes are said to operate at the level of the sentence, indicating syntactic and/or semantic relations; the functions of language is said to be exhaustively described in this way.

But in the past fifteen years many linguists have discovered that discourse cannot be reduced to the level of the sentence. There are both structures and functions at the level of discourse which are not derivative from the traditional descriptions of language at the sentence level. Over the past ten years, Susan Ervin-Tripp and her students have begun to explore what this discovery in linguistics means for language acquisition. One aspect of this discovery concerns a class of morphemes called discourse markers (what we have been calling "little words"; see Schiffrin, 1987). Discourse markers are pragmatically plurifunctional; they index the structure or flow of discourse and index the underlying interactional factors that organize social behavior. We have chosen discourse markers to study because the constellation of pragmatic, semantic, and syntactic features which define them allow us to examine the interactions between discourse and syntax. The examples below demonstrate the markers' pragmatic plurifunctionality; in addition, markers have syntactic characteristics, such as forming questions (tags), marking subordi-nate and coordinate clause structure (connectives), and participating in different paradigm-atic categories (*okay* used as adjective, verb, and noun). Many of the semantic character-istics of discourse markers are weak (e.g., *now, and, okay*) or opaque (e.g., *well*), but they sometimes distinguish certain classes of markers from each other (e.g., causal connectives from additive connectives).

The particular markers which are the focus of our review include: *okay, and then, then, because, so,* and *yah*.

FUNCTIONS OF DISCOURSE MARKERS

Discourse markers index two dimensions of organization simultaneously: the organization of discourse into coherent structures and the organization of people's behavior into socially meaningful events, such as play, narratives, or disputes. Although these dimen-sions overlap and influence each other, it is helpful to describe them initially as separate domains.

Discourse structures involve several planes of coherence simultaneously: the message level of ideas or propositions (ideational level), the instrumental level of speech acts or conversational moves (action level), and the mechanical level of turn-taking (exchange level). In addition, discourse can be described in terms of a speaker's changing informa-tion states as the conversation unfolds, and the manner in which speakers relate to each other in an interaction (participation frameworks, Schiffrin, 1987). The exchange, action, and participation framework levels of discourse can be grouped together, denoting the **interactional** level of discourse structure, as opposed to the representative or **ideational** level. Here are some examples of discourse functions and structures:

Example 1
KE (3;10) and CO (3;10) are two girls playing in a "house" area of a preschool class-room. They have just entered the area:

1	KE:	I'm gonna play Sleeping Beauty!
2	CO:	I'm gonna play Sleeping Beauty!
3	KE:	I wanna be Sleeping Beauty!
4	CO:	I wanna be Sleeping *Beauty:\
5	KE:	I don't wanna be- I don't wanna be a *boy:\
6		I don't wanna be a *prince\
7		a prince is a boy:\
8	CO:	I don't want to be the boy *or prince\
9		Sleeping *Beauty:\
10	KE:	me *too:\
11		<2 seconds of silence>
12	KE:	now first Sleeping Beauty has to fall asleep - she falls asleep\
13	CO:	(xx and-)
14	KE:	she close her eyeses like this\
15		[KE gets into play bed; CO follows]
16	CO:	no\ no, the- the bad *witch is coming:\
17	KE:	yeah, and the bad *witch (is called) her to sleep\
18		but the prince has to kill, *kiss her\
19	CO:	yeah, and she's like *this\
20		[closes her eyes, falls asleep with arms crossed]
21	KE:	and then she *opens her eyes: and saw the prince\
22		<1>
23		here, what happened\ [something in environment]
24		a *very pretty movie- Sleeping Beauty is a very pretty movie, *isn't it\
25		[no answer from CO]
26	KE:	my daddy *loves Sleeping Beauty\
27	CO:	==Sleeping Beauty is the *best movie\
28	KE:	so first I'm gonna fall asleep\
29		[nonverbal playing; CO giggles]

Lines 1 to 10 contain a negotiation exchange between the two girls as they decide the roles for the pretend play activity. After a few moments of silence, KE begins planning the sequence of the pretend play in line 12. In line 16 CO introduces a new character and a complicating action, which KE and CO then jointly elaborate in lines 17 to 21, bringing in the role of the prince. After a distraction in line 23, KE changes topic and speech event as she shares an evaluation of the movie which they are enacting. After getting an agreement from CO in line 27, KE returns to the narrative activity. Each of these new speech events (negotiation → narrative → assessment → narrative) changes the participation framework for the two children. Their relation as speakers changes from negotiators to co-constructors of a narrative to casual conversationalists and back to co-constructors of the pretend play. At the level of speech events, "little words" like *now* introduce the narrative and *so* returns to the narrative after the intervening assessment. Examining the internal structure of each speech event, it is evident that the narratives contain many connectives: *and, but, and then,* and *so* in this example. The connectives are used collaboratively by the children to co-construct the narrative and mark its coherence on the interactional and ideational level. For example, the uses of *and* in lines 17 and 19 mark an addition to the pretend play scene, elaborating the idea further, while simultaneously marking the coordination of the two speakers' actions to create the pretend play scene. The negotiation speech event relies primarily on the exchange and action levels for its coherence, marked by repetition and rapid turn-taking. The assessment speech event contains the only tag question, explicitly signaling a response and marking coherence on the exchange and action levels of discourse.

The discourse analysis of this example highlights many functions and structures marked by words which are not part of traditional syntactic and semantic analyses. Children's interactions can also be analyzed in terms of their **social organization**. Parker and Gottman (1989) suggest that the organization of young children's peer interactions reflects the children's desire to maximize excitement, entertainment, and affect levels in play. This underlying developmental theme is manifested in affective and conversational processes observable in young children's peer interactions.

Affective developments at this age involve learning to manage one's emotional states in ways that allow one to achieve higher levels of coordination in play. Concomitantly, conversational processes relevant to this interactional concern include those used for coordinating play and the escalation and de-escalation of involvement in an interaction, and also those involved in social comparison and "gossip," talk about others that establishes a climate of agreement and solidarity.

An example from Gottman's data serves to illustrate the steps taken by young children towards higher levels of coordination in play:

Example 2:
```
1          [Two young friends are playing in parallel]
2    J:    I got a fruit cutter plate
3    D:    Mine's white.
```

4   J: You got white playdough and this color and that color.
5   D: Every color. That's the colors we got.
6
7   [They continue playing, escalating the responsiveness demand
8   directly to one another, ultimately moving toward doing the
9   same thing together (true collaborative activity):]
10 D: And you make those after we get it together, okay?
11 J: 'Kay.
12 D: Have to make these.
13 J: Pretend like those little roll cookies too, okay?
14 D: And make, um, make a, um, pancake, too.
15 J: Oh rats. This is a little pancake.
16 D: Okay. Make, make me, um, make two flat cookies.
17   Cause I'm I'm cutting any, I'm cutting this. My snake.
18
19   [When a joint activity is introduced, they begin using "we"
20   terms in describing the activity:]
21 D: Put this the right way, okay?
22   We're making supper, huh?
23 J: We're making supper. Maybe we could use, if you get
24   white, we could use that too maybe.
25 D: I don't have any white.
26   Yes, we, yes, I do.
27 J: If you got some white, we could have some, y'know.
28
29   [As they continue to play, they employ occasional contextual
30   reminders that this is a joint activity:]
31 D: Oh, we've got to have our dinner. Try to make some.

                            (Parker & Gottman, 1989, pp. 108-109)

Note that with the movement of the activity towards higher levels of coordination, many of the same discourse markers that index discourse structure also serve social-inter-actional functions such as signaling plans and intentions and ensuring the coherence of play. The tag *okay* figures prominently both in the initial escalation into true collabora-tive activity (line 10), as well as in maintaining the activity and introducing new activities (lines 13, 20). Connectives also play a role in establishing and maintaining coordinated play; they coordinate current actions with previous actions (lines 10, 14) and they justify actions that have an impact on how the interaction unfolds (line 17).

The two dimensions of discourse structures and social organization influence each other but do not fully determine each other. We have discussed both dimensions separately to highlight the distinction between functions related to organizing talk as text and functions related to organizing social interaction. But ultimately talk is social, so when we discuss the interactional functions of markers, we mean functions related to both the interactional level of discourse structure and to the organization of social behavior.

HYPOTHESES

Our exploratory research in this area has prompted us to form two hypotheses about the acquisition of discourse markers. The first is the **interactional functions hypothesis**: Given the great concern children show in organizing their social worlds (Corsaro, 1985; Parker & Gottman, 1989), we predict that the markers' initial uses will be in service of the functions related to organizing social behavior, and functions that are less related to the organization of face-to-face interactions will appear later. The later functions include marking purely representational or ideational relations and discourse structures, and syntactic functions which may rely on ideational relations (see Gerhardt, 1990, and Guo, 1994, for detailed analyses).

Further, we believe that the markers are first used in limited contexts, and later spread to other contexts, reflecting greater flexibility in use of the forms. The **limited context hypothesis**[1] predicts that children acquire markers in highly constrained discourse and social environments, such as adjacency pair discourse formats (question–answer), speech events (narratives), and social routines (gaining access to play). The increase in flexibility in the use of markers reflects changes in the constellation of social, pragmatic, semantic, and syntactic functions which define the use of the form. As the child develops, different pragmatic functions become available (such as topic-shifting within one speech event), the markers become more and more defined by semantic and ideational features, and the markers become more syntactically complex, as they are used in new syntactic frames or for different syntactic functions.

These two hypotheses describe an underlying continuity between early language use and later adult–like language use. We, therefore, presuppose a theory of linguistic structure different from the formalist belief in syntax as autonomous in both structure and process. We believe that the child's acquisition of language involves constructing schemata for each form and combining these schemata; the schemata are constructed through a combination of pragmatic, semantic, and syntactic information, as has been suggested by different theories in cognitive linguistics (Fillmore, Kay & O'Connor, 1988; Givón, 1989; Langacker, 1987). In addition, we believe the language acquisition process

---

[1] Many researchers have suggested similar hypotheses regarding the relation between competencies and their particular contexts of acquisition, both in language acquisition and in nonlinguistic cognitive and social competencies.

is shaped by the child's emerging concerns in the socioemotional realm. We believe the need for social participation through language goes beyond the desire to achieve instrumental goals. In addition to communicating individual wants, needs, and desires, language enables individuals to establish a collective focus, and to jointly construct an interaction with collaborative themes and ideas as well as collaborative physical activity. In fact, with very young children, it is often the use of language that transforms a play episode from a loose alliance in which space and goods are shared into a deliberate collaboration in which these items and the children's interactions become part of a shared system of ideas, beliefs and rules. In this way the social bases of language go beyond immediate communicative needs.

The remainder of this chapter briefly describes several studies which examine discourse markers in child language. These studies provide support for the hypotheses we have advanced.

OKAY

The word okay defies definition because of its multiple functions; the most common definition attempt is that it means "yes," but the marker is not interchangeable with the word *yes*. It is a specialized affirmative which incorporates other functions which *yes* does not contain (Bolinger, 1957; Merritt, 1984).

The uses of *okay* by children in the Family database collected by Susan Ervin-Tripp were analyzed for their functions (Escalera, 1989). Records from five families were used, with children ranging in age from 1;5 to 7;5.

The children in this database used six different functions for *okay*. The functions differed in the degree to which they index interactional, discourse, and syntactic structures. The functions were coded using the scheme described in Table 18.1.

Recall that the interactional functions hypothesis predicts that markers will at first code functions related to the maintenance and structuring of face-to-face social interaction. Only later will markers be used for functions unrelated to the online concerns of social interaction. For the functions indicated above, the hypothesis predicts that functions related to discourse structures at the action and exchange levels will be acquired first, and then functions which rely on ideational content only, such as syntactic functions, will be acquired later.

Pearson correlations were performed to determine the relation between age and kind of function used, with tags and compliance uses grouped together due to their role in structuring adjacency pairs; approbative uses, turn exchange and action/participation framework uses grouped together due to their role in marking discourse structures at levels higher than adjacency pairs; and syntactic integration by itself due to its reliance on knowledge of paradigmatic categories and on purely ideational content. Results were significant (Pearson's $R = .228$, p < .001). Table 18.2 presents the results by noting the age of onset of each of these functions.

TABLE 18.1. Functions of *Okay*

Function	Definition	Example
Compliance Use	used to signal acceptance of offers and compliance with requests	B: (showing A where to put the propeller on plane) Right in here. A: *Okay*. (A puts propeller in front).
Tag Question	used to elicit responses from addressee	A: Get your gear on when I be lazy, *okay*? B: *Okay*.
Approbative Use	used to signal agreement and verification, acknowledgments and approvals	M: I'll put it in the oven. G: *Okay*. B: Oh good, *okay*.
Turn Exchange Use	used to signal the beginning of a speaker's turn	A: We had a machine and =( )= T: =*okay*, here it goes!=
Action/Participation Framework Use	used to signal a change in activity or phase of activity or change in speaker's role	J: Just take one of them then *okay* now I'm gonna put the flour in.
Syntactic Integration	used as adjective, noun or transitive verb	A: I need your *okay* on this. B: Are you *okay*?

TABLE 18.2.
Age of First Uses of Each of the Functions Marked by *Okay*.

Function	Compliance	Tags	Approbative	Turn Exchange	Action/ Participation	Syntactic Integration
Age	1;3	2;6	3;9	3;9	4;0	4;4

In addition to demonstrating the importance of the interactional level of discourse in the first stages of acquisition of discourse markers, these results also highlight the importance of limited contexts as the framework in which this acquisition occurs. *Okay* is first acquired in the highly constrained discourse context of adjacency pairs, where answering requests with compliance is highly salient, and where a little later using the marker as a tag to set up the second part of adjacency pairs is also highly salient. As children develop at the level of discourse, other functions relevant to discourse structure emerge, such as marking action and participation frameworks within speech events, and marking turn exchanges beyond adjacency pair structures. Consequently, these functions become part of the discourse marker. In later stages, the marker interacts with other aspects of syntactic knowledge and other syntactic frames which are more ideationally based than interactionally based.

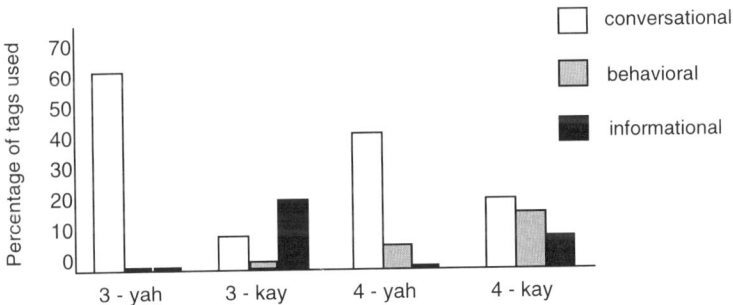

FIG. 18.1. The functions of *kay* and *yah* in three- and four-year-olds

TAG QUESTIONS

Studies of patterns of co-occurrence of certain forms with certain functions also provide converging evidence for our hypotheses. Pak (1990) analyzed the functions of the tag forms *yah* and *kay* by 3- and 4-year-old speakers of Hawai'i Creole English. The functions fell into three primary categories: conversational, behavioral, and informational. The conversational function occurs when a speaker's primary goal centers around continuing a verbal interaction. No new information is added in the response, nor does the speaker expect any. The behavioral function occurs when the speaker makes a request for action, either direct or indirect, on the part of the addressee. The informational function occurs when the speaker makes a request for new information.

Among 3-year-olds, 61% of all tag questions used *yah* as the tag and all of these served the conversational function. Conversely, 36% of questions with tags involved *kay*, and predominantly served the informational or behavioral functions. Among 4-year-olds, the association of specific tags with a limited range of functions becomes less obvious.

It is likely that the conversational function appears early because it most directly attains young children's goals in terms of organizing social interaction. According to Parker and Gottman (1989), young children's primary social concern is to maximize collaborative action. An early vehicle for this concern is the use of interactional routines. Interactional routines are sequences of conversational exchanges in which certain utterances and nonverbal behavior produce a limited set of responses. The effectiveness of these routines as language learning devices lies in their predictability, simplicity and salience to the participants. "Specific configurations of time, place, participants and goals tend to recur, leading the child to expect particular verbal and non-verbal behaviors." (Peters & Boggs, 1986; p. 84). The children in these data first begin to use questions to peers as part of an interactional routine, using the least complex, most predictable forms and functions. The 3-year-olds, for example, use tag questions with no subject–verb inversion serving the conversational function:

Example 3
A: And (-) wake up in the hospital and it was a (bad) time, *yah*?
B: You didn't cry, *yah*?
C: You didn't be bad, *yah*?
B: We saw the snake at the hospital, *yah*?
    And it was alive, *yah*?
C: Yah?
B: We went to a different hospital, *yah* girl baby?
    Yah because the — a different one.

The use of tag questions in the conversational function is highly effective because it seems to impose fixedness and routinizes the exchange for children. In this case, the placement of tags seems to facilitate turn-taking in the exchange, and yet verbal or physical responses to the questions do not seem to be expected. The tag *yah* is used by all three participants as a means of maintaining the interaction and organizing discourse.

Four-year-olds have a greater repertoire of strategies for maintaining conversational coherence. The use of specific tags to serve specific functions in the control of interactive episodes becomes less common. The child may use only parts of routines to maintain an interaction through changes in activity or setting. Here, Ju uses a vocative (*sweetie*) to maintain an interaction in spite of a change in location and activity:

Example 4
>[Je and Ju are playing in the upper level of the playhouse]
>Ju: I need to go make decorations downstairs in the pantry, just a minute.
>[Ju goes downstairs to the activity table]
>Ju: [to Je, who is still upstairs]
>Sweetie? I'm down here making decorations.

In fact, some of the older 4-year-olds demonstrate considerable skill in their construction of interactions that span a range of changes in participants and themes, even without the use of markers or routines to maintain interactional coherence. Here, a 4-year-old girl manages to negotiate and maintain an interaction which continues even after her initial partner leaves, and the new participants are playing in a different area.

Example 5
>[S and L are engaged in role play in the block area; they have constructed a house and are negotiating roles. L's sister comes to pick L up for a doctor's appointment, so S is left alone in the area.]
>S: [calling to D, who is playing outside with J and SW]
>D, D, could you play with me?
>[D consents, but remains outside. S continues to play in the block area]
>[about five minutes later Ju and A approach S]
>Ju: Can I - can we play with you?
>A: Can we play with you?
>S: [looks outside to where other girls are playing]
>Ask J and SW and (.) D.

As predicted by the interactional functions hypothesis, tags, which were initially used only as a means of maintaining an interaction, begin to be used for functions that are less related to interactional collaboration. In the following example, a tag question is used to perform an implicit control act. A child has been trying to gain access to some toys in the dress-up area for several minutes. Implicit in her utterance is a reminder to the teacher of the class rule of only four people at a time in the dress-up area, and a request that the teacher invoke the rule in her favor.

Example 6
M: No, only four people.
    Teacher, this much peoples supposed to be in here, *yah*?
    [pointing to the play area while looking towards teacher]

Note that while the child's use of *yah* serves a speech act function which doesn't directly contribute to the coordination of play in the episode, it still maintains its function of organizing interaction at the discourse level, as a turn taking device. In addition, neither the 3- nor the 4-year-olds used *yah* to mark a purely ideational shift in discourse structure.

In summary, the use of tags starts out in limited contexts, defined by social interactional functions. Gradually, as tags spread to other contexts and functions, the relation between discourse structure and social organization becomes less direct. Initially, however, the social organizational functions of the markers overshadow other functions less related to face-to-face interaction.

CONNECTIVES

Two studies (Sprott, 1992, 1993) have examined the discourse functions and the limited contexts of connectives. These studies have contrasted children's narratives and verbal disputes, because discourse coherence in narratives relies primarily on the ideational level and discourse coherence in disputes relies primarily on the interactional level.

Sprott (1992) examined the use of *because, so, and*, and *but* as discourse markers in 128 verbal disputes between peers, siblings, and adults during play activities and mealtime at home, the same database Escalera (1989) used. The 23 children ranged in age from 2;7 to 9;6. Table 18.3 displays the developmental trends for particular connectives to mark different levels of discourse coherence; the table records the first instance of each connective to have a particular function. In addition to **Exchange** and **Action** functions referred to in the above studies, this study also investigated local vs. global ideational relations. **Local ideational** refers to the use of connectives to indicate a propositional relation between two clauses. **Global ideational** refers to the use of connectives to mark shifts in argumentative tactic or the introduction of a subunit of an argument. The distinction between local and global levels of discourse has implications for the interactional functions hypothesis, since global factors such as topic play a role in the organization of discourse and the development of interactional functions.

While markers are plurifunctional, for this analysis each marker was given one primary coding, following systematically the function definitions in the order reflected in Table 18.3; this allows for a conservative identification of instances of connective use which are only ideational, in order to capture when such uses are clearly acquired. For instance, if a marker began a turn and signaled a semantic relation between two clauses across speaker turns, it was coded as having an exchange function primarily; any marker serving both interactional and ideational functions was coded either as action or exchange.

TABLE 18.3. Age-Related Differences in the Form–Function
Relations of Connectives in Verbal Disputes

	2;7 - 3;6	3;7 - 6;6	6;7 - 9;6	adults
Exchange	because and but	because and but	because and	because
Action		so and but	so and but	so and but
Local Ideational		because so and	because so and but	because so and but
Global Ideational		because	because but	because so and but

In spite of being in verbal disputes often, children between 2;7 and 3;6 hardly used connectives in this context. The specific forms under study were used at least once by the youngest children in the corpus, except *so*. Table 18.3 shows that the youngest children do not use connectives for purely ideational functions, although the markers may have ideational functions concurrent with interactional functions. As predicted by the interactional functions hypothesis, the early uses of the connectives mark the exchange structure of the interaction. For example, the youngest children used *because* only to mark the "answer" part of a question–answer adjacency pair. At later stages of acquisition, the older children used *because* to mark semantic relations between clauses within a single turn. The older children also marked shifts in argumentative tactic which did not coincide with exchange structures with *because*.

In a different study, Sprott (1993) examined connectives in both verbal disputes and spontaneous narratives in twelve 3-year-old and twelve 4-year-old children. A total of 138 discourse markers were identified from the three-year-old narratives and disputes; these came from 33 narratives and 30 disputes in 15 hours of taping. For the 4-year-old narratives and disputes, a total of 87 discourse markers were identified; there were 16 narratives and 23 disputes in ten hours of taping. Tables 4 and 5 display a full plurifunctional analysis of the functions of the connectives *and then, then, because,* and *so* drawn from these data. In addition to their discourse marking functions, the markers were also coded for their use as subordinate and coordinate conjunctions. These particular markers were chosen in order to compare syntactic characteristics, since *and then* and *then* can be used for similar coordinate clauses and *because* and *so* can be used for similar subordinate clauses.

Because versus *so*

Because versus *so* demonstrate the limited contexts associated with discourse markers. Chi-square tests of the contexts of the causal connectives show a significant difference: *because* is used more in disputes and *so* is used more in narratives (chi-square $X^2 = 13.472, df = 3, p < .01$). Further tests show that this contextual effect is significant for the 3-year-olds but not for the 4-year-olds (three: chi-square $X^2 = 10.769, df = 1, p < .01$; four: chi-square $X^2 = 2.213, df = 1, p = .1368,$ n.s.).

As predicted by the interactional functions hypothesis, the ideational and syntactic functions come later, as evidenced by comparing the functions of *so*, which is acquired later in development, to the functions of *because*, which is acquired earlier. The 3-year-olds combine clauses with *because* in eight out of thirteen cases, with only three out of the thirteen cases used for interactional functions; it clearly has ideational and syntactic functions. However, the ideational and syntactic functions are not automatically extended to *so*. The 3-year-olds used *so* to mark a definite causal relation between two propositions in only one out of seven cases, and there are no examples of clause combining. *So* was used primarily to mark changes in speech events, reorientations to different talk activities, and marking shifts in the episodic structure of narratives. It appears that each discourse marker undergoes its own development from interactional to ideational functions with little influence from other, closely related markers.

TABLE 18.4. Functions and Contexts of Causal Connectives
Produced by the 3- and 4-year-olds

		Exchange	Action	Local Ideational	Global Ideational	Clause-Combining
because	Narrative	3	-	3,4	-	3,4
	Dispute	3,4	3	3,4	-	3,4
so	Narrative	3,4	3	3,4	3,4	4
	Dispute	-	4	4	-	-

And then vs. then

Table 18.5 shows the functions of the temporal connectives in two different speech contexts at two different ages. The number of cases for these markers are too small to test statistically, but there are some suggestive patterns in them. For the 3-year-olds, *and then* was used to combine clauses in only seven out of 18 instances, while the 4-year-olds always used *and then* to combine clauses (four out of four instances). Three-year-olds used this marker for interactional functions in six out of 18 cases, the 4-year-olds never. The rest of the 3-year-old cases were markers of ideational relations without clause combination. Again, for both 3- and 4-year-olds this marker was only used in narratives, not in disputes.

TABLE 18.5. Functions and contexts of temporal connectives
produced by the 3- and 4-year-olds

		Exchange	Action	Local Ideational	Global Ideational	Clause-Combining
and then	Narrative	3	3	3,4	-	3,4
	Dispute	-	-	-	-	-
then	Narrative	4	-	4	-	-
	Dispute	4	-	4	4	-

Four-year-olds used *then* as a marker in five cases, most of which were in verbal disputes. In all of these cases the marker was used for interactional functions, especially to mark turn exchanges:

Example 7
(#) JS and DE (both boys, 4;6) are arguing about taking turns at a typewriter:
DE: *I do all of them and *you do all of them\
JS: No it's not fair\
DE: **Then** you can do it again\
JS: Okay ... not sure\

The comparison of *and then* versus *then* shows us that the syntactic function of combining clauses does not directly translate between the two connectives. While the syntactic function is definitely a part of the *and then* construction for 3-year-olds, it is not the dominant function, as it is for 4-year-olds. The use of *then* as a discourse marker is just being acquired between 3 and 4, and at this initial stage the interactional functions completely determine its use. The syntactic function comes later with the ideational functions.

It is unclear at this time why particular markers are associated with particular contexts for children, such as *because* with disputes and *so* with narratives. Children could be reflecting distributional characteristics of adult language in this respect, albeit in an "intensified" way. It is clear that children acquire each discourse marker in a particular social context to mark interactional functions and do not go beyond these contexts and functions until other linguistic, cognitive, and social developments occur.

CONCLUSION

In this chapter, we have presented data that suggest, at least for some linguistic forms, early uses occur in limited, socially defined contexts, serving interactional functions before ideational functions. These findings raise questions about language acquisition:

1.   *What is the significance of limited contexts and interactional functions in the initial stages of the acquisition of discourse markers?*

Our investigation of discourse markers and their functions has led us to postulate a theory of language acquisition in which the child acquires language in a problem solving space that simultaneously addresses the interrelated domains of language and social interaction.

The notions of limited contexts and interactional functions are central to this theory. Recall that the developmental theme underlying the organization of children's social worlds is the desire to maximize excitement, entertainment, and affect levels in play. In order to achieve these ends, children must achieve a certain level of social, affective, and linguistic competence. Our observations in 3- and 4-year-old classrooms show remarkable differences between these two age groups in ability to maintain complex interactions without the help of an adult, and in the range of linguistic forms and functions used by children at each age to support various activities in which they are engaged.

What is surprising (and elegant) about the cognitive and social constraints that structurally define young children's interactions at each stage is that they may also constrain how children solve the form–function puzzles presented to them as they acquire discourse markers.

2. *If discourse markers are initially determined by limited, socially defined contexts, when and how do children start to use them for non-interactional functions?*

What we are calling "noninteractional" functions are the meanings and the constraints on discourse markers which are not tied directly to the immediate speech context; for example, the use of *okay* as a verb or noun is not constrained by speaker turn exchanges, shifts in topic or phases of activity, or concerns about social interaction. Its approbative meaning is at the core of its presence in different paradigmatic categories.

Non-interactional functions may be considered the decontextualized uses of forms which comprise their semantic and syntactic characteristics (Langacker, 1987). The process of decontextualization, relying on cognitive capacities to create schemas based on language use and to categorize these schemas, can describe the acquisition process we have observed in these studies.

When do non-interactional functions of discourse markers come in? While each marker has a different developmental history in its details, all of our studies indicate radical changes between age 3 and 4, related to changes in discourse and social abilities. During this period children's talk begins to incorporate complex discourse structures, which in turn support complex social interactions. The give-and-take reciprocity of earlier interactions develops into higher forms of cooperation and coordination which rely on the sharing of ideas, beliefs, plans, and stories. These higher levels of cooperation and coordination demand that language become a tool for self-regulation, not just communication (Mead, 1962; Vygotsky, 1978). Language begins to be used for its ideational capacities, not just interactional capacities. In this way, the social and the discursive aspects of language use demand more schematic, decontextualized, noninteractional functions for markers.

As discourse markers begin to incorporate non-interactional functions, they begin to interact with other aspects of the child's knowledge about grammar. Specifically, connectives begin to mark coordinate and subordinate clause structure, and *okay* becomes a noun or verb or adjective. This, then, is how discourse and syntax interact, at least in this part of grammar: the communicative, interactional functions of discourse markers become the basis for the self-regulatory, ideational functions, part of which is expressed syntactically.

3. *Can the emerging pattern of discourse markers moving from interactional functions defined by limited contexts to more abstract symbolic representation observed in our data be extended to explain the acquisition of other forms? Especially forms that are viewed as central to syntax in traditional generative linguistic theories?*

These questions are the next step in exploring the relations between discourse and syntax. Having examined a particular part of linguistic ability, the use of discourse markers, we have seen how the social, pragmatic, semantic, and syntactic aspects of linguistic forms interact over the course of acquisition. These investigations promise to be a model for understanding language acquisition in its full cognitive and social contexts of development.

As language acquisition explorers, we overlook a new uncharted territory; all that we have discovered about social development, cognitive abilities, discourse, and linguistics seem to meet at some point on the horizon. We are thankful that Susan Ervin-Tripp has pointed us in this direction.

REFERENCES

Bolinger, D. (1957). *Interrogative structure of American English: The direct question.* Alabama University Press.

Corsaro, W. (1985). *Friendship and peer culture in the early years.* Norwood, NJ: Ablex.

Escalera, E. (1989). Child*ren's use of* Okay. Unpublished manuscript, University of California, Berkeley.

Fillmore, C., Kay, P., & O'Connor, M. (1988). Regularity and idiomaticity in grammatical constructions: The case of *let alone. Language,* **64**, 501-538.

Gerhardt, J. (1990). The relation of language to context in children's speech: The role of HAFTA statements in structuring 3-year-olds' discourse. *Papers in Pragmatics,* **4**:(1/2), 1-57.

Givón, T. (1989). *Mind, code and context: Essays in pragmatics.* Hillsdale, NJ: Lawrence Erlbaum Associates.

Guo, J. (1994). *Social interaction, meaning, and grammatical form: Children's development and use of modal auxiliaries in Mandarin Chinese.* Unpublished doctoral dissertation, University of California, Berkeley.

Langacker, R. (1987). *Foundations of cognitive grammar: Vol. 1, Theoretical prerequisites.* Stanford: Stanford University Press.

Mead, G. H. (1962). *Mind, self and society.* Chicago: University of Chicago Press.

Merritt, M. (1984). On the use of *okay* in service encounters. In J. Baugh & J. Sherzer (Eds.), *Language in use* (pp. 139-147). Englewood Cliffs, NJ: Prentice-Hall.

Pak, M. (1990, July). *"This much peoples supposed to be in here, yah?": Cognitive and social effects on children's use of questions.* Paper presented at the 3rd International Pragmatics Conference, Barcelona, Spain.

Parker, J., & Gottman, J. (1989). Social and emotional development in a relational context. In T. J. Berndt, & G. W. Ladd (Eds.), *Peer Relationships in Child Development* (pp. 95-132). New York: Wiley.

Peters, A. M. & Boggs, S. T. (1986). Interactional routines as cultural influences upon language acquisition. In B. B. Schieffelin & E. Ochs (Eds.), *Language socialization across cultures* (pp. 80-96). New York: Cambridge University Press.

Schiffrin, D. (1987). *Discourse markers.* New York: Cambridge University Press.

Sprott, R. A. (1992). Children's use of discourse markers in disputes: Form-function relations and discourse in child language. *Discourse Processes*, **15**, 423-439.

Sprott, R. A. (1993, March). *The development of conversational skills: Contextual and functional analyses of children's discourse markers.* Paper presented at the SRCD Biennial Meeting, New Orleans.

Vygotsky, L. S. (1978). *Mind in society.* Cambridge: Harvard University Press.

PART FOUR: NARRATIVE

19 FRAMES OF MIND THROUGH NARRATIVE DISCOURSE

Ayhan Aksu-Koç
Boğaziçi University, Istanbul

Narratives are cultural as well as individual affairs. To the extent that the entry of an individual into his or her culture is mediated by language, any personal narrative, account, or other kind of monologic text will be reflective of prior dialogic processes in the history of the narrator. Thus, a piece of narrative discourse can be taken as a context where the culture embodied by the individual unfolds simultaneously. In this study I investigate the ways in which the socioculturally determined individual comes through in the creation of a text.

The notion of cultural implies a shared perspective regarding ways of life and symbolic systems maintained within a social group, or in LeVine's terms, "an inherited system of ideas that structures the subjective experience of individuals" (1984, p. 20). Furthermore, within a culture there are subcultures, groups, or communities definable in terms of an intersection of properties such as ethnicity, gender, education, and economic standing. Almost everywhere, gender plays a role in the determination of the individual consciousness since socialization proceeds in accordance with behavior patterns and norms deemed appropriate for males and females. A self which is the product of socialization into a given sex role, then, is a member of a subculture or group. Similarly, education, which involves socialization in a formal institutional context, will have determining effects on the individual's level of literacy, cognitive skills, the extent to which these are used in everyday life, as well as his social standing (Cole & Scribner, 1984). The various constellations of these properties are expressed in the perception and interpretation of experience as well as practices of everyday life associated with different social groups. Each individual, then, experiences and interprets the world collectively within the interpretive frames of given subcultures as well as singularly as his or hers. It can therefore be assumed that when individuals create or interpret texts, the product is a function of the "frame of mind" which is determined by individual as well as sociocultural variables. In other words, every narrative has to be regarded as "contingent on a wider set of narratives" (Gee, 1991, p.3).

NARRATIVE DISCOURSE

Narrative is a genre of discourse generated in oral or written language. Students of narrative in different disciplines adopt different approaches: linguistic analyses focus on structures that create cohesion in discourse (Halliday & Hasan, 1976), or on structures functional in the differentiation of temporal perspective into foreground and background (Labov, 1972; Polanyi, 1989; Hopper & Thompson, 1980; Thompson, 1987). Cognitive approaches look at the episodic structure of stories, analyzing the development of and memory for such schemas (Stein, 1982; Stein & Glenn, 1982), or at the causal relations that underlie the plot (Trabasso & van den Broek, 1985). Psycholinguistic studies investigate the relationship between forms and functions in the expression of episodic structure, temporal perspective, and coherence in stories (Bamberg & Marchman, 1990; Aksu-Koç, 1992, 1994; Berman & Slobin, 1994).

Common to all approaches is the assumption that a narrative is organized in accordance with a universal schema which has a beginning, a conflict and a resolution. Furthermore, narrative events are organized in a sequential way, in accordance with a guiding theme which renders them meaningful. A narrative, then, is simultaneously structured at (i) the *linear* level where events are ordered temporally, yielding the local structure of the plot, and (ii) the *thematic* level where episodic units constituted of linear sequences are organized hierarchically in terms of a given goal, yielding the macrostructure of the story (Bamberg & Marchman, 1990). This multilayered structure allows the narrator to present events from different perspectives or in different voices, sometimes as a *narrator* moving with events in narrative time, sometimes as an *author,* regarding events from the temporal axis of discourse; and sometimes as one of the *characters* experiencing the narrative events. The intersection of different voices and shifts between them allows the teller to recount an event from within the narrative line and to comment on it from without at the same time, thus contributing to the weaving of a rich and colorful story. Such multivoicedness, generally regarded as a property of the written genre (Olson, 1977; Tannen, 1982, 1984) has been recognized to be a characteristic of oral narratives as well (Wolff & Hicks, 1989).

GENDER-RELATED CULTURAL CODES
IN TURKISH SOCIETY

The present study looks at narratives produced by Turkish adults after viewing a short film excerpt with a content equally familiar but of different degrees of relevance to members of different social milieus. It is assumed that the actual text of the film can potentially trigger different interpretations in different minds, which will in turn determine its retelling (Bruner, 1986). An analysis of the newly created texts, then, can reveal the interpretive schemas in terms of which the original readings were done. The question of how narrators with different conditions of sociocultural determination structure their narratives calls for a brief description of the society in terms of the characteristics relevant to interpretive schemes of its members.

"Patriarchy or gender hierarchy along with generational hierarchy" (Fişek, 1993, p. 3) are among the most frequently cited features of Turkish society and culture in general. However, gender and socioeconomic standing interact to yield less rigid sex role stereotypes in the urban context, particularly among upper income groups. In her review of the gender research in Turkey, Fişek (1993) reports that the values fostered in socialization for both males and females are obedience, dependency, and conformity, with more allowance for aggressive and assertive behavior in boys than girls and for increased autonomy and democratic expectations in urban middle and upper classes than in traditional families (Kağıtçıbaşı & Sunar, in press).   Same-sex socialization is fostered, although mixed-sex socialization is increasingly common for urban youth.   Among low income segments of the population the youth is oriented toward technical or occupational training to prepare for adult life, whereas in the urban upper and middle classes sons and daughters are equally directed toward education.   In terms of employment status and work related values, women from urban elite backgrounds are highly motivated to work and succeed in male dominated jobs as compared to their counterparts from lower strata who work because of economic need.

In rural areas as well as among recent migrants to larger cities, marriage is still a social and economic transaction between families, and arranged marriages continue to be the norm.   In marital relationships, high education, high income, urban groups show more egalitarian attitudes regarding spousal relationships, division of labor and intrafamily status than do low education, low income groups (Imamoğlu, 1991).   Among the less urbanized low income strata, cultural codes of "honor" and "shame" operate as an important mechanism of social control.   "A man's honor and social prestige are intimately linked to the sexual chastity of his female relatives; therefore, in order to preserve his place in the community of men, he has to impose strict controls over the conduct of his women" (Fişek, 1993, p. 12; Kandiyoti, 1987).   A woman's *namus* 'honor' is defined in negative terms — the loss and not the attainment of it is a matter of concern, for once it is lost, it can never be regained (Belbez, 1979).   Differences in the definition of *namus* by middle versus lower class subjects point toward a broader conceptualization that includes wider issues of moral conduct, thus suggesting that the concept of *namus* extends beyond gender relations, specially for the middle classes (Belbez, 1979, p. 106).   In short, gender hierarchy with its associated controls prevails, but with much weaker determining effects among the educated urban elite (Fişek, 1993).

METHOD

Sample

The data consist of narratives in the form of film retellings obtained from 24 adults within the 18 to 25 year age range.   The sample is constituted of two groups of 12 subjects who differ in terms of years of education (primary school graduates and high school drop outs vs. university graduates), area of residence (low vs. upper income neighborhoods), and occupation (in jobs with low level of professionalism vs. graduate student at the university) with equal number of females and males (6 males and 6 females) in each group.[1]

Although both groups represent urban youth, they are from different sociocultural milieus of the metropolis. Both exist in a society changing from a "traditional, rural, agricultural, patriarchal to an increasingly modern, urban, industrial and egalitarian" one, with corresponding changes in interpersonal relations dominated by familial and relational values (Fişek, 1993). However, as was noted above, the psychological world of the less educated, less professionalized, low income groups is more tightly organized by more conservative cultural codes, modes of conduct, and everyday practices as compared to the higher educated, high income groups.

Procedure

A 14-minute film piece edited from the Turkish movie *Fahriye Abla*, focusing on some culturally stereotyped events was used to elicit the narratives. The subjects were shown the film on video in a room at the Boğaziçi University by a female assistant who watched the film with them. They were then asked to narrate the film as if telling it to someone who had not seen it before, with the following instruction: "Now I would like you to tell me what happened, what you have seen as if you were telling it to someone who has not seen the film before." In this way an attempt was made to overcome the problem of shared perception and knowledge.[2] With these standard procedures the content of the story as well as the context and motivation for its telling were kept constant across narrators. None of the narrators had seen the commercial version of the film at the time of data collection. All the narratives were audiotaped. The texts were later transcribed and coded.

Materials

A summary of the excerpt from the movie *Fahriye Abla* is given below. The material in the square brackets represents the codes used in the breakdown of the plot into episodes and subepisodes as will be discussed in the next section.

Setting

Fahriye, her family, and some visitors are having coffee in the drawing room. The characters and the physical setting typify a lower middle class, relatively traditional sector of society.

---

[1] The data were collected for the project "A Literary and Linguistic Analysis of Narrative Discourse" conducted by D. Doltaş, C. Sevgen, E. Erguvanlı-Taylan, and A. Aksu-Koç, and supported by the Boğaziçi University Research Fund (Project #85 B 0414).

[2] An additional set of data where the listener did not watch the film with the narrator was collected after the completion of the original project. A comparison of these data which have not been analyzed yet will be particularly informative for questions about differences in the task frame adopted by the subjects.

Episode I

Initiating Event:
[EP1:IE]   Neighbors visit Fahriye and her family, proposing an arranged marriage for her with a rich jeweler who lives in Erzincan, a city in eastern Turkey. Fahriye's family appears to consent.
Internal Response:
[EP1:IR]   Fahriye, opposed to this marriage, sends word to her lover Mustafa.
Action:
[EP1:AA] Fahriye and Mustafa meet in a forsaken old house. She informs him about the situation; they decide to elope that night and make love.
Consequence:
[EP1:CQ] Fahriye waits all night but Mustafa does not come. In the morning he sends a letter explaining he can't marry her because he is still economically dependent on his father, and that she should decide for her future.
Reaction:
[EP1:RE] Fahriye marries the rich man from Erzincan.

Episode II:

Initiating Event:
[EP2:IE]   Fahriye's family wave goodbye as she leaves with her husband for Erzincan.
Internal Response:
[EP2:IR]   Fahriye is not happy.
Action:
[EP2:AA] Fahriye faints away in her bedroom. An empty bottle of pills on the table suggests suicide. She is saved by her husband, and admits that there was someone else in her life. Her husband is furious.
Consequence:
[EP2:CQ] The husband brings Fahriye back to her father's house, noting the daughter was "spoiled" and divorces her. Fahriye admits to her family that all is true.

Episode III:

Initiating Event:
[EP3:IE]   Fahriye visits Mustafa in his father's carpentry shop where he works. Mustafa is engaged to another woman, Gülay, but claims he did so under pressure from his father. He promises to leave his fiancee and marry Fahriye, they make love.
Internal Response:
[EP3:IR]   There is gossip about Fahriye and Mustafa in the neighborhood and Gülay comes to Fahriye to reproach her. Fahriye, who believes Mustafa, says he will marry her.

Action:

[EP3:AA] The two women go to the coffee shop to ask Mustafa whom he will marry.

Consequence:

[EP3:CQ] Mustafa, scared of his father who enters the shop that moment, disclaims his promise, says he will marry his fiancee and tells Fahriye to leave.

Reaction:

[EP3:RE] Fahriye grabs a screwdriver lying on the counter and stabs Mustafa.

Episode IV:

Conclusion:

[EP4:CN] Fahriye, with a small case in her hand, enters through big doors into the courtyard of a penitentiary.

This excerpt is from the beginning of the movie, which is the story of Fahriye's emancipation. Fahriye presents a strong character in all phases of the story. In the rest of the film not viewed by the subjects, she serves her term in jail, starts working in a factory, overcomes her love for Mustafa and becomes autonomous in every sense. In the edited excerpt, *namus* 'honor' is thematized from the perspectives of different characters: the husband's honor is lost because of his bride, Fahriye's honor is lost because of her lover's betrayal, and Fahriye's family's honor is lost because of their daughter. Fahriye's final act of violence is legitimate in view of the fact that it is a response to betrayal.

Framework for Analysis

Among various models, the story schema proposed by Stein and Glenn (1982; Stein, 1982) was adopted for the analysis. In this view, a story is composed of (a) a setting and (b) one or more episodes. The episode in turn has the following structural components: (i) initiating event, (ii) internal response, (iii) action, (iv) consequence, and (v) reaction. The film segment was analyzed into episodes and subepisodes in accordance with this schema by four judges after several sessions of viewing the film. This was then cross-checked with a breakdown obtained from 14 students which showed a high degree of overlap, providing support for the reliability of the original breakdown. This procedure resulted in the division of the film into three episodes with subepisodes and a fourth concluding episode. These divisions have been indicated in the above summary.

In the analysis, the clause was taken as the basic unit. Each clause was coded according to a coding scheme designed to capture: (a) the extent to which a text follows or diverges from the temporal sequence of events as presented in the film, and (b) the narrator's choice of particular voices at different points in the story.[3] Thus each clause

---

[3] This coding scheme was developed with Eser E. Taylan.

was coded for its referential position in the episodic structure, for its discourse function, and for its grammatical type, in terms of six parameters.[4] These designate:

(i)   the episode and subepisode the clause refers to [e.g., EPI:IE], and evaluative statements which do not refer to any episode [EPO:0];

(ii)   the information the clause gives about the setting [G:ST], the characters [G:CH], or a retrospective or prospective time perspective [G:RT];

(iii) the voice represented in the clause: the unmarked narrator's voice just reporting events [E:0], the narrator's voice interpreting events from inside the narrative line [E:IN]; the author's voice evaluating events from a personal or social–normative perspective external to the narrative line [E:DG], or the voice of a character taking part in narrative events [S:DIR];

(iv) information the clause gives about the task frame: that of a neutral narrator [F:0], a film spectator [F:FF], or an experimental subject [F:TF];

(v)   information that is not veridical in terms of what is represented in the film [DV:!]; and

(vi) information about the grammatical function of the clause (independent: [S:0], adverbial: [S:ADV], complement: [S:CMP], direct speech: [S:DIR], relative: [S:REL], main: [S:MC]).

RESULTS

The main question of interest is on the characteristics that unify the stories of narrators from the same sociocultural milieu. I thus focus on differences in episodic content, perspectives voiced, and structural organization that can inform us about the different interpretive frames from which the story is told. As noted above, content of story and context of storytelling were controlled by using a film piece as a standard stimulus. For the effects of variables such as gender and socioeducational status analyses of variance (ANOVA) were carried out on the data: Number of clauses, number of episodes, or proportion of clauses with a given code were entered into the analyses. In the following section I first consider differences in content and voice, showing the effects of socioeducational standing and gender in making relevant different aspects of the story and activating different perspectives. I then argue that the relevance of story content and the perspective adopted have determining effects on the structural organization of the narratives that result.

Differences in Content

The narratives of tellers from the two sociocultural milieus differ in terms of content: the majority of stories from the high education — high income group ("HEL" here onwards) are good copies of the film excerpt and focus on **event** representation, whereas the

---

[4]   A more detailed grammatical coding with particular attention to categories of temporality such as tense, aspect, and modality is in progress.

majority of the stories from the low education — low income group ("LEL" here onwards) focus on what they take to be the **message** of the story.   The difference in the
amount and type of content included in the retellings of the same story by the two groups
is best illustrated with the following examples, (1) from an HEL and (2) from an LEL
female narrator.[5]

(1)   Önce Fahriye Abla, babası, annesi sanıyorum kayınbiraderi ya da kardeşi
olabilir, onun karısı bir evde oturuyorlar.   Komşulardan birisi Fahriyeyi
hamamda görüp beğeniyor, ve ıı, Erzincanlı bir kuyumcuya istemeye geliyor.
Kahve ikramı sahnesiyle başlıyor.   Ailesi veriyor Fahriye Abla'yı.   Fakat Fahriye
Abla mahalledeki sevgilisi Mustafa'ya bir mektup gönderiyor bir çocuk
aracılığıyla.   *Buluşuyorlar.   Ve Mustafa onu bırakmıyacağını kaçacaklarını
söylüyor.*   Fakat o akşam Mustafa gelmiyor.   O çocukla yine sabah mektup
yolluyor.   Parasız olduğu için onu kaçıramıyacağını, bu işten vazgeçmesini
söylüyor.   Ve Fahriye Abla Erzincanlı ile evleniyor, gidiyorlar Erzincan'a.   O ilk
gece Fahriye Abla optalidon içerek intihar etmeye kalkıyor, fakat yapamıyor.
Kurtarıyorlar.   Fakat, ııı, intihar etmesinin nedeni "özürlü" olması olduğu için
Erzincanlı onu geri getiriyor ve, ailesine teslim ediyor.   Ailesi, babası büyük
tepkiyle karşılıyorlar.   Fahriye Mustafaya gidiyor ve onun nişanlandığını
öğreniyor, onun yokluğunda.   *Fakat Mustafa nişanlısını bırakıp, babasını
zoruyla nişanlandığını söyleyip, onunla evleneceğini söylüyor.*   Bu nişanlının
kulağına gidiyor ve kızla annesi geliyorlar.   Doğruluğunu ispat etmek için
Mustafa'nın ev, ııı, kahveye gidiyorlar ve orada Mustafa reddediyor.   Babasının
varlığı nedeniyle herhalde.   Fahriye Abla Mustafayı öldürüyor ve hapse giriyor.
Bu kadar.

{HEDYF1}

First, Fahriye Abla (F.A.), her father, mother, I think brother-in-law or it could
be her brother, his wife are living in a house [EP1:IE]. One of the neighbors
sees F. in the Turkish bath [EP1:IE] and likes her [EP1:IE], and, iii, comes
[EP1:IE] to ask for her hand for a jeweler from Erzincan {a city in Eastern
Turkey} [EP1:IE]. [The film] begins with the scene of offering coffee [EP1:IE]
[F:FF]. Her family gives F.A away in marriage [EP1:IE] [E:IN]. But F.A.
sends a letter to her lover in the neighborhood with a boy [EP1:IR]. *They meet*
[EP1:AA]. *And Mustafa (M) tells her* [EP1:AA] *he won't leave her* [EP1:AA]
and they will elope [EP1:AA]. But that night M. doesn't come [EP1:CQ]. He
sends a letter with the same boy in the morning [EP1:CQ]. He says [EP1:CQ]
he can't elope [EP1:CQ] because he doesn't have money [EP1:CQ] and that she
should give up [EP1:CQ]. And F.A. marries the man from Erzincan [EP1:RE].
They go to Erzincan [EP2:IE]. That first night F.A. attempts [EP2:AA] suicide
[EP2:AA]. by taking pills [EP2:AA]. Bu she can't [EP2:AA]. They save her
[EP2:AA]. But, iii, because the reason for her suicide is [EP2:AA] her being

---

[5] The codes that are relevant to the present discussion are given after each clause in the English
translation of the texts. Material in { } brackets are my additions for the sake of clarity.

"defective" [EP2:AA] [E:IN], the man from Erzincan brings [EP2:CQ] and gives her back to her family [EP2:CQ]. Her family, her father react strongly [EP2:CQ]. F. goes to M. [EP3:IE] and learns [EP3:IE] that he got engaged in her absence [EP3:IE]. *But M. tells her* [EP3:IE] *that he'll leave his fiancee* [EP3:IE], *that he got engaged because his father forced him* [EP3:IE], *that he'll marry her* [EP3:IE]. The fiancee hears this [EP3:IR] and the girl and her mother come [EP3:IR]. To prove it is true [EP3:IR] they go to M.'s house, to the coffee shop [EP3:AA] and there M. denies (his promises) [EP3:CQ]. Probably because of his father's presence [EP3:CQ] [E:IN]. F.A. kills M. [EP3:RE] and enters jail [EP4:CN]. That is all [EPO:0] [F:FF].

In this quite typical HEL narrative, events are reconstructed in accordance with their order in the film and each subepisode is mentioned with at least one clause. The narrator remains true to what was observed and heard, contributing almost nothing of herself. Thus it is not possible to identify a special, individual anchoring point from which her story is told. Consider in contrast text (2):

(2) Fahriye Abla hamama gitti, kızı, kızı hamam gitti. Hamamda başkasıyla bir ilişki kurdu. O ilişkiyi kurunca "kız bozuk çıktı" dediler. Oradan başka yere geldi. Başka birisiyle ilişki kurdu. Ondan sonra o çocuğun da nişanlısı varmış, *ama onu seveceğini söyledi. Kız onlan arkadaşlık yaptı. Sonra da {nişan- }* *"sizi seviyorum" dedi. Sevmediğine söz verdi.* {Baş- } nişanlısı olduğunun dolayısıyla kızdan vazgeçti. Kız kahretti. Ondan sonra annesine, ailesine yakaladı. Kızı babası dövdü, "bizi namus ettin diye." Kız kahroldu. Üzüntü duydu bu olayları duyunca. Tabii annesini babasını duyunca. Kız utanca haline geldi.{....Bu kadar.}

{LEDYF2}

F. A. went to the (Turkish) bath [EP1:IE], the girl, the girl went to the bath [EP1:IE]. At the bath she got into a relationship with someone else [EP1:AA].When she got into that relationship [EP1:AA] they said "the girl is defective" [EP1:CQ]. She came to someplace else from there [EP3:IE]. She established another relationship [EP3:IE]. And then that man had a fiancee [EP3:IE], but *he said* [EP3:IE] *that he would love her* [EP3:IE]. *The girl was friendly with him* [EP3:IE]. *Then [he] said* [EP3:IE]*"I love you"* [EP3:IE]. *[He] promised* [EP3:IE] *he didn't love anybody else* [EP3:IE]. {Some--} Because there was someone else [EP3:CQ] he gave the girl up [EP3:CQ]. The girl felt great distress [EP3:CQ] [E:IN]. And then was caught by her mother, her family [EP3:IR]. Her father hit her [EP3:IR], saying [EP3:IR] "you destroyed our honor" [EP3:IR]. The girl felt crushed [EP3:IR] [E:IN]. She felt sorrow [EP3:IR] [E:IN] when she heard all this [EP3:IR]. Of course, when she heard her mother and father [EP3:IR]. She became embarrassed [EP3:IR] [E:IN].{........   ....that is all}.

In this case, focus is not on the events but on the interplay between the protagonist's emotional responses to events and the social environment's evaluations. Although the marriage, the plan to elope, the attack on the lover and the entry to jail episodes are omitted, the narrator conveys what is worth telling for her. The three events of loss of honor are thematized, differentiating the social stigma due to being "defective," the personal distress due to betrayal by loved one, and the public shame experienced by the family. In short, this narrator's response to the film is in terms "loss of honor," which suggests that this concept is culturally significant for her.

The two groups differ consistently in regard to which subepisodes they include or exclude in their stories. In the film segment, the interpretive context for the story is framed with the Initiating Event [EP1:IE] where Fahriye's arranged marriage is planned, and with the Concluding episode [EP4:CN] where she enters jail. The texts differ in the extent to which they use these framing episodes: while both are almost always referred to in the HEL narratives (11 out of 12 cases for each episode), the initial scene is mentioned in about half the LEL narratives and the Concluding episode in only two, as if the film ends before the scene in which Fahriye enters jail (see text [2]). The difference between groups for the first episode only approaches significance ($p < .08$) while for the Concluding episode it is significant at $p < .01$ level ($F = 6.82$; $df = 1$; see Table 19.1 for the means).

TABLE 19.1.
Proportion of clauses that refer to [EP1:IE] and [EP4:CN] by
socioeducational level (HEL and LEL) and sex (M and F)

	HEL		LEL	
	M	F	M	F
[EP1:IE]	.06	.01	.03	.05
[EP4:CN]	.02	.02	.01	.00

One reason why LEL narrators do not integrate the Conclusion into their telling could be the operation of a schema that does not admit "entry to jail" as an event type appropriate to females. In a culture of male domination where women are not expected to be self-assertive, the "strong woman" image portrayed by Fahriye going to jail appears not to be as readily assimilable by individuals from some sociocultural milieus as by others. Put differently, other schemas representing "appropriate" behavior may be operative in blocking the telling of this episode. Although the difference between groups is not statistically significant for the stabbing scene [EP3:RE], only five LEL narrators refer to it as compared to all the HEL narrators, supporting this interpretation.

The difference between groups in interpretive frames becomes apparent also in the themes abstracted by narrators who have a message-focused approach. In all such LEL texts the concept of "honor" is expounded as the important social principle determining the course of events. In the two HEL texts of this kind, on the other hand, the strength or weakness of character, and the lack of economic power are treated as the important themes. For instance, in text (2) the sorrow and the shame consequent to loss of honor are centrally important for the LEL female narrator. In contrast, in example (3) the excerpt from an HEL male narrative shows that lack of economic independence due to inadequate education is identified as the cause of the ensuing dramatic events.

(3) .... Fahriye'yle ıı, Mustafa, ...ɪIkisi de ıı ekonomik olarak ıı kendi kendilerine yeterli değiller.   Bunların sebebi de gene sanırım ailelerinin başlangıçta onlara yeterli eğitim imkanı sağlayamaması. Eğer öyle bir imkanları olsaydı herhalde kendi kendilerine yetecek kadar parasal yönden kazanç sağlayabilirlerdi. .... Mustafa, o da onların dediklerine uymak zorunda kalıyor; *verdiği sözü tutamıyor.* ɪIkisi için de kötü oluyor. Sonunda, birisi ölüyor, birisi de hapse düşüyor. Bu kadar.

{HEDYM10}

.................Fahriye and Mustafa............neither of them are [EP1:0] [E:IN] economically self-sufficient [EP1:0] [E:IN]. The reason for this I think is [EP1:0] [E:DG] again the fact that their families could not give them enough education at the beginning. If they had had such an option [EP1:0] [E:DG] , they would probably have had earnings [EP1:0] [E:DG] to be self-sufficient [EP1:0] [E:DG]. ....Mustafa, he also has to oblige [EP3:CQ] [E:IN] with what they say [EP3:CQ] [E:IN]. He cannot keep [EP3:CQ] the promise he gave [EP3:CQ]. This is bad for both of them [EP3:RE] [E:IN]. In the end one dies [EP3:RE], one goes to jail [EP4:CN]. That's all [EPO:0] [F:FF].

These differences suggest that members of different sociocultural milieus, despite their shared focus on the message, differ in frames of mind, since they make relevant the same narrative events from quite different anchoring points, abstracting different messages from the same content.

Other differences in content are gender related. Two subepisodes where Fahriye meets her lover, one before and the other after her marriage (in EP1:AA and EP3:IE, respectively), are emphasized more systematically by female as compared to male narrators. The difference in the proportion of clauses that refer to the second meeting is significant ($F = 5.36$; $df = 1,23$, $p < .03$), while the first approaches significance at $p < .08$ level (see Table 19.2 for the means).

TABLE 19.2. Proportion of clauses that refer to [EP1:AA] and [EP3:IE] by socioeducational level (HEL and LEL) and sex (M and F)

	HEL		LEL	
	M	F	M	F
[EP1:AA]	.03	.07	.02	.04
[EP3:IE]	.11	.14	.10	.22

In both episodes the young man promises to marry her but later does not keep his word. All women talk explicitly about the promises given but not kept (see the italicized clauses in examples (1) and (2)), as if to justify Fahriye's subsequent actions which do not fit the cultural stereotype of the female role — obedient and nonaggressive. Men, on the other hand, either totally ignore, or reduce the importance of these events (e.g., 'the two young people are in love', 'they decide to run away'), or at best make an indirect reference by mention of an unkept promise (see examples [3] and [4]). These findings suggest the operation of a gender-linked interpretive frame which leads the female narrators to identify with and defend the woman protagonist. They in a way make accountable what turns out to be an unacceptable situation, on behalf of Fahriye.

Such different accounts, I think, reflect the cultural contexts and practices of which different narrators are a product. They disclose the "frame of mind" that comes from "history, traditions, socialization" or "practices of a group of people" (Gee, 1991, p. 3).

Voices in Discourse

Differences in the tendency to shift between narrative and discourse worlds by using different voices were found to be mostly gender related. Descriptive or evaluative statements that stand outside the narrative line, or clauses that don't refer to any particular episode but to the story globally ([EPO:0]), as well as clauses that relate narrative events to the narrator's own experiences, putting them in an evaluative framework ([E:DG]) represent the **author's voice.** Clauses that express the narrators interpretive inferences of events within the storyline [E:IN] represent the interactive use of the **narrator - author's voice.** The proportion of clauses that express a descriptive or evaluative author perspective [EPO:0] is significantly higher in the LEL male stories ($F = 5.47$, $df = 1,23$, $p < .03$, see Table 19.3 for the means) than in others. The proportion of clauses that present narrative events while simultaneously evaluating them from an external framework [E:DG] also shows a tendency to be higher in male than in female narratives, the difference approaching significance at $p < .09$ level.

TABLE 19.3. Proportion of Clauses that Express Author's Voice: [EPO:0] and [E:DG] by Socioeducational Level (HEL and LEL) and Sex (M and F)

	HEL		LEL	
	M	F	M	F
[EPO:0]	.06	.04	.26	.03
[E:DG]	.10	.05	.16	.03

If it is assumed that in narrative, the unmarked voice is that of the **narrator,** then the **character's** or the **author's** voices are marked. In the present data, males from the LEL group tend to adopt the marked perspective, strongly bringing to fore their own evaluative frameworks. This is not surprising since the film which treats the cultural stereotypes supportive of male domination as an organizing principle of community life may be read as justifying this world view. It thus provides a context, in particular to the LEL male tellers, to legitimately own the authorship of what is voiced. Example (4) is from an LEL male narrator whose narration is more in the author's than in the narrator's voice.

(4) {fiimdi şöyle.} Türkiye'deki yapım yani şey olarak geliyor, tabii normal bir film gibi. Türk standartları dışındaki değil de yani Batı ve Doğu olarak ayırım yapılıyor. Yani kırsal kesimle zengin kesimin bir parçası. [E: neler oldu filmde?] Film şöyle: fiimdi çocuk zengin diyelim, kız fakir. Yani bunun öncüsünde de namus girebilir ortaya. Yani normaldir. Doğu töreleri böyle şey yapıyor. Hepsi öyle, yani film şey değildir. Yani kızla birbirine aşık oluyorlar. Kızı zorla evlendiriyorlar. Tabii daha önce kızla erkek ilişkisi olduğu dolayından kız geri geliyor. Doğuda bu normaldir. Tabiii ki namusunu korumak için çocuğu öldürüyor ve hapse düşüyor.

{LEDYM6}

{Now it is like this} The production in Turkey, I mean it comes [EPO:0] [E:DG] like..of course, like a normal film [EPO:0] [E:DG]. Not beyond Turkish standards [EPO:0] [E:DG], but I mean a distinction between East and West is being made [EPO:0] [E:DG]. That is a sector of the rural and the urban regions [EPO:0] [E:DG]. {E: What happened in the film?} The film is like this [EPO:0] [F:FF]: Let's say the boy is rich [EP1:IE] [E:IN] and the girl is poor [EP1:IE] [E:IN]. I mean before this, "honor" may be at issue [EPO:0] [E:DG]. That is, it is normal [EPO:0] [E:DG]. The Eastern norms do things like this [EPO:0] [E:DG]. All is like that [EPO:0] [E:DG]... That is the film is not [EPO:0] [E:DG]... I mean they fall in love [EP1:AA]. They force the girl into a marriage [EP1:RE]. Of course, because the girl and the boy had a relationship beforehand [EP1:AA] [G:RT], the girl comes back [EP2:CQ]. This is normal in the East [EPO:0] [E:DG]. Of course,to save her honor [EP3:RE] [E:IN] she kills the boy [EP3:RE] [E:IN], and goes to jail [EP4:CN].

This narrator asserts in the author's voice the cultural code that governs the course of events to be valid at least in the larger cultural context of one sector of society (*Yani normaldir, doğu töreleri böyle şey yapıyor* 'I mean it is normal, Eastern norms do things like that'). When asked about the narrative events he gives a brief but evaluative summary. He accepts "loss of honor" as a legitimate problem both for the husband and the girl, noting that it is "normal" for him to bring her back, and that it is "normal" for her to kill the young man, both to save face. The following excerpt from an HEL male narrator also illustrates the author's perspective, which, however, interacts with the narrator's voice in making judgments about narrative events. The author's voice is disguised in the lexical–grammatical structures chosen rather than being explicitly stated.

(5) Olay İstanbul'un eski semtlerinden birinde geçiyor. Yoksul ailelerin oturduğu bir semt burası. Iıı, ... birbirini seven iki genç var. Bir tanesi işs..., işsiz bir çocuk, bir tanesi de Müjde Ar. Iıı, birbirlerini seviyor ama, tabii Türkiye'deki bir çok genç kızın kaderi gibi, kız bir nevi pazarlanıyor. Zengin ancak, ancak Erzincanlı birine gitmek zorunda kalıyor. .... Fakat, ıı gerdek gecesinde Erzincanlı kocasına, ıı, durumu açıklıyor, ve tabii ar ve namus sorunu. Adam kızı kaptığı gibi İstanbul'a geri getiriyor. Bozuk bir mal, kendisine verildiğini ileri sürerekten

kızı yaka paça evine bırakıp geri dönüyor. .... *Fakat nedendir bilinmez, çocuk sanki Müjde Ar'a hiç bir ümit vermemiş gibi,* o sırada kahvehaneye babası geliyor, çocuk da tabii bozuntuya vermemek için "Güler'i seviyorum, onunla nişanlanacağım. Unut beni artık" filan diyor. O sırada tesadüfen orada bırakılmış bir tornavidayı alan Müjde Ar çocuğun karnına ufak bir delik açıyor ve ondan sonraki sahnede de kodes kapıları açılıyor tabii. Müjde Ar içeri transfer oluyor. Buraya kadardı film.

{HEDYM9}

Events take place in an old area of Istanbul [EP1:0] [G:ST]. This is an area [EP1:0] [G:ST] [E:IN] where poor families live [EP1:0] [G:ST] [E:IN]. Iıı, there are two young people [EP1:0] who love each other [EP1:0]. One of them is unemp...an unemployed boy [EP1:0] [G:CH] [E:IN], the other is Müjde Ar [EP1:0] [G:CH] [F:FF] {the name of the film star} Iı›, they love each other but [EP1:AA], like the fate of many other young girls in Turkey, the girl is marketed in a way [EP1:IE] [E:IN]. She is obliged to go [EP1:IE] to a rich man who, however, is from Erzincan [EP1:IE] [G:CH]. .... But, ııı... on the first night she explains the situation to her husband from Erzincan [EP1:AA] and of course it is a matter of honor and pride [EP2:0] [E:DG]. The man, grabbing the girl [EP2:CQ], brings her back to Istanbul [EP2:CQ]. Claiming [EP2:CQ] that a defective product was given to him [EP2:CQ] he leaves the dishevelled girl [EP2:CQ] and goes back [EP2:CQ]. .... *But nobody knows* [EP3:AA] [E:IN] why *it is* [EP3:AA] [E:IN], *as if the boy hasn't raised the hopes of Müjde Ar* [EP3:AA] [G:RT] [F:FF], at that moment his father comes to the coffee shop [EP3:AA], and of course the boy, in order not to mess things up [EP3:CQ], says [EP3:CQ] "I love Güler [EP3:CQ], I'm going to get engaged to her [EP3:CQ]. Forget about me [EP3:CQ]." At that moment Müjde Ar [EP3:RE] [F:FF] who takes a screwdriver [EP3:RE] which was by chance left there [EP3:RE], makes a small hole in the stomach of the boy [EP3:RE], and of course in the next scene the jail doors are opened [EP4:CN] [F:FF], Müjde Ar is transferred inside [EP4:CN] [F:FF]. The film was up to here [EPO:0] [F:FF].

In the above excerpt, it is the author's voice which typifies the setting in terms of its socioeconomic dimensions ('an old area of the city where poor families live') and the arranged marriage as an institution of economic exchange ('the girl is being marketed in a way'). To keep apart the author's and the narrator's voices, or the narrator's and the character's voices a variety of modality markers are used. The nonfactive modal verb *ileri sürmek* 'to claim' used in the main clause of a complement construction (*Bozuk bir mal kendisine verildiğini ileri sürerekten* 'claiming that a defective product was given to him') signals that the analogy 'defective product' belongs to the character who makes the claim but not to the narrator who reports this. The modal *tabii* 'of course' used to underscore the importance of 'honor and pride', marks their presupposed status as social codes. The final events are dramatized as 'making a small hole in the stomach of the boy....and being transferred inside (the jail)' in a marked register with a jargon specific to a world of crimes and jail terms. In short, while recounting successive events the narrator also works on situating the underlying themes in the cultural context they arise from as well as in his own evaluative framework with an interactive use of the narrator's and the author's voices.

The author's voice expressed in male narratives differs for the two sociocultural groups. All males tend to introduce their own judgments and evaluations into the scene. However, the HEL males do so keeping the social and the personal evaluative frameworks distinct. They distantiate themselves by using modal markers which are dependent on contextual inferences from nonverbal indicators such as tone of voice, facial expression or even social status. They use marked registers which express the voice of an author who does not identify with the norms and values of the protagonists but maintains a critical or distant attitude. LEL men, on the other hand, take a stance from within the evaluative framework they use to interpret the narrative events: The congruence between the normative structure portrayed in the film and their own norms, values and experiences becomes evident in explicit statements of judgment that assert opinions as fact.

Women, on the other hand, express the author's voice interactively with the narrator's in statements that make interpretive inferences about narrative events [E:IN]. They use evaluative statements from a personal or societal point of view less often. In the HEL female narrative in (1) the story is told in the narrator's voice, and a distant author's perspective is conveyed by the use of lexical-grammatical strategies similar to those discussed above. These are devices like nominal phrases for typification of situations as culturally symbolic categories (*kahve ikramı sahnesi* 'the scene of coffee serving'), and factive versus nonfactive contrasts to keep apart character vs. narrator voices (*Fakat intihar etmesinin nedeni özürlü olması* {nonfactive} *olduğu* {factive} *için Erzincanlı onu geri getiriyor.* 'But because her being defective is the reason for her attempt at suicide, the man from Erzincan brings her back'). The use of the author's voice in other female texts may not be so subtle. The modalized statements in the following excerpt from an LEL female text express judgments by an author who regards events from the female protagonist's point of view.

(6) Çünkü onlar, şimdi babası o adama verdi. Zorla verdi. *Kızın almaması lazımdı. Madem istemiyorsun, onu almaması lazımdı. Çünkü boşuna kendi namusunu kirletti. Boşuna haplar içip de kızlığını da namusunu kirletmemesi lazımdı....*

{LEDYF12}{LEDYF12}

Because they, now, her father gave her to that man [EP1:RE]. He gave by force [EP1:RE]. *The girl shouldn't have* [EP1:RE] [E:IN] *taken him* [EP1:RE] [E:IN]. *Since you don't want* [EP1:RE] [E:IN], *she shouldn't have* [EP1:RE] [E:IN] *taken him* [EP1:RE] [E:IN]. *Because she lost her honor for no reason* [EP2:0] [E:IN]. *She shouldn't have* [EP2:AA] [E:DG] taken *pills* [EP2:AA] *and lost her virginity* [EP2:AA] [E:DG] *and lost her honor for nothing* [EP2:AA] [E:DG].

Women thus prefer to stay within the narrative line and express their point of view on that platform. Just like men, they differ in the degree of loudness they are willing to give their voice, some prefer to remain subtle while others can be very explicit. The marked author's perspective evaluating events from an external point of view is the male strategy. Men pull the narrative events to a real world platform and express judgments on a wider scale. They too may choose an implicit or a loud voice in doing so. In summary, use of the author's voice in the present narratives is more typical of narrators from the low education-low income traditional milieus in terms of sociocultural background, and more typical of males, in terms of gender.

Consequences for Structure

The analyses of the content and discourse features of our narratives revealed differences between groups in the "degree of relevance" of story content to the teller, and in the prevalence of different voices in discourse. It was observed that the content of the film evoked culturally specific social-interpretive schemas in narrators from low education-low income urban milieus presumably because it was closer to their everyday life experiences. These schemas, or "frames of mind" functioned selectively in determining what is worth telling and rendered their telling more personal. It could be said that this group, experiencing more directly the rigid and conservative cultural codes, took the film content more seriously or more individually. The texts of narrators from high education-high income milieus, on the other hand, gave evidence for the operation of an interpretive schema abstracted from the film itself, resulting in quite standard stories and a distantiated stance. Again, this was presumably because the content of the film was not as significant for the everyday practices of this group as it was for the former. As was noted in the introduction, the effects of gender and generational hierarchy governing the social relations and practices at issue in the film are much weaker for the educated urban elite as compared to the less educated-low income urban groups.

Another factor that could have a bearing on the anchoring points from which the subjects related to the film content is the stance adopted in the experimental context. High education subjects, given their long years of formal schooling, could easily adopt an objective stance that allows the performance of whatever behavior is required in a task situation, whereas low-education subjects experienced difficulty in doing so. The HEL narrators could assume a hypothetical audience and behaved like experienced film tellers. The LEL narrators, on the other hand, performed in a context of face-to-face interaction from which they did not seem to abstract themselves. These observations suggest that level of education, by mediating this task attitude, could have been partially functional in the adoption of the interpretive frame provided in the film by the HEL group.[6]

Altogether, these differences result in different ways of structuring the same story as reflected in the number of clauses per text and the number of subepisodes that contribute to plot development. The HEL narratives are longer than LEL narratives ($F = 6.51$; $df = 1,23$; $p < .01$). Correlatively, the number of subepisodes referred to is high er in the HEL than in the LEL narratives ($F = 19.84$, $df = 1,23$, $p < .00$) (See Table 19.4 for the means).

The high education-high income texts present narrative events in a sequentially organized way. The temporal–causal relations between events follow the order given in

---

[6] The linguistic consequences of this difficulty LEL narrators experienced in abstracting themselves from the context of face-to-face interaction is a topic for another discussion.

the original film, and each episode is given its due weight in the plot, without much addition or subtraction. The LEL narrators, on the other hand, focus on a subset of the constitutive events, include those that are deemed important and ignore others. They single out a dominant theme such as "loss of honor" to guide the story, and only those events that contribute to this theme are elaborated. Events regarded to have marginal relevance to the point within the chosen interpretive frame are either mentioned in passing or totally left out. In short, in HEL narratives (10 out of 12), the plotline of the film is closely followed and subthemes within each episode are developed locally, whereas in most LEL narratives (8 out of 12) only about half of the subepisodes are referred to, with emphasis on those events carrying significance for the global theme.

TABLE 19.4. Mean Number of Clauses and Subepisodes Per Pext
by Socioeducational Level (HEL and LEL) and Sex (M and F)

	HEL		LEL	
	M	F	M	F
Clauses	118.33	77.67	46.33	40.00
Subeps[1]	11.83	13.17	7.17	8.17

[1] maximum number of subepisodes = 15

The first type of narratives are thus characterizable as **linearly organized** and the second type as **thematically organized**. There are of course exceptions in each case, there being sequentially organized texts in the LEL group and thematically organized ones in the HEL group. Furthermore, this is not to mean that linearly organized narratives are devoid of a thematic structure or that thematically organized ones lack a sequential ordering. As was laid out in the introduction, linear and thematic refer to two levels of organization within the narrative. Nevertheless, the structure of the narratives of the present groups is best definable as such, with one level of organization having primacy at the expense of the other, particularly in the case of the thematically organized LEL texts. In fact, our content related analyses have revealed that many of the LEL stories are lacking in terms of the events that constitute the plot, which can potentially lead to difficulties of comprehensibility if the listener cannot supply the missing information. In contrast, what may be missing in the HEL stories is at worst the author's voice bringing in the subjectivity of the teller because the sequential organization of the tale ultimately renders the theme inferable. In any case, the present findings are suggestive of the ways in which every viewer's interpretation is structured in part by the same text and in part by their own "interpretive frames that permit the use of" their cultured or gendered experiences (de Vault, 1990, p. 897).

CONCLUDING REMARKS

In the present data, the sociocultural formation of the narrator emerged as a complex determinant that has a bearing on the structural organization of narratives: It was observed that in low education-low income narratives the theme is taken as primary and determines the events to be included into the narrative because they are necessary for its development. In high education-high income narratives the sequence of events is taken as essential and the global theme is developed with the development of local themes around successive events. Furthermore, in low education-low income narratives the author's voice is activated more often, suggesting a high level of subjectification, while in high education-high income narratives the voice of a relatively distant author or observant narrator comes to fore. These differences appear accountable in terms of the relatively distinct set of codes and practices of individuals from different milieus. As Bruner notes (1986), specific aspects of the content to be narrated evoke different styles or genres in different narrators, which results in different renderings of the story. Here, the piece from a Turkish film was interpreted at different degrees of relevance by subjects of different sociocultural formations, which resulted in the adoption of different structural compositions.

Other studies by researchers such as Tannen (1984) and Liebes (1988) have obtained similar findings pointing to the close relations between ethnicity, culture, subculture or education, and narrative styles. For example, Tannen (1984) found differences between American and Greek adults. Operating more within the oral than the written style, Greek narrators adopted a more subjective perspective and provided more interpretations and evaluations as compared to Americans. In Liebes' (1988) study, narrators from different ethnic, social, and cultural backgrounds displayed different genres in the retelling of an episode from the television series *Dallas*. Subjects with traditional backgrounds and fewer years of education preferred a linear style of narrative organization, those with higher education and more critical outlook preferred a thematic-ideological style, and a third group with higher education but a more modern orientation chose a psychological genre focusing on the characters and their determinative powers on events. Our findings, together with those of Tannen and Liebes, suggest that the question of what determines narrative style is a matter of complex interactions between level of education, the subculture that is associated with it, and the relevance of the tale from the point of view of the teller.

The effects of gender were found to be more determining at the level of content than structure. Men and women differed particularly in what they found worthwhile and relevant for telling in their stories. They also displayed a difference in terms of the voice adopted for doing so. While women chose to use the author's and the narrator's voices interactively, men preferred a stance outside of the narrative events from which they could easily display an evaluative and knowing attitude. These findings show that multivoicedness is indeed also a quality of oral narratives as of written. The observed gender differences are not surprising in the light of findings by Nicolopoulou, Scales, and

Wientraub (in press) that the spontaneous stories of children as young as four years of age display gender-related differences both in structure and content. These findings then show that there are different interpretive frames maintained by males and females which arise from different kinds of socially organized activity and collective discourse practices. The present analysis, by showing that both the structure and the content of the story provide options in what is to be thematized and how this is to be marked, revealed that the question of how the socioculturally determined individual comes through in narrative is a complex one. And it has demonstrated, I hope, that the combined use of interpretive and quantitative analyses can be fruitful in showing more reliably how the cultural embodied in the individual can be captured in narrative.

REFERENCES

Aksu-Koç, A. A. (1992). Eğitim düzeyinin anlatı yapısına etkisi. *VI. Dilbilim Sempozyumu Bildirileri Kitabı.* Gazi Üniversitesi, Ankara.

Aksu-Koç, A. A. (1994). Development of linguistic forms: Turkish. In R. Berman, & D. I. Slobin, *Relating events in narrative: A crosslinguistic developmental study* (pp. 217-255). Hillsdale, NJ: Lawrence Erlbaum Associates.

Berman, R. A., & Slobin, D. I. (1994). *Relating events in narrative: A crosslinguistic developmental study.* Hillsdale, NJ: Lawrence Erlbaum Associates.

Bamberg, M., & Marchman, V. (1990). What holds a narrative together? The linguistic encoding of episode boundaries. *Papers in Pragmatics,* **4,** 58-121.

Belbez, B. (1979). *A study on namus, dürüstlük and şeref as social values.* Unpublished master's thesis. Boğaziçi University, Istanbul.

Bruner, J. (1986). *Actual minds, possible worlds.* Cambridge, MA: Harvard University Press.

Cole, M., & Scribner, S. (1984). *The psychology of literacy.* Cambridge, MA: Harvard University Press.

De Vault, M. L. (1990). Novel readings: the social organization of interpretation. *American Journal of Sociology,* **95,** 887-921.

Fişek, G. O. (1993). Life in Turkey. In L. L. Adler (Ed.), *International handbook on gender roles.* Westport, CT: Greenwood Publishing Group.

Imamoğlu, O. (1991). Changing intrafamily roles in a changing world. Paper presented at *The seminar on the individual, the family and the society in a changing world.* Istanbul.

Gee, J. P. (1991). Memory and myth: a perspective on narrative. In A. McCabe, & C. Peterson (Eds.), *Developing narrative structure* (pp. 1-25). Hillsdale, NJ: Lawrence Erlbaum Associates.

Halliday, M. A. K., & Hasan, R. (1976). *Cohesion in English.* London: Longman.

Hopper, P. J., & Thompson, S.A. (1980). Transitivity in grammar and discourse. *Language,* **56,** 251-299.

Kağıtçıbaşı, Ç., & Sunar, D. (in press). Family and socialization in Turkey. In J. P. Roopnarine & D. B. Carter (Eds.), *Parent-child relations in diverse cultural settings: socialization for instrumental competency.* Norwood, NJ: Ablex.

Kandiyoti, D. (1987). Emancipated but unliberated? Reflections on the Turkish case. *Feminist Studies,* **43,** 317-339.

Labov, W. (1972). *Language in the inner city: Studies in the Black English vernacular*. Philadelphia: University of Pennsylvania Press.

LeVine, R. (1984). Properties of culture: An ethnographic view. In R. Shweder & R. LeVine (Eds.), *Cultural theory*. Cambridge, England: Cambridge University Press.

Liebes, T. (1988). Cultural differences in retelling of television fiction. *Critical Studies in Mass Communication*, **5**, 272-292.

Nicolopoulou, A., Scales, B., & Wientraub, J. (in press). Gender differences in symbolic imagination in the stories of four-year-olds. In A. H. Dyson, & C. Genishi (Eds.), *The need for story: Cultural diversity in classroom and community*. National Council of Teachers of English.

Olson, D. (1977). From utterance to text: The bias of language in speech and writing. *Harvard Educational Review*, **47**, 257-281.

Polanyi, L. (1989). *Telling the American story*. Cambridge, MA: MIT Press.

Stein, N. L. (1982). The definition of a story. *Journal of Pragmatics*, **6**, 487-507.

Stein, N.L., & Glenn, C. G. (1982). Children's concept of time: The development of a story schema. In W. J. Friedman (Ed.), *The development of the psychology of time*. New York: Academic.

Tannen, D. (1982). The oral / literate continuum in discourse. In D. Tannen (Ed.), *Spoken and written language: Exploring orality and literacy*. Norwood, NJ: Ablex.

Tannen, D. (1984). Spoken and written narrative in English and Greek. In D. Tannen (Ed.), *Coherence in spoken and written discourse*. Norwood, NJ: Ablex.

Thompson, S. (1987). Subordination and narrative event structure. In R. S. Tomlin (Ed.), *Coherence and grounding in discourse* (pp. 435-454). Amsterdam: John Benjamins.

Trabasso, T., & van den Broek, P. (1985). Causal thinking and the representation of narrative events. *Journal of Memory and Language*, **24**, 612-630.

Wolf, D., & Hicks, D. (1989). The voices within narratives: The development of intertextuality in young children's stories. *Discourse Processes*, **12**, 329-351.

20 EMOTION, NARRATIVE, AND AFFECT: HOW CHILDREN DISCOVER THE RELATIONSHIP BETWEEN WHAT TO SAY AND HOW TO SAY IT[1]

Michael Bamberg
Clark University

Judy Reilly
San Diego State University

In narrative presentations of personal experiences, it is often assumed that narrators relive their past emotional experience, i.e., that they feel parts or shades of the originally felt emotion, and that these feelings are expressed in the act of performing the narrative. In such situations, it may be said that the presentation of the narrator reflects an involved attitude towards his or her original experience.[2] However, the issue of involvement is not unique to self-experienced events. The emotional significance of a sequence of events for another person is usually also presented with a certain amount of feeling or involvement in the narrative performance. Again, the narrator can signal an affiliation with or a distance from the way the protagonist in the story felt at that particular time. This affiliating or distancing stance usually is marked by particular evaluative devices. This way the audience learns and is educated about who are the "good guys" and who are the "bad guys." In the same breath, the narrator legitimates — or might try to challenge —

---

[1] This contribution to the festschrift for Susan Ervin-Tripp was originally presented under the title "The expression of affect in narratives" at the 5th Congress of the International Association for the Study of Child Language, held in Budapest in July 1990. Dr. Ervin-Tripp was present at our presentation at that Congress, and with her — usual — insightful comments has helped shape our original brief paper into its now — we hope — more complete form. Parts of the research presented here were supported by a two-year National Academy of Education Spencer Fellowship to the first author, and by the National Institutes of Health FIRST award # 5R29 DC00539 and BRSG # S07 RR 07004-15 to the second author.

[2] Of course, it is possible that a narrator takes a reflective and distanced attitude toward a once experienced emotion, such as in situations where the interpretation or significance of the once experienced constellation of events has changed, and the narrator tries to claim a newly developed evaluative stance (e.g., That's how I felt then, but THIS is how I feel about it now, or even more drastically: *That's how I felt then, but I realized soon thereafter, that I SHOULD HAVE felt differently in that situation*).

basic moral and educational values that are assumed to be shared with his/her culture and society.

In our contribution to this festschrift, we want to focus on how young narrators learn to integrate message content (more concretely, the emotional significance of a sequence of events for a [third-person] story character) and the way this content is presented, i.e., the actual emotional/affective performance of the telling. In other words, we want to explore how young narrators learn to tie the referential plane of story content and the activity of story performance into a bounded (integrated) structural unit, one that considers the perspective of a generalized audience. With this in mind, we will try to transcend our original starting point, which began with the assumption that there is something "natural" in the experience of emotions that is **subsequently** "expressed" in speech performance.[3] In contrast to this widespread folk model of the relationship between emotions and their expressions, we will argue for a broader conceptualization of the relationship between language and emotion(s), one that views them as interdependent and mutually constituting each other (see, in addition, Bamberg, 1993; Bamberg, Ammirati, & Shea, in press).

Our discussion is based on two studies; both used a 24-page picture book titled *Frog, Where are You?* (Mayer, 1969). The story depicted in the pictures is as follows: A boy, a dog, and their pet frog are happily together. At night, while the boy and the dog are asleep, the frog escapes. The next morning, after the discovery of the loss, the boy and the dog begin to look for the frog. During their search they meet with several adventures and obstacles, mainly with other animals in the forest, but finally they find their frog, and — on the last picture of the book — turn happily homeward with a frog in the boy's hand. Within this goal-directed sequence, there is a short digression, within which the dog gets a jar stuck on his head and falls out of a window, shattering the jar into fragments.[4] The picture depicting this scene (picture 7) will be of special relevance in the course of our later analyses, concerning where children and adults locate their references to emotions that they assume to occur (or have occurred) in the third-person protagonist of the story, i.e., in the boy.

Before our subjects were asked to narrate the picture book, they were given time to

---

[3] Much of the theorizing and subsequent empirical analyses of narratives seems to be based on exactly this assumption, which also may have led Labov and Waletzky to their highly consequential definition of narrative "as one method to *recapitulate past experience* by matching a verbal sequence of clauses to the sequence of *events which actually occurred*" (Labov & Waletzky, 1967, p. 20 — our own highlighting). From our point of view today, more than 25 years after this statement appeared in print, it is fascinating to see how this assumption of a one-to-one correspondence of "events" expressed in clauses and "events" occurring in reality, could open the door to an abundance of stimulating research, particularly on the development of narrative competence in children, but at the same time could block a good deal of probably even more productive research.

[4] Note how this presentation of the sequence of events by use of the form *shattering* assigned more "agency" to the dog than other potential characterizations of the same scene — such as for instance in terms of *resulting in the jar being shattered into fragments*. This latter form of presentation, focusing more on the resultant state, would have de-emphasized the dog as the probable willful — and as such responsible — agent.

look through the book in order to get a sense of the plot. We elicited the narratives by having subjects hold the book and turn the pages on their own. All stories were audio-taped and the stories for Study 1 were also video-recorded. The transcripts were originally coded into clauses (predicate-argument structures) in order to get a measure of story-length. Transcriptions also denoted the pertinent pictures in order to have a more precise measure of which clause corresponded to which particular story-event.

STUDY 1

To assess storytelling performance (details of this study are reported in Reilly, 1992), we drew from both Labov and Waletzky's (1967) classification and the categories specified by Ross (1980), tallying the following instances of affective expression:

(1) number of propositions

(2) story components

(3) characterization or quoted speech: the child speaks for one of the characters, e.g., *he said, "Froggie, come back again."*

(4) evaluative comments: these include situations in which the child attributes emotions to the characters, e.g., *an' when he woke up he was very sad* or *he was crying*; other such examples can include the evaluation of an action or a character (from the point of view of the narrator), e.g., *he was a nasty owl.* In addition, mental verbs were also included in this category, e.g., *he was wondering where that frog had gone.*

(5) facial expressions: e.g., smile, frown

<u>   smile   </u>
he went boing right out of the jar

(6) gestures: those that appeared to be related to a particular utterance, e.g., covering the head to demonstrate hiding from the (apparently) attacking owl

(7) prosodic features: pitch, length, volume, and voice quality:
"he said, '((*Fro:ggie*, come back again/))'" ((high))
(( )) = pitch/voice quality (specified at utterance end)
: = lengthened vowel
italics = increased volume

(8) lexical/phonological stress:
he said, "Froggie, come back# again".
= stress on the preceding syllable

These eight codes revealed the following (here generalized) findings:

(a) There is an increase in both story length and story complexity from 3–4 to 7–8 years. Although story length does not increase from 7–8 to 10–11, stories are more complete in the 10- to 11-year-olds.

(b) In contrast to their structural incompleteness, the narratives of the 3—4-year-olds are affectively quite rich. They recruit their full repertoire of paralinguistic affective expression, relying especially on vocal prosody. Seven and 8-year-olds' stories incorporate significantly fewer devices and are affectively flat. Those of the 10- to

11-year-olds once again recruit affective expression into their narratives.

(c) The youngest age group makes few references to emotions; however there is a significant increase in the oldest group.

Although the narratives of the youngest and the oldest age group look similar when compared to the narratives of the 7- to 8-year-old children (when analyzed for the amount of affective expression), they nevertheless reveal striking differences. It appears that the preschoolers are using affective expression to comment on the discourse activity (e.g., "I am not done yet" or "there is more to come") and to compensate for their lack of linguistic sophistication; 10- to 11-year-olds use them as decentering devices, displaying an awareness of the episodic structure of the narrative and reflecting a greater awareness of recipient design.

It also should be mentioned that these findings held up irrespective of the audience, i.e., irrespective of whether children told the story to an unknowledgeable, slightly younger peer, or to the adult interviewer who had brought the book along and could be assumed (by the child narrator) to "know" the book before the child's telling.

STUDY 2

In the second study (reported in full detail in Bamberg & Damrad-Frye, 1991), we coded children's and adults' narratives for explicit use of linguistic evaluative devices only. These included:

(1)   number of propositions
(2)   characters' speech (direct and indirect)
(3)   negations
(4)   causal connectors
(5)   hedges (i.e., "distancing devices" — e.g., *probably, might, maybe*)
(6)   "frames of mind" (here especially: references to emotions)

Here, we will focus primarily on the references to frames of mind: 20% were references to purely mental states (such as *thinking*), and about 80% were references to emotions. We should also mention that we compared slightly different age groups in this second study, namely ages 5–6, 9–10, and adult English speakers. A brief synopsis of the findings is as follows:

(a) Story length: no differences between the 5–6 and the 9–10-year-olds; however, there was a significant increase between the 9- to 10-year-olds and the adults.

(b) Frames of mind: no significant difference between 5- to 6- and 9- to 10-year-olds; however, we found significant differences between the adult narrators and the two younger age groups.

(c) A comparison of the use of all evaluative devices showed that references to frames of mind (though already well established in the 5- to 6-year-olds' narratives) became increasingly prevalent with development.

In a second analysis of the same data, we focused on the use of frame of mind devices, especially the references to the emotions of the characters in the story. Specifically, we wanted to investigate their narrative functions — and whether there were any changes in function across age groups.

This analysis revealed that in adult English narratives of this particular picture book, references to emotions typically cluster with pictures 1–3 (the setting or orientation of the story), and pictures 22–24 (the happy ending), and to a lesser degree also with picture 7 (the ending of the aside, resulting in the shattered jar). The following example illustrates a typical adult narrative response to picture 7:

(1) the boy is *angry*
     that the dog broke the jar
     but he's also *happy*
     because his dog didn't get hurt
     so they jointly continue the search ...

In contrast to the adult narrators who cluster their references to emotions around setting and happy ending, 5- to 6-year-olds use 40% of their references to emotions for picture 7, commenting, some of them repeatedly, on the negative emotion expressed by the boy (*sad* and/or *angry*). There are no instances of conveying the happy ending, and only a few for the setting of the story. The 9- to 10-year-old children range in their use of references to emotions somewhere in the middle between the 5- to 6-year-olds' and adults' performances: They still cluster their emotion references more strongly around picture 7 than the adults, but, at the same time, they clearly begin to mark the setting and the happy ending with references to emotions.

SUMMARY OF FINDINGS

What the two studies thus far have shown should first be understood as three unrelated sequences of changes over time:

(1) A. Between 3 and 7 years, the length of children's narratives (measured in numbers of propositions per story) increased significantly.
     B. Between the ages of 6 to 9 there was no further increase in story length.
     C. Starting around 8–9 years, children's narrative productions again began to pick up in length.

The question that emerged from these observations centers on the phase in the middle of this process: Why is the increase in story length not a continuous process from early on till adulthood? What is happening between ages 6 and 9 that holds children from expanding their narratives in length?

Before presenting the remaining two sequences of changes, a note of caution is appropriate: Our presentation thus far may be interpreted as if all age groups, in particular our adult sample, present their narratives in a unique and homogeneous fashion. This, however, is not the case, particularly for the adult narratives. As has been reported elsewhere (Bamberg, 1994b, p. 154), posttest interviews of adult narrators of the frogstory revealed that narrators placed themselves in two distinct groups, one imagining a child-like audience of the narrative, the other presenting the narrative to the actual adult interviewer. This difference in "audience construction" correlated strongly with increased story length and increased use of evaluative devices for the imagined child audience group, and a decrease in both measures in the group that simply told the story to the adult interviewer (who could be supposed to be already familiar with the story).

(2) At about the same age we found the stagnation in story length, i.e., around age 6 to 9, there was a significant drop in affective expression, while for younger and older children the expression of affect seemed to play a much more dominant role in how to tell a good story.

(3) Children younger than 8–9 if they used references to third-person characters' emotional states, are generally concerned with local aspects of the story, such as facial or behavioral aspects which are seemingly more accessible from the pictures themselves. In contrast, older children as well as adults (and this process seems not to begin to kick in before the age of 8–9) use references to emotional states in third-person characters to signal the relevance of individual story events from a more global story-telling perspective.

THREE PHASES OF NARRATIVE ABILITY

Pulling these three aspects of story-telling changes together in an attempt to integrate them into a more coherent developmental picture, we would like to put forth a three-phase model of the development of story-telling ability.

(I) **Early phase**: Children start from the assumption that a story is a whole at the level of *story-telling activity*. Neither are the units held together very well at the horizontal (cohesive) level, nor is their vertical, hierarchical organization coherent. Rather, they use paralinguistic affective expression to bolster their unsophisticated linguistic narrative abilities. It may be that children in this phase have filtered from their parental input the affective expressive message as the most meaningful, and have generalized this as "the stuff" that makes "good story telling." In other words, it is the expression of affect that marks the activity of story telling as a type of global genre marking. This phase is characteristic for children in our samples between 3 and 6 years of age.

(II) **Middle phase**: At around the age of 6 years, children begin to concentrate their efforts on the establishment of horizontal, intersentential cohesion.

(a) Signaling the wholeness of the narrative activity is no longer central to structuring the child's story performance. Rather, children at this age begin to use linguistic references to emotions (and references to internal states in general) to signal their evaluations of particular story events. More specifically, references to third-person characters' feelings reflect the ability to tie story happenings to story characters' internal states from a narrator's point of view. However, in this case, the narrator's point of view does not reflect an overall perspective on the story as a whole. Rather, it reflects a particular, single focus on the local connection between a particular precipitating story event and its internal (evaluative) outcome "in" one of the story characters.

(b) This focus on the particular keeps the child in this "middle" phase from using paralinguistic expressions of affect (since the narrative whole is of no interest at this time), and at the same time from elaborating on longer stories. For the child this age, it is not more content or more affect that makes a better story, but rather the local links that tie characters' evaluations and motivations to the story events precipitating (or following) them.

(III) **Final phase**: In this phase, the two different levels of narrative structuring that were separate in each of the previous phases, become integrated into *one* story telling activity/performance.

(a) Linguistic references to emotions (and other internal states) become *evaluative* from a more *global* perspective, i.e., they increasingly index the overarching orientation from which events are connected into a plot line. From this perspective, the setting of the story events (i.e., the construction of a loving and caring relationship between the boy and his two animal friends) becomes relevant for the motivations of the protagonist(s) to go on a search for their lost frog, resulting in a solution that presents a happy ending. In other words, the horizontal and the hierarchical levels of story organization are increasingly integrated.

(b) Being freed from the level of the particular, i.e., being now able to present third persons' inner states as outcomes of story happenings, and story happenings as outcomes of the story characters' emotions and motivations, children around the age of 8–9 years are able to tie emotions, motivations, and story events together from a more global level of story organization. Instead of moving horizontally from one local perspective to the next, the child now is able to "reorient" himself or herself and

(a) elaborate quantitatively with more affective expression;
(b) increase (quantitatively and at more strategic points in the narrative) the use of linguistic references to emotions; and
(c) elaborate quantitatively in terms of overall story length.

In summary, en route to becoming a "good" story teller, children at a relatively early age, i.e., around 3–4 years of age, are perfectly able to focus on narrating as a (global level — in the sense of a wholistic) organizing activity. However, using affective expression to direct the audience in their understanding of the story (and as such, in the understanding of the narrator), undergoes reconstruction. Around the age of 6 years, children shift their focus to more local level details of content organization. This shift enables them to emphasize more directly the connection between story events and the motivations of the actors of the story (here: third person protagonists and antagonists). This connection is clearly signaled by the emergence of references to emotions and other internal states. Later, around the age of 9 years, children begin to integrate their earlier focus on telling the story as a wholistic unit, with their, by this time, more fully acquired ability to signal motivations for story events. At this point, the use of references to emotions as well as the expression of affect are beginning to orient the audience in a more integrated fashion toward the story and its narrator as a unit. As such, both forms of presentation, namely establishing a referential plane of what is depicted as emotionally and motivationally relevant, as well as the activity of story performance by means of affective expression, are functionally united.

CONCLUSIONS

In the remainder of this chapter, we will discuss our findings in light of two general considerations. The first concerns the relationship of story content and story performance. Here we will try to use the above findings to reconsider the common separation between *what* is said (story content) and *how* it is said (story performance). Our call for questioning the well-accepted boundary between what language refers to (its referential function) and how language is used interpersonally (its communicative function) — however useful this distinction may have been for other purposes — has far reaching implications for our second general consideration, namely how to view *emotion(s)* and *affect*. Here, we will try to extend an orientation that has been central to Ervin-Tripp's research in language development, and to apply it to the two domains of emotion(s) and affect. Specifically, we will put forth the view that such *objects* as emotions and affect are best understood as meaningful interpersonal relationships that are *discursively* constituted.

Narrative Structure, Content, and Performance

While at a purely referential level emotion terms refer to another's inner, psychological state, the actual employment of such terms is organized by other principles than the other's assumed feelings. As our studies show, with children at as early as 5 years of age, emotion terms are employed as evaluative stances from a narrator's perspective. The changes over time from the age of about 5 to adulthood, however, reveal the underlying organizing principles for their deployment. With increasing age, references to emotions become increasingly motivated by textual assumptions, i.e., the narrator's attempts to organize and to give shape to the plot (in light of an assumed dramatic relationship) becomes the organizing force for the deployment of emotion terms. Thus, in the course of linguistic/discourse development, references to emotions for American English-speaking children take on an indexing function that gives events and happenings their grounding in human motivation and action. As such, references to emotions provide local motives within the more global forces of the human drama.

The development of how the tellings are performed appears to follow similar organizing principles: With increasing age, the paralinguistic expression of affect becomes subjected to textual principles in the service of an overall recipient orientation. While early on, it was the activity of narrating which served as the global organizing principle for the deployment of affect use, with development, affective expression takes on a similar indexing function as references to emotions at the plane of content. Thus, the boundaries between content organization and the organization of story performance become obliterated in their joint goal to orient the audience.

Considering the way both story content and story performance develop in response to the addressee, we are now in a position to give more developmental credit to what we called *recipient design*. Realizing that the orientation toward being understood presents the governing force for the organization of content and performance, and at the same time their mutual integration, shifts the view of what develops in the process of narrative development. The development of narrative structure, content, and performance are no longer the units out of which a social orientation can developmentally "evolve." Rather, they are developmental products, emerging out of activities that have interpersonal (pragmatic) orientations at their core. Consequently, our construction of the developmental process no longer needs to rely on the assumption that either events, processes, states, or the self pre-exist as units out of which stories, plots, and the drama are constructed. Rather, the self as the narrator, as well as the events (including processes and states) that are reported in the narrative, *emerge* in the interaction; they are jointly co-constructed.[5] Content and performance both are contextualization factors[6] in the process of how narrators intend to be understood in interaction, and how they ultimately constitute their self-understanding.

Another way of understanding this process of orchestrating what we talk **about** and how we say it, is in terms of speakers' **involvement**. Involvement here first of all is understood as the construction of a relationship between the narrator and his or her audience (cf. Bamberg, 1992; Bamberg et al., in press; Chafe, 1982; Tannen, 1985, 1989). The pictured material that we used in our studies as elicitation material seemed to lend itself (at least for our subjects from Western, industrialized cultures) to being narrated from a somewhat involved third-person perspective. This means that our subjects did not choose to construct the story events and processes from the first person I-perspective, merging the boy-protagonist of the story and the narrating self into a (linguistically) indistinguishable unit. Neither did any of our subjects choose a totally detached perspective by staying outside the minds of all the story participants, reducing the narrator's role as informant to eyewitness or commentating chorus. The perspective from which story and content are organized is through the "mind" of the protagonist (i.e., the boy). Actually, to be more precise, in the process of story formation, children learn how to choose linguistic forms that instruct the recipient to take a similar perspective; and in this process **the mind** of the third-person character becomes "visible." As a consequence of this process, something like a *protagonist* is called into existence. Again, these units do not pre-exist outside or prior to the narrative or the interactive situation. Rather, they emerge within the interaction as part of the narrator-audience involvement.

From this perspective, an analysis that focuses on the "aboutness" or theme of the narrative, in the sense that the booklet we used is about "a lost frog" or "a boy's search for his run-away pet," has missed the point that the narrator's contribution does not consist in talking *about* this topic or theme. Rather, the "aboutness" or theme is a product of the activity of telling *through* the central protagonist's (in this story: the boy's) "intelligence," i.e., his perceptions, desires, and his consciousness. Consequently, any

---

[5] This does not imply that projects of "selfhood" (or "personality") — and, as such, "forms of identity" — cannot be projected out of re-emerging contours in interactions; and similarly, that a "past" cannot be constructed in terms of key events and key processes that prolong the project of identity formation from a constructed past into an imagined future.

[6] We are borrowing though also extending John Gumperz's notion of "contextualization cues" (Gumperz, 1982, 1992).

analysis that starts from the identification of the narrative by delineating the narrative clauses in their sequential order,[7] has lost sight of what is central to narrating as a discourse activity. *Narrating* means giving instructions to the recipient as to how to construct motives and actions through slipping into the protagonist's intelligence, and this activity is not to be confused with the theme (or topic) of the narrative. Again, the entity of the search theme (resulting in the [happy] finding of the lost frog) is best understood as emerging from the narrative activity that takes place between narrator and recipient, and not as anything that has an existence prior to the narrating activity "in the story." Reading the picture book *Frog, Where Are You?* by oneself, and presumably "discovering" the narrative structure (of the complicating action, the search theme, and its resolution) still requires the differentiation of the self into the narrator *and* the recipient, i.e., even the private activity of reading presupposes a narrating activity to let characters, scenes and events emerge in story form. As such, nothing can be taken as preexisting "in the story" without the (linguistic) **activity** of narrating.

Consequently, the emerging characteristics of the narrative activity, which are the narrative structure, the narrative content, and along the same line, the narrative performance,[8] are closely intertwined in terms of their orientation toward the recipient. In light of this (functional) interrelationship of narrative structure, content, and performance, it should not come as a surprise that the process of learning how to organize structure, content, and performance presents surprising parallels.[9] In sum then, it seems as if the pragmatic orientation of the narrative activity presents the driving organizing force for the development of narrative.

Toward a Narrative Constitution of Emotions

Attempting to draw any conclusions from the above-reported studies regarding the notion of what "emotions" are (or better: what they might "mean" to our narrators), we have to realize first of all, that the narrators are not reporting their feelings or emotions. The task of narrating *Frog, Where Are You?* from the picture book requires differentiating between

---

[7] Filtering the narrative for narrative clauses in order to arrive at the core narrative, and thereby distilling the events in the order they *actually happened* (cf. footnote 2 above), are the supposed means that lead to the narrative structure. In the particular cases of verbal presentations of the picture book *Frog, Where Are You?*, they are most likely to reveal the complicating action (the frog's departure), leading to several attempts to find the frog (the search theme), leading to the resolution in the form of the (happy) finding of the frog.

[8] At this point it may have become clear why it may be misleading to view "the performance" and "the activity" of narrating as one and the same entity.

[9] The same point was made in some earlier work (Bamberg, 1987) using a similar elicitation technique with the same picture book *Frog, Where Are You?*. There it was reported that children undergo organization and reorganization processes in two seemingly independent linguistic domains, that of learning how to use full determining nominal expressions versus pronouns and that of learning language specific tense–aspect differentiations. The fact that noun–pronoun and tense–aspect forms both instruct discourse participants how to construct, subjects the seemingly independent two linguistic "domains" to the same developmental organizing principles, suggesting that the development of linguistic forms be viewed as governed by discourse (organizing) activity.

the author, the narrator, and the characters, integrating them in the way they emerge in the narrative. References to emotions were used to attribute feelings as outcomes of actions (usually of others than the protagonist), and as motivations to act (usually for the protagonist) in order to "glue" or "transfix" the sequence of actions into an understandable, coherent whole. As such, our narrators were able to engage the story recipient in the protagonist's intelligence, and by doing so, in the narrator's own intelligence of how a world of actors, motives, and actions are viewed in their coexistence.

Along these lines, we have to clarify a second point, namely that neither the picture book, nor the narratives that are "taken" from the picture book, are explicitly thematizing emotions.[10] Though, as we have pointed out in the previous sections, the construction of action sequences and the construction of the "glue" that holds these actions together, form a unit, the actions and processes that are reported for protagonist as well as for the antagonists only make sense from a motivational "basis." At the same time, the motives that are attributed to the story characters only make sense from the assumption that certain things are happening "in" the story. Thus, the shift in perspective from reporting happenings to the report of actions brings in issues of volition, intention, and responsibility, i.e., a system of human, culturally-shared virtues which are possibly best viewed in the frame of the "human drama" (cf. Bamberg, 1994a; and particularly Burke, 1968, and 1969, for further elaborations on this issue).

Revealing how the mutual constitution of actions and motivations is linked to the understanding of persons seems to present a special case in the presentation of third-person narratives, particularly the way they are told from a picture book. Taking another's point of view is often assumed to be a product of transference from what is called self-experience onto a concrete third person or onto generalized others; or it is assumed to be a specific instantiation of general, cultural expectations that follow from scripts or schemata (at the cognitive plane) or norms (at the social/institutional plane) outside and prior to the individual. In the former case, actions and emotions are assumed to be experienced by a "self" that has privileged access to his or her experience. According to this view, emotions and actions have a factual existence before they can become linguistically expressed and communicated. According to the latter view, scripts and norms impose themselves due to their social, institutional force onto the forms of interactions between individuals. In both cases, language is viewed as the tool for prior existing conceptualizations to be communicated.

However, as has been convincingly shown by Hopper (in press) for first-person narratives, events and actions are the products of particular linguistic choices. They emerge at the level of narrativization due to a persona that intervenes between whatever

---

[10] Emotions are *explicitly* thematized when subjects are asked to report a time when they were particularly "happy" or "sad," or to explain what it means to be "scared" or "angry." It is interesting to see that these kinds of interview questions elicit a sequence of reported actions — usually those that are assumed to have led to the experience of an emotion. However, when asked in interviews for the action sequence, subjects are much more likely to report the feeling-state that they believe held for the time of the happening that is central to the action sequence (see Bamberg, Ammirati, & Shea, 1995, for further discussion of this relationship).

("really") happened and the act of narrating. According to Hopper, to assume that narratives account for the factuality of what happened (or for a memorized record of it) fails to take note of the constitutive role of language in the process of narrating.[11]   A similar argument has been put forth for what has often been called *dual* or *mixed* emotions (Bamberg et al., in press). From our analyses of self-reports (first-person narratives) of American English-speaking subjects between 5 years and college age to the request to share a time when they felt two simultaneous emotions (eg. *happy* & *angry*, or *scared* & *sad*), we could conclude that it is the merging of two different aspectual (=linguistic) systems that bring about the impression of the "same" situation as "causing" two different, simultaneously felt emotions. Whatever the subjects may have "really" felt, a dual emotion is clearly a retrospective, *linguistic* construction. Harré and Gillet (1994) make a similar point with regard to the construction of single emotions by assuming that references to emotions function as directives to bring to bear the local taxonomy of judgments that obtain as discursive practices at a particular time. As such, references to emotions are in a close functional proximity with how feelings are expressed and displayed: Both are discursively used to express judgments and to perform social acts (Harré & Gillet, 1994, pp. 153ff.).

A similar tack underpinning the role of language in the constitution of events and actions on the one hand, and of emotions on the other, has been taken by philosophers such as MacIntyre (1984), Taylor (1985), and more recently Kerby (1991). Kerby for instance argues that "the narration of events is not a simple description of 'facts' but an interpretive activity. . . . Prior to some degree of narration, the meaning of human events for us is obscure or simply absent" (Kerby, 1991, p. 48). Taylor claims in a similar vein: "To say that language is constitutive of emotion is to say that experiencing an emotion essentially involves seeing that certain descriptions apply" (Taylor, 1985, p. 71).

In sum, we do not mean to imply that emotions only exist in language and/or discourse. However, it is our contention that emotions are part of our capacity to self-interpret (Taylor, 1985), i.e., they are regulated by our awareness of the roles of self and other in social situations. And a central component of this awareness is the ability to view one's own behavior from the perspective of others (Averill, 1980, p.314; Bamberg, 1993). With the narrative approach to the understanding of emotions that we have put forth in this chapter, and with our corresponding focus on the narrating *activity*, we hope we have also contributed to a more refined understanding how emotions are socially *constructed*. In addition, we also hope that our call for a revision of the common separation between the referential plane and the performative plane of language functioning will lead to a renewed interest to explore the relationships between discourse, language, affect, and emotions — particularly in child discourse.

---

[11] Compare Edwards and Potter (1992) for a similar position regarding the role of discourse activity in the constitution of form-function relationships.

REFERENCES

Averill, J.A. (1980). A constructivist view of emotion. In R. Plutchick & H. Kellerman (Eds.), *Emotion: Theory, research, and experience: Volume 1. Theories of emotion* (pp. 305-339). New York: Academic.

Bamberg, M. (1987). *The acquisition of narratives*. Berlin: Mouton de Gruyter.

Bamberg, M. (1992). Binding and unfolding: Establishing viewpoint in oral and written discourse. In M. Kohrt & A. Wrobel (Eds.), *Schreibprozesse — Schreibprodukte* (pp. 1-24). Hildesheim, Germany: Georg Olms Verlag.

Bamberg, M. (1993). Communication and internal states: What is their relationship? — Commentary on D. Lubinski & T. Thompson "Species and individual differences in communication based on private states." *Behavioral and Brain Sciences*, **16**, 643-644.

Bamberg, M. (1994a). Actions, events, scenes, plots and the drama: Language and the constitution of part-whole relationships. *Language Sciences*, **16**, 39-79.

Bamberg, M. (1994b). Development of linguistic forms: German. In R. Berman & D. I. Slobin, *Different ways of relating events in narrative: A crosslinguistic developmental study* (pp. 189-238). Hillsdale, NJ: Lawrence Erlbaum Associates.

Bamberg, M., Ammirati, D.L., & Shea, S. (1995). What constitutes "good" data for the study of language development? — How children learn to talk about things with no name: "Double emotions." In P. W. Davis (Ed.), *Alternative Linguistics: Descriptive and theoretical modes* (pp. 1-43). Amsterdam, The Netherlands: John Benjamins.

Bamberg, M., & Damrad-Frye, R. (1991). On the ability to provide evaluative comments: Further explorations of children's narrative competencies. *Journal of Child Language*, **18**, 689-710.

Burke, K. (1968). *Counter-statement*. Berkeley: University of California Press.

Burke, K. (1969). *A grammar of motives*. Berkeley: University of California Press.

Chafe, W. (1982). Integration and involvement in speaking, writing, and oral literature. In D. Tannen (Ed.), *Spoken and written language: Exploring orality and literacy* (pp. 35-54). Norwood, NJ: Ablex.

Edwards, D., & Potter, J. (1992). *Discursive psychology*. London: Sage.

Gumperz, J. J. (1982). *Discourse strategies*. Cambridge, England: Cambridge University Press.

Gumperz, J. J. (1992). Contextualizing and understanding. In A. Duranti & C. Goodwin (Eds.), *Rethinking context. Language as an interactive phenomenon* (pp. 229-252). Cambridge, England: Cambridge University Press.

Harré, R., & Gillet, G. (1994) . *The discursive mind*. Thousand Oaks, CA: Sage.

Hopper, P. (in press). The English verbal expression in written discourse. In P. W. Davis (Ed.), *Descriptive and theoretical modes in the alternative linguistics*. Amsterdam: John Benjamins.

Kerby, A. P. (1991). *Narrative and the self*. Bloomington: Indiana University Press.

Labov, W., & Waletzky, J. (1967). Narrative analysis: Oral versions of personal experience. In J. Helm (Ed.), *Essays on the verbal and visual arts* (pp. 17-35). Seattle: University of Washington Press.

MacIntyre, A. (1984). *After virtue: A study in moral theory*. Notre Dame, IN: University of Notre Dame Press.

Mayer, M. (1969). *Frog, where are you?* New York: Dial Books for Young Readers.

Reilly, J. S. (1992). How to tell a good story: The intersection of language and affect in children's narratives. *Journal of Narrative and Life History*, **2**, 355-377.

Ross, R. (1980). *Storyteller*. New York: Merrill.

Tannen, D. (1985). Relative focus on involvement in oral and written discourse. In D. Olson, N. Torrance, & A. Hildyard (Eds.), *Literacy, language, and learning: The nature and consequences of reading and writing* (pp. 67-88). Cambridge, England: Cambridge University Press.

Tannen, D. (1989). *Talking voices: Repetition, dialogue, and imagery in conversational discourse* (Studies in Interactional Sociolinguistics, 6). Cambridge, England: Cambridge University Press.

Taylor, C. (1985). *Human agency and language: Philosophical papers I*. Cambridge, England: Cambridge University Press.

21 FORM AND FUNCTION IN DEVELOPING NARRATIVE ABILITIES[1]

Ruth A. Berman
Tel Aviv University

The title of this chapter acknowledges the contribution of Susan Ervin-Tripp to the study of children's language. She started out by focusing on form, then moved on to function, with her current work reflecting an insightful integration between the two (e.g., in Ervin-Tripp, 1989). The present study considers the relationship between form and function in language acquisition and language development through analysis of the Hebrew morpheme *ve*, the counterpart of English *and*, in early conversational interaction and in the narratives of children aged 3 to 9 compared with adults.

1. FORM – FUNCTION RELATIONS

In this context, the term "form" refers to closed-class lexical items such as conjunctions, prepositions, and pronouns; but it also applies to bound affixal morphemes, both inflectional and derivational (e.g., the English suffixes *-ing* or *-ic(al)*); to syntactic constructions such as relative clauses or passive voice; to syntactic operations such as left-dislocation or subject ellipsis; and to lexical expressions with modifying functions such as temporal adverbials, intensifiers, and floating operators like *also, even*. More problematic is the question of what constitutes a "function," in linguistic analysis as in the study of language development.[2] The "function" of a linguistic form has been used to apply to any or all of the following: knowledge of discourse-sensitive factors such as maintaining and shifting reference, focus, and contrast (Karmiloff-Smith, 1981; Wigglesworth, 1990); level

[1] This chapter is a revised and extended version of a paper presented to the International Pragmatics Conference, Barcelona, July 1990. Collection of the longitudinal data was supported by a grant from the G.I.F., the German-Israeli Foundation for Scientific Research and Development to the author with Juergen Weissenborn of the Max-Planck Institute for Psycholinguistics, Nijmegen, Holland. The Hebrew narrative materials are part of a project with Dan I. Slobin of the University of California at Berkeley, supported by the United States-Israel Binational Science Foundation (BSF), Jerusalem, Israel, and the National Science Foundation. The chapter relies heavily on insights derived from work with Slobin in coauthoring a crosslinguistic study of narrative development (Berman & Slobin, 1994).

[2] The varied construals of this topic are reflected in the title of the special edition of the journal *First Language* devoted to "Functional Approaches to Child Language" (Budwig, 1991). Very different approaches are articulated there from the point of view of developmental psycholinguistics by researchers dealing with the acquisition of verb categorization, passive voice, epistemic modals, and pronominal usage and from the perspective of linguistic analysis by Silverstein (1991) and Van Valin (1991). In the present study, the term "function" is used without commitment to a particular functionalist view of linguistic analysis (see, further, Nichols, 1984; Bates & MacWhinney, 1982).

of informativeness and organization of information in the text (Giora, 1983, 1985); or conditions governing the pragmatics of assertion and presupposition at the level of a single sentence (Crain & Nakayama, 1987). In the present context, the term "function" applies to the semantic import and/or to the discourse role served by a variety of forms in the construction of a linguistic text. For instance, the function of **object-specification** is served by nominal modifiers such as adjectives, adjunct nouns in compounds, relative clauses, and prepositional phrases (Dasinger & Toupin, 1994); and temporal notions such as **simultaneity** and **retrospection** in ongoing discourse are expressed by morphological markers of verb aspect, by lexical adverbials, and by clause-sequencing (Aksu-Koç & von Stutterheim, 1994). The grammatical and lexical forms of a language provide speakers with an array of different "expressive options" or "rhetorical choices" for verbalizing particular concepts and relations in ongoing discourse (Berman, 1993c, 1993b; Berman & Slobin, 1994).

The way and extent to which these options are deployed by speakers of different languages and at different developmental phases is affected by the "functionality" of a given construction within a language to achieve goals of the kind noted above (Slobin, 1987). Here, "functionality" refers to (1) how obligatory a particular option is for expressing a given form-meaning relationship, (2) the availability of other forms for the same purpose, and (3) the range of different levels of usage which it serves (for instance, forms restricted to academic discourse are less functional in this sense than ones which can also serve in everyday conversation). For instance, Demuth (1992) suggests that young Sesotho speakers use relative clauses very early in part because their language lacks a rich system of adjectives for expressing nominal attribution. I have argued that although passives are syntactically quite productive in Hebrew, speakers use them relatively little because the language has a wide range of other, more favored devices for downgrading the agent and focusing on the patient of an action (Berman, 1979). Similarly, out of the entire range of morphological devices available for new-word formation in a language, speakers will exploit mainly those which have a high degree of productivity in current usage (Berman, 1993b). Linguists working in different research paradigms agree on the lack of perfect fit between form and function, whatever sense they attach to the term "function" (see footnote 1). Psychologists identified with a functionalist orientation, on the other hand, have tended to take "a view of language acquisition and use that posits priorities for communicative functions over forms" (Muma, 1986, p. xv). The present study involves no commitment to whether forms are "more important" than functions or vice versa. Rather, concern is with the way in which the two interact in language acquisition and in language use. From a developmental perspective, the aim of the present study is to re-examine Slobin's oft-cited claim that: "New forms first express old functions, and new functions are first expressed by old forms" (1973, p. 184). Underlying this analysis is the assumption that the initial phase of language acquisition manifests a one-to-one mapping between form and function, in both directions. Children start by assigning one particular function to each new form they learn. And they do so in one of two ways: Either they restrict each form to a single function out of several it has in the endstate grammar, or they assign a nonconventional function to a given form.[3] In the opposite direction, children may initially use one particular form to express a given function; for example, iterativity or recurrence might first be expressed by repetition of the same lexical items, subsequently by derivational morphology, and eventually by extending the use of progressive aspect (e.g., with *always* in a language like English).

Detailed analysis of the developmental route followed by particular linguistic forms reveals yet another facet of the notion "function." Across time, use of any given form is extended and hence reconstrued in a variety of interrelated ways. It may be used (1) with different **semantic** denotations (e.g., *after* first occurs in children's narratives in spatial contexts such as *run after*, later takes on a temporal sense as in *after that*); (2) in extended **syntactic** contexts (e.g., *after* first functions as a preposition, later as a sequential marker as in *after that*, then as a subordinating conjunction in finite clauses, e.g., *after he left*, and only later in nonfinite contexts, e.g., *after leaving*); (3) with different **discourse roles** in connecting parts of a text as a thematically related whole (e.g., in picture book description, *now* first functions as a means of spatial deixis moving from one picture to the next, later it is replaced by nonspatial temporal expressions such as *afterwards* relating between events in the evolving plot, while mature speakers use *now* to mark narrative sequentiality in the sense of 'at this point in the story' or for logical inference, as in *now that he sees what has happened ...*); and (4) with different stylistic levels or **usage registers** (for instance, familiar spatial terms like *here* or *far* are used to mark temporal and logical relations between parts of a text in academic discourse, in expressions like archaic *heretofore* or formal *thus far* or contrasting with colloquial *up to here, so far*).

Analysis of English picture book narratives elicited from children aged 3, 5, and 9 years old compared with adults (Berman & Slobin, 1994) reveals numerous instances of such extensions and changes in use as new functions are added to old forms. Different linguistic domains reveal parallel developmental trends, for instance: (1) a grammatical inflection like the suffix *-ing* starts out as the means favored for referring to deictic speech time in the sense of an immediate present tense, then marks progressive aspect — initially only in the present, subsequently in past-tense contexts too, later it is used in verb complement constructions, and finally as a nonfinite subordinator in modifying, relative-clause-like or adverbial constructions; (2) closed class items like the prepositions *in* or *after* progress from static and dynamic locative to temporal marking, to adverbial use with nonfinite verbs and with abstract derived nominals (e.g., *in despair, in amazement*); (3) a syntactic construction like passive voice, develops from use with dynamic activity verbs to stative predicates, and from describing change-of-state situations to marking shifts in narrative perspective from an agentive-actor to a patient-undergoer orientation; and (4) a syntactic operation such as subject ellipsis, which in English

---

[3] An example of children's restricted use of a form are early past tense or perfective markings limited to achievement-type verbs denoting perceptible changes-of-state. Instances where children assign to a form a function it does not serve in the endstate grammar are provided by Gee and Savasir's (1985) analysis of early uses of *will* versus *gonna* for marking different modalities and by Budwig's (1989) study of young children's use of *I*, *me*, and *my* for self-reference.

initially merely indicates illformed simple-clause construction, later serves for clause-linkage through syntactic coordination, and finally functions to achieve discourse connectivity through an implicit, shared discourse topic.

The central theme of the present study is to demonstrate that while knowledge of linguistic forms is evident from a very young age, this knowledge is only partial since, with age, these forms take on different functions. The analysis thus focuses on the first of two complementary facets of the form–function relation in language acquisition. Order of **development** across time is determined by the development of more functions for the same form, in this case, the Hebrew coordinating conjunction *ve* 'and'. Order of **emergence**, which is determined by the development of new forms for a particular function, lies outside the domain of the present study.

2. COORDINATION AS A LINGUISTIC FORM

The Hebrew morpheme *ve* is syntactically similar to its English counterpart *and* in most respects relevant to the present analysis.[4] Both forms join two propositions in a type of clause-linkage or nexus which represents a whole-whole equivalence relation between two independent clauses (Van Valin, 1993), more formally defined as an S, which "consists of two or more Ss and a conjunction, with the Ss being sisters of one another" (McCawley, 1988, p. 263). The acquisition of conjoined structures has been analyzed for different languages in relation to developing syntax (e.g., Ardery, 1979; Halkiadakis-Delidakis & Tager-Flusberg, 1985; Lust, 1977, 1980; Lust & Y-Chien, 1984) as well as semantics (e.g., Bloom, Lahey, Hood, Lifter, & Fiess, 1980; Tager-Flusberg, de Villiers, & Hakuta, 1982).[5]   Recently, researchers have also become increasingly concerned with how *and* is used in children's extended discourse, alone or together with other markers of connectivity (Jisa, 1987; Laubitz, 1987; Peterson & McCabe, 1987, 1988, 1991; and Slobin, 1993). These studies provide important insights into the use of connectives in children's extended discourse in the context of developing narrative abilities (e.g., Peterson & McCabe, 1991) and of crosslinguistic comparisons (Slobin, 1989). The present study, in contrast, focuses rather narrowly on the one form, *ve*, in a single language, Hebrew, in the framework of an overall model of language acquisition and language use. Its aim is to analyze children's use of coordination from the combined

---

[4] The morpheme *ve* is prefixed to the following item as part of the same orthographic word; in normative usage it alternates with the vowel /u/ before labials, e.g., *Kara ve Sara u Mara* 'Kara and Sara and Mara'. The form patterns syntactically much like its English counterpart, although when used for conjoining subjects, it may entail changes in the number and/or gender agreement on verbs. Hebrew has the same basic SVO word order as English and Spanish, and it lies between these two in the extent to which the repeated subject may or must be elided under coordination (e.g., "The boy ran and he fell" compared with "The boy ran and fell"). In terms of the requirement of same-subject elision under coordination, Hebrew lies between a subject-requiring language like English and a freely subject-eliding language like Spanish (Berman, 1990).

[5] Findings for semantics are well summed up in Peterson and McCabe (1991, p. 33).

perspective of the relation between form and function in emerging discourse abilities, on the one hand, and the place of coordination in a general model of language acquisition and language development, on the other. As background, I hypothesized that children's use of the coordinating conjunction *ve* would proceed through three general phases, as shown in (1). To start with, they will use *ve* as an empty discourse filler, a kind of narrative "glue" (Peterson & McCabe, 1988). As they gain mastery of the syntax of coordination, older children will use *ve* to mark temporal sequentiality between events. Eventually, mature speakers will deploy the term selectively, as one out of a range of devices available to them for narrative cohesion. These predictions were tested in two types of data: Longitudinal records of 2-year-olds in conversation with their parents, and narratives produced by children from age 3 compared with adults.

(1) Phases in emerging use of the marker *ve* 'and':

Phase	Position / Function	Intention Signaled
1	Utterance-initial "announcing"	I have more to say (in the same conversational turn)
2	Clause-initial "chaining"	Something else / more happened (in chronological sequence)
3	Text-embedded "chunking"	Events or states are related (within a discourse theme)

3. COORDINATION
IN EARLY PARENT–CHILD CONVERSATION

Early use of *ve* as an utterance-initial means of announcing that the child has more to say is illustrated by the little girl Naama in (2), with her mother and a little boy called Uri. Transcription is broad phonetic, following the CHILDES convention (MacWhinney & Snow, 1990), with CHI standing for the child, MOT for the mother, FAT for the father.

(2) **Naama, aged 2;2,12**

    CHI: *Ani roca calaxat gdola.*
           'I want (a) big dish.'
    MOT: *Roca te?*
           'Want+FEM tea?' = 'Do you want tea?'
    CHI: *Lo, lo raca.*
           'No, no want.' = 'No, I don't.'
           ***Ve** le Uri gam calaxat gdola.*
           '**And** for Uri also (a) big dish.'
           Le Uri gam.
           'For Uri also.'

Naama is not yet capable of syntactic coordination, but she can use *ve* to start the second utterance out of the three which form her response to the mother's query. With regard to this example note, first, that this child was soon afterwards able to make use of syntactic coordination; for example, at age 2;3,2, she said *hayom yarad geshem **ve** lo yaradeti* 'Today it rained **and** I didn't go-down [= out]'. Second, her use of the floating operator *gam*, meaning 'also, too', suggests that this form functions as a **precursor** of *ve*, as an immature, pregrammatical device for expressing the notion of conjoining.[6] This claim is supported by narrative usage of both Hebrew- and German-speaking 3-year-olds, who rely heavily on *gam* and *auch* respectively as an utterance-linking device (Bamberg, 1994; Berman & Neeman, 1994).

The following conversational interchanges between parents and their 2-year-old daughters, illustrate utterance-initial *ve* — in (3a) and (3b) — compared with early clause-chaining — (5a) and (5b). As with Naama, the period between exclusive reliance on utterance-initial *ve* and a more syntactically motivated use of this form for combining clauses is quite short: a couple of months in the case of Hagar, a week or two for the precocious Smadar.

(3a) **Hagar, aged 2;5,1:**

    CHI: *Tesapri li al ha-ze'ev*
           'Tell me about the-wolf.'

    MOT: *Ma asa ha-ze'ev?*
           'What did the-wolf (do)?'
           [a few utterances are interchanged]
           Ma ha-ze'ev omer?
           'What the-wolf says?'

    CHI: *Hu omer lax: telex habayta,*
           'He tells you: you-go home'
           ***ve, ve** ...*
           '**and, and** ...'

    MOT: ***Ve?***
           '**And?**'

    CHI: ***Ve** ha-xamor taraf otax.*
           '**And** the-donkey ate you (up).'

---

[6] The term "pregrammatical" is used in a highly specific sense, to refer to use of language that precedes initial marking of grammatical distinctions and reliance on structural categories (Berman, 1986). Another example of *gam* 'also' as a precursor of coordination is provided by the boy, Leor, aged 2;3.

(i)   LEOR: *Yesh, doda Ogi poteax [sic] po*
              There's, Aunt Orly opens+MASC here
      AUNT: *Doda Orly potaxat po et hateyp?*
              Aunt Orly opens+FEM [= turns on] the tape here?
      LEOR: *Ve **gam** po.*
              And here also.

Note that *gam* does not typically occur in the one-word stage of Hebrew language use, when the terms *od* 'more' and *od-paam* 'again' are used to indicate addition or repetition.

(3b) **Smadar, aged 2;2,10:**

MOT: *Eyfo hayinu hayom?*
'Where were we [= did we go] today?'

CHI: *Ani agid laxem ey(fo).*
'I'll tell you (all) whe(re).'

MOT: *Nu?*
'Well?'

CHI: *Be gan Erela.*
At Erella's nursery (school).

MOT: *Ve az?*
'**And** then?'

CHI: *Ve az xazarnu ha-bayta*
'**And** then we came back home.'

MOT: *Ken.*
'Yes.'

CHI: *Ve shamanu oti ba-teyp.*
'**And** we heard me on the tape.

MOT: *Kvar shamanu otax bateyp?*
'Did we hear you on the tape already?'

CHI: *Ve hishkat-, ani hishketi et ha'acicim.*
'**And** wate-, and I watered the plants.'

Example (3a) is of one-turn interchanges. Here, *ve* is used by the adult as a prompt-ing device to indicate that she is waiting for more to come, and by the child Hagar as an utterance-initiator to inform the interlocutor that she has more to tell. Similarly, in (3b), Smadar, a very advanced 2-year-old, introduces new pieces of information by *ve*. The mothers' prompts suggest that children have ample evidence for their early construal of *ve* as utterance-initial from adult input, where this morpheme prods the child to continue with his or her story, indicating that the interlocutor is willing and ready to hear more. This type of cooperative prompting is by no means restricted to juvenile discourse; it is common in adult conversations, encouraging speakers to go on with their accounts by such prods as *and . . . , so then what happened?*. Besides, in picture-description tasks, adults typically prompt children by saying *ve ma ro'im po?* 'And what do we see here?', or in scaffolding early narratives, by saying *ve ma kara az?* 'and what happened then?' The following examples are from maternal interchanges with the same two girls, well before the children used *ve* as in (3a) and (3b) above.

(4a) **Hagar 2;0,1:**

FAT: *Mi kofets lamayim?*
'Who jumps into the water?'

CHI: *K(r)uvi.*
'Cabbage' [= name of pet]

FAT: *Naxon, ve eyfo Shoshi?*
'Right, **and** where's Shoshi?'

CHI: *Al akavish yashav, tafasnu oto ...*
'On a spider (he) sat, we caught him ...' [based on familiar song]

MOT: *Ve ma asinu lo axrey she tafasnu oto?*
      '**And** what did we do after we caught him?'
      Natanu lo lalexet, naxon?
      'We let him go, right [= didn't we]?'

(4b) **Smadar 1;6,14**:
MOT: *Smadari yoshevet al hateyp?*
      'Is Smadari sitting on the tape?'
CHI: *Teyp!*
      'Tape.'
MOT: *Eyfo ha-teyp?*
      'Where's the tape?'
CHI: *Hine, hine!*
      'Here, here!'
MOT: *Ken. Ve ma at osa axshav?*
      'Yes. **And** what are you doing now?'

The utterance-initial use of *ve* in (3a, 3b), possibly triggered by parental prompts as shown in (4a, 4b), is soon followed by **clause-chaining**. In (5a), the child is telling her parents what she has been playing at, and in (5b), what she did with her sisters at the playground. At this phase, *ve* alternates with other sequential markers such as *az* 'then', to indicate that another event is about to be described, and the child has advanced beyond producing only a single utterance or predication per turn. By now, both children can chain two or more events within a single sequence, uninterrupted by parental prompts.

(5a) **Hagar, aged 2;7,23**:
FAT: *Banit, banitem bayit shel gamadim im kubiyot?*
      'Did you, did you make a house of dwarfs from blocks?'
CHI: *Kubiyot, babayit, ... shel gamadim, ve ba arye,*
      az ciyarnu arye.
      'Blocks, in the house ... of dwarfs, **and** a lion came,
      so we drew a lion.'
MOT: *Ciyartem arye? Bimkom livnot oto mikubiyot,*
      ciyartem arye?
      'You drew a lion? Instead of making it from blocks?'
CHI: *Ken, az hu gam, lakaxnu et ha-mocecim shelanu ve,*
      hixnasnu la-pe, ve lakaxnu et babakbuk shelanu.
      'Yes, **so** he also, we took our pacifiers **and**,
      we put (them) in our mouths, **and** we took our bottle.'

(5b) **Smadar, aged 2;2,19**:
MOT: *Ve ma od at roca lesaper le'ima?*
      '**And** what else do you want to tell me (about)?'
CHI: *Al hagan shaashuim she halaxnu im banot?*
      'About the playground that [= where/when]
      we went with the girls?'
MOT: *Ken.*
      'Yes.'

CHI: [in singsong, storytelling intonation, with syllable-lengthening]
    She *hayinu bagan shashuim im habanot,*
    az *halaxanu ve axarkax halaxnu lanadneda,*
    ve *axarkax halaxnu lamaglesha haktana*
    'That [= when] we were at the playground with the girls,
    then [= so] we went and afterwards we went to the swing,
    and afterwards went to the small slide.'

These examples bear out the predictions in (1): Initially, *ve* serves as an empty discourse filler, and is typically utterance initial. This *ve* is "empty" in the sense that it lacks both normative syntactic structure and conventional semantic content. And its use as utterance initiating is consistent with what has been noted for early subordinate clauses as "truncated." At first, the complementizer *she-* 'that' typically introduces an utterance which is a lone clause; the associated matrix clause is either not specified at all, or occurs in the preceding utterance of another speaker. However, immature *ve* does serve a specific discourse function, one which is interpersonal rather than intratextual: It tells the interlocutor that "more is to come," and so is interactional in motivation and function. And this *ve* is mirrored by use of the same morpheme as a "prompt" in adult scaffolding of early narratives: For adults, *ve* serves to inform the child that "more should be coming."

The examples in (5a) and (5b) show how this use of *ve* as an interactive discourse-marker evolves into the syntactically and semantically more conventional function of chaining clauses in temporal sequence.   These instances of conversational discourse reflect the early, interactive origins of narrative abilities (Miller & Sperry, 1988; Ninio, 1988), since they meet the most rudimentary requirement of narrative discourse: to produce "a sequence of two clauses that are temporally ordered" (Labov, 1972, p. 360).   And they provide support for what Susan Ervin-Tripp has so cogently argued: that grammatical forms deployed in narrative discourse occur at an earlier age in conversational interaction.

4. COORDINATION AND CONNECTIVITY IN EXTENDED NARRATIVES

In the context of more extended narrative texts which lack the "ping-pong" type of scaffolding afforded by adult input queries and other prompts, the same two phases in the use of *ve* — first as a marker of "more to say" and then as a marker of "something else happened" — characterize the usage of older children, too.[7]   The examples in (6) are taken from a crosslinguistic study by Slobin (1989), comparing the use of three superficially similar forms by children of different language backgrounds.   These excerpts

---

[7] The term "phases" is used here rather than "stages," since the same developmental patterning may be manifested at different ages (hence at different maturational stages) in relation to different types of cognitive and linguistic tasks (see Berman, 1986; Karmiloff-Smith, 1986).

illustrate the use of morphemes meaning 'and' in stories told by 3-year-old children in four languages.[8]

(6) 3-year olds' use of *and* for describing pictures in a story book
(from Slobin, 1989):

English, aged 3;1 -	A owl. Flew out of here. **And** he's running away.
German, aged 3;3 -	*Da kommt ein Vogel. **Und** da rennt er.*
	'There comes a bird. **And** there he runs.'
Spanish, aged 3;3 -	*Salió un pájaro immenso. **Y** un niñito se*
	cayó de cabeza así.
	'An immense bird came out. **And** a little boy fell
	on his head like this.'
Hebrew, aged 3;6 -	*Hine yanshuf. **Ve** hine hayeled nafal.*
	'Here's an owl. **And** here the boy fell (down).'

In the examples in (6), the first clause ends with a period, which marks utterance-final intonation. In other words, the *and* of the second clause is utterance-initial, and it meets the criteria for an "empty discourse filler": It does not express an established semantic relation for conjoining temporally or causally related events; nor does it manifest syntactic coordination of two clauses within a single sentence. These are immature uses of *and*: They merely indicate that the speaker has something more to say about the same picture.

Two sets of narrative texts were analyzed for the present study: (1) picture-book-based narrations of 36 Hebrew-speaking children aged 3, 5, and 9 compared with 12 adults, who were asked to tell a story while looking through a book depicting the adventures of a boy and his dog in search of their pet frog which has escaped from the jar in which it was held — the "frog" story (*Frog, Where Are You?*, by Mercer Mayer, New York, 1969);[9] and (2) free narrations of ten Hebrew-speaking children at each of the ages 3, 5, 7, and 9, compared with 10 adults, who were asked if they had ever been in a fight or had a quarrel, and to tell what happened — the "fight" story.

4.1   Chaining Functions of *ve*

Examination of extended narrative discourse leads to a refining of the distinctions between different types of "chaining" expressed by *ve* as set out in (1) above. The "chaining" function of the *and* conjunction seems to follow three steps: listing of objects, introducing new clauses, linking states or events. These are shown in (7), in describing the opening scene of the picture book story.

(7)   Development of chaining functions of *ve*:

    a.   **Chaining objects = LISTER** — e.g., Child #3F, aged 3;7

---

[8]   The excerpts describe a two-page picture which shows an owl coming out of a hole in a tree and a boy falling down at the bottom of the tree on the left hand side, with a dog running away from a swarm of bees on the right hand side.

[9]   These materials form part of a larger crosslinguistic project conducted with Dan I. Slobin of Berkeley (Berman, 1988; Berman & Slobin, 1994; Slobin, 1990, 1991).

Yesh   yeled ... ve   yareax ve kelev ve tsfardea
'There's (a) boy ... **and** (a) moon **and** (a) dog **and** (a) frog'

b.   **Chaining clauses = INTRODUCER** — e.g., Child #4B, aged 4;2
Hatsfardea em ... hi hayta kan, ve - gam hu histakel aleha,
'The frog er ... it was here, **and** *- he also looked at it,'*
ve haya layla.
'**and** (it) was night.'

c-i   **Chaining (related) states = LINKER** — e.g., Child #7A, aged 7;1
Pa'am axat haya yeled, ve hayta lo tsfardea betox tsinsenet.
'Once (there) was (a) boy, **and** he had (a) frog inside (a) jar.'

c-ii   **Chaining (related) events = LINKER** — e.g., Child #9B, aged 9;2
Yeled exad matsa tsfardea ve hem sixku ita.
'A boy found (a) frog **and** they played with it.'

The Hebrew stories revealed a clear developmental pattern starting with the youngest narrators, aged 3 years, who were typically beyond the first step in (7). (The child whose text is excerpted in (7a) told a particularly immature story.) Most 3-year-olds used *ve* as a next-clause introducer, as in (7b), while 5- and 9-year olds used it to chain events in sequence, as in (7c). In the much shorter narratives produced by children asked to tell about a fight they had been involved in, *ve* functions for chaining in the sense of linking events in sequence even among some 3-year-olds, as shown in (8a). In contrast, (8b) shows a mixture of initial temporal chaining of events in sequence followed by a less motivated, "additive" use of *ve* — merely to add one clause to the next.

(8a)   **Adi, girl, aged 3;5**:
Ravti im El'ad ve baxiti.
'I quarreled with Elad and I cried.'
Hu hipil oti, ve hu hirbic ba-rosh
'He pushed me, **and** he hit me in the head'
ve mashax li ta sa'arot. Ve hu gam shavar li et ha-rosh.
'**and** pulled my hair. **And** he also broke (sic) my head.'
Ve yarad li dam, ve samu li yod ba'ayin.
'**And** it bled, **and** they put iodine on.'

(8b)   **Pe'er, boy, aged 3;7**:
Paam haya yeled, she kar'u lo Eytan.
'Once there was a boy who was called Eytan.'
Ve Dotan zarak alav xol ba-panim
'**And** Dotan threw sand in his face.'
ve gam al harosh ve btox ha-enayim.
'**and** also on his head and in his eyes.'
Ve axarkax hu ba,
'**And** afterwards he came,'
ve hasheni baxa,
'**and** the other one cried,'
ve hayalda amra lahem "al tivke, Rami."
'**and** the girl said "don't cry, Rami,"'

Ve Tali, hi amra le-Riba she telex
'**And** Tali, she told Riba to go to'
labayit shela ve gam kol habanim
'to her house, **and** all the boys also'
ve Riba tishaer lvad bli hagananot
'**and** Riba will stay alone without the teachers'
ve rak bat axat tishaer ve gam ben exad.
'**and** only one girl will stay, and one boy also.'
Ve sham kulam yelxu ve ben exad yisha'er
'**And** there everyone will go **and** one boy will stay'
ve gam hem racu lizrok od pa'am xol.
'**and** they also wanted to throw sand again.'

In (8a), 3-year-old Adi uses *ve* to link each one in a series of events making up a single-episode narrative. Although her constant repetition of *ve* creates a mechanical progression from one clause to the next, without any global-level hierarchical structuring, her use of *ve* serves to mark off each subsequent clause as the next in a temporally organized successive chain of events. In (8b), after the two initial introductory, background clauses, Pe'er also links one event to the next in a linear succession; but this breaks down when the episode-structure becomes more complex, more protagonists are introduced, and simple linear chaining is not sufficient to describe the consequences of the initial sand-throwing episode. In other words, as shown in the conversational interchanges analyzed in Section 3, among younger children, *ve* functions for event-chaining on a strictly local level, adding one clause to the next within a single **turn** among 2-year-olds, and linking pairs of clauses within a single **episode** in the narrative texts of children from around age 3.

These observations are consistent with what was found for the 16 picture book narrations produced by 3-year-olds, as shown in example (9). Although the "frog story" has a quite complicated episode structure, the linear flow of narrative is facilitated by the spatio-visual prop of successive pictures which children had before their eyes while producing their narrations. The text in (9) is a translation of a typical 3-year-old Hebrew narrative, set out consecutively by clauses.

(9) Hebrew 3-year old story translated into English [Child 3G, aged 3;8]:

A frog went into the jar,
and then the ... the boy fell,
and the frog went out.
And the dog put its head inside the jar.
The boy took the dog in his arms [= picked up the dog].
And the boy calls for the frog.
And the dog wants to climb up [= the tree].
And ... and here a mouse goes inside the hole.
Here the dog fell.
And the dog ran [= was running away from the bees].
And then the bird came.
And the boy went up the mountain [= a rock].

And the deer up ... and the deer went up the mountain.
And here the deer also went up the mountain.
And the boy went to the sky.
And the boy went into the sea [= a lake] with his shoes [on].
And here's the boy.
Here the dog goes into the sea.
Here are frogs.
Here's the dog and frogs.

70% of the 20 clauses in this child's narrative start with *and*, the same proportion as out of the 19 clauses in 3-year-old Pe'er's "fight" story in (8b): The difference is that most of the remaining clauses in the "frog story" text in (9) start with the spatial deictic *hine* 'here('s)', which has a sense close to French *voici*, indicative of the picture-pointing nature of these narrations. The next section examines whether the same high proportion of *and*-introduced clauses applies equally across children, across age-groups, and across the two narrative elicitations.

4.2   Quantitative Distribution of *ve* in Narrative Texts

The following analysis of the proportion of *ve*-introduced clauses was undertaken in the conviction that the quantitative distribution of forms must be supplemented by an analysis of their function, both alone and in relation to other forms with which they compete. Nonetheless, it is worth noting that overall amount of clause-initial *ve* reveals clear age-related differences across both types of narratives investigated, as shown in Table 21.1.

TABLE 21.1.   Percentage of Clauses Introduced by *ve* Out of Total Number of Clauses in Two Types of Narrative Texts, by Age

Age-Group	3 yrs	5 yrs	7 yrs	9 yrs	Adults
"Frog" [N=12]					
#Clauses	356	634	---	740	725
+ *ve*	60.2%	59.4%	---	47.0%	30.0%
"Fight" [N = 10]					
#Clauses	148	99	88	84	288
+ *ve*	35.8%	62.6%	48.9%	51.2%	18.4%

Sixty percent of the total narrative clauses produced by the 3-year-olds in the picture-book-based "frog story" sample were initiated by *ve*. And all 12 children in this group use *ve* at the beginning of at least one-quarter of their clauses. That is, mechanical, semantically and syntactically unmotivated, repetition of *ve* to mark a new predication, as in (9), is common in the 3-year-old texts. In this setting, *ve* is one of several different indicators of the younger child's immature mode of relating to each picture in isolation, rather than embedding it in a global thematic organization of the narrative as a whole (Berman, 1988).   In contrast, only around one-third of all clauses produced by the 3-year-olds in the "fight" story setting start with *ve*. The main reason for this discrepancy is that a number of these children, unlike any of the older age-groups, required heavy input prompting from the investigators to sustain the narrative flow (e.g., "why?"; "and what did you do then?"; "did you hit him back?"; "was she mad at you?"), creating a context where *ve* could not be used felicitously to introduce a response, so lowering the overall proportion of *ve* introduced clauses in this group.

As against this discrepancy in amount of *ve*-initial clauses in the two narrative settings among 3-year-old children, in both settings the older children use *ve* to introduce a very large proportion of their clauses: nearly two-thirds among 5-year-olds, going down to around one-half among school-age children. Even in the relatively very short "fight-story" texts (averaging between 9.9 clauses per 5-year-old texts to 8.4 for 9-year-olds, compared with "frog-story" averages of 53.3 and 61.7 clauses respectively), all the children from age 5 years up use *ve* at least once, in contrast to several 3-year-olds. Moreover, use of *ve* drops dramatically among the adults, down to less than one-third of their "frog-story" clauses, and under one-fifth in the "fight-stories." To support the assumptions underlying this study, the following section examines what, if any, developmental changes in the function of *ve* can explain these findings for its quantitative distribution.

4.3 *And* as a Narrative Connectivity Marker

The following analysis attempts to resolve the contradictions which Peterson and McCabe (1991, p. 36) note in the literature "about whether or not *and* becomes replaced by more semantically specific connectives as children get older." They cite investigators such as Jisa (1987), Laubitz (1987), Martin (1983), and Scott (1984) as having suggested that "with age, connective variety in any discourse increases while dependence on *and* decreases", and compare them with research like that of Kernan (1977) or McCutchen and Perfetti (1982) who have suggested that the change in children's narratives "from an early dependence on temporal relationships between events to more causally linked chains of events . . . is reflected in a relative decrease of the connectives *and, then*, and *and then*, while there is a simultaneous increase in *so, and so, and so then* and other causal connectors" (pp. 36-37). The present study aims to reexamine these claims by comparing (1) two types of narrative discourse and (2) adult versus children's use of *ve* in the same settings.

First, the present study confirms findings from other languages for an age-related increase in variety of connectivity markers. Table 21.2 presents the breakdown of markers of sequentiality such as *az* 'then', *axarkax* 'afterwards', *axarey ze* 'after that' and of other temporal and logical relations, e.g., *ad she* 'until', *kdey she* 'so that', *aval* 'but', *ki* 'because' in the two types of narratives.

TABLE 21.2.   Percentage of clauses introduced by sequential and other markers of connectivity out of total clauses in two narrative samples by age

Age-Group	3 yrs	5 yrs	9 yrs	Adults
"Frog" [N = 12]				
#Clauses	356	634	740	725
SEQ %	13	22	14	2.5
CON %	5	12	18	23
TOTAL %	18	34	32	25
"Fight" [N = 10]				
#Clauses	148	99	84	288
SEQ %	11	29	38	3.8
CON %	6	2	3	10
TOTAL %	17	31	41	13.8

SEQ = sequential;   CON = connectivity

Table 21.2 shows that in both narrative samples, older children use relatively more lexical markers of sequentiality (i.e., sentence-modifiers meaning 'then', 'after that', or 'afterwards') than the 3-year-olds, so confirming that, with age, these forms are used as well as 'and' for the purpose of clause chaining. This trend is particularly marked in the shorter, less complex "fight-stories," but even in the elaborate "frog-story" sample, such expressions, alone or preceded by the conjunction *ve*, account for fully **one-quarter** of the "free" or independent clauses — i.e., single-clause sentences or the main clause syntactically in multiclause constructions — in the 5- and 9-year-old texts (25% and 26% respectively, compared with only 13% in the 3-year-old texts). This increased reliance on overt markers of temporally sequenced chaining is reflected in the examples of 5- and 9-year-old texts in (10) and (11) respectively.

(10a) Part of Hebrew 5-year-old "frog" story translated into English
    [Ben, age 5;3]:
There was a boy that er ... that he caught a frog!!
And afterwards he slept,
And suddenly did not see it
And then he said to the dog ...
And - and - he also went outside with his dog to search.
And afterwards he took it
And - he said (something) like this
And they called for it, for the frog!
And afterwards he went down, told him [=the dog] to go down,
Then he caught him [=the dog]
And he [=the boy] thought he [=the dog] (had) chased it away.

He told him [=the dog] to go outside.

And afterwards they walked and walked until they came to a place
where they wanted to see if it [= the frog] was there.

(10b) Hebrew 5-year old "fight" story translated into English
[Meital, age 5;3]:

Yesterday at nursery-school I quarreled with my friend Roni,

My friend took the doll (away) from me by force

And afterwards (she) threw it (away).

And then (she) laughed and said that I had it coming to me.

Afterwards I got upset, and cried.

And afterwards I told (about) her to the teacher.

The texts in (10) are typical of the 5-year-old stories: Nearly every clause has a sequential introducer, with or without the conjunction *and*. These mark event-chaining, the fact that the next step in the story is about to be described. This contrasts with the "announcing" mode of the 3- year-olds, as in example (8). They use few terms marking sequentiality, and for them *ve* signifies that another picture is about to be described (in the "frog" story), or that another utterance is to follow (in the "fight" sample). The 9-year old narratives are illustrated in (11). These also rely heavily on sequentials, but they use *ve* somewhat less than the 5-year-olds and, as shown in Table 21.2, they make more use of other connective devices such as those meaning 'because', 'but', 'in order to', or 'until' and 'meanwhile' to mark not only sequential, but also logical and other temporal relations between events in the unfolding narrative.

(11a) Part of Hebrew 9-year old "frog" story translated into English
[Dan, age 9;5]:

Once there was a boy, and he had a dog.

The boy looked inside the jar

And inside the jar was a frog.

Afterwards the dog ... er afterwards the boy went to sleep
and the dog climbed on top of him to sleep together,

And meanwhile the frog went out of the jar.

Next morning the boy got up, and the dog ... as well.

When they looked at the jar, they didn't see the frog.

And then they started looking for it all over the place,
and inside the jar that was there.

Afterwards the boy went outside, and the dog as well.

When they looked at the jar, they didn't see the frog.

And so they started looking for it all over the place, inside
shoes and inside the jar where it was [= had been].

Afterwards the boy went outside, and the dog as well.

(11b) Hebrew 9-year old "fight" story translated into English [Tsvi, age 9;2]:

Every night I fight with my brother

Because he says that only he should take the dog downstairs.

One night he pushed me

And afterwards ran away quickly to his room,

And after that I went downstairs with the dog.
[The family lives in an apartment building of several floors]

The Hebrew narratives demonstrate that as use of utterance-initial *ve* decreases with age, its function is taken over by lexically specific markers of sequentiality, and these are supplemented increasingly from age 5 to age 9 by use of nonsequential connectives. The excerpts in (8) and (9) from 3-year-olds compared with the 5- and 9-year-olds illustrated in (10) and (11) reveal two complementary age-related trends. The coordinator *ve* starts out as a preferred means for announcing that more is to come, another picture is about to be described or another utterance articulated, and the speaker is still in the "telling" mode. Subsequently, it is used to produce syntactic coordination at the level of adjacent clauses, or to indicate that another event follows in a narrative sequence which may extend for several clauses at a time.

The quantitative findings presented in Tables 1 and 2 for distribution of forms thus need to be interpreted in light of the function which these forms serve in different narrative settings, and at different phases of development. For instance, in the "frog story" sample, children from age 5 use initial *ve* about the same **amount** as do the 3-year-olds: around 60% to 50% respectively. But the same form serves a different function in the narrations of older children; they use it for syntactic coordination and for narrative "event-chaining," as follows. In syntactic terms, older children tend to delete the repeated subject noun phrase (e.g., "My friend took the doll away from me by force and afterwards threw it away"; "One night he [my brother] pushed me and afterwards ran quickly to his room") rather than merely repeating it as do 3-year-olds ("Here the dog fell. And the dog ran") or using a pronoun the second time ("There was a boy that he caught a frog and afterwards he slept"). That is, increased command of syntactic coordination with *ve* accompanied by same-subject ellipsis serves the discourse function of increased connectivity and text cohesiveness. In terms of narrative "event-chaining," older children often go beyond "chaining" of single events in two or at most three adjacent clauses to some "chunking" of several events within a single syntactic package. That is, they begin to move from a strictly linear chaining of single clauses in succession to a more tightly packaged, interwoven discourse texture, in which coordination is only one means of relating between events in narrative. This is reflected in the fact that with age, *ve* in its clause-chaining function is increasingly accompanied or replaced by other markers of sequentiality, such as those meaning *then, afterwards, suddenly* or *next morning, later on,* as well as clause-internal markers of temporality such as *meanwhile* (typically nonclause-initial in Hebrew) and other markers of textual cohesiveness, including logical connectors and subordinating conjunctions.

These developments taken together mark a progression in narrative competence from **pointing** to single pictures (in the "frog story" task) or isolated responses to input utterances (in the "fight" story task) to **chaining** of linearly ordered adjacent clauses to **chunking** of discourse segments. That is, in place of the seemingly contradictory findings perceptively noted in the literature by Peterson and McCabe (1991), changes in the function of *ve* across time can be related to broader developmental advances in text-construction in general (i.e., in the domains of discourse coherence and cohesivity) and in narrative competence in particular. Analyses of narrative structure reveal a continuum of organizational principles, each of which is subsumed by the next, proceeding from (1) the local level of individual events to (2) temporal and (3) subsequently causal relations between contiguous events — typically in adjacent pairs or strings of clauses — to (4) more global command of causal networks (Trabasso & van den Broek, 1985) and of hierarchical "action structure" (Shen, 1988). An analogous progression can be traced in the development of children's storytelling abilities (Berman & Slobin, 1994; McCabe & Peterson, 1991). It is this progression from local to global connectivity, from coherence at the level of single scenes or episodes to embedding these within overall plot construction, which is expressed in the use of *ve*, first for joining utterances, then for chaining clauses, then for chunking segments of an integrated discourse.

The quantitative findings for distribution of *ve* and other connective forms are thus indicative of children's relative command of a "narrative flow." Even the youngest children in these samples, aged 3 to 4, attend in some degree to the principle of linear ordering of events in time, with *ve* indicating that something is to follow. A higher level chaining of events in narrative is manifested by most 5-year-olds and all 9-year-olds in our sample, reflected in their use of *ve* along with more explicit markers of connectivity. Moreover, children's use of *ve* is more selective, and less mechanical, in the shorter, more compact "fight" story texts than in the longer, more elaborate picture book stories. In the former, the 5-year-olds almost all manifest a well-motivated action-structure in describing one single episode. The same level of organization, and less automatic reliance on clause-initial *ve* is revealed by only a few of the preschoolers in relating the different episodes which make up their frog story texts.

4.4   Evidence from Adults of Endstate Narrative Abilities

The patterns of usage observed among preschool and school-age children contrast with the **adult** narratives in several ways, as revealed by the figures in Tables 1 and 2. First, in the "frog-story" sample, only one-third of the adult clauses are introduced by *ve*, a figure which drops to under 20% in the "fight-stories," compared with around **half** the clauses of the school-age children in both samples. Second, adults use very few sequential conjunctions like those meaning 'then', or 'afterwards' compared with the older children. Third, adults relied on **other** connectives, marking nonsequential temporal or logical relations between events far more than did the children. Fourth, adults often do without explicit means for marking temporal and other relations between successive clauses; only 55% of the adult "frog" clauses and 30% of their "fight-story" clauses are introduced by some such device. In contrast, the older children (5- and 9-year-olds) mark their move to the next picture or to the next event overtly most of the time; around three-quarters of all their clauses in both samples are initiated by means of *ve* or a semantically more specific connective form.

The adult frog-story texts excerpted in (12), in English translation, reflect three different ways of expressing narrative connectivity. The first relies on syntactic coordination with *ve* for packaging together related events, without any lexical marking of new events in the sequence; the second favors subordination with long chunks of embedded clauses and elision of the subject pronoun functioning as topic;[10] the third relies largely on subject-elision with occasional coordination.

(12) a. **Adult 20G — Syntactic Coordination with *ve*:**
   Okay. Danny was a boy.
   Danny found a frog **and** put it in ... er ... a glass jar.
   Danny had a dog called Yoye.
   At night Danny slept **and** the frog got out of the jar **and** ran away.
   In the morning Danny got up **and** did not find the frog.
   Danny and Yoye started looking for ... the frog.
   Danny looked in his boot,
   Yoye looked inside the glass pail, **and** his head got stuck there.

 b. **Adult 20H — Syntactic Embedding and Subject Elision [= 0]:**
   Once there's a boy, a boy **that** has a dog has a frog in his room.
   He keeps the frog in a jar.
   He and the dog enjoy watching the frog **which** is inside a closed jar
   While they are asleep, the dog and the boy together in bed,
   The frog runs away, 0 climbs out of the jar and runs away.
   After the boy and the dog find **that** the frog is gone, 0 has disappeared,
   0 go-out [+Plural] to look for it.

 c. **Adult 20F — Syntactic Coordination and Subject Elision:**
   The boy Yoram had a cute little room, he and a dog and a frog in a jar,
   and he liked playing with them a lot.
   At night, **when** 0 went to sleep, the frog jumped out **and** ran away.
   Next morning Yoram awoke, **and** behold the jar was empty.
   0 searched [+Singular] in the room,
   0 searched [+Singular] inside his boots,
   And his dog helped him to search inside the jar, under the bed,
   and 0 did not find [+Plural].
   0 went-outside [+Plural] to seek.
   0 searched [+Plural], 0 searched [+Plural], **and** did not find [+Plural].

An effect of tight packaging of entire segments of a narrative is achieved by similar means in the adult fight-story texts, with 1st-person reference inflectionally suffixed to the verb in past tense (see fn. 9), as in (13).

(13) a. **Yair, man aged 28** — entire text:
   At grade school there once was a boy **who** hassled me. His name was Zohar S. He used to run after me and harrass me. **One day, when** he kept hassling me, 0 got-mad-1sg [=*hit'acbanti*] at him, 0 pushed-1sg [=*hipalti*] him down to the ground, 0 grabbed [=*tafasti*] him, and 0 told-1sg [=*amarti*] him that if he ever bothered me again, **I** [= *ani*] would-break his face. More he never bothered me.

---

[10] This violates Hebrew sentence-level grammatical constraints, since 3rd person verbs like those in (12) are not inflected for person agreement (Berman, 1990).

b. **Hanan, man aged 24** — first part of text:
Yesterday 0 went-1sg [=*halaxti*] to fill [= put] gas into the yellow car, and 0 got-1sg [=*higati*] there. Usually I fill, **because** the guys that work at the gas station can't be bothered to do their job. So 0 got-out-1sg [=*yacati*] of the car **and** 0 took-1sg [=*lakaxti*] the hose and 0 put-1sg [=*samti*] it inside the car. 0 began-1sg [=*hitxalti*] to fill up with gas **and** he looks at me like this. 0 told+1sg [=*amarti*] him also that I wanted to put in oil. 0 helped me to put in gas. 0 asked-1sg [=*bikashti*] him for two cans of oil, 0 gave me. **After that** I go to pay with my credit card, **like** I usually do ...

The cohesiveness achieved by adults through these various devices for chunking whole sections of the narrative was not revealed by even the oldest children in our sample (9-year-old second graders and even some 11-year-old sixth graders). This leads to a conclusion which is strongly borne out by other analyses of narrative development. The older children in our sample know about the "grammar" or structure of storytelling. They can construct narratives sequentially in relation to an overall plot; but they are not yet capable of making fully flexible use of the various rhetorical options available in their language for packaging together parts of the unfolding narrative sequence by selective deployment of such means as: coordination, subordination, elision, or a combination of all three .[11]

With respect to *ve*, the older children in our sample have mastered the grammar of coordination, both its syntax and semantics, **and** they also know that in stories, events follow one another in narrative sequence. Consequently, they use the coordinator *ve* along with other devices for marking the unfolding chain of events. Mature narrators know this is unnecessary, since one event after another constitutes the **default** case in narrative. They use *and* primarily as a syntactic coordinator; they rarely use either *ve* or other means for explicit marking of chronological sequence; and they have recourse to other devices for embedding related events within thematically related discourse frames.

Another development evidenced by mature language users relates to progression in form-function correspondences. The Hebrew connective *az* is ambiguous between sequential 'then' and consequential 'so'; that is, like French *puis*, it can mark either temporal or logical relations between clauses. In the 3-year-old narratives in (9), it is not clear what function this form fulfills, whether it marks sequentiality or merely indicates utterance-chaining as does *ve*. Among the 5-year-olds, in the examples in (10), this form clearly serves as a temporal marker of the next event in sequence; in the 9-year-old texts in (11), it sometimes appears to express the logical relation of *so* = 'therefore'. Adults, in contrast, use this form predominantly for this purpose, reserving some more explicitly temporal term for sequentiality, e.g., *axarkax* 'afterwards', *axarey ze* 'after that' (for instance, Yuval, aged 22, says "Well, I never actually fought physically, **if** I got around to quarreling with someone, **then** [= *az*] I would just give him a shove ..."). Moreover,

---

[11] These options will differ from one language to another. For instance, mature English narrators rely widely on participial and gerundive -*ing* forms for this type of packaging, Hebrew narrators may use nominalizations (e.g., *xipus* 'search, seeking', *vikuax* 'argument, arguing'), while Turkish relies on nonfinite embeddings for subordination (Berman & Slobin, 1994).

adults, and they alone, use this connective as a means for segmenting off their narration into its component parts, e.g., Hanan, in the continuation of the 80-clause-long hassle story excerpted in (13b), uses the form no less than six times when saying the equivalent of "so I told him ...," "so he said to me ...," ending his account as follows:

(13) c. **End of narrative excerpted in (13b):**

So [=*az*] he said to me that he could talk to the boss and all that, but the owner (of the gas-station) wasn't there and all kind of stuff like that. **That's it**, the argument went on like **until** I saw there was no point arguing any more, **so** [=*az*] I signed the bill, and got back my change.Packaging of this type indicates that the text is organized within a global thematic structure, in which one episode follows from and is embedded with the next. Such a use of connectives like *ve* and *az* requires mature command of their full range of rhetorical functions, integrated within the process of online production of a hierarchically organized narrative.

5. CONCLUSION

This study has aimed to show that in early conversational interchanges as well as subsequently, in more extended narratives, 'and' first serves as an empty discourse filler, indicating merely that more is to come; subsequently it is used for linear chaining of events along the time line, together with, and increasingly replaced by, explicit markers of sequentiality such as 'after that'; only adults dispense with any overt marking, as the default option for connecting temporally sequential clauses in narrative. This progression is highly consistent with a more general view of the development of both grammar and discourse which I have argued for elsewhere (Berman, 1986, 1990): Children's knowledge of language structure and language use proceeds from an initial, "pre-grammatical" phase, of the kind characterized in much of Ervin-Tripp's work on early conversational interaction (in the present context, *ve* is utterance-initial, communicatively motivated) to structure-bound knowledge (*ve* serves for syntactic coordination, and for chaining clauses in temporal sequence), and on to flexible integration of *ve* as one of a range of formal means meeting the rhetorical purpose of discourse connectivity, initially at a local, and subsequently at a more global, level of text structure.

Within this model, acquisition of *ve* as a marker of clause coordination can be reinterpreted as marking a specific phase in the development of sentence-level grammar. It constitutes a syntactic link between simple-clause structure and the more complex grammar of complementation and embedding by subordination, just as it forms a semantic link between isolated and interdependent propositions, first as temporal sequentially and then for logical relations (Berman, 1993a).

Finally, this study reflects a more general, cognitively driven reorganization of discourse abilities. Its findings are consistent with Ervin-Tripp's analysis of local-to-global development in the sphere of language acquisition, and they support Karmiloff-Smith's (1979, 1986) three-phased analysis of development from initial data-driven or item-based performances, which evolve into top-down metaprocedural operations, and eventually into fully integrated conceptually-driven representations.   In the case in point, use of the morpheme *ve* at each phase of development is based on a given level of knowledge, which will subsequently be extended and reorganized, at different periods in children's development: at first, in question-and-answer interchanges, where each child-turn provides only a single comment on the same topic; then in short two to three-clause narratives that are embedded in heavily scaffolded ongoing conversational interaction; only later in the more complex cognitive task of producing lengthier and textually elaborate narratives in noninteractive discourse setting.   These findings also accord with Slobin's (1994) analysis of the development of perfect aspect in different languages, as proceeding from a directly referential function to inferences from nonvisible situations, and from there to "textual" meanings.   Language development is thus seen to evolve from an immature pragmatic basis, which is communicatively and interaction-driven — telling the hearer more is to come; it proceeds to a semantically appropriate, propositionally-based use of syntactic constructions — conjoining sequentially related events; and it culminates in a discourse-motivated, global organization of speech output — selective use of elision, conjoining, and embedding in constructing a thematically integrated extended text.

REFERENCES

Aksu-Koç, A., & von Stutterheim, C. (1994). Temporal relations in narrative: Simultaneity.   In R. A. Berman & D. I. Slobin.   *Different ways of relating events in narrative: A crosslinguistic developmental study* (pp. 393-455). Hillsdale, NJ: Lawrence Erlbaum Associates.

Ardery, G. (1979). The development of coordination in child language.   *Journal of Verbal Learning and Verbal Behavior, 18,* 745-756.

Bamberg, M. (1994).   Development of linguistic forms: German.   In R. A. Berman & D. I. Slobin (1994).   *Different ways of relating events in narrative: A crosslinguistic developmental study.* Hillsdale, NJ: Lawrence Erlbaum Associates.

Bates, E., & MacWhinney, B.   (1982).   Functionalist approaches to grammar.   In E. Wanner & L. Gleitman (Eds.), *Language acquisition: The state of the art* (pp. 173-218). New York: Cambridge University Press.

Berman, R. A. (1979).   Form and function: Passives, middles, and impersonal in modern Hebrew.   *Berkeley Linguistic Society, 5,* 1-27.

Berman, R. A. (1986).   A step-by-step model of language development. In I. Levin (Ed.), *Stage and structure: Reopening the debate* (pp. 191-219). Norwood, NJ: Ablex.

Berman, R. A. (1988).   On the ability to relate events in narrative.   *Discourse Processes, 11,* 469-497.

Berman, R. A. (1990).   Acquiring an (S)VO language: Subjectless sentences in children's Hebrew.   *Linguistics, 28,* 1135-1166.

Berman, R. A. (1993a).   Crosslinguistic perspectives on native language acquisition.   In K. Hyltenstam & A. Viberg (Eds.), *Progression and Regression in Language* (pp. 245-266). Cambridge, England: Cambridge University Press.

Berman, R. A. (1993b). Developmental perspectives on transitivity: A confluence of cues. In Y. Levy (Ed.), *Other children, other languages: Issues in the theory of language acquisition* (pp. 189-241). Hillsdale, NJ: Lawrence Erlbaum Associates.

Berman, R. A. (1993c). The development of language use: Expressing perspectives on a scene. In E. Dromi (Ed.), *Language and cognition: A developmental perspective* (pp. 172-201). Norwood, NJ: Ablex.

Berman, R. A., & Neeman, Y. (1994). Development of linguistic forms: Hebrew. In R. A. Berman & D. I. Slobin. *Different ways of relating events in narrative: A crosslinguistic developmental study* (pp. 285-328). Hillsdale, NJ: Lawrence Erlbaum Associates.

Berman, R. A., & Slobin, D. I. (1994). Development of linguistic forms: English. In R. A. Berman & D. I. Slobin. *Different ways of relating events in narrative: A crosslinguistic developmental study* (pp. 127-188). Hillsdale, NJ: Lawrence Erlbaum Associates.

Berman, R. A., & Slobin, D. I. (1994). *Different ways of relating events in narrative: A crosslinguistic developmental study.* Hillsdale, NJ: Lawrence Erlbaum Associates.

Bloom, L., Lahey, M., Hood, L., Lifter, K., & Fiess, K. J. (1980). Complex sentences: Acquisition of syntactic connectives and the semantic relations they encode. *Journal of Child Language, 7,* 235-361.

Budwig, N. (1989). The linguistic marking of agentivity and control in child language. *Journal of Child Language, 16,* 263-284.

Budwig, N. (1991). Editorial introduction to "Functional Approaches to Child Language." *First Language, 11,* 1-5.

Crain, S., & Nakayama, M. (1987). Structure-dependence in grammar formation. *Language, 63,* 522-543.

Dasinger, L., & Toupin, C. (1994). The development of relative clause functions in narrative. In R. A. Berman & D. I. Slobin. *Different ways of relating events in narrative: A crosslinguistic developmental study* (pp. 457-514). Hillsdale, NJ: Lawrence Erlbaum Associates.

Demuth, K. (1992). Acquisition of Sesotho. In D. I. Slobin (Ed.), *The crosslinguistic study of language acquisition, Vol. 3* (pp. 557-638). Hillsdale, NJ: Lawrence Erlbaum Associates.

Ervin-Tripp, S. (1989). *Speech acts and syntactic development: Linked or independent?* (Berkeley Cognitive Science Report, No. 61.) University of California, Berkeley, Institute of Cognitive Studies.

Gee, J. G., & Savasir, I. (1985). On the use of *will* and *gonna*: Toward a description of activity-types for child language. *Discourse Processes, 8,* 143-175.

Giora, R. (1983). Segmentation and segment cohesion: On the thematic organization of the text. *Text, 3,* 155-182.

Giora, R. (1985). What's a coherent text? In E. Sozer (Ed.), *Text connexity, text coherence: aspects, methods, results* (pp. 16-35). Hamburg: Buske.

Halkiadakis-Delidakis, S. & Tager-Flusberg, H. (1985, October). A crosslinguistic study of the acquisition of syntactic coordination in Greek, English, and Japanese. Paper given at Boston University Conference on Language Development, Boston, MA.

Jisa, H. (1987). Sentence connectors in French children's monologue performance. *Journal of Pragmatics, 11,* 607-621.

Karmiloff-Smith, A. (1979). Micro- and macrodevelopmental changes in language acquisition and other representational systems. *Cognitive Science, 3,* 91-118.

Karmiloff-Smith, A. (1981). The grammatical marking of thematic structure in the development of language production. In W. Deutsch (Ed.), *The child's construction of language* (pp. 121-147). London: Academic.

Karmiloff-Smith, A. (1986). Stage/structure versus phase/process in modelling linguistic and cognitive structure. In I. Levin (Ed.), *Stage and structure: Reopening the debate* (pp. 164-190). Norwood, NJ: Ablex.

Kernan, K.T. (1977) Semantic and expressive elaboration in children's narratives. In S. Ervin-Tripp & C. Mitchell-Kernan (Eds.), *Child discourse* (pp. 91-102). New York: Academic Press.

Laubitz, Z. (1987). Conjunction in children's discourse. *Papers and Reports on Child Language Development, 26,* 64-71.

Labov, W. (1972). The transformation of experience in narrative syntax. In W. Labov, *Language in the inner city* (pp. 354-396). Philadelphia: University of Pennsylvania Press.

Lust, B. (1977). Conjunction reduction in child language. *Journal of Child Language, 4*, 257-287.

Lust, B. (1980). Development of coordination in the natural speech of two and three year olds. *Journal of Child Language, 7*, 1-26.

Lust, B., & Chien, Y.-C. (1984). The structure of coordination in first language acquisition of Mandarin Chinese: Evidence for a universal. *Cognition, 17*, 49-83.

MacWhinney, B., & Snow, C. (1990). The Child Language Data Exchange System: An update. *Journal of Child Language, 17*, 457-472.

Martin, J. R. (1983). The development of register. In J. Fine & R. Freedle (Eds.), *Developmental Issues in Discourse* (pp. 1-39). Norwood, NJ: Ablex.

Mayer, M. (1969). *Frog, where are you?* New York: Dial Books for Young Readers.

McCawley, J. (1988). *The syntactic phenomena of English.* Chicago University Press

McCutchen, D., & Perfetti, C. (1982). Coherence and connectedness in the development of discourse production. *Text, 2*, 113-139.

Miller, P., & Sperry, L. (1988). Early talk about the past: The origins of conversational stories of personal experience. *Journal of Child Language, 15*, 293-315.

Muma, J. R. (1986). *Language acquisition: A functionalist perspective.* Austin, Texas: Pro-ed, Inc.

Nichols, J. (1984). Functional theories of grammar. *Annual Review of Anthropology, 13*, 97-117.

Ninio, A. (1988). The roots of narrative: Discussing recent events with very young children. *Language Sciences, 10*(1), 35-52.

Peterson, C., & McCabe, A. (1987). The connective "and": Do older children use it less as they learn other connectives? *Journal of Child Language, 14*, 375-381.

Peterson, C., & McCabe, A. (1988). The connective *and* as discourse glue. *First Language, 8*, 19-28.

Peterson, C., & McCabe, A. (1991). Linking children's connective use and narrative macrostructure. In A. McCabe & C. Peterson (Eds.), *Developing narrative structure* (pp. 29-54). Hillsdale, NJ: Lawrence Erlbaum.

Scott, C. (1984). Adverbial connectivity in conversations of children 6-12. *Journal of Child Language, 11*, 423-452.

Shen, Y. (1988). The X-bar grammar for stories: Story grammar revisited. *Text, 9*, 415-467.

Silverstein, M. (1991). A funny thing happened on the way to the form: A functionalist critique of functionalist developmentalism. *First Language, 11*, 143-180.

Slobin, D. I. (1973). Cognitive prerequisites for the development of grammar. In C. A. Ferguson & D. I. Slobin (Eds.), *Studies of child language development* (pp. 175-208). New York: Holt, Rinehart, & Winston.

Slobin, D. I. (1987, January). Frequency reflects function. Paper presented at Conference on Interaction of Form and Function in Language, University of California at Davis.

Slobin, D. I. (1989, July). Factors of language typology in the crosslinguistic study of acquisition. Paper presented at Biennial Meeting of the International Society for the Study of Behavioral Development. Jyvaskyla, Finland.

Slobin, D. I. (1990). The development from child speaker to native speaker. In J. W. Stigler, R. A. Shweder & G. Herdt (Eds.), *Cultural psychology: Essays on comparative human development* (pp. 233-256). Cambridge, England: Cambridge University Press.

Slobin, D. I. (1991). Learning to think for speaking: Native language, cognition, and rhetorical style. *Pragmatics, 1*, 7-26.

Slobin, D. I. (1993). Converbs in Turkish child language: The grammaticalization of event coherence. In M. Haspelmath & E. Konig (Eds.), *Converbs (adverbial participles, gerunds) in crosslinguistic perspective* (pp. 349-371). Berlin: Mouton de Gruyter.

Slobin, D. I. (1994). Talking perfectly: Discourse origins of the present perfect. In W. Pagliuca & G. Davis (Eds.), *Perspectives on grammaticalization* (pp. 119-133). Amsterdam: John Benjamins.

Tager-Flusberg, H., de Villiers, J., & Hakuta, K. (1982). The development of sentence coordination. In S. Kuczaj (Ed.), *Language development. Vol 1: Syntax and semantics* (pp. 201-244). Hillsdale, NJ: Lawrence Erlbaum Associates.

Trabasso, T., & van den Broek, P. (1985). Causal thinking and the representation of narrative events. *Journal of Memory and Language,* **24**, 612-630.

Van Valin, R. D., Jr. (1991). Functionalist theory. *First Language*, **11**, 7-40.

Van Valin, R. D., Jr. (1993). A synopsis of Role and Reference Grammar. In R. Van Valin, Jr. (Ed.), *Advances in Role and Reference Grammar.* Amsterdam: John Benjamins.

Wigglesworth, G. (1990). Children's narrative acquisition: A study of some aspects of reference and anaphora. *First Language,* **10**, 105-126.

22 NARRATIVE DEVELOPMENT IN SOCIAL CONTEXT[1]

Ageliki Nicolopoulou
Smith College

An important teacher often plants seeds that take years to come to fruition. I am increasingly struck, in retrospect, by how much this pattern applies to my long-term association with Sue Ervin-Tripp. As a graduate student at Berkeley in the late 70s and early 80s, I found it hard to make up my mind whether to focus my dissertation research on cognitive or language development (or to combine them, in the Berkeley style, in some sort of grand synthesis). I eventually opted for cognitive development, but in the meantime this indecision led me — along with much of the rest of my cohort — to attend every seminar offered by the department in both areas. These included several seminars with Sue Ervin-Tripp, which stood out because of her emphasis on the need to situate the acquisition and uses of language in sociocultural context. I was also struck by her occasional favorable references to Freud (who was otherwise pretty much a Great Unmentionable in our department), and, more generally, her suggestions that developmental research should take account of the role of children's emotional life. These were messages I duly noted at the time but (I now see) appreciated only imperfectly. For the last several years, however, as much of my work has involved the effort to integrate the study of children's cognitive development with the analysis of their narrative activity, the significance and value of these themes have now fully come home to me.

In a somewhat complex and indirect way, Sue also influenced this more recent turn toward narrative in my work. A few years after I finished graduate school, I had the good fortune to be involved in a project along with Sue   and Barbara Scales and Millie Almy — that focused on the role of play in children's development. (One result was the publication of Scales, Almy, Nicolopoulou, & Ervin-Tripp, 1991.) In the process, I became increasingly dissatisfied with what seemed to me both the conceptual limitations and the mutual isolation of the dominant approaches to play in developmental research;

[1] The research presented here was supported in part by a Picker Fellowship Award to the author from Smith College. I would like to thank Yoon-Joo Lee, Maureen Carney, and Paula Desjarlais for their careful and diligent work in helping me analyze the data. I am also indebted to Jeff Weintraub for extensive advice, constructive criticism, and theoretical inspiration. An earlier version of the argument in this chapter was advanced in "The active interplay of social-relational and cognitive/symbolic factors in the development of children's narrative activity," a paper presented as part of an invited symposium at the 1994 annual meeting of the Jean Piaget Society (Chicago, IL: June 2-4).

and I began to see how we might build on unexplored possibilities offered by both Piaget and Vygotsky, as well as insights derived from the broad "interpretive turn" in the human sciences, to move toward an approach that could more powerfully illuminate the cognitive significance of play by grasping it as a fundamentally sociocultural and imaginative activity. (For an orienting statement, see Nicolopoulou, 1993.) Sue encouraged me to pursue this line of inquiry further, and her encouragement very much influenced my decision to do so, so I hope she is not too taken aback by the long-term results. At the same time, a side-effect of the play project was to start me on the analysis of preschool children's spontaneous stories, composed and acted out in a practice that straddled the line between play and narrative activity. I thus became aware of the close affinity and interdependence between the discursive exposition of narratives in children's storytelling and their enactment in fantasy play; of the relevance of my emerging theoretical concerns to narrative as well as play research; and of the need to integrate the study of young children's play and narrative activities much more fully and systematically than is usually the case. I arrived, in short, at the conclusion that developmental research should treat play and narrative as parallel, and often interwoven, forms of socioculturally situated symbolic action. (For some of the arguments behind these remarks, see Nicolopoulou, in press.)

Since the research that I am about to discuss brings together all these different strands that lead back, one way or another, to Sue Ervin-Tripp, I am especially pleased to have the opportunity to present it in this volume.

INTRODUCTION

Based on my ongoing study of preschool children's spontaneous storytelling, this chapter advances two interconnected arguments that, taken together, have some broad programmatic implications for the conduct of developmental research on narrative: (1) First, I present evidence suggesting that participation in certain forms of socially-structured peer-group activity can contribute dramatically to advancing the complexity and sophistication of young children's narrative activity. These results strongly suggest, in turn, that the main body of current research in narrative development has tended to underestimate significantly both (a) the potential narrative capabilities of preschool children and (b) the role of social context in the development of these capabilities. (2) At the same time, we need to reconsider and refine the conceptions of "social context" and its effects that predominate in much socially-situated research, to avoid (a) reducing "social context" to dyadic interaction, and/or (b) constructing one-sided models that neglect the child's own agency and motivations. In particular, I argue that one of the key ways that socially structured practices influence and activate individual development is by simultaneously drawing on and shaping the inner motivations that drive and direct this development; and I offer an exploratory analysis of some of the socially-situated motivations which appear to be most crucial in this respect. Specifically, I suggest that the patterns of narrative development displayed by the children in my sample emerge, in large part, from the complex interaction of two related but analytically distinct kinds of motivating concerns that I have termed (for reasons to be explained below) "social–relational" and "aesthetic" concerns. In general, this chapter urges that development be seen as involving an active interplay between the "internal" dynamics of the individual's cognitive structures and the impact of sociocultural context.

Children and Narratives: The Research Terrain

Let me begin with some necessarily brief and schematic remarks about the main tendencies in current research that can help locate the distinctive emphases of the work discussed here. The first point to note is that, while there is an enormous volume of research on children and narratives being carried out in the overlapping disciplines of psychology and linguistics, studies of spontaneous stories composed by children themselves are decidedly in the minority, and this is especially true for preschool children. A great deal of this research focuses on children's comprehension of stories read by or told to them. And, when studies do deal with children's production of their own stories, they are most likely to be conducted in experimental or quasi-experimental settings, where the stories are generated under conditions that more or less sharply limit their spontaneous character. (For an overview of these general tendencies, as well as some important exceptions, see Nicolopoulou, in press.) For example, children may be presented with preselected topics, with story stems to complete, or with picture books on which to base their stories.

There are often well-considered methodological reasons for these choices; but, as I will try to make clear, they also entail important limitations. Children's storytelling is generally richer and more ambitious when they are following their own narrative agendas rather than those shaped by adults. (This is true even of picture-based elicitations, which allow more flexibility than some other techniques. In a systematic comparison, Wellhousen, 1993, found that the quality of kindergarten children's oral stories, as measured by a number of indices, was higher when they told a story without any props than when they told a story from a picture or were asked to draw a picture to accompany the story.) And while research in experimental settings can of course yield valuable results, an exclusive reliance on experimental techniques has the practical effect of excluding any systematic consideration of the sociocultural contexts within which actual learning and development take place (a point made especially well by Heath, 1983). As Sutton-Smith has argued (1986), the study of children's narrative activity forfeits much of its potential to deepen our understanding of their experience and development "if it is constrained by artificial situations" and by interpretive lenses that obscure those elements of narrative that make it most engaging and significant for the children themselves.

Bringing Social Context Back In: The Missing Peer Group and the Limits of Interactional Reductionism

A recognition of these limitations has helped give rise to a variety of more socially situated approaches. In the field of language acquisition and development, there is in fact a growing body of research that seeks to specify those features of adult–child interaction (in practice, usually mother–child interaction) that most effectively promote and facilitate the development of linguistic skills.   Most of this work has focused on very young children that are either preverbal or at the one- or two-word stage (for a useful review see Snow, 1989).   More recently, there have been increasing attempts to extend this type of research to language development in later years, including narrative development.   One impetus for this kind of investigation has been a series of findings suggesting that the early mastery of narrative skills is an especially good predictor of later language and school achievement (Snow, 1983, 1989; Snow, Cancini, Gonzalez, & Shriberg, 1989; Sulzby, 1985).   These studies have established the importance of social context for narrative development, and have begun to delineate the interactional styles that best facilitate this development (for a review, see McCabe & Peterson, 1991).   But so far the focus of these studies has also been limited in two key respects: (a) they have dealt fairly exclusively with children's "factual" narratives of past experiences and not fictional or fantasy narratives; (b) and the "social" context of narrative development has, with rare exceptions, been conceived only in terms of adult–child interaction, to the exclusion of such other elements as children's peer relationships and group life.

While an exclusive focus on dyadic adult–child interaction is understandable for studying very young children, it is both puzzling and unfortunate in research on narrative development in older preschool children.   From the age of 2 on, children begin to devote increasing time and attention to other children; and ethnographic research in preschool settings has underlined the significance of peer relations and peer culture among preschoolers (Corsaro, 1985; Davies, 1989).

Several factors in combination seem to have contributed to the relative neglect of peer-group activity in narrative research.   In the work that has studied preschool children's peer interaction and its role in cognitive development, the most vigorous tendencies have generally been those inspired, directly or indirectly, by Piaget's seminal insight that the developmental significance of adult–child relations — necessarily asymmetric and hierarchical — is in important ways qualitatively different from that of peer-group relations, which are potentially more egalitarian and cooperative (Piaget, 1923/1959, 1932/1965; for an exceptionally sophisticated treatment of the field from an essentially Piagetian perspective, see Musatti, 1986; for a useful critical overview of developmental peer-interaction research that compares the influence of Piagetian and Vygotskian perspectives, see Tudge & Rogoff, 1989).   For reasons of historical accident, these research tendencies have generally focused on children's play (e.g., Garvey, 1990; Stambak & Sinclair, 1993) rather than narrative activity, and these two fields of investigation are rarely integrated.

Some of the reasons why this integration would be useful are suggested by the work of Garvey, which — aside from its exemplary combination of theoretical eclecticism with analytical coherence — has examined both child–caregiver and child–child interaction, and has extended her play-research concerns to issues of language development and communication (1984).   As Garvey's synthesis of the relevant research (1986) makes clear, in interacting with peers children encounter distinctive challenges, but also special opportunities.   At the very least, children learn different things from each other — in different ways — than what they learn from adults (see also Paley, 1984).   For example, even 2-year-olds "work" harder at maintaining conversations with peers than they do in their interactions with adults, who assume greater responsibility for maintaining and regulating conversations; in the process, they often use and develop techniques they are rarely required to employ in adult–child interactions. However, even Garvey's work does not systematically address **narrative** activity and development, and her analysis tends to stay largely at the level of dyadic interaction, with only scattered attention to group life and peer culture.

On the other hand, much of the research investigating the role of social interaction in narrative development has drawn theoretically on a Vygotskian perspective. But there is a certain irony about the results of this Vygotskian influence. Vygotsky himself was excited by Piaget's insight regarding the distinctive possibilities inherent in children's autonomous peer-directed activity, and incorporated it into his developmental theory, particularly his seminal treatment of children's play (see especially Vygotsky, 1967; Nicolopoulou, 1993). Furthermore, his theory of play is actually more sociocultural in orientation than Piaget's, emphasizes the cognitive significance of children's imaginative and symbolic activity, and offers a natural bridge between the study of play and narrative (as I argue in Nicolopoulou, in press, from which I draw in the present discussion). However, these promising leads have largely not been followed up. Most Vygotskian-inspired narrative research has tended to interpret his key notion of the "zone of proximal development" rather narrowly, in terms of the direct effects of dyadic interaction between the developing child and either adults or more knowledgeable children — usually the former. And even in research on peer collaboration linked with this paradigm — primarily examining its effects on cognitive development — peer relations have, in effect, been conceptually assimilated to the model of dyadic adult–child interaction. In most of these studies, to borrow a formulation from Tudge and Rogoff (1989, p. 32), "although the interaction is between peers in the sense of age-mates, their relation might be better thought of as a relationship between an expert and a novice than between two equals." (As Tudge, cited in Tudge & Rogoff, 1989, p. 32, perceptively notes, this has also been true, in practice, of much Piagetian-inspired research.)

Reconceptualizing "Social Context": Toward a More Sociocultural Perspective

A different, and less restricted, vision is suggested by Vygotsky's assertion — often noted, but not always pondered — that, in the preschool years, "**Play** is the source of development and **creates** the zone of proximal development" (1967, p. 16; emphases added). That is, it is a form of activity that pushes the child beyond the limits of development that have already been achieved, and provides an opportunity to expand the world of mental possibility. In saying this, Vygotsky is **not** referring to assisted problem-solving in expert–novice interaction. Rather, the crucial feature of play from a developmental perspective is that, in play, children collaborate in constructing and maintaining a shared "imaginary situation" in an activity that is simultaneously voluntary, open to spontaneity, and structured by rules — but these are rules recognized and accepted as necessary by the children themselves, not handed down from above by adults. That is, in play the child confronts a situation where the rules are not so much externally imposed as inherent in the structure of the activity itself, and are necessary in order to be able to carry out a practice or form of activity that is valued by its participants; thus, Vygotsky argues (following Piaget), the child begins to separate the notion of rule-governed practice from that of adult authority. The shared symbolic space of the play-world (to use the term of Huizinga, 1955) creates a field of activity for children's symbolic imagination that generates both opportunities and motivations for development.

What Vygotsky says of children's play applies equally to their narrative activity: both represent the union of expressive imagination with rule-governed form. And in both, as Vygotsky emphasizes with regard to play, the elements of fantasy and imagination are central to the **cognitive** significance of the activity, in terms of both its motivations and its developmental value. It is through the creation and elaboration — in imagination — of a symbolic world dominated by meanings, with its own inner logic, that children are first able to emancipate their thinking from the constraints of their immediate external environment and, thus, to take the first steps toward organizing thought in a coherent and independent way. But the creation of this autonomous world of imagination also leads the child, paradoxically, back to reality. Inserting elements from the larger culture into the symbolic universe of the "make-believe" forces the child to try to make sense of them, even as they are stylized and transformed. In short, it is precisely by fostering the development of children's symbolic imagination and providing a field for its exercise that fantasy play — and, we can add, narrative activity — prepares the way for the development of abstract thinking and "higher mental processes." As children come to realize the possible purposes and satisfactions that can be pursued in narrative activity — which are symbolic, expressive, and emotional as well as instrumental — they are driven to learn and appropriate the narrative forms culturally available to them and to turn these to their own ends; and they gradually discover that, in order to do so, they must attend to and grasp the (mostly implicit) rule-governed structures inherent in these narrative forms. Children are both impelled and enabled to do this through their participation in practices of shared symbolic activity that serve as collectively constituted fields within which to use and master these narrative forms, to explore and extend their inherent possibilities through performance and experimentation, and to push on to greater narrative range and proficiency. It is in this sense, if we follow Vygotsky, that certain types of peer-group activity can serve as especially powerful contexts promoting development.

None of this is to deny the critical role that various forms of educative and socializing relations between unequals play in the process of development. But that should not be allowed to eclipse the potential complementary contributions of peer-group activity, beginning in the preschool years. An exclusive focus on one-way transmission (or facilitation) in the acquisition of skills and information overlooks the real possibilities offered by the shared construction of reality in various forms of genuine peer collaboration (noted by Tudge & Rogoff, 1989, pp. 32-33; see Damon, 1984, for a useful analysis of this complementarity; see Forman & McPhail, 1993, for a promising Vygotskian approach to egalitarian peer collaboration).

Even more important, the methodological temptation to reduce the "social" context of development to dyadic (or triadic) interaction entails the neglect (or even the conceptual invisibility) of the larger sociocultural frameworks within which these interactions are embedded, and which structure their nature, meaning, and impact. To move from the isolated individual to the interactional pair (or triad) as the unit of analysis is a useful first step in the direction of a more socially situated perspective, but taken by itself it is incomplete and misleading. Such sociocultural frameworks as institutions, communities, classroom mini-cultures, socially structured practices and activity systems — or, for that matter, the shared symbolic space of the play-world — have to be understood as genuinely **collective** realities which, in manifold ways, shape the actions and experiences of those who participate in them. To take one example, different educational settings may be more or less successful in fostering a culture of collaborative learning, which will then affect both the frequency and the quality of problem-solving interaction within these settings (see Nicolopoulou & Cole, 1993, which also offers a more general critique of the tendency toward interactional reductionism in much Vygotskian-inspired research). In addition, young children's peer-group activities can generate rich fields of symbolic action that provide critical arenas for the shared use, appropriation, and working-over of cultural resources. Thus, both narrative research and educational practice should treat children's group life as a developmental context of prime importance and great potential, and should seek to identify, understand, and facilitate those forms of peer-group activity that can most effectively engage children in ways that promote their narrative development.

The preceding discussion should also make clear why we need to avoid a one-sided concentration on children's "factual" narratives of past experience (ranging from adult–child conversations to everyday anecdotes to classroom "sharing time") of the kind that has marked the bulk of current narrative research conducted in naturalistic settings — important as these narrative genres undoubtedly are for children. In another ironic twist, part of the impetus for this turn to narratives of personal experience was a reaction against what many of these researchers took to be an excessive preoccupation, in previous work, with fantasy narratives elicited by adults in semi-experimental contexts. Indeed, in summing up her particularly illuminating study of children's conversational narratives — one of the few, incidentally, that deals with spontaneous conversations between children rather than adult–child conversations — Preece (1987) comments that "make-believe" stories actually make up a very small proportion of the repertoire of narrative forms that children employ when left to their own devices, with the implication that these should be regarded as being of limited significance for narrative research. But, while these proportions no doubt hold true for the particular situation in which her study was conducted (young children in the back seat of a car being driven to and from school), the general conclusion is unwarranted, and represents an overreaction. For one thing, it overlooks the enormous field of children's pretend play, which is dominated by the composition and enactment of fictional or fantasy narratives. Furthermore, there is abundant evidence that, when children are offered the right kinds of context, they plunge into fantasy storytelling with great enthusiasm, energy, and creativity (e.g., Paley, 1984, 1988, 1990; I can also attest to this from personal experience in helping to introduce spontaneous storytelling practices into several preschool classrooms). And it is of great importance, both theoretically and practically, not to neglect or undervalue those forms of narrative activity that most effectively nourish and educate children's symbolic imagination.

A final word is in order regarding the theoretical concerns informing the analysis in this chapter, so that my emphasis on the need for a sociocultural approach not be misunderstood. Despite some notable attempts to bridge the gap, it remains true that much developmental research in psychology falls into two sharply polarized camps. One focuses more or less exclusively on individuals' cognitive structures and their inner tendencies toward development, while the other focuses on the sociocultural contexts and practices within which development occurs. The first body of research was, for a long time, primarily Piagetian in its orientation, but it is now also increasingly influenced by perspectives rooted in biology or cognitive science. A key limitation of this approach, whatever specific form it takes, is that it tends to neglect or deny the significance of sociocultural contexts in providing both **resources** and **motivation** for development and in shaping its direction; furthermore, it finds it difficult to capture important aspects of change and variation that are socioculturally specific.

The second approach, which has been especially stimulated by the influence of Vygotsky and the Vygotskian school, has properly emphasized the need to situate the individual mind and self in sociocultural context. In practice, however, it has often tended to go beyond this to **dissolve** the individual in his or her sociocultural context. Thus, even when it claims to be Vygotskian in inspiration, it is often in danger of sliding into a new form of simple learning theory. Substantively, one result is that, while it can account for **change**, it often has difficulty formulating a strong concept of **development**.

Accounts of development that focus one-sidedly on either of these dimensions are necessarily truncated and misleading; rather, both are mutually and intricately implicated in the process of development, and their interplay helps to motivate development and contributes to shaping its form and direction. In recent years there have been increasing attempts to overcome these limitations by finding ways to integrate a socially informed perspective with a constructivist one (see, e.g., Forman, Minick, & Stone, 1993). I see my own work as offering a contribution to this larger project.

YOUNG CHILDREN'S SPONTANEOUS STORYTELLING IN A PEER-GROUP CONTEXT: POSING THE PROBLEM

The stories analyzed here are drawn from a multi-year project that examines the development of children's narrative activity and attempts to situate it in the context of their group life. The children in this sample were a class of 28 four-year-olds, 14 boys and 14 girls, who attended a half-day nursery school affiliated with the Child Study Center of the University of California at Berkeley during the academic year 1988-1989. At the beginning of the year, the ages of the children ranged from 3;10 to 4;9 (with a mean of 4;2 each for both the boys and the girls). The family backgrounds of the children in this group were primarily middle- to upper-middle-class, mostly professional or academic.

The stories were generated and collected as part of a storytelling and story-acting practice, pioneered by Vivian Paley (1984, 1988, 1990), that is a regular component of the preschool curriculum. One optional activity in which any child in the school can choose to participate every day is to dictate a story to a designated teacher, who records the story as the child tells it. At the end of each day, all the stories dictated during that day are read aloud to the entire class at "circle time" by the same teacher; while the story is being read, the child/author and other children, whom he or she chooses, act out the story. One result is that children tell these stories, not only to adults, but primarily to each other. Furthermore, the children's storytelling activity is embedded in the ongoing framework of their everyday group life — in the "real world" of their classroom mini-culture.

The analysis is based on the complete set of 582 stories collected during the entire academic year 1988-1989, which included stories told by all 28 children. About 60% (347) of these stories were dictated by girls and about 40% (235) by boys. (This corpus of stories is drawn from the "Child Study Center Archives of Children's Play Narratives" at the Institute of Human Development of the University of California, Berkeley.)

I am presently extending this line of research by collecting further data in collaboration with teachers at two preschools in western Massachusetts who use the same storytelling and story-acting activity in their classrooms. At several points in this chapter, I will draw on observations from my current research to support and supplement the analysis presented here.

The Development of Children's Narrative Activity: A Case Study

As the year went on, the stories told by all of the children became more complex and sophisticated, manifesting significant advances in both narrative competence and cognitive abilities. To illustrate some features of this development, let me begin with three of the stories told by a girl in the group whom I will call Nora.[2] Nora was a frequent storyteller (she told 28 stories over the course of the year, 14 in the fall and 14 in the spring), and her stories exemplify a number of typical patterns. The first story quoted here was dictated toward the middle of October, the second and third toward the end of January. Nora turned 5 shortly before the second story.

> Once upon a time there was a **bunny** and a **duck** and they played in the park on
> the swing. And then they went back to their house and there was a **monster**.
> And then they were into their room there was **another monster**. The end.
>
> (Nora, 4;9; 10/18/88)

This was Nora's fourth story of the year. Now let's jump ahead three months (and ten stories) to the following, which she told in sequence:

> Once upon a time there was a **mom** and a **dad** and a **sister**. They lived in a
> house in the forest. And one morning the sun came up and they weren't awake
> yet. But then a **fox** came looking for food. But then the sister woke up, and
> she heard the fox. And then the fox came knocking in her door. Then the sister
> peeked out the door. And then she slammed it closed. And then she ran to tell
> her mommy and dad. They opened the door and the fox ran away.

---

[2] Pseudonyms have been assigned to the children whose stories are quoted. Characters in the stories are marked by boldface.

(Nora, 5;0; 1/26/89)

Once upon a time in a forest there was a **tiger** and a **bunny**. They played hide and seek. And then they found a **person** and they thought it was a stranger. They ran and then got up a tree, and then the person ran away. They were all scared. And then came a whole **family**. Then they took the bunny back to their house. And they had dinner there. And then all went to bed. And then in the morning, they woke up. And then they looked out the window. And then they saw snow falling down.

(Nora, 5;0; 1/29/89)

Many of Nora's most interesting stories actually came later in the year, but these are sufficient to bring out certain key contrasts. Without going into a full-scale analysis, let me just note some of the most important differences we can see when we compare the first story with the second and third. In all three stories the number of characters per story remains roughly the same (about four characters, with the last story introducing a "family" as a collective character whose members remain unspecified), but there is a significant difference in the length and quality of the stories. In a pattern that is not uncommon among the children, Nora tends to re-use and recombine certain basic themes and characters in many of her stories, but gradually works over this material so as to produce stories of increasing narrative complexity and sophistication.

The first story is brief, and each character performs a limited number of actions that are described in generic terms (e.g., they played, they went back home). The second and third stories have much more specificity and complexity: A background is established, and then an interrelated sequence of actions is initiated and elaborated (with the second story combining a general and a specific temporal marking device, "once upon a time" and "one morning"). In addition, the characters are more fully developed, with a number of specific actions attributed to each, and the relations between the characters are more clearly and carefully worked out. Furthermore, we see the attribution of motives and the development of focalization, or an "internal" point of view, whereby scenes in the story are related from the perspective of one or more of the characters (e.g., the girl hears, then sees, the fox; the tiger and bunny think the person is a stranger and are scared, etc.). Above all, the different characters and activities in each story are organized into an inter-connected **plot**. Note, for example, that in the second and third stories a series of dramatic **problems** are posed (the fox goes looking for food, then the sister hears the fox at the door, etc.), which are then **resolved**. In the third story, which has a looser form than the second, elements from two episodes are nevertheless coordinated into a continuous story.

Reconsidering Preschool Children's Narrative Capabilities

The kind of movement toward greater narrative competence, richness, and complexity demonstrated in Nora's storytelling is generally typical of the children in the sample — though, it should be noted, the precise patterns of development vary from case to case. The most striking implication of these results is that the stories of almost all the children involved come to display a degree of narrative complexity and sophistication that, according to the overwhelming consensus of mainstream research in narrative development, 4- to 5-year-old children should simply not be able to achieve. This research consistently reports, for example, that preschool children are not able to go beyond simple event descriptions or scripts. As Hudson and Shapiro (1991) emphasize in their useful summation of the predominant point of view in current research — backed by an extensive range of supporting references — there is widespread accord that the construction of plot structures with clear initiating events, dramatic problems and their resolution, internal points of view, and formal ending devices should not emerge until "much later" than 4 years of age; and children should not be able to integrate the full range of these characteristics until "around 8 years" (Hudson & Shapiro, 1991, pp. 100-101; similar arguments are made by McKeough, 1992; Stein, 1988.) But in fact by the end of the year **all** these characteristics can be found in at least some of the stories told by **all** of the 4- to 5-year-olds in the classrooms I have been studying (and they can also be discerned, for example, in a number of stories told by children of similar ages that are reported in Paley's books). With many of the children in my sample, a high proportion of their stories meet these criteria beginning quite early in the school year.

This marked discrepancy in results can be readily demonstrated. As a first step, the entire corpus of stories was coded for their level of structural complexity using the criteria provided by Hudson and Shapiro's study (1991), since these are broadly representative. (While I will later raise some questions, on conceptual grounds, about whether this set of criteria needs to be refined, taking it over directly provides the most convenient basis for an initial comparison.) "Despite some variations," Hudson and Shapiro note, "there is considerable agreement on the minimally acceptable characteristics of the structure for a single episode story" (p. 100). For fictional or make-believe stories, the "checklist" consists of the following structural characteristics (pp. 108-109): (1) "a **setting statement** such as 'Once upon a time', 'once...' or 'one time...'"; (2) using "a **fictional character**" such as animals, monsters, giants, queens and kings, princesses and princes, or cartoon characters, as well as using the self as a fictional character; (3) "[e]xplicit **temporal sequencing**"; (4) including "a **problem** or **surprise** action"; (5) a "**resolution** of" or "**reaction** to a problem or surprise action"; and (6) an "**ending marker** such as 'The end', 'they all went home', and 'they all lived happily ever after'."

Hudson and Shapiro use this scheme to measure the percentages of children who included each of these structural elements in their stories. When a direct comparison is carried out with the stories in the present sample, the results are overwhelmingly different. Hudson and Shapiro found that when 37 preschoolers (mean age 4;8) were asked to tell make-believe stories about four separate events (birthday party, doctor's, Halloween, and trip) only 17% of them ever used a setting statement, 14% used fictional characters, 41% used temporal sequence, 30% used problem/surprise, 20% used resolution/reaction, and 16% used an ending statement (pp. 107ff). In striking contrast, the results for the present study reveal that **all** 28 children in this group used **all** of these structural elements sometime during the year. In fact, even when percentages are calculated based only on stories told during the fall, they remain much higher than those reported by Hudson and Shapiro: 96% of the children used a setting statement, 100% used fictional characters, 96% used explicit temporal sequence, 100% used problem/surprise, 81% used resolution/reaction, and 96% used an ending statement. (And these more stringent measures include three children who told only one story apiece in the fall — which means they did not really get started in their storytelling until the spring.) What is even more striking is that almost half of these children combined **all** of these structural elements in at least one of the first five stories they told.

Given the very high percentages of children who used these structural elements at some point, it seemed worthwhile to probe the data a bit further by using a finer and more demanding measure. Thus, I calculated the percentage of stories **per child** that used each of these structural elements. Fig. 22.1(a) and Fig. 22.1(b) summarize the mean percentages, listing results separately for stories told by the girls and by the boys, respectively, as well as by semester.

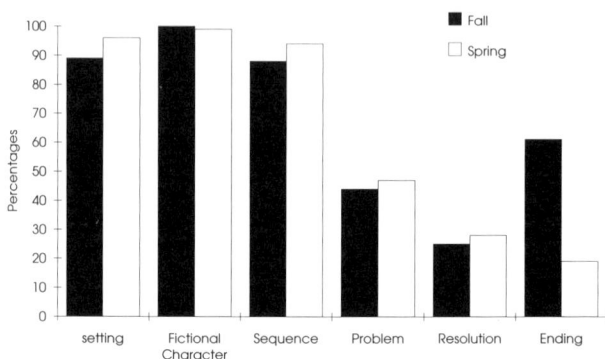

FIG. 22.1(a).
Mean Percentages of Stories by Girls that Include Specified Structural Elements

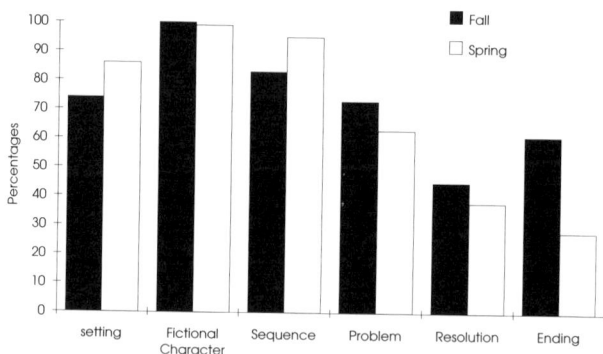

FIG. 22.1(b).
Mean Percentages of Stories by Boys that Include Specified Structural Elements

The results remain fairly high, though now a slightly more differentiated picture begins to emerge. The children in this sample used all the designated structural elements in a substantial proportion of their stories. This is particularly true for the use of a setting statement, fictional characters, and explicit temporal sequence (93%, 100%, and 91% respectively for the girls; and 80%, 100% and 89% respectively for the boys). The introduction of problem/surprise and resolution/reaction is higher for the boys than for the girls (68% and 42% respectively for the boys; and, 46% and 27% respectively for the girls). This result accords with an earlier interpretive analysis of these stories (Nicolopoulou, Scales, & Weintraub, 1994), in which we argue that girls' stories are more likely to portray images of order while boys' stories are more likely to portray images of disorder (and it suggests that this particular criterion may be weighted toward the boys' preferred storytelling style).

However, a puzzling result is that while the girls' scores generally increased during the spring semester, particularly for their use of problem/surprise and resolution/reaction, in the case of the boys' stories the use of these two structural elements decreased (see Fig. 22.1[a] and Fig. 22.1[b]). Similarly, both boys and girls decreased dramatically in their use of a formal ending statement (from 61% to 28% for the boys and from 61% to 19% for the girls).

The results I have outlined so far raise two sorts of questions: (1) On the basis of a number of the standard indicators used in research on narrative development, it is clear that this group of preschoolers performed at a far more advanced level than the bulk of current research would lead us to expect. What kinds of factors might account for this discrepancy? (2) At the same time, certain features of the results raise questions about the conceptual adequacy of these indicators themselves. In particular, the scores for several of these criteria do not increase in either a uniform or unilinear way. This fact is already apparent from the illustrations presented schematically in the previous paragraph, and it is brought out even more strongly by detailed analysis. These and other anomalies pose the issue of whether the criteria being employed are fully adequate to capture the developmental patterns in young children's narrative activity — in part because the criteria may often be more oriented to operationalizing the adult researcher's picture of a good story than to elucidating the narrative elements that the children themselves are trying to achieve. To take the simplest and most obvious example: It seems implausible that the children's decreased use of formal ending statements represents a developmental regression; it is more likely that, having mastered the use of these devices, they gradually find them less necessary or assign higher priority to other concerns in constructing their narratives. Similarly, my own analysis of young children's narrative styles suggests that the different ways that girls and boys use certain structural elements has less to do with their having reached different developmental levels than with the fact that they are using their narratives to pursue different symbolic purposes.

To be sure, the kinds of developmental criteria examined so far remain useful and important, though they often require some refinement. But they also need to be supplemented — and informed — by a more systematic effort to reconstruct the underlying purposes and motivations that actually drive and direct young children's narrative activity and development. This is especially necessary if we wish to understand the factors that most effectively promote or facilitate this development.

EXPLAINING YOUNG CHILDREN'S
NARRATIVE DEVELOPMENT: CONTEXTS AND MOTIVATIONS

The Peer-Group as Social Context: Beyond Interactional Reductionism

What accounts for the striking disparity between the findings of the present study and those that predominate in the research literature? Part of the answer certainly lies in the very different **contexts** within which the children's narrative activity is being examined. The great bulk of current research in the field of children and narratives, as I have emphasized, is conducted in more or less isolated experimental settings; whereas, in the case of the children I am studying, the narrative activity is carried out in the context of a storytelling and story-acting practice that is embedded in the context of their everyday classroom life.   The conclusion is inescapable that this socially structured practice significantly enhances the development of the children's narrative abilities — which drives home, at the same time, the crucial significance of sociocultural context for the process of development.

This being the case, the next questions are: Which features of this sociocultural context are decisive, and how do they achieve their effects?

It is not yet possible to resolve all the relevant issues (especially in the limited space available here), but I will try to highlight some of the most important. In thinking about how a classroom setting might influence children's narrative development, two factors that often occur first to people are (1) the stories that are read or told to the children as part of the curriculum and (2) the feedback and encouragement they receive from the teachers concerning their own stories. These factors clearly play a role; but, in fact, there is considerable evidence that they are of secondary importance. While the children obviously draw symbolic themes and other elements from what is taught or read to them in the classroom, they also draw heavily on popular culture; and, in both cases, it is clear that they draw selectively, so that the impact of these elements is heavily mediated by the children's own preoccupations and by the narrative forms they develop (for a more extended discussion, see Nicolopoulou et al., 1994). And the teachers' prime concerns are not to have the children tell "better stories," but rather to facilitate the storytelling practice as a way of building up a common culture in the classroom; their direct intervention to improve the **quality** of the children's stories is negligible.

In both the northern California preschool from which the stories in this chapter are drawn and the western Massachusetts preschools I have been observing, the teachers write down the story as the child tells it and generally give very little feedback. On the whole, the only kind of probing that I have (occasionally) observed is for the teacher to ask, when the cues are ambiguous, whether the child had something more to say or whether he or she is "done." Rather rarely, if a child has listed a string of characters and stopped (most typical of the younger children toward the beginning of the year), the teacher might ask whether the characters "do something?" (This kind of question doesn't necessarily elicit any further elaboration from the child.) In short, the input that the children get from the teachers is minimal and non-directive, and cannot go very far to explain the dramatic changes we observe in the children's narrative activity.

In addition, one indirect — but telling — piece of evidence that the teachers are not systematically guiding the development of the children's narrative forms is that they are often not clearly aware of such development when it does occur. As I noted earlier, some children tell stories that use the same or similar characters over and over again, but if one follows the pattern of these stories over time it is clear that they are methodically working through the formal possibilities of the material and gradually producing more complex and effective narratives. However, what the teachers notice in these cases is that the stories are getting monotonous, and in fact they often complain to me that these children are "stuck in telling the same stories." Whatever the children's motivations for developing the formal structure of their narratives this way, they are evidently not doing it for the teacher's benefit.

Of course, teachers influence children in many ways other than direct intervention; but, even in this respect, another interesting piece of evidence from my current research suggests the limits of their impact on children's narrative activity. In one school, I am observing two preschool classrooms with children of the same ages. In one of these classrooms, the teacher is herself a vivid and imaginative storyteller, who does try to use her stories to provide models for the children's narrative activity (and particularly to influence their content). The children love her stories, constantly press her to tell more, and hang on her every word. However, her stories have no obvious effect on either the form or the content of the children's stories; nor is the quality of their stories noticeably different from those told in the other classroom, where the teacher does not tell her own stories.

Thus, rather than focusing on the interactions between the children and the teachers, it seems more fruitful in this case to focus on the dynamics of the children's peer-group relations, and on the experience of this narrative practice itself. The evidence suggests that the children's mastery of narrative form is advanced most effectively not by **listening** to stories alone, but by **telling** stories as well; in fact, the best predictor of a given child's improvement in narrative ability over the course of the year is the number of stories he or she told. Furthermore, a close analysis makes it clear that the children are highly attentive to each other's stories, and influence each other extensively — in ways, I should add, that are intricately mediated by friendship ties, subgroup formation, gender, and so on.

In short, it appears that a key matrix for the children's narrative development is a **socially structured practice** which is, in turn, deeply embedded in the sociocultural fabric of the children's group life. But recognizing this does not, by itself, fully explain the kinds of **motivations** that shape the pace and direction of development within this context.

Social–Relational and Aesthetic Concerns

I submit that these motivations are complex — which helps to explain why individual children's patterns of development are themselves complex, rather than simple or unilinear. Elucidating them and grasping their interrelations remains a long-term challenge for developmental research, but at this point I can offer a first step in that direction. Building on an extensive, though still exploratory, analysis whose results I can only summarize here, I would suggest that the process of the children's narrative development appears to be driven, to a great degree, by the ongoing interplay of two interrelated but analytically distinct kinds of motivating concerns. Each of these sets of concerns is influenced by, and at the same time helps to sustain, the sociocultural context of the children's narrative activity.

(1) First, there are what might be called **social–relational** concerns. Since the stories that the children tell are acted out every day in a group context, and the author of the story chooses the other children who will help act it out, the stories are used as vehicles for seeking or expressing friendship, group affiliation, and prestige. These social–relational concerns affect the character of stories in a number of ways, most of which will have to be neglected here. For example, in composing stories a child may be inclined to include specific characters that his or her friends like to act out, as well as using themes that will appeal to them or which mark the clique to which he or she belongs; and so on.

Here I will focus on one relatively simple, but generally quite significant, index of social–relational concerns, namely the inclusion of large numbers of characters in a story. Everything else being equal, multiplying the number of characters gives children the chance to include all their friends in the story, as well as potential friends and playmates who will then owe them a favor in return.[3] In addition, it often gives them a feeling of power and influence, since it allows them to control the situation and to bring many other children on stage under their direction.

(2) At the same time, it is clear that the children's construction of narratives is also guided, to varying degrees, by intrinsically cognitive, symbolic, and formal concerns, including the mastery of narrative form for its own sake. Certain children seem especially preoccupied with developing a greater control of characters and their interrelations, in working through specific formal problems through repeated efforts, in attaining more coherent plot structure, in achieving more powerful or satisfying symbolic effects, and so on. In short, the motivations driving the children's narrative activity include what must be seen as genuinely **aesthetic** concerns, strange as it may seem to assert this of 4-year-olds.[4]

The two sets of concerns may be in tension — for example, when a child's desire to multiply characters is limited by the number that he or she can effectively handle — but in the long run they are also complementary. The different ways that children manage this interplay helps to produce a range of subtly distinctive routes to narrative development.

---

[3] On the other hand, restricting the number of characters sometimes allows children to express special bonds with close friends — and perhaps to **exclude** others — but these tendencies seem to be less significant at the preschool level.

[4] I have also emphasized the motivating significance of the aesthetic dimension in children's symbolic imagination, in two somewhat different contexts, in Nicolopoulou, 1991; Nicolopoulou et al., 1994.

The Interplay of Social–Relational and Aesthetic Concerns:
A Longitudinal Illustration

To examine fully the working-out of these two analytically distinct yet interrelated concerns for the entire sample would require a lengthy discussion. But their interplay is illustrated in a particularly revealing way by the stories of another child in the group, a boy whom we can call Mickey. At the beginning of the year, he was 4 years and 5 months old, and he told 28 stories throughout the year (17 in the fall and 11 in the spring). What makes the pattern of Mickey's storytelling especially illuminating in this respect is that it seems to involve a partial differentiation, and then a gradual reintegration, of social–relational and aesthetic concerns.

Mickey's first two stories contained a large number of characters (ten and eight, respectively) and were relatively unstructured and disconnected. Here is one of them:

> There is a **horse** and a building (a clock tower). The horse was standing near the building. There was a little fire in the building. Then a **whale** came and sprayed the fire out with his blowhole. The horse just watched. Then there was a farm and it had lots of kinds of animals from the forest, a **fox**, a **bear**, a **deer**, a **woodpecker,** and **horse**. A **tiger** owned the farm. The tiger took them all to the zoo.
>
> (Mickey, 4;5; 9/12/88)

This story displays a vivid imagination, but not a very coherent narrative structure. In fact, there are two separate stories, which are juxtaposed rather than integrated. There are eight characters in all, each of which performs at most one action.

We then see a striking shift. Mickey begins to tell stories that have very few characters (sometimes only one), but uses them to generate stories that have increasing narrative complexity and density of character development. The following is an example of such a story:

> Once upon a time there was a **dinosaur**. The dinosaur gets under a tree. Then the leaves fell off the tree and the leaves buried the dinosaur. Then the dinosaur unburied himself. He ate the leaves. And then painted a picture of all the horses, all the stores, all the schools, and he painted himself. Then he painted all the barns. The end.
>
> (Mickey, 4;5; 9/21/88)

As the year goes on, he once again gradually begins to compose stories with larger numbers of characters; but now he is able to manage them within a coherent and effective plot structure. I would argue that, while social–relational concerns predominated in Mickey's first stories, he then gave an overriding priority to addressing aesthetic concerns. In the long run, however, he is increasingly able to integrate these two concerns. The result is the overall pattern shown in Fig. 22.2.

After experimenting extensively with stories that have a few characters, toward the end of the fall Mickey can tell a story with a moderate number of characters that are well-related to each other:

> Once upon a time there was a **man** and one **girl**. They found some dinosaurs

in the stick house and they were **Tyrannosaurus Rex** and **Packiasefalasaurus**. They rode on them and the man was bad and the woman was good. The woman was on Packiasefalasaurus and the man rode Tyrannosaurus Rex. And they fighted while they were on the dinosaurs. Packi bited Tyrannosaurus with his head. And Tyrannosaurus bit him with his teeth. And Packi won the fight.

(Mickey, 4;7; 12/1/88)

Then, in the second semester, there are some remarkably elaborate constructions:

Once upon a time there was a **cat** and a **bunny** and a **dog**. They all lived together in a backyard. One day a **rag man** came along. He said, "Any rags today? Any rags today?" It was a chilly day and the rag man began to sneeze. "Ah-ah-choo!" "Ke-choo! Ke-choo! Ke-choo!" The bunny had the cat's ears! And the cat had the bunny's ears. And the cat had the dog's bark. So the bunny tried to run over and pull his ears off. And the dog had the kitty's meow. They walked around looking for the rag man. Then they met a **goose** with her feathers off, and she was carrying her feathers in a little basket. So then, the cat and the bunny all said to the goose, "Did you see a rag man go by?" "Yes," said the goose, stomping her foot. Then they went on walking, and they met a **rooster** with a comb and a beak and his tail feathers on top of his head. Then they went on walking and they met a **boy** with a shoe on top of his head and his [?] the rag man. Ah-choo! Ah-choo! Ah-choo!

(Mickey, 4;9; 1-27-89)

It has undoubtedly occurred to some readers that Mickey probably based this story on something he had heard. However, it needs to be emphasized that, for these children, hearing stories does not necessarily imply being able to reproduce or adapt them. (In the same way, some of us can't manage to tell jokes however many times we've heard them.)

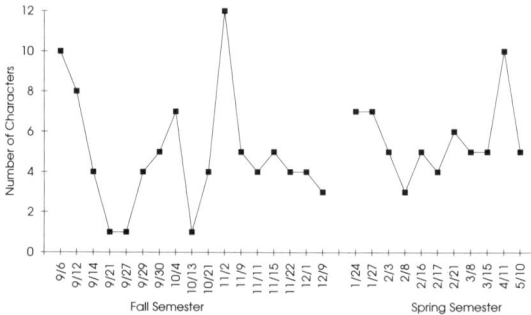

FIG. 22.2. Characters per Story in Stories by Mickey

In short, the overall pattern of Mickey's stories during the year demonstrates both the distinction between social-relational and aesthetic concerns and their ultimate interrelatedness. Once again, it should be noted that different children emphasize and blend these concerns in different ways, depending on variations in temperament and situation, thus yielding distinctive rhythms and configurations of narrative development. But in the end their patterns of development express, in one mode or another, the structuring interplay of both types of motivating concerns.

CONCLUDING REMARKS

The present study demonstrates that an ongoing storytelling and story-acting practice such as the one examined here, which integrates individual spontaneity with group participation, creates a powerful context for enhancing preschool children's narrative development. This practice draws on preschoolers' existing ability and inclination to tell and enact make-believe stories, and helps these develop by providing the children with continual opportunities for narrative performance and cross-fertilization in composing their own stories, acting in each others' stories, or simply listening to and watching the stories of others. Furthermore, since this practice is integrated into the preschool curriculum and the children are given control over what stories to tell, when to tell them, and who should act in their stories, it provides children with the opportunities to use and elaborate their narratives for their own purposes, which are both symbolic and social–relational (in complex combinations). Over time, this practice helps to create and sustain a common culture in the classroom (as well as an arena for the articulation of differences within this common culture) woven together by an ongoing framework of shared narrative activity in which all the children participate according to their own pace, rhythm, and inclination.

As a consequence, children become enthusiastically involved in this practice, and bring considerable energy and creativity to their narrative activity. And this results, in turn, in their generating stories of increasing variety, complexity, ambition, and sophistication. Not only does this rich body of spontaneous stories provide us with an invaluable window into the mind of the preschooler; the stories of these preschoolers also indicate that they have achieved levels of narrative capability and proficiency that go well beyond what the great bulk of current research in this area would lead us to expect for children of their age.

These results have some important implications for the study of development in general and of narrative development in particular. First, they strongly suggest that studies conducted in experimental and semi-experimental settings, which predominate in current narrative research, systematically underestimate the potential narrative capabilities of young children. Not only are these studies not well suited to tap the full extent of children's actual capabilities. More crucially, since they necessarily exclude the examination of the sociocultural contexts within which actual learning and development take place, they are also not well suited to understand many of the factors that are most important in promoting and facilitating this development.

These limitations are only partly overcome by many of the more socially-situated approaches in research on narrative development, because (among other reasons) they tend to conceive of the "social" context of development rather narrowly in terms of the direct effects of dyadic (or occasionally triadic) interaction, usually adult–child interaction. Such interactions are of course important; but when they are examined exclusively and in isolation, the result is a truncated and misleading picture of the social embeddedness of thought and development. As I have argued (here and elsewhere), it is also necessary to situate these interactions in the larger sociocultural contexts — ranging from classroom mini-cultures and socially structured play-worlds to communities and institutional frameworks — that shape the nature, meaning, and impact of these interactions.

In short, this study demonstrates the crucial importance of social context for narrative development; and, at the same time, it suggests the need for a more comprehensive and genuinely sociocultural understanding of "social context" and its impact than those which currently inform most narrative research (and developmental research in general). The social contexts of development cannot be reduced (conceptually or in practice) to simple aggregations of dyadic (or triadic) interactions; they consist above all of cultural and institutional frameworks that need to be grasped and analyzed as genuinely **collective** realities which, in manifold ways, structure, enable, and constrain the actions and experiences of those who participate in them. In the present case, the social context most critical for the children's narrative development consists of a socially structured practice of ongoing shared activity which simultaneously offers them opportunities and resources for development (including the mastery of narrative skills) and serves to motivate this development.

This study also provides strong evidence for the importance, both theoretical and practical, of peer relations and peer-group activity in young children's learning and development. Practices that build effectively on children's group life, and on the spontaneous exercise of their symbolic imagination, can significantly promote their narrative development. In educational contexts, the role of adults in this connection — which remains a vital one — lies in facilitating these practices and in helping to create, maintain, and support the kinds of social environments in which these forms of activity can flourish. This role complements, rather than replacing or undermining, the more direct role of the teacher as a transmitter of skills and information.

In the present case, a still exploratory analysis suggests that the storytelling and story-acting practice being examined is successful, in part, because it is able to draw on, and integrate, two interrelated but analytically distinct kinds of concerns that are especially important in motivating and directing young children's activity: (a) social–relational concerns, rooted in the children's group life and expressed in their preoccupation with issues of friendship, affiliation, status, group membership, and so on; and (b) more intrinsically aesthetic concerns, including the mastery of (culturally elaborated) narrative form for its own sake and the effort to use it for a variety of symbolic purposes. Both types of motivating concerns are socially situated, but each child in the study pursued, emphasized, and combined them in a different pattern; and, in the process of the child's narrative performance, experimentation, and increasing proficiency, the two concerns acted on and reshaped each other as well. Thus, while both of these motivating concerns seem to be present in all cases, their complex interplay produced a variety of distinctive patterns of narrative development over the course of the year.

The theoretical perspective underlying this exploratory argument stems from an effort to delineate and understand the reciprocal links between sociocultural context and individual motivation in the process of development. That is, I argue that one of the key ways that socially structured practices influence and activate individual development is by simultaneously drawing on and shaping the inner motivations that drive and direct this development. This argument bears, in turn, on a larger theoretical agenda that has informed this chapter as a whole. An effective approach to understanding individual development requires a genuine integration of sociocultural with constructivist perspectives (as the Piagetian tradition has termed them), and such an integration is not only necessary but eminently feasible. Any approach to development that does not systematically address the embeddedness of human thought and action in sociocultural contexts will necessarily be incomplete and misleading. But, on the other hand, an approach that simply dissolves the individual in his or her sociocultural context is in danger of forfeiting any genuine conception of **development**. The analysis offered in the present chapter has attempted to suggest some concrete ways that we can move toward overcoming this damaging and unnecessary polarization.

REFERENCES

Bruner, J.S., Jolly, A., & Sylva, K. (Eds.). (1976). *Play: Its role in development and evolution.* New York: Basic Books.

Corsaro, W.A. (1985). *Friendship and peer culture in the early years.* Norwood, NJ: Ablex.

Damon, W. (1984). Peer education: The untapped potential. *Journal of Applied Developmental Psychology, 5,* 331-343.

Davies, B. (1989). *Frogs and snails and feminist tales: Preschool children and gender.* North Sydney: Allen & Unwin.

Forman, E. A., & McPhail, J. (1993). Vygotskian perspective on children's collaborative problem-solving activities. In E. A. Forman, N. Minick, & C. A. Stone (Eds.), *Contexts for learning: Sociocultural dynamics in children's development* (213-229). New York: Oxford University Press.

Forman, E. A., Minick, N., & Stone, C. A. (Eds.). (1993). *Contexts for learning: Sociocultural dynamics in children's development.* New York: Oxford University Press.

Garvey, C. (1984). *Children's talk.* Cambridge, MA: Harvard University Press.

Garvey, C. (1986). Peer relations and the growth of communication. In E. C. Mueller & C. R. Cooper (Eds.), *Process and outcome in peer relationships* (pp. 329-345). Orlando, FL: Academic.

Garvey, C. (1990). *Play.* Cambridge, MA: Harvard University Press. (2nd ed.; original work published 1977)

Heath, S. B. (1983). *Ways with words: Language, life, and work in communities and classrooms.* New York: Cambridge University Press, 1983.

Hudson, J. A., & Shapiro, L. R. (1991). From knowing to telling: The development of children's scripts, stories, and personal narratives. In A. McCabe & C. Peterson (Eds.), *Developing narrative structure* (pp. 89-136). Hillsdale, NJ: Lawrence Erlbaum Associates.

Huizinga, J. (1955). *Homo ludens: A study of the play element in culture.* Boston: Beacon Press. (Original work published in 1944)

McCabe, A., & Peterson, C. (1991). Getting the story: A longitudinal study of parental styles in eliciting narratives and developing narrative skill. In A. McCabe & C. Peterson (Eds.), *Developing narrative structure* (pp. 217-253). Hillsdale, NJ: Lawrence Erlbaum Associates.

McKeough, A. (1992). A neo-structural analysis of children's narrative and its development. In R. Case (Ed.), *The mind's staircase: Exploring the conceptual underpinnings of children's thought and knowledge.* Hillsdale, NJ: Lawrence Erlbaum Associates.

Musatti, T. (1986). Early peer relations: Views of Piaget and Vygotsky. In E.C. Mueller & C. R. Cooper (Eds.), *Process and outcome in peer relationships* (pp. 25-53). Orlando, FL: Academic.

Nicolopoulou, A. (1991). Constructive play: A window into the mind of the preschooler. In B. Scales,

M. Almy, A. Nicolopoulou, & S. Ervin-Tripp (Eds.), *Play and the social context of development in early care and education* (pp. 173-191). New York: Teachers College Press.

Nicolopoulou, A. (1993). Play, cognitive development, and the social world: Piaget, Vygotsky, and beyond. *Human Development*, **36**, 1-23.

Nicolopoulou, A. (in press). Children and narratives: Toward an interpretive and sociocultural approach. In M. Bamberg (Ed.), *Narrative development: Six approaches*. Hillsdale, NJ: Lawrence Erlbaum Associates.

Nicolopoulou, A., & Cole, M. (1993). The generation and transmission of shared knowledge in the culture of collaborative learning: The Fifth Dimension, its play-world, and its institutional contexts. In E. A. Forman, N. Minick, & C. A. Stone (Eds.), *Contexts for learning: Sociocultural dynamics in children's development* (pp. 283-314). New York: Oxford University Press.

Nicolopoulou, A., Scales, B., & Weintraub, J. (1994). Gender differences and symbolic imagination in the stories of four-year-olds. In A. H. Dyson & C. Genishi (Eds.), *The need for story: Cultural diversity in classroom and community* (pp. 102-123). Urbana, IL: NCTE.

Paley, V. (1984). *Mollie is three: Growing up in school*. Chicago: The University of Chicago Press.

Paley, V. (1988). *Bad guys don't have birthdays*. Chicago: The University of Chicago Press.

Paley, V. (1990). *The boy who would be a helicopter: The uses of storytelling in the classroom*. Cambridge, MA: Harvard University Press.

Piaget, J. (1959). *The language and thought of the child*. London: Routledge. (Original work published 1923, 3rd. ed. 1945)

Piaget, J. (1965). *The moral judgment of the child*. New York: Free Press. (Original work published 1932)

Preece, A. (1987). The range of narrative forms conversationally produced by young children. *Journal of Child Language*, **14**, 353-373.

Scales, B., Almy, M., Nicolopoulou, A., & Ervin-Tripp, S. (Eds.). (1991). *Play and the social context of development in early care and education*. New York: Teachers College Press.

Snow, C. E. (1983). Literacy and Language: Relationships during the preschool years. *Harvard Educational Review*, **53**, 165-189.

Snow, C. E. (1989). Understanding social interaction and language acquisition: Sentences are not enough. In M. H. Bornstein & J. S. Bruner (Eds.), *Interaction in human development* (pp. 83-103). Hillsdale, NJ: Lawrence Erlbaum Associates.

Snow, C. E., Cancini, H., Gonzalez, P. & Shriberg, E. (1989). Giving formal definitions: An oral language correlate of school literacy. In D. Bloome (Ed.), *Classrooms and literacy* (pp. 233-249). Norwood, NJ: Ablex.

Stambak, M., & Sinclair, H. (Eds.). (1993). *Pretend play among 3-year-olds*. Hillsdale, NJ: Lawrence Erlbaum Associates.

Stein, N.L. (1988). The development of children's storytelling skill. In M. B. Franklin & S. S. Barten (Eds.), *Child language: A reader* (pp. 282-297). New York: Oxford University Press.

Sulzby, E. (1985). Children's emergent reading of favorite storybooks: A developmental study. *Reading Research Quarterly*, **20**, 458-481.

Sutton-Smith, B. (1986). The development of fictional narrative performances. *Topics in Language Disorders*, **7**, 1-10.

Tudge, J., & Rogoff, B. (1989). Peer influences on cognitive development: Piagetian and Vygotskian perspectives. In M. H. Bornstein & J. S. Bruner (Eds.), *Interaction in human development* (pp. 17-40). Hillsdale, NJ: Lawrence Erlbaum Associates.

Vygotsky, L. S. (1967). Play and its role in the mental development of the child. *Soviet Psychology*, **12**, 6-18. (Translation of a stenographic record of a lecture given, in Russian, in 1933; included in J. S. Bruner, A. Jolly, & K. Sylva (Eds.), 1976; **partly** reproduced in Vygotsky, 1978.)

Vygotsky, L. S. (1978). *Mind in society: The development of higher psychological processes*. Edited by M. Cole, V. John-Steiner, S. Scribner, & E. Souberman. Cambridge, MA: Harvard University Press.

Wellhousen, K. (1993). Eliciting and examining young children's storytelling. *Journal of Research in Childhood Education*, **7**, 62-66.

23 THE DEVELOPMENT OF COLLABORATIVE STORY RETELLING BY A TWO-YEAR-OLD BLIND CHILD AND HIS FATHER[1]

Ann M. Peters
University of Hawai'i

INTRODUCTION

An important part of the process of socializing young children lies in the transfer of cultural knowledge from caregiver to child. Vygotsky (1962, 1978) has emphasized the social (as opposed to the cognitive) nature of such transfer, together with the notion that, with the interactive help of a caregiver, the child must reconstruct such knowledge for himself at the same time as he internalizes it. Vygotsky's focus on the interpersonal context in which sociocultural knowledge is transferred lends itself to the metaphor of apprenticeship even where very young children are involved: the caregiver can be seen as assuming the role of cultural expert while the child takes the role of cultural novice. Adopting such a viewpoint makes us particularly aware of the context dependent nature of cognitive learning.

Once we accept this view of socialization, two important questions arise. First, what do both participants do to ensure that the sociocultural knowledge which the caregiver/expert wishes to transfer is made available to the child/novice in a usable form? Second, how do they see to it that the child has an opportunity to interact with this knowledge in such a way that it can be internalized? Rogoff (1990; Rogoff & Gauvain, 1986; Rogoff, Malkin, & Gilbride, 1984) has repeatedly reminded us that both partici- pants actively work at such tasks, and that we must look both at what the adult does to promote the learning as well as at what the child does to involve herself in the learning activity. Furthermore, we must concern ourselves not only with the transfer of the knowledge, but also with the transfer of the responsibility for making use of the knowl-

[1] Preparation of this paper was supported in part by NSF grant BNS-8418272, the Social Science Research Institute of the University of Hawai'i, the MIT Center for Cognitive Science under a grant from the A. P. Sloan Foundation's program in cognitive science, and the Institute for Cognitive Science, University of Colorado at Boulder. I wish to thank Alison Adams, Betsy Brandt, and Herb Roitblat for their helpful comments and suggestions when I was first trying to analyze the story data, and Patricia Donegan, Barbara Fox and Lise Menn for comments on various drafts, as well as the editors of the present volume.

edge (Rogoff & Wertsch, 1984). This last concern will lead us to consider how the actual performance of the task is shifted from expert to novice during the learning process.

The decision to try to understand learning within its social context raises methodological questions. In particular, we must develop ways to collect and analyze data that will shed light on developmental processes, i.e., on what is changing and how it is changing over the course of the teaching and learning. Vygotsky (1962) has pointed out the need to study the dynamics of the genesis of thought — how it originates and develops — rather than focusing on the description of static stages. He has suggested that this can be done in laboratory situations by setting up tasks that "artificially provoke and create a process of psychological development" (Vygotsky, 1978, p. 61). This proposal is the essence of the research method that has come to be called microgenetic, in which a teaching and learning situation is set up and data are collected on a succession of attempts at this task, typically within a single recording session. (See, for example, the puzzle-copy studies by Wertsch and his colleagues; e.g., Wertsch, McNamee, McLane, & Budwig, 1980.)

It is rare, however, for studies of the transfer of knowledge to be carried out over a lengthy time period. A truly "genetic" study would follow development over as long a period as needed to trace the complete transfer and internalization of the knowledge in question — to the point where the novice is capable of carrying out the target task completely on her own (Brandt, 1987). The data reported on here begin to fit the requirements of a truly genetic study because they cover multiple attempts at a single task in a natural setting over an eight-month period. They fall short in that data collection stopped before the child could do the task all alone. They do, however, afford an opportunity to trace developmental change over an extended period.

Before proceeding to look at these data I would like to sound a cautionary note about the way "development" may look to a researcher. The performance of any task (even in the laboratory!) is necessarily embedded in a complex web of social interactions which involve multiple goals — not only getting the focal task done, but also maintaining social relations among the participants and fulfilling social expectations. This is particularly true of parent–child interactions in the home: considerations of hunger, hygiene, safety, tiredness, mood (among others) may intervene, causing different goals to become primary at different times. This inevitably leads to variability from one episode to the next: rather than a monotonic increase in level of performance from one session to the next, we can only expect general increase across time. (See Valsiner, 1984, for further discussion.)

The particular study to be reported on here relates to the ways in which children learn about the story forms of their culture. This is an important activity for children growing up in both literate and nonliterate societies, and may involve oral, written and/or read-aloud stories, depending on the particular society. For any of these genres the child must internalize several kinds of knowledge including: (1) the appropriate interactional (dialog) patterns, (2) the accepted story-structural forms, and (3) any specific language, such as Once upon a time. Through participation in culturally defined story events the child also gradually internalizes the "meaning" these activities have for members of his cultural group.

The present chapter looks at the natural development of collaborative oral story-retelling in a single parent–child dyad over a period of eight months. Its purpose is to investigate the mechanisms by which the turntaking rules of this particular "language game" are made available to and internalized by the child in the course of multiple retellings of two stories. Although the two stories in my data were not read but told orally, they are consistent enough from one telling to the next to be considered as relatively fixed scripts. While Chomsky (1965) and other generative linguists have emphasized the creative nature of language, researchers in language acquisition have lately become increasingly aware of the central role of what are variously called **scripts**, **routines**, or **formats** in at least the early stages of language acquisition (Bruner, 1983; Nelson, 1986; Ninio & Bruner, 1978; Peters, 1987, 1993; Peters & Boggs, 1986; Ratner & Bruner, 1978; Snow, Nathan, & Perlman, 1985). Although some of these scripts are fairly loosely constructed, others have portions which are quite fixed, such as bookreading sessions where the text of the book is central (Snow, Dubber, & deBlauw, 1982), or collaborative performances of nursery rhymes and songs (Miller, 1982). While a study of the acquisition of a fixed script may not shed direct light on the development of the more creative aspects of language, the very fixedness of the target does give the researcher a firmer purchase on when deviations occur. This, in turn, allows more confident inferences about the nature of the processes underlying acquisition, including the kinds of errors that are produced, their developmental order, and their possible causes.

An exploration of these data is of particular interest for two reasons. First, as has already been noted, we have no genetic studies of the transfer of knowledge over such a long time period. In the present case it is possible to trace the process of transfer over an eight-month period and to explore how the transfer mechanisms change alongside the development of both the child's global understanding of story retelling and his ability to participate in it. Second, Seth's visual handicap helps keep him on task longer than would probably be the case for a sighted child. This is because he is not distracted by the sight of interesting objects in the environment. His desire for social interaction with Dad (he does have Dad's undivided attention on these occasions) also helps keep him focused on this highly verbal task. Although these storytelling sessions may not be typical of interactions involving young sighted children, they are extreme in an interesting way: Just those elements (of negotiation of transfer of verbal knowledge) on which child language research might like to focus are present here in a highly concentrated form, affording a clearer view of mechanisms that would tend to be present but less noticeable in other dyads.

Because quantitative and qualitative analyses complement each other, both kinds will be presented. The quantitative analyses will orient us to the big picture by providing a view of the proportional shifts in responsibility for performance over the developmental period. The qualitative analyses, on the other hand, will allow us to focus more closely on expert's and novice's specific strategies: what these are like, how they subserve the goal of transfer of knowledge, and how they change with development. (For some discussion of quantitative vs. qualitative analyses of development see Rogoff & Gauvain, 1986; Valsiner, 1986, 1987.)

THE DATA

The subjects of this study are Seth, a severely visually impaired child between 23 and 31 months of age, and his father, here referred to as Dad. Seth's extremely limited access to visual information makes him more dependent than a sighted child on the speech channel as a source of information about the world "out there" — that part of the world which he can neither see nor touch at a given moment. Because he has no access to eye contact and shared gaze, he must also depend on language as a means of initiating and maintaining social contact, for which he seems very eager (Peters, 1987, 1993).

Dad began telling Seth two folk stories, The Rabbit and the Hyena and The Crocodile and the Monkey (see appendix), when Seth was about 18 months. Dad's purpose was at least dual: to interact with Seth in some verbal way (because visual ways were precluded), and to amuse Seth during routine activities such as bathing and feeding. By the time Seth was 23 months old (the first recorded story) he was beginning to chime in as Dad went along; by 31 months he was able to repeat a good deal of each story from memory — with judicious prompting from Dad.

The data consist of audio-tape recordings of what is probably a representative sequence of these collaborative story retellings which starts when Seth was 23 months old. Table 23.1 gives Seth's age for each recorded story, along with his mean length of utterance in words (MLUw) as calculated from full half-hour transcripts at approximately the same ages. The number of clauses per story (shown in Table 23.1) indicates how complete/elaborated a particular retelling was. The tapes were all made by Seth's father (at that time a graduate student in linguistics at the University of Hawai'i), as part of a project in which he recorded a sample of their daily interactions for at least one hour per week. Sometimes the samples happened to include story tellings. During the period when Seth was between 23 and 31 months there are nine recordings of the Crocodile story and eight recordings of the Hyena story (plus one or more abortive attempts at each story). It is important to keep in mind that, although I have analyzed all the stories that were recorded, not all the story telling sessions occur on the tapes.

TABLE 23.1.   Ages of Recordings and Number of Clauses/Retelling

Age	23;0	23;2	23;3	24;0	24;1	24;3	25;0	25;3	28;1	28;2	29;0	30;0	30;3
MLUw	1.78	1.63	---	1.49	1.99[a]	---	2.02	2.4	4.44	---	4.08	3.24	4.57
Croc.	---	39	---	40	38	39	32[b]	---	37	39	39	40	39
Hyen.	74	75	15[b]	---	---	---	---	56[b]	56[b]	67[b]	76	74	69[c]

Age: months.weeks   MLUw: Mean length of utterance in words

a: MLU calculated at 24.2   b: re-telling not finished   c: part of story was skipped

TURNTAKING AND THE NEGOTIATION OF PERFORMANCE

What evidence can we find here regarding the way in which Seth learns the most global "performance" aspects of the storytelling "language game?" To what extent and in what ways does he come to share his father's (and ultimately his culture's) definition of this activity? The kinds of things that he needs to learn include: how stories are framed (i.e., begun, ended, broken into and resumed, Goffman, 1974); the extent to which each participant is expected to perform (both alone and in collaboration); and the turntaking structure, including what to do when it is somehow violated.

Because assumptions about performances of this kind are a fairly deeply ingrained part of our culture, they are rarely made explicit under ordinary circumstances. Even in the present learning situation, Seth and Dad already seem to share a number of these assumptions — at least they are almost never explicitly negotiated. Therefore we have to look very closely at the data in order to glean any information about how they may be learned in the first place, and how that knowledge comes to be refined. Aside from fairly obvious procedures like counting the ways in which stories are started or ended, there are two kinds of evidence that are particularly useful: explicit comments or corrections by Dad, and more implicit work to repair the performance when it has somehow gotten off track.[2]

How the Stories are Framed and Defined

What can we discover about how Dad and Seth define this story retelling activity? What are their expectations about how this activity is supposed to proceed, i.e., to begin, to continue and to terminate? What subset of the component activities is each participant responsible for? How do these activities change as Seth's ability to participate increases? In what ways?

TABLE 23.2.   Initiation and Termination of Stories

	Initiates	Interrupts	Terminates
Seth	14	29	2
Dad	6	9	2

Starting at the most obvious level of framing, how do the stories get started, ended, interrupted? Who takes the initiative for each of these steps? Table 23.2 shows that, for

---

[2] Because in our society we usually operate on the assumption that only one person speaks at a time, the single most useful clue as to where repairs might be found is an overlap in speech. This is not infallible, however, since co-speaking is acceptable under some circumstances, as illustrated in example (6). See Sacks, Schegeloff, & Jefferson, 1974, for a discussion of work and repair.

those stories that were recorded,[3] Seth initiates them some 70% of the time, usually by requesting "Tell story!" In a few cases Dad initiates the telling, usually in order to record Seth's progress on tape.

Because most of the stories were told to completion (see Table 23.1), the closing of the story frame was usually accomplished by saying the last line of the story.[4] For the four stories for which the retelling was aborted,[5] they each terminated two: Seth by getting distracted by other activities; Dad by diverting the telling into sound play once, and by refusing to continue once (see example 1). They also each interrupted the telling (broke frame) a number of times (Seth three times as often as Dad), but the frame was subsequently repaired and the retelling resumed. (These repairs are discussed under repairs of interruptions.)

A culturally defined activity such as story telling includes more than merely getting started or stopped. In particular, there is an associated participant structure, which determines who participates and in what ways (speaker, cospeaker, audience). For Dad and Seth there is evidence that their expectations about participant structure were renegotiated when Seth was about 23 months old. Earlier than this we must assume that Dad takes the role of teller and that Seth is audience, but with privileges of interruption that reflect his tender age and short attention span. Once Seth begins to indicate (certainly by the tapes at 23.2) that he has learned bits of the stories and is willing and able to chime in at these points, Dad's expectations change. From this point on, Dad makes his own part of the retelling contingent on Seth's willingness to "help Daddy tell the story." Example 1 shows a crucial episode in which Dad actually refuses to continue unless Seth agrees to become a co-narrator. Evidently the negotiation was successful because the situation never recurs.

(1) Necessity for Seth to "Help" — Hyena story at 23.3 months[6]

D: and hyena said, Rabbit has stopped...

S: tape recorder. [y]ou cwose it?

D: n'the hyena said, Rabbit has stopped...

S: [y]ou cwose it?

D: ya wanta help Daddy an' tell Daddy the story? [REQUESTS HELP]

S: [y]ou cwose 'is? [y]ou cwose it?

D: okay, Daddy's gonna stop tellin' you story   [THREATENS TO QUIT]
       if you don't wanna hear it,

---

[3] Bear in mind that Dad had been telling Seth these stories for some months before they begin appearing on tape, and that at first they must have been entirely initiated by Dad.

[4] It is interesting that, while both stories have clear closing lines, the end of the hyena story (But that's another story.) may have more highly salient closing properties, since Seth eventually imported it as a closing line for the crocodile story as well. See example (16).

[5] The tape ran out in the middle of a fifth one.

[6] Boldface indicates the crucial lines or words of the example; underline marks a major stress; intonation is indicated as follows: . = falling, ? = rising, ... = "waiting"; { marks simultaneous speech; comments are in parentheses; material in / / is in broad phonetic transcription; D is a dental flap; analyses/interpretations are in square brackets.

	because I got things ta do. (firmly)	
S:	copodile. (good humored statement; 3 sec)	
	tell s'owy! (shouts)	
D:	okay. okay then.	[CONCEDES]
	so help Daddy with the story.	
	the rabbit has stopped. let's...	[PROMPTS]
S:	/diyt/-- (almost a grunt)	[barely contributes]
D:	okay, I don't wanta tell you story.	[QUITS]
	you don't wanta help.	[INVOKES "HELP"]

Even though the primary goal of these interactions seems to be to recite or perform these stories, other subgoals can be detected whenever their presence affects the course of the interaction. In fact, as mentioned in the introduction, it sometimes transpires that one or another subgoal will assume priority. For instance, sometimes Dad gets set on finishing the story in spite of the fact that Seth is repeatedly getting distracted; at other times Dad seems concerned that Seth continue to perceive storytelling as "fun" rather than "work" and lets him have "timeouts" for soundplay and other kinds of verbal interchanges; once Dad himself seems to be getting bored and introduces the sound play that terminates the retelling.

Evidence that Dad and Seth both construe this activity as "fun" is seen both in the increasingly snappy pace of their performance (see below) and in Dad's allowance for digressions such as the sound play in (2):

(2) "Timeout" for Sound Play Hyena at 30.0 months

D:	the rabbit said...	
S:	/les iyDling./	[starts sound play]
D:	/les iiyDling./	[GOES ALONG]
	the rab {bit said...	[RE-PROMPTS]
S:	{/s iiyDling/.	[still playing]
D:	/iyDling-ng./	[PLAYS ALONG]
S:	/iyDling./ }	
D:	{ /iyDling./	
S:	we wen' ta the meedling.	[keeps the lead]
D:	we wen' ta the meedling-ng.	[PLAYS ALONG]
S:	we wen' ta the meedling- {ng.	
D:	{meedling.	
S:	we went ta the cemetery.	
D:	we went to the cemetery.	
	but you know what that rabbit said —	[BACK TO STORY]
	he said, ehe...	[RE-PROMPTS, ADDS 1 WORD]
S:	tikada daroma.	[contributes to story]

(This example also shows Dad trying to make a repair after an interruption — see further discussion below.)

Expectations about Turntaking

Another aspect of what Dad and Seth seem to have negotiated about how their story retellings are to proceed involves the turntaking structure. Once it becomes accepted that Seth will also be an active participant, the expected procedure seems to be as follows: Dad tells those parts that he thinks that Seth does not know, but when he thinks Seth can contribute to a particular line he initiates the line, Seth participates to the extent of his ability, and Dad then confirms Seth's performance.[7] Example 3 shows how this normal sequence proceeds.

(3) Normal Turntaking Sequence — Crocodile at 24.1 months

D:	and his wife said...	[PROMPTS]
S:	ohhh!	[contributes]
D:	ohh.	[CONFIRMS]
	your friend the...	[PROMPTS]
S:	/mah-giy?/	[contributes]
D:	monkey,	[CONFIRMS]
	who lives in a...	[PROMPTS]
S:	/twuw-wey?/	[contributes]
D:	tree,	[CONFIRMS]
	and he eats...	[PROMPTS]
S:	mangos.	[contributes]
D:	mangos alll...	[CONFIRMS, PROMPTS FOR MORE]
S:	day! (very final)	[contributes]
D:	all day, long.	[CONFIRMS AND CORRECTS]

Because confirmations of this sort are not part of typical conversations, it is not obvious how Seth has learned their function. The most likely explanation lies in the long history of "fill-in-the-blank" (or "3-dot") prompts that occur in their everyday interactions. In these contexts, too, Dad is trying to elicit some knowledge that he knows that Seth knows, and when Seth produces it Dad confirms it.[8]

Evidence that prompt-contribute-confirm is indeed the expected norm comes from the repairs that must be made when the sequence is violated. For example, in at least two instances Dad fails to confirm Seth's contribution and this leads Seth to repeat his contribution.

(4) Failure to Confirm and Resultant Repair — Crocodile at 29.0

D:	and allll... (prolonged)	
S:	day..	
	day?	[repeats, higher pitch]
D:	all day?...	[PROMPTS FOR MORE]

---

[7] Note the similarity to the schoolteacher's Initiation-Response-Evaluation sequences as discussed, e.g., by Mehan (1979).

[8] As shown in Wilson and Peters (1988), at 18.3 Seth has not yet learned to respond to such prompts; at 19.1 Dad is still working on shaping Seth's responses; by 24.2 Seth knows how to fill in the blank.

later in the same retelling:

D:	we'll swim in the river.	[CONFIRMS PREVIOUS LINE]
	and I'll...	[PROMPTS FOR NEXT]
S:	give you a wide.	[finishes line]
D:	(2 sec silence)	[FAILS TO CONFIRM]
S:	{ ride.	[repeats]
D:	{ so-- so the ma--	[STARTS TO CONTINUE]
	give you a ride, that's right.	[BACKS UP TO CONFIRM]

It is, however, possible for Dad to skip his confirmation without necessitating a repair if his next prompt comes fast enough for it to be perceived as serving simultaneously as an implicit confirmation. This contributes to what was referred to earlier as "snappy" performance, and it seems be another indication of their perception of this activity as "fun."

(5) Skipping of Confirmation   Crocodile at 25.0 months

D:	I left my...	[PROMPTS]
S:	heart?	[contributes]
D:	hanging...	[PROMPTS W/O CONFIRMING]
S:	in tree.	[contributes]
D:	we have to...	[PROMPTS W/O CONFIRMING]
S:	back an' get it.	[finishes line]

Snappy performance can also lead to collaborative production of certain lines (cospeaking). Although this causes overlaps, they do not need repairs because the speakers are cooperating in performance rather than competing for the floor — because each knows what the other intends to say, no clarification is necessary.

(6) Co-speaking — Crocodile at 24.3 months

D:	once'a...	[PROMPTS]
S:	pa-a time?	[contributes]
D:	'pon'a time	[confirms]
	there was a...	[PROMPTS NEXT LINE]
S:	cop {adile.	[contributes]
D:	{crocodile.	[OVERLAPPING CONFIRMATION]
	and he lived in {n...	[PROMPTS]
S:	{da rip{per!	[chimes right in]
D:	{the river.	[OVERLAPPING CONFIRMATION]

Repairs of Interruptions

We have already seen that Seth interrupts the story tellings some 29 times. Whenever this happens, Dad has to go to some trouble to pick up the thread of the story in a clear manner. This usually involves some backtracking and the replacement of a pronoun with a noun. For example:

(7) Interruption and Resumption — Hyena at 30 months

D:	and he...	[PROMPTS NEXT LINE]
S:	m' we saw th' geese?	[distraction]

D: yeah, we saw the geese, Bird.   [ACKNOWLEDGES]
      well, what did the rabbit do.   [RETURNS TO STORY]
      the rabbit...   [MORE EXPLICIT PROMPT]

An example of this kind of repair also occurs in (2).

A more interesting situation in which Dad seems to feel that repair work is needed occurs when Seth unexpectedly volunteers a line. This causes an overlap that is unanticipated (as opposed to collaborative cospeaking), which Dad usually repairs by pausing and then saying his line again.

(8) Volunteer and Repair — Crocodile at 23.2 months

D: he told him the whole story.
S: 'n   { muhgey — ['and monkey']   [volunteers line]
D: { an' —   [OVERLAPS]
      an' the monkey said,   [RESTARTS]

Crocodile at 25.0 months

D: we'll swim in the... (3 sec)   [PROMPTS]
      { river,   [ADDS 1 WORD]
S: { a give [y]ou wi- {ide.   [starts next line as D finishes his]
D: {an' I'll give you a ride.

Hyena at 28.1 months

D: I...   [PROMPTS]
S: stoppi, {I —   [finishes line, starts next]
D: {I wasn't stopping,...   [STARTS CONFIRM, LETS S GO ON]
S: I was finking.   [gives line]
D: I was thinking.   [CONFIRMS]

Developmental Changes

How does their joint idea of collaborative performance evolve over the period in question? On the whole, there is relatively little explicit indication of what Seth was "supposed to do." Such indications as occur, however, do turn out to be most frequent in the earliest tellings, peaking in the abortive telling at 23.3 (see Table 23.3). They take the form of three kinds of requests by Dad: for "help" in telling the story, for the next line, and for imitation. These then disappear for a while, suggesting that the routine is fairly well established.

In the later tapes we find Dad making different kinds of explicit comments — about the contents of the lines rather than about how they are performed. These include: several explicit disconfirmations of lines ("No" plus the correct line); a few explicit confirmations of lines ("Give you a ride, that's right," "This time you got 'again' in the right place. Good"); and one laughing comment that Seth's performance had deteriorated ("Oh you turkey, you forgot all your lines!"[9]).

---

[9] It is interesting that this occurred during the last taping we have, when Seth was 30.3. Although he was making quite a few errors in which he confused one line with another, he was also taking on much more responsibility for initiating lines (see Table 23.5 and discussion of shifts of responsibility). In this

TABLE 23.3.   Explicit Negotiations by Dad

Age	23;0	23;2	23;3	24;0	24;1	24;3	25;0	25;3	28;1	28;2	29;0	30;0	30;3
R-N		4	1*										
H-D		1	2*					1					
R-I		2										1	
Stop			3*				1		1				
E-D									1	1	1	1	1
E-F										1		2	
E-M													1

R-N: explicit requests next line   H-D: asks for Seth's help   R-I: requests imitation

Stop: suggests stopping   E-D: explicitly disconfirms   E-F: explicitly confirms

E-M: explicitly comments   *: unfinished story

THE TRANSFER
OF KNOWLEDGE AND RESPONSIBILITY

In this section we will look at the ways in which each of the two participants involves himself in the work of learning/ teaching the language of the two stories and how these kinds of involvement change over time. Because the only observable evidence of such involvement comes from the amount and ways in which each performs in the storytelling task, we must first look at how they divide the responsibility for performance, and at how this division shifts over time.

The Shift in Responsibility for Performing Individual Lines

A Quantitative View

Let us first take a quantitative look at how the responsibility for performance of a story shifts over the eight-month period for which we have data. See Table 23.4.

In the first four recorded stories (all at 23 months) Dad takes almost full responsibility for the retelling, producing over 90% of the lines by himself (D-solo). Seth does try to take on a little of the responsibility (S-participate) by chiming in at places he knows: in the first story he even manages to "solo" (S-solo) on three lines (all of which involve the same set of words). By the final recordings at 30.3, Dad is soloing on only 13% (Crocodile) and 22% (Hyena) of the lines (mostly those with the form and the [animal name] said) while Seth's proportion of solos has risen to 28% and 41%, respectively.

Much more predominant than solo performance, however, is collaborative performance and how this changes. "Collaboration" involves one of the pair beginning a line and

---

sense his performance could be said to be much improved!

the other continuing or finishing it. Sometimes a single line is produced in four or more pieces — we will see examples when we get to the qualitative analyses. Who takes the responsibility for initiating a collaborative line? To begin with Dad accomplishes this by use of what Wilson & Peters (1988) call the "3-dot prompt," whereby he begins the line but then stops in the middle with a "fill in the blank" intonation (transcribed with 3 dots). For example: "and he would eat...." Table 23.4 shows that Dad so prompts (D-3dot) less than 15% of the lines in the first four stories, increasing to a maximum of 64/82% when Seth is 30 months old. On his part, Seth initiates (S-beg) less than 10% of the collaborative lines in the early stories, but this increases to around 50% in the final recordings.

A last quantitative measure of the change in Seth's participation is the proportion of lines he participates in at all (S-part). This rises from less than 5% to nearly 80% across the time period.[10]

TABLE 23.4.   Division of Labor   (percent lines/performance)

Age	23;0	23;2	23;3	24;0	24;1	24;3	25;0	25;3	28;1	28;2	29;0	30;0	30;3
Crocodile													
D-solo		95		68	39	33	34		19	21	15	10	13
S-solo				2	3		3		27	21	31	12	28
D-3dot			3	32	45	74	56		62	64	69	82	51
S-beg			3	5	13	10	22		30	31	33	15	46
S-part			5	32	61	59	56		78	79	79	82	79
Hyena													
D-solo	94	91	93					47	43	37	28	36	22
S-solo	4								20	25	24	18	41
D-3dot	4	9	13					67	46	57	51	64	49
S-beg	5	3	7						23	30	38	20	54
S-part	5	3	7					53	57	63	72	64	78

A Qualitative View

Now let us take a more qualitative look at the shift in the division of storytelling work. Here we will follow the shift in responsibility for performance of a single line. Example (9) shows the development of the line and all day long he ate mangos. (Note that in the first recording the words and all day long were omitted.)

(9) Shifting Responsibility for Performance of a Line

TARGET:	and all day long he ate mangos.	
24.0	D:	an' he would eat... mangos. [D GIVES LINE IN 2 PARTS]
	S:	meengos.
24.1	D:	aaand, all day long, he ate... [COLLABORATION: 2 PARTS]

---

[10] Note that since S-part represents the total amount of Seth's participation, it includes both S-solo and S-beg. Similarly, since S-beg is a count of all the lines which Seth initiates, it includes both those which he also finishes (S-solo) and those on which he needs help.

	S:	mango.	
	D:	mangos.	
24.3	D:	and all day...	[COLLABORATION: PART 2 GROWS]
	S:	hy'et mango {s.	
	D:	{he ate — sweet mangos.	
		(pause emphasizes the added "sweet")	
25.0	D:	and all...	[COLLABORATION: 4 PARTS]
	S:	dey.	
	D:	day, he...	
	S:	ey' { beyngos.	
	D:	{ ate — ate mangoes.	
28.1	S:	all day...	[S INITIATES: 2+ PIECES]
	D:	all day long...	
	S:	e — he et mengos.	
	D:	he ate mangos.	
28.2	S:	(breath) and all day...	[S INITIATES: PART 1 GROWS]
	D:	all day...	
	S:	he ate- mangos.	
	D:	he ate mangos.	
29.0	D:	and allll... (prolonged)	["RELAPSE": D INITIATES]
	S:	day...	[D FAILS TO CONFIRM]
		day? (repeats, higher pitch)	
	D:	all day?...	[CONFIRMS/PROMPTS REST]
	S:	he ate (ma —) (whispers "ma")	
	D:	he ate...	[CONFIRMS/PROMPTS REST]
	S:	mangos.	[gets it]
	D:	he ate mangos.	[CONFIRMS]
30.0	S:	'a' all day long...	[S INITIATES: PART 1LONGER]
	D:	all day long...	
	S:	he ate man-gos.	
	D:	he ate mangos.	
30.3	D:	all day long { —	[VARIABILITY: D INITIATES]
	S:	{long, he ate mango.	
	D:	he ate mangos.	

In the first retelling Dad ends up having to do all the work, even though he does try to involve Seth by using a 3-dot prompt. In the second recording Seth is able to provide the missing piece, which grows larger in the third telling. By the fourth recording (25 months) Seth begins to take responsibility for initiating this line. The 29 month performance shows an example of the nonmonotonically increasing nature of this kind of development — not only does Dad have to initiate the line, but he has to use quite a bit of effort to extract pieces which Seth was easily producing earlier.

Mechanisms of Transfer

To what specific mechanisms can we attribute the kind of shift we have just seen? On Seth's part, he increases his capacity to play this game both through increased participation (contributing more words per line, to more lines of each story, and initiating certain lines himself) and through active work in imitating Dad's corrections, rehearsing bits outside of the storytelling context, and reconstructing the language of a line for himself. In complement to Seth's progress, Dad develops increased expectations of Seth's ability to contribute, leading to escalations in his attempts to encourage Seth to perform at as advanced a level as possible within his current capabilities. In order to understand the complex changes in the interaction of these two participants we need to move to a different kind of qualitative analysis and ask: how does this dyad capitalize on Seth's current abilities so as to enable him to perform at maximum capacity? There are two ways to look at this: (1) what kinds of involvement does each participant show? and (2) what kinds of interdependent changes does the dyad show? (See Rogoff & Gauvain, 1986, for a discussion of the implications of looking at individual vs. dyadic contributions to such interactions.) Let us look at individual changes first. We will begin with Dad because understanding Seth's strategies depends on understanding Dad's.

Dad's mechanisms of transfer

As a prelude to the discussion which follows I would like to briefly review two key concepts from the developmental literature. The first of these is Vygotsky's zone of proximal development which refers to "the distance between the actual developmental level as determined by independent problem solving and the level of potential development as determined through problem solving under adult guidance or in collaboration with more capable peers" (Vygotsky, 1978, p. 86). The second, related concept is the metaphor of a teacher/expert who scaffolds the performance of a learner/novice by providing just enough support to allow the performance to take place. As the learner's competence increases the teacher descaffolds by offering less support in just such a way as to allow the learner to perform at maximum capacity (e.g., Bruner, 1975; Wood, 1980). Descaffolding has two facets: the first is the concern not to let the learner's performance slip below levels already attained, the other is the effort to advance the learner's performance a notch. Bruner uses the apt metaphor of the ratchet which advances things a notch without allowing slippage.

If we now ask what Dad does to try to insure that Seth performs at or near maximum capacity, we can look first for the strategies he uses to maintain Seth's performance at previously established levels (keeping the standards high), and then for the strategies he uses for helping Seth to advance the level of his performance another notch.

Maintenance.   First, what does Dad do in order to maintain Seth at a previously established level of performance? I have found three strategies adapted to this purpose: (1) he does not give prompts that are more elaborated than they were the previous time; (2) he reiterates his prompt when he knows Seth knows a particular line, as if to say, "I know you can do this;" and (3) he shifts from an implicit prompt to a more explicit question (for instance by asking "what") when he knows Seth knows the prompted-for piece. Let us look at some examples.

(1) By looking back at Dad's sequence of prompts in (9) we can see how he tries not to give a more elaborated prompt at time N than he did at time N-1.

(2) The two examples in (10) show how Dad reiterates his prompt when Seth does not perform up to Dad's expectations.

(10) Repeated Prompt when Performance is not Adequate

Hyena at 28.1:

D:	the animals all said,...	
S:	what w'you finking.	[wrong line]
D:	no, the animals said...	[EXPLICIT "NO," RE-PROMPTS]
S:	e tii didum!	[succeeds]
D:	e tii dhero.	[CONFIRMS]

Crocodile at 29.0:

D:	h'eats mangos. (4 sec)	[PROMPTS]
S:	heart ve-er' /jenmeyk/.	[testing D?]
D:	his heart...	[PROMPTS FOR BETTER]
S:	ver' sweet. (a bit mushy)	[complying to a degree]
D:	very...	[KEEPS STANDARDS HIGH]
S:	sweet. (quite clear)	[complies]
D:	(silence)	[FAILS TO CONFIRM]
S:	{sw--	[starts to repeat]
D:	{mus' be very sweet.	[CONFIRMS]

(3) The next example shows Dad shifting from an implicit to an explicit prompt when he thinks Seth knows the next piece.

(11) 3-Dot Prompt Backed up by a More Explicit Question — Crocodile at 23.2

D:	an' he told the monkey...	[PROMPTS]
	wha'did he tell her.	[EXPLICIT QUESTION]
S:	ho' zowiy. (enthusiastically)	
D:	the whole story.	[CONFIRMS]

Advancement.   Next, what does Dad do in order to try to advance Seth's performance a notch? I have found four such strategies: (1) he requests imitations; (2) he starts a line with a minimal prompt (as if to say, "can you do it with this small a hint?") and adds hints as necessary until Seth can perform; (3) he confirms "pretty good" performance, but also expands and corrects, as if saying, "that's okay, but here's how to improve this"; and (4) if Seth seems to be having too much difficulty he provides the piece he is trying to get Seth to produce. Let us look at some examples.

(1) Example (12) shows Dad explicitly requesting Seth to imitate a particular piece of language. (Table 23.3 shows that in the recordings requests for imitation only occur at 23.2.)

(12) Elicited Imitation — Crocodile at 23.2 months

D:	once upon a time...	[PROMPTS]
	c'n you say "once upon a time?"	[REQUESTS IMITATION]
S:	huh vas. (promptly, as if complying)	

D: once upon a time, there was a monkey, (and continues)

(2) The two examples in (13) show how Dad may start a line with a minimal prompt and then add hints a bit at a time until they reach the point at which Seth can contribute.

(13) Minimal Prompt Followed by Hints — Crocodile at 24.3

D: an' the crocodile... (3 sec)   [3-DOT PROMPT]
        swam...   [ADDS ONE MORE WORD]
S: uh wibba.   [gets some of the next phrase]
D: in the river,   [CONFIRMS]

Crocodile at 30.0:

D: the monkey...   [3-DOT PROMPT]
S: twas a fruz a eever after.   [wrong line: they were
                                            friends for ever after]
D: the monkey said...   [RE-RUNS, ADDS 1 WORD]
        that's...   [ADDS 1 MORE WORD]
S: s'okay.   [succeeds]
D: that's okay.   [CONFIRM, EXPAND]

(3) Example (14) illustrates of the way in which Dad confirms "pretty good" performance, but at the same time expands and corrects it.

(14) Confirmation Plus Expansion — Crocodile at 25.0

D: but he couldn't...   [PROMPTS]
S: 'a 'ers.   ou' it.   [approximates talk her out
                                            of it]
D: couldn't talk 'er out of it.   [CONFIRMS, CLARIFIES]

Crocodile at 28.1

D: and he said...
S: stole my   heart. (staccato)
D: somebody stole my   heart.   [CONFIRMS, ADDS MISSING WORD]
        and the monkey and the crocodile...
S: live a ever after.
D: were friends fer ever after.   [CONFIRMS, CORRECTS]

(4) In (15) we see Dad providing the piece he is trying to get Seth to produce when Seth seems to be having too much difficulty. (There is another instance at the beginning of example (9).) Sensitivity as to when to hold out for a hoped for level of performance and when to provide the information in question is helpful in avoiding frustration on the learner's part. Dad seems to be very good at this because he rarely loses Seth's interest by pushing him too hard. As a complement to Dad's provision of new information, Seth often works at the "uptake" of the new piece by spontaneously imitating the chunk which Dad has just provided.

(15) Provision of Prompted-for Piece — Crocodile at 28.1

D: the monkey said...
S: ohhh no!   [wrong line]
D: the monkey said, that's okay,   [PROVIDES CORRECT LINE]
S: that's okay!   [imitates]

Crocodile at 28.2:

D: the monkey threw the mangos down to his friend...

S: the monkey? (unsure at end)   [guessing]

D: the crocodile. (smiling)   [PROVIDES CORRECT WORD]

S: crocodal.   [imitates]

Dad even provides some help at the phonological level. The hyena story contains the phonologically similar forms eaten and eat'im,[11] which Seth confuses at around 30 months.[12] At both 30.0 and 30.3 we find a combination of pronunciation drill and sound play which seems to be aimed at trying to help Seth distinguish these two phrases. For instance, at 30.0 Seth pronounces eaten quite clearly as /iyt 'n/ (with two very distinct syllables). This is confirmed by Dad. In the first episode of the hyena story Seth says: "let's /iidliyn/", which Dad confirms and corrects with: "Let's eat him." In the second episode of the story Seth produces "let /iiyDlt/" which Dad corrects to "Let's eat'im." This is immediately followed by the sound play episode already shown in (2). In the third episode we find the following exchange, which even includes articulatory instructions:

(16) Sound Play with Pronunciation Drill — Hyena at 30.0

S: let's /iyDl/.

D: let's eat'im.   [CONFIRMS, CORRECTS]

        { so the hyena said...

S: { /iyDling/.   [sound play? work on last

                                syllable?]

        /iyDling/.

D: /iydlim/.   [SAME INTON. BUT FINAL /M/]

S: /iyling/.   [no change in nasal]

        { I wa' te' sto'--   [trying to resume: I want tell story]

D: { close yer mouth, Bird,   [ARTICULATORY INSTRUCTIONS]

        an' say /iyDlimm/.   [MODELING THE /M/]

        say /iyDlim, iyDlim/.   [REQUESTS IMITATION]

S: okay (whispered)

        /iiy liiy/. (same intonation, [trying to comply?]

        stretched out, no nasal)

D: /iyDlimm/. (long /m/)   [MODELING]

S: /iyDling iyling ying-ng/. [still doesn't get the point?]

D: you silly goose?   [GIVES UP?]

        so the hyena said...   [RESUMES STORY]

Thus it seems that by making shrewd use of sound play Dad is able to bring a phonological error to Seth's attention and Seth does slowly acquire the requisite distinction.

---

[11] The actual lines are: "Whoever stops along the way will be eaten." (which occurs in the introductory part), and "Let's eat'im." (which occurs in each of the three episodes). To add to the confusion, the crocodile story contains the line "I want to eat it."

[12] At 29.0 he pronounces eaten correctly, but eat'im comes out as /iyDln/ all three times.

Seth's Involvement in the Learning Process.   Turning now to Seth, let us look at the ways in which he engages himself in both the story performance and in the learning process. Rogoff (1990) has observed that even very young children seem to be prepared to involve themselves actively in learning situations, both by trying to participate in interesting situations and by attending to any instruction provided in such contexts. In these ways the child helps the adult calibrate his zone of proximal development — the level at which the child can reasonably be expected to perform, both with and without help. And sure enough, there are a number of ways in which Seth actively works at both the participatory and the learning aspects of this task. We have seen the following participatory strategies: contributing when prompted, volunteering lines or chiming in even when not prompted (8), and repeating his contribution when Dad fails to confirm it (4). One learning strategy that we have seen is imitation after Dad has provided some kind of correction or expansion (12). Other learning strategies to be discussed and illustrated below include: spontaneous "rehearsing" of a bit of a story sometime after a telling has been completed (17), confusing lines within a particular story (18), bringing in lines from other stories that he knows (19), attempting to reconcile the language of the story with his own developing grammatical system (20), and correcting himself when he perceives he has made an error (21). Table 23.5 gives a quantitative summary of the development of some of these strategies.

TABLE 23.5.   Evidence of Seth's Active Involvement (numbers of occurrences)

Age	23;0	23;2	23;3	24;0	24;1	24;3	25;0	25;3	28;1	28;2	29;0	30;0	30;3
Rehearse	1			1									
Imitate	4	4		2	1		1		4	1	4	8 .	5
Vol.-New	4	1	1	1	3	2	4	1	11	3	6	1	13
Vol.-Old									3	10	10	9	18
Oth. Story									5	4	5	6	6
Nov.Synt.											5	6	
Self.-Corr.										1	2	1	

Rehearse: rehearses later   Imitate: spontaneous immediate imitation

Vol.-New: volunteers line he hasn't initiated on tapes before

Vol.-Old: volunteers line he has initiated before

Oth.Story: brings in hits from some other story

Nov.Synt.: produces novel syntax   Self-Corr.: self-corrects

Certain strategies appear early and die out, others are present across the whole time span, and some only appear in the later recordings. Let us consider how Seth seems to utilize them in his learning process.

Several times early in the sequence of retellings Seth initiates "rehearsal" of a bit of a story outside of the actual telling context, suggesting some sort of active involvement in recalling the rehearsed portion. This is illustrated in example (17).

(17) Spontaneous Rehearsal by Seth — Crocodile at 24.0

S: un te' sowiy?   [want tell story? trying to reinitiate]
D: (10 sec silence)   [NO RESPONSE]
S: uncha cwa-ay.   [rehearsing: he started to cry]
D: crocodile started to cry.   [PICKS UP, CONFIRMS, EXPANDS]
S: n sta' cwy.   [imitates/rehearses]
D: an' he told the monkey...   [PROMPTS FOR MORE]
S: hoo' s'ory.   [responds to prompt]
D: the whole story.   (4 sec silence; story dropped)

Another indication of active involvement in trying to recall/reconstruct a portion of a story appears when Seth confuses lines that start in similar ways. In fact, most of his errors are due to such confusions and, as his knowledge of the language of the stories grows, the number of lines on which he makes errors also grows. For the crocodile story such confusions peak at 30 months when he makes errors on one third of the lines.

(18) Confusion of Similar Lines — Crocodile at 28.1 months
Target line: and the crocodile started to cry.
Confusion line: and the crocodile said,
D: an' the crocodile...   [IMPLICIT PROMPT]
S: said...   [wrong line; only gives 1 word]
D: started to...   [ADD 2 WDS, CORRECT, PROMPT]
S: cwy!   [succeeds]
D: cry.

Not only does Seth confuse lines within a particular story, he also actively draws on his growing knowledge of other stories, at times bringing in lines both from the other of these two stories and lines from entirely different stories. Example (19) illustrates how he employs both of these sources of knowledge.

(19) Lines from Other Stories — Crocodile at 28.1
D: and the monkey and the crocodile...
S: live a ever after.   [from some other story]
D: were friends fer ever after.   [CORRECTS]
S: dat's aner stowy —   [end of hyena story]
D: that's a nice story.   [DOESN'T PICK UP ON IT]

In the later tapes Seth also seems to be working hard at reconciling the language of the stories with his own developing syntactic system. Starting at 29 months he produces a number of constructions that are clearly his own. Several examples are given in (20).

(20) Use of his Own Syntax — Hyena at 29.0
D: why are all the little rocks...
S: on toppa on big rocks.   [own construction]
D: on top of all the big rocks.

Hyena at 30.0:
D: rocks...
S: on de top on th' big rocks.   [own construction]
D: on top of all the big rocks.
        ...
D: what...

S:	do you finking.	[own construction]
D:	what were you thinking.	

...

D:	no, the animals said, what...	
S:	da you fink.	[own construction]
D:	what were you thinking.	

Another late strategy, which appears when Seth's idea of the appropriate target is sufficiently developed, is self-correction. This is illustrated in (21).

(21) Self-correction by Seth — Hyena at 30.0

D:	The hy-ayena said...	[PROMPTING]
	{ I...	[ADDS A WORD]
S:	{ /a ʼ s/ —	[I (w)as; wrong line]
	forgot.	[remembers, self-corrects]
D:	I forgot.	[CONFIRMS]

A final way in which Seth actively works at absorbing crucial information is by imitating Dad just after the latter has produced some kind of correction (whether implicit or explicit). Although Seth does not imitate very much in this context (there are only 36 imitations across all the recordings of both stories)[13], half of these occur just after Dad has produced one of the following: an overt correction, a confirmation with expansion, or the provision of a piece that Seth could not remember. We have already seen two examples in (15). We can presume that under these conditions Dad's language is particularly "in focus" for Seth and that imitation is one way of internalizing it. Kagan (1981, p. 94) believes that "the probability of imitation is a function of the state of response uncertainty generated in the child," pointing out that "acts that are too easy or too difficult to assimilate and to perform are not likely to be imitated." He also suggests that "events in the environment representing responses which are in the process of being mastered by the child function as incentives that alert or excite the child. The reaction to that arousal is the attempt to reproduce the act" (Kagan, 1981, p. 97). Although Kagan does not take a Vygotskyan view of child development, it seems to me that these remarks are very relevant to Rogoff's suggestion that the child as well as the adult actively works in the process of trying to operate within the boundaries of the zone of proximal development. Spontaneous imitation of new but performable material is yet another way in which the child can take responsibility for his own learning and for moving forward the boundary of what is next to be achieved.

TRANSFER MECHANISMS IN THE DYAD

As we have looked separately at Dad's and Seth's transfer strategies we have seen some hints that, rather than operating independently, they are, in fact, quite interdependent —

---

[13] This is in contrast to his overall rate of imitation in all contexts, which varies between 7% and 30% in the age range of these story retellings. See Peters (1987).

such as when Seth spontaneously imitates after Dad offers a correction. Now let us consider how the actions of these two participants complement each other to produce what is, on the whole, a harmonious learning situation. It is as if, when one of them decides to push the other agrees to pull, and vice versa. Rarely do they push or pull against each other. When they do, the story telling may stop, as it does in a number of the middle tapes (see Table 23.1).

A useful point of view to adopt here is a functional one: How does the interplay of strategies in the dyad function to promote the following four goals: (1) story telling performance, (2) maintenance of the previously achieved level of performance, (3) advancement to a new level, (4) absorption of new material?

Dyadic Management of Story Performance

As we saw in Table 23.4, in the earliest tapes Dad has to assume almost total responsibility for getting a story told: he "solos" on most of the lines and does not even bother with a 3-dot prompt very often. But Seth is already trying to participate — by chiming in even when Dad does not expect it. This causes an overlap in their speech which Dad has to repair (see examples in [8]). By volunteering in this way Seth helps Dad find the present boundary of his zone of proximal development. As Dad learns what Seth can do he gradually relinquishes responsibility for the retelling, both by increasing his use of 3-dot prompts and by expecting Seth to begin certain lines. While Seth is still learning the performance management convention of the 3-dot prompt Dad may revert to more explicit prompts (as in [11]), but these disappear as Seth learns his role. As the tapes progress it appears that Seth himself sometimes tries beginning a line with a 3-dot prompt and then waits for Dad to fill in the blank. This occurs in (9) at both 28.2 and 30.0. Dad, however, believes that it is not his job but Seth's to fill in blanks, and does not let Seth get away with this role reversal — Dad's response is to take back the lead by repeating/confirming what Seth has just said using a 3-dot intonation and then to wait for Seth to continue.[14]

Seth also gradually learns that a contribution on his part will normally be followed by a confirmation or correction by Dad. We have seen his awareness of this pattern in the repair work he does when Dad fails either to confirm or to move immediately to the next line (4). On the other hand, when they are in "snappy pace" mode, Seth does not require a confirmation ([5] – [6]).

Cooperative Maintenance of Established Performance Levels

In this regard, too, Dad initially takes most of the responsibility by encouraging Seth to contribute what he knows. If Seth does not comply, Dad often either gives a more explicit prompt (as in [11]) or reiterates his prompt (as in [10]). Explicit prompts appear only in the earliest tapes, while reiterated prompts appear primarily from 28 months, after Seth's ability to contribute, as well as Dad's expectations regarding this have had a

---

[14] Wilson and Peters (1988) discuss at some length Seth's attempts to reverse roles in 3-dot routines.

chance to develop. After a reiteration by Dad, Seth often does produce the expected material. If he does not, the whole performance is in jeopardy. Dad may then decide that Seth is not interested and discontinue the retelling (as happened at 23.3 months, [1]) or he may decide not to push Seth too hard and provide the material himself (as in [15]).[15] Such a juncture is one at which factors such as mood or environmental distractions can enter in to produce apparent nonmonotonicity in development.

Collaborative Advancement of Performance Level

This is the area in which Dad and Seth are most actively negotiating the edges of Seth's zone of proximal development, in terms of both what he can do without help and what he can now do with Dad's support. We have already looked in some detail at how each participant takes some of the responsibility for transfer of the performance of particular lines. Now we may ask: how do their individual efforts mesh; that is, how do they collaborate to transfer the requisite linguistic knowledge? An early strategy, which has a long previous history with this dyad (Peters, 1987), is elicited imitation: Dad requests and Seth complies, as in (12). More important is the minimal 3-dot prompt followed by hints (13). Success of this strategy depends on Seth's willingness to contribute as soon as he can. On the whole he seems quite eager to do so. As a consequence, when Seth shows he is having difficulties, by either making mistakes or failing to contribute, Dad is usually ready to provide the missing language (15).

Collaboration in Helping Seth Integrate New Material

It is not enough, however, for Dad merely to provide new material — in order for transfer to be complete Seth must actively work at internalizing it, and Dad helps him at this task. In Table 23.5 and (17)–(21) we saw examples of the ways in which Seth indicates that he is working at absorption; for each of these Dad provides a supportive response. When Seth initiates "rehearsal" of a bit of a story outside of the retelling context, Dad picks up on it and collaborates (17). When Seth confuses lines within a particular story, Dad corrects and works to get the story back on track (18). When Seth imports lines from other stories, Dad corrects and works to get the story back on track (19). When Seth reconstructs a sentence using his own syntax, Dad accepts (confirms) but also provides the correct version (expands/clarifies) (20). When Seth corrects himself, Dad confirms the right line (21). Dad also tries to help Seth learn the phonological distinction between eat'im and eaten by using sound plays which Seth willingly enters into (16).

---

[15] A complete Mehan-type analysis (1979) would entail accounting for what happens after every one of the iterated prompts.

CONCLUSIONS

In trying to understand the development inherent in this sequence of story retellings, the metaphor of apprenticeship has been useful because it has helped us focus on the mechanisms by which both the knowledge and the responsibility for language use were transferred from the parent/expert to the child/novice. We have identified a number of strategies adopted by each participant that not only allow Seth to participate at a previously established level, but also help him advance his level a notch. We have looked at these strategies in two ways: how they function for the individual and how they interact in complementary ways to promote development.

The data presented here involve a fairly young child in a fairly complex task over quite a long time span. They show us an interactive routine that, on the whole, functions quite smoothly. (The repair situations we have seen show some of the times where it goes awry.) In this situation it has been relatively easy to isolate transfer mechanisms that seem to function effectively for this dyad. It now remains to look for these same kinds of mechanisms, and the interactions thereof, in different kinds of developmental situations.

REFERENCES

Brandt, M. E. (1987, January). *Issues in apprenticeship: Explorations and implications.* Paper presented at Third International Conference on Thinking, Honolulu.

Bruner, J. S. (1975). From communication to language: A psychological perspective. *Cognition, 3,* 255-287.

Bruner, J. S. (1983). *Child's talk: Learning to use language.* New York: Norton.

Chomsky, N. (1965). *Aspects of the theory of syntax.* Cambridge, MA: MIT Press.

Goffman, E. (1974). *Frame analysis.* Cambridge, MA: Harvard University Press.

Kagan, J. (1981). *The second year: The emergence of self-awareness.* Cambridge, MA: Harvard University Press.

Mehan, H. (1979). *Learning lessons.* Cambridge, MA: Harvard University Press.

Miller, P. J. (1982). *Amy, Wendy and Beth: Learning language in South Baltimore.* Austin: University of Texas Press.

Nelson, K. (1986). *Event knowledge: Structure and function in development.* Hillsdale, NJ: Lawrence Erlbaum Associates.

Ninio, A., & Bruner, J. S. (1978). The achievement and antecedents of labelling. *Journal of Child Language, 5,* 1-15.

Peters, A. M. (1987). The role of imitation in the developing syntax of a blind child, *Text, 7,* 289-311.

Peters, A. M. (1993). The interdependence of social, cognitive and linguistic development: Evidence from a visually-impaired child. In H. Tager-Flusberg (Ed.), *Constraints on language acquisition: Studies of atypical children* (pp. 195-219). Hillsdale, NJ: Lawrence Erlbaum Associates.

Peters, A. M., & Boggs, S. T. (1986). Interactional routines as cultural influences upon language acquisition. In B. B. Schieffelin & E. Ochs (Eds.), *Language socialization across cultures* (pp. 80-96). Cambridge, MA: Cambridge University Press.

Ratner, N., & Bruner, J. S. (1978). Games, social exchange, and the acquisition of language. *Journal of Child Language*, **5**, 391-402.

Rogoff, B. (1990). *Apprenticeship in thinking: Cognitive development in social context*. New York: Oxford University Press.

Rogoff, B., & Gauvain, M. (1986). A method for the analysis of patterns, illustrated with data on mother-child instructional interaction. In J. Valsiner (Ed.), *The individual subject and scientific psychology* (pp. 261-289). New York: Plenum Press.

Rogoff, B., Malkin, C., & Gilbride, K. (1984). Interaction with babies as guidance in development. In B. Rogoff & J. V. Wertsch (Eds.), *Children's learning in the "zone of proximal development"* (pp. 31-44). San Francisco: Jossey-Bass.

Rogoff, B., & Wertsch, J. V. (Eds). (1984). *Children's learning in the "zone of proximal development."* San Francisco: Jossey-Bass.

Sacks, H., Schegeloff, E. A., & Jefferson, G. (1974). A simplest systematics for the organization of turn-taking for conversation. *Language*, **50**, 696-735.

Snow, C. E., Dubber, C., & deBlauw, A. (1982). Routines in mother-child interaction. In L. Feagans, & D. Farran (Eds.), *The language of children reared in poverty* (pp. 53-72). New York: Academic.

Snow, C. E., Nathan, D., & Perlman, R. (1985). Assessing children's knowledge about book reading. In L. Galda, & A. Pellegrini (Eds.), *Play, language and stories: The development of children's literate behavior* (pp. 167-181). Norwood, NJ: Ablex.

Valsiner, J. (1984). Construction of the zone of proximal development in adult-child joint action: The socialization of meals. In B. Rogoff & J. ,V. Wertsch (Eds.), *Children's learning in the "zone of proximal development"* (pp. 65-76). San Francisco: Jossey-Bass.

Valsiner, J. (1986). Between groups and individuals: psychologists' and laypersons' interpretations of correlational findings. In J. Valsiner (Ed.) *The individual subject and scientific psychology* (pp. 113-151). New York: Plenum.

Valsiner, J. (1987). *Culture and the development of children's action*. New York: Wiley.

Vygotsky, L. S. (1962). *Thought and language*. Cambridge, MIT Press.

Vygotsky, L. S. (1978). *Mind in society: The development of higher psychological processes*. Cambridge, MA: Harvard University Press.

Wertsch, J. V., McNamee, G. D., McLane, J. B., & Budwig, N. (1980). The adult-child dyad as a problem-solving system. *Child Development*, **51**, 1215-1221

Wilson, B., & Peters, A. M. (1988). "What are you cooking on a hot?": A 3-year-old blind child's "violation" of universal constraints on constituent movement. *Language*, **64**, 249-273.

Wood, D. J. (1980). Teaching the young child: Some relationships between social interaction, language, and thought. In D. R. Olson (Ed.), *The social foundations of language and thought* (pp. 280-296). New York: Norton.

APPENDIX: STORY SCRIPTS

The Crocodile and the Monkey

Once upon a time, there was a crocodile, who lived in a river. And his friend the monkey lived in a tree. And all day he ate mangos. And sometimes the monkey threw the mangos down to his friend the crocodile. And sometimes the crocodile would take the mangos home to his wife.

And his wife said, "Ohh, your friend the monkey who lives in the tree, and eats those mangos all day long, his heart must be very sweet. I want to eat it." And the crocodile said, "Oh no!" And he tried to talk her out of it. But he couldn't talk her out of it. She made him trick the monkey.

So he went to the monkey and he said, "If you'll come down from the tree and jump up on my back, we'll swim out in the river and I'll give you a ride." And so the monkey climbed down out of the tree and jumped up on the crocodile's back, and they swam out in the river.

Well, they got out into the middle of the river, and the crocodile started to cry. And he told the monkey the whole story. And the monkey said, "Oh that's okay, but I left my heart hanging in the tree!" And the crocodile said, "Oh we hafta go back and get it!"

And so they swam back to the river bank, and the monkey jumped off the crocodile's back, and ran up the tree, and he said, "Somebody stole my heart!"

And the monkey and the crocodile were friends forever after.

The Rabbit and the Hyena

(Underlined words are routinely given extra/contrastive stress by Dad; italicized words are reportedly in Kikuyu)

Prologue.

Once upon a time, the lion was king of the jungle. And he told all the animals, "Tomorrow, we're going on a **long** journey to a **far** country, and whoever stops along the way will be eaten."

Episode 1.

And so the next morning they got up and they started to walk. And they walked and they walked. And the sun came up. And it was hot. And rabbit's legs were short. And rabbit got so tired. And he **stopped**.

And the hyena said, "Rabbit has stopped. Let's **eat**'im."

And the rabbit said, "Ehe, tikaroma ndaroma ningwashira ngwashiraga. I wasn't **stopping**, I was **thinking**."

And the animals all said, "What were you thinking?"

And the rabbit said, "I was wondering, where do all the old clothes go when they wear out?"

And the animals all said, "E tii dhero! That's something to think about." And meanwhile the rabbit had had his rest.

Episode 2.

And so they walked on and on. And it was noontime. And it was so hot, and rabbit got so tired. And so he stopped again.

And the hyena said, "Rabbit has stopped, let's eat'im."

But the **rabbit** said, "Ehe, tikaroma ndaroma ningwashia ngwashiraga. I wasn't stopping, I was **thinking**."

And the animals all said, "What were you thinking?"

And the rabbit said, "I was wondering, why are all the little rocks on top of all the **big** rocks?"

And the animals all said, "E tii dhero! That's something to think about." Meanwhile the rabbit had gotten his rest.

Episode 3.

And so they walked **on** and on. And it was afternoon. And the sun was so hot. The hyena's legs were short, and he got **so** tired. And he stopped. He had seen the rabbit get away with it.

And the **lion** said, "Hyena has stopped, let's eat'im!"

But the hyena said, "Ehe tikaroma ndaroma ningwashira ngwashiraga. I wasn't stopping, I was thinking."

And the animals all said, "What were you thinking?"

And the hyena said, "I forgot."

And the animals ate him up!

Coda.

And that's why the Kikuyu(s) say, "Imitation is how the frogs lost their tails." But that's another story.

PART FIVE: BILINGUALISM

24 BILINGUALISM: SOME PERSONALITY AND CULTURAL ISSUES

Philip V. Hull
American School of Professional Psychology, Hawaii

Human personality is typically considered to reflect a person's "true" self or "core" identity, stable and unique relative to other measures of behavior over time. This concept of personality makes it difficult to envision a healthy person having two personalities. On the other hand, personality is also considered to be an attribute of groups and societies. Thus, people might talk about an "Anglo," a "Mexican," or a "Chinese" personality when trying to categorize the types of behaviors believed to be characteristic of these ethnic groups.

Susan Ervin-Tripp was one of the first to distinguish between COORDINATE bilinguals (those who have learned and continue to use their two languages in separate and distinct cultural contexts) and COMPOUND bilinguals (those who have learned their second language in the same cultural context as their first language). The Chinese immigrant who learns English after arriving in the United States at age 10 is an example of a coordinate bilingual, whereas individuals who learn a foreign language in college or from bilingual parents are examples of compound bilinguals. As Susan Ervin-Tripp further pointed out more than three decades ago (Ervin, 1961), in switching from one language to another, coordinate bilinguals may also be choosing or shifting from one array of topics and/or meanings to another. Ervin-Tripp's pioneering interest in psycho- and sociolinguistics and her important contributions to these fields inspired the conceptual development and the execution of the research reported in this chapter. It is thus particularly appropriate to dedicate this chapter to her.

Bilingual immigrants continue to provide a very useful focus for research into the social and psychological meaning of language because immigrants often speak languages associated with different cultural systems. Many bilinguals report that they think and/or feel differently depending on the linguistic context. The research reported here attempts to determine whether bilingual individuals have access to culturally different modes of thought, and, if so, whether this implies the existence of two different personalities within the same individual, each associated with one of the bilingual's two languages. Two questions were particularly relevant to this study: (a) To the extent that human personality is learned, are any language-associated differences between verbal memory systems in bilinguals reflected in similar differences between dimensions of personality in bilinguals? (b) Should such differences exist, can they be tapped in the same way that differences in verbal memory processes are tapped?

   Personality questionnaires were administered to three groups of coordinate bilinguals in both their first (L1) and second languages (L2). The California Psychological Inventory (CPI) was chosen as a more reliable and empirically valid measure than the personality questionnaires used in previous studies, and the experiment was carried out with larger subject groups. The CPI demonstrated clear and meaningful differences among the three cultural groups studied: Chinese, Korean, and Mexican-Americans. Within-group, between-language differences were also found for all three groups demonstrating that coordinate bilinguals provide predictably different responses when alternately tested in their first and second languages. This implies the existence within these bilinguals of distinct personalities, each associated with one of the bilinguals' two languages.

METHOD

In an effort to ascertain whether verbal memory systems mirror personality structures in bilinguals, responses to a personality-descriptive stimulus in a bilingual's L1 were compared with responses to the same stimulus presented in L2. It was expected that differences would be most evident among a population of coordinate bilinguals because they were hypothesized to have two distinct and clearly delineated cultural affiliations, each accessible through the language in which specific cultural knowledge was learned or was associated.

SUBJECTS

Subjects for this study were immigrants to the United States who were bilingual in English and either Spanish, Chinese, or Korean. The Spanish-English bilinguals (N = 74) were from Mexico, and the Cantonese-English and Mandarin-English bilinguals (N = 57) came from Hong Kong and Taiwan. The Korean-English bilinguals were all born in South Korea (N = 17). Subjects were selected who had learned English naturalistically after the age of eight, following their arrival in the U.S., to ensure that the L1 of each subject was firmly established. Because past and present use of each language may be an important variable in determining the social and cultural role of the languages, only subjects who currently used both languages were eligible. All subjects reported currently using their L1 with their parents and, in many cases, their siblings and peers. All had successfully completed one or more semesters of undergraduate study at Berkeley. Those subject to English language testing requirements for admission to the University of California had scored above 550 on the Test of English as a Foreign Language. Those not subject to this requirement demonstrate equivalent English language proficiency in other ways.

INSTRUMENT

The measure used was the CPI. The CPI was preferred because it is the most reliable and widely-used measure of personality for non-pathological populations both within the U.S. and overseas. Although the CPI has been criticized as lacking a factorial base (e.g., Baucom, 1985; Domino, 1985; Eysenk, 1985; Goldberg, 1972), no other measure of personality for normal populations has been so thoroughly validated with external criteria. The CPI has been translated into more than 20 languages and is used in as many countries. The Chinese, Korean, and particularly the (Mexican) Spanish translations have been refined over many years to a level of reliability among educated monolingual populations similar to that of the U.S. edition. In particular, care has been taken to ensure that individual items have similar cultural significance and response patterns to permit valid cross-cultural comparisons to be made. Although the cross-cultural use of the CPI belongs in the category of ETIC approaches to investigation, research has demonstrated that the ETIC[1] categories used have more than roughly equivalent meanings in a variety of cultures (e.g., Adis, 1967; Gough, 1960; Gough & Sandhu, 1964; Mizushima & DeVos, 1967).

The CPI is also a suitable instrument for measuring personality in a cross-cultural context because it was constructed using the EMPIRICAL-CRITERION method; consequently, its scales are reflective of behavioral tendencies rather than self-concept. This ensures that the responses are predictive of actual behavior rather than self-presentation, avoiding problems of interpretation arising from questions about which frame(s) of reference subjects might be using to make their judgments. Due to the nature of the items on the CPI, the questionnaire is also likely to tap into old and long-established memory stores. Thus, the CPI is likely to draw upon the so-called DUAL STORES of memory, hypothesized in a population of bilinguals, to a greater extent than would be the case on other self-report measures or with a single, limited behavioral sample.

The CPI is a self-administered paper-and-pencil personality test which takes approximately an hour to complete. Its content is geared more to middle-class students and young adults than to older individuals or other socioeconomic groups. The questionnaire asks respondents to indicate whether they agree or disagree with 480 statements. Most of the statements report on typical behavior patterns and customary feelings, opinions, and attitudes about social, ethical, and family matters. Item scores are converted into 18 separate scores on scales that represent what Gough (1956) has called folk concepts of personality (see Fig. 24.1). These 18 folk concepts have been validated in many different countries and appear to have universal validity. This does not mean that different cultures assign the same values to the concepts, merely that the concepts themselves have

---

[1] Emic approaches use the insider's cultural categories for description of belief and behavior, while etic approaches use a single --and presumed universal-- set of categories for describing belief and behavior in every culture (LeVine, 1974, 1982; Pike, 1950, 1979).

cross-cultural meaning. In other words, all cultures make distinctions between individuals on the dimensions of the scales but each may place different values on any particular dimension.

FIG. 24.1. The 18 CPI Scales

CLASS I SCALES:

1. **(Do) DOMINANCE** - assesses social ascendancy, leadership and self-confidence.

2. **(Cs) CAPACITY FOR STATUS** - predicts social status and prestige.

3. **(Sy) SOCIABILITY** - measures extroversion, degree of social participation.

4. **(Sp) SOCIAL PRESENCE** - measures poise, self-confidence, and spontaneity.

5. **(Sa) SELF ACCEPTANCE** - measures sense of personal worth.

6. **(Wb) SENSE OF WELL-BEING** - measures sense of physical and mental health and vitality.

CLASS II SCALES:

7. **(Re) RESPONSIBILITY** - social responsibility and personal dependability.

8. **(So) SOCIALIZATION** - measures social conformity and norm-following.

9. **(Sc) SELF-CONTROL** - measures self-restraint and self-regulation. Freedom from impulsivity.

10. **(To) TOLERANCE** - measures social tolerance and lack of ethnocentrism.

11. **(Gi) GOOD IMPRESSION** - measures concern about how others react to oneself.

12. **(Cm) COMMUNALITY** - measures willingness to admit to minor social transgressions.

CLASS III SCALES:

13. **(Ac) ACHIEVEMENT VIA CONFORMANCE** - measures need and ability to achieve and succeed in socially-constrained situations.

14. **(Ai) ACHIEVEMENT VIA INDEPENDENCE** - predicts need for/success in independent, creative endeavors.

15. **(Ie) INTELLECTUAL EFFICIENCY** - correlates highly with standard measures of IQ.

CLASS IV SCALES:

16. **(Py) PSYCHOLOGICAL-MINDEDNESS** - measures insight into others' needs and motives.

17. **(Fx) FLEXIBILITY** - measures flexibility/rigidity.

18. **(Fe) FEMININITY** - measures degree of conformance to stereotypically masculine and feminine attitudes and behavior.

Gough (1956) originally classified the scales into four classes to facilitate interpretation:

Class I: These scales measure poise, social ascendancy, self-assurance, and interpersonal adequacy. These scales are *Dominance* (*Do*), *Capacity for Status* (*Cs*), *Sociability* (*Sy*), *Social Presence* (*Sp*), *Self-Acceptance* (*Sa*), and sense of *Well-Being* (*Wb*).

Class II: These scales assess socialization, maturity, intrapersonal structuring of values and include the scales of *Responsibility (Re)*, *Socialization (So)*, *Self-Control (Sc)*, *Tolerance (To)*, *Good Impression (Gi)*, and *Communality (Cm)*.

Class III: These scales measure *Achievement via Conformance (Ac)*, *Achievement via Independence (Ai)*, and *Intellectual Efficiency (Ie)*.

Class IV: This is somewhat of a residual class, containing the three scales of *Psychological-Mindedness (Py)*, *Flexibility (Fx)*, and *Femininity (Fe)*. The adjectival correlates of these scales will be outlined in the *Results* section.

DESIGN AND PROCEDURE

The design was of a simple within-subjects repeated-measures type. Subjects completed the CPI twice, once in their native language and once in English, with 5 to 15 days between sessions. Subjects were permitted to complete the inventory on their own time and to return the completed answer sheet within 2 days.

RESULTS AND DISCUSSION

Although a considerable number of cross-cultural studies have demonstrated the accuracy of the CPI in predicting behavior in different societies, it remained questionable whether the CPI could distinguish between groups of Mexican, Chinese, and Korean-Americans. It was therefore necessary to verify that the cultural groups under review had distinctive CPI profiles before attempting to use culture-based interpretations (such as the *dual-self hypothesis*, Dinges & Hull, 1992) to explain within-group, between-language differences. Because translation-inequivalence is not an issue when a single measure is given to different groups in the same language, differences in the scores on the English version of the test from group to group could, with some degree of certainty, be attributed to cultural differences. Accordingly, the English-language responses of the three groups were compared to determine whether relatively pure cultural differences could be observed. The results of these analyses are displayed in Tables 24.1, 24.2, and 24.3. An initial analysis of variance revealed no significant differences between the mean scores of the Mandarin-speaking group and those of the Cantonese-speaking group. For this reason, these two groups were treated as a single "Chinese" group.

As the data in Table 24.1 demonstrate, there were significant differences on most of the scales between the Mexican and Chinese groups. The Mexican-Korean and Chinese-Korean comparisons displayed in Tables 2 and 3 revealed far fewer between-group differences than the Mexican-Chinese comparison in Table 24.1.

The Mexican group scored significantly higher means than its Chinese counterpart on all scales except *Socialization*, *Self-Control*, and *Communality*. These between-group patterns are consistent with the between-language data discussed in the next section and with the cultural differences documented in the minority group literature. For instance, Chinese-Americans scored lower than Mexican-Americans on the CPI scales with a surgency (or extraversion) component, a finding consistent with previous studies that have shown that Chinese-Americans exhibit less dominance, aggression, and autonomy than Anglo-Americans (Sue & Morishima, 1982). One empiricallydocumented feature of Chinese culture that may be uniquely salient among the three is its emphasis on self-abasement and self-effacement (Sue & Morishima, 1982). The higher scale scores of the Mexican-Americans relative to the Chinese-Americans, indicative of a more socially desirable self-presentation, demonstrate the greater self-abasement of the Chinese group. The high social desirability of self-effacement for the Chinese, however, limits the accuracy of predictions about actual behavior. Because scales are scored in the socially desired direction, behavioral correlates may be less pronounced than the between-group scale differences would indicate.

The lack of significant differences on the *Socialization, Self-Control,* and *Communality* scales suggests that, on these dimensions, Mexican and Chinese-Americans display a similar level of acculturation when they are using English. Framing this in terms of the *dual-self hypothesis* (Dinges & Hull, 1992), the "English-language selves" of both groups seem to be similar in terms of their internalization of mainstream American culture and in the degree to which they constrain their self-expression to conform to its norms and expectations.

Fifteen of the eighteen scales in the Mexican-Chinese comparison differed significantly, whereas only four differences were evident in the Mexican-Korean comparison and seven in the Chinese-Korean comparison. These correspondences indicate that, in the areas measured by the CPI, Chinese culture differs more from Mexican culture than either culture differs from the Korean culture. In addition, there was a complete overlap in the particular scales that deviated significantly from culture to culture. The four scales that differentiated the Mexican group from the Korean group overlapped with the seven scales differentiating the Chinese and Korean groups and with the fifteen scales differentiating the Chinese and Mexican groups. This distributional pattern implies that Korean culture represents a type of "middle-ground" between Chinese and Mexican culture on the personality dimensions measured by the CPI.

A coherent picture of cultural differences emerged when adjectival correlates of the scales were considered. The adjectival correlates of the CPI scales (Gough, 1975) suggest that, relative to the Chinese, people socialized in the Mexican culture judge themselves to be more aggressive and persuasive (*Do*); active and forceful (*Cs*); outgoing and enterprising (*Sy*); clever and enthusiastic (*Sp*); outspoken and self-confident (*Sa*); energetic and free from self-doubt (*Wb*); planful and independent (*Re*); informal and tolerant (*To*); sociable and warm (*Gi*); co-operative and sincere (*Ac*); independent and self-reliant (*Ai*); energetic and resourceful (*Ie*); perceptive and rebellious (*Py*); informal and adventurous (*Fx*). Conversely, the adjectival correlates suggest that, relative to people in Mexican culture, people in Chinese culture consider themselves more often as retiring and inhibited (*Do*); shy and conventional (*Cs*); awkward and quiet (*Sy*); deliberate and moderate (*Sp*); methodical and conservative (*Sa*); cautious and self-defensive (*Wb*); immature and moody (*Re*); suspicious and narrow (*To*); inhibited and shrewd (*Gi*); stubborn and aloof (*Ac*); inhibited and anxious (*Ai*); cautious and defensive (*Ie*); apathetic and serious (*Py*); deliberate and worrying (*Fx*).

TABLE 24.1. Comparison of English CPI Means: Mexican x Chinese

CPI SCALE:	MEXICAN (N = 74)	CHINESE (N = 57)	MEXICAN x CHINESE
Dominance (Do)	27.6	25.0	$t = 3.5, p < .01$
Capacity for Status (Cs)	18.0	15.8	$t = 4.5, p < .01$
Sociability (Sy)	23.6	20.3	$t = 5.9, p < .01$
Social Presence (Sp)	34.0	31.0	$t = 4.2, p < .01$
Self Acceptance (Sa)	21.3	19.0	$t = 5.3, p < .01$
Well Being (Wb)	30.4	27.8	$t = 4.6, p < .01$
Responsibility (Re)	27.2	25.1	$t = 3.6, p < .01$
Socialization (So)	35.4	36.0	n.s.
Self Control (Sc)	24.8	24.7	n.s.
Tolerance (To)	18.3	15.5	$t = 5.0, p < .01$
Good Impression (Gi)	16.0	14.3	$t = 2.2, p < .05$
Communality (Cm)	24.5	24.0	n.s.
Achievement via Conformance (Ac)	25.0	23.7	$t = 2.5, p < .05$
Achievement via Independence (Ai)	18.3	16.7	$t = 3.2, p < .01$
Intellectual Efficiency (Ie)	34.6	31.1	$t = 6.3, p < .05$
Psychological Mindedness (Py)	10.5	9.0	$t = 4.3, p < .05$
Flexibility (Fx)	9.6	8.3	$t = 2.6, p < .05$

TABLE 24.2. Comparison of English CPI Means: Mexican x Korean

CPI SCALE:	MEXICAN (N = 74)	KOREAN (N = 17)	MEXICAN x KOREAN
Dominance (Do)	27.6	26.5	n.s.
Capacity for Status (Cs)	18.0	18.1	n.s.
Sociability (Sy)	23.6	21.7	$t = 2.4, p < .05$
Social Presence (Sp)	34.0	32.3	$t = 1.75, p < .10$
Self Acceptance (Sa)	21.3	19.19	$t = 2.3, p < .05$
Well Being (Wb)	30.4	29.9	n.s.
Responsibility (Re)	27.2	26.1	n.s.
Socialization (So)	35.4	35.0	n.s.
Self Control (Sc)	24.8	24.1	n.s.
Tolerance (To)	18.3	17.8	n.s.
Good Impression (Gi)	16.0	14.8	n.s.
Communality (Cm)	24.5	24.1	n.s.
Achievement via Conformance (Ac)	25.0	24.5	n.s.
Achievement via Independence (Ai)	18.3	18.3	n.s.
Intellectual Efficiency (Ie)	34.6	33.0	$t = 1.9, p < .10$
Psychological Mindedness (Py)	10.5	10.1	n.s.
Flexibility (Fx)	9.6	9.6	n.s.

TABLE 24.3. Comparison of English CPI Means: Chinese x Korean

CPI SCALE:	CHINESE (N = 57)	KOREAN (N = 17)	CHINESE x KOREAN
Dominance (Do)	25.0	26.5	n.s.
Capacity for Status (Cs)	15.8	18.1	$t = 3.31, p < .01$
Sociability (Sy)	20.3	21.7	n.s.
Social Presence (Sp)	31.0	32.3	n.s.
Self Acceptance (Sa)	19.0	19.19	n.s.
Well Being (Wb)	27.8	29.9	$t = 2.7, p < .05$
Responsibility (Re)	25.1	26.1	n.s.
Socialization (So)	36.0	35.0	n.s.
Self Control (Sc)	24.7	24.1	n.s.
Tolerance (To)	15.5	17.8	$t = 2.7, p < .05$
Good Impression (Gi)	14.3	14.8	n.s.
Communality (Cm)	24.0	24.1	n.s.
Achievement via Conformance (Ac)	23.7	24.5	n.s.
Achievement via Independence (Ai)	16.7	18.3	$t = 2.1, p < .05$
Intellectual Efficiency (Ie)	31.1	33.0	$t = 2.1, p < .05$
Psychological Mindedness (Py)	9.0	10.1	$t = 2.1, p < .05$
Flexibility (Fx)	8.3	9.6	$t = 1.9, p < .05$

In the Mexican-Korean comparison, the Mexican group means were higher than those of the Koreans on all four of the scales that showed significant differences: *Capacity for Status*, *Well-Being*, *Intellectual Efficiency*, and *Tolerance*. When adjectival correlates of these scales are examined, a similarly coherent picture of cultural differences emerges despite the relatively few scale differences. The first three of these scales have the common underlying dimension of surgency. Relative to Korean culture, Mexican culture could thus be characterized as active, forceful, versatile (*Cs*); Energetic, free from self-doubt, active (*Wb*); capable, resourceful, and energetic (*Ie*). Relative to Mexican culture, Korean culture would thus be conventional, shy, narrow-thinking (*Cs*); cautious, conventional, self-defensive (*Wb*); cautious, defensive, and conventional (*Ie*).

With respect to the Mexican group's higher mean on *Tolerance*, the adjectival scale correlates suggest that, relative to that of the Koreans, Mexican culture might be characterized as informal, tolerant, and verbally fluent, while Korean culture relative to Mexican culture would be characterized as aloof, retiring, and suspicious.

The Korean means were higher than those of the Chinese on all seven of the scales that showed significant differences; *Capacity for Status, Well-Being, Intellectual Efficiency, Achievement via Independence, Tolerance, Psychological-Mindedness,* and *Flexibility.* The first four scales have the common underlying dimension of surgency. When adjectival correlates of the scales are examined, a similarly coherent picture of cultural differences emerges. Relative to Chinese culture, Korean culture could thus be characterized as active, forceful, and versatile (*Cs*); energetic, free from self-doubt, active (*Wb*); capable, resourceful, energetic (*Ie*); dominant, independent, and self-reliant (*Ai*). Relative to Korean culture, these correlates suggest that Chinese culture could be described as conventional, shy, narrow-thinking (*Cs*); cautious, conventional, self-defensive (*Wb*); cautious, defensive, conventional (*Ie*); inhibited, compliant before authority, and lacking in self-insight. The last three scales (*Tolerance, Psychological-Mindedness,* and *Flexibility*) define a dimension of openness to experience and are positively correlated with each other and with *Achievement via Independence.* This implies that, relative to Chinese culture, Korean culture could be characterized as informal, tolerant, and verbally fluent (*To*); observant, perceptive, rebellious (*Py*); insightful, informal, and adventurous (*Fx*). The adjectival correlates also suggest that, relative to Korean culture, Chinese culture could thus be characterized as aloof, retiring, and suspicious (*To*); apathetic, conforming, and conventional (*Py*); guarded, pedantic, and deferential (*Fx*).

The next question addressed by this study is the extent to which between-language, within-group differences might be detected comparable to those measured on the English tests. This was achieved by analyzing the data using the *Wilcox Matched-Pairs Signed-Ranks Test.* The between-language means for the three cultural groups are displayed in Table 24.4. The results are also displayed graphically in Fig. 24.2 in three grids, similar to those used to display the CPI profiles of individuals.

The top grid contains the results for the Spanish-English bilinguals, the center grid those for the Chinese-English bilinguals, and the bottom grid those for the Korean-English bilinguals. Results were collapsed across sex; therefore the *Femininity* scale, which is scored and interpreted differently for males and females, was eliminated. Significant between-language differences were noted on several scales of each cultural group. Those scales asterisked (*) at the top and bottom of each grid showed statistically significant (*p* < .05) differences in response between the two languages, strongly implying that coordinate bilinguals function differently depending on their current linguistic context.

Two things should be kept in mind while considering these results:

(i)   One should not expect to find large personality differences since the scales measure personal style, which can remain the same across a wide variety of environments.

(ii) Group profiles show a remarkable stability compared to individual profiles, so relatively small differences are meaningful.

The Mexican bilinguals (N=74) scored higher in English on the following scales: *Capacity for Status* (interpersonal prestige); *Social Presence* (impression on others); *Self-Acceptance* (self-criticism); *Well-Being* (physical and emotional robustness and lack of extreme anxiety); *Responsibility*; *Achievement via Conformance* and *Achievement via Independence* (drive towards achievement expressed in a socially confined or a more individualistic environment), and *Intellectual Efficiency*.

TABLE 24.4. Between-Language CPI Means for 3 Cultural Groups

CPI SCALE:	MEXICAN GROUP (N = 74) LANGUAGE:		CHINESE GROUP (N = 57) LANGUAGE:		KOREAN GROUP (N = 17) LANGUAGE:	
	Spa.	Eng.	Chi.	Eng.	Kor.	Eng.
Dominance (Do)	26.9	27.6	23.7	25.0*	27.3	26.5
Capacity for Status (Cs)	17.3	18.0*	15.0	15.8	17.6	18.1
Sociability (Sy)	23.1	23.6	20.6	20.3	21.4	21.7
Social Presence (Sp)	32.4	34.0*	29.4	31.0*	31.4	32.3
Self Acceptance (Sa)	20.2	21.3*	19.3	19.0	19.8	19.9
Well Being (Wb)	28.9	30.4*	26.7	27.8	29.5	29.9
Responsibility (Re)	26.3	27.2*	25.5	25.1	26.1	26.1
Socialization (So)	35.3	35.4	34.1	36.0*	36.4	35.0
Self Control (Sc)	25.5	24.8	24.1	24.7	25.2	24.1
Tolerance (To)	18.7	18.3	15.1	15.5	18.5	17.8
Good Impression (Gi)	17.4	16.0*	16.4	14.3*	17.3	14.8*
Communality (Cm)	22.1	24.5*	21.7	24.0*	22.4	24.1
Achievement via Conformance (Ac)	23.5	25.0*	22.1	23.7*	22.4	24.5*
Achievement via Independence (Ai)	16.6	18.3*	16.7	16.7	17.6	18.3
Intellectual Efficiency (Ie)	32.9	34.6*	30.9	31.1	34.0	33.0
Psychological Mindedness (Py)	10.5	10.5	8.9	9.0	10.9	10.1
Flexibility (Fx)	9.8	9.6	7.9	8.3	9.6	9.6
	* $p < .05$					

Figure 2:   Between-Language *C.P.I.* Profiles for 3 Cultural Groups

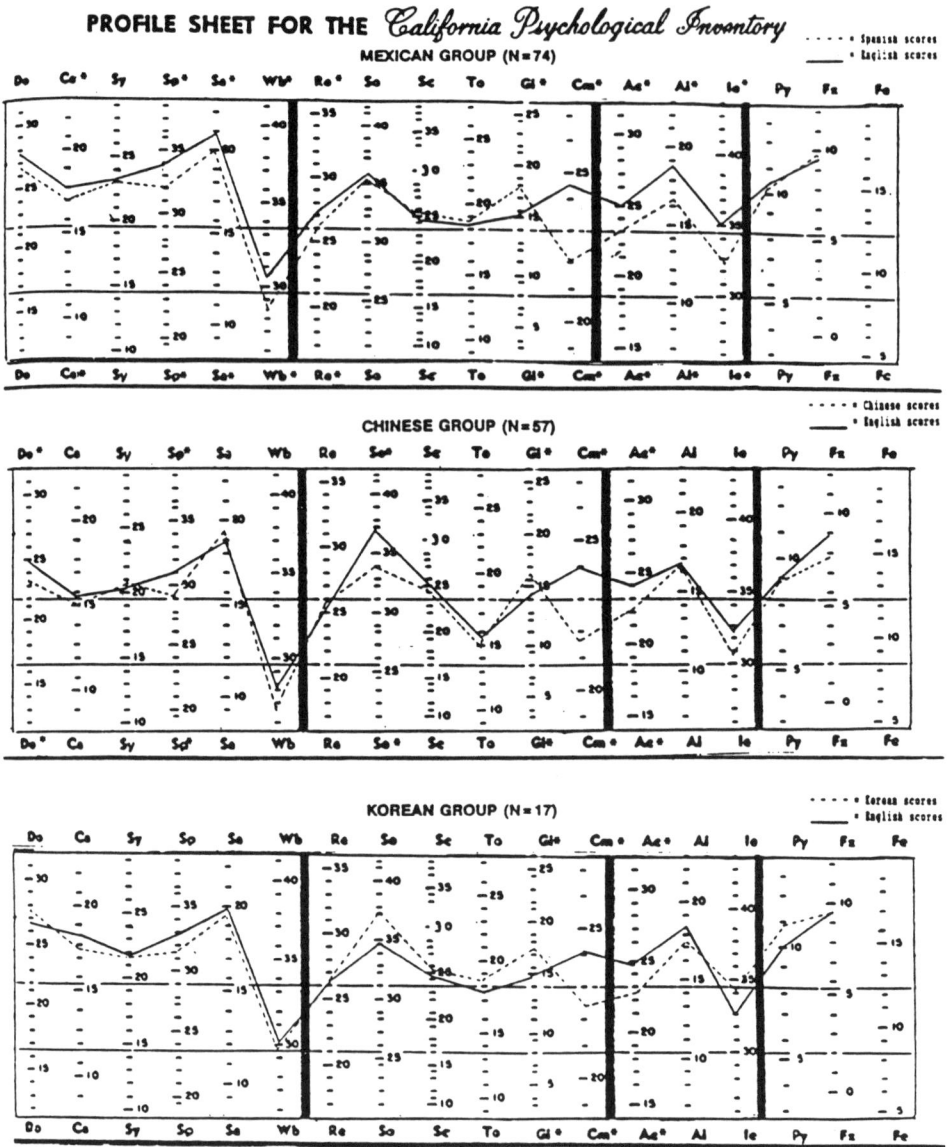

PROFILE SHEET FOR THE *California Psychological Inventory*

ASTERISKED (•) SCALES: p < .05

It has been observed (e.g., Ruiz, 1982) that it is often more appropriate in the dominant, English-speaking "mainstream" U.S. culture than in Mexican culture to present oneself in a positive manner, displaying perceived successes and achievements and downplaying aspects considered to be negative. Kagen and Madsen (1971) found that, compared to Anglo-American children (i.e., those born and raised in the U.S. as part of the dominant, English-speaking "mainstream" U.S. and without significant affiliations to another culture), Mexican-American children demonstrated a preference for cooperative over competitive behavior. In this regard, the CPI differences might result from Mexican-American subjects identifying more closely with "Anglo-American" norms of behavior (an "Anglo-American" is defined loosely as one born and raised as part of the dominant, English-speaking "mainstream" U.S.) when responding to the CPI in English and more closely with Mexican norms and expectations of behavior when responding to the CPI in Spanish. Given the lower self-esteem of Mexican-Americans as a minority group (compared with other Americans, cf., Ogbu, 1974), such differences could also reflect the subjects' stronger self-identification as members of a Mexican-American minority when responding in Spanish. The lower score in Spanish on *Intellectual Efficiency* is interesting in light of the common stereotyping by American schoolteachers that Mexican-American students have lower achievement aspirations than Asian-American or Anglo-American students (Fishman, 1977) and raises the issue of language and self-esteem. Using English language assessment materials, Fernandez and Nielsen (1986) found that Mexican immigrants' length of residence in the U.S. was inversely correlated with their expectations of scholastic achievement. It is intriguing to speculate whether Mexican-Americans might have become gradually acculturated to the majority culture's view that Hispanics have low academic aspirations. In any event, if self-stereotyping plays a role in the between-language CPI differences on *Intellectual Efficiency*, subjects may have tended to identify with members of the majority American culture more often when responding in English.

The Mexican group scored higher in Spanish on *Good Impression*, which suggests a greater concern about other people's reactions to oneself and perhaps a greater sense of group affiliation when responding in Spanish. This is consistent with findings (e.g., Ruiz, 1982; Bach-y-Rita, 1982) that family and other social networks are more important to the Mexican-American than to mainstream Americans, and that this cultural group values cooperation over competition (Kagen & Madsen, 1971). Subjects also scored higher in Spanish on *Self-Control* and *Communality*. The latter is a validity or truthfulness scale that includes items indicating the degree to which an individual is willing to admit to minor and common social transgressions. As with the other differences, a possible explanation is that of cultural affiliation. The "culture affiliation" hypothesis proposed here would suggest coordinate bilinguals will identify with the culture associated with the language currently utilized, independently of social context. Thus, according to this view, when tested in Spanish, subjects may have identified with a Mexican culture that values self-restraint and conformity to group values over individualism.

Chinese bilinguals (N = 57) scored higher in English on *Dominance, Social Presence, Socialization, Communality,* and *Achievement via Conformance*. They scored higher in

Chinese on *Good Impression*. When responding in Chinese, subjects exhibited values closer to those that have been found to be common among Chinese-Americans. Chinese-Americans as a group exhibit greater deference, abasement, external locus of control, and less dominance, aggression, preference for ambiguity, and autonomy than other Americans (Sue & Morishima, 1982). The importance placed on *mentz* (shame or loss of face) in Chinese culture (Kim, 1978) may account for subjects' greater concern with creating a *Good Impression* when tested in Chinese. However, it is difficult to make interpretations similar to those for the Spanish-English data because many subjects reported that their families had previously emigrated from different parts of Mainland China, raising the possibility that the Hong Kong and Taiwanese cultures may be more heterodox than Mexican culture.

The Korean-English bilinguals (N = 17) scored higher in English on *Communality* and *Achievement via Conformance* and higher in Korean on *Good Impression*. Because Sue and Morishima (1982) have suggested many similarities in Korean and Japanese family roles and expectations, studies of Japanese behavior might possibly provide insight into the Korean group's responses. DeVos' (1978) observation that conformity to social role expectations is a better measure of sincerity in Japanese culture than how individuals respond to their own inner feelings and needs may indicate that revealing common and minor social transgressions (*Communality*) could be regarded in a much more negative light in Korean culture than in Anglo-American culture, where transgressions in the pursuit of individualism may be viewed as heroic. The "culture-affiliation" hypothesis could therefore account for the score differential demonstrated in these data.

The score differential on *Achievement via Conformance* is less easy to explain. At least at first glance, it appears to be counter-intuitive since the culture-affiliation hypothesis would predict a reverse differential. If the Korean-American subjects identify strongly with the values of Korean culture when responding in Korean, their scores on this scale should be higher in Korean than in English. However, the Korean subjects' higher score in English could reflect the Korean culture's emphasis on meeting social role obligations through social conformance. Another possibility is that Korean-American subjects may have adopted an Anglo-American stereotype that Koreans are socially conformist, interpreting their own behavior in this light.

The importance of *chaemyun* (shame or loss of face, a similar concept to the Chinese notion of *mentz*, Kim, 1978) in Korean culture may account for the greater concern with creating a *Good Impression* noted in the Korean responses. However, on the whole, the Korean-English data obtained in this study need to be evaluated cautiously because the Korean-English group included fewer subjects than the other groups. Earlier analyses performed on small sample sizes of Spanish and Chinese data produced data similar to the low levels of significance obtained in the Korean-English sample; thus, the size of the Korean-American sample may have been too small to determine between-language personality differences with any degree of certainty.

CONCLUSION

Given that repeated-measures of personality questionnaires on monolingual populations have not detected the variations observed in this study, the importance of the present findings lies less in the number of differences detected than in the discovery that measurable differences can be observed. The between-group (English-language) differences argue for a strong cultural influence on CPI responses. There is at present no obvious reason to doubt that cultural influences are a significant factor in accounting for the within-group (between-language) differences measured in this study.

A question remains whether within-group, between-language differences reflect between-language personality differences. If the between-language, within-group differences in scores on the CPI scales are due solely to differences in cultural norms, then the difference between L1 and English on any scale should correspond to the difference between the L1 score on that scale and the English norm. Similarly, the difference between English and L1 on any scale should correspond to the difference between the English score and the L1 norm for that scale. Correlations between these differences were calculated and no significant relationships were found. We can thus conclude that the differing cultural norms of each of the differing versions of the CPI used did not produce the within-group, between-language differences noted. That similar data exist using a markedly different measure of personality (Hull, 1990) suggests that these findings are robust and one is thus left with the conclusion that these differences **must** reflect language-related differences in personality.

REFERENCES

Adis, C. G. (1957). *A study of selected personality dimensions by means of the questionnaire method in a Latin American culture.* Unpublished doctoral dissertation, University of California, Berkeley, California.

Bach-y-Rita, G. (1982). The Mexican-American: Religious and cultural influences. In R. M. Becerra, M. Karno, & J. I. Escobar (Eds.), *Mental health and Hispanic Americans: Clinical perspectives.* New York: Grune & Stratton.

Baucom, D. (1985). Review of the California Psychological Inventory. In J. V. Mitchell, Jr. (Ed.), *The Ninth Mental Measurements Yearbook*, (Vol. 1, pp. 250-252). Lincoln, NE: University of Nebraska Press, 1985.

Dinges, N. G., & Hull, P. V. (1992) Personality, culture, and international studies. In D. Lieberman, & M. Gurtov (Eds.), *Revealing the world: An interdisciplinary reader for international studies.* Dubuque, IO: Kendall-Hunt, Inc.

Domino, G. (1985). A review of the California Psychological Inventory. In D. J. Keyser, & R. C. Sweetland (Eds.), *Test Critiques*, 1(1), (pp. 46-157). Kansas City, MO: Test Corporation of America.

Ervin, S. M. (1961). Semantic shift in bilingualism. *The American Journal of Psychology*, 74(2), 233-241.

Eysenk, H. (1985). Review of the California Psychological Inventory. In J. V. Mitchell, Jr. (Ed.), *The Ninth Mental Measurements Yearbook* (Vol. 1, pp.) Lincoln, NE: University of Nebraska Press.

Fernandez, R. M., & Nielsen, F. (1986). Bilingualism and Hispanic scholastic achievement: Some baseline results. *Social Science Research,* **15**, 43-70.

Fishman, J. A. (1977). Language and ethnicity. In H. Giles (Ed.), *Language, ethnicity, and intergroup relations.* London: Academic.

Goldberg, L. R. (1972). Some recent trends in personality assessment. *Journal of Personality Assessment,* **36**, 547-560.

Gough, H. G. (1956). *California Psychological Inventory.* Palo Alto, CA: Consulting Psychologists Press.

Gough, H. G. (1960). Cross-cultural studies of the socialization continuum. *American Psychologist,* **15**, 410-411.

Gough, H. G. (1975). *Manual for the California Psychological Inventory.* Palo Alto: Consulting Psychologists' Press.

Gough, H. G., & Sandhu, H. S. (1964). Validation of the CPI socialization scale in India. *Journal of Abnormal and Social Psychology,* **68**, 544-547.

Hull, P. V. (1990). *Two languages, two personalities?* Unpublished doctoral dissertation, University of California, Berkeley.

Kagen, S., & Madsen, M. C. (1971). Competition of Mexican, Mexican-American, and Anglo children of two ages. *Developmental Psychology,* **5**, 32-39.

Kim, B. L. C. (1978). *The Asian Americans: Changing patterns, changing needs.* Montclair, NJ: Association of Korean Christian Scholars in North America.

LeVine, R. A. (Ed.) (1974). *Culture and personality.* Chicago: Aldine.

LeVine, R. A. (Ed.). (1982). *Culture, behavior, and personality.* 2nd edition. New York: Aldine.

Mizushima, K., & DeVos, G. (1967). An application of the California Psychological Inventory in a study of Japanese delinquency. *Journal of Social Psychology,* **71**, 45-51.

Ogbu, J. U. (1974). *The next generation: An ethnography of education in an urban neighborhood.* New York: Academic.

Pike, K. L. (1950). *Axioms and procedures for reconstructions in comparative linguistics: An experimental syllabus.* Glendale, CA: Summer Institute of Linguistics.

Pike, K. L. (1979). *On the extension of etic-emic anthropological methodology to referential units-in-context.* Denpasar, Bali, Indonesia: Lembaran Pengkajian Budaya.

Ruiz, P. (1982). The hispanic patient: Sociocultural perspectives. In R. M. Becerra, M. Karno, & J. I. Escobar (Eds.), *Mental health and Hispanic Americans: Clinical perspectives.* New York: Grune & Stratton.

Sue, S., & Morishima, J. K. (1982). *The mental health of Asian Americans.* San Francisco, CA: Jossey-Bass.

25 WHAT HAPPENS WHEN LANGUAGES ARE LOST? AN ESSAY ON LANGUAGE ASSIMILATION AND CULTURAL IDENTITY[1]

Lily Wong Fillmore
University of California, Berkeley

Language figures in any discussion of cultural identity, which is not surprising, since the two are closely connected. The language of a people evolves out of their experience: it reflects, not only their origins, but their history, their perspectives, their relationships to other peoples, and their uniqueness as well. In fact, for many people, language is inseparable from cultural identity since it is the means by which members of communities communicate with one another, and how individuals establish that they are, in fact, members of the same cultural community.

In our society, the question of language and cultural identity is often a painful one. American society is composed of peoples from diverse linguistic and cultural origins, both native and immigrant. We are an English-speaking society, but for many Americans, English does not reflect our heritage or our primary cultural affiliation. The language is someone else's. It evolved, in the sense that I have characterized the connection between language and culture, out of someone else's experience; it reflects their history and relationships, not our own. This may not be problematic for some people, but it is for many others. It is especially so for those who have lost their own languages, and who feel less connected to their heritage than they would like to be. This is often the case for second generation Americans, especially those who lose their primary languages in the process of learning English. It is a problem that is felt keenly by many American natives, people who lost their languages through the process of forced linguistic assimilation. For them, the question of language and cultural identity is a particularly painful one. Can a people really be connected to its culture, its history, its heritage without its language? What does it mean to lose a language?

That question is the subject of this essay; it is a subject that touches on the experience of many Americans, in one way or another. Let us begin by considering a unique

---

[1] My work in bilingualism and in the social factors that affect language learning and behavior owes much to the pioneering work of Susan Ervin-Tripp (1954, 1967, 1972, 1974, 1986). I have been inspired and influenced by her work in these areas. This chapter in particular recognizes her work on language behavior in the Southwest.

435

but troubling aspect of our society. We Americans take pride in our diverse immigrant origins,[2] but we are, at the same time, troubled by that diversity. In fact, our society has never tolerated cultural or linguistic diversity very well. We have dealt with it by denying it, and by insisting on conformity and uniformity in speech and outlook.

Recognizing the relationship between language and cultural identity, this society has always tried to attack both whenever it has been faced with a group within it that is different. Its aim has been, and is now, to diminish or neutralize the cultural identity of groups that fall outside its core. How it has tried to do this invariably begins with getting people to put aside their own languages, and to adopt English instead. It is unquestionably useful for everyone in this society to know English — but the issue here is the societal policy of forced assimilation.

American natives, especially, know about this policy. They have had ample first-hand experience with forced assimilation. The first step in the process has always been to wipe out the languages they spoke. This policy was enunciated in an 1868 federal commission report on the "condition of Indian tribes": "Schools should be established which [Indian] children should be required to attend; their barbarous dialects should be blotted out and the English language substituted. . ." (Atkins, 1887/1992). This policy became required practice in public and parochial schools serving Indian reservations, but even with compulsory school attendance beginning in 1891, it was thought that the policy was not effective enough as long as the children remained in their own communities and homes.

Boarding schools for Native American children were established, not for the purpose of providing children with a better education than they might have gotten in day schools near their homes, but for the purpose of getting them away from their families and communities where they would continue speaking their own languages and living in their traditional ways. It was the surest way to break down their cultural identities. At such schools, children were required to speak English and not permitted to use their own languages. The justification given for requiring Native American children to learn English was so they would have a common language, a means by which they could talk with one another and with anyone else they might encounter in the society. In these situations, bilingualism — whereby children maintained their first language as they learned English — was never the goal. English monolingualism was. That was the prime reason for keeping children at boarding school, away from their families and their communities, sometimes for years at a time. The policy and practice were inhumane, and downright cruel. Consider the following description of the boarding school experience:

> We were told never to talk Indian and if we were caught, we got a strapping
> with a leather belt. I remember one evening when we were all lined up in a
> room and one of the boys said something in Indian to another boy. The man in
> charge of us pounced on the boy, caught him by the shirt, and threw him across

---

[2] Our national motto, after all, is *E pluribus unum*: 'out of many (peoples), one (people)'; or is it, 'out of many nations, one nation'?

the room. Later we found out that his collar-bone was broken.

(Lone Wolf, Blackfoot, 1972/1991)

People knew that if the children were kept from using and hearing their languages, they would forget and lose them. Unable to speak their languages, they would find it hard to relate to family members, even after they were allowed to go home. And this, of course meant that the children would be estranged from family and members of their own communities, and they would be cut off from cultural support. A member of Taos Pueblo described the process of being cut off from his people, and then attempting after seven years away of trying to return to the cultural world of his community:

They told us that Indian ways were bad. They said we must get civilized. I remember that word too. It means "be like the white man." I am willing to be like the white man, but I did not believe Indian ways were wrong. But they kept teaching us for seven years. And the books told how bad the Indians had been to the white men — burning their towns and killing their women. and children. But I had seen white men do that to Indians. We all wore white man's clothes and ate white man's food and went to white man's churches and spoke white man's talk. And so after a while we also began to say Indians were bad. We laughed at our own people and their blankets and cooking pots and sacred societies and dances. I tried to learn the lessons — and after seven years I came home. . . .

(Sun Elk, Taos Pueblo, 1939)

Unable to speak the language of his community, the returnee with his now foreign ways, soon discovered that he no longer fit into his own community. He had lost in the process of becoming assimilated to the non-Indian world, not only his language but his Indian identity as he soon learned. He tells of the tribal leaders coming to his home to speak to his father:

The chiefs said to my father, "Your son who calls himself Rafael has lived with the white men. He has been far away from the pueblo. He has not lived in the kiva nor learned the things that Indian boys should learn. He has no hair. He has no blankets. He cannot even speak our language and he has a strange smell. He is not one of us."

(Sun Elk, Taos Pueblo, 1939)

The policy and practice of cutting children off from their languages and cultures were the same, both where native **and** immigrant children were concerned. The only difference was that no one took immigrant children away from their families and communities to insure that the process would take place. And tragically, it continues to be the educational policy even now. It continues to endanger the languages of Native American children and families in those few communities where the native languages somehow escaped being stripped completely in the past. There are few indigenous groups — precious few — where the languages that evolved on this continent still have young native speakers. A language doesn't have much of a chance of surviving unless many children are being socialized in it, and children are encouraged to see it as a useful communicative tool and an important part of who they are. It is children who keep a language alive, just as it is children who keep a community alive.

Although I do not work on Native American languages, I do work with members of Native American communities, especially from the Pueblos of New Mexico, who are interested in preserving their languages or in revitalizing them. My work has focused on language learning and language maintenance. Over the past several years, it has been devoted to supporting communities in their fight against educational programs that are detrimental to families and children. I have been fighting efforts to force-feed young children English before they have mastered the languages their parents speak at home. When children are in such programs they tend to abandon the use of their home language as soon as they learn a little English, and they lose it. The loss of a language — especially when it is the only language spoken by parents — can have a drastic effect on subsequent social, emotional, intellectual, and cultural development. Parents can not then easily teach their children all the things that parents must teach them; they can no longer inculcate their children in the cultural values and beliefs that are important to the family and group; and they can no longer support their children in their development of a strong sense of self or culture. These educational policies, especially that of teaching young children English in Head Start — a preschool program most people regard as benevolent or at least benign, if not positive — might be justified if only they increased the likelihood of later school success, and did not affect children's ability to relate to their families and communities. But they do not insure anything at all — not school success, nor even an easier adjustment to school. And they do gravely affect the well-being of families and communities. Over the past ten years, there has been in a number of Native American communities a rapid deterioration of primary language skills among the children and young people as a result of such programs. Whereas ten years ago children in those communities came to school speaking the indigenous language, they no longer do.[3] Or in the case of those who come to school speaking their native languages, one year of school — especially preschool — can wipe it out.

My work over the past several years has been to document the effects of this highly damaging policy, to warn educators of the harm they are doing in carrying it out, and to work with families and communities in defending themselves against this kind of attack on family languages, cultural identity, and family communication.[4] These efforts to influence policy at the professional or the societal levels are a long shot at best, since there are too many vested interests at stake there. The community, I believe, is where the battle line must be drawn.

It is at the community level that people in this society must defend their rights to their own languages and cultures. Members of American native groups that have somehow managed to preserve their tribal languages in spite of all the efforts that have been

---

[3] This is the case in Zuni Pueblo (Hayes Lewis, former Superintendent of the Zuni Public Schools, and Kirby Gchachu, former Associate Superintendent of Schools, personal communication) and in several Yupik communities in western Alaska (Anthony Woodbury and Roy Iutzi-Mitchell, personal communication).

[4] A group of children's advocates, including Susan Ervin-Tripp, conducted a study investigating the effects on language retention and use in families with children who had been in early childhood programs for the purpose of learning English. Some findings of that study are reported in Wong Fillmore (1991).

made over the years to wipe them out, must take a close look at what is happening in their communities and homes. Are families still using the tribal language for everyday communicative purposes? Are they teaching it to their children? Are they telling their children the stories that must be told in the language? Are they using it for the conduct of community affairs? If not, then community members must work with one another to try to turn things around. Language loss is not inevitable, especially when the people who speak a particular language believe that it is essential to maintain and preserve it.[5]

But what about people whose languages are already lost? In fact, most native groups no longer speak their ancestral languages. The process of forced assimilation worked all too well a long time ago. What about communities and people for whom the indigenous language is just a memory — a relic of the past? What about people in communities where only the oldest generation still knows the language, but even they don't really use it much anymore since English is the language of everyday discourse? Language, after all, like any other human artifact, has got to be constantly practiced and passed on or it will be forgotten and lost forever.

Can languages be revived? The answer is: It's difficult but it **can** be done. The Maoris of New Zealand have shown what is possible, through community effort.

Some twenty years ago when the Maori language was essentially moribund (the youngest native speakers were then in their fifties),[6] a group of women realized that if something was not done to rescue it, it would be lost. The situation for their community, they realized, was critical. The language erosion and loss among the younger generations was accompanied by an overall breakdown of the extended family and clan structure that is at the core of Maori culture. The younger generations were caught in the cycle of despair that so many American native people have experienced in schools that educated them according to hegemonic and racist policies. Many young people had left their communities and tried to make it with success in the cities. Like young American natives, they were poorly educated, poorly prepared for jobs, and not coping well with life in cities. There were high rates of alcoholism, drug use, unemployment, single-parent families, and child abuse among them.

To the women[7] involved in what came to be known as the Kohonga Reo movement, the loss of the language was just one aspect of the problem facing the community. The women, a group of grandmothers, realized, however, that language is a critical aspect of their way of life. To save the culture required attention to the language. They estab-

---

[5] Consider, for example, the preservation of Hebrew over several thousand years of diaspora. It was kept alive through its continued use in religious observances, and once the people who spoke it had a homeland once again, it was possible to reestablish it as a language of everyday use.

[6] A language can be considered moribund when it is no longer being learned by children. When members of the community who are in their child-bearing and rearing years are unable to speak the language, they can't socialize their children in that language. According to Michael Krauss (1992), 80% of the 187 indigenous languages that are still spoken in the U. S. and Canada, can be considered moribund.

[7] Katarina Mataira, from Wellington, NZ, personal communication. She was the driving force behind the Maori women who started Te Kohanga Reo, the language nest program.

lished the Kohanga Reo Program, child care centers, where young parents could leave their children in the care of older women who would socialize them in Maori language and culture. Over the period of a decade, the number of "language nests," which were staffed by volunteers, women of the grandparent generation, grew from five to over five hundred. For the first time in decades, there were young native speakers of the language again. For the Maori people, the Kohanga Reos have brought new hope for the survival of the language. Survival is not assured, but there is cause for hope.

But what of the communities where the language is too far gone for efforts like the Maoris'?[8] There is perhaps another way to think about language and cultural identity. It is especially relevant to those of us, American natives and immigrants alike, for whom English — if it is not the only language we speak — is the one we know best: the one in which we can most easily express ourselves, or is the only language in which we can communicate with the other members of our communities and families. What does it mean to speak someone else's language?

Let's consider what language is. The language systems we use are human creations. And like the humans out of whose experiences they evolved, the languages we speak are diverse and complex, and they are "living" things. Like all living things, they do not stay the same — they change over time, reflecting the changing circumstances of the people who speak them. Over time, the sounds of a given language, the words spoken, the structures used, the way meanings are communicated, all of these aspects of language change. What a language was like, how it was spoken, say, three or four hundred years ago, and what it is like now can be quite dramatically different. The English spoken in America three hundred years ago was not like the English spoken now. Of course, America several hundred years ago was not like the America of today. The most notable changes have been in the make-up of the society. We are an infinitely more diverse people than we were even then. At that time there were native peoples belonging to many different tribes and nations; there were the first "boat people" — the European colonizers; there were the peoples they brought as slaves; there were soldiers and missionaries. American society began with those people, but it grew each decade as tide after tide brought more people to the shores of this continent.

And while those of us who went through the process of assimilation to become members of American society have been profoundly changed — so too, have we changed American society and the English language. We learned English, and for many of us, after displacing our primary languages, English became our only language. But because it was a foreign tongue, and not our own, it didn't at first allow us to express ourselves as we wished — and so we changed it. If the words didn't quite work — didn't allow us to express those little nuances of meanings that were important to us — we looked for words that would work better. We added new ones, changed others,

---

[8] As long as there are speakers who are willing to support the efforts of those who want to learn a language, there is hope for the language. Leanne Hinton (1994) has been helping American Indian communities in which the only remaining speakers of the indigenous languages are in their seventies and eighties, to establish master–apprentice programs whereby an elder teaches a younger member of the community to speak the language.

invented some, and we gradually reworked the vocabulary until it did what we wanted it to do. If the sounds didn't quite suit us — they were too harsh on our ears, or required our tongues to work in ways that they were unaccustomed to working — we changed them too. We smoothed sounds out, jazzed them up a bit, slipped in a vowel or consonant here, dropped something out there, until the language suited our ears and mouths better. And if English was too laid back for us, or it seemed too busy, we changed its rhythm until it matched our sense of timing, our preferred tempo. The truth is, languages are recreated in the mouths of new speakers. They may start out as languages that reflect someone else's cultural experience and history, but in time, we can and do reshape them to fit our own realities and needs.

One might counter-argue that this makes language change sound a lot more teleological than it really is: Change surely takes place, but is there that much intentionality and purpose involved in the process? My response would be this: It may not be all that intentional in the beginning, but as people put languages that they learn to communicative use, change can certainly become purposeful.

One of the most striking examples of this has been the evolution of so-called Black Dialect, the varieties of English spoken by many African-Americans across the country. Like American natives, African-Americans have had first-hand experience with forced assimilation. The Africans who were brought as unwilling immigrants to America came from many different parts of Africa, and they spoke many different languages. Their languages were quickly replaced by a variety of English that was created out of communicative necessity. The English they adopted was a kind of pidgin that develops when people find themselves having to devise a common language in order to communicate with one another. They needed one because the slave traders and owners tended to separate people who spoke the same language, so they would not be able to talk to one another in private. The African newcomers were required to learn English, but most of them were not around their English-speaking owners enough to do so. The ones who worked in people's homes were better able to learn English than the field hands were. And so, as often happens in such situations, they created a language out of the English they heard; they added to it words and forms from their various African languages, and they invented forms as needed. They did so out of their need to express themselves, and to communicate to one another who they were, where they came from, and what was important to them. In short, the language they created enabled them to form a community with their fellows. The language is English, but its sound system, the way meaning is conveyed, its vocabulary, its rhythm and intonation have all been reconfigured and recreated in the making of this language. This process of development has gone on over several hundred years, and Black Dialect has a distinctive character and a grammar of its own — it is as rich, varied and complex as any human language, and it is in keeping with the cultural sensibilities of the people who speak it.

There are people in our society, including some Blacks, who regard Black Dialect[9] as a corrupted, bastardized form of "real English." People who speak it are put down, and are told that they have to learn "standard English" if they want to get anywhere. At school, children who speak dialect are corrected, and they are urged to switch to standard English. But even where the schools succeed in getting some of these kids to use standard dialect sometimes (which can be taken as evidence that they know it), they will not switch over to it entirely. Many speakers of dialect prefer dialect. And they continue to prefer it in adulthood, even though they may use a standard variety of English in their workplaces. When they are with members of their own communities, when it is important to them to express who they really are, they speak dialect. This language is more resistant to change than most, as it often is with hybrid languages which evolve out of people's need to maintain a sense of peoplehood in spite of the hateful discrimination and dehumanizing treatment they are getting.

And now back to the case of the native peoples on this continent. I have visited a number of American Indian and Alaskan Native communities where varieties of English were spoken — so-called "reservation English," "boarding school English," "bush English," and so on. These dialects developed in ways that were not greatly different from the way Black Dialect evolved. The boarding schools in which many native children were educated in the not too distant past attempted to separate children who spoke the same language. The idea was to force them to learn English. And again, as in the case of the Africans who had to learn English in order to communicate with each other but who were not given adequate support for learning the variety spoken by English speakers, so too did Native American children learn English based on limited support, because there were more of them than there were teachers who might have given them full access to the target language. They found themselves having to create a language out of the English they heard; they added to it the sounds and intonations of their native languages, and they devised ways to say what they needed to say to one another. Children are as creative as anyone in this regard,[10] and they came up with varieties of English which were similar, but not identical to the variety used by their teachers. They created from the English they heard a language that worked for them; they then added their own spin to it and molded it until it allowed them to express who they were, what they believed in, and what they valued. The language they devised allowed them to establish relationships with one another, and a community for mutual support.

In many of the places where I have encountered these varieties of English, the people

---

[9] There are actually many quite different varieties of Black Dialect, but they all developed in a similar fashion. And like all languages, each variety comprises, not just one register, but many. Linguistic studies of Black Dialect have frequently been based on just one or another of the registers of a particular variety, say, like the language spoken by adolescent members of street gangs, or the casual speech of young adults in the drug culture. Their speech is just about as representative of the community's language as you would expect the casual speech of any rebellious group of kids to be of theirs.

[10] Susan Ervin-Tripp (1974) documented the process by which English-speaking children learning French as a second language created French-sounding words when their communicative needs outstripped the words they knew in French.

who spoke them were second, third, or even fourth generation speakers of English. Their tribal languages were just cultural memories. If anyone spoke these languages, it was the oldest members of the community. The young people knew nothing more than a word or two, if that. But life went on in their communities. The young people might or might not have been participating in any of the traditional practices of their people — their tastes and interests seemed to run more along MTV lines. In their dress and demeanor, they looked pretty much as kids their age do everywhere — slouched, cool, and imperturbable in their shades and de rigeur baggy garb and footwear — but by their language, they let you know definitively that you were dealing with a unique group of young people.

Actually, my dealings in these communities have mostly been with the educators. And in their attitudes they are not all that different from teachers I meet in inner city schools that serve African-American children. The prevailing attitude toward the varieties of English spoken by native children, if it differs even slightly from standard English, is that it isn't a real language. What the children speak is deplored as a degenerate form of English, a patois, a pastiche of "this and that," having no structure, incapable of logic or of expressing even the simplest of thoughts. No wonder, I am told, these kids can't learn: They are alingual! And believing this, the teachers treat the children as if they are incapable of learning, and they don't attempt to teach materials that are sufficiently challenging to hold their interest in school. The teachers concentrate their efforts on teaching them standard English. Like the African-American children I mentioned earlier, the Native American children who speak these varieties of English also resist efforts to get them to change — and for the same reasons, I believe. Yes, these young people need to learn standard English, as anyone must, in order to do well in school. But by denying the validity of the language they speak, their teachers deny the validity of the children's experiences and their identities. And there is no more effective way to turn them off to school than by doing just that.

So where does this all lead? I want to go back to the statement made earlier in this chapter regarding the hard time American society has always had dealing with its diversity. As I said, despite our diversity, our society has never been tolerant about or accepting of differences. In our educational policies, we have always tried to do away with cultural and linguistic differences by getting children to abandon their native languages and adopt English as quickly as possible.

These policies have been quite effectively carried out in our schools — group after group, whether Native American or new Americans, have lost their ethnic languages, and have been converted into English speakers. Most of us, willingly or not, have become assimilated into the common culture to one degree or another. But it has not been without cost. Many people in this society do not feel whole. There are many who feel that they do not belong anywhere — not to any definable group, not to their families, not to American society. And the ranks of those who are intolerant of differences grow, even as the society grows more diverse. The cost — I believe has been a psychic one.

The question we must ask, as Americans, is: Why — how come — in a society that is so diverse in origins — we are so intolerant of differences? Why do we despise that which makes us unique — our own diversity? Why do we reject the very source of our strength and creativity? How is it that we — and I mean most of us in this society, having undergone the process of linguistic assimilation, having our native languages replaced by English, can now be so intolerant of non-English speaking newcomers who do not immediately abandon their languages in favor of English? How can native communities even, when faced with the question of whether or not to support bilingual education for their own children, argue that such programs are bad, they hold children back, and the schools should concentrate on English and forget about the native language? How can they agree to the adoption of programs in which children are taught English at ages 3 or 4, knowing that it will very likely displace the family language?

The reader needs no reminder that the U.S. English movement, the effort to establish English as the one and only language for public use (as if it weren't already) is going strong. While its proponents sometimes argue that in proposing that the U. S. Constitution be changed to make English the official language of the society, we would be doing no more than we already have done in adopting the bald eagle as the national bird, and *E Pluribus Unum* as our national motto. But that is disingenuous, of course. Although the bald eagle is our national bird, we do not prohibit other birds from flying in our air space, nor do we force seagulls and ravens to be bald eagles. And although E pluribus unum is our national motto, we do not put in jail anyone who decides to adopt instead "There is no such thing as a free lunch," as a personal motto.

The U.S. English movement would have us abandon the use of languages other than English in public affairs: Communities might not then use Cantonese or Navaho or Spanish on 911 emergency lines, use multilingual ballots so that American citizens who are more literate in a language other than English might vote intelligently, or teach children in Spanish or Yupik or Tlingit in a public school program.

I have tried hard to understand why we Americans do as we do, why we are what we are. How do people who are former immigrants themselves, who surely must have experienced discrimination after coming to the U.S., become ardent supporters of a movement like U. S. English?[11] How did they become so intolerant of newcomers to this society or be so hard on people who don't speak English perfectly? Did they, in becoming English monolinguals, take on the prejudices that made them give up their native languages? Why do we deny that part of us that makes us special, that gives us substance, that connects us with others? Why do we judge each other by what we are or are not? Listen to kids from immigrant backgrounds: "Hey FOB, go back to where you came from," Chinese-American children will say to newcomers who are not more than half-a-generation behind them (FOB means "Fresh-Off-the-Boat" in the parlance of ABCs or "American-Born-Chinese"; it is the nastiest thing someone can say to a compatriot).

---

[11] A major spokesperson for U. S. English, Gerda Bekalis, is herself an immigrant from Hungary. Linda Chavez, a one time officer of U. S. English, is an immigrant from Cuba. The late S. I. Hayakawa, one of the founders of U. S. English, was himself either an immigrant or the son of Japanese immigrants. In California, where a substantial proportion of the population are first, second, and third generation Americans, a state with the greatest number of immigrants, the voters approved Proposition 63, the English Only amendment in 1963 by a 3 to 1 margin. In 1994, they approved Proposition 187, an amendment that would deny all public services to undocumented immigrants.

We judge each other by appearances, dress, by the language we speak: "How can you be an Indian — you don't talk Indian," or, "you don't look Indian," or, "You call that English? That's nothing but slang, street talk," and on and on.

I think the reason we do these things to each other must be because many of us have been deeply wounded in the process of becoming Americans. A Chinese immigrant high school student described the experiences that are shaping her notions about how Americans judge and treat newcomers in the following way:

> The kind of thing that American people laugh at immigrants are their ways of talking in English. Because like Chinese people talk different ways of English that Americans couldn't understand. They make fun of the English and laugh at them. They pretend to say the same words that Chinese people say and make it funny and tell other Americans and laugh together at us. Immigrant peoples are very embarrassed in front of American people. It is because of the English.[12]   (Olsen, 1995, p.)

It should be noted that the Americans of whom she is speaking are, for the most part, themselves the children of immigrants or former immigrants. One hopes this student will become an American without adopting all of the behaviors by which she herself was socialized as an American. Newcomers are oppressed, wounded, diminished in the process of becoming Americans — and so too often we oppress, hurt and cut one another down. In order for this society as a whole to become a better, healthier, stronger one, it has got to do something about damage that has been done to people. There has got to be a healing process. Such a process has got to take place in communities — but it must start with individuals and families. Those of us who have lost our languages and cultures must recognize that in fact we are not cut loose from our moorings: Human culture goes on, and if we think about what we are doing as constantly recreating culture as we live our lives, if we think about how we affect others by how we relate to them, if we think about our place and responsibilities to the others in our communities, if we show tolerance in accepting differences among our fellows — we can begin to create a culture for this society that will be a whole lot more humane than the one we have right now. The place to begin is here, now, in us. It begins with tolerance and acceptance of ourselves, our fellows, and our communities. It can only lead to a healthier and stronger society.

---

[12] This text comes from Laurie Olsen's (1995) ethnographic study of the social and political forces operating on immigrant students and their teachers in an urban high school. It was written by one of the students in her study.

REFERENCES

Atkins, J. D. C. (1992). *Annual report of the Federal Commissioner of Indian Affairs.* Excerpted in J. Crawford (Ed.), *Language loyalties: A source book on the official English controversy.* Chicago: The University of Chicago Press. (Original work published 1887)

Ervin (Tripp), S. M., & Osgood, C. E. (1954). Second language learning and bilingualism. *Journal of Abnormal and Social Psychology, 49,* 139-146.

Ervin-Tripp, S. M. (1967). An Issei learns English. *Journal of Social Issues, 23,* 78-90.

Ervin-Tripp, S. M. (1972). Children's sociolinguistic competence and dialect diversity. In I. J. Gordon (Ed.), *Early childhood education.* Chicago: University of Chicago Press.

Ervin-Tripp, S. M. (1974). Is second language learning like the first? *TESOL Quarterly, 8,* 111-127.

Ervin-Tripp, S. M. (1986). Activity types and the structure of talk in second language learning. In J. A. Fishman, et al. (Eds.), *The Fergusonian impact, Vol. I: From phonology to society.* Berlin: Mouton de Gruyter.

Hinton, L. (1994). Rebuilding the fire. In *Flutes of fire: Essays on California Indian languages.* Berkeley, CA: Heyday Books.

Krauss, M. (1992). The world's languages in crisis [one of several essays on endangered languages] *Language, 68,* 4-10.

Lone Wolf, Blackfoot. (1991). School wasn't for me. In P. Nabokov (Ed.), *Native American testimony: A chronicle of Indian/White relations from prophecy to present, 1492-1992.* New York: Viking/Penguin. (Original work published 1972)

Olsen, L. (1995). *From nation to race: The Americanization of immigrants in the high school of the 1990s.* Unpublished doctoral dissertation, University of California, Berkeley.

Sun Elk, Taos Pueblo. (1939). He is not one of us. In P. Nabokov (Ed.), *Native American testimony: A chronicle of Indian/White relations from prophecy to present, 1492-1992.* New York: Viking/Penguin. (Original work published 1939)

Wong Fillmore, L. (1991). When learning a second language means losing the first. *Early Childhood Research Quarterly, 6,* 323-346.

PART SIX:
DISCOURSE IN INSTITUTIONAL SETTINGS

26 THE THERAPEUTIC ENCOUNTER: NEUTRAL CONTEXT OR SOCIAL CONSTRUCTION?[1]

Julie Gerhardt
California Institute of Integral Studies

Charles Stinson
University of California, San Francisco

How better to pay tribute to Susan Ervin-Tripp than to examine a context heretofore considered recalcitrant to contextual analysis (but see Gaik, 1992; Labov & Fanshell, 1977; Lakoff, 1990, for some exceptions to this claim) and suggest that even here interactive, socially-constructive processes are at play? Thus, in this chapter, we briefly examine some features of the context of the psychoanalytically-based therapeutic encounter where the myth of the "neutral context" — in which the therapist is said to function as a "blank screen" or "mirror" — is finally having its day and suggest that far from being neutral, the context is in fact organized around a set of value-laden, ideological assumptions about the nature of mental health in general, and the role of the twin processes of self-investigation and conceptual understanding in particular, as ameliorative processes. In other words, the therapist's belief in the role of "insight" (or "secondary process") as curative functions to establish a very select context which is designed to lead the client to a conceptual understanding of her own unconscious subjective experience.

In reconstructing the source of this deeply entrenched conceptual bias, which, according to Lear (1990) reaches its apogee in Freud, Lear (1990) locates its origin in Platonic philosophy by reminding us, in anecdotal form, of the aspersions Socrates cast against the renown poets of his day due to their metaphoric, experiential mode of knowledge in contrast to the explicit, conceptual mode favored by philosophers. As Lear points out, "for Socrates, understanding and wisdom require that one be able to express one's thoughts in *conceptualized* explanations [*emphasis* added]" rather than poetic metaphors, and he urges us to consider whether psychoanalysis shares this very same "Socratic

[1] The research upon which this paper is based was, in part, supported by The Program on Conscious and Unconscious Mental Processes directed by Mardi Horowitz, MD and Charles Stinson, MD and funded by the John D. and Catherine T. MacArthur Foundation. A more elaborate version of this chapter will appear as "'I don't know': Resistance or Groping for Words? The Construction of Analytic Subjectivity' (Gerhardt & Stinson, in press).

prejudice" and, as such, functions as one of the quintessential expressions of the conceptual turn inherent to Western thought. To no one's surprise, our claim is, along with Lear's, that it does, and thus it follows that the task of explicating the context of this rather curious enterprise must take the form of an inquiry into how this rather tendentious trope toward self-scrutiny and self-reflection which purports to result in a conceptual understanding of the self is brought about. Moreover, only by analyzing the context in such terms can the linguistic goal of determining the relation between the use of particular forms and the discursive purposes they serve in particular contexts of use be adequately addressed.

This chapter builds on an assumption about the nature of psychoanalytically oriented psychotherapy as a mode of therapy which is based on the exploration of the client's subjectivity and the consequent attempt to foster the self-reflexive stance of what we call "analytic subjectivity." The primary agenda consists in the mutual attempt by the therapist and client to understand the client's subjective experience. Though given the current Zeitgeist, this agenda tends to be carried out with reference to various psychoanalytically-based interpretive models (Pine, 1990), according to Loewald (1971), one assumption is "fundamental" and underlies all modes of psychoanalytic interpretation: In short, that "whatever transpires is personally motivated" — an assumption which directs the interpretation of the client's associative material in terms of its personal meaning and personal motivation.

Now, with this agenda in mind, the point we wish to make here is that in order to succeed, a particular **stance** on the client's part must be brought about: Namely, the client must come to adopt a self-reflexive stance in which one part of the self observes and reflects on other parts of the self. Indeed, the crucial feature of analytic work, and thus analytic subjectivity, is its **reflexivity**: The object of scrutiny is one's self. Based on this claim, the problem which is raised is how the client of a psychoanalytically based therapy comes to be constituted as an analytic subject who participates in the psychodynamic project, i.e., the self-reflexive quest for personal meanings. That is, how does the client come to scrutinize him- or herself in order to explore problematic emotional material and to construct new understandings of it? If we assume that such a stance is a cultural construction and not an ontological given and has come about through an array of historically based social practices such as those documented in Foucault's account of the "cultivation of the self" (1977, 1979, 1985, 1986), the question which is raised is how in any particular context — such as psychodynamic psychotherapy — attention to the self is brought about.

To address this issue requires that the blank screen model of the psychodynamic encounter be abandoned in favor of a more dialogic or "social constructivist" model in Hoffman's terms (1991). That is, rather than assume that the therapeutic environment functions as a neutral context in which the therapist adopts the role of mirror and merely reflects back the client's own conflicts expressed in the form of transferences, recent psychoanalytic theorizing recognizes the role of the therapist's participation in the intersubjective context. In other words, the therapist's own affective experience of the client is claimed to inevitably result in countertransference enactments, and, as such, serves as a major determinant of the client's subjective experience, and ultimately the transference (Aron, 1991; Heimann, 1950; Jacobs, 1986; Renik, 1993; Tansey, 1992).

In the present chapter, however, we shall focus on another dimension of the psycho-dynamic context which also plays a role in organizing the therapeutic interaction: Name-ly, the particular set of **analytically-based theoretical assumptions** which constitute the therapist's professionally-grounded preconceptions about the nature of psychological distress. Our claim is that such preconceptions play a role in structuring the therapist's particular mode of intervention which contributes to the establishment of an analytic frame so that these interventions ultimately play a role in organizing the client's experi-ence and mode of participation in the therapy. We conceive of these preconceptions as **demand characteristics** of an analytically based therapy in that they determine how the analytic work is carried out. For example, the belief in the role of the unconscious in bringing about psychological distress guides the therapist to intervene in such a way that will induce the client to go beyond her initial consciously formulated account to consider alternate, possibly disavowed meanings. From this perspective, even the standard exploratory interventions — "What comes to mind?" or "Do you have any thoughts or feelings about that?" — as well as the more individually fashioned interpretive interven-tions are not innocent probes or mirrors as the scientism in the field would have it. Rather, such interventions need to be viewed as **analytic techniques** which let the client know what is expected of her, and thus function to bring about the client's stance of self-inspection and self-investigation. Put more generally, such analytically-informed inter-ventions need to be viewed as modes of discursive production in Foucault's sense (1972, 1979) — whose effect is to establish a particular stance on the client's part, i.e., a particular mode of self-scrutiny (which we are calling "analytic subjectivity") which is embodied in a particular mode of discourse.

In a previous paper, it was suggested that the mode of discourse which the psychody-namic encounter gives rise to is a form of "account-giving," specifically, "accounts of the self" (Gerhardt & Stinson, 1994). This proposal was intended as a further development of the claim that the life-history material which emerges in psychotherapy is narrative in nature (Schafer, 1983; Spence, 1982, 1987). Our point was that even if we accept the idea of the irreducibly narrative character of client talk as a way of acknowledging its problematic relation to "historical truth" (Spence, 1982), the inclusion of this mode of discourse in the genre of narration does not do justice to the unique type of intention which organizes the communication in this context. Instead, based on Loewald's (1971) claim about the centrality of "personal motivation" as an interpretive principle in analytic therapy, the argument was made that in virtue of this very distinct theoretically-based interpretive bias — which tends to portray psychic distress as the outcome of predomi-nantly endogenous factors (see Greenberg, 1991, for a critique) — over time, material of a particular sort will tend to be produced — material which in some way references the self. As such, a distinct mode of talk develops which revolves around self-expression, self-evaluation, and self-assessment such that even if narrative material is introduced, it functions as part of a self-account — often as a mode of illustration.

In contrast, here we focus on a different dimension of the therapeutic encounter: Namely, the construction of what we call the stance of "analytic subjectivity." To address the development of this stance fully would require a head-on analysis of the therapeutic context as a determining context in its own right, and would include both the "distal" and the "proximate" context in Schegloff's (1992) sense; that is, both (a) the role of therapy as an historically-grounded institution about which members have constructed a set of beliefs in terms of its efficacy as a mental health service (Foucault, 1965, 1973; R. Lakoff, 1990; Masson, 1988; Reiff, 1968; Oremland, 1991), as well as (b) the role of the local interactional context (the therapist's interventions, etc.) in bringing about a particular mode of participation on the client's part. For example, it might be shown how the seemingly neutral intervention — "Tell me what you were thinking and feeling" — after a client's account functions strategically as a means of creating an interactively grounded associative space for the client to get in touch with any associated thought and feeling content. As such, the metamessage which is conveyed is that there is more to the story than meets the eye, and that this latent material may bear on the client's puzzlement or distress. The point is that even such a seemingly benign intervention as this needs to be conceived as a particular "technique of the self" (Foucault, 1986), since it draws the client into an actively self-inspecting stance and as such shapes the client's understanding of her distress as a problem of the self.

In this paper, however, rather than focus on the determining role of the therapist's interventions per se, we will take a step back and consider a set of *four assumptions* which, we claim, are inherent to the psychoanalytically based enterprise, and as such, provide part of the rationale for the interventions themselves. As noted above, we think of these assumptions as *demand characteristics* of the therapeutic encounter in that they play a formative role in structuring the therapist's distinct mode of intervention as well as the client's response. Though at first blush, the particular assumptions appear too benign to cause any trouble, it is argued that far from constituting a neutral set of discursive assumptions, they are actually quite tendentious and thus play a formative role in constituting the psychodynamic encounter as an encounter of a particular kind, i.e., one which promotes the analytic stance of self-reflection. Indeed, our claim is that it is precisely on the basis of these assumptions — and *not* on the amount of primary process material which obtains (Reynes, Martindale, & Dahl, 1984) — that therapeutic discourse differs from other genres of speech: For example, the genre of "troubles talk" among friends (Jefferson, 1988), the genre of "painful self-disclosure" between acquaintances (Coupland, Coupland, Giles, Henwood, & Wiemann, 1988), the "conversation of intimate friendship" (R. Lakoff, 1990), etc. It follows that only by understanding these assumptions and the way they operate as constraints on the meaning-making process will certain features of the talk which occurs therein begin to make sense.

Then, after presenting these assumptions, we turn to some examples from a particular client's discourse from a single case psychotherapy study and attempt to show how certain features of her speech play a reciprocal role in helping to carry out the therapeutic task as defined by these assumptions. Specifically, we will focus on the client's use of the two discourse markers — *I mean* and *I don't know* — and suggest that they function as part of the client's involvement in the reflexive task of self-investigation — what we are calling "analytic subjectivity." In other words, the client's use of *I mean* and *I don't know* in the therapeutic encounter functions as a means of responding to and wrestling with the demand characteristics in terms of which analytic subjectivity is brought about.

FOUR ASSUMPTIONS-QUA-DEMAND CHARACTERISTICS OF OF PSYCHOANALYTIC PSYCHOTHERAPY

1. It is better to know than not to know

Corollary: Knowing involves conceptual knowledge captured in the container metaphor
of putting one's thoughts/feelings into words

This assumption is stated quite clearly in a recent book by Oremland in which he distinguishes psychoanalytically oriented psychotherapy from more "supportive" or "interactive" variants. According to Oremland, "that it is better to know is the singular value of the psychoanalytic orientation" (1991, p. 12) from which he concludes that the aim of an interpretation is "to add explicit knowledge" — an aim which is contrasted with that of a more "interactive intervention" whose aim is "largely experiential" (p. 10). In other words, the crucial feature of the psychoanalytic approach is the belief in the primacy of knowledge as a means of relieving psychic distress. Interpretations attempt to provide such knowledge by translating content theretofore unclear by means of a conceptual statement. To emphasize the conceptual orientation of psychoanalysis over more supportive approaches, Oremland suggests that we think of it as primarily "investigative" rather than "therapeutic." It is for this reason that the psychoanalytic orientation is said to offer "insight" or "understanding" over, or as a means of, "cure."

One of the first attempts to spell out this bias toward conceptual knowledge over behavioral enactment can be found in Freud's original paper "Recollection, Repetition, and Working Through" (1914). In this essay, Freud explicitly contrasts the conceptual act of remembering with the behavioral act of repetition, and claims that the latter functions as a defense against the former. Indeed, transference itself is conceived of as "only a bit of repetition" since it functions by "replacing the impulse to remember" (p. 161) with a behavioral enactment. Based on this characterization of the dynamic relation between repetition and recollection, Freud maintains that the goal of analysis is "recollection in the old style, reproduction in the mind" (p. 163) by which is meant converting symptomatic acts into verbal expression which provides the basis for increased self-knowledge.

In short, analytically based psychotherapy rests on the premise, "It is better to know than not to know" where knowing involves the translation of the subject's thoughts, feelings, and actions into explicit, conceptual statements. Our point is that this belief plays a fundamental role in organizing the therapist's particular mode of intervention — which for present purposes can be glossed as aiming to "Make the unconscious conscious" — and thus ultimately, the client's mode of response.

2. It is important to observe and reflect on oneself

Corollary: A virtual separation needs to be established in the client's self between an
observing part and an experiencing part, and the observing part needs to

reflect on the experiencing part

Analytically-oriented psychotherapy is based on a multiple selves or divided self model in which the separation of the self into subject and object is viewed as central: The self-as-observer needs to separate from the stream-of-consciousness mode characteristic of the self-as-experiencer and reflect on the latter's mode of functioning. In other words, to even engage in a psychodynamic therapy requires that the client be able to detach from her experiencing self and assume the roles of observer and narrator. This requirement is due to the fact that typically, when a person seeks therapy, something has gone awry in that person's life which she wants to understand and/or change. What is involved is the forging of a separation between different parts of the self whereby the observing part is induced to grasp an aspect of its own activity: That is, to think about, question, evaluate and understand the purpose, motivation, etc. of certain problematic forms of behavior. Our claim is that the forging of such a separation between different parts of the self is brought about by the therapist's distinct mode of intervention.

From a literary perspective, according to Freccero (1986), the structure of a divided self is inherent to all autobiographical accounts, i.e., all representations of the self from a retrospective stance require a separation between the self-as-narrator from the self-as-character. As Freccero puts it, the separation of the self into narrator and character "springs from the formal exigencies of telling one's life story" (1986, p. 16), i.e., fashioning an historical portrait of the self. Accordingly, Freccero suggests that even the narrative of conversion found in Augustine's *Confessions* — from sinner to saint — needs to be viewed as an instance of, and metaphor for, the transformation of the self, represented in this genre in a theological guise. Our claim is that therapeutic discourse is another type of autobiographic activity in which one part of the self not only narrates other parts of the self, but observes, reflects on, evaluates, criticizes, censors and reveals other parts of the self for the purpose of achieving some kind of self-transformation.

In fact, the self-as-observer separate from the self-as-experiencer forms the basis for certain technical recommendations which draw upon the metaphor of a "divided self" — or a "dissociation within the ego" as Sterba (1934) would have it. For example, proposals concerning the "therapeutic alliance" (Zetzel, 1956) or "working alliance" (Greenson, 1967) are based on a model of a divided self in which the observing self is assumed to separate from the observed self and form an identification with the therapist. Note that both of these technical formulations presupposes an ego [self] capable of assuming the heterogeneous roles of observer and observed — a phenomenon which, according to Sterba, is brought about by means of the therapist's transference interpretations.

3. There is more to the story than meets the eye

Corollary: Certain forms of expression manifest different levels of meaning: A primary meaning and a more indirectly conveyed symbolic meaning; primary meanings function as a means of both revealing and concealing latent secondary meanings

According to Spence (1987), psychoanalysis rests on the assumption that things are not what they seem, and thus surface meanings are considered suspect in favor of more abiding latent meanings. From this perspective, the client's account of his or her experience is assumed to represent something other (more) than what is said: Specifically, surface meanings are viewed as derivative of some piece of the client's unconscious. It follows that the therapist needs to cultivate a distinct mode of listening which translates surface into depth.

Moreover, though the assumption of there being more to the story than meets the eye typically rests on a surface-depth model in which the mind is conceived as a layered set of representations which require spade work, it need not. An alternate formulation is offered by Ricoeur (1970) who argues that the psychoanalytic program is situated with respect to the problem of "double meaning" by which is meant the designation of an indirect meaning in and through a direct meaning. For Ricoeur, the dream serves as a prototype for all disguised expressions of desire. Accordingly, the manifest level of behavior is viewed as the locus of a complex set of significations in which one meaning is both given by and hidden in another meaning. "To mean something other than what is said" is, according to Ricoeur, the essence of the psychoanalytic problematic and as such, provides the basis for the analyst's particular mode of depth interpretation.

In addition, Ricoeur observes that psychoanalysis actually differs from other modes of interpretation in that the manifest level of meaning is viewed not only as an expression of the latent, but also as a "motivated distortion." In other words, surface meaning is viewed as a defensive distortion of a more basic level of meaning. It follows that the purpose of an interpretation is not just to penetrate the surface, but to expose it as a tactical cover-up. The problematic Ricoeur outlines gives rise to a unique mode of inquiry which he calls the "hermeneutics of suspicion" which takes to the extreme the premise "There is more to the story than meets the eye."

For present purposes, what is important to recognize is how the assumption of surplus meaning (i.e., there being other levels of meaning than the conscious reflective level) has almost axiomatic status in psychodynamic thinking, and as such, forms the basis for many of the therapist's interventions which aim to induce the client to go beyond her consciously fashioned account.

4. It is necessary to get to the level of personal motivation or personal significance when interpreting problematic forms of behavior

Corollary: The level or kind of meaning which is important to interpret is that which has been referred to as the level of "personal motivation" by Loewald (1971). The level of "personal motivation" not only includes the personal meaning of a particular action or event, but also the client's investment in viewing herself in particular ways.

According to Loewald, psychoanalytic interpretation can be distinguished from other interpretive endeavors in terms of the basic or, in his words, "fundamental" assumption upon which it is based: Namely, that "whatever transpires is personally motivated" (1971, p. 103). This means that both the content of the client's material as well as its occurrence at a particular moment in the hour have a personal meaning for the client. In Loewald's terms, "what the patient reveals is motivated [from] within and not simply [a] chance occurrence or merely determined by forces external to him" (p. 103). Loewald illustrates his claim with the case of a woman who feels plagued by a compulsion to murder her child — a compulsion which is initially viewed as a strange, impersonal force, but which comes to be understood as a means for the gratification of hostile feelings harbored toward her spouse, and ultimately, her father. In Loewald's words, "what was an impersonal, unrelated compelling force becomes inserted in a linkage of personal motivation" (p. 105). In this context, "personal motivation" refers to a particular unconscious fantasy of a wishful aggressive impulse allegedly being gratified by the otherwise opaque symptom.

In a somewhat similar vein, Schafer has suggested that "in the course of analysis, the analysand comes to construct narratives of personal agency ever more readily, independently, convincingly, and securely. The important questions to be answered . . . concern personal agency, and the important answers reallocate the attributions of activity and passivity" (1983, p. 226). Note that whereas Loewald's interpretive principle is stated in terms of the client's "personal motivation" or "personal meaning," Schafer's focuses on the client's "agency" in bringing about the situations which distress her. Whatever variant one chooses, the point is that the principles of interpretation of analytically oriented psychotherapy are *not* neutral, but revolve around a core set of personal or subject-centered meanings. Our claim is that these core meanings structure the therapist's particular mode of intervention, and as such, function as implicit contextual demands which play a role in organizing the client's experience and mode of response.

In terms of the specific content covered by the principle of "personal motivation," interpretations tend to be pitched at the level of wishes and impulses, i.e., endogenous factors (see Greenberg, 1991, for an explication and critique). More specifically, interpretations of unconscious content are typically made in terms of unconscious affects and impulses. It is assumed that certain affects and impulses have been stifled from expression and as such, have taken up residence within the unconscious. Because, however, out of sight does not mean out of mind, the repressed material persists though remaining unacknowledged, and thus constitutes the source of the client's distress.

The point is that the psychoanalytic paradigm rests on a very distinct interpretive bias whereby "personal motivation" in Loewald's terms translates into the internal vicissitudes of fantasy and desire. This bias is the basis for a standard set of interpretive assumptions which are projected onto the client's material by means of the therapist's distinct mode of intervention. (For an alternate set of interpretive possibilities see Greenberg, 1991). One outcome of a successful therapy is that the client's narrative accounts come to be retold — first by the therapist, then by the client — by incorporating aspects of the psychodynamic themes of personal meaning and endogenous motivation (Schafer, 1992).

To summarize the first part of our paper, recently there has been a trend toward more interactive and dialogically conceived accounts of the psychoanalytically based therapeutic encounter which recognizes the reciprocal influence between therapist and client — even if that influence is asymmetrical in nature (Aron, 1991). We have attempted to join forces with this paradigm shift by examining a set of implicit assumptions which analytically trained therapists share which function to structure their mode of listening and evaluation, as well as their mode of intervention. As such, our claim is that these assumptions play a role in shaping the client's experience and mode of response.

At this point, however, rather than continue to examine the particularities of the therapeutic context or therapeutic frame, we turn, very briefly, to particular events embedded within this frame. That is, we shall consider an example of a particular client's use of the markers *I mean* and *I don't know* from a single psychotherapy session and suggest that, the literal meaning of these markers notwithstanding, they function as attempts to grapple with the demand characteristics listed above: That is, "It is better to know than not to know"; "It is important to observe and reflect on oneself"; "There is more to the story than meets the eye"; and "It is necessary to get to the personal significance of the matter." Indeed, we suggest that the entire system of markers referred to as "discourse markers" by Schiffrin (1987) plays a special role in analytic therapy: Namely, they function to engage in, and thus help to bring about, the particular self-inspecting/self-reflective stance upon which analytic therapy is based. A similar claim is made for the use of irrealis modality in therapy by Gaik (1992).

The client, whom we will refer to as P, is a woman in her early 40s who responded to a public notice seeking volunteers for a research and therapy study on "unresolved grief."[2] Though P's husband had died in a traumatic accident about a year and a half before she presented herself to the research and therapy program, P felt that she was not recovering from her loss. P described herself as being very happily married to James, her deceased husband, whose sudden and violent death stunned her. This resulted in a chaotic experience of alternating states of either intrusion (intrusive, dysphoric thoughts and images of James) or avoidance (numbness and denial). P came to therapy after a few months of dating Sydney, a kind and stable man, at the point when their relationship had begun to deepen. While her intimacy with Sydney was comforting, it also made her feel guilty and anxious, especially when she thought of herself as the devoted wife of James. Thus, P tended to avoid talking about her relationships, shifting her attention to the travails of daily life. P's continual avoidance of these emotion-laden topics, however, disrupted the working-through process of mourning and contributed to her intense anxiety. (See Horowitz, et al., 1991, for an analysis of this case according to Horowitz's theory of pathological grief; also Horowitz, 1990).

The data to be examined consist of the use of the markers *I mean* and *I don't know* during P's twelfth therapy session. This particular session was selected since it appears to contain significant breakthroughs. Both *I mean* and *I don't know* can be considered "discourse markers" by Schiffrin's criteria, i.e., "sequentially dependent elements which bracket units of talk" (1987, p. 31) and thereby provide "contextual coordinates for ongoing talk" (1987, p. 41). As situated forms, discourse markers depend on and help to realize certain meanings in the discourse situation in terms of how the content is to be understood. Based on the characterization of the therapeutic context presented above, we suggest that in order to account for most of the occurrences of these two markers in an analytic therapy, they need to be viewed as particular devices which **lock into** the assumptions-qua-demand characteristics of the context. In other words, the function of

---

[2] The data for the present research are taken from a larger program of research on the nature of grief reactions directed by Mardi Horowitz, MD and Charles Stinson, MD.

these markers in therapeutic discourse is to help bring about the analytic stance of self-reflection and self-investigation which is the essence of the analytic orientation. The pragmatic value of these markers is such that the context not only pulls for their use and places constraints on their meaning, but they also can be viewed as "contextualization cues" in Gumperz's (1982) sense, in that they signal the client's adoption of the self-reflexive analytic stance.

I mean

According to Schiffrin (1987), *I mean* is used when the speaker orients to her prior talk and proposes a modification or reformulation of what she has just said. Hence, *I mean* functions as a metalinguistic device whose focus is talk itself and not some state of affairs in the world. Due to the self-reflexive stance inherent in the use of *I mean*, we suggest that this marker lends itself well to the analytic task of self-reflection and self-investigation, and as such, when used in the therapeutic context, will be pressed into service for this self-analytic purpose.

Appendix 1 presents a transcript of the first few minutes of P's twelfth therapy session. Names and other identifying information have been altered, and thus the client is referred to as P, her deceased husband as James, and her current significant other as Sydney. Unit #15 contains the first occurrence of *I mean* in session 12. Prior to its use, P begins the session by describing the trajectory of her emotional states over the week: "anxiety attack," "going to go out of my mind," "chaotic," "a wreck," "sick," etc. While P announces her decision to marry Sydney, no connection is made between her decision and her apparent distress. Instead, in units #1 through 14, P merely *expresses* or *reports* her distress.

By contrast, in units #15 and #16, *I mean* is used as a means of taking up a different stance to her distress: one of *self-reflection* and *evaluation.* That is, P begins to consider the reasons for her distress. Though she is not able to figure herself out ("I don't know why I'm so distraught"), the point is that the problem is made explicit for the first time (the first time in her therapy) and is done so through the use of the metalinguistic marker *I mean.* For present purposes, what is important to observe is that the *I mean* utterances are used not only to organize a shift in narrative perspective — from reporting to evaluating — but also to organize a shift within the self. It is as if P steps up to a different level and adopts an observational stance to begin to reflect on her own experiential states. In other words, when *I mean* is used, P appears to step out of the experiential self mode she initially presents with and assumes the role of the reflective/evaluative subject who begins to consider the reasons for her own distress. (See G. Lakoff, 1992, on the distinction between "self" vs. "subject").

Moreover, note how both occurrences of *I mean* preface utterances which convey significant evaluative material on P's part, namely, her conflict about marrying Sydney. In unit #15, while the occurrence of *I mean* suggests that P is oriented to her prior talk and intends to elaborate it in a meaningful way, the subsequent occurrence of *I don't know why* suggests that P quickly becomes defensive at the moment of self-revelation and thus uses this marker as a means of warding off self-knowledge. Hence, P's conflict is manifest in this on-line production of multiple and contradictory voices. Similarly, note the marked syntactic construction which *I mean* introduces in unit #16 (*I mean it was not like . . .*) which also expresses P's conflict about marrying Sydney. Moreover, the utterance is highly "presuppositional" in Givón's (1982) sense. That is, for the utterance even to make sense, the corresponding affirmative is implied: That is, P does have to decide whether or not she is free to marry Sydney. And indeed, as we learn in the course of the hour, P is actually quite conflicted about whether she is free to marry Sydney. Though up until this point in her therapy, P has presented her relationship with her deceased husband James as the most perfect, most ideal relationship, later in this session she suddenly expresses "guilt" that her love for Sydney may be actually greater than her love was for James. In her own words: "I even feel a little guilty because I think maybe I love Sydney more than I did James — and that makes me feel horrible . . . I feel kind of unfaithful." According to various theories of unresolved grief (Parkes & Weiss, 1983), the harboring of such guilt based on ambivalence and conflicted feelings toward the deceased predisposes the individual to remain unconsciously tied to the deceased and thus unable to move forward.

Our point is that the *I mean* marker can be viewed as a naturally occurring device which is deployed in this context to respond to the inducements or pressure, so to speak, of the implicit injunctions listed above ("It is better to know," "It is important to observe and reflect on oneself," "There's more to the story than meets the eye," and "It's necessary to get to the level of personal meaning"). As such, the marker is used by P as a means of adopting a self-reflective stance toward her own emotional states. As a result, what we observe is that the *I mean* marker isn't used to preface just any old material, but material which results in significant self-disclosure. In fact, analysis of the entire therapy suggests that the various discourse markers tend to cluster at moments of greater self-disclosure on P's part (Stinson, et al., 1996). This is especially true for the use of *I don't know* — the marker to which we now turn.

I don't know

Turning to the use of the response marker *I don't know*, we shall suggest that its seemingly refractory appearance notwithstanding, it also functions as part of P's involvement in the reflexive task of self-investigation. That is, what appears to motivate P's extensive use of the *I don't know* marker in the therapeutic context is that the pressure, if you will, of the demand characteristics has begun to kick in, yet for various reasons, certain emotional/ideational content of P's subjective experience has not yet been formulated or has been disavowed. More specifically, the *I don't know* marker is used in such a way by P which suggests that it goes beyond its literal semantic-level meaning — as a clausal marker indicating the speaker's lack of knowledge about a particular state of affairs — and instead is most often used to convey a more specific contextually situated meaning. Based on the putative demand characteristics presented above, we propose that the therapeutic context provides an interpretive frame for the semantic meaning of *I don't know* to license the following pragmatic inference: "the presence of something absent." That is, whether it is used to express P's own reluctance to self-explore, or as an intimation of something yet "unknown" or not completely conceptualized, *I don't know* is used when the client senses and marks what Ogden (1992a) refers to as "presence in absence and absence in presence." In other words, the use of *I don't know* functions as a means of marking something as present yet unknown — almost like a variable in an algebra problem — which then generates a collaborative search for a solution.

Appendix II presents a segment from a later moment in P's twelfth therapy session. There are 11 instances of *I don't know* in this passage. Prior to the segment in Appendix II, recall that at the beginning of the hour, P describes herself as extremely anxious, reports that she has been so all week, and then announces that she and her significant other have decided to get married. She then expresses her confusion about the source of her distress since, she claims, she has known all along that she desires to marry Sydney. After P goes on to give an example of the extremity of her distress during the week, stressing her puzzlement as to its source, T issues the standard exploratory injunction — "Tell me what you were thinking and feeling" — to induce P to reflect on her own inner processes and experiences. In response to T's request, P quickly changes the topic and reveals that she has had dysphoric, intrusive thoughts about her deceased husband James. However, she then quickly curtails this disclosure, thereby avoiding the anxiety it raises, and begins.to expatiate on the travails of everyday life. Finally, after characterizing a friend's reaction to her engagement as both "happy and sad," P concludes her narrative with an account of her own multifaceted reaction: "I think that's the way I feel about it, you know? Happy and sad." At this point, T attempts to induce P to explore her own feelings of sadness using the standard injunction to translate emotions into words (#207 at the start of Appendix II): "Well, I can see you feeling some of the sadness. Can you .. try to put it into words?"

What follows is an account of P's relationship with James which contrasts dramatically with the previous accounts heretofore given. That is, until session 12, P has presented different versions of what we might think of as "the perfect relationship narrative." The relationship with James was portrayed as ideal. For example, in session 1, the relationship is described as "the perfect picture" where "everything was perfect." In accord with this portrait, P elaborates, "All I knew was uh, you know, love and trust and commitment and devotion." Similarly, in session 4, P expresses her concern that her feelings for Sydney will never equal her feelings for James: "I'm just afraid I'd always compare, you know, any relationship to that one and it would fall short."

In view of the consistency of this portrait up to now, it is quite striking that in session 12, an alternate version of the relationship emerges. That is, in response to T's inquiry in #207, P expresses feelings of conflict due to the intensity of her feelings for Sydney, and consequent fear of betraying James. She states that it is "overwhelming" to think of being someone else's wife and the corresponding change in identity which is required. She then begins to focus on her feelings for Sydney: In short, she reports feeling "a little guilty" that she may actually love Sydney more than she ever loved James, adding that her preference for Sydney makes her feel "horrible" as it leads her to feel "kind of unfaithful" to James. Though the relationship with James is depicted as having been "very comfortable and happy," she now claims that even at the beginning it "was never anything intense or passionate or horribly exciting" as it now is with Sydney.

Though James is characterized as a "wonderful person," the relationship with Sydney "feels so much more intense" which makes P feel "a little guilty." Nevertheless, P reassures T that had James not died, she would have "been with him forever." By the end of the hour (the transcript for this segment is not included), P reveals that she "went through a period of really resenting" James since he had loved her more than she ever loved him "There was no question about James loving me. Um, I mean I always knew he loved me more than I loved him," and describes herself as having been quite "stricken" before the wedding, fearing "that [she] didn't love him quite enough." Despite her misgivings, since her father prevailed upon her to follow through with her wedding plans, she did so, and insists that during her marriage she "never had any regrets." However, in light of the intensity of her current feelings for Sydney, P acknowledges, somewhat sadly, that she "might have been right" back then: "You know, I might have not have loved him as much."

This segment of P's discourse qualifies as an episode of what has been called "painful self-disclosure" (Coupland, Coupland, Giles, Henwood, & Wiemann, 1988). Not only does P fashion a new, less appealing version of her relationship with James as less than perfect ("never anything intense or passionate"), but she also provides a negative assessment of herself (feeling "guilty") for having had such longstanding misgivings about James — especially, in contrast to her strong feelings in the present for Sydney. For our purposes, however, what is most striking about this segment is that accompanying P's painful self-disclosure is the *prolific* use of the disclaimer *I don't know*.

Now, at first blush, this use of *I don't know* merely seems to corroborate an observation of Freud's that "the content of a repressed image or idea can make its way into consciousness on condition that it is negated" (1925, p. 55). Under this interpretation, the negative marker is viewed as actually enabling the disclosing process. To explain this seeming paradox, Freud states that "with the help of the symbol of negation, thinking frees itself from the restrictions of repression and enriches itself with material that is indispensable for its proper functioning" (p. 55) meaning that through the act of negation, the erstwhile repressed content is sufficiently repudiated so as to be able to cross the repression barrier into conscious awareness.

The problem with this interpretation, however, is that the metaphor on which it is based — thought breaking free from the clutches of repression — rests on a binary or "linear model" (Ogden, 1992a) in which the negative marker is viewed as an index of the repressed, i.e., repressed content which is finally able to emerge into consciousness. According to this way of thinking, the negative marker functions as a kind of passport for the erstwhile repressed material to gain access to consciousness. The picture that emerges is one where heretofore hidden, repressed material, or an aspect of P's interior self, finally emerges. Within this "romanticist model" of the self (Gergen, 1991), the belief in a single truth — the deep interior self — is accepted a priori.

Instead, we suggest that this passage is better understood in terms of a dialectical model of the sort proposed by Ogden (1992a, 1992b). According to Ogden, the subject which is constructed through the psychoanalytic process is "dialectically constituted" meaning that the person's full subjectivity comes into being through "the dialectical interplay of consciousness and unconsciousness" (1992a, p. 517). That is, the distinct mode of subjectivity which develops is one which comes into emergence through a process in which both systems "create, preserve and negate the other; each stands in a dynamic ever-changing relationship to the other" (p. 517). In Ogden's view, Freud's formulations which bear on the subject are often obscured by his reliance on goal-directed, ego-centered linear models (e.g., from unconscious to conscious, pleasure principle to reality principle, primary process to secondary process, etc.) which lead to an essentialist construal of the subject (the ego) in terms of the dominance of rational, conscious thought processes. Instead, Ogden ventures a new, more subtle reading of Freud based on his belief in "the radical nature of the psychoanalytic project, i.e., the notion that the experiencing subject is simultaneously constituted and decentered from itself by means of the negating and preserving dialectical interplay of consciousness and unconsciousness" (p. 518).

The picture which emerges from Ogden's account is one which recognizes the possibility of variations in perspectives and thus allows for the coexistence of two (or more) disparate, even contradictory, forms of experience. In line with this relatively more, if you will, post-modern formulation, we suggest that the target occurrences of *I don't know* function as more than just negative operators whose purpose is to disguise the entry of the repressed into consciousness. Rather, the continued use of this device indicates *the on-line process of shifting between perspectives — and thus that work is being done on the self.* Indeed, our reason for referring to this type of use as "the groping use" is to counter the very tempting assumption that P's disclosure in this passage represents the final, heretofore hidden, truth about her relationship with James which should now replace the earlier versions. Instead, according to the reading being put forth here, the use of *I don't know* in this passage functions as an index that P is in the process of shifting from one perspective to another where the different perspectives are not wholly commensurate, yet neither can they be viewed as false. Accordingly, the prolific use of *I don't know* gives the impression of a *struggle* within the self and suggests that P is dealing with conflicting states of consciousness: Or, in more textual terms, the movement between different voices of the self.

In support of this interpretation, note that the majority of occurrences of *I don't know* are not explicitly dialogic; they do not occur as direct responses to the therapist's inquiry as in the literal use of the clause. Nevertheless, despite the absence of overt dialogue, because of its association with a question–answer format, we suggest that the use of *I don't know* retains the status of a rejoinder whether or not the speaker is directly responding to the other. In Bakhtin's (1981) terms, the use of *I don't know* functions as a marker which is "internally dialogic" and thus is directed as a rejoinder to, or comment upon, something outside of its own use.

Based on this claim, the use of *I don't know* in this passage can be viewed as one side of an intrapsychic dialogue in which one part of P's self responds to material which is coming up in another part of P's self in response to the earlier request by T. Specifically, it is as if the prefabricated good-girl side of P (that part of P who remains loyal to the unconscious fantasy of being a devoted wife and obedient daughter) attempts to push away the questioning, open-to-a-new-experience side of P (that part of P who has been "resentful" toward James for not being the passionate man she wanted and who now finds delight in her relationship with Sydney as well as vindication for her misgivings about James ["I might have been right"]). In other words, once again, the use of *I don't know* presupposes a split within the self in which, using G. Lakoff's (1992) terminology, P-qua-reflective Subject evaluates the experiences of P-qua-experiencing Self and simultaneously invites and disavows the Self's experience.

Indeed, we suggest that at this point in her therapy, a definitive version (or resolution of the conflicting versions) of P's relationship with James is beyond her grasp. Therefore, not having worked out an integrated version of the relationship based on an interaction of the different perspectives — what Burke (1945) calls a "perspective of perspectives" — P adopts various procedures to move from one perspective to another, and hence speaks with a fragmented voice. Among these different procedures is the "groping use" of *I don't know*. This use of *I don't know* is based on the existence of unresolved conflict which is expressed at the level of discourse through the method of juxtaposition: That is, incommensurable versions which are juxtaposed, thus giving rise to sharp discontinuities in the representation of self and other. Based on theories of unresolved grief (Freud, 1917; Parkes & Weiss, 1983; Horowitz, 1990), P's mode of juxtaposing opposing contents without an attempt at synthesis can be viewed as an index of a lack of resolution of pre-existent (to the death) relationship conflict. Once a level of integration is attained, which involves accepting the different versions of her own emotional experience with James, the dialectic of disclosure and disavowal (enacted through the use of *I don't know*) can be replaced by a less fragmented mode of presentation. In other words, once a meta-narrative is developed based on the recognition of local/partial versions, the use of *I don't know* to signal "absent presence" will no longer be required.

In summary, in this passage, the use of *I don't know* functions as an index of the analytic stance — what we have been calling "analytic subjectivity." At this point, the focus of P's gaze is reflexive: P takes her self as the object of scrutiny and the character of her narrative. All non-literal uses of *I don't know* in the therapy transcripts follow suit: Namely, the use of *I don't know* is mediated by an awareness of self-as-subject and self-as-object. Moreover, our claim is that it is only because P has some prescient awareness of the four context defining demand characteristics presented above (i.e., that she is supposed to know [I], to reflect on and evaluate her own behaviors [II], to figure out their deeper meanings [III], and to figure out their personal meanings [IV]) that *I don't know* is used as a means of acknowledging these demands — each of which requires the separation of self-as-subject from self-as-object.

In conclusion, our interest in the context of analytic therapy stems from two sources. First, when we examine studies within the past two decades on the relation of language, or any other type of socially organized activity, to context in various social science disciplines, what we see is a trend toward more interactive and dialogically based descriptions of context, as well as more contextually situated descriptions of the target event being studied. Rather than view context as simply a static backdrop to a particular focal event, context is viewed as a frame which pulls for the occurrence of certain events and provides the resources for their appropriate interpretation (Goodwin & Duranti, 1992).

Hence, with respect to the problem of genre analysis — What sets psychoanalytically-based therapy (or therapeutic discourse) apart from other modes of therapy (or other modes of discourse)? — we have tried to approach this problem through an analysis of certain dimensions of the context. Thus, a set of four assumptions were proposed which are claimed to constitute the core of psychoanalytically oriented psychotherapy and as such play a role in structuring the types of interventions which are made, and thus ultimately, the client's mode of response. It should be mentioned that the assumptions listed are not intended to be exhaustive. For example, no mention is made of the various assumptions about the asymmetry of knowledge and power which play a role in structuring certain nonreciprocal aspects of the psychodynamic encounter (e.g., the fact that the therapist has authority in interpreting the meaning of the client's behavior, but not vice versa, see R. Lakoff, 1990). Instead, we have narrowed our focus to only those assumptions which are claimed to play a role in bringing about the self-reflexive analytic stance. It was proposed that based on these assumptions, the therapist intervenes in such a way which serves to induce the client to turn her attention to the vicissitudes of her subjective experience. Indeed, our interest in the discourse markers *I mean* and *I don't know* is precisely due to their putative role in helping to carry out the therapeutic task as defined by these assumptions. In other words, our claim has been that the client's use of *I mean* and *I don't know* functions as a means of acknowledging, responding to, and wrestling with the therapist's direct or indirect requests to examine her self.

REFERENCES

Aron, L. (1991). The patient's experience of the analyst's subjectivity. *Psychoanalytic Dialogues*, **1**, 29-51.

Bakhtin, M. (1981). Discourse in the novel. In M. Holquist (Ed.), *The dialogic imagination: Four essays by M. M. Bakhtin*. Austin: University of Texas Press.

Burke, K. (1945). *A grammar of motives*. New York: Prentice-Hall.

Coupland, N., Coupland, J., Giles, H., Henwood K., & Wiemann, J. (1988). Elderly self-disclosure: Interactional and intergroup issues. *Language and Communication*, **8**, 109-133.

Duranti, A., & Goodwin, C. (1992). *Rethinking context*. Cambridge, England: Cambridge University Press.

Foucault, M. (1965). *Madness and civilization: A history of insanity in the age of reason*. New York: Random House.

Foucault, M. (1972). *The archeology of knowledge*. New York: Harper Colophon.

Foucault, M. (1977). *Discipline and punish*. Harmodsworth, Penguin.

Foucault, M. (1979). *The history of sexuality, Vol. I: An introduction*. New York: Random House.

Freccero, J. (1986). Autobiography and narrative. In T. Heller, M. Sosna, & D. Wellbery (Eds.), *Reconstructing individualism: Autonomy, individuality and self in western thought*. Stanford: Stanford University Press.

Freud, S. (1914). Remembering, repeating and working through. *Standard Edition*, **12**, 145-156.

Freud, S. (1917). Mourning and melanchoia. *Standard Edition*, **14**, 237-258.

Gaik, R. (1992). Radio talk-show therapy. In A. Duranti, & C. Goodwin (Eds.), *Rethinking context*. Cambridge, England: Cambridge University Press.

Gergen, K. (1991). *The saturated self: Dilemmas of identity in contemporary life*. New York: Basic Books.

Gerhardt, J., & Stinson, C. (1994). The nature of therapeutic discourse: Accounts of the self. *Journal of Narrative and Life History*, **4**(3), 151-191.

Gerhardt, J., & Stinson, C. (in press). "I don't know": Resistance or groping for words? The construction of analytic subjectivity. *Psychoanalytic Dialogues*.

Greenberg, J. (1991). Countertransference and reality. *Psychoanalytic Dialogues*, **1**, 52-73.

Greenson, R. (1967). *The technique and practice of psychoanalysis.* New York: International Universities Press.

Gumperz, J. J. (1982). *Discourse strategies.* Cambridge, England: Cambridge University Press.

Heimann, P. (1950). On counter-transference. *International Journal of Psycho-Analysis*, **31**, 81-84.

Hoffman, I. (1991). Discussion: Toward a social-constructivist view of the psychoanalytic situation. *Psychoanalytic Dialogues*, **1**, 74-105.

Horowitz, M. (1990). A model of mourning: Changes in schemas of self and other. *Journal of American Psychoanalysis Association*, **38**(2), 297-324.

Horowitz, M., Stinson, C., Fridhandler, B., Milbrath, C., Redington, D., & Ewert, M. (in press). Pathological grief: An intensive case study. *Psychiatry*.

Jacobs, T. (1986). On countertransference enactments. *Journal of American Psychoanalytic Association*, **13**, 38-56.

Labov, W., & Fanshell, D. (1977). *Therapeutic discourse: Psychotherapy as conversation.* New York: Academic Press.

Lakoff, G. (1992). Multiple selves: The metaphoric models of the self inherent in our conceptual system. Paper presented at the Conference of the Mellon Colloquium on the Self.

Lakoff, R. (1990). The talking cure. In R. Lakoff (Ed.), *Talking power: The politics of language in our lives.* New York: Basic Books.

Lear, J. (1990). *Love and its place in nature: A philosophical interpretation of freudian psychoanalysis.* New York: Farrar, Straus and Giroux.

Loewald, H. W. (1980). On motivation and instinct theory. In H. W. Loewald (Ed.), *Papers on Psychoanalysis* (pp. 102-137). New Haven: Yale University Press.

Masson, J. (1988). *Against therapy.* New York: Atheneum.

Ogden, T. (1992a). The dialectically constituted/decentered subject of psychoanalysis: I. The Freudian subject. *International Journal of Psychoanalysis*, **73**, 517-526.

Ogden, T. (1992b). The dialectically constituted/decentered subject of psychoanalysis: II. The contributions of Klein and Winnicott. *International Journal of Psychoanalysis*, **73**, 613-626.

Oremland, J. (1991). *Interpretation and interaction: Psychoanalysis or psychotherapy?* Hillsdale, NJ: The Analytic Press.

Parkes, C. M., & Weiss, R. S. (1983). *Recovery from bereavement.* New York: Basic Books.

Pine, F. (1990). *Drive, ego, object and self: A synthesis for clinical work.* New York: Basic Books.

Reiff, P. (1966). *The triumph of the therapeutic: Uses of faith after Freud.* Chicago: University of Chicago Press.

Renik, O. (1993). Countertransference enactment and the psychoanalytic process. In M. Horowitz, O. Kernberg, & E. Weinshel (Eds.), *Psychic Structure and Psychic Change* (pp. 137-160). Connecticut: International Universities Press.

Reynes, R., Martindale, C., & Dahl, H. (1984). Lexical differences between working and resistance session in psychoanalysis. *Journal of Clinical Psychology*, **40**, 733-737.

Ricoeur, P. (1970). *Freud and philosophy: An essay on interpretation.* New Haven: Yale University Press.

Schafer, R. (1983). *The analytic attitude.* New York: Basic Books.

Schegloff, E. (1992). In another context. In A. Duranti, & C. Goodwin (Eds.), *Rethinking context.* Cambridge, England: Cambridge University Press.

Schiffrin, D. (1987). *Discourse markers.* Cambridge, England: Cambridge University Press.

Spence, D. P. (1982). *Narrative truth and historical truth: Meaning and interpretation in psychoanalysis.* New York: Norton.

Spence, D. P. (1987). *The Freudian metaphor: Toward paradigm change in psychoanalysis.* New York: Norton.

Sterba, R. (1934). The fate of the ego in analytic therapy. *International Journal of Psycho-Analysis,* **15**, 117-126.

Stinson, C., Eells, T., Mergenthaler, E., Gerhardt, J., Horowitz, M., Milbrath, C. (1996). *Computer transcript measures of dysfluency and hedging: Correlated with information production and avoidance.* Unpublished manuscript.

Tansey, M. J. (1992). Psychoanalytic expertise. *Psychoanalytic Dialogues,* **2**, 305-316.

Zetzel, E. R. (1956). Current concepts of transference. *International Journal of Psycho-Analysis,* **37**, 369-376.

APPENDIX I

P: (1) I'm having an anxiety attack. (laugh)

T: (2) at this moment?

P: (3) oh — oh this whole morning. (4) God I feel like I was just going to go out of my mind. (5) actually for about twenty-four hours.

T: (6) mm

P: (7) it's just been chaotic. Um, Sydney and I have decided to get married. (3 second pause) and uh we decided this Saturday.

T: (9) uh-huh

P: (10) and I have been a wreck ever since.

T: (11) oh

P: (12) um Sunday I was absolutely, I — I was sick, I was so — such a wreck I was sick to my stomach the whole day.

T: (13) hm

P: (14) um I finally started calming down about it by Sunday evening. **I mean** I don't know why I'm so distraught about it. (16) **I mean** it was not like I had to make this decision but once I agreed, I was like panicked.

T: (17) yeah

P: (18) um I'm sort of starting to relax and you know get used to the idea a little but I'm still just — I don't know. (19) I came home Sunday night. (20) His mother is still here.

T: (21) uh-huh

APPENDIX II

T: (207) well I can see you feeling some of the sadness. (208) Can you -

P: (209) yeah (cry)

T: (210) try to put it into words?

P: (211) um, oh **I don't know**. it's real conflicting. (212) I mean I feel happy just because I do love Sydney terribly. (213) um and just sad that I'm going to be someone else's wife. (214) I mean it's just overwhelming to think I'm not going to be PQ anymore. (215) I'm not going to be, I mean I'm just — it's a tri- it's a big change. (216) it's kind of the way I felt when James died. I felt like my identity had changed drastically. (217) and now it's -

T: (218) mm-hm

P: (219) going to change again (cry).

T: (220) mm-hm

P: (221) and **I don't know**. somehow I feel like I'm getting a little lost in the shuffle. (222) (sigh) **I don't know**. and I just never I mean I never dreamed I'd be anybody else (223) (sigh) I even feel a little guilty because sometimes I think maybe I love Sydney more than I did James.

T: (224) mm-hm

P: (225) and that makes me feel horrible.

T: (226) why?

P: (227) why do I feel horrible?

T: (228) yeah

P: (229) **I don't know**. I feel kind of unfaithful.

T: (230) uh-huh

P: (231) um I never questioned my love for James when he was alive.

T: (232) yeah

P: (233) I mean it was just there. (234) but my feelings for Sydney seem **I don't know** more intense.

T: (235) mm-hm

P: (236) and uh **I don't know** — just it's different. (237) and it makes me wonder what it was. (238) **I don't know**, maybe you just love people differently. (239) I don't quite understand it but I know it feels different.

T: (240) yeah

P: (241) it's certainly, **I don't know**. it's somehow more exciting. (242) James and I were very comfortable and happy and —

T: (243) mm-hm

P: (244) um but and it was that way from the very beginning. I mean it was, you know **I don't know** we just sort of started dating and kind of, he grew on me. (245) and you know that was never anything terribly intense or passionate or horribly exciting.

T: (246) mm-hm

P: (247) I just loved him. (248) **I don't know**. I thought he was terribly you know he was a wonderful person. (249) but this feels so much more intense. (250) and it makes me feel a little guilty.

T: (251) mm-hm

P: (252) although I, you know if James hadn't been killed I would have I'm sure been with him forever.

T: (253) mm-hm (pause) but you kind of feel unfaithful in your heart?

P: (254) mm-hm (pause) yeah (pause) Sydney's mother was telling me that, of course she's terribly biased thinking her son is the best thing that ever walked the earth. (255) but you know she was saying how it was unfortunate that my husband had to be killed but this is the way obviously it was meant to be. (256) **I don't know**. it made me feel funny.

27 ON TEACHING LANGUAGE IN ITS SOCIOCULTURAL CONTEXT

John J. Gumperz
University of California, Berkeley

After many years when second language teaching specialists were primarily concerned with instructional technology, the question of introducing cultural content into second language instruction curricula has once more begun to receive a great deal of attention. A frequently heard argument is that, in today's global economy, where international organizations proliferate and multinational organizations have come to assume ever increasing importance, mere instrumental control of foreign languages is no longer enough. Increasingly, individuals who grew up in different parts of the world under historically and culturally quite distinct circumstances must work together and cooperate as equal partners in the same enterprises. It can readily be shown that (a) cooperating in a foreign language requires more than just knowledge of grammar and lexicon, and, (b) to the extent that cultures differ, communication tends to become more and more problematic (Gumperz, 1982). Thus interlocutors should have at least some understanding of their audience's cultural background to make themselves understood. Yet so far foreign language courses have made no systematic efforts to deal with this issue.

Language and Culture is one of a series of topics brought up in a special issue of *The Annals of the American Academy of Arts and Sciences*, which brings together a number of articles concerned with "strengthening our language teaching capacity to meet current national needs" (Lambert, 1987). Some of the program improvements proposed there have been criticized because, while they call for more attention to native-like verbal ability in the foreign language, they take an overly instrumental, technical approach to teaching and fail to take account of the real difficulties that language curricula encounter when faced with our pervasively monolingual ideology and the resultant ambivalence towards the immigrant languages in our midst. I agree with such criticisms. It is difficult to see how culturally sensitive foreign language teaching can flourish in an "English-only" atmosphere which, while paying lip service to tolerance and social equity decries the linguistic and cultural heritage of our immigrant past. Language teaching cannot be divorced from intrasocietal issues of linguistic diversity. But, assuming we accept this point and decide to incorporate culture into our foreign language curricula, what do we teach? With a very few exceptions, the literature on language pedagogy is of very little help here.

If we consider the innovations proposed in the Lambert volume, it becomes evident that, in spite of many shortcomings, discussion of purely linguistic matters such as grammar, lexicon and speech acts, and matters of pedagogical strategy are at least presented in sufficiently concrete detail to enable us to obtain some idea as to what it is that is to be taught. This is far from true about culture. What we find are a series of statements such as the following, taken from Larsen-Freeman's (1987) survey of innovations in language teaching. "The culture of the speakers is inextricably woven into the language" (Lambert, 1987, p. 56); "Culture is integrated with the language" (p. 58); "Culture is the everyday lifestyle of the people who speak the foreign language natively"(p. 63). If, as the first two citations suggest, culture is "in languages," how is it represented linguistically? How does it enter into our lifestyles? Is it through the content of what we say or is it reflected in linguistic form? How do we distinguish culturally shared from individual characteristics or from pan-human universals? Another contributor to the Lambert volume, Lange (1987), who writes on the language teaching curriculum, cites suggestions to the effect that "the cultural syllabus should contain elements that can be observed, examined and analyzed"; and that, "there are three or four possible approaches, one is the adoption of classification schemes of cultural information and behavior, another could be developed from those topics said to have particular educational value, from student interests or both." No additional details about either classification schemes or relevant topics are given. In a paper that deals explicitly with making language teaching culturally relevant, Lehman (Lambert, 1987, pp. 186ff.) leans heavily on the writings of linguist Eugene A. Nida, whom he quotes as classifying "problems of cultural equivalence across languages" under five rubrics: (1) ecology, (2) material culture, (3) social culture, (4) religious culture, (5) linguistic culture. Lehman describes variation in material culture in terms of lexical expressions for, among other things, "telling time," "meals," and the like. Social culture is said to be "so complex that the handbooks may be excused from attempting even an elementary presentation."

The best one can say for such statements is that they treat culture almost exclusively in programmatic terms. To the extent that it is discussed at all, culture becomes identified with descriptive information about lexical usage, ways of living (whatever that means), geographical environments, beliefs. customs, and an indeterminate array of other matters. No wonder that "social culture" is hard to fit into this perspective. What is completely left out of this debate is the linguistic anthropologists' suggestions that we approach culture in ways akin to the linguists' approach to grammar and treat it as a form of knowledge that, along with other factors, determines the way we react to and interpret what we see and hear. On this view we would learn about culture, not by classifying what people report about their own or others' beliefs, but primarily through discourse analysis that seeks to lay bare the mostly unstated, taken for granted and subconsciously internalized presuppositions that guide the way we interpret talk.

I would like to argue that it is this perspective on culture — as implicit knowledge we rely on to interact with others in daily life — that language teaching programs need to adopt or at least consider if they are to give learners access to the native's world. But before going on to illustrate what I mean, let me add some additional remarks concerning the notion of *cultural differences* and the distribution of cultural knowledge in human populations. In the pedagogical literature, the phrase "cultural differences" commonly refers to distinctions among geographically separate populations whose ways of living and viewing the world have been established and reinforced through years of historically specific experience. I do not need to argue that this is no longer the case. There is abundant evidence around us to show that the urban environments in which we live are by no means culturally uniform. We are all aware that our own formerly relatively homogeneous and largely monolingual European-based societies are well on their way to being transformed into systems resembling the multicultural environments known to us from the anthropological descriptions of Caribbean, Southeast Asian, or African societies. To quote just one set of demographic projections from California which are beginning to assume more and more importance in local educational planning: By the year 2000, linguistic minorities will outnumber monolingual English speakers among school populations so that more than fifty per cent of our students will have encountered more than one grammatical and cultural system as part of their home or peer group socialization experience.

What is true of industrialized environments is also true of previously isolated Third and Fourth World settings. As populations become integrated into national and world market systems, and English and other regional languages spread as media of education and official communication and as the influence and homogenization of radio, television, and other mass media increases, internal cultural diversity becomes a major issue. People adapt to such changes in sociocultural environments by adapting their lifestyles and acquiring new languages or new modes of discourse. Surface symbols of linguistic and cultural distinctness may disappear. But behavior becomes situationally differentiated and significant differences in underlying cultural assumptions may remain and give rise to serious, often undiagnosed, communicative problems.

Learning a foreign language is not merely something we do to travel and interact abroad. We need to know how language and cultural differences work to deal with communicative problems in our own, as well as in other, societies. How do we isolate underlying differences in cultural assumptions from everyday discourse? My own work on this question focuses directly on indepth conversational analysis of situations of interethnic and intercultural contact. The data collection strategy is akin to that of the linguist who compares grammatical with ungrammatical utterances. But rather than asking participants to assess samples of speech, I take advantage of the fact that intercultural communication is often plagued with misunderstandings. By systematic comparisons of such situations with similar encounters where culture is shared, it is possible to derive stable hypotheses about what cultural differences are involved and how they affect the outcome of the encounter. Let me now turn to some concrete examples.

The first set of examples comes from a dissertation by Charles Underwood, *The Indian Witness: Narrative Style in Courtroom Testimony*, University of California, Berkeley (1986).

Testimony in direct examination of Native American elders not thoroughly familiar with courtroom discourse style in court case involving land rights:

Ex. 1

Q: What I want to know . . . what is, what is the meaning of the sacred hoop, to the best of your understanding?

A: The best of my understanding is that my grandfather told me when I was a boy, when I was still very young, back when I was first hearing about these things, my grandfather told me about the meaning of the hoop.

Compare the answer (A) with the attorney's question (Q). The elder begins by repeating part of the attorney's last phrase as if he were about to respond as expected, but then he launches into a seemingly rambling and somewhat repetitive narrative which, when judged in terms of our own middle class American standards, is clearly not responsive to the attorney's question. If this were an isolated case, one might assume that the witness simply did not understand the question, although his English is quite grammatical. But let us look at the next few examples:

Ex. 2 Second witness (similar background).

Q: We have been using the word Sioux and the word Lakota. Will you tell us what you understand them to mean?

A: First of all, I've heard from the grandparents that the Sioux word was really not a word. The word was more or less given to us by identifying us . . the white people. But we are Lakota, which is the Sioux nation now known . . Lakota nation.

Ex. 3 Third witness.

Q: Now what did that treaty mean to the persons who signed it, according to your oral history?

A: From what was told to me is that the Lakota nation as what it was known at the time — we were a nation — we are a nation and the government had attempted prior before various things. These are — I think some of those were mentioned already, but as far as the 1968 treaty, it was a treaty between the United States government and our Lakota nation.

Ex. 4 Fourth witness.

Q: Will you tell us what the oral history is that you have been given?

A: Well, when I was a child and my mother died and my grandfolks were raising me, and I used to go around with them; and this treaty was signed by the chiefs and the government promised to support the Indians, lay down their arms and there would be peace.

And the government promised the Indians that they will support them, send them to schools, and feed them until the last Indian survived and not even a, and even their animals which they left in their homestead were still alive until the rest of them, until the end of the world would come, that's what they told me.

These are just a few extracts from the lengthy transcript of testimony by Indian witnesses delivered on separate days over a considerable period of time. Note that all passages show considerable similarities, that is, they fall roughly into a general pattern of delivery. Each answer is couched in the form of a narrative which begins with a reference to how the knowledge was acquired and by whom the witness was told, as if the speaker needed to cite authority for each statement. Those parts of the answer that contain material relevant to the question that was asked are embedded in the narrative, as if responsibility for the answer were not the individual's but the group's. The first witness's initial phrase is interesting in this respect. The speaker begins as if he were about to respond directly but, after repeating the attorney's phrase, he immediately and without lexically marked transition shifts into a narrative which is similar in form to that of the other witnesses.

Now consider some answers by outside experts.

Ex. 5 Professional anthropologist of Native American parentage.

Q: And in the course of the learning of your oral history and your studies, can you tell us what the tradition — well, putting it in its simplest terms, tell us what is meant by a phrase "the Lakota way of life"?

A: This is a life style that has allowed my people to maintain their integrity and their way of living as a distinct culture despite various efforts to change us. Our maintenance as an ongoing cultural group in our own way we see our life style is what we know as the Lakota way of life, and we call it Lakota — we live this a Lakota people.

Ex. 6 American anthropologist.

Q: Well what do you think the Indians understood it when they said they acknowledged themselves to be under the protection of the United States?

A: It is my understanding that they simply understood this to be the same kind of kinship metaphor which they used in any kind of interaction between human beings, whereas the government was using it as a cliche in the most offhanded manner and not really meaning anything by it, not implying a moral relationship between a grandparent and grandson that would be implied in the relationship as the Sioux understood it.

The two answers differ in that the Native American clearly signals his identification with his people while the other anthropologist refers to them as "they." Yet both provide some insights into what the court's "folk model" is, i.e., what the court expects and what the standards are by which it is likely to judge the witness's testimony. One way to characterize the expert testimony is by the old adage, "Say what you're going to say, say it, and say what you said." There is a preamble which acknowledges the question, then an explanation, and then a summary. Moreover, each speaker uses covert lexical devices to distinguish between his own understanding and what has been heard from others. This contrasts with the Native American lay witnesses' way of embedding the entire testimony in narrative and leaving the listener to infer whose opinion and conclusion are being expressed.

To some extent, the first expert's explanation to the effect that, for the Native Americans concerned, the words used have different meaning than for the governmental officials captures what is involved here. But this is not everything. It does not account for lay witnesses' seeming unwillingness to say what they themselves think, and their tendency to put their answers into other's mouths. Native American culture, as reflected here, seems to have its own norms as to who can make public statements and how they are to be made. The unstated assumption is that such statements must reflect the authority of the group and must be ratified with reference to that group and cannot be given by any one individual. Narrative forms here serve as a verbal strategy to conform to such norms, a conventional rhetorical means of foregrounding the fact that what is said reflects the tribe's position, not any one person's beliefs or opinion.

Support for the view that Native Americans have culturally specific ways of defining interactive situations comes from independent work by anthropological linguists like Sally McLendon (1982), Tedlock (1983), and others. Scollon and Scollon (1981), in their work on narrative literacy and face in interethnic communication, furthermore, point out that Native Americans, including those who no longer speak their own language well, frequently transfer rhetorical preferences characteristic of their own native language into their English. What is at issue in this case, therefore, is not that one set of speakers, the Native Americans, talks oddly, but that both sets, legal professionals and laymen, rely on their own culturally determined standards for deciding what to say and how to behave in these situations and that what these standards are can be inferred from systematic differences in their choice of discourse strategies.

The second set of examples comes from a study of the English communication styles of overseas Chinese entitled *Crosstalk in Sino-American Relations* by Linda Young (1994).

Ex. 7

Tape recording of a discussion, part of a management training sessions in Hong Kong. The chair is Chinese, as are the other discussants. The topic is, "What qualities are desirable in a good salesperson?"

Chair: Oscar, anything else to add? Your line of business is, again, quite different from what PK and Tony have. And, in your line of business, I presume market information will be quite important.

Oscar: . . . My business is textile, the salesman is . . . the quality of the salesman, need something different. Because the volume of making a sale is about, at least to over ten thousand U.S. dollars, sometimes. So that is the problem. That is, whenever anybody who makes a decision to buy such . . willing to pay such amount, we'll make sure their financial aid is strong and, then, such . . sometimes the market may suddenly drop in textile. Maybe we're willing to buy one month ago, but may not be buying . . . want to buy . . things like that. So, the, so, for a salesman, always have to understand about the financial situation and things like that.

Ex. 8 Management training: budget meeting.

Chair: I would like to have your opinion on how we should utilize the extra amount of one hundred eighty thousand pounds to improve . . .
          (Beta is the second participant to offer a suggestion.)

Beta: As you know, I have spent five hundred and seventy thousand pounds last year to on the machinery and components. And, ah, if, ah, if Mr., ah, Lincoln would like to increase the, ah, production in ha, through the coming year, I think we have to make our budget ten per cent on top of the amount five hundred and seventy thousand pounds because there will be ten per cent on uh increase in price on average. And, uh, in other words, I need another sixty thousand pounds to buy the same materials to buy the same material and quality.
          And, as you know, whenever there's a shortage of components on the ( ) amount of time, and, ah, although we have arranged delivery of normal supplies for for for at least six months, but we still need ah an extra money

to buy ah the replacement, which cost us five hundred more. So, in other words, I need at least six hundred thousand, sorry, six hundred thousand pounds for an extra uh extra money for the for the new ah budget for for our component.

Ex. 9

Tape recording of a discussion following a public talk at the University of California at Berkeley. The speaker (C) is Chinese; the audience (A) is American.

A: How does the Nutritional Institute decide what topics to study? How do you decide what topics to do research on?

C: Because, now, period get change. It's different from past time. In past time, we emphasize how to solve practical problems. Nutrition must know how to solve some deficiency diseases. In our country, we have some nutritional diseases, such X, Y, Z. But, now, it is important that we must do some basic research. So, we must take into account fundamental problems. We must concentrate our research to study some fundamental research.

Ex. 10

Tape recording of an oral history interview with (C), a Chinese man in his seventies, resident in the U.S. for more than forty years. The interviewer (A) is American.

A: Do you have any opinions about intermarriage or interracial dating and marriage?

C: Ah well, this is very hard to say. Because to Chinese, if you want to keep it to the Chinese culture. . . . I am in favor of the Chinese married to the Chinese. But, on the other hand, to the individual, for the one that you love, it doesn't make any difference. Ah, because if you find a Chinese wife, and if she doesn't love each other, well, it's not going to be a happy family. So, the intermarriage will come in, ah, much better. So, it depends on which point.

As with the first set of examples, it is not easy to see at first how the answers and questions are related. Respondents seem to rely on listing facts which, while loosely related to the question's topic, do not overtly respond to what the questioner wants to know. Note that in each case this listing concludes with the conjunction "so," which is then followed without any additional overtly lexicalized transition by a generalization which more directly responds to the question. This last generalization is what, based on our own conventions, we would expect to see at the beginning of the answer rather than at the end. Young's study provides detailed evidence to show that verbal strategies like the above directly reflect Chinese norms of rhetoric embodied, for example, in the well-known "eight legged essay" (Kaplan 1968) and folk sayings such as, "When you paint a dragon, you start with the tail and end with the eye," as well as the Chinese view of how interpersonal relations are to be articulated. She goes on to say, "What matters above all to the Chinese is the ritual playing out of interpersonal relations," that is to say, there seems to be a rhetorical principle to the effect that face preserving strategies must be put on record. Thus, the emphasis is on providing background information, and the seeming failure to come to the point in the above examples can be seen simply as a conventionalized way of conforming to these norms. The strategy is frequently used by native Chinese working in the United States whose English is otherwise excellent. When presented with alternate ways of saying the same thing, informants report that they know what the relevant American English strategy is, but they claim they prefer their own practice, which comes more naturally to them.

The third and last set of examples consists of extracts from counseling sessions recorded in England involving native speakers of South Asian languages communicating with native English speaking counselors.

Ex. 11

Interview between Indian English speaking man (A) and a female native British counselor (B). The recording begins almost immediately after the initial greetings. B has just asked A for permission to record the interview, and A's first utterance is in reply to her request (Gumperz, 1982).

    1. A: exactly the same way as you, as you would like = to put on
    2. B: = Oh no, no
    3. A: there will be some of = the things you would like to
    4. B: = yes
    5. A: write it down
    6. B: that's right, that's right [laughs]
    7. A: but, uh . . . anyway it's up to you
          <1 sec>
    8. B: um, [high pitch] . . . well . . . = I miss C.
    9. A: = first of all
 10. B: hasn't said anything to me you see
          <2 sec>
 11. A: I am very sorry if = she hasn't spoken anything
 12. B: = [softly] doesn't matter
 13. A: on the telephone at least,
 14. B: doesn't matter
 15. A: but ah . . . it was very important uh thing for me
 16. B: ye:s. Tell, tell me what it = is you want
 17. A: = umm
 18.   Um, may I first of all request for the introduction please
 19. B: Oh yes sorry
 20. A: == I am sorry
          <1 sec>
 21. B: I am E.
 22. A: Oh yes = [breathy] I see . . oh yes . . . very nice
 23. B: = and I am a teacher here in the Center
 24. A: very nice
 25. B: == and we run
 26. A: == pleased to meet you [laughs]
 27. B: == different courses [A laughs] yes, and you are Mr. A?
 28. A: N.A.
 29. B: N.A. yes, yes, I see [laughs]. Okay, that's the introduction [laughs]
 30. A: Would it be enough introduction?

The example has been transcribed in some detail, using a transcription system that reveals how speakers use pausing and prosody to chunk their talk into clauses to indicate inter-clausal coherence and to mark transitions between turns.   If we look at the interactional dynamics of the encounter, we see clear signs to the effect that both speakers are relatively ill at ease.   There is a great deal of overlap, and speakers frequently interrupt each other.   The initial sequences are devoted to B's attempt to secure permission to record.   Beginning in turn 9, B seeks to open the interview by mentioning that Miss C. (the person who referred A to her) has not told her anything about the case.   A's answer, "I'm very sorry . . .," sounds odd, to say the least.   He insists on continuing to express his disappointment even though B keeps saying it does not matter.   When B then asks, "tell me what it is you want," A asks for an introduction in a way which, from a native English speaking perspective, sounds odd for someone who is seeking advice.   B then gives her name and A replies with "I see, oh yes, very nice," which is again not the kind of response a native English speaker would give in a counseling situation.   There follows a rather tense sequence which ends with A's question, "Would it be enough introduction?"   The evidence here shows that, in spite of several attempts, both interactants fail to negotiate a suitable relationship for the conduct of the interview.

Why the Indian English speaker is behaving in a way that native English speakers find odd and inconsistent is hard to explain.   Are we dealing with systematic crosscultural differences?   The following example suggests that this may indeed be the case, and gives some illustration of how South Asian bilinguals may view such situations.

Ex. 12

Recorded in an advice center associated with a neighborhood housing association in an industrial city in the English midlands.   Speaker A, a South Asian native who has lived in Britain for about ten years, is a householder whose property adjoins the housing association.   He is coming to report that the boundary wall which he shares with the association has been blown down in a storm and to find out if the association is willing to share the costs of the reconstruction.   Speaker B is an employee of the advice center whose family is of North Indian origin but who is a native speaker of English.

1. A: (name) Arundel Street
2. B: 39 Arundel Street
3. A: — yes/ I got walls, tumble down/ . . . Friday . . eh, Saturday night yeah/
4. B: the walls tumble down, you mean they fell down/
5. A: fell down yeah/ . . fell down/ but could you tell me which/
      . . that's my wall, ya somebody else wall/
6. B: hm well is your wall here?
7. A: both sides/ . . and the front of that/
8. B: here here and here/
9. A: hm yes/
10. B: aha um there would be a party wall between you and your next door
      neighbor here/
      this guy here and this guy here/
11. A: yes but see next door/ . . I think is your house/ . . Calmore's center's/

12. B: Calmore center/
13. A: yes, . . forty-one/ . . and thirty-nine mine/
14. B: hm
15. A: but that up there, Lisit . . Lisit's garden/
16. B: you want to know who's responsible to put them back up/
17. A: up for this front one/
18. B: I see/ . . so if you want that/
         . . . so if you want that, . . un that wall to be put up/
19. A: only here/
20. B: this one here/
21. A: un up there yes/
22. B: you want to know if you are the only one who is liable to pay for
         it/
23. A: pay for it/ that's what I want to know//

Speaker A begins with a brief narrative account of what happened on the night of the storm. B counters by repeating A's statement and asking for clarification. A answers and then goes on with a question of fact about the owner of the wall. There follows an exchange in which B seeks to find out where the wall is located. The exchange continues until B takes the initiative and poses the question which is the one A had come to the center to ask in the first place. As in example 11, the client's verbal behavior seems at first quite odd. Without stating his problem, he begins with factual matter the relevance of which is hard to see. He then asks a question about the ownership of a wall — something that he as a local property owner should certainly know. Whereas the first counselor had refused to respond to her client's odd answers and countered with new questions of her own, the second counselor, by repeating his client's words, seems to accept the answers and then proceeds to make his own inference as to what the relevant issue is. Note moreover that, while the first interaction is marred by interruptions and a great deal of excessively long conversational overlap, the second proceeds quite smoothly and the two participants clearly understand each other. This type of exchange is typical of a number of counseling exchanges involving speakers of South Asian languages I have studied. These exchanges are marked by strict role separation between client and counselor. It is the client who presents facts and the counselor who defines the problem at hand. In our American tradition, this is done in medical diagnosis, but in counseling clients are expected to present their own problems and the counselors are discouraged from making indirect inferences lest they be accused of putting words into the client's mouth.

Let me point out that these are not isolated anecdotes. The transcripts come from a large body of case study analyses collected through long-term ethnographic fieldwork in the Goffmanian tradition, where participant observation is employed to discover key interactive situations that demonstrably play an important role in the populations' daily life. What occurs in such situations and how interactants deal with them thus has clear cultural relevance.

The significance of such analyses for second language instruction becomes apparent if we consider that the language is English and look at individual participants as learners in different stages of language acquisition. The bilinguals have good working control of English grammar but they rely on rhetorical conventions characteristic of their own native languages and distinct from those used by native English speakers in similar settings. Such rhetorical conventions constitute systems of structural principles which, on the one hand, closely reflect basic cultural norms while at the same time governing everyday language use and discourse interpretation. By learning what these conventions are and how they differ, learners not only improve their ability to communicate but also acquire something of an implicit understanding of how the culture works.

We can understand what kind of learning is involved here, if, instead of looking at communication from the perspective of individuals conveying information or producing grammatical or situationally appropriate utterances, we adopt a dialogic perspective of speakers cooperating in the production of conversational exchanges, by means of strategies similar to those of musicians playing ensemble or ball players moving the ball across the field. Participants in such team endeavors must, of course, know the basic rules before they can take part. But once the play begins, any one individual's moves are made in concert with or in relation to other players' moves. This requires timing and strategic planning in the sense of predicting what is to come. Conversing, when seen in this perspective, is not simply a matter of putting one's ideas into words; what is communicated or accomplished in any one encounter is significantly affected by how others interpret one's words and by what can be achieved under the prevailing circumstances.

There is one important respect in which the conversationalists' task differs from the game players'. In a game we can assume that the basic rules are known to all and that role allocation is agreed on beforehand. In conversation this is the case only for the most formal situations. Elsewhere, rules and expectations are negotiated as part of the interaction. To be sure, we do not enter into an encounter without at least some knowledge of what to expect. The schemata we have learned through previous socialization prepare us for what is to come. But such expectations are always subject to change through negotiation. Negotiation processes are in turn cued by means of verbal, prosodic, and nonverbal signs or contextualization cues which function as part of the rhetorical system (Gumperz, 1982). The "so" examples (7-10) are examples of such cues. Note that their use to indicate that the main point is about to come is a peculiarity of Chinese-English strategies. When knowledge of contextualization cues is not shared, communication can become difficult and encounters are often unsuccessful (Gumperz, Jupp, & Roberts, 1979). This is the case in example 12. A closer analysis of the two participants' use of pausing and stress shows they interpret individual cues quite differently. Consequently, smooth turn-taking is impaired and misunderstanding, as a result of different culturally based presuppositions, is aggravated.

Because of their highly context sensitive character, rhetorical strategies must, for the most part, be acquired through interpersonal contact. It is only through conversation that the relevant strategies are learned. They cannot be taught through formal instruction. Perhaps this is the reason why language learners vary so greatly in the extent to which they manage to acquire nativelike proficiency in discursive practices. The bilinguals in our examples are typical of large classes of language learners who, although they have an instrumental control of the second language, for a variety of reasons never acquire the ability to enter into intensive close contact with natives.

I believe it is possible to give even beginning students some sense of rhetorical strategies with instructional materials that are properly selected to reflect events typical of experiences that learners and those who must interact with them encounter. Through discussion and through systematic analysis of one's own interaction in culturally diverse situations, one can become aware of differences in rhetorical strategies. In the most general terms, what this analysis involves is learning to separate discourse level form from discourse level content, somewhat in the way that I have tried to do it in my examples. There is some evidence, however, to suggest that by having been exposed to language learning experiences a person gains a better sense of how to go about doing this and thus to learn from interactive experience. It is in this sense that language instruction may prepare us for meeting the cognitive demands of multicultural environments.

REFERENCES

Gumperz, J. J. (1982). *Discourse strategies.* Cambridge, England: Cambridge University Press.

Gumperz, J. J., Jupp, T. C., & Roberts, C. (1979). *Crosstalk: A study of cross-cultural communication.* Southall, England: National Centre for Industrial Language Training.

Kaplan, R. B. (1968). Contrastive grammar: Teaching composition to the Chinese student. *Journal of English as a Second Language,* 3(1), 1-13.

Lambert, R. (Ed.). (1987). *Foreign language instruction: A national agenda. The Annals of the American Academy of Political and Social Sciences,* **490**.

Lange, D. L. (1987). The language teaching curriculum and a national agenda. In R. Lambert (Ed.), *Foreign language instruction: A national agenda. The Annals of the American Academy of Political and Social Sciences,* **490**.

Larsen-Freeman, D. (1987). Recent innovations in language teaching methodology. In R. Lambert (ed.), *Foreign language instruction: A national agenda. The Annals of the American Academy of Political and Social Sciences,* **490**.

Lehmann, W. P., & Jones, R. L. (1987). The humanistic basis of second language learning. In R. Lambert (Ed.), *Foreign language instruction: A national agenda. The Annals of the American Academy of Political and Social Sciences,* **490**.

McLendon, S. (1982). Meaning, rhetorical structure and discourse organization in myth. In D. Tannen (Ed.), *Analyzing discourse: Text and talk* (pp. 284-305). Washington, D.C.: Georgetown University Press.

Scollon, R., & Scollon, S. (1981). *Narrative literacy and face in interethnic communication.* Norwood, NJ: Ablex.

Tedlock, D. (1983). *Spoken word and the work of interpretation.* Philadelphia: University of Pennsylvania Press.

Underwood, C. F. (1986). *The Indian witness: Narrative style in courtroom testimony.* Unpublished doctoral dissertation, University of California, Berkeley.

Young, L. (1994). *Crosstalk in Sino-American relations.* New York: Cambridge University Press.

28 TRUE CONFESSIONS? PRAGMATIC COMPETENCE AND CRIMINAL CONFESSION

Robin Tolmach Lakoff
University of California, Berkeley

1. INTRODUCTION

There are two especially difficult problems for pragmatics and sociolinguistics. One is the connection between purely linguistic form (phonology, syntax, morphology) and discourse function. Eventually we must, however reluctantly, consider to what degree and in what ways real-world situations and communicative needs of speakers govern syntactic form; and the sense in which syntax, semantics, and pragmatics are truly, bidirectionally, interdependent. The second is the definition of "pragmatic" or "communicative" competence: What does the normally competent speaker know?

The case I will discuss here raises another issue of interest to linguistics and other social sciences. Over the last fifteen years or so, there has been much discussion in several fields concerning the nature and/or reality, of the "self." Some of the data we will be examining provide more evidence of the tenuousness and fuzziness of that concept.

The examples I will use are drawn from a pair of criminal confessions in a death penalty case currently (June, 1993) under appellate review. I was asked as an expert by the defense to review the confessions to assess the linguistic (or communicative) capacities of their client. Since I was asked by counsel to use a pseudonym in referring to the defendant, I shall refer to him as Virgil Reilly (or VR).

2. FACTS OF THE CASE

The facts of the case are briefly these. When the crimes were committed, in November, 1984, Virgil Reilly was a black male of 25, who had never been in any previous legal trouble.

VR's IQ falls between the mid-60s and mid-70s — borderline or "dull normal." Psychological testing reveals an array of impairments — particularly relevant to our concerns are verbal deficits, including "severe impairment in attention, memory for verbally presented material, verbal fluency, cognitive flexibility, and adaptability to novel cognitive tasks."[1] He is a native speaker of English, and has attended high school. He reports, prior to receiving a Miranda warning during one of his confessions, that while he "know[s] how to read," he doesn't read "that good you know." (SB 2:5,7)[2]

VR's life prior to the crimes to which he is confessing was typical for a defendant convicted of a capital crime. His mother used alcohol rather heavily during her pregnancy. She was 20 when VR was born, three months prematurely, after a difficult pregnancy, the first of eight children born over a twelve-year period. VR was regularly abused by his father and other relatives (physically and sexually) and neglected by his mother. He also displayed, from early childhood, a variety of physical and psychological problems, created or exacerbated by the abuse.

In October of 1984 he had begun to use large quantities of over-the-counter and prescription analgesic drugs (especially Tylenol with codeine) to self-medicate a variety of complaints, including but not restricted to persistent headaches and pain from dental procedures. He was also drinking large quantities of wine.

On the night of November 16 in Riverside, he abducted two children, raping the girl and killing the boy. The next night, in San Bernardino, he abducted and raped two young women. He was arrested by the Riverside police on November 22, and was interrogated later that night; he was interrogated by the San Bernardino police on November 27. In both interrogations he ultimately made full confession.

There is little doubt that VR is guilty of the crimes for which he was given the death penalty: Physical evidence incontrovertibly connects him to both crimes. So the problem with these confessions is not that an innocent man may die for crimes he did not commit. Rather, the ethical question that my discussion poses concerns a possible conflict in our present culture between our desire to see ourselves as a humane people who require that criminal confessions be extracted humanely — that is, fully in compliance with the intentions and instructions of the Supreme Court in *Miranda*,[3] that is, with the subject's informed consent — and our equally pressing and valid need to feel secure from violence in our daily lives, and therefore the government's obligation to pursue and convict malefactors with dispatch (or risk a general perception of the erosion of the social contract, with consequent chaos). What constitutes "informed consent" to a criminal confession? Does VR's situation meet that standard?

---

[1] Report of UCLA Neuropsychiatric Assessment Laboratory, 9/26/85

[2] References to the two confessions will be indicated throughout the text as follows: SB = San Bernardino confession, 11/27/84. R = Riverside confession, 11/22/84. Numbers preceding a colon refer to pages of each confession; numbers following the colon refer to conversational turns on each page. Thus, the foregoing quotations are taken from page 2 of the San Bernardino confession and represent the fifth and seventh turns on that page.

[3] 384 US 436 (1966). At 479, *Miranda* states that the suspect "must be warned prior to any questioning that he has the right to remain silent, that anything he says can be used against him in a court of law, that he has the right to the presence of an attorney, and that if he cannot afford an attorney one will be appointed for him prior to any questioning if he so desires." Receiving these warnings will enable him to "knowingly and intelligently waive these rights."

3. COMMUNICATIVE COMPETENCE IN THIS CASE

As I noted, I was asked by the defense to evaluate the defendant's pragmatic competence to make a valid (under *Miranda*) confession. Did he understand what a "confession" is? What confessing meant for him?

We can define **full pragmatic competence** as including (but not limited to) a knowledge of the felicity, or preparatory and essential, conditions necessary for the appropriate performance of any speech act in which the person being evaluated is involved (in any capacity), an appreciation of conversational logic, and an understanding of the rules and forms of dyadic conversation.[4] It is essential that a suspect understand not only the literal wording of a *Miranda* warning, but its discourse function as marking a boundary between essentially harmless conversation and discourse in which serious self-damage can be done by helping the interrogator. The Supreme Court has been quite clear on this: Several opinions since the original 1966 ruling have required that a suspect demonstrate explicitly a fluency in English equal to eighth-grade capacity (necessary to understand words like "attorney"). They have acknowledged that this capacity may be fatally compromised either by nonnative speaker status or by demonstrated subnormal mental capacity. In either of these cases, a confession would be inadmissible at trial, and if such a confession was used by the prosecution as a crucial part of its case, a guilty verdict (and/or a death sentence) would likely be overturned.

To demonstrate full pragmatic, or communicative, competence in this discourse context, VR would have to possess several forms of communicative knowledge, which could be assessed by observing, from tapes or transcripts of his verbal productions, his conversational behavior. The evaluator would look for (1) an ability to respond to interrogations, directives, and other speech acts in a manner consistent with a normally fluent speaker's understanding of speech act theory and conversational logic; (2) an understanding of his role in the discourse more generally: what it means to be under criminal interrogation; and (3) evidence of competence, active and passive, in the rules of conversational interchange: indications that his turns represented preferred, or at least dispreferred but permissible seconds. Additionally, as essential underpinnings of pragmatic competence, VR would have to demonstrate other forms of linguistic competence: knowledge of relevant English vocabulary, the ability to construct and parse sentences of the appropriate complexity, knowledge of the relationship between linguistic forms and their real-world referents. It is my belief that VR demonstrated anomalies or failures of all of these capacities to some degree, though not so utterly as to show unequivocal absence of the communicative competence to make a meaningful and consensual confession. Rather, these confessions represent an intriguing and ultimately unresolvable gray area, showing that language and communicative capacity are infinitely complex and

---

[4] For the definitions and functions of these terms, cf. Austin (1962) and Searle (1969, 1979); for conversational logic, Grice (1975), and for conversational structure, Sacks, Schegloff, & Jefferson (1974).

ambiguous. We must confront these uncertainties as such: we cannot dismiss examples like these as uninteresting or meaningless merely because we cannot be sure what they mean. Here as often in linguistics, it is the shadowy cases, the borderline examples, that have the most to teach us about our subject.

4. CONFESSION:
WHAT THE CONFESSOR NEEDS TO KNOW

Several specific sorts of knowledge are needed to make a fully meaningful, informed, and consensual criminal confession, including an awareness of the following properties of the speech act of confession:

1.   Because confession is a truth-seeking discourse genre[5] (different, therefore, from an informal conversation), contributions must be directed toward a mutually agreed-upon point: Did you or didn't you, and if you did, how did you? Expatiation and irrelevancy are marked as (at best) requiring special interpretation (beyond the normal bounds of conversational implicature) in a truth-seeking discourse genre.   That is, deviations of these kinds tend to suggest to hearers that the speaker either has something to hide, or is seriously communicatively incompetent.

2. The participants in a confessional speech act are unequal in power, before, during, and after the discourse. But the making of a confession increases a suspect's vulnerability still further. The interrogator has significantly more power through institutional status, as well as the ability to use the confession in ways that will hurt its producer in the future.   Additionally, interrogators often get extra power in more subtle ways: The interrogation is done on their turf, at their chosen time (often late at night, when the suspect has been isolated in a holding cell for many hours); they ask the questions, and are free to withhold benefits of various sorts (water, coffee, food, sleep, access to family members) until satisfied. They have training and formal experience in this discourse genre; they make judgments on suspects' productions. They are often of a higher social class, better educated, and more likely to be speakers of the standard dialect.

3. The confessors (a term I will use here to mean "speakers of confessions") must be acknowledging behavior committed previously by themselves (or at least, someone closely connected to them).   A confession must therefore acknowledge an identity between speaker and performer — explicitly or otherwise.

4. In order for the confession to be informedly consensual, the agreement must be fully responsive. That is, the suspect must explicitly indicate understanding of the circumstances and willingness to participate. Mere indication of compliance is insufficient.

5. To demonstrate communicative competence in this context, a speaker must show an understanding of conversational structure: specifically, turn-taking and preference organization.

---

[5] For discussion of this term, as well as the notion of truth-seeking vs. other discourse genres, cf. Lakoff (1990).

6. Finally, to confess appropriately, the confessor must agree with the hearer (and the culture at large) that the behavior in question was "bad." This does not necessarily imply a sense of remorse: The confession need not be, in this sense, "sincere," any more than an apology. But if we were to find that a subject was totally, and genuinely, unaware that the act that he acknowledged committing was one that was considered "bad" by his society, we would have to set the confession aside; indeed, under current definitions of criminal insanity, if the suspect could be shown not to recognize the badness of the act, he would have to be declared "not guilty by reason of insanity."

The texts suggest failures by VR in the first five categories, to be illustrated in the remaining sections of this paper.

5. THE TRUTH-SEEKING NATURE OF CRIMINAL CONFESSIONS

VR repeatedly flouts or violates Gricean maxims, in a discourse context in which strict adherence should be the norm. Actually, the latter statement should be qualified. It is not infrequent (indeed it is expected) that a suspect violates certain of the maxims (especially Quality) especially early on in the process. But conversational implicature makes sense of these floutings, with the understanding that they are to the speaker's benefit (that is, politeness, or at least defensiveness, here as elsewhere may supersede strict informativeness). But what is unusual about VR's performance is that the particular ways in which he flouts the maxims cannot be seen as working, or even intended to work, in his interests: they are violations largely of Relevance, and neither supply requested information nor attempt to withhold it.

In example (1), the interrogator (RM) is trying to establish VR's whereabouts on the morning after one of the crimes (SB 28:11-29:1):

(1) VR: What time I get up Saturday mornin'? Uh Saturday mornin' 'round about uh nine or ten o'clock.

RM: Nine or ten o'clock. What time did you go to L.A.?

VR: Time I went to L.A.? Close to twelve. I'd say about quarter to twelve, usually.

RM: Did you get up in between there and take off and get something or do something?

VR: No.

RM: Before you went to L.A.?

VR: Before I went to L.A.?

RM: Uh huh.

VR: Well the only time I went and took off is when I woke up uh with me and my wife both woke up and uh we sat down in the livin' room. I had the TV on.

RM: What time was that?

VR: It was 'round about uh ten o'clock. We was watchin' the, uh, what's the show called? Uh, she was watchin', uh, what's that show? Uh not uh I watched the Gong Show, that come on around eleven, and movie usually come on after that. The uh thing where they mash down, that game goes around uh you get so many points, you get the whammy, uh you get the whammy. You gets money. If you don't get the money, you get the wham- my. That, the show come or it and it usually stays on around a half hour and the Gong Show come on after that. I have a swelling here, in the top on down behind my ear.

And another in the same vein, from the Riverside confession (R 26-7:14-15):

(2) CORNEJO (an interrogator): Okay. Tell us what you have on your mind [Virgil].

    VR: Okay. Uh, going to work on the evening, I guess that last night.... (crying)... I woke up this morning [unintelligible for several seconds] guarded my hand.... I didn't know where it come, you know, I had it out in the truck or in the house. Half the time I don't know where, how I got the gun. And I get these, I don't know if it's tumor, or pains in my head. I tell my wife everytime it happens and she always say, "Check it out, dear." "Check it out." So I.... they haven't tell me anything about...pain still there. Before I came to work, when I was down at the place, the store, okay, I fell I had an attack or something, and when I left the coffee.... you know I had coffee, I was shaking and was spilling half the coffee and all I remember was getting in the truck. I was going back to the place and I had this gun in my hand. I don't know if I walked in the store with it or what. I don't know. And when... next thing I know I was back at the site, and I was hearing shots ... some banging noise. And I don't know if I was scared, or what. I was just as calm, you know, like I was earlier. And different people come to me, you know, and I was there. And they were [unintelligible] wasn't there. You know, I don't know if I killed anybody or not. I never killed anybody. You understand?

And shortly later (R 28:2-3):

(3) BOWEN (another interrogator): Where did you shoot him [Virgil]?

    VR: I don't know. All, I just opened fire and shot. I wasn't even aiming, you know, even when I'm practicing or something I usually take my time, aim, you know, even when I'm with my wife, I tried to show her how to use the gun, how to prop it up, you know. But when I get in these, these stages or something, the change, and nobody doesn't listen to me or what's happening to me, and sometime, I be mad myself. I be want to do things to myself and things I don't even know that I'm doing it. You understand? Like my wife one day, I had a beard and I was just went in the kitchen and shaved it all off. And she says, "Whys you do that? " I says, "Just something to do." Shave my mustache off. I usually don't shave my mustache off.

It is essential here to draw a distinction between utterances that, while not strictly relevant, would be perfectly appropriate under the more relaxed expectations of ordinary conversation (as is probably true of all the examples above), and utterances occurring in the strict truth-telling frame of a criminal confession, in which each of the examples above is aberrant to some degree. In each, unnecessary and irrelevant information is supplied at considerable length (violating the maxims of Quantity, Relevance, and

Manner). VR merely seems not to know how to "keep to the point," or perhaps even does not understand what "the point" is, what his interlocutors want to know, what the discourse as a whole is about. It might be argued that VR is merely trying to throw his questioners off by irrelevance and longwindedness. But many of his expatiations occur **after** he has essentially made full confession: he has nothing to gain from temporizing at that point. And it is questionable whether someone with an IQ barely above the level of retardation, and significant verbal and cognitive deficits, could consistently play a deliberate game of this kind — or even understand the advantage of playing such a game. These examples supply evidence of other problems with this discourse as a true "confession." For instance, VR's failure to adhere to the Gricean Maxims suggests a failure to perceive the adversarial nature of the conversation.

6. THE NON-EGALITARIAN NATURE OF THE CONFESSIONAL DISCOURSE

For a confession to have been made with informed consent, the suspect must realize that the confessional frame itself places the confessor in jeopardy, and that that risk is the interrogator's desired outcome: it is a win–lose situation. Since as a criminal suspect VR enters the discourse under a disadvantage, full understanding would make clear to him the necessity of keeping up the boundaries, maintaining distance and formality at all points, giving no more information than is essential, and not expecting the interlocutors to do anything to his advantage. This is the reason why *Miranda* requires interrogators to offer suspects explicitly the right to have an attorney present, and also why interrogators do their best to discourage suspects from invoking those rights[6]: the presence of an attorney would substantially equalize the participants. In VR's case, the waiver was almost too easily accomplished. In the SB confession, for example, the *Miranda* statement is read rapidly and without inflection, in long phrases. So while VR might have understood all or most of the **words** used, in isolation, it is very possible that the warning as uttered, presented to him in a state of agitation and exhaustion, might not have been fully comprehended. He answers "uh huh," but it's not clear whether this response signifies understanding or merely compliance: "just do what you like, fine with me." In the Riverside confession, after the detective has read VR his rights, he asks (R 2:10): "Having these rights in mind, [Virgil], do you wish to talk to us now?" There follows a four-second pause on the tape, an indication that VR fails to understand fully the requirement that, at this explicit TRP, he take a turn. As the silence lengthens, the second interrogator takes over. There is a marked stylistic shift between Cornejo, who speaks first, and Ferguson: the former is formal and distant, the latter spontaneous-sounding and colloquial. VR responds inappropriately to Ferguson quite possibly because of his apparent friendliness, especially after Cornejo's distance: VR may confuse the appearance of friendliness with true "friendship," mutuality of interests. To make the case more

---

[6] Ainsworth (1993) discusses some of these methods.

strongly, Ferguson makes VR's waiver something Ferguson would like VR to do **so that** Ferguson, true friend that he is, will be enabled to do something for VR in return. (R 2:10-11):

(4) CORNEJO: Having these rights in mind, [Virgil], do you wish to talk to us now?

   [4 seconds of silence]

   FERGUSON: Well, you can stop talking anytime you want to and you don't have to answer any question that you do not want to but there's two sides to every story. And for us to hear your side you have to acknowledge that your rights have been read to you and that you waive your rights.

   VR: Well, what do I say? I don't know.

At this point, Cornejo takes over again and makes VR's role in the confession into a kind of voluntary game (R 2:13): "Well, I'll ask you a question. If you want to answer it, answer it." Although VR has never explicitly in so many words indicated his willingness to give a confession, he is now locked into a discourse frame in which he would have to aggressively perform an active (rather than passive) violation of conversational preference rules: refuse to carry out a directive. For someone who has been repeatedly diagnosed as having a compliant personality (and someone with few communicative skills), this would be particularly difficult. From VR's subsequent behavior, it seems clear that, rather than recognizing Cornejo's *Miranda* warning as a statement of a boundary, as the beginning of an adversarial and high-risk interrogation frame, VR is encouraged by Ferguson's quasi-offer of help to see the ensuing discourse as collaborative, win-win: a safe place wherein he can ask for advice, or openly digress about things that trouble him, in the hope of getting help or clarification, as in Examples 1–3 above, and his repeated questions such as "What should I do?" "What should I say?"

7. THE PROBLEM OF CONFESSIONAL RECOGNITION OF IDENTITY, AND THE SELF

As noted above, an essential presupposition governing the felicity of the speech act of confession is the recognition by all participants that the speaker making the confession is the same person as the one who performed the action being acknowledged.[7] That is, an identity relation is presupposed between the two: They are, in some sense, "the same" person. So stated, the relationship seems simple and unambiguous: Either A1 = A2, and (other things being equal) the confession is appropriate; or A1 ≠ A2, in which case it is aberrant — both semantically meaningless and pragmatically nonfunctional. The clearest cases of the latter are literally false confessions, in which speakers "confess" to deeds

---

[7] This definition is somewhat too narrow as stated, in that under some conditions it is possible to "confess" appropriately to an act performed by someone with a close connection to the confessor, and for whom the confessor has some degree of responsibility or control — rather like the case of apology. For instance, a mother might confess that her small child had damaged a neighbor's property. But even in this case there is still a presumptive identity relation between the confessor and the doer of the action, albeit at one remove.

they have not done. Such cases are recognized as inappropriate speech acts, and have no further legal or moral status as confessions.

That is the simplest and most obvious problem case. It suggests that identity relations are analyzable dichotomously: A1 = A2, or the reverse. But in fact, both in human life and in syntactic construction, there exist numerous intermediate possibilities: Possibilities abhorred alike by linguists, psychologists, and legal scholars, but nonetheless very real. Because both our minds and (therefore) our language seem to demand strictly delimited categories rather than continua, we either refuse to recognize such cases, or relegate them to the margins of our analytic systems as "special cases," willfully refusing to recognize them as central and highly significant. Yet these cases define us and are crucial to our language, and which must be acknowledged, and eventually accounted for, in a complete theory linking language, mind, and the real world in which and on which they operate.

At this time, in Western culture, it is commonplace to feel that "normal" human beings possess a unified and cohesive "self" — a persona that is felt to be constant over time as a cohesive and rational agent, a person more or less consistent at all times, under all conditions. These definitions seem to us basic, self-evident, and eternal, as aspects of the human condition.

Over the last dozen years or so, postmodernist scholars in a diverse array of fields have questioned and largely discarded the certainty and universality of the concept of selfhood.[8] This research demonstrates persuasively that the "self" is only a convenient organizing fiction of the post-Renaissance West, no more basic, universal, or eternal than (say) Calvinist notions of predestination.

As participants in real life, however (whatever our theoretical beliefs), we must act and believe as if we possessed selves that provide coherency across space and time. Our language reflects that purported certainty not only through the existence of lexical items like *self, selfish, self-esteem* (and so on), but through syntactic processes that involve a notion of coherent identity. Some devices found in English are represented in the examples of (5) and (6) — first, in (5)(i)-(ii), "true reflexives":

(5) (i)   I know myself.

     (ii)   I stuck myself with a pin.

It might be argued that even in these "simple" cases, there are two distinct notions of "identity" operating: in (i) it is psychological, but in (ii) physical. The problem only worsens with

(5) (iii)   I forced myself to speak,

in which the obvious identity of subject and object implied in (i) and (ii) gives way to a split between the interests and perspectives of subject and object, yet not a complete schism. The complexity increases in (5)(iv),

(5) (iv)   I dreamed that I had eaten New York.

---

[8] For example: in history, work by Davis and Starn (e.g., 1988); in anthropology, perhaps the earliest and most influential discussion is that of Geertz (1983, ch. 3); in discourse analysis, cf. Linde (1993); in the field of ethics, cf. the collection edited by Johnson (1993); and in psychology, cf. Sass (1992).

in which there is still a notion of identity between the subjects of the two clauses, but not the complete merger assumed in (v):

(5) (v)   I know I can't eat the whole thing.

Things get worse still, in the cases exemplified in (6):

(6) (i)   (a) I disapprove of me.

    (b) myself.

(6) (ii)   (a) In my dream, I saw me eating ice cream.

    (b) myself

(6) (iii) (a) I expected myself to be nominated.

    (b) Ø

In each of the sets in (6), both examples represent some sense of identity between the subject and direct object of the clause. If identity, or selfhood, were a single, undifferentiable, dichotomous concept, the possibilities of choice represented in the examples of (6) would not exist.[9] What we see in (6) are three options: (1) fully-merged and presupposed identity as in (6)(iii)(b), in which the identification is so complete that there is no need for even pronominal mention; (2), almost complete merger, with reflexive pronouns, in which the presence of the explicit reflexive **asserts** (rather than presupposing) full identity, as in (6)(i)(b), (6)(ii)(b), and (6)(iii)(a); and (3), partial nonidentity, in the cases with the objective pronouns, in which there is a sense of the subject-I looking out at the direct object-I as distinct yet a part of itself, as in (6)(i)(a) and (6)(ii)(a).

These shorthand devices of the syntactic grammar represent the subtler continua of reality. It is true that we generally construe psychological "normality" as coinciding with a sense of complete identity of personality. But psychopathology recognizes a wide range of distinct problems in the construction of "selfhood" — a continuum that indicates how complex and multiplicitous the cohesive self really is. We can set up such a continuum:

full recog. — "neurotic"   — mult. pers. — retro. — schizo-
of ID   non-cohesion   disorder   amn.   phrenia[10]

Along this continuum, VR falls somewhere between "neurotic" noncohesion and

---

[9] For extensive and interesting discussion of several problems of this kind, see Lakoff and Becker (1991).

[10] Some clarification of the points on this scale may be helpful. The second point, "'neurotic' non-cohesion," refers to the argument in much recent psychoanalytic writing that what brings people into therapy is a disorganized or incoherent life story narrative. Therapy, then, consists of restoring the narrative to coherency. In this situation, the patient senses gaps and discrepancies among points in the narrative, but recognizes him or herself as its subject throughout. "Multiple Personality Disorder" (MPD), a condition in which, as a result of early and persistent abuse, patients experience themselves as fragmented into multiple discrete personalities with no continuity of memory or personality among them. Each one typically maintains its own continuity across time; but synchronically the patient feels divided into multiple selves, rather than selfless. Retrograde amnesia is that rare state beloved by writers of soap opera in which, as a result of physical or mental trauma, memory of all past history is lost. Hence the individual has no "self" at all, no memory providing an identity and a means of predicting and stabilizing future behavior. Finally in schizophrenia, especially as interpreted by Sass (1992), the individual's total sense of self, synchronic and diachronic, is shattered and boundaries between the self (physical and psychological) and other individuals and the outside world cease to exist.

multiple personality disorder: his "selves" are not disparate enough from our normal assumptions to qualify him as "psychotic," and still less as legally "insane"; he does not clearly fail to identify a cohesive self (but does not clearly identify one, either). The problem (academically if not jurisprudentially) is: If it is not fully clear to VR that VR the confessor = VR the doer of the deeds confessed to, is the confession valid (since one of its felicity conditions is disputable)?

Consider a few of many examples illustrating the problem. At first VR strongly denies remembering any of the actions his interrogators question him about (e.g., (7), R 23:1-2):

(7) CORNEJO: You don't sound like [you're upset]. I've accused you of killing a little boy and you haven't yelled at me and said "You're a goddamned liar," or nothing. You just sit there as calm as can be. I don't understand your attitude.

VR: Well, I've never, you know, there's something that I did, I know I didn't do it, you know.

But under repeated assault, VR gets flustered (R 23:9-10):

(8) CORNEJO: When we're accusing you of killing a little boy? Me arresting you hasn't upset you?

VR: Well, I'm in shock. I don't know what to say. I don't know what to say or do.

After much more of the same, he begins to waver (R 27:8)

(9) VR: But, but if I killed somebody I am deeply, deeply sorry that I've done it. By being knowing myself, I probably did kill somebody.

And he speaks similarly later on (R 50:10-11), even though by that point a more adequate "confession" had already been obtained:

(10)CORNEJO: Were you talking to the little girl [Virgil]?

VR: I probably was or didn't know what I was doing or something like that. I don't know.

VR's "confessional" statements here sound (especially in their use of words like "probably") like those of someone who is trying to make sense of someone else's actions or motives, rather than remembering his own. That suggests that VR's self-identification is at least problematic, if it exists at all to the degree necessary to validate a confession. Ultimately, VR finds it easier (especially being a "compliant" personality) to incorporate his interrogator's plausible narrative into his own "identity": better to have a clear identity (even if it gets him into the gas chamber) than the fuzziness VR seems to have been living with. Dubious identity for VR is a fate worse than death (R 30:17-22):

(11)CORNEJO: This is the little boy right here. Handsome little boy, isn't he? Eleven years old. A handsome eleven year old little boy.

VR: I killed him?

CORNEJO: You killed him [Virgil]?

VR: I killed him?

CORNEJO: Uh-hum.

VR: I don't know why I killed him.

While that is taken as a virtual confession by his interrogators, it is certainly arguable that it represents a failure of the requisite conditions for that speech act, rendering it, in Austin's terms, void. Examples have already been given that illustrate failures in all the other significant aspects of the confessional interaction: The rules of conversational behavior are frequently violated by VR: He fails to answer when an answer is mandatory; his answers are frequently dispreferred — for instance, compliant rather than responsive. He fails to grasp the discourse frame of confession: The power imbalance, his jeopardy, the truth-seeking nature of the discourse. While he may technically "understand" the language of the *Miranda* warning, and technically "participate" in the confessional discourse, it is far from clear that he is pragmatically competent to understand what is happening — the subject matter of the talk, his situation, the probable consequences. His uncertainty about identity further casts doubt on the validity of his "confession" as a whole.

8. CONCLUSIONS AND DILEMMAS

Within the safe confines of academic interchange, the examples discussed here are intriguing but not seriously problematic. They suggest a link which any coherent theory of language must represent, between syntactic form, psychological perception, and the real world both seek to capture. There are fuzzinesses and uncertainties in the syntax of reflexivization in English because the self (which that grammatical process implies or asserts), is by no means a clear or certain construct in our psychologies or our daily inter- (and intra-) actions. Language, as linguists love to claim, is important because it informs and creates our physical and psychological reality: If pragmatic analysis represents confession as complex and subtle interactive behavior, and shows that many interactions that might be labeled "confession" fail to meet the pragmatic criteria for the valid performance of that act, does that force nonlinguists — ethicists, lawmakers and legal scholars — to re-evaluate the rules of criminal interrogation? Does it force all of us to re-evaluate our belief in ourselves (late twentieth century Americans) as humane people committed to the vision of the Founders embodied in the Bill of Rights — in this case, the Fifth Amendment protection against self-incrimination as represented in the *Miranda* decision's requirement of informed consent? If we question the admissibility at trial of confessions as dubious as this one (but "dubious," rather than unambiguously coerced), where will our good intentions leave our society? If the construct of "selfhood" is as tenuous as data of this kind suggest, and if the admissibility of confessions rests on this and other problematic grounds — might it not be argued that **no** confession is legally admissible? Then what becomes of criminal trial procedure, since convictions often depend significantly if not crucially on confessions? How can we feel comfortable about consigning defendants to long sentences — even to death — on the basis of evidence acquired — we must finally admit — fraudulently? Unthinkable!

So examples like VR's confession force us to rethink the use of criminal confessions altogether, as a great many obtained under these (quite typical) conditions would be found to be tainted. But many convictions — perhaps most — especially in the most serious crimes depend on the availability of a confession to the jury. Were this option to be lost, convictions would surely become harder to secure. And — in America's favorite nightmare — criminals might go free to walk the streets. And if the government were seen as a result to be helpless to ensure the security of the citizens, the social contract might well be abrogated — an invitation, as the Founders would be the first to tell us, to revolution. Intolerable!

I for one am happy that, as an academic linguist rather than a jurist, I don't have to make real-life Solomonic decisions of this kind. If I had to, though, I might suggest as a first step what has already been suggested by prominent legal scholars: that convictions, and certainly capital sentences, never be based totally on a defendant's confession (as is not infrequently the current case), since confession as a speech act and a discourse genre is notoriously subject to abuse.

REFERENCES

Ainsworth, J. (1993). In a different register: The pragmatics of powerlessness in police interrogation. *Yale Law Journal*, **103**, 259-322.

Austin, J. L. (1962). *How to do things with words*. Oxford: Clarendon.

Davis, N., & Starn, R. (1989). Introduction. *Memory and Countermemory*. Special issue of *Representations*, **26**, 1-6.

Geertz, C. (1983). *Local knowledge*. New York: Basic Books.

Grice, H. P. (1975). Logic and conversation. In P. Cole & J. L. Morgan (Eds.), *Syntax and semantics 3: Speech acts* (pp. 41-58). New York: Academic.

Johnson, B. (ed.) (1993). *Freedom and interpretation*. New York: Basic Books.

Lakoff, A., & Becker, M. (1991). *Me, myself and I: Spatial metaphors for the self*. Unpublished manuscript.

Lakoff, R. (1990). *Talking power*. New York: Basic Books.

Linde, C. (1993). *Life stories: The creation of coherence*. Oxford: Oxford University Press.

Sacks, H., Schegloff, E., & Jefferson, G. (1974). A simplest systematics for the analysis of turn-taking in conversation. *Language*, **50**, 696-735.

Sass, L. A. (1992). *Madness and modernism*. New York: Basic Books.

Searle, J. R. (1969). *Speech acts*. Cambridge, England: Cambridge University Press.

Searle, J. R. (1979) *Expression and meaning*. Cambridge, England: Cambridge University Press.

29 MANAGING THE INTERMENTAL: CLASSROOM GROUP DISCUSSION AND THE SOCIAL CONTEXT OF LEARNING[1]

Mary Catherine O'Connor
Boston University

In recent work on classroom group discussion and its role in learning[2] an idealized view of classroom discourse frequently appears. In this idealization, content-related meaning is continually negotiated and created in the moment by peers who respect each others' views. Within the participant structure of small or large group discussion, students purposefully appropriate each others' ideas and utterances to further their own thinking and that of the group. In this scenario, students have the right and responsibility to function as equal members in a "discourse community" characterized by frequent instances of dialogic discourse.

While the supposed social benefits of such participant structures are sometimes emphasized, the usual focus is on the cognitive benefits. "Whole-class discussions enable students to pool and evaluate ideas, record data, share solution strategies, summarize collected data, invent notations, hypothesize, and construct simple arguments" (National Council of Teachers of Mathematics [NCTM], 1989, p. 79). Small group discussions are believed to confer similar benefits. These beliefs about classroom discussions are generally buttressed by reference to Vygotskyan theory, in that collaborative or joint reasoning, the "intermental" plane of cognition, is viewed as the genesis of a child's individual "intramental" functioning.

[1] A version of this paper was presented at the Annual Meeting of the American Educational Research Association, April 1991. Support for the data and analysis presented here was partially provided by a postdoctoral Spencer fellowship from the National Academy of Education, and by a grant to the Literacies Institute from the Mellon Foundation. The views expressed here are mine alone and are not intended to represent those of either organization. Special thanks are due to Lynne Godfrey, Sarah Michaels, Pamela Paternoster, and Amy Strage. Susan Ervin-Tripp deserves more tribute than a paper of mine can offer. Her vital, curious, and wide-ranging mind and her accepting, gentle nature have been crucial ingredients in the intellectual development of many students. She has created a research environment in which many people have been able to find their own way, due to her benign scholarly mentoring. Finally, she has made more visible to many the complex and beautiful social fabric that we are all weaving and rending with our every use of language.

[2] A partially random sample might include Yackel, Cobb, & Wood, 1991; O'Connor & Michaels, 1993; Chang-Wells & Wells, 1993; Gray, 1993; Hatano & Inagaki, 1991; Forman & Cazden, 1985; Lampert 1990; Brown et al., 1993; Pontecorvo & Girardet, 1993.

For a variety of reasons this ideal is seldom visible in real classrooms; it's easy to understand, however, why it appears in writings on classroom teaching and learning. There are good reasons to think that the ideal is a worthwhile target for research and practice. Unfortunately, the idealization itself, however heartening, may do a disservice to teachers and students alike, in that it encourages us to avoid serious examination of the complexities posed by classroom group discussion and group learning. As soon as one spends time in an actual classroom where group discussion is part of the instructional panoply, a less than ideal reality emerges, one in which social and interpersonal factors work their often unwelcome way into the group learning and thinking that is supposed to be taking place. Stone (1993), in a paper that invites the reader to reconsider the notion of scaffolding, makes a relevant observation:

> The social relationships within a scaffolding situation can be seen as involving both a subjective relation defined by the current activity (the "here-and-now") and symbolic qualities of social interchange crystallized out of past interactions. This complex interpersonal context acts as a filter through which an individual's learning opportunities via scaffolding must be viewed. (p. 179)

Stone's point, made in relation to the prototypical expert–novice scaffolding situation, is pertinent to the context of peer interactions in group discussion. Put less elegantly, social relationships of various kinds can work against the desiderata of "group sense-making" and "negotiation of meaning." In this realist scenario, students' good ideas and insights may die aborning, squelched by disrespect or animosities that are generated on the playground or spawned within society's many varieties of group conflict. In these cases peers do not respect each others' points of view, but rather ignore them or even expend energy defeating them, not for any intrinsic lack of merit, but solely because of their sources. Less obvious but no less problematic is the fact that even problem-solving activities or pedagogical practices themselves, as implemented by the teacher, can be resisted by students for vague reasons having to do with their symbolic qualities or their perceived social histories.

In short, implementing the classroom discourse practices intended to create a "community of learners" or a "discourse community" or a "thinking curriculum" is not for the faint-hearted. These practices and participant structures require individuals to interact with each other in ways that depart from the social norms they adhere to in most other areas of life. This fact has so far gone largely unexamined in the literature on classroom discourse and teacher talk (but see Lampert, Rittenhouse, & Crumbaugh, in press, for a notable exception). Yet the increasing emphasis on classroom discourse as a context that fosters learning requires a serious examination of these factors.

For these reasons, a theoretical framework that views classroom discussion as an unproblematic pathway to higher-order thinking practices is naive and will ultimately be of limited utility. The putative relationships between cognitive processes and classroom discussion cannot be easily separated from the social processes that are embodied in language use in those settings. Moreover, to understand the nature of the task facing teachers who adopt group discussion as a pedagogical tool, the multilayered nature of talk as social action between individuals must form a permanent part of our analytic framework for classroom discourse.

James Wertsch, in his many writings exploring and extending the work of Vygotsky and colleagues (e.g., Wertsch, 1985, 1991, Wertsch & Rupert, 1993), discusses the genetic relationship between the intermental and intramental. He argues that the intermental can only be studied and understood in its own terms in light of the social and cultural context in which a specific intermental activity is embedded — the setting in which individuals are in action, participating in the creation of their own and others' understanding as they interact in the social world around them.   These contextual dimensions of social and cultural forms of organization will necessarily then shape the outcome for intramental learning.   The issue of Stone's "filter" thus has relevance to the theorizing about the relationship between the intermental and the intramental.

In this chapter I will explore these issues in the context of an example of group discussion, finally posing a question about the use of language in group reasoning and the social processes that underlie the surface structure of the discourse. This example reveals some of the complexity facing a teacher in such a setting: the teacher must in some sense orchestrate the group's intermental functioning through orchestrating their language use. Given a realistic view of the social processes being played out within group discussion, what does management of that intermental context entail?

BACKGROUND

The episode described here took place in an urban public school. All names have been changed.[3]   While conducting a study of language use and mathematics learning, I was a participant observer in a sixth grade math class over a period of two years. Each year the math class consisted of 20 to 25 sixth graders, representing a wide range of ethnic, sociocultural and socioeconomic backgrounds.   The curriculum included units from the Algebra Project Transition Curriculum which are based on concrete experiences of various kinds that are "mathematized" through a cyclic, recurring five-step process (see Moses, Kamii, Swap, & Howard, 1989, for an extended description).

Group discussion is a central part of the curriculum, and students in this class were fairly adept at discussing their views and experiences. They were completely familiar with two participant structures that recurred frequently: (i) a large group discussion, in which all students sat down on a rug, roughly in a circle, and generally bid for turns by raising hands, and (ii) small group work, in which hands-on activities were carried out over periods of 30 minutes to an hour in an informal conversational setting involving assigned groups of three to five students (who usually worked together over the period of one to three months).

In the particular case to be described, the students were engaged in a pilot unit on

---

[3] I began observing in this sixth grade classroom in a public school in January and continued through the end of June of that year, and continued to observe frequently during the following school year. During that twenty-four month period, I made audiotapes and field notes of approximately 125 math class meetings and held regular discussions with the two teachers.

ratios and proportional reasoning, designed by Robert Moses. In this unit, students working in small groups mixed together various quantities of sugar and lemon juice to make a lemonade concentrate. They would then rate the concentrate on a sweetness scale, as in Fig. 29.1.

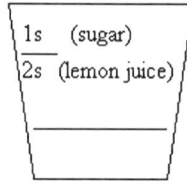

$$\frac{1s}{2s} \quad \text{(sugar)} \atop \text{(lemon juice)}$$

very sweet   sweet   neither sweet nor sour   sour   very sour

FIG. 29.1.

Each student mixed one strength of their choosing. For example, one student might mix two spoonfuls of sugar and five spoonfuls of lemon juice. Another might mix six spoons of sugar and three spoons of lemon juice. The students noted in writing how many spoonfuls of each they had used, tasted each other's concentrates, rated them for sweetness and wrote about it. Later the class created more concentrates, comparing tastes and using the concentrate values as data for various graphing activities, exploration of ratios, and the fractions representation of ratio situations. The following episodes take place during the days in which this curriculum was carried out.

Two students are the focus of this account: Ted and Tony. Ted's parents are both professionals. He, like approximately four fifths of the class, is a native speaker of American English. He appears to be influential among his peers; observations and discussions with his teacher suggest that many of the students treat him as a high status individual both in sports activities outside the classroom and in academic domains. For example, he is often cited as the source of opinions or views in group discussions when in fact the ideas originated with someone else.

Tony is a fairly recent immigrant from the Caribbean, staying with relatives in the area who provide support and careful guidance in his educational life. While expansive and seemingly fully incorporated in group activities such as sports with the boys in the class, he does not have Ted's influence in group discussions on academic matters. Moreover, his contributions are sometimes difficult for both adults and students to understand, and tend not to be picked up or extended by other students. Nevertheless he does not shrink from entering either large or small group discussion, and often tries to explain himself when he is not understood, gamely continuing to rephrase and re-explain, often at considerable length. On more than one occasion I observed students (girls) complaining to each other expressly about the length and intelligibility of Tony's turns.

The following two vignettes, taken from observations of small group work, are representative in a number of ways of the two boys' stances and roles in the classroom. They also exemplify the ways that ideas are often subordinated to social processes arising out of past interactions, the complex interpersonal context through which learning opportunities are "filtered."

1. Tony: "Oh, he always does this."

Group A is composed of two girls (Sarita and Jane) and two boys (Tony and Leon). Group A decides that it needs to make more of its lemonade concentrate, which is a 1/2 mixture (one spoonful of sugar to two spoonfuls of lemon juice). The small quantity they have (only one spoon of sugar and two of lemon juice in a little plastic cup) is not enough for the tasting procedure. But the group encounters a dilemma: If they mix another batch of 1/2, consisting of one spoonful of sugar and two spoonfuls of lemon juice, and add it to the one they have, they will then have two and four spoonfuls, or a 2/4 mixture. Is this the same mixture?

Jane argues heatedly that two batches of 1/2 would taste the same as one batch of 2/4. The fractions are equivalent; the mixtures will taste the same.[4] Sarita maintains that they are different mixtures and will not taste the same. Finally they decide to prepare both and conduct a taste test, but Jane says that Sarita cannot be the judge, since she would be "prejudiced," interested only in supporting her own hypothesis. The teacher, called in to their dispute, suggests that Tony serve as taste-tester. Tony, with a flourish, drinks both and pronounces the 1/2 mixture and the 2/4 mixture "different. They taste different."

Jane is disappointed, but even Sarita, whose hypothesis is affirmed, does not accept the judgment as reliable. They both immediately begin to discuss what is potentially wrong with the result. They tell me "Oh, Tony always does this. He just wants to say what Sarita wants to hear. He doesn't know." They begin to discuss ways to expose Tony's unreliability as a taster and as a reporter of his experiences. No energy is put into looking for other sources of error, for example, measurement error (a topic the class subsequently spends a great deal of time on, and which is clearly within the grasp of both girls).

In this group, a spontaneous dilemma did lead to some important attempts at sense-making. The small group intermental context seemed here to be fostering some authentic "horizontal" group thinking: peers working together to try to figure something out. But in this case, one participant in the context is disqualified from any role in furthering the thinking, due to his putative unreliability, a property "crystallized out of past interactions" (Stone, 1993, p. 179) by his peers, Jane and Sarita. For reasons that can only be surmised, Tony is not accepted as a legitimate participant within the context of problem solving.

2. Ted: "Look, this doesn't matter."

Group E was composed of three girls, Jennifer, Chloe, and Sarah, and one boy, Ted.

---

[4] This paper does not afford me the space to discuss the fascinating process whereby some students came to understand the physical and mathematical equivalence of various ratios through this extended experience with lemonade concentrates.

One day the four wanted to mix a new lemonade concentrate, in the ratio of four spoons of sugar to five spoons of lemon juice, in order to explore how different the taste would be from their previous mixture, a 3/5 mixture. This group already had decided that mixtures labelled by equivalent fractions were "the same," and now they wanted to explore what they were calling "similar fractions," those only one numerator or denominator unit away from their concentrate ratio. They decided to add one teaspoon of sugar to a mixture they already had — a 3/5 mixture — to create the new 4/5 mixture. Just as the group was adding the spoonful of sugar, Sarah announced that she saw a problem: since all four group members had taken tastes of the concentrate, they would be adding the extra spoonful of sugar to a cup containing an unknown quantity.

At first the others had trouble understanding this, then Ted leaped in with an objection. If they took Sarah's point into account, it would take "too much time" to remix the concentrate, they'd get behind — it was "not an important point." The disagreement escalated. Sarah, Chloe, and Jennifer all became angry at Ted, and their conflict suddenly resonated above the background noise. All heads turned towards Group E as Ted finally yelled "Look! I'm not getting a million dollars from the government to do this! This is a half hour math class!" A few seconds of complete silence followed this shouted declaration, then other groups turned back to their work.

Sarah's intuition was a good one, and if taken up could have generated some important sense-making.[5] Whether or not the students decided to start with a new concentrate, this is the type of spontaneous observation that indicates to cognitive theorists that the speaker is actively and mindfully thinking about what she is doing. It's an opportunity for learning, driven by a real dilemma. Ted's dismissal of it is unfortunate from that perspective. What drove him to react so vehemently?

The incident might be construed as a personal attack on Sarah by Ted, like the fairly personal dismissal of Tony in the previous example. But here Ted goes somewhat further than to devalue Sarah's observation. He deems it irrelevant, but his reasons for doing so are not stated in terms of its lack of merit, nor in terms of any intellectual lack of Sarah's. His reasons are stated within a dismissal of the entire context. For Sarah, the context requires intermental work. For Ted, this intermental work is not real. For him there is no obligation — or motivation — to truly explore beyond that which is most easily accessible. This is "just a math class."

Yet Ted is not intellectually lazy, as evidenced by his explorations in many other

---

[5] To understand the potential power of Sarah's intuition, consider the slightly simpler case of adding one teaspoon of sugar to a 2/4 concentrate — one consisting of two spoons of sugar and four of lemon juice. The resulting mixture will be in a ratio of three sugar to four lemon juice, and 3/4 is an appropriate label for any amount of the concentrate. Now if we take a cup of the same 2/4 concentrate, but three of the six teaspoons of concentrate mixture have already been drunk by tasters, then adding one teaspoon of sugar will result in a mixture that has sugar and lemon juice in a 2/2 (or 1/1) ratio, not 3/4. This event provides a good example of the ways that "hands-on" or "inquiry" science and mathematics can lead students to grapple with the complex linkages among mathematical relationships, the physical reality that is being "mathematized" within the problem-solving context, language that represents the physical situation, and mathematical language.

classes observed over the year. Nor does he normally seem to dislike interacting with his classmates. Rather, he seems here to question the legitimacy of the "inquiry" classroom as a whole. This stance was revealed in other contexts as well: in the aftermath of the incident mentioned above a group discussion was held about how to resolve problems that emerge during small group work. In this and other group conversations later in the year, Ted expressed the view that "all this talk is really a waste of time."

So here is the teacher's dilemma, a dilemma that the learning theorist and the curriculum designer rarely must deal with. Current progressive pedagogies (e.g., the "thinking curriculum" and "communities of learners" *inter alia*) aim to foster higher order intellectual development through the use of specific participant structures, and their concomitant discourse practices. Yet these practices bring with them nontrivial interactional consequences. Namely, all students, at least in principle, have the right to contribute, and all students, at least in principle, have the responsibility to entertain the contributions of their fellow students. The two phenomena described above — the discounting or dismissal of individuals' contributions, and resistance to the spirit of the entire enterprise — emerge (perhaps unavoidably) out of the classroom arrangements entailed by these pedagogies. Therefore the teacher in such a classroom is faced with a much more difficult task than in a traditional classroom, with its emphasis on students learning in relative isolation.

Without group interaction, students cannot cooperatively engage in the construction of joint meaning; neither, however, can they engage in the destruction of joint meaning. With group interaction, the teacher must manage the intermental context in such a way that the desired curricular outcome is reached, while also maintaining the rights and responsibilities of students within the group participant structures and maintaining the spirit of the enterprise. This is far more complex than traditional instruction because it requires socializing students into new ways of dealing with each other as intellectual companions or coworkers. If students do not voluntarily accept the ethos of such a classroom, it is virtually impossible to make them do so.

If a student does not complete a traditional assignment there are a variety of ways to persuade him to carry out that action; "you don't have to like it, but you have to do it." If a student does not accept the rights and responsibilities of a "dialogic" classroom participant structure, there are perhaps hundreds of points during a week where that student can bring productive work to a halt. The teacher is left in the untenable position of trying to persuade him to become part of a different culture. Perhaps most difficult is the fact that such resistance is often completely off-record, and thus nearly impossible to address directly.

MANAGING THE INTERMENTAL
IN LARGE GROUP DISCUSSION

In the remainder of this paper I will describe another incident within this curriculum, one that took place in a large group discussion. It is an incident that brings together several of the problems mentioned earlier, and to some extent centers around the two individuals previously described, Tony and Ted. It's important to note that in some ways this classroom provides a best-case scenario. Most of the students have been in this school for years, and have therefore become completely familiar with the discourse norms of an inquiry classroom. There is very little open hostility beyond what one normally finds in the volatile middle school years, and the students generally seem to get along well with each other and with their teacher. Yet this episode illustrates how subtle are the strands of resistance to the social norms the teacher attempts to install.

When this episode begins, the class is recording, for every class member, the values of sugar and lemon juice used by each class member in the making of his or her first lemonade concentrate. As the group checks its data, Paulina discovers that she has not recorded the number of spoons of lemon juice she used in her first concentrate. She remembers only that her first concentrate tasted sour, and that it was two and a half spoonfuls of sugar and between 10 and 22 spoonfuls of lemon juice. This presents a problem: Her first concentrate was mixed a month or more ago. There is no direct way to retrieve the actual value for lemon juice.

Several students begin to worry about this, and Claire, the teacher, invites them to discuss what to do. Over the course of the hour, four suggestions emerge and their merits are debated vigorously.

1) The class should leave Paulina's lemonade concentrate out of the data set.
2) Paulina should use the average of 10 and 22 for her lemon juice value.
3) Paulina should make a new lemonade concentrate mixture and those values should be used in the data set.
4) Paulina should try to reconstruct how many spoons of lemon juice she had originally by mixing up all the potential concentrates she might have originally mixed (2.5 spoons of sugar to 10 spoons of lemon juice, 2.5 spoons of sugar to 11 spoons of lemon juice, etc.). Then she should try each one, seeing if her memory is jogged by any concentrate in particular.

The 20 sixth-grade math class members, seated on the floor in a small area (10' x 8') discuss this topic for approximately 35 minutes, through 184 turns. The discussion continues into the next day's math class, and then a vote is taken. A great deal of active participation takes place, and intensity of interest is high. Interestingly, only two people suggest that the decision does not matter, and these two change their minds later, taking strong positions on what should be done.

When we join this episode, a number of students have been questioning whether strategies that substitute a new value for Paulina's old concentrate value are really legitimate, since they will not be her "real" first value. Ted is one of the students who is exploring this most actively. Tony then offers his suggestion, (4) above. His suggestion is delivered within a long and circuitous turn. (The two dot sequences indicate the excision of hesitations and false starts, which were quite frequent.)[6] Nevertheless Claire hears it, reframes it, and by reframing, offers it to the group for its consideration.

---

[6] Prosodic prominence is indicated by bold face. Contiguous utterances are indicated by "=". Overlaps are indicated by "[".

98 Tony: Um well I don't agree with um doing the testing, um like . . making another concentrate, but if . .it came down and we **did** have to do that, then
we would have to like do that . . choice thing again,
like when we . .were blindfolded and then we'll say like "which is
which?" and maybe it might gradually come back to us.
She'll remember, cause if . .she blanks out **all** the rest of the concentrates
that she tasted then and then she drank **this** certain one,
then she tried **all** through ten and twenty-two, maybe . .
After, we'll give it like five minutes so the taste would um disappear.
And then it might come **back** to her and and she might say well um it
was it was sort of like **this** but it was more on **this** side of =
99 Claire: = M-mm
100 Tony: of . . how it tasted than **this** one, and then . .we would skip this part. This
one would be **out** of it so that'd be one **less**. . .Then you narrow it down
until you get one that she says "Well **this** is what it tasted like, and so I
think . .it's going to be **hard** for me but I can . .if I can just remember a
little more about what I did, and I know I have like two and . . . . so if
ѕhe thinks a little more harder about it maybe it might come **back** to her,
and she'd remember it because that happens to me, too.
Claire enlists another student's support, and then reframes:
101 Claire: Leon, what do you think about Tony's idea?
102 Leon: I think it's a really good idea
103 Claire: So let me just repeat Tony's idea again, which was if Paulina was **blind**-
folded and we made up concentrates, . .that would have two and a half
spoonfuls of sugar — because that's what she had in her **first** concentrate.
And then there would be a concentrate that had two and a half spoonfuls
of sugar and ten spoonfuls of lemon juice, then the **n**ext one would be two
and a half spoonfuls of sugar — **eleven** spoonfuls of lemon juice, and so
on, Tony, all the way up to twenty-two spoonfuls of lemon juice? And
she'd keep tasting each one, and like between each one she'd [taste some]
water or wait a few minutes before she tasted the next one to see which
one reminds her the most of the one that she made in the **first** place?
104 Tony: . . Yea::h and . . . then she'd say m-mm "well **this** one, . . it's coming
back to me" and then we'd try to . . get all the . . books and people
around her in a group, and . . with **that** and with this **my** idea and . . with
help from her teammates that what she wrote where they wrote it down
and stuff maybe that might give us a clue of . . . .

Tony's suggestion is the only one of the four which involves the group in collaborative action to help Paulina reconstruct her concentrate value. It is an exercise in intermental memory: All students must bring their memory and records to bear on the problem, and together, maybe, as Tony says, "that might give us a clue." His statement of
the group strategy is formulated in terms of group goals: There are first person plural
pronouns throughout — "maybe it might gradually come back to us."

At this point Claire is faced with leading a group discussion in which one of the least academically persuasive students has made an interesting proposal (albeit not very clearly), a proposal that embodies many of the principles of the curriculum Claire is trying to support: It involves real inquiry, the answer is unknown, it will require collaboration between students, and it may include many students in the set-up and solution of the procedure. It has the disadvantage that it will require some time and effort, as Paulina will have to mix and then taste the range of concentrates between ten spoons of lemon juice and 22 spoons of lemon juice. The other suggestions would each have their own advantages and disadvantages, and Claire told me that she would have been willing to accept any of them, had the group converged on one of them.[7]

What happens next is that a number of students take up the idea and challenge it. Many of them attempt to dismiss it by raising various objections, most of which amount to questioning its plausibility as an approach — in various ways, they say "it just won't work." The politeness with which they say this is striking. As striking is the single-mindedness of their objections. In many discussions through the year, students would change sides, reconsider their position, state that they had changed their minds, and so on. In this discussion, the students who started out to defeat Tony's proposal stuck to their positions until an unexpected turn near the end of the second day's discussion.

Immediately after Tony finishes several more long turns about his Proustian idea, Miriam is called on. Her "thank you" and laughter are lightly poking fun at Tony's long-windedness, as though she is saying "well, it's about time."

108 Miriam: [to Claire] Thank-you [laughs] um well I have something to say . .
about **Ted**'s which was a **long** time ago.   And **that** is that um, I agree
that what he was saying was um, that if she um . . . but I remember
what **I** was going to say I was going to say that um she um that you that
you couldn't ask her to, I — this is also for Tony — You couldn't **ask**
her to remember what it tasted like?
Because it was like, **month**s ago.

109 Paulina: [mutters to no one in particular] I can't remember

Miriam begins her turn by citing Ted, something she does frequently, although she fails to construct a coherent account of what it was he said that she is citing. Notice also that Miriam has not addressed Tony directly, but directs all her utterances to Claire. She barely concedes that her objection is for Tony to address; halfway through her turn she says "this is also for Tony." Tony, however, immediately offers her a response directly.

110 Tony: [addressing Miriam] I know, but if if you get all . . **everything** from
everybody in the group, right? . . like you take um every idea that can
help her to go **back**wards like it's like going **back** in time . . . We'll be
going back in time by using all the um papers and sheets and studies
that she did and then that'd narrow it **down**.
And then we'd come to this point that says — well we know it wouldn't
be like two and fourteen or two and eighteen or something, . . and we'd

---

[7] An obvious question is why does it matter what happens with this data point? Why spend the time discussing it or trying to reconstruct the actual value? I take up this point at length in a forthcoming paper.

do much **bet**ter because then we won't have to use like **those** concentrates that we would have to um but we'd we might be able — we might um have to **do** that cause we'd have to bring it back

Miriam finally acknowledges Tony at this point: Laughing lightly she says "OK, I get it." She then immediately turns back to Claire and goes back to an earlier point in the discussion, before Tony had made his suggestion. She is polite in the way one is polite to a stranger who has done something embarrassing in public, polite, but clearly signaling to other bystanders that one is not "with" the stranger, in Goffman's sense.

Paulina, on the other hand, herself the focus of the day's discussion, does directly address her evaluation to Tony. She is the only person to use direct address to Tony without Tony first establishing direct student-to-student talk. Yet she challenges his idea, expressing doubt that other students' memories could be of help. She cites a previous comment of Miriam, who remembered having heard Paulina say, on that distant day when they first mixed the concentrates, "Ugh, it's sour."

127 Paulina: [to Claire] O.K. can I make a comment?

[to Tony] Um, I think your idea is a pretty good one, but ya know, . . if Miriam overheard me saying "well this is sour" um, it could have easily been ten [spoons of lemon juice] but then it could have also easily been twenty-two if it were sour.

128 Tony: Yes but what I'm saying is. . **you** make the decision. Like um you'd have to think you know how you . . remembered how it was between ten and twenty-two? then you'd have to um say, ya have to think real hard and say m-mm [gestures as though tasting]

[six turns deleted, Paulina and Tony continue to argue back and forth]

135 Paulina: Yeah well if I did . . it's hard to believe that I can recall it. Y'know, if I couldn't remember minutes after I did it, how I could remember **months** after I did it. I think your suggestion is pretty good, but there's **still** some **ob**stacles.

136 Tony: Well you try to, you try to do the best that you can **do**, by putting the obstacles out of your way.

A short time later, Ted weighs in with his view of Tony's plan. He addresses Claire, not Tony. When Tony directly responds to his comments, he talks briefly to Tony, but then turns again to address Claire.

142 Ted: I have a comment

143 Claire: Yes

144 Ted: [to Claire] because um I don't think it's going to work because if it was me, I'm **su**rely not going to remember how my concentrate tasted a long time ago and I **cer**tainly wouldn't be able to remember it if I had no idea of what one of the numbers was of the amount **use**d. And I think it's a good suggestion but it's too big of a time period, like if she had made it a **we**ek ago I think it would be a good suggestion . . but it was like a month or two or so and I don't think she would remember what it tasted like.

145 Tony: [to Ted] well you see how you had just said how it would be like um a

week ago and then you're . . finding a strategy to . . say well **this** was a week ago but I'm trying to find a strategy to say well this was like two months ago.

146 Ted: [to Tony] I know but still I don't think it would, I don't think it would — like I don't think she could remember.   I don't think her taste buds could remember that well what it tasted like.

147 Tony: [to Ted] well it's not only her taste buds that's going to have to work and she =

148 Ted: [to Tony] = Right but what I'm saying is like, well [to Claire] Can I ask Paulina a question?

Claire does not respond to this request, but instead takes a few more comments, and then asks Paulina whether she would be willing to try Tony's suggestion, no matter what the outcome of the class decision. Paulina agrees. This is a skillful move: Claire maintains Tony's suggestion as an interesting question in its own right, while being fully responsive to the comments that "it won't work."   By getting Paulina to say she will try it in addition to whatever the class decides on, Claire avoids the possibility that its defeat in a vote will constitute a complete loss for Tony.

In the literature on the cognitive outcomes of group discussion, one reads of good ideas that get developed, and less good ideas that get winnowed out. One rarely reads of good ideas that didn't make it through the process, and even less frequently of the individual consequences of putting an idea out for consideration only to see it dismissed without cause. But these are things that this teacher remembers long after the discussion is over. Yet Claire cannot openly demand that students adopt Tony's idea. The social norms that she has put in place for this classroom require individuals to argue for their ideas, and to motivate their decisions on the basis of negotiated understandings. Any direct support of Tony's idea from Claire would undermine his role as an equal participant in this classroom culture. His idea must stand or fall on its own.

Through the next 28 turns, Ted intermittently tries to get air time to ask his question of Paulina. Claire is trying to move the conversation forward, and Paulina has now agreed to try Tony's experiment, whether or not the group votes for it. If Ted's agenda is to defeat Tony's proposal, one might argue that that is now superfluous, since Paulina has expressed an interest in finding out, on her own time as it were, whether she will actually recognize the original concentrate when she tastes it. Ted, however, continues in this line of argumentation. With the authority of an attorney cross-examining a witness, he addresses Paulina, trying to establish the inadequacy of her memorial representation of the original concentrate taste, thus proving his point that Tony's experiment in memory is not worth doing.

171 Claire: O.K. let's make a decision here. Ted — what?

172 Ted: [to Claire] Awright I have a question for Paulina.
             [to Paulina]   Do you have **any** remembering, remembrance or whatever, of what your first concentrate tasted like or do you just like have **no** idea?=

173 Paulina: = yea::h I . . [*Paulina consults her incomplete notes taken when she first mixed her original concentrate*]

It says I tasted my lemonade concentrate and that it is. . and I had=

174 Ted: = No but not, **not** what your paper says.

175 Paulina: Alright

176 Ted: What do you think — do you have **any** idea what it tasted like?

177 Paulina: yea::h it tasted **strong** and that's what I put down. I said good but **too**
             strong.

178 Ted: Well, but like I mean — not like using one word, "strong."   Would you
             remember what it tasted like? Do you — not just if it's sour or not just
             if it's strong or a little sour=

179 Claire: =why why you asking her that [Ted?

180 Ted: [because if she has no idea, I don't think Tony's suggestion is going to
             work.

Claire ends the class soon after this interchange. The next day, after further discussion,
an amendment is proposed to Tony's plan. Another student proposes what is in effect a
binary search algorithm as an improvement to Tony's proposal: Make up a concentrate
using the middle value, two and a half spoons of sugar and sixteen spoons of lemon juice
(the"average") and give that to Paulina to taste. If she thinks her original concentrate
was sweeter than that, then her potential set of concentrate samples would be cut in half:
She would only have to taste the values of lemon juice lower than sixteen spoons. If she
thought her original concentrate was more sour than the middle concentrate, she would
only have to try the concentrates in the upper half of the range of lemon juice values.
Students responded in a very positive manner to this proposal: It would support the goal
of reconstructing the actual value, and it would not be as laborious as the solution Tony
originally proposed.   In fact, over two thirds of the students voted for the modified
version of Tony's proposal. When Paulina carried it out, everyone was somewhat shocked
to learn that it worked: She recognized her original concentrate upon tasting it.

CONCLUSION

What is the value of thinking about the fairly well-hidden animosities or personal agendas
that may, if my observations are well-founded, be taking place in these episodes? After
all, as adults we do not expect task-related interactions to be free of hidden agendas and
the sequelae of past interpersonal experiences. If we are primarily concerned with
individual cognitive development and learning in classrooms such as these, why focus on
what is usually just an undercurrent?

First, discussions with expert teachers quickly reveal that these social phenomena are
a major part of what must be managed in the moment to moment work of teaching. If
they are ignored, no veridical account of the work of teaching is possible. Moreover,
from the perspective of neo-Vygotskyan research on the genesis of learning, these
phenomena may be central to further development of the theoretical framework. Wertsch
and Rupert (1993) argue that although cognitively oriented Vygotskyan research assumes
that individual mental functioning (the intramental) is formed through an internalization
of social discourse, social discourse itself is fundamentally organized by issues of

authority and value. In the episodes reported here, students held clearly different views about who is inherently suited to contribute an idea, and what kinds of activities are truly productive. Tensions about authority and value recur throughout this and other episodes. Wertsch and Rupert argue that authority and value dimensions of social processes do not disappear in the process of internalization, rather "they are essential properties of *both* intermental and intramental functioning" (Wertsch & Rupert, 1993, pp. 236-237). If this is so, then the task as set out by Wertsch above, to study the intermental in its own terms, in light of the social and cultural context in which a specific intermental activity is embedded, requires that we pay attention to these troublesome aspects of interaction.

We can see in the example discussed here a tension growing out of the teacher's goals and the students' attitudes. The students hold divergent views about who is a real thinker, about who can legitimately contribute to the investigation. This teacher wants to legitimate the participation of all the students, to treat every student as a real thinker. The students also hold divergent views about the current activity: Is it real investigation, real intellectual work, or is it "doing school"? This teacher wants these students to treat the work as real — she wants them to engage in real exploration and sense-making. Yet there is a sense in which these two goals — the legitimation of all students' participation, and the orchestration of real, non-ritualized intellectual activity — sometimes undercut one another. And this is the real challenge of managing the intermental context: Some students see the exploration of a problem as less real, less intellectually compelling, due to the participation of other students whose views they do not value. The teacher cannot legislate or demand compliance, interest or participation. Instead, she must find ways to work always towards both goals, without sacrificing either.

This episode is particularly striking to some observers because of its length (almost two class periods) and the fact that it arose spontaneously; it is not part of the required curriculum. Many people ask "why did she take so long with that missing data point? They were really off track. What was she trying to do?" In the view put forth here, when Claire makes the decision to follow a spontaneous problem like this, she is directly addressing both the goal of legitimating all participants and the problem of supporting real inquiry. The length of the episode emerges out of her pursuit of these two aims. First, these "off-road" excursions into group problem solving often evoke contributions from students who do not put themselves forward during strictly curriculum-related discussions. Second, by making an investment of time in the question of the missing data point, she is working on the long-term project of enlisting students in the curriculum as a real enterprise. They learn that when a real problem arises, she will follow it, take it seriously, and insist that they do the same. And she will listen to their views about it, attempting to give equal consideration to all. The discussion I've presented here is intended as a caution against underestimating the complexity of that work.

REFERENCES

Brown, A. L., Ash, D., Rutherford, M., Nakagawa, K., Gordon, A., & Campione, J. (1993). Distributed expertise in the classroom. In G. Salamon (Ed.), *Distributed cognitions* (pp. 188-228). New York: Cambridge University Press.

Chang-Wells, G.L., & Wells, G. (1993). Dynamics of discourse: Literacy and the construction of knowledge. In E. A. Forman, N. Minick, & C. A. Stone (Eds.), *Contexts for learning: Sociocultural dynamics in children's development* (pp. 58-89). New York: Oxford University Press.

Forman, E., & Cazden, C. 1985. Exploring Vygotskian perspectives in education: The cognitive value of peer interaction. In J. V. Wetsch (Ed.), *Culture, Communication and Cognition: Vygotskian Perspectives* (pp. 323-347). Cambridge, England: Cambridge University Press.

Gray, L. (1993). *Large group discussion in a 3rd/4th grade classroom: A sociolinguistic case study.* Unpublished doctoral dissertation, Boston University.

Hatano, G., & Inagaki, K. (1991). Sharing cognition through collective comprehension activity. In L. Resnick, R. Levine, & S. Teasley (Eds.), *Perspectives on socially shared cognition* (pp. 331-348). Washington, DC: American Psychological Association.

Lampert, M. (1990, September). *Practices and problems in teaching authentic mathematics in school.* Plenary address, International Symposium "Research on Effective and Responsible Teaching." Fribourg, Switzerland.

Lampert, M., Rittenhouse, P., & Crumbaugh, C. (in press). Agreeing to disagree: Developing sociable mathematical discourse in school. In D. R. Olson & N. Torrance (Eds.), *Handbook of psychology and education: New models of learning, teaching and schooling.* Oxford: Basil Blackwell.

Moses, R. P., Kamii, M., Swap, S. M., & Howard, J. (1989). The algebra project: Organizing in the spirit of Ella. *Harvard Educational Review, 59,* 423-443.

National Council of Teachers of Mathematics. (1989). *Curriculum evaluation standards for school mathematics.* Reston, VA: National Council of Teachers of Mathematics.

O'Connor, M. C., & Michaels, S. (1993). Aligning academic task and participation status through revoicing: Analysis of a classroom discourse strategy. *Anthropology and Education Quarterly, 24,* 318-335.

Pontecorvo, C., & Girardet, H. (1993). Arguing and reasoning in understanding historical topics. *Cognition and Instruction, 11,* 365-395.

Stone, C. A. (1993). What is missing in the metaphor of scaffolding? In E. A. Forman, N. Minick, & C. A. Stone (Eds.), *Contexts for learning: Sociocultural dynamics in children's development* (pp. 169-183). New York: Oxford University Press.

Wertsch, J. (1985). *Vygotsky and the social formation of mind.* Cambridge, MA: Harvard University Press.

Wertsch, J. (1991). *Voices of the mind: A sociocultural approach to mediated action.* Cambridge, MA: Harvard University Press.

Wertsch, J. V., & Rupert, L. J. (1993). The authority of cultural tools in a sociocultural approach to mediated agency. *Cognition and Instruction, 11,* 227-240.

Yackel, E., Cobb, P., & Wood, T. (1991). Small-group interactions as a source of learning opportunities in second-grade mathematics. *Journal for Research in Mathematics Education, 22,* 390-408.

PART SEVEN:
GENDER DIFFERENCE
IN LANGUAGE ACQUISITION AND USE

30 GIRLS, BOYS AND JUST PEOPLE: THE INTERACTIONAL ACCOMPLISHMENT OF GENDER IN THE DISCOURSE OF THE NURSERY SCHOOL

Jenny Cook-Gumperz
University of California, Santa Barbara

Barbara Scales
University of California, Berkeley

The continued reproduction of unambiguously differentiated gender roles by children, evident from kindergarten play, through the gender separation of middle school into the highly genderized life of high school students, presents a puzzle to all those concerned with gender socialization. Despite major changes in power relationships between the genders in contemporary society and the influence of these on adult lives, children continue to reproduce behaviors evocative of earlier social arrangements. Recent work in elementary school shows that children insist on a clearcut separation of gender roles in elementary school life and tease their peers who want to crossboundaries (Thorne, 1993). Such boundary drawing becomes even stronger in high school with its ritual divisions between boys and girls, who often belong to separate, named groups, and where such group divisions have persisted through several generational cohorts of students (Eckert, 1988). Psychologists and sociologists who long ago rejected a simplistic biological determinism as the explanation for gender differentiated roles find these phenomena particularly challenging.

Gender reproduction theory in its strongest form, argues that the social roles of women and men, girls and boys cannot change in substantial ways until gender specific, stereotypic behaviors no longer exist. In this view gender differentiated behaviors will need to be eradicated before a cognitive and emotional basis for social change can be established (Connell, 1987; Holland & Skinner, 1990). Traditional views of social gender distinctions assume fundamental nature–nurture differences common to all and built into the very origins of human society (Rosaldo, 1974; Ortner, 1974). Such views propose that any changes in the social arrangements of gender would require a complete reversal of the given social order and the adoption of an "ideology of opposites" such that, for example, girls should hunt and fight, and boys should hoe and cook. Exploring such gender ideological views in contemporary classrooms, Bronwyn Davies found in her study of middle school children, "Frogs and Snails and Feminist Tales" (1987), that children were resistant to the idea of exchanging gendered behaviors, preferring differenc-

513

es to remain clear cut. She concludes that gender inequalities will continue to be reproduced until girls and boys are able to view each other as capable of the opposite behavior, with boys becoming nurturant and caring and girls becoming challenging and adven-
turesome.

As an alternative, what can be called the "weak" reproduction thesis takes the
position that task sharing and cooperation between the genders will weaken the reproductive links. Gender equality will come about through the withering away of distinctions.
This state of affairs can arise in a social environment of public gender neutrality where
women and men are able to achieve equity of tasks and positions in the social world
(Epstein, 1988). It is this latter view of the desirable benefits of gender neutrality that is
at the center of current political thinking and current school practice (Delamont, 1980;
Epstein, 1988).

Both views, however, present the problem of gender difference in terms of the need
for equity that will result from a redistribution of social roles and genderized tasks that
will bring about necessary social change. Both views see the continuance of social
gender as evidence of the need for ideological manipulation of what are considered to be
desirable activities for the two genders. Neither suggest the possibility of a move away
from an oppositional view of gender roles. More importantly, reproductive theories do
not deal with the more fundamental issues addressed by some feminist theory: whether
"the social organization of gender requires that there is a theory as to how we become
sexed and gendered . . . and that while biology informs notions of both sexuality and
gender these are not immutable givens" (Chodorow, 1989, p. 168). That is, the idea that
gender, as a set of interactionally constructed social categories, does not stand in opposition to the biological bases of human sexuality, but rather in complementary alignment
with it.

In a recent article, Cynthia Fuchs Epstein (1988) explores a social constructive
perspective on gender. In synthesizing two decades of research on gender difference, she
provides support for the view that gender roles are socially constructed by concluding, in
contradistinction to those who use a sociobiological explanation of gender, that the
reasons for the continuance of gender distinctions lies in the human need for organiza-
tionally powerful social categories. She suggests that social ideological categories are
most powerful when they are simple and clear-cut, and gender difference therefore,
provides us with one of the most powerful and available organizing categories.

In this chapter, we show how studies of children's early social gender learning
reinforces such a view of gender as a powerful and available organizing category. In
research on how children's social gender roles are communicated, we can see that from
early childhood to late adolescence and beyond, children interactionally construct gender
distinctions as important categories in terms of which they carry on their daily lives.
Work on children's styles of conflict and cooperation shows that the patterns of communication in girls and boys groups are essentially dissimilar (Goodwin, 1990; Sheldon,
1990; Tannen, 1990). Boys' and girls' groups are maintained through different ways of
organizing common activities through talk, talk that reveals how the social goals of the
two groups differ. Children from very early in their school career become part of a
communicatively realized, productive–reproductive social cycle. The main goal of this

chapter is to explore these ideas in the discourse of nursery school children.

In our recent work, we have found that even in the earliest years of preschool, gender is an important factor in children's construction of their social identity, one which has great organizational power in their daily lives (Cook-Gumperz & Scales, 1986; Scales & Cook-Gumperz, 1993). Though important throughout school activities, gender rarely receives explicit acknowledgment. In fact, gender neutrality is operative as an official curricular ideology in many school settings. Thus, the organizational force of gender remains active but hidden in the interactional and discourse practices of school activities. Our observations are supported by those of Vivian Paley (1984), who describes kindergarten teachers' attempts to avoid sex-stereotyped play by making the traditional areas of the nursery school — -the doll corner and the block area — into gender neutral zones. She shows that these efforts are defeated, however, by children's persistence in maintaining domains of conventionalized interactional and discourse practice (Cook-Gumperz & Corsaro, 1977). Despite teacher efforts to neutralize gender, Paley found that stereotyping by gender was well established in children's play activities by the time they reach the age of 5. For these reasons, attempts to neutralize or eliminate gender expression from classrooms neglect the significance of gender in the over-all development of the child.

In this chapter we describe our current exploration of how children use gender constructs interactionally in the discourse of their play. The data being used here are collected in a university-based preschool of 4- and 5-year-old children, and include ethnographic observation and video recording of interactional play episodes, narrative tellings, and interviews. Initially we explored the preschool children's conceptualization of gender differences using interviews to elicit the children's notions of common genderized object or activities. Photographs of familiar settings and objects were discussed with the children using settings both from preschool play areas which we knew to attract gender distinct groups, such as the climbing structure and the playhouse, and photographs of adult settings: kitchens and offices and objects associated with adult usage — typewriters, stoves, trucks, cars and vans. The results of these interviews showed that, as could be expected from other research on children conceptual development (Carey, 1987), preschool children found the task of talking about gender as an abstract category difficult or puzzling.

While gender is potentially one of the most accessible social categories available to children, situated at the junction of the biologically given and the socially communicated, what makes gender a powerful social construct is its use in discursive practices. How gender becomes central to the children's construction of a social self in interaction and discourse with others has so far been discussed only as a part of the experimental literature on child sociolinguistics (Andersen, Chapter 8, this volume; Ervin-Tripp & Mitchell-Kernan, 1977). Children begin to express some perceptions of social gender difference as early as the age of 4 (Lloyd & Duveen, 1991). However, developmentally, this awareness of gender as a separate category can be seen as a consequence of cognitive advances in children's ability to classify objects in terms of similarities and differences, and at this age the constructs are not well equilibrated (Van Hoorn, Nourot, Scales, & Alward, 1993). As a result of this lack of equilibration, children tend to see the two genders as polar extremes, with girls and boys perceived as the opposites of each other.

Teachers and parents are often dismayed by the stereotypic form that a child's social awareness of gender differences seem to take. However, when children use gender categories as active social guides to their own behavior, their adoption of such aspects of gendered categories may enable them to achieve social goals for themselves within the emerging peer culture. Corsaro, in a sociological study of preschools (1992), reports that certain roles carry more status than others; for example, "mommies" and "big sisters" or "super heroes" and "bad guys" are higher status categories than pets or animals. It is clear from teacher reports that some of these categories are also part of a genderized world, the higher status being more genderized and the lower status less so. Many of these roles will not only be expressed in stereotypic form but may also emerge in uniquely original forms as well, especially if they realize a given child's social goals. For example, one shy but imaginative and articulate 4-year-old girl recently took on the role of a "super cat" in her thematic play. As a consequence, within the space of a few weeks, she moved from a peripheral member of the group to one who suddenly had many friends and play partners and could competently engage in dramatic role play across gender in diverse configurations. The in-depth study of such discrepant cases may shed light on how interventions to assure gender equity can proceed in the classroom.

Moreover, children's gender perceptions often reflect aspects of the culture at large, which at present, even for adults, frequently defines gender in terms of opposing groups (Faludi, 1992). For some researchers, these childhood representations of difference are seen as both contributing to and consequent of a dichotomy in which the sexes operate as two different cultures (Maltz & Borker, 1982), and children's development of gender roles is a playing out of this adult script. Some recent research suggests that the differential between the boys' and girls' groups may both mimic and reflect the adult culture's predominant notions about management of power (Kyratzis, 1992). According to this view, men and women occupy separate cultural spheres and wherein the different evolutions and natures of these two can be accounted for by society's existing power relationships (Tannen, 1990). From this point of view, gender identity for children, as manifested in differences between girls' and boys' social choices, while not biologically determined, becomes activated through the interactional experience of children. Childhood experience continues to consolidate many genderized practices under peer pressure.

However, from our own research, we see that gender differentials are more fluid and dynamic than is allowed for in any single-script view. Taking the perspective that children define themselves with respect to others and are subject to both cultural and developmental influences, we see that gender differentials are continuously being negotiated and vary in differing contexts. What distinguishes gender is not an *a priori* script provided to a child at birth in each culture or society. Instead, the distinctive characteristics of gendered action are the product of *particular* interactions over time. The identity choices that emerge will be to some extent unique. That is, they will be influenced by particular constellations of the child's personal social context, for example, the gender of siblings, the child's birth order and place in the family, the presence or absence of two parents in the home, and the presence or absence of step family, as Dunn and Plomin (1990) have argued. We are suggesting that analysis of the processes by which gender is achieved and interpreted in early schooling reveals a more complicated picture of how social gender is constructed than either a simplified reproduction theory or biological determinism would allow.

By looking at how children talk about gender as they attempted to solve everyday problems in their own world, we see that while their views may reflect some stereotypic models, they also appear to be sensitive to local social and family contexts, drawing upon multiple sources as they put together their own social constructs. In the following example from one of our interviews, a 4-year-old boy is discussing with a researcher some pictures of things that adults do, in this case, drive cars and trucks. In a way common to many children of his age, he uses gender differences as a category that must be distributed fairly between the objects and persons, and he demonstrates an awareness of order relations involving categories of age, people, and objects, that is "big girls" can drive trucks but "little girls" can not. In the transcript excerpt below we can see how he attempts to explain how the adults he knows actually behave. Realizing that he is dealing with a discrepant case, Matt begins to reason out the problem but his attempts are interrupted by the interviewer just as he makes the discovery that as "Suburban," being minivans are neither trucks nor cars, they can "belong" in either category and thus can be driven by either men or women.

Example One: Matt's interview

Matt   Yeah, when I grow up I'm gonna learn how to drive a car.

Res   Okay. And how about a truck?

Matt   A truck?

Res   Will you drive that, too, do you think, or not?

Matt   Yeah, I can drive either one [truck or car].

Res   Okay. Now, when girls grow up, do you think they'll drive one of these things?

Matt   Yeah, but they only grow up to moms, and boys grow up to dads.

Res   Uh huh.

Matt   Dads can drive trucks and girls can drive cars. But sometimes dads can drive cars and moms can drive trucks.

Res   They can do that?

Matt   Yeah, but if we have a Suburban, which . . .

Res   What's that?

Matt   It's not a truck.

Res   Oh. When girls in this school grow up, do you think they'll be able to drive trucks?

Matt   Uh, our mom know how to drive trucks.

Res   Do you think that means that other girls can drive trucks?

Matt   Yeah, other big girls.

In this interview, a 4-year-old child is attempting to reason about gender as a social category, adapting it to his understanding of the specific circumstances of his own life but when his reasoning is interrupted he seems to contradict himself. Matt's problem is one of categorization. The cognitive reasoning processes that occur in the development of gender categories when explored through hypothetical situations, have always been an issue in research on children's cognitive change (Carey, 1987). By contrast, the children in the next example are talking about play activities with which they are involved in their everyday play experiences.

Two little girls, Kristine and Chloe were asked about their accustomed expectations for who plays in the various play sites in the preschool yard. By "accustomed expectations" we mean those expectations that arise through patterns of use over time of the school's various social ecologies. As such, these expectations are part of accumulated social experience in a particular setting and particular set of social relationships (Cook-Gumperz & Corsaro, 1977). As the remarks of Kristine and Chloe reveal, the two little girls were aware of gender-defined boundaries, but were also aware that these boundaries could be transcended (Ruggles, 1989).

Example Two: Kristine and Chloe's Interview

Res Who would you go on the big structure with?

Kris Ummm . . . we like to stoled it from the bad guys.

Res You like what?

Kris We like to stoled it . . . cause we never been there.

Res Oh, Kristine, what did you say about the bad guys?

Kris Ummm . . . oh. We'd like to stoled it from the bad guys, because they have it every time of the day.

Chlo So, we have to take care of it. But we didn't take care of it yesterday.

Res Who are the bad guys?

Kris They just play.

Chlo They're all David's friends and David.

Res Oooh.

Chlo My brother David.

Res You steal it. . .you steal the big structure from the bad guys?

Chlo Yeaaaa . . . then they leave.

Kris Yea! They chase us . . . but I try to get 'um away.

What is at issue here is possession of the play site: The boys customarily use the climbing structure as a frame for their games of chase and catch. The girls are unlikely to be invited to participate in these games and the two girls interviewed suggest that they would like to appropriate it for themselves, although in reality they have never been observed doing this. If Chloe seems a bit more intrepid about possibly invading the "boys' territory," perhaps it is because the David she refers to is in fact her own twin brother, someone with whom she has a very familiar relationship. The effect of sibling relationships on a child's definition of his or her gender identity and personal power is only beginning to be investigated (Yeatman & Reifel, 1992). It has been observed, however, that a child's search for personal power is reflected partly in a gender-differentiated desire to affiliate and win acceptance within his or her peer group. Clearly, the gender category holds great significance for children, and we see its more stereotypic or one-dimensional forms surface in talk about gender as a generalized, abstract category, such as girls become "Moms" and boys become "Dads."

However, we found unmistakable evidence that children use gender differentiations in distinctive ways in managing their social world when we analyzed an extensive collection of children's narratives dictated to teachers at this university preschool over a one-year period. In these stories it was found that the narrative forms developed by children divided overwhelmingly along gender lines. This division was reflected in both form and content (Nicolopoulou, Scales, & Weintraub, 1993; Nicolopoulou, Chapter 22, this volume; Scales & Cook-Gumperz, 1993). Even though all the stories told by the children were regularly enacted as story plays for all the children in the group at circle time each day these differences nevertheless emerged.

Both in the dictated narratives (or story-plays) and in video-taped observations of children's spontaneous dramatic play, we saw the organizational power of gender as a category. We suggest, however, that utilization of gendered categories does more than merely mimic adult forms, it also provides a vehicle for the child to articulate relationships within the peer-group, social fabric of the classroom. As Helen Schwartzman (1978) noted in her daycare study, a strategy for establishing a niche for themselves is found in the uptake of roles which are part of a child's fantasy and play life as we described above with the episode of the shy little girl as "super cat." Schwartzman asserts that roles assumed by children in dramatic play often reflect their perception of power relations in the group.

In the examples from a collection of group play episodes reproduced below, we found that the genderized nature of the play appeared to be most highlighted when the two groups were playing in close proximity rather than any interaction between gender different individuals. There is therefore a distinct interactional dimension to the expression of gendered behavior. These episodes demonstrate the organizational power of gender in children's interactive play, even in the relatively gender neutral setting of a university-based preschool classroom. Such gendered play commonly goes on unnoticed, continuing to exist as a hidden curriculum, unless it takes an overtly aggressive form (such as rough and tumble play on the part of boys). In this latter case teachers are likely to intervene or attempt to prohibit rather than seek to understand such incidents, as Vivian Paley (1984), describes in her preschool studies.

As the play episodes begin, the three girls, Jennifer, age 4;9, Emily, age 3;10, and Alicia, age 4;5, enter a carpeted area of the classroom. They gather around a small sand tray with such accessories as miniature people and animals on the right and an array of variously sized blocks to the rear of the area. The three girls start a play episode typical of the play in the sand box. They begin by constructing a house setting into which animal characters are introduced.

The girls establish the outlines of a scenario involving making food, tending and feeding pets, and tidying the area. Alicia introduces a topic: "Sweep our roads, sweep our roads, everybody sweep here." Jennifer follows with a topic about making rice, which Alicia takes up also. After several minutes, the single boy, James, comes and sits next to the shelves to the right of the girls.

Close examination of the unfolding sequences of the interactional episodes reveals the way in which gender categories affect players and the course of their play. The scenario develops from a play episode between three girls who are using both blocks and miniature animals at a sand tray. Two different interruptions occur in the course of the play, one by a **single** boy who begins to play nearby and a second involving a **group** of boys who come by and then return to set up a block structure adjacent to the girls. The first

interruption by the lone boy is quickly negotiated. When in response to the girls challenge he quietly asserts: "I'm not bothering you," his talk is reclassified into a nonthreatening action which can be explained away by saying: "He is a just being a next-
door neighbor." In this way, James becomes a warranted part of play and his actions are
not treated as gender specific. He remains nearby as just a "person," not a gendered
individual. The girls are therefore able to continue alongside their "neighbor" without
changing the character of their play.

Example Three

176	Jam	(making weird noises.)	
177	Jen	If you will not please, don't bother us!	
178	Jam	I'm not bothering you.	
179	Jen	OK - well then don't trip the horses or the dogs or the zebras.	
180	Jam	I wasn't doing that.	
181	Jen	What?	
182	Jam	I wasn't doing that.	
183	Jen	Oh good- good. He's just	

183 Jen Oh good- good. He's just
             being a next-door neighbor   James playing by himself,
             or something because we have   talking quietly.
             a house.

With the arrival of a **group** of boys, however, the play changes. The fact that the
boys form a group introduces the possibility of genderized action as a salient feature, a
possibility that did not arise with the single boy. Since the new arrivals are a **group**, the
three original girl players become a **group** of girls rather than continue as gender unspe-
cific "animal organizers." Gender rapidly becomes the controlling issue in the play
discourse for both groups, realized both in the thematic content and in the action. As the
two collections of boys and girls evolve into oppositional groups, they take on new
socially organized identities which have a life of their own for the duration of the
activities. From this point onward, additional candidate members will need to be induct-
ed into the group as gendered members. While the single boy could potentially have
been adopted into the girls' play, and is in fact treated as a marginal occupant of the
girls' play space, after group consciousness is raised neither boys nor girls could enter
into each other's world.

Some moments later the four boys, Marc, age 4;5, Nathan, age 4;1, and twins Colin
and Stewart, age 4;3, stride into the block play area where the three girls have now
moved their play. The boys are swinging lassos and chanting, "Looking for a lost bunny.
Looking for a lost bunny." They stop in front of the girls' block structure and ask if they
have seen a bunny. As the boys leave, the girls pause to watch intently without moving,
then resume their play. James' status apparently remains unchanged on the periphery of
the action.

However, now the girls' play theme is somewhat altered as Jennifer's high pitched
play-voice is heard calling, "Help, help." Alicia expands the theme with her own
contribution: "Help, mommy; help, mommy." As can be seen in the final portions of
excerpt four, the arrival of a group of boys has begun to transform the play theme of a
quiet animal play. The girls have incorporated their anxiety over the boys' actions into

their play characters' utterances [lines 231-236]:
Example four

221	Mar	Come on, you guys.	Marc comes in, speaks to others (**not** to Alicia, Emily, Jennifer).
222	Nat	Looking for a lost bunny. Looking for a lost bunny - for a lost bunny - looking for a lost bunny.	Boys come through - Nathan, Colin, Stewart - Marc continues on/off screen. All are swinging lassos.
223	Mar	Put that in the box.	
224	Nat	(You know) have you seen a bunny?	
225	Emi	No	
226	Jen	No/no bunny at all.	The group of boys stop in front of Jennifer & Emily
227	Mar	Well, if you see one - call us.	
228	Nat	If you see one, call us.	
229	Col	If you see one, call us.	
230	Jen	(XXX)	
231	Emi	Kitty chase - chase any animal it wants to eat anybody or (be anything back).	Marc goes off. Nathan follows.
232	Ali	Can these persons have a tall bridge	Colin and Stewart follow.
233	Jen	Help! Help!	
234	Ali	Look, I covered it with a block.	Alicia and Jennifer watch after the boys.
235	Emi	Great can this kitty	Jennifer goes to large blocks
236	Ali	Help mommy, help mommy.	Jennifer comes back.

At this stage, as the following segment demonstrates in keeping with the somewhat more ominous tone of the domestic play just prior to the boys' second entrance, Emily, the youngest, introduces two new topics: "bad guys" and "traps." Efforts are made by the three interactants to integrate the various new topics. After the considerably more intrusive foray by the boys into the block area, the themes of "traps," being "caught," and needing "help" begin to multiply.

This final sequence begins when Nathan, Marc, and a new player, Darrel, age 4;4, come into the area and begin to play very near the girls, repeatedly passing behind the girls' play space in order to obtain blocks to build a "hideout." In a loud voice, Marc is alternately singing, "We're working" or "We're walking," as the boys pass back and forth to obtain large blocks for an adjacent area. The girls attempt to ignore the boys and continue their play despite the disruption of the boys' repeatedly passing nearby to select blocks and on occasion furtively stealing blocks from the girls' structure. In excerpt five, we see the girls' play become more and more involved in the "trap" theme: being "stuck in the trap" and needing "help." The girls seem intent on ignoring the boys' rather obtrusive play until Jennifer, coming out of role, says, "See those two boys." The boys now are loudly and repeatedly chanting, "Keep on working," varied sometimes as "Keep on walking," as they continue to pass near the girls to obtain more and more blocks. At this point the youngest of the girls is distracted and picks up the boys' theme when she discovers a microphone in the area and begins to speak into it, "Work, hello, keep on work//work. I have to work. I have to go to work, Jennifer."

Example five

471	Ali	That would look excellent	Nathan comes in for another block.
472	Jen	Alicia look it. I found	
473	Emi	Pretend the girl tail got stuck in here.	While walking very near the girls, Nathan's block slips and he catches it.
474	Nat	Gotcha, gotcha, gotcha, boom.	
475	Emi	Jennifer, Alicia pretend this girl tail got stuck in here.	Marc comes by, walks
476	Jen	Hey! Hey, I'm stuck in the trap. Hey, there's a trap here, there's a trap here. Ah, help, help, help, help	around Alicia, Emily, and Jennifer
477	Emi	In the house	
478	Jen	Help, help, some horse help	Nathan comes around to get another block.
479	Ali	Ahhh (sound high & babyish)	
480	Nat	Doie, doie, doie, (etc. . .)	
481	Ali	Oh, I need to get my pony.	
482	Jen	I'll stay right here.	Alicia crosses around and gets her toy.
483	Emi	(XXX)	
484	Ali	(XXX)	
485	Jen	Who's that // // (xx) Oww/ // I'm going for a long walk.	

486	Emi	where that place (xx)	Teacher goes over to boys and talks with them.
487	Emi	She can jump down from the water	Jennifer gets up, gets a block. Darrel and Nathan come over to shelves.
488	Mar	(off screen) Come on, we need a bit more.	
489	Nat	Quick, Darrel.	
490	Emi	slide down a fall	Gets blocks.
491	Jen	see those two boys.	
492	Emi	We're having fun with the (xxx) because you can slide down and land on here // OK? OK?	
493	Jen	Open this gate door and let me out.	
494	Ali	Oww, oww, oww	
495	Emi	Let's play with my(xx) these three ponies, OK? These three ponies, OK// // We're playing with these three ponies, OK?	Emily gets to other side of Alicia and Jennifer.
496	Jen	now, now	The three boys come in behind sandbox and start singing, "Keep on working," sometimes
497	Mar	Let's go to working Keep on working.	"Keep on walking," repeated approximately 25 times.
	Emi	Work, hello, keep on worker// //(un ko)I have to go work, I have to go work, Jennifer	Emily finds mike and speaks directly into it, then to Alicia and Jennifer.

Finally, in example six, Jennifer, coming out of role again, attempts to control the unruly situation that is developing by calling out a suggested ultra-polite request which could be addressed by her two friends to the boys, but also said loud enough so that the boys can immediately overhear, "and we should say to be quiet":

Example six

| 499 | Jen | And we should say to be quiet we should say you should be quiet, we should say be quiet, we should say you should be quiet. | Three boys continue singing, as above. Emily leaves. Teacher interrupts, talks to boys. They start singing again. |

500	Emi	Do you want to see a ring? Do you want to see a ring.	Boys still singing. Alicia covers her ears. [some whispering here]
501	Jen	Hey, look it. Hey, are you dead?	
502	Ali	No, I'm not.	Boys still singing.
503	Jen	Well, I don't mean to interrupt you.	
504	Emi	This, this girl (kept on) walking and walking and walking and walking.	
505	Jen	Pretend she was walking this way.	
506	Emi	And she fell off here.	Alicia and Emily come behind Jennifer.
507	Ali	( )	
508	Jen	[sings]	
509	Ali	( )	
510	Emi	And she had no ( )	
511	Ali	( ) her space.	
512	Jen	Hey look out // I'm just hurting myself ( ) like this, and I don't want to fall down and hurt myself (again).	
513	Emi	( )	
514	Ali	Help, help! ( )	
515	Emi	We're just walking her and walking and walking and walking.	
516	Jen	Help me. I'm in the hole, help me, I'm in the hole ( ).	Alicia and Emily come over.
517	Ali	Be careful because there's a cliff and right here and you could fall off and hurt yourself.	
518	Jen	Maybe I'll just leave her right here.	
519	Ali	OK, maybe not too close.	
520	Emi	Pretend she fell off // OK / OK	
521	Jen	( ) her girlfriend.	

522	Ali	Ah, Ah, help us quick. I'm falling. See ( )	
523	Emi	Oh ah we're knocking through that's okay, the whole bridge this this made their own house, (right here).	Emily brings some blocks over.

We note in this long passage from the videotaped episode that at the point that Jennifer, coming out of roleplay, asserts that they should say "be quiet," the theme of "walking" that the boys have utilized in their play finally gets incorporated into the girls' play. Emily says, "This, this girl kept on walking and walking and walking and walking and walking," and Jennifer incorporates the walking topic by saying, "Pretend she was **walking** this way." Emily follows with her own theme expansion: " . . . and she fell off here." It is from this point on that themes of **danger, falling,** become more intense and cohesive among the girls. Here, Emily has become much more assertive by repeating the boys' theme of "working" and "walking" and by attempting to develop more aggressive activities, such as knocking over blocks.

These episodes can be seen as the playing out of a psychodrama, in which tension is built up as the two gender different groups establish themselves in juxtaposition and begin to define themselves through their talk and actions. The existence of the other is clearly thematized as both have become oppositional gendered groups. Although this does not initially disturb the rhythm of the girls' activities, gradually the girls treat the boys' activities both as a threat and a challenge and the girls' topics of talk move into some synchrony with the boys'. The themes of talk move from those of danger and helplessness and incorporate the same chants and words as the boys are using. The transcript shows how the boys' attempt to invade the girls' enclosed world, first by creating a diversion through the development of the rabbit theme and then by positioning their play in juxtaposition to the girls' domain. Further into the episode we can see that both groups have influenced each other's talk and activities to a point where the original themes of their separate play breaks down, and both parties finally leave the scene.

We suggest that by establishing a presence within proximity of each other, both the girls and boys begin to realize themes by which they define themselves collectively as gendered beings, who then engage in a power struggle for control of their own play scenario. While the girls' original play theme of tending animals could be seen as more "girlish" in its emphasis on care-taking, the data show that the girls' own awareness of gender as an oppositional category begins only when the boys' proximal presence influences their domain. The existence of the boys' activities both in walking by the girls and then settling to play in close proximity to them makes it necessary for them to establish a distinctive, shared **group** identity of a "girls' world," if their play is to continue at all. This accommodation is at first expressed by ignoring the intruders and then by introducing themes of potential danger and helplessness into the animal play. Later, after a studied attempt to ignore the boys, the girls one by one finally acknowledge their presence. In doing so, they open the way for further accommodation by attempting to incorporate some of the boys' themes into their play. The boys' awareness of the girls is revealed mainly in genderized displays of activity using a challenging "macho" style of action-filled play themes such as, "hunting" for bunnies, singing about "working" and "walking" in a loud voice and marching to the singing tempo. The initial style of their attempts at entrance into the girls' territorial domain in a rear section of the large classroom seems to be more of a bid for a take-over than an accommodation. Not surprisingly, no interactive themes are established across the gender groups by the boys who continue to show their awareness of the girls by challenging themes and activities that keep them in close physical proximity. At the end of the play session the girls give up their efforts to maintain their play and leave the scene. As they do so, the boys' group also abandons the block structure they have been building and move off. Perhaps most revealing of the power of the group creation of a gendered identity is the fact that as Jennifer, the final girl to quit the play area leaves, she looks over to the lone boy, James, who has resumed his play nearby and says: "We don't need this any more, you can have it." James's identity as just a "person" not a member of a gendered group is maintained by his single status.

The dynamics of the play sequences analyzed here shows how the organizational power of the children's "hidden agenda" of gender is manifested in their free play activities. Gender becomes an active part of the children's discursive practice in a preschool setting and enters into all their activities. It is when gender neutrality operates as an official curricular ideology in an attempt to ensure gender equity in school settings, that the organizational force of gender can be hidden, continuing to exercise influence in many unnoticed peer interactional discursive practices. The children's interest in, and need to use gender as a category in the realization of a personal social self may become neglected. Because the young child's notion of gender does not coincide with the adult ideological world view it tends to be ignored. Yet the notion of gender remains important to children and often emerges in forms that are not subject to adult supervision, as we described in the young girls adoption of her play symbolic play roles as "supercat and superdog." Through their own construction of gender roles and gender categories, children, in their play activities, may interactionally realize a view of gender that will both challenge the older ideas of gender determinism and at the same time, make possible the creation of new gendered scenarios.

REFERENCES

Carey, S. (1987). *Conceptual change in childhood.* Cambridge, MA: MIT Press

Chodorow, N. J. (1989). *Feminism and psychoanalytic theory.* New Haven, CT: Yale University Press.

Connell, R. W. (1987). *Gender and power: Society, the person, and sexual politics.* Stanford, CA: Stanford University Press.

Cook-Gumperz, J., & Corsaro, W. (1977). Socio-ecological constraints on children's communicative strategies. *Sociology,* **11,** 411-435.

Cook-Gumperz, J., & Scales, B. (1986). *Gender in the nursery school: Final report to the Chancellor's Committee on Women.* Berkeley, CA: University of California at Berkeley.

Corsaro, W. (1992). The interpretive study of children's play. In W. A. Corsaro & P. J. Miller, *Interpretive approaches to children's socialization* (pp. 66-81). San Francisco: Jossey-Bass.

Davies, B. (1989). *Frogs and snails and feminist tales: Preschool children and gender.* Sydney: Allen and Unwin.

Delamont, S. (1980). *Sex roles and the school.* London: Methuen.

Dunn, J,, &. Plomin, R. (1990). *Separate lives: Why siblings are so different.* New York: Basic Books.

Eckert, P. (1988). *Jocks and Burnouts: Social categories and identity in high school.* New York: Teachers College Press.

Epstein, C. F. (1988). *Deceptive distinctions: Sex, gender, and the social order.* New Haven, CT: Yale University Press.

Ervin-Tripp, S., & Mitchell-Kernan, C. (1977). *Child discourse.* New York: Academic.

Faludi, S. (1992). *Backlash: The undeclared war against American women.* New York: Doubleday.

Gilligan, C. (1982). *In a different voice: Psychological theory and women's development.* Cambridge, MA: Harvard University Press.

Goodwin, M. H. (1990). *He-said-she-said: Talk as social organization among Black children.* Bloomington, IN: Indiana University Press.

Holland, D., & Skinner, D. (1990). Prestige and intimacy. In D. Holland & N. Quinn (Eds.), *Cultural Models* (pp.78-111). New York: Cambridge University Press.

Kyratzis, A. (1992). Gender differences in the use of persuasive justification in children's pretend play. In *Locating Power: Proceedings of the Second Berkeley Women and Langue Conference* (pp. 326-337). Berkeley, CA: Berkeley Linguistics Society.

Lloyd, B., & Duveen, G. (1990). *Social representations and the development of knowledge.* Cambridge, England: Cambridge University Press.

Maltz, D., & Borker, R. (1982). A cultural approach to male-female miscommunication. In J. Gumperz (Ed.), *Language and social identity* (pp. 196-216). Cambridge, England: Cambridge University Press.

Nicolopoulou, A., Scales, B., & Weintraub, J. (1994). Gender differences and symbolic imagination in the stories of four-year-olds. In A. H. Dyson & C. Genishi (Eds.), *The need for story: Cultural diversity in classroom and community* (pp. 102-123). National Council of Teachers of English.

Ortner, S. (1974). Is female to male as nature is to culture? In M. Z. Rosaldo & L. Lamphere (Eds.), *Women, culture and society* (pp. 67-88). Stanford: Stanford University Press.

Paley, V. G. (1984). *Boys and girls: Superheroes in the doll corner.* Chicago: University of Chicago Press.

Rosaldo, M. Z. (1974). Introduction. In M. Z. Rosaldo & L. Lamphere (Eds.), *Woman, culture, and society* (pp. 17-42). Stanford: Stanford University Press.

Ruggles, C. (1989). *Entering the child's world: Gender identity in young children.* Unpublished manuscript. University of California, Berkeley.

Scales, B., & Cook-Gumperz, J. (1993). Gender and play in nursery and preschool: A view from the frontier. In S. Reifel (Ed.), *Advances in early education and day care, Vol. 5* (pp. 167-195). Greenwich, CT: JAI Press, Inc.

Schwartzman, H. (1978). *Transformations: The anthropology of children's play.* New York: Plenum Press.

Sheldon, A. (1990). Pickle fights: Gendered talk in preschool disputes. *Discourse Processes, 13,* 5-31.

Tannen, D. (1990). Gender differences in topical coherence: Creating involvement in best friends talk. *Discourse Processes, 13,* 73-90.

Thorne, B. (1993). *Gender play: Girls and boys in school.* New Brunswick, NJ: Rutgers University Press.

Van Hoorn, J., Nourot, P., Scales, B., & Alward, K. R. (1993). *Play at the center of the curriculum.* New York: Macmillan.

Yeatman, M., & Riefel, S. (1992). Sibling play and learning. *Play and Culture, 5,* 141-158.

31 THE NEW OLD LADIES' SONGS: FUNCTIONAL ADAPTATION OF HUALAPAI MUSIC TO MODERN CONTEXTS

Leanne Hinton
University of California, Berkeley

1. INTRODUCTION

The topic of this paper is a new genre of song developed in the Hualapai school (Peach Springs, Arizona)[1] as a tool for teaching Hualapai language and culture. It is a genre which bears many traits of traditional Hualapai songs but also has characteristics and functions that are not traditional at all. The new genre has been influenced strongly by non-Indian culture. The songs bear features adopted from Western music, and features that reinforce modern western values; yet at the same time, the new songs express love of Hualapai land and history, and Hualapai pride and social unity. The result, then, is a form of *syncretic* music — a new kind of music that arises at the interface of cultures in contact.

1.1. Background

In the last two decades, there has been a flowering of school programs in Native American communities aimed at maintaining the viability of Native American languages and cultures. In some of these programs, songs in the native language are used as one means of increasing native language use among the children. For various reasons, traditional songs are usually inappropriate for this function: Often the traditional songs are sacred and not to be sung out of their appropriate context. In other cases, the songs contain few or no real words; they are still taught to children for their cultural value, but they are not of direct use as a language teaching tool. A fairly common practice in many communities is to translate common nursery songs and Christmas carols into the native language,

---

[1] The Hualapai Indians are a Yuman tribe, closely related to the Havasupais who live nearby. Before the present day tribal designations were established, there were seven loosely-associated bands that were linguistically close to identical and had social relations, but went to different locations to plant their summer gardens. Six of these seven bands now share the Hualapai reservation, and one band became the Havasupais. Even now, the tribes have close kinship ties and sing the same kinds of songs.

which does give the desired language practice to the children. But the problem with these songs, of course, is that they have no traditional cultural significance.

This chapter records an attempt by the staff of the Hualapai Bilingual Education Program to recreate a traditional Hualapai song genre, and what happened in the process. As a consultant to the Hualapai Bilingual Education Program, I was asked to work with the Hualapai staff to confront the problem of how to find appropriate songs for the classroom. The result, it should be pointed out immediately, was not what we expected.

The Hualapai Bilingual Education staff had begun to translate nursery songs and Christmas carols into Hualapai to teach to the school children, but were also interested in the prospect of finding traditional forms of music appropriate to the school setting. Circle dance songs were already being taught, but since they have only a few words embedded in a network of vocables, they were not ideal for language teaching. What was needed was a genre of songs which consisted of real words and at the same time one which was not at all sacred in nature — not, for example, the medicine songs, which should be sung only by medicine men in the curing context, or narrative songs, which can only be sung certain times of year.

I suggested to the staff a traditional genre of song that had once been very common, but was now so rare that most of the staff members had never heard of them. These were the Women's songs, often called the Old Ladies' songs. Until the early twentieth century, the composition of Old Ladies' songs was very common, probably practiced by the majority of women and many men as well (in which case they would be labelled "Old Men's Songs"). The songs were secular in nature, usually having quite personal subject matter. Usually the song was about a family member or a suitor, sometimes teasing and humorous in nature, sometimes caustic, sometimes loving. Sexuality was also a common theme (as in example 2). The songs served an important social function: They advertised to the community the composer's feelings about some person's qualities or behavior, and could shape the community's attitudes as a result. These songs could put considerable social pressure on the persons they were about. More important, however, was that the songs were a major vehicle of personal self-expression. They were also often beautiful poetry.

Such songs have not been composed since the early twentieth century among the Havasupais, and even earlier than that among the Hualapais. Their demise is of course related to the severe cultural and physical disruption created by the white invasion. But while these songs are no longer composed, many are remembered by the older Havasupai and Hualapai singers. During the 1960's several Havasupai singers provided me with a collection of these women's songs, which are referred to in this study. Some of the same songs are known by the older Hualapais.

Since most of the staff, who consist of younger Hualapais, had not heard women's songs before, they asked one of the older Hualapai consultants to come in and sing some. It was obvious to the staff that the subject matter of women's songs was too personal, often too sexual, to be appropriate for the classroom. Thus while the genre was appropriate for teaching language, the specific songs within the genre were not appropriate. It appeared that if Old Ladies' songs were going to be taught to the children, new songs would have to be composed that befitted the classroom.

The prospect of composing new songs was very significant. With a few exceptions, no living person in the two tribes had ever composed a song in a traditional genre. Havasupai and Hualapai songs have been a closed and diminishing corpus since the early twentieth century. The possibility of reviving an active composing tradition was attractive to all the staff members.

However, perhaps the most important finding in this experiment in composition was that the new Old Ladies' songs composed by the staff were so different from the old ones that they cannot be called members of the same genre. It has been maintained by some researchers that song function shapes song form (Lomax, 1968; Hinton, 1984). The functions to be served by the new women's songs were very different from the function of the old ones, and as a result, rather than a revival, the creation of a new genre occurred. I will show below some of the differences between the old and new women's songs, and will attempt to explain how these differences derive from functional differences.

2. THE OLD LADIES' SONGS, AND THEIR RELATION TO OTHER GENRES

There are many different genres of Havasupai and Hualapai songs, each having its own diagnostic musical and text characteristics. Most of the genres are so rarely sung today that young adults are completely or almost completely unfamiliar with them. There are two genres that the younger generations hear commonly: the funeral songs and the circle dance songs. The funeral songs include such song cycles as the Bird Songs and Tomant, which came to the Hualapais and Havasupais from the Mojaves; these exhibit the "rise,"[2] a melodic device common to Mojaves and other Yuman tribes as well as most tribes in Southern and Central California (Nettl, 1954). Hualapais and Havasupais do not utilize the rise in their native music (Hinton, 1984). Very few Hualapais and Havasupais sing the funeral songs proficiently. Mojave singers are often hired to lead the singing at a funeral, with Havasupai or Hualapai assistant singers.

The circle dance songs are much better known than the funeral songs, and are often sung in the schools. They were composed by the Hualapais and Havasupais, but inspired by Great Basin music: The genre was adopted as part of the 1890 Ghost Dance religion, which was spread to the Hualapais and Havasupais by the Southern Paiutes. These songs reflect their Great Basin inspiration by the strong paired-phrase patterning,[3] generally with all phrases having equal length (Nettl, 1954). Unlike the funeral songs, the circle dance songs are widely sung. Most Havasupai and Hualapai children and adults can sing a few

---

[2] The rise is a phrase or set of phrases of higher melodic material that is sung after a lower section has been repeated several times. A typical form would be: A A A A A A A R A A A A R A A A . . . where A represents the lower section and R the rise.

[3] Paired phrase patterning is the pattern of repeating each phrase twice, for example A A B B C C D D.

circle dance songs well, although it is primarily the professional singers who have large repertoires.

2.1. Melodic form

Unlike the popular genres, the women's songs exhibit neither the rise nor predominant paired-phrase patterning. Instead, the melody (consisting of a short repeated strophe averaging about seven seconds in length) is always divisible into two parts, the first containing slightly higher melodic material than the second. The tonal center of the first part is usually a half tone or whole tone higher than that of the second part. Both parts are descending. A typical melodic contour for a women's song might look something like this:

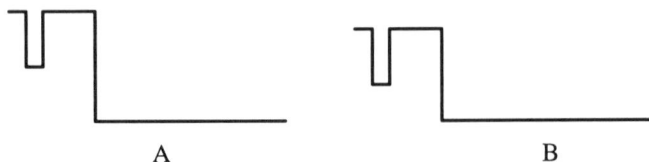

A   B

(A will always refer to the first, higher part, and B to the lower part.) The melody is always made up of between two and four different tones. Most frequently the melodic form is simply AB — of the eleven traditional Old Ladies' songs analyzed for this chapter, seven have the AB form. (Two are shown as examples in the appendix to this chapter.) Of the other four, one has a strict AABB form, the only example of paired phrase patterning in the women's songs; but very similar to that is another that has the form $A_1A_2B_1B_2$, where A_2 varies from A_1 only by a half tone in the first tone of the phrase. A third song can also be represented as $A_1A_2B_1B_2$, where the difference is that A_2 and B_2 are a beat longer than A_1 and B_1. The fourth nonstandard form is A followed variably by from two to four Bs.

In a couple of songs, the A and B phrases are particularly long with an internal structure of their own, and so can be subdivided into shorter phrases; this subdivision is corroborated by the text, which takes as the repeatable unit the smaller subdivisions. Example 2 is a case in point: A consists of 5 phrases (labelled lower-case c c d e f) and B of a repetition of d e f, as diagrammed below:[4]

---

[4] An alternative would be to analyze the higher structure as paired phrase patterning:

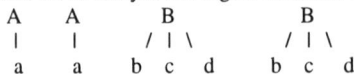

```
A    A      B        B
|    |     / | \     / | \
a    a    b  c  d   b  c  d
```

However, this is misleading, because in typical paired phrase patterning all phrases are of equal or near-equal length, which is not the case here. The decision to analyze the song as AB is further strengthened by the fact that the resulting overlying structure is typical of women's songs in having higher tonal material in A than B.

```
         A                    B
       /|\\                   /|\
      / | \ \                / | \
     /  |  \ \              /  |  \
    a  a  b  c  d          b  c  d
```

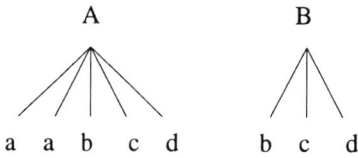

2.2. Rhythm and meter

The rhythm of women's songs is somewhat loose — that is, there is no notably strong beat. Nevertheless, there is almost always a regular pattern to the meter. Most women's songs have alternating meters. The two traditional women's songs in the appendix exemplify these alternating patterns: Example 1 alternates between 4/8 and 6/8, and example 2 between 7/8 and 6/8.

2.3. Text

Among the Havasupais and Hualapais, songs may be compartmentalized according to the degree to which they utilize real words as opposed to vocables (Hinton, 1984). The women's songs are one genre that utilized real words primarily, with only a few vocables inserted to fill out the meter of lines.

The text is characterized by a fair number of repeated lines; usually the first line, which states the topic — most often the name of the person the song is about — is repeated several times. From then on, lines may be repeated once, more rarely several times, and commonly not repeated at all. A typical text is song 1, consisting of eight four-line verses (three lines in the first verse of this performance). The first line is sung seven times, and subsequent verses have one line repeated (either the first or last) with two others not repeated; and the last verse has no repeated lines. Thus the pattern:

```
            TEXT
             A A A
             A A A A
             B B C D
             E E F G
             H I J J
             K K L M
             N O P P
             Q R S T
```

The other texts also show varying patterns of repetition with the greatest degree of repetition at the beginning, and often with an increase in repetition toward the end as well, as exemplified in the text of song 2:

```
            A A A B B C D E
            F C G H I J K L
            M N O O P Q R R
```

It is also strongly characteristic of the old women's songs that they are partially improvised. Each singing of the song, even by the same singer, shows a good deal of variation in the text. Lines of text may be inserted or deleted at various singings, and which lines are repeated, and how many repetitions occur, vary from performance to performance.

2.4. Phonological characteristics of the text

Phonological differences between sung and spoken words have been described in detail before, in Hinton (1980, 1984). They will be summarized here.

2.4.1. Canon

In spoken Havasupai, vowels are inserted between consonants in many environments; the vowels are very short, usually devoiced between voiceless segments, usually phonetically [ə] or [ɨ], often [i] next to a palatal, [u] next to a labial, sometimes [a] next to a glottal stop. In sung Havasupai, vowel insertion is even more prominent: Almost no consonant clusters are allowed at all, and the epenthetic vowel is usually full — a, e, i, o, or u.

2.4.2. Vowel harmony

The epenthetic vowel in songs optionally follows rules of vowel harmony — it takes on the features of a nearby vowel. Thus in song 1 /hu g-lum-ñ/ (head relativizer-wrinkled-demonstrative, "Wrinkled Head") becomes [ho golonomo] (epenthetic vowels underlined; the form also exhibits metathesis and vowel lowering, discussed below). If the vowel harmony option is not followed, then the quality of the inserted vowel will be [e], [o] or [a] if the tone it falls on is on a beat; and [i], [u] or [ə] in the rare off-beat syllables.

2.4.3. Vowel lowering

Underlying /i/ and /u/ are often lowered to [e] and [o] in song, as illustrated in the example in the previous paragraph. Two more examples:

> /va wi-g-a/[5]
> (demonstrative do-same:subject:marker-augment,
> "That's what he did")
>
> > [va wega]

---

[5] The alphabet used here to represent Havasupai and Hualapai is similar to the Havasupai and Hualapai practical orthographies with three differences: I use /ə/ in the representation of sung words; this sound was unwritten in the Havasupai practical orthography and written by a variety of standard vowels in the Hualapai system; and I use the symbol /t̪/ for the dental stop and /ʔ/ for glottal stop, in place of the less commonly known symbols used in the practical orthographies.

/ñu-l/ (demonstrative-in, "in there")
>   [ñol]

2.4.4. Consonantal changes

Most sung consonants remain as they are in speaking. However, once in a while we find a process of lenition: most commonly /v/ to [w], as in

/ʔ-t-svo-g/

(I-plural-wait-same:subject,

"I wait (for a long time)")

>   [ʔatəswoga]

In some songs, the first, oft-repeated line of a song may exhibit some consonantal changes. For example, the first verse of song 1 shows that the name *hu g-lum-ñ* is metathesized to *ho golonomo* (with /ñ/ also changed to n); some other consonantal changes in that song include h > g and m > ŋ.

2.4.5. Vocables

Vocables (sometimes called "nonsense syllables") are common in all Havasupai songs, although they are least frequent in songs such as the women's songs where the text plays a prominent role. But still, in women's songs it is common to find an added meaningless syllable here and there, usually at the beginning or end of a line. Examples from song 1:

ho ñiyegitə   "early in the morning"

gwe giñe*wama*   "he went hunting"

va wega *ŋa*   "that's what he did"

Vocables generally have the shape CV where V is *o, a,* or *e*, and C is a sonorant (usually a nasal), semivowel or *h* or *ʔ.* A full discussion of vocables can be found in Hinton (1980, 1992).

2.4.6. Syntax

A line of text in Havasupai and Hualapai generally consists of a single fully stressed lexical item with affixes. This may be preceded by a member of a class of pronouns and particles, which may carry case markers, are one to two syllables long, and bear secondary stress. In the first example below we find a single word with no pronoun or particle in front. The second and third examples exhibit pronouns in front of the main lexical items.

1.   [tevgyaliyo]
        (/tvgyal-yo/, saddle-vocable "saddle")
2.   [gwe giñewama]
        (/gwe g-ñe-o-m/, something g-hunt-applicative-m,
         "he went hunting")
3.   [ñoliyama]

(/ñu-l ya:m/, pronoun-in go,
"in there [my heart, I'd like to] go")
The use of pronouns and particles is much more common in sung language than in spoken language. In large part, their presence or absence is a function of meter.

3. THE NEW OLD LADIES' SONGS

Two of the new songs created by the staff of the Hualapai Bilingual Education Program are given in the appendix as examples 3 and 4. From virtually every point of view, they are different from the old songs.

The first part of song creation is to figure out the topic. When the personal songs were a living genre of self-expression, the knowledge of the topic usually preceded the urge to compose. The way Havasupai singers described composition, women were thinking about someone and the song would come to mind as a result of the thought. In the present situation, on the other hand, the desire to compose precedes the topic: The goal is to create songs for the school children to sing. The problem then is to find the thought that can be turned into a song.

Linguistic consultant Akira Yamamoto[6] has worked with the Hualapai bilingual staff on the writing of poetry in Hualapai. He taught them how to compose short poems in the style of Japanese Haiku, and the staff found that the poems the staff had written under his guidance provided a fine basis for song writing. Each poem provided the topic and basic wording from which the song text could be derived.

The next step was to extend the text to have the appropriate form and meter for a women's song. Songs 3 and 4 along with others were composed by the staff during the workshop. The poems that had been written previously with Dr. Yamamoto were now adapted to musical form. The insertion of vowels and vocables, and the division of the poetic lines into shorter song lines when necessary presented little problem for the staff. Besides the phonological changes, the most marked change from poem to song is the use in the latter of repeated lines. Pronouns were also added for metric purposes, such as the addition of the second person pronoun (maj) in example 4.

3.1. Differences between the old and new Old Ladies' songs.

The songs created during the workshop were very different from the traditional songs, in several important ways. First, of course, the subject matter was of a different and more expurgated nature. While all the old songs dealt with people, the songs composed at the workshop were primarily about the physical environment — one about snow, one (this one being an especially beautiful creation) about the rock walls of the Colorado River and the ruins in them. In terms of subject matter, the songs were more like circle dance

---

[6] Professor Yamamoto (University of Kansas) is a linguist who has done research for many years on the Hualapai language, and is the main linguistic consultant for the bilingual program.

songs, which rarely discussed people, but instead referred to the environment or to cultural objects.

I have previously written about the relation between content and function in Havasupai songs (Hinton, 1984), noting that the difference in content between women's songs and circle dance songs is strongly related to differing functions of the songs: The women's songs were individualistic expressions of the composers' feelings, often a complaint or a negative attitude toward another individual, and often used to create social pressure on someone. The circle dance songs, on the other hand, were a part of a ceremony of community solidarity, and the subject matter was correspondingly benign and noncontroversial.

For the present revival, the new women's songs, like the circle dance songs, have a functional component of *solidarity*. Community solidarity is a major aim of all that the Hualapai Bilingual Program does. Schools in general also aim for student body solidarity. This goes against the original aim of the women's songs. Lomax (1968 and elsewhere) points out the close relationship between form and function. It can be predicted that with such a strong difference between the primary function of the old and new women's songs, form and content will be forced by necessity into very different molds — and in fact, it might be predicted that the new women's songs would converge strongly in form and content with the circle dance songs, because they have the same function. But at the same time, while the circle dance songs are characterized by having very short texts with only a few isolated words embedded in vocables, the new women's songs fulfill their other intended function of teaching language by maintaining the characteristic of the original women's songs of having relatively long, rich texts with complete sentences.

The melodies of the new songs are very different from the old women's songs, none of them bearing the AB descending pattern of typical of the old ones.. Example 3 is almost paired phrase patterning: its melodic form can be represented as $A_1A_2B_1B_2$. Another song, not included here, is strict paired phrase patterning (AABB). Both these melodies are much more like the circle dance songs than they are like the typical style of the old women's songs. Example 4 is unique in Hualapai music in that each of the first three phrases introduces a tone higher than the previous phrase. This is counter to the traditional descending tonal center, and is representative of a more Western musical style, where tunes tend toward a high point late in the verse, rather than the Hualapai and Havasupai custom of having the high point early in the verse.

Another innovation is that the new songs have a stricter rhythm and meter, and lack the complex metric alternation of the old songs. All the songs created by the staff were sung in strict 4/4 time with a beat that could be clapped to. This is quite distinct from the old songs, which have a loose rhythm and alternating meter. The change is also in keeping with the model of song function developed in Lomax (1968) and, for Havasupai, Hinton (1984): Songs designed for solidarity have a strong beat that allows the audience or singing group to unify rhythmically. The staff, designing their songs with group learning and singing in mind, have adhered to this rule.

Also like the circle dance songs, the new women's songs are sung the same way every time. Having a predictable pattern of repetition is another essential part of group singing. Related to this is the fact that the songs are written down. Their creation and remembrance has been strongly dependent on the use of the Hualapai writing system. The original poems were created in written form; during the song composition, the poems were written on the blackboard, and as lines of the song were discussed, they were written beside the poem. Each staff member then wrote down his or her own copy of the song, and later on a final typewritten version was reproduced and passed around. When taught to children, written versions of songs are passed out to them. The learning of a song from a written form, as well as group singing, constrains the song to be sung the same way every time. Further support to learnability is lent by the increase and regularization of repetition in contrast to the old women's songs. In the songs created by the bilingual education staff each line is sung an even number of times. In example 3 each line is sung twice. Example 4 has a pleasant mirror imagery, with the first and last lines each sung 6 times, and the middle lines twice. This is in contrast to the old women's songs where many lines are sung only once, even though in those songs too there is a pattern of repetition at the beginning and usually the end. The regularized repetition in the new women's songs aids song memorization and enhances the language lesson embedded in the song.

The one aspect of the women's songs that is more or less similar to the traditional ones is the line form of the text. Each line has one linguistic primary stress. When a line of the poem has more than one primary stress, it is divided into more than one line of the song. The introduction of inserted vowels and vocables also follows the same general form as the traditional songs: It was easy for the staff to decide which vowel to insert, following both lexical rules and vowel harmony rules, despite the fact that none of them had ever composed a Hualapai song before. In fact, these poetic devices are to a large extent extensions of phonological rules existing in everyday speech. Because everyday speaking has vowel-insertion rules and, to a limited extent, vowel harmony (for example, the inserted vowel after a glottal stop will be identical to the vowel preceding glottal stop), it is quite easy even for novice composers who are native speakers to apply these rules appropriately in song-making.

4. CONCLUSION

In sum, the main similarities between the old and new women's songs are the use of vowel and vocable insertion and the rich poetic text. Otherwise we find that there is some similarity to Western songs (such as in the use of higher tonal material late in the verse in song 5, and in the fixing of the text), and a great similarity to the circle dance songs, in terms of meter, musical form and subject matter, and a regularized pattern of repetition.

We might draw the conclusion that it is simply impossible to recreate an old tradition. What began as an attempt to create new songs in an old genre resulted in a new genre instead. To a large extent, the musical differences between the old and new women's songs are due to the functional differences, with new educational functions and new values being reinforced in these songs. Where the old women's songs are to be sung solo in an informal setting, with few people present, the new songs are sung by the group, in the more formal context of the school, teaching unified group behavior, and memorization skills.   While the old women's songs express a traditional attitude of relative sexual freedom, the subject matter of most of the new songs help reinforce the Western notion that sex is a taboo topic.   The new songs were created with the conscious goal of teaching children about their language and culture as a contrastive unit to the more general Western, English-speaking curriculum that pervades the school in other subjects, while the old women's songs had no such aim, but simply express the language and culture directly without self-consciousness.   New Hualapai values are also expressed in these songs: where the old women's songs are individual expressions of positive or negative feeling for another person, the new songs are expressive of Hualapai pride and social unity.   The choice of song topics that express love of Hualapai land and history display and reinforce this group consciousness, as does the strict meter, which allows group singing and rhythmic unity.

This is not to say, of course, that the staff attempt to create Hualapai songs for the classroom was in any sense a failure.   The songs serve the functions they are supposed to serve.   But using traditional genres to serve all these functions turned out to be impossible; what was created instead was a new genre — a new Hualapai song tradition for a new Hualapai culture that combines a European and Native American cultural heritage.

REFERENCES

Hinton, L. (1984). *Havasupai songs: A linguistic perspective.* Berlin: Gunther Narr.

Hinton, L. (1980). Vocables in Havasupai song. In C. J. Frisbie (Ed.), *Southwestern Indian ritual drama* (pp. 275-306). Albuquerque: University of New Mexico Press.

Hinton, L. (1992). Songs without words. *News from Native California*, 6(3), 34-36.

Lomax, A. (1968). *Folk song style and culture.* Washington, DC: American Association for the Advancement of Science.

Nettl, B. (1954). *North American Indian musical styles.* Philadelphia: American Folklore Society.

Example 1

	Song text	Spoken equivalent	Gloss
1.	golonoma	(hu) glumñu[7]	Wrinkled Head (name)
	ho golonoma	hu glumñu	Wrinkled Head
	ho golonoŋoja	hu glumñu	Wrinkled Head
2.	ho golonomo	hu glumñu	Wrinkled Head
	go golonomo	hu glumñu	Wrinkled Head
	ho golonomo	hu glumñu	Wrinkled Head
	go golonomo	hu glumñu	Wrinkled Head
3.	ho ñiʔegitə	ñiyegtg	Early in the morning
	lo ñiʔegitəge	ñiyegtge	Early in the morning
	ñe məʔomoni	ñi ʔolo	His horse
	mwa yogana	wa yog	He takes it
4.	tevəgyavo	tvgyavo	The saddle
	tevəgyavomogə	tvgyavomg	He saddled it
	va vidobo	va vdobg	He went out
	va ñitibeŋe	va ñtbem	He was gone

---

[7] I do not provide morpheme glosses here. See Hinton (1984) for a morphological analysis of Havasupai.

5.	gwe giñewama	gwe gñe	To go hunting
	gwe giñewaŋañi	gwe gñe	To go hunting
	vaməwegañə	vlwig	Like that
	vawegaŋa	vlwig	Like that
6.	atəswogomə	ʔsvog	I waited
	atəswotememe	ʔsvo-t	I waited, until
	ña odwobigə	ña dob-g	The sun went out
	ña bemememe	ña bem	Until the sun was gone
7.	tevgyaliyo	tvgyal	The saddle
	bitanaʔa	bite	Only that (did he bring back)
	wawvtagəgə	wa vtag	He threw it at the house
	wawtageŋeʔemu	wa vtag	He threw it at the house
8.	gagəʔana	gag hana	No good,
	ha ʔobeme	tʔobm	No.
	ñoli yama	ñulʔyaam	I (want to) leave here,
	yegiyomoŋəʔ	yigʔyu	I feel like doing that.

Example 2.

Song text	Spoken equivalent	Gloss
1. a ñevo gud govotye	?	Hair-tied-back
ñevud vovotye	?	Hair-tied-back
ñevuvud vovo-otye	?	Hair-tied-back

ve yañi-i ga	viya ñi?ig	That's what they call him
veyə ?iga-a-ha	viya ?ig	That they call him
ñigamiyume	gamiyum	You are some way
gavumiwijehañu	gavmuwij	You do it some way[8]
wijigiñije ?eme	wij gñi?ijm	That's what they say.

2.
mayugwi yo yo	myug yu	You are
ñegamiyome	ñigamiyum	Some way you are,
gavañiwiño	gavñiwiñ	Do it to me like that,
gowalə yigaha	gwal yig	I want it!
viya giyomowa	viya gyum	(That is,
matowi dava	mat wi dava	I don't mean it,
gavañuwehaga	gavñuwihg	Don't do it to me,
vi?ete	vi?ete	Not really!)

3.
besa sitem	bees sitm	One dollar
walijiwóga	wal jwog	I have in there
awigi emboma	?	In my pocket
awigi emboma	?	In my pocket
iñigaaha	nyig aa	I have in here
vi iñya iga	vña ñi?ig	So I say
viñanivi	vñya n~iv?i	So I say
viñiña ithe əm?	vñya ?ithm	So I say

Example 3

Example 3
VERSE ①
a- ha-ni-ba-chu-wa   a- ha-ni-ba-chu-wa
nyim-sa-va da- va   nyim-sa-va da

---

[8] i.e., "You are something! You are *some* lover!"

The poem

han bach	snow
nyimsav dav	white-very
thugway vʔim	light so-be
hachv hach	melts, melts

	Song text	Spoken equivalent	Gloss
1.	ahani bachuwa	han bach	snow
	ahani bachuwa	han bach	snow
	nyimsava dava	nyimsav dav	very white
	nyimsava dava	nyimsav dav	very white
2.	thugway viʔime	thugway vʔim	It's so light
	thugway viʔime	thugway vʔim	It's so light
	hachava hacha	hachv hach	It melts, melts
	hachava ha	hachv hach	It melts, melts

Example 4

The poem

ha gaʔa:məl nya ya:mk	To the Colorado River I went
wi ham gaʔa:ma nya ʔu:k	The rock walls going along I see
gud ba guvwavach gayuk vam	Long ago the ancient people were here
wayok ya bay gayuk yuyik wasi:v	I wonder how it is they lived?

	Song text	Spoken equivalent	Gloss
1.	ha ga amale	ha gaʔa:məl	The Colorado River
	ha ga amale	ha gaʔa:məl	The Colorado River
	ha ga amale	ha gaʔa:məl	The Colorado River
	ha ga amale	ha gaʔa:məl	The Colorado River
2.	ha ga amale	ha gaʔa:məl	The Colorado River
	ha ga amale	ha gaʔa:məl	The Colorado River
	nyaj nyaya:maka	nyaj nyaya:mk	I went there
	nyaj nyaya:maka	nyaj nyaya:mk	I went there
3.	wi ham gaʔa:ma	wi ham gaʔa:ma	The rock walls going along
	wi ham gaʔa:ma	wi ham gaʔa:ma	The rock walls going along
	nyaje nya ukuwu	nyaj nya ʔu:k	I saw them
	nyaje nya ukuwu	nyaj nya ʔu:k	I saw them
4.	gud ba guvwavacha	gud ba guvwavach	The ancient people
	gud ba guvwavacha	gud ba guvwavach	The ancient people
	ga yuku vama	gayuk vam	Those who were here
	ga yuku vama	gayuk vam	Those who were here
5.	wayoka ya bay	wayok yabay	The way they lived
	wayoka ya bay	wayok yabay	The way they lived
	gayuku yumo	gayuk yum	What was it like?
	gayuku yumo	gayuk yum	What was it like?
6.	nyayik wasi:va	nyayik wasi:v	I wonder
	nyayik wasi:va	nyayik wasi:v	I wonder
	gayuku yumo	gayuk yum	What was it like?
	gayuku yumo	gayuk yum	What was it like?
7.	gayuku yumo	gayuk yum	What was it like?
	gayuku yumo	gayuk yum	What was it like?
	gayuku yumo	gayuk yum	What was it like?
	gayuku yumo	gayuk yum	What was it like?

32 WOMEN'S COLLABORATIVE INTERACTIONS

Vera John-Steiner
University of New Mexico

Creative and intellectual partnerships are motivated and sustained along a variety of dimensions. One of these is the need for affirmation. The hard effort involved in sustained, productive work requires a sense of trust in oneself. The ability to develop such a sense is nourished and sustained in certain effective collaborative partnerships.

Another important dimension of collaborative work is linked to developments in one's domain of endeavor. When scientists or artists are engaged in re-examining theories which are in conflict with new discoveries, insights, or perspectives, they find "thinking together" particularly productive. I have suggested that thinking collaboratively is particularly prevalent in the construction of a new framework. "In this way, researchers can overcome the grip of a dominant perspective" (John-Steiner, 1992, p. 103). The new jointly constructed framework can become the foundation of each individual's own novel directions of thought. Such a process is effectively described by Vygotsky's frequently quoted notion of the shift from the interpersonal to the intrapersonal level of functioning. In developing Vygotsky's sociogenetic notions further, Van der Veer and Valsiner (1991) suggest:

> If we were to try to understand the processes of scientific discovery from a purely sociogenetic perspective then we would have to accept that no innovative scientist can create any new ideas independently from the collective cultural processes that surround him, the cultural history in which his life-course is embedded, and the particular interpersonal relationships of his life course. Or in other terms, it is the **intellectual interdependency** of the scientist or artist that sets up conditions under which novel ideas or expressions can come into being [emphasis added]. (p. 393)

Jointly constructed thinking is particularly important when a governing perspective within a domain of thinking is changing. Conversations which provide thoughtful articulation of new insights become more intense and frequent. This process has been particularly interesting to writers documenting the changes in physics during the 1920s, (cf. Heisenberg, 1971). Less is known of the establishment of discourse communities during periods of paradigmatic changes in the social sciences and of the role of women in these communities.

In thinking about communities of thinkers, I have relied to a great extent on Ludwik Fleck's (1979) ideas. He wrote about thought collectives and collaboration as central facts in creative scientific work. His claim that cognition is "the most socially conditioned activity of man" has recently been echoed by Levine, Resnick, and Higgins (1993):

At work and in civic and personal life, each person's ability to function successfully depends upon coordinated cognitive interactions with others, and the cognitive "products" that emerge from these interactions cannot be attributed to single individuals. (pp. 599-600)

Our work on collaboration is based on similar assumptions. (My partners in this project include Kathryn Miller and Michele Minnis.) We have been particularly interested in studying dyads and small working groups engaged in developing novel approaches in their disciplines. In studying how they interact to overcome their own disciplinary socialization, we have relied upon sociocultural theory (including the works of Bakhtin, Holquist, & Emerson, 1986; Rogoff, 1990; Vygotsky, 1989; and Wertsch, 1991), on Fleck's thinking, and on the work of feminists and discourse theorists.

Collaboration has been of interest to the sociologists of science (Knorr-Cetina & Mulkay, 1983; Latour & Woolgar, 1979; Zuckerman, 1977) and to anthropologists. Among the latter, Traweek (1988) examined the world of high energy physics, of which she wrote that it is "a culture of no culture, which longs passionately for a world without loose ends, without temperament, gender, nationalism, or other sources of discord — for a world outside human space and time" (p. 162). In describing the high energy physics community, she brings to it a feminist perspective when she comments that "the denial of human agency in the construction of science coexists with the imaging of scientists as male and nature as female" (p. 158). The issues raised by Traweek are of interest to feminist scholars, many of whom are engaged in studies of "career patterns of women attempting to do science, studies of the history of exclusion of women, studies of the content of particular sciences both in their formative periods and in their contemporary manifestations" (Longino & Hammond, 1990, p. 164). The discussions themselves carry with them seeds of conflict based, in part, on the disciplinary position of the women who are exploring issues confronting women in science. (The different perspectives of philosophers of science versus practicing scientists is one such issue.)

While much of the work has focused on large, competitive laboratories, including Traweek's research, our interest is in the ways in which social scientists and mathematicians think together. Our focus is on "high conceptual collaboration," a term used by Michael Schrage (1990) who defines it as "when people work together to devise concepts, ideas, themes, metaphors, analogies." (p. 61). Our interest is the role women play in these kinds of collaborations.

Some of our questions include: How do collaborators create their communities of discourse? What are their patterns of thinking and working together? Are these based upon complementarity of skills and knowledge? How is a division of labor achieved? Do the collaborators share a commitment to construct a community with shared beliefs? Are there different phases in collaborative endeavors?

At the start of this project we conducted interviews based on twelve broad, open-ended questions. A number of recurrent themes were identified in these interviews including: various motives for collaboration; identification of complementary working and cognitive styles of the collaborators; and a specification of settings they construct for their work. From these interviews we have constructed a Q-sort for collaboration (Block, 1961).

In our most recent work, we combined the Q-sort with interviews: the statements from the sort provide the participants with a quick view of some of the relevant aspects of collaborations. Usually, collaborators meet with the researcher individually, and they comment on their partnership during and after completing the Q-sort. Once the similarities and differences in the sorts are identified, a joint meeting is arranged. There, the partners' perceptions of their common work is discussed. Partners have differed in their ranking of statements concerning the importance of creating a shared community; they frequently differ in their use of visual and/or verbal representation and communication of their ideas. They may have different expectations about deadlines and different commitments to a single, encompassing endeavor versus concurrent engagement in a number of projects.

This work on intellectual collaboration is in process. In this chapter, I present some examples of different collaborative partnerships, primarily among women. (In our ongoing work, the Q-sort data are analyzed statistically. We are also examining the discourse features of the interviews. These include functional analyses, patterns of turn-taking, interruptions, and elaborations; the use of conceptual "short-hands" and other indices of communicative efficacy; and patterns of pronoun use.)

In examining dyads and small groups, we have looked at the ways in which female participants envisage collaboration. To date, women have placed Q-sort items at the high end of their distributions more consistently than have men, such as: "By the time we have finished a project, we do not know from whom the ideas came"; or, "Among my collaborators there is a sense of mission to establish a community in which we can participate"; and "In a good collaborative environment one's ideas can be made explicit through questioning and dialogue."

Valuing these items as descriptive of why and how women collaborate is further elaborated upon in their interviews. The reliance upon verbally negotiated ideas is a comfortable mode for women as conversations play a crucial role in female socialization. Girls tend to rely upon "best friends" as their resource for self-understanding and the development of identity (Rubin & Shenker, 1978). As writers on women's language have shown (Lakoff, 1975; Penfield, 1987; Tannen, 1990), women's interactional styles support the tentative exchange of ideas which become more clearly shaped in a course of dialogue. In collaborations involving same-sex dyads and small groups, women report their pleasure in sustained, free-flowing, mutually trusting explorations of ideas. Some women writers who have deeply influenced each others' work, also benefit from sustained caring interaction. In a chapter on Virginia Woolf and Vita Sackville-West, Louise De Salvo writes:

> In conversations, letters, and in their novels, they explored their own and each other's pasts and came to far more realistic assessments of their family histories. Woolf wrote *To the Lighthouse*, *The Waves*, and *The Years*, novels that examined her childhood in the Stephen family, a childhood riddled with violence, sexual abuse, and emotional neglect. She wrote *Orlando*, which examined

Vita's. Sackville-West wrote *The Edwardians*, based upon her childhood, and *Family History*, which to some extent examined Virginia's. (1993, p. 91)

Jill Tarule, a coauthor of *Women's ways of knowing: The development of self, voice and mind* (Belenky, Clinchy, Goldberger, & Tarule,et al., 1986), ranked the item about dialogue very highly in interview.[1] She wrote in a recent paper (Parule, 1992) that conversation for adults is a way of knowing:

> The returning or re-entry students' experience usually includes having lived in dialogue-rich environments: work, church, community, home, friendships. (p. 12).

She further wrote:

> Students define the ability to feel "safe" as they speak, to be voiced, to listen and to be heard, and "to explore ideas" not as **part** of their learning, but **as** their learning. (p. 14)

Some of the women of whom she writes are "Connected Knowers." "Authority" for these women "rests not on power or status or certification but on commonality of experience" (Belenky et al., 1986, p. 118). The women collaborators with whom we have worked integrated connected knowledge — which is contextually and relationally oriented — with constructed knowledge. Belenky et al. wrote of "weaving together the strands of rational and emotive thought and of integrating objective and subjective knowing" (1986, p. 134). The participants in this study spoke of voicing and shaping their thoughts through dialogue, through a multiplicity of voices and "ways of knowing." They deepen, criticize, elaborate and join their ideas through solo or joint writing.

Tarule makes a powerful case for the role of dialogue in knowledge construction, and our research seems to indicate that it plays a particularly significant role for women. But there are many situations where women still find it difficult to articulate ideas while they are in a formative stage, to have full equality in discussion settings, or to have their ideas considered as precise as those of men.

In a study of computer discussion groups using e-mail exchanges, Selfe and Meyer (1991) analyzed discourse for gender and status differences. They found that while there was fairly equal access to participation by men and women and by high and low status participants in the groups, nevertheless the discussion tended to be dominated by the high-status males:

> This paradox may be partly explained by differences in linguistic style and behavior . . . These behaviors included contributing more messages, introducing more new topics, and disagreeing more frequently with others. (p. 187)

Criticism, disagreement, and attribution of styles of thought were interesting themes that emerged from our own interviews. During a thoughtful and very candid discussion, a French mathematical physicist, Cécile DeWitt-Morette, whose work has received many honors, describes her way of talking about her ideas as different from that of her physicist husband:

> When he says, "I understand," we don't mean the same thing at all. When I say,

---

1. The interviews from which the quotes have been drawn were conducted between 1990 and 1993.

"I understand," I speak of an idea that I like, that seems promising, and I like it enough to make that decision. When he says, "I understand," it means that he has looked at it this way and that way, looked at it in all the little corners. (personal communication, 15, March, 1992)

Professor DeWitt-Morette spoke further about the broad range of her attention, which is linked in part to her role as a mother. It was interesting that a scientist as successful as DeWitt-Morette saw an important connection between her maternal role and her working style. She provided an excellent example of a recurrent theme in these interviews, namely the need of many women and some men to overcome long-standing dichotomies between work and family responsibilities.

Comfort with interdependency emerged as another important feature of women's talk about collaboration. The ability to articulate ideas a-borning, to participate in an intensely experienced co-construction of thoughts, and the willingness to speak of them to others is richly illustrated in my joint interview with the social psychologist Michelle Fine and her co-author, the writer, Pat MacPherson. They described their interactions as intensely dialogic. They both placed the card "With my collaborator I can talk at the speed of thinking" as characteristic of their exchanges. When I interviewed them recently they were drafting a new, joint publication.

The day before MacPherson was to join Fine in New York (she lives in Philadelphia), Fine called her to check out some ideas she was "cooking." It was important to her to be able to make a connection and to have her partner's reaction while her thoughts were fresh and percolating: "If I am cooking this idea, I just need to know if it is a rotten egg, and I think we tell each other."

When I asked MacPherson how she feels about the urgency of her partner's need to make contact, she responded:

I was happy to have her say "I want you to think about this coming up on the train." I was happy to hear what direction she was coming in from. And I have come up with my own contribution to this outline last week after two days of deep thinking by myself. And then I wrote that out, saw Michelle the next morning, talked her through my notes and felt that we got into sync about that. So she was getting back to me with something else that can bolster this draft. (personal communication, 10, April, 1993)

Fine and MacPherson have a well-developed routine in their collaboration. It is not only based on their deep enjoyment of each others' thinking and their effective ways of dialoguing face-to-face, or on the phone, or through successive drafts of their joint articles, but also because they share a lot of their values as committed, feminist scholars. At the same time, they are quite aware of some interesting differences in their styles of working. MacPherson is a writer, while Fine is a charismatic teacher who presents ideas with force and self-confidence. She relies upon her working partner to deepen her thinking.

While MacPherson uses extended notes, Fine writes her drafts quickly and then rewrites them many times. In characterizing her friend's method of working, she says:

Pat will do many detailed, wonderful notes and then she will produce a draft...
My experience with really fine writers is that they do a lot of interior work and

then a production. And I do threads, and spit something out and then I work it, and work it... I really do 10 to 15 drafts. That is where I really do my work. I really don't know what I am thinking until I have written a draft of it. (personal communication, 10, April, 1993))

Their current method of working has taken some time to develop. In the beginning, MacPherson tried to work too closely with Fine's early drafts which were like an exploration of the territory. Fine says:

Its much more like a map, all the ideas that I have. I assume that it is the wrong draft, but I got to get them all out there. And Pat was taking them too seriously. Conversation and getting them out into early drafts is what I need to do.

After the two of them have come to understand their patterns better, Pat has learned "to lift the ideas out of the text" and she feels free to reorganize them, and Michelle is comfortable in staying with her partner's language. "I will touch the ideas but not the language."

The anthropologists Elinor Ochs and Bambi Schieffelin are another dyad of women whose collaboration weaves together friendship, shared values, and an enormously successful common working style. They met at a conference and recognized very quickly how similar their ideas were and how much they needed to explore them in dialogue. Their shared enterprise was symbolized from the very beginning by putting all their notes together "into a green canvas bag." They carried this bag and a small portable typewriter with them to any quiet place where they could work. Their basic working pattern has not changed much throughout the years:

We always talked each line through. We did not ever allocate parts of the paper to one person or to the other person. Every single sentence we discussed. The typewriter was between the two of us, and we put our chairs so that we could both see the text. While saying one sentence, we would think of the next one to write. It was definitely constructed on the phrasal level, together. Sometimes we used the blackboard to plan ahead. (personal communication, 6, April, 1990)

The green canvas bag remained with the stationary partner when the other went on a field trip. It served as the repository of their common data and thoughts.

After completing several articles and an edited book together, they identified their central theme as "language socialization." Having achieved clarity about their own theoretical direction, Ochs and Schieffelin decided to try to broaden their "thought community." In order to achieve that, they taught courses covering similar topics, and they organized symposia on language socialization:

We wanted to encourage this emerging enterprise, we wanted to get more people involved. This has been a sustaining strategy...to try to nurture a community of people, not just the two of us. To fill out this enterprise, to make it healthier.

The sustaining power of these carefully shaped and joyously nurtured collaborations of women social scientists is recognized by the participants. But it is not equally valued by others in their field who prefer solo endeavors. Tenure committees frequently question jointly authored papers, reflecting a broad cultural commitment to individualism and autonomy.

Full intellectual equality in academia still eludes us. In part, this is due to the legacy of nepotism rules: DeWitt-Morette described how she (as the wife of a physics professor) taught part-time and worked on soft money for 16 years. Then a French woman mathematician, Yvonne Choquet-Bruhat, invited her to give three lectures in Paris. That invitation revitalized her career and was the beginning of a long collaboration which produced two influential volumes on *Analysis, Manifolds, and Physics.* Since that time, each of the two women have also had other intellectual partners, but their work together has a very special role in their lives.

A strong emphasis on mutuality which includes cognitive and affective elements characterizes a number of the Q-sorts and interviews which we have collected. We refer to this approach as the *inclusive pattern of collaboration.* Such a relationship is sustaining to women who frequently experience marginality, who love to collaborate, and who speak with pride of their partner's mind. One woman described collaboration as "the affair of the mind." Jean Baker Miller and Janet L. Surrey — members of the Stone Center group of psychotherapists who are exploring a relational theory of development — write of "agency in community." Judith Jordan, another participant in the group, describes mutuality as follows: "In intersubjective mutuality, then, we not only find the opportunity of extending our understanding of the other, we also enhance awareness of ourselves" (1991, p. 96).

Dyadic collaboration between women has many sources and causes. Women who like to collaborate do not limit themselves to women partners. But when they choose males to work with, their choice is carefully made: Jill Tarule commented in her interview that the classic gender stereotypes could not work in her partnerships. Many women rejected the Q-sort card that expressed a generalization which they considered too simplistic: "The female collaborators with whom I work are more nurturing and relationship oriented than male collaborators." The women who placed this item as relevant to their own experience are women who have worked in highly competitive environments such as corporations. They expressed the pain of not being fully heard by men, being given caretaking jobs (keeping track of materials), and finding that whatever women did, it was devalued because it was done by women.

On the other hand, women who have had successful collaborations with men describe two different patterns. One of them is a situation of clear role definitions, where each collaborator is an expert who complements the skills of the others performing the joint task. These *collaborations of complementarity* are very wide-spread, and they vary considerably in the way in which women are treated within them.

In this paper, I have focused more on dyads who **think together**, who are jointly engaged in generating new ideas, new approaches, new theories. In these dyads, the relationships are inclusive and mutual. While complementarity of skills exists, the bonds are deeper. To create these bonds when the partners are both men and women is a more complex and demanding task. But some of the participant dyads and groups in this project did achieve this elusive objective. These were partnerships in which the men worked hard to implement their deeply held beliefs in "agency in community."

Thus, a commitment to dialogue and community is not exclusive to women, although it occurred with greater consistency among female participants interviewed to date. Men who have ranked highly some of the items dealing with interdependence and mutuality on the Q-sort, have also spoken of their conscious commitment to an ideology of working, caring communities. The sociolinguist John Dore was quite clear in his interview when he spoke of inclusive and dialogic communities: "I am now aware at this stage of my career that a sense of mission is absolutely imperative, in the sense that it is the overarching vision of what one is doing. The only way it can really get done is with the help of a community of co-participants" (personal communication, February, 1993)

Not all women see collaboration among women, not even among feminists, as conflict-free. Hirsch and Keller (1990) edited an important volume titled *Conflicts in Feminism*. They write of a "decade of intense mutual criticism and internal divisiveness"; a decade in which "the dream of a common language" gave way to "the realities of fractured discourses" (p. 1). They are writing of the 1980s.

In this work the participants did not express much conflict among themselves. They represent social scientists whose commitment to collaboration is powerful and who have relied upon "agency in community" as a way to break new ground in intellectual work. These women and men have gained a sense of fulfillment in their relationships with their partners. These psychologists, linguists, mathematicians, and anthropologists have been successful in creating small communities within the larger, frequently impersonal world of academia. They reject many features of the dominant model of intellectual work — a model of excessive objectivity and impersonality. Instead, they are reaching towards new possibilities of human interdependence and shared creativity.

REFERENCES

Bakhtin, M. M., Holquist, M., & Emerson, C. (1986). *Speech genres and other late essays.* Austin: University of Texas Press.

Belenky, M. F., Clinchy, B., Goldberger, N, & Tarule, N. (1986). *Women's ways of knowing: The development of self, voice, and mind.* New York: Basic Books.

Block, J. (1961). *The Q-sort method in personality assessment and psychiatric research.* Charles C. Thomas.

Chadwick, W., & Courtivron, I. (1993). *Significant others: Creativity and intimate partnership.* London: Thames & Hudson.

De Salvo, L. (1993). "Tinder-and-flint": Virginia Woolf and Vita Sackville-West. In W. Chadwick, & I. Courtivron (Eds.), *Significant others: Creativity and intimate partnership* (pp. 83-95). London: Thames & Hudson.

Fleck, L. (1979). *Genesis and development of a scientific fact.* Chicago: University of Chicago Press.

Heisenberg, W. (1971). *Physics and beyond: Encounters and conversation.* New York: Harper & Row.

Hirsch, M., & Keller, E. F. (1990). *Conflicts in feminism.* New York & London: Routledge.

John-Steiner, V. (1987). *Notebooks of the mind: Explorations of thinking.* New York: Harper & Collins.

John-Steiner, V. (1992). Creative lives, creative tensions. *Creativity Research Journal, 1,* 99-108.

Jordan, J. (1991). The meaning of mutuality. In J. Jordan, A. G. Kaplan, J. B. Miller, I. P. Striver, & J. L. Surrey (Eds.), *Women's growth in connection: Writings from the Stone Center* (pp. 81-96). New York: Guilford Press.

Knorr-Cetina, K. D., & Mulkay, M. (1983). *Science observed: Perspectives on the social study of science.* Beverly Hills, CA: Sage.

Lakoff, R. (1975). *Language and women's place.* New York: Harper & Row.

Latour, B., & Woolgar, S. (1979). *Laboratory life: The social construction of scientific facts.* Beverly Hills, CA: Sage.

Levine, J. M., Resnick, L., & Higgins, E. T. (1993). Social foundations of cognition. *Annual Review of Psychology, 44,* 585-612.

Longino, H. E., & Hammond, E. (1990). Conflicts and interactions in the feminist study of gender and science. In M. Hirsch & E. F. Keller (Eds.), *Conflicts in feminism* (pp. 164-183). New York: Routledge.

Miller, J. B. (1991). The development of women's sense of self. In J. Jordan, A. G. Kaplan, J. B. Miller, I. P. Striver, & J. L. Surrey (Eds.), *Women's growth in connection: Writings from the Stone Center* (pp. 11-26). New York: Guilford Press.

Penfield, J. (1987). *Women and language in transition.* State University of New York Press.

Rogoff, B. (1990). *Apprenticeship in thinking: Cognitive development in social contexts.* New York: Oxford University Press.

Rubin, Z., & Shenker, S. (1978). Friendship, proximity and self-disclosure. *Journal of Personality and Social Psychology, 46,* 1-22.

Schrage, M. (1990). *Shared minds: New technologies of collaboration.* New York: Random House.

Selfe, C. L., & Meyer, P. R. (1991). Testing claims for online conferences. *Written Communication, 8,* 163-192.

Tannen, D. (1990). *You just don't understand: Women and men in conversation.* New York: Ballantine Books.

Tarule, J. (1992). Dialogue and adult learning. *American Association of Colleges of Liberal Education, 78*(4), 12-19.

Traweek, S. (1988). *Beamtimes and lifetimes: The world of high energy physicists.* Cambridge, MA: Harvard University Press.

Van der Veer, R., & Valsiner, J. (1991). *Understanding Vygotsky: A quest for synthesis.* Oxford, UK: Blackwell.

Vygotsky, L. S. (1989). *Thought and language.* Cambridge, MA: MIT Press.

Wertsch, J. V. (1991). *Voices of the mind: A sociocultural approach to mediated action.* Cambridge, MA: Harvard University Press.

Zuckerman, H. (1977). *Scientific elite: Nobel laureates in the United States.* New York: Free Press.

33 "SEPARATE WORLDS FOR GIRLS AND BOYS"? VIEWS FROM U.S. AND CHINESE MIXED-SEX FRIENDSHIP GROUPS[1]

Amy Kyratzis
University of California, Santa Barbara

Jiansheng Guo
Victoria University of Wellington

INTRODUCTION

Issues of gender, from both an academic and political standpoint, have concerned Sue Ervin-Tripp through much of her research career (Ervin-Tripp, O'Connor, & Rosenberg, 1984; Ervin-Tripp & Lampert, 1992). Both in her research and political life, Ervin-Tripp has been concerned with power differentials existing between females and males in U.S. society, how these are created in talk, and how they are socialized. As a tribute to Sue, we take on here an important and controversial claim that has been made in the literature on the socialization of gender differences — the "Separate Worlds Hypothesis." According to this hypothesis, girls and boys spend much of their time during the preschool and elementary school years in same-sex friendship groups, with boys playing mainly with other boys and girls playing mainly with other girls (Maccoby, 1990; Maltz & Borker, 1982). As a result, girls and boys evolve very separate and different "cultures," involving different interaction styles and goals for interactive exchanges (Maltz & Borker, 1982; Tannen, 1990). Girls' interactive style focuses on the goal of intimacy establishment and maintenance. When girls get together, they make suggestions and are concerned with group rather than self goals. They tend to avoid conflict and competition, at least in an explicit, unmitigated form (Sheldon, 1992). Boys' interactive style focuses on the goal of one-upsmanship and hierarchy-establishment. When boys get together, they give orders rather than make suggestions, are explicitly contentious, and are concerned with

[1] We gratefully acknowledge the helpful comments and insights about their native cultures of Qing Xiao (Clark University) and Li-ling Sun (University of California, Santa Barbara), and those of Sikhung Ng, Ann Weatherall (both of Victoria University of Wellington), and the social psychology research group of Victoria University of Wellington.

self rather than group goals (Goodwin, 1980; Kyratzis, 1992; Sheldon, 1990; Tannen, 1990). This view is a rather widely held and popular one in the literature on gender differences today, although many critiques of it have been raised. For example, Barrie Thorne (1993) has argued that "separate worlds" is not the reality for all children, that the concept characterizes only about half the children in many classrooms, and in fact does not at all characterize the make-up of friendship groups in many other classrooms. Class size, teachers' encouragement of spontaneous peer friendship groups, and the ethnic-gender-age make-up of the classroom student body all affect whether girl–girl and boy–boy friendship groups will emerge. Moreover, engagement in play with same-sex peers is not an across-the-board quality even of girls and boys who mainly play in same-sex friendship groups at school (Thorne, 1993).[2]

Despite the fact that "separate worlds" may not be the reality for all children in all classrooms at all times, it does appear to be the reality for many children in many U.S. classrooms for much of the time. And such gender segregation for many hours of each day may lead many boys and girls to develop quite gendered ways of interacting, along the lines described above. According to Maltz and Borker (1982) and Tannen (1990), one ramification of this is for cross-gender interaction. The two cultures "clash," with the same behaviors meaning very different things in the two "cultures."[3]

Relevant here is Lakoff's discussion (1975) of "bilingualism" — to what extent can men and women and boys and girls shift to the opposite sex's way of speaking when it is appropriate to do so in mixed gender talk? The findings from observations of mixed-gender interactions in experimental studies are that, although there is some shift to the opposite-sex's ways of talking (e.g., less directness in men and boys, more direct-ness in women and girls), there are still apparent "culture clashes." For women, "There is . . . evidence that they carry over some of their well-practiced female-style behaviors, sometimes in exaggerated form. Women may wait for a turn to speak that does not come, and thus may end up talking less than they would in a women's group. They smile more than the men do, agree more often with what others have said, and give nonverbal signals of attentiveness to what others, perhaps especially the men, are saying" (Duncan & Fiske, 1977; cited in Maccoby, 1990, p. 518). In some writings this female behavior has been referred to as 'silent applause' (Maccoby, 1990, p. 519). Importantly, "there is evidence that women feel at a disadvantage in mixed-sex interaction," (Maccoby, 1990, p. 519) — not surprising, given the above description.

To date, there is not much data on the extent to which such culture clashes and male-domination occur in spontaneous mixed-sex interactions involving children. Docu-mentation of such features would provide some support for the "separate worlds" hypoth-

---

[2] The Separate Worlds Hypothesis has also been challenged elsewhere, for example, in the literature on gender differences in interruptions in adult speech, where contextual influences are frequently found (see James & Clarke, 1993, for a review).

[3] Witness Tannen's poignant examples of the female spouse who relates her problematic day to her partner, in an attempt to share troubles, only to have him solve her problem for her, leading her to feel he is insensitive; the male driver who frustrates his female partner by refusing to ask for directions, finding it a sign of weakness and being one-down.

esis. Moreover, there has been little research examining the reality of **separate worlds** and gender segregation in early and middle childhood cross-culturally. If gender segregation is sensitive to the plethora of influences described by Thorne, it is likely to be affected by cultural views and values as well. This is important to study, given many researchers' concern to point out that gender is socially constructed (see Cook-Gumperz & Scales, Chapter 30, this volume) and may be constructed differently in different cultures (Goodwin 1990, 1995). The present study attempts to examine both phenomena — male-domination in mixed-sex interactions in U.S. samples and cross-cultural variation in this phenomenon — by comparing mixed-sex interactions occurring among children at two schools, one a public school in Worcester, Massachusetts, and the other a school in Beijing, China.

HISTORY OF THIS STUDY

The question of cross-cultural variation in gender segregation and gender construction first came up for the present authors in a research group discussion with Sue Ervin-Tripp. We were simultaneously collecting data for separate studies: Kyratzis' was on talk in friendship dyads in the U.S. and Guo's was on talk in friendship triads in Beijing. The foci of the two studies were different. Kyratzis was interested in stylistic features of reason-giving and justifications in boy–boy, girl–girl, and boy–girl friendship dyads. Guo was interested in spontaneous uses of Mandarin modal forms in peer exchanges. However, both authors were using similar materials: Scenario toys involving either doll play with action figures (e.g., Playmobile's medical scenario) or materials allowing children to take on character roles themselves (e.g., Fisher-Price medical kit), which were intended to elicit rich interaction among peers. Interestingly, Kyratzis began to notice during her pilot that while interactions over these materials involving boy–boy and girl–girl friendship dyads were very rich, it was nearly impossible to get mixed-sex pairs of friends to play together. Boys and girls rarely named opposite-sex classmates as their "best friends." When Kyratzis attempted to pair boys and girls together who were not best friends, the children (especially boys) would often refuse to play with the opposite sex peer, and when forced, would play separately, dividing the toys in half. This looked quite a bit like "separate worlds."

In contrast, Guo reported that he had encountered no difficulty constructing mixed-sex triads of children from the Chinese classroom. Boys readily played with girls, and vice versa. Moreover, the children did not divide up the toys and play separately. Ervin-Tripp found this to be a fascinating comparative difference. She suspected from this that same-sex interactions would not yield as strong differences in China as they characteristically do in the U.S., and lamented the fact that Kyratzis and Guo did not have comparable data (Kyratzis' were of same-sex interactions and Guo's were of mixed-sex). Later, Kyratzis collected some mixed-sex interactions in a U.S. school to look at the "separate worlds" question from the angle of miscommunications and male-domination in mixed-sex talk among U.S. children. With the set of new data, this cross-cultural comparative analysis of mixed-sex interactions was undertaken.

THE U.S. STUDY

METHOD

Subjects

The U.S. sample was collected as follows. Kyratzis taught a course on Gender Development in Fall, 1994. The course project consisted of a semi-ethnographic study of prekindergarten and kindergarten classrooms in a public school in Worcester, Massachusetts. The age range of the children was between 4 and 6 years. The school had children from middle class, lower middle class, and poor families and many ethnic groups. Each class had about 55% European-American children and 45% children of non-Anglo ethnic groups.

The data were collected as follows. Each pair of seminar students chose one classroom to work in. Here, they had to conduct a mini-ethnography with the goal of identifying two friendship groups in the class based on biweekly observations of the class over a two-month period. The two friendship groups had to represent a comparison between an all-boy and all-girl friendship group or between a mixed-sex and same-sex friendship group. Many of the students chose the latter comparison because interaction within mixed-sex groups had come to be a topic of interest in the class. In most of these cases, a mixed-gender friendship group was compared to an all-girl friendship group.

The mini-ethnography was conducted as follows. Observations were made during the free-play period of each day, since this was when classroom friendship groups were most clearly in evidence. Field notes were taken of whom the children in the class played with, what activities they shared, and how they played and interacted within friendship groups. Field notes were shored up with interviews querying teachers' and children's impressions of the friendship groups in the class, as well as their characteristic activities and interaction styles. After the friendship groups were identified, one interaction within each group was audiorecorded. The audiorecording was made within an activity that was typical for the particular friendship group (e.g., dollhouse play, block play).

Interactions from seven different mixed-sex friendship groups were audiorecorded. Six of these were from pre-K classrooms. The majority of classrooms chosen for observation were pre-K because these classes are the most unstructured by teachers and afford the best observation of spontaneous classroom friendship groups.

Members of some of these are overlapping. The groups are as follows: Stanley-Holly-Bert; Mickey-Jenny; Patrick-Calvin-Alissa; Patrick-Calvin-Anita-Fred; Drake-Norman-Erin-Amy; Norman-Bess-Jessie; Norman-Sally.[4]

Transcription and Coding

The interactions were transcribed according to a transcription system developed by John Gumperz and his colleagues (Gumperz & Berenz, 1993). These transcripts were then

---

[4] The names are changed to protect the children's identities.

analyzed for various features, including: requests (direct and indirect, question and nonquestion forms), conflicts, challenges, refusals, uptakes and complying moves, justifications, and other features. The seminar students analyzed the features they thought differentiated the mixed-gender and comparison (same-sex) group. These features are described in the coding scheme in the appendix.

RESULTS

Student wrote reports of the results of their mini-ethnographies, including the field notes and discourse analysis.[5] The first result indicated that the mixed-sex groups were quite unstable. For each of the seven of the mixed-sex friendship groups identified, the same-sex group to which it was compared was more stable. That is, the same-sex group was more frequently observed during the two-month period than the corresponding mixed-sex group — it convened more frequently. Moreover, within each class, there were fewer mixed-sex friendship groups identified than same-sex groups. Consistent with the Kyratzis pilot study results reported above, in U.S. classrooms, mixed-sex friendship groups tend to be less frequent and less stable than same-sex friendship groups. This finding provides some support for the reality of "separate worlds" in U.S. classrooms.

The second set of results concerns the activity settings which were characteristic for the two kinds of friendship group, mixed-sex and same-sex. (In all but one case, same-sex groups were all-girl). The mixed-sex friendship groups characteristically played in the block area of each classroom; the all-girl friendship groups characteristically played in the dollhouse area. The all-boy friendship group identified also played in the block area. In other studies as well as in this one, block-play is more frequently chosen by boys' groups while dollhouse play is more frequently chosen by girls' groups (Paley, 1984). The selection of block area play in the mixed-gender groups here is one indication that boys are setting the agenda in mixed-gender play.

The third set of results concerns the analysis of the discourse in the mixed-gender friendship groups. Here, boys seemed to dominate the interaction. For all of the seven mixed-sex friendship groups, at least two of the following four patterns indicating domination of the interaction by boys was found: (1) boys made more power-asserting moves than girls (commands, challenges, and attention-getters); (2) girls more often complied with boys' moves than vice versa; (3) girls asked boys questions and made opinion- and permission-requests of boys more than vice versa; and (4) girls explained more than boys did. So, reminiscent of the characterization of mixed-sex interaction for adults by Duncan & Fiske (1977), boys ended up doing the agenda-controlling in the interaction and girls complied with boys' moves. These discourse features can be seen in the examples below.

---

[5] We gratefully acknowledge the contributions of the seminar students: Andrea Caporrella, Diane Ferragamo, Ciji Jones, Julian Jung, Regina Kursten, Julia Lacks, Anabel Lago, Linda Luthi, Elizabeth Miller, William Penuel, Cindy Sierakowski, Kim Tyszkowski, and Qing Xiao to these research results.

In (1), Mickey is continually challenging Jenny (e.g., line 02: *You can't put it in the hole*). She complies with his moves (line 02: *here*; line 10, *okay*) and defers to him by seeking out his help (line 07: *it's stuck, Mickey*) and permission (line 10: *can I have it now?*).

(1) Boy Challenging and Girl Agreeing and Deferring (Jenny(G)-Mickey(B)):

01 [The two children are sitting at a small pegboard]
02 Mi: You can't put it in the hole, *you have to put it in here! [Jenny has been try-
        ing to place plastic cube into a hole; she's been struggling. Mickey points up
        an alternative hole]
03 Je: here [moves it to another hole, as Mickey suggested]
04   here.
05 Mi: yes, yes, here [interrupts Jenny, pointing up yet another hole]
07 Je: it's stuck, Mickey, I can't get it out.
08 Mi: no that's not right, let *me have it, I'll try [tries to free cube] see, I got it
        [giggles].
10 Je: okay, Mickey, can I have it now?

In (2), Drake continually challenges the correctness of Amy's moves (e.g. line 04: *no, don't touch it*; line 09: *too late*; line 12: *that's too wide*). He seems to be quite concerned about being right and gaining one-upsmanship. Amy complies with his moves and, seemingly deferring to him, requests his opinion at several points in the exchange (e.g., line 12: *"okay? can we tunnel?"*; line 33: *"and these?"*). She defers to him even further by inviting him to her birthday party, a matter which he treats in a pragmatic and cursory fashion rather than dwelling on the theme, as she apparently would like to do. This exchange calls to mind Tannen's (1990) description of male–female miscommunications that occur when women want to share feelings and men simply want to solve problems — the women report dissatisfaction in such exchanges.

**(2) Boys give orders and challenge, girls comply and try to accommodate boys
    (ask them questions)** (Drake(B)-Norman(B)-Erin(G)-Amy(G)):

01 [Playing blocks]
02 Dr: [speaking to Amy] you do that. you do that.
03 Am: here, touch it.
04 Dr: no, don't touch it!
05 Er: [carrying some blocks over] here?
06 Dr: what? what? what?
07 Am: [speaking to boy behind her] you can play. (xxx) my last summer...(xx).
09 Dr: too late? too late? too late!
10 No: no, this is mine! [loud noise as block drops]
11 Am: okay? can we tunnel?
12 Dr: we turn, turn, turn. no! that's too wide!
13 Am: here Drake! Here Drake! [hands Drake blocks]
14 Dr: you can't have a car!
15 Er: well?
16 Dr: you dropped it
17 No: you take all of these! take 'um!

18 Am: Drake? Are you coming to my birthday party?
19 Dr: I'll come
20 Am: Na uh. You didn't come last year...for my first burfday (birthday). You
          didn't came...
22 Dr: I wasn't in school yet..(xxx)...we have to turn! We have to turn! see? see?
          it's too big!
24 Am: my burfday (birthday)? Are you comin' (coming) Drake?
25 Dr: uh huh! we have to turn.
26 Am: like this?
27 Er: do you wanna (want to) make a house?
28 Am: i'm buildin' the maze like this...and then you can make a house like this.
30 Dr: Turn it! to the market! turn the maze to the market!
31 No: Hey! you're in my way! build it over there!
32 Dr: up! up! this way....(xxx)...
33 Am: and these other ones? and these...(xxx)...
34 Dr: and these ones! now we can make it our maze. this is how we make it.
          [all the.kids scream 'wow!']
36 Er: no! the other one! the other car! [sound of cars crashing]
38 Dr: turn it like that! turn it like that! [to Amy] not that, that!
40 Am: it's too fat?
41 Dr: turn it now...turn it!
42 No: no! there's no room! go overa (over) there!
43 Dr: turn it.
44 Am: that's okay?
45 Er: it's too fat?
46 Am: can I have it?
47 Dr: (xxx)...this way. Why don't you turn it this way!

What is significant in Examples 1 and 2 is that the boys are setting the agenda and challenging and the girls are agreeing and deferring. One comes away with the feeling that the girls cannot be too satisfied in such exchanges. In the all-girl friendship groups that comprise many U.S. girls' peer culture, girls are used to deferring to their conversational partner and seeking out the partner's involvement — a large body of research has shown this (e.g., Kyratzis, 1992; Sheldon, 1990; Tannen, 1990). But there, such moves are reciprocated in kind. Here, in the mixed-sex exchanges, girls' open, partner-involving moves are not reciprocated.

Duncan and Fiske (1977) report that in mixed-sex exchanges, what can happen is that rather than adapting to the style of the conversational partner and meeting them halfway, girls intensify the features of girls' style as boys intensify the features of boys' style. Such an example can be seen (3), where Holly is making an excessively deferent move — apologizing to her conversational partner. Apologies are not frequently seen in all-girl exchanges. However, in mixed-sex exchanges, because the two styles when pitted against each other create such a power differential between the partners, quite deferent moves on the part of girls may become consistent with the agenda of the interaction.

(3) Boy Challenging and Girl Apologizing (Holly(G)-Stan(B)-Bert (B)):
01 St: My pencil! You have my pencil! Give me my pencil!
02 Ho: Oh Jeez, sorry
03   I didn't know it was yours/
04 St: That's okay. I don't care.

Girls did not frequently challenge boys' moves in our observed classrooms. However, when girls challenged boys, challenge was usually accompanied by extensive reason-giving, as in (4). Reason-giving represents girls' attempt to be open to and involve the conversational partner by incorporating her perspective in the joint decision-making process (Kyratzis, 1992). But in the context of boys' one-upsmanship agenda, where reasons are viewed as capitulation, such moves made by girls can render them one-down in the interaction.

(4) Boys Challenging and Girl Trying to Reason (Holly(G)-Stan(B)-Bert(B)):
01 St: The chicken is...[sounding out for journal] chicken.
02 Ho: turkey.
03 St: Not jerky! Mrs. Smith! [Telling on Ho]
04 Ho: What [whiny]? I said 'turkey'.
                    ---
05 Ho: Do you know what 'jerk' means?
06 Be: What?
07 Ho: It means when you're pulling something
08 Be: No, it's 'you're a jerk!'
09 St: Jerk, jerk, jerk, jerk!
10 Ho: Jerk means, like you're driving along and then you
11   suddenly go, EEEH, and stop like that. that's 'jerk'.
12 Be: Okay
13 St: O::ou! [escalating into shriek]
14 Ho: Jerk is not a swear
15 St: O::ou!
16 Ho: it's not a swear!

Although domination of girls by boys was the predominant pattern seen in our U.S. classroom friendship groups, it was not the exclusive one. In the ethnographic phase of the study, some less well established groupings of girls with boys were identified. In these, boys were sometimes seen to comply with girls' moves and ask them questions. This result points up again the contextual restrictedness of Separate Worlds, as noted in the past research cited, and the need to study the situations that promote greater gender equity in the classroom (see Cook-Gumperz & Scales, Chapter 30, this volume, for further discussion of this point). However, the fact that more stable friendships are associated with more gendered patterns in our sample suggests that taking on gendered styles of behavior may be a way for U.S. children to organize their social networks and create lasting friendships. In other words, it may be functional in children's social lives. This, in turn, may explain the frequent presence of gendered interaction patterns in U.S. classrooms.

CONCLUSIONS — THE U.S. STUDY

In sum, girls' moves seen in these mixed-sex exchanges — not challenging, agreeing, questioning and opinion-seeking, apologizing, and reasoning — are moves which render girls equal in exchanges with other girls but which in this mixed-sex context render them one-down in the interaction. Hence, it is not surprising that girls frequently report dissatisfaction in mixed-sex interactions. The Relativistic model of inter-cultural communication put forth by Maltz and Borker (1982) and Tannen (1990) — **Separate Worlds** — whereby the same moves mean different things in men's and women's "cultures" leading to communicative problems in cross-sex communication, seems to apply to children in the U.S. classrooms studied here. Consistent with Duncan and Fiske's (1977) finding, boys and girls did not much adapt to one another's style in playing together — boys did not hesitate to challenge and girls did not hesitate to agree and question. As a result, girls were dominated by boys. The dynamic of boys dominating girls could also be seen in the activity settings selected by mixed-sex friendship groups, which tended to be male- typed activities (block-play). That this dynamic was the prevalent pattern in the better-formed mixed-friendship groups we observed suggests that gendered patterns may be strategies for sustaining mixed-sex friendships.

THE CHINESE STUDY

METHOD

The data of the Chinese study were taken from the corpus of a larger study examining the relationship between social interaction and language development by Mandarin speaking children in China (Guo, 1994). Transcripts of two triads were selected, one consisting of two boys and one girl, and the other two girls and one boy. A half-hour sample of transcribed interactive speech for each triad was included in the analysis, yielding about five hundred utterances for each.

Subjects

Six children were involved in the current study. The children were 5-year-olds (ranging in age from 5;0 to 5;4) who attended a daycare center associated with a university. All had attended the daycare center for at least 2.5 years. Two mixed-sex triads were involved in this study, one boy (C11) and two girls (C12, C13) in Triad 1 and two boys (C21, C22) and one girl (C23) in Triad 2. The triads were selected from a class of 26 children on the basis of their "compatibility" as assessed by their teacher. More specifically, the teacher was asked to recommend two groups of three children who could play together and get along well. She was not asked to choose children who were "good friends" in their class. Normally, activities in Chinese daycare classrooms are heavily structured by the teacher and the concept of friendship is not viewed as a basis for children's play groups.

Procedure

The triads were taken to a separate classroom in the school for recording. They were given a set of miniature playhouse toys and were instructed to play together for about an hour. Usually, children assigned themselves roles, such as mom, dad, child, etc., at the beginning of the recording session. Sometimes they changed these roles later in the session. The experimenter sat in the corner of the room, trying to avoid contact with the children. He only spoke to the children when they addressed him or when the children were misbehaving.

RESULTS

All "interactive utterances" were extracted from the transcripts and coded for various features. "Interactive utterances" were defined as utterances that attempted to elicit responses, either verbal or nonverbal, from the conversational partner. They included various kinds of control moves (e.g., direct and indirect requests, prohibitions, and scoldings), requests for information, short anecdotes, and pretense statements that were intended to elicit teasing or laughter from the partner. Utterances in an extended monologic narrative or those intended for self-regulative purposes (e.g., to think aloud) were excluded. The number of interactive utterances by each child is reported in Table 33.1.

TABLE 33.1.
Mean number of interactive utterances by gender and triad

	Triad 1 Mean	Triad 2 Mean	Total Mean
Male	122.0	89.5	100.3
Female	82.5	78.0	81.0
Total	95.7	85.7	90.7

The total number of utterances of the two triads are quite comparable, despite the different gender composition of the two groups. However, there was a slight tendency for boys to produce more interactive utterances than girls in both groups, whether there was only one boy or two boys in the triad.

The interactive utterances were coded for type of speech act: challenge (insults, refusals to comply with a request, scoldings), direct request, indirect request, and agreements (e.g., *okay*). In addition, the type of exchange in which the interactive utterance occurred was coded. There were four types. **Cooperative xchanges** were exchanges involving complying with or building upon partners' suggestions. **Conflicts** were short exchanges (i.e., fewer than three turns) involving partners refusing to comply with one another's requests or proposals or insulting one another. **Extended conflicts** were long exchanges (i.e., three turns and more) involving partners refusing to comply with one another's requests or proposals or insulting one another. **Unresolved conflicts** were conflicts having no resolution with respect to the initiating move.

Conflicts, Challenges, and Compliance in Chinese Mixed-Sex Groups

As shown in Table 33.2, about half of each speaker's interactive utterances occurred in conflicts.

TABLE 33.2.   Proportions of exchange types by each speaker

Subject	C11	C12	C13	C21	C22	C23	Male Mean	Female Mean
Sex	M	F	F	M	M	F		
COOP	58.2	55.9	51.5	48.1	42.0	55.1	49.4	54.2
CONF	32.0	33.8	39.2	40.0	45.0	41.0	39.0	38.0
EXTE	9.8	10.3	9.3	13.9	13.0	3.8	12.2	7.8
UNRE	0.8	1.5	0.0	0.0	0.0	0.0	0.3	0.5

Conflicts flourished in the Chinese mixed-sex triads; unlike their U.S. counterparts, Chinese girls did not acquiesce to their partners' challenges and conflicts were sustained.

Also unlike their U.S. counterparts, the Chinese mixed-sex play groups readily took on the domestic theme for their pretend play. Remember that the U.S. mixed-sex groups tended to engage in block play; they never played house, apparently due to the influence of the boys, for whom playing house is negatively valued. Conflicts for the Chinese children focused around violations of the domestic theme, as in Example (5) below. In this episode, the two boys of the triad are in conflict. C22 is angry at C21's insult ("you stupid thing") and draws upon the domestic theme to challenge C21, complaining to the researcher that C21 is in violation of his child role. A boy drawing on the domestic theme in this way would be quite an anomaly in U.S. mixed-sex interactions.

(5)

0484 C22: (looks for lid)

　　　　　guō gàir ne? guō gàir ne?

　　　　　'Where is the pot lid? Where is the pot lid?'

0485 C21: (points)

bèndàn, guō gàir zài zhèr.
'You stupid thing. The pot lid is over there.'[6]
0486 C22: (puts it aside)
wǒ bù yào le. shǎguā.
'I don't want it anymore, you fool.'
0487 C22: (a little annoyed, points at C1 to Guo)
shūshū, tā, shūshū, nèige, LU MIAO, LU MIAO zhèi
0488 C22: *háizi lǎo shì, tā bù tīng bàba māma de huà,*
0489 C22: *LU MIAO.*
'Uncle, he, uncle, he, Lu Miao, Lu Miao, the child never listens to the parents.'
0490 GU: *nà zěnme bàn ne?*
'Then, what can be done?'
0491 C21: (to Guo, pretends to bite the plates)
wǒ zài chī diézi ne.
'I'm eating the plates now.'
0492 C23: (totally surprised expression, giggles)
aa?
'What?'
(all laugh)   (tr5li5)

In Example 6 as well, the boys are in conflict with one another and C22 again draws upon norms surrounding family life to challenge C21 (the child character cannot eat things at his will).

(6)

0460 C21: (dishes food out from C22's pot, pretends eating)
chī yú.
'Eat fish.'
0461 C22: (to C21)
gàn má ni, LU MIAO. tǎoyàn.
'What are you doing, Lu Miao. You are a nuisance.'
0462 C21: *wǒ shì háizi ya.*
'I'm the child.'
(giggles)
0463 C22: *nà, nèige, nà nǐ bù néng suíbiàn chī a.*
'But, but you can't eat things at your will.'
0464 C22: *bàba hái děi chī ne.*
'Daddy has to eat, too.'
0465 C21: *wǒ xiǎng chī.*
'I want to eat.'

---

[6] In Mandarin Chinese, the use of insulting words such as *bèndàn* or *shǎguā* with an impatient intonation to refer to another person's failure to perform an obviously easy task usually indicates intimacy and solidarity rather than real insult. But repeated use of such expressions runs the risk of making the addressee annoyed, as evidenced in this episode.

0466 C22: *bàba gěi nǐ zuò a, shǎguā.*
          'Daddy will make it for you, you fool.'
0467 C21: *nà nǐ gěi wǒ zuò ma.*
          'Then please make it for me.'
0468 C22: *lái, gěi nǐ. bàba gěi nǐ yī ge rén. gàosù nǐ,*
0469 C22: *bàba yǒu liǎng tiáo yú le.* (give pot to C21) *gěi nǐ,*
0470 C22: *chī ba.*
          'OK, here you are. Daddy makes it for you alone. Let me tell you, daddy
          has two fish now. Here is one for you. Eat it now.'
0471 C21: (takes pot and pretends to eat)   (tr5li5)

What is particularly interesting is C22's calling C21 a "nuisance." Several conflicts in the Chinese mixed-sex interactions focused around acts which were deemed "silly" or "nuisance-ish" from the perspective of subverting norms of family life. Even more significant in the use of domestic themes in Chinese children's friendship groups is the fact that **all** participants **willingly** conform to the domestic roles they take, rather than merely exploiting their advantageous role to compete for one-upsmanship. As shown in Example 6, C21 first (in line 462) used his child role to counter C22's nuisance accusation. But then, in line 465, he did not hesitate to take the subordinate role of the child and tries to appeal to C22 for food, effectively acknowledging C22's authority in the father role. In return, C22 did not exploit the father's authoritative role, but rather, took the father's nurturing role and complied with C21's request. This way of employing domestic themes and roles clearly indicates that the domestic themes are not utilized primarily in the service of one-upsmanship, but rather to sustain the interaction in the "correct" way according to the conventional cultural scripts of such scenarios. The domestic themes are used in managing **both** conflicts and cooperations among the Chinese children. The importance of domestic themes in organizing mixed-sex interactions among the Chinese children is in striking contrast to the absence of such themes in the U.S. mixed-sex interactions.

An important ramification of the seriousness with which the domestic theme was taken in the Chinese mixed-sex groups is the gender dynamic which resulted. Boys more often than girls were perpetrators of the silly and naughty acts (see Table 33.3). Girls, who often had the mother-role with the associated responsibility of upholding norms of family life, often got to boss the boys around and have their way over the boys, while boys very often ended up complying with girls' commands. These two trends can be seen in Tables 33.3 and 33.4 and in the examples that follow.

Table 33.4 shows that all three boys in the two triads made these silly and naughty moves quite frequently, and more often than girls did. This style was intensified by the presence of two boys in a group, and this intensified atmosphere was contagious — the girl in Triad 2 committed these silly acts to a greater extent than her counterparts in Triad 1, who were not outnumbered by boys. In addition, this type of move was directed to both the same-sex and opposite-sex partners, but more so to opposite-sex partners.

The fact that the silly acts were more likely to be addressed to the opposite sex indicates that these children, boys in particular, were not just silly or naughty by nature. Rather, these acts were used to serve certain social functions. In fact, boys seemed to deliberately initiate some silly and naughty acts in order to elicit scolding and nuisance-accusations from girls. This is evidenced by the fact that when the boys were scolded by girls for these acts, they never fought back, but rather, either laughed together with the girls (as in Example 7) or performed some additional silly acts that conformed to the scenario as arranged by the girls (as in Example 8).

TABLE 33.3.   Proportions of silly and naughty moves by individual speakers

	Boys			Girls		
	C11	C21	C22	C12	C13	C23
Frequency	12	20	15	---	---	9
Proportion of silly moves of total utterance	10%	25%	15%	---	---	11.5%
Proportion of silly moves addressed to girls	100%	45%	40%	---	---	---
Proportion of silly moves addressed to boys	---	10%	33%	---	---	67%
Proportion of silly moves addressed to both	---	45%	27%	---	---	33%

(7)
0445 C12: (plays with a doll by herself, takes off doll head, laughs)
0446 C11: *ou, wáwa tóu,*
           'Oh, the head of the doll.'
           (throws doll head to floor)
           méi le.
           'It's no more.'
0447 C13: (goes to pick it up)
           gàn má nǐ, tǎoyàn de, tǎoyàn de.
           'what are you doing, nuisance, nuisance.'
0448 C13: *LU JIN , nǐ zěnme zènme tǎoyàn na.*
           'Lu Jin, how come you are such a nuisance.'
0449 C12: (giggles)
0450 C13: (holds up toy)
           bǎ zhèi wǎn gěi nòng dào chuáng dǐ xià qù le.
           'You pushed the bowl under the bed.'
           (all three children laugh)   (tr5ba5)

(8)

0615 C11: (suddenly jumps up, to C13)
    wǒ zá sǐ nǐ.
    'I'll smash you.'

0616 C13: (to C11, scoldingly)
    nǐ shì bù shì shénjīng bù zhèngcháng le, nǐ.
    'Are you a little crazy?'

0617 C11: (turns to C13)
    wǒ zá nǐ.
    'I'll smash you.'

0618 C13: (loud, challengingly)
    nǐ zá wǒ ya nǐ?
    'Are you going to smash me? You?'

0619 C12: (laughs)
    nǐ zá LU XIN, wǒ bǎ nǐ nǎobēnr gěi zá chū lái.
    'If you smash Lu Xin, then I'll knock your brain off your forehead.'

0620 C11: (stands, making silly posture, as if being killed)

0621 C13: (pretends hitting C11's bottom)
    ei, ei, ei.
    'Spank, spank, spank.'

0622 C12: (to C11 and C13)
    kuài wár ba, dāi huǐr jiù méi le.
    'Better hurry up and play. There won't be much time left.'   (tr5ba5)

The scenario involving boys being a nuisance with respect to subverting the domestic theme often resulted in girls getting the upper hand over the boys. Table 33.4 shows that boys were somewhat more likely to comply to girls in the mixed-sex interactions than were girls to boys. In the first triad, the proportion of compliance by the only boy (C11) to the two girls (C12 and C13) is comparable to that of the only girl (C23) to the two boys (C21 and C22) in the second triad. However, the two boys (C21 and C22) complied to the only girl (C23) in the second triad more frequently than did the two (C12 and C13) girls to the only boy (C11) in the first triad. This is quite unexpected from the perspective of what went on in our U.S. mixed-sex play groups.

TABLE 33.4.   Proportion of compliant moves to male and female partners

Male partners comply with female partners	C11→C12		C11→C13		C21→C23		C22→C23		Mean
	M	F	M	F	M	F	M	F	
	29.4%		40%		25%		29.7%		31%

Female partners comply with male partners	C12→C11		C13→C11		C23→C21		C23→C22		Mean
	F	M	F	M	F	M	F	M	
	21.9%		15.8%		48%		33%		29.6%

Not only do boys tend to comply more to girls in Chinese mixed-sex interactions by virtue of conforming to domestic themes, but also girls are extremely skillful in employing the domestic themes in taming the boys. Example (9) demonstrates boys having to comply to girls by virtue of the power accorded girls by the domestic theme. C22 joined C21's fooling around and said a taboo word "bottom." C21 elicited the experimenter's prohibition to C22. Then the girl (C23) also scolded C22 for using a bad word. C22 tried to defend himself by telling the experimenter that C21 had done an equally wrong thing, that is, using the scale as a toy, and tried to talk back to the girl by telling her the rule, that is, "The scale is for adults to use, not for children" (implying that C21 was wrong since he was playing the child role but was nonetheless playing with the scale). As C22 was correct about the rule, C23 could not counter him on those grounds. However, the girl used a different tactic to challenge C22. She shifted the frame to the playhouse scene involving feeding the child, where the mother (role played by C23) could order the father (role played by C22) around for the benefit of the child (role played by C21). What is remarkable here is that the girl made the command in a harsh tone and the boy readily complied. In real-life Chinese families, mothers officiate over family matters and this powerful female role is duplicated and utilized in children's play surrounding the domestic theme.

(9)

0588 C21: *mài bàba le.*
    'selling daddy.'

0589 C22: (giggle with C3)

0590 C21: *mài háizi dàng qiūqiān le. mài xiā tiáo le.*
    'selling children and swings. selling prawn chips.'

0591 C21: *mài jù le. mài chāzi le.*
    'selling saws. selling forks.'

0592 C22: *mài pìgǔ le.*
    'selling bottoms.'

0593 C21: *mài, shūshū, LU CHAO shuō, mài pìgǔ.*
    'selling, uncle, LU CHAO said, selling bottoms.'

0594 GU: *bù néng xiā shuō a.*
    'You can't say bad words.'

0595 C23: (to C22)
    nǐ qiáo, shūshū shuō nǐ le ba.
    'See. Uncle has scolded you for it.'

0596 C22: *shūshū, nà LU MIAO ná chèng dāng nèige, bǎ chèng*
0597 C22: *dāng wánr de dōngxi.*
    'Uncle, but Lu Miao took the scale as a toy.'

0599 GU: *mm.*
    'Mh Hum.'

0600 C22: (to C23)
    gàosù nǐ, chèng shì dà rén yòng de.
    'I tell you. The scale is for adults to use,'

0601 C22: *bù shì xiǎohái yòng de.*
       'not for children to play with.'
0602 C23: (ignore C22, then to C22 commandingly)
       zánmen gěi háizi chī fàn ba.
       'We should feed the child now.'
0604 C22: (turns to C21, and gives C21 food)
       háizi,
       'Child.'
0605 C21: (waves toy to C23, being silly)   (tr5li5)
     Girls can take on a quite domineering and harsh style when interacting with boys.
Girls in our data sometimes used extra-harsh language to boys, ordered them around, and
even created unreasonable obstacles for boys. The following example illustrates how
difficult girls could be to their boy partners, and concommitantly, how willingly compliant boys could be to their girl partners.

(10)
       (C11 plays the role of father, C13 plays the role of the child)
0192 C13: (to C11) *lián yú, hái yǒu shuǐguǒ, zhèige làjiāo dōu*
0193 C13: *méi yǒu xǐ. táozi méi xǐ jiù gěi wǒ chī ya?*
       'These fruit are not washed yet. How come you simply give them to me?'
0194 C13: (commanding)
       kuài qù gěi wǒ xǐ xǐ.
       'Hurry and go wash them for me.'
0195 C11: (pretends washing food, then gives it to C13)
       shuǐ. xǐ wán le.
       'Water. They are all washed now.'
0196 C13: (to C11)
       kuài qù gěi wǒ xǐ xǐ qù.
       'Hurry and go wash them for me.'
0197 C11: *xǐ wán le, xǐ wán le, xǐ wán le.*
       'They are all washed. They are all washed.'
0198 C13: *yòng xǐjiéméi. gē xǐdílíng.*
       'You have to use detergent. Put in detergent.'
0199 C11: (pretends washing)
0200 C13: *nǐ zhèige bàba.*
       'What a lousy father you are.'
0204 C11:   (gives C13 toy)
       ei , xǐ wán le.
       'Hey, they are washed now.'
0205 C13: *you , nà nǐ xǐdílíng jiù gěi wǒ hē, jiù ràng wǒ*
0206 C13: *chī ya?*
       'Hey, you simply give it to me to eat with detergent?'
       (gives toy back to C11)
       kuài qù gěi wǒ chōng chōng.
       'Hurry and go rinse it for me.'

0207 C11: (surprised, funny face)
    a?
    'What?'
0208 C13: (commandingly)
    kuài qù gěi wǒ chōng chōng.
    'Hurry and go rinse it for me.'
0209 C11: (pretends washing, then gives C3)
    hǎo le.
    'Ok, it's done.'
0210 C13: (complainingly)
    zěnme hái yǒu a?
    'How come there is still some detergent on them?'
0211 C11: (washes again, etc.)   (tr5ba5)

From the perspective of U.S. mixed-sex exchanges, it is extremely unlikely to encounter this kind of dialogue. The girl (C13) used direct and aggravated commands repeatedly, such as *kuài* 'hurry' and *gěi wǒ* 'for me' and kept ordering the boy around. In addition, she was unreasonably picky. First she criticized the boy for not having the food washed, and then for not having used detergent while washing, and after that, for not having rinsed the food. No matter what the boy did there was something wrong with it, and she was never satisfied. The boy continually complied. It appears that it is the dominant role accorded women in the sphere of Chinese domestic life that sanctioned the domineering role that the girl took over the boy in this mixed-sex interaction.

CONCLUSIONS — THE CHINESE STUDY

To summarize, our Chinese mixed-sex play groups utilized domestic scenarios in their play and, because women dominate in this sphere of influence in the adult culture, girls were afforded a powerful role in the play. They are the protectors of the norms surrounding domestic life, while boys are the subverters, often becoming a **nuisance**. For this, they must be scolded and ordered around by the girls.

Most striking in the Chinese data is that the domestic themes are not merely employed by girls unilaterally in order to gain the upper hand in the mixed-sex interactions. Rather, boys, along with girls, willingly comply with the norms as prescribed by the domestic scripts even when they have much to "lose" and nothing to "gain" in terms of social status and control. In addition to being perfectly happy with the subservient roles (child or father) they were assigned by virtue of the domestic scenarios, boys often initiated silly and naughty acts in order to elicit scolding and accusations, which would put them in a subordinate position in relation to girls. And they had no problem with being scolded and ordered around by girls, not even when the girls were unreasonably harsh in their commands.

OVERALL CONCLUSIONS: COMPARING THE SEPARATE-NESS OF WOMEN'S AND MEN'S WORLDS IN THE U.S. AND CHINA THROUGH THE WINDOW OF CHILDREN'S PLAY

In U.S. mixed-sex interactions, boys dominate, while in Chinese mixed-sex interactions, boys do not dominate; in fact, they are often dominated by girls. How can we account for this difference in gender hierarchy? The key to the question here, it seems, lies in the different values placed on the family as a fundamental social unit and the position of the individual in the two different cultures. In Chinese culture, domestic life is a highly valued social domain. In addition, great emphasis and value is placed on collectivism and interdependence of individuals, whose relationships are specified according to the positions people take in locally defined social groups, such as the family, work place, and peer groups (Bond, 1986; Brown, Chapter 2, this volume; Hsu, 1970; Markus & Kitayama, 1991). Once in the context of family life, men, powerful though they are in the sphere of influence outside the home (e.g, in the work place), are nonetheless evaluated in terms of their role in the family unit of which they are a part. Hence, what goes on inside the home is important for personal definition, independent of one's position in other social domains. Women, who officiate in the sphere of family life, are therefore accorded considerable power, at least within the family unit, although they may have a quite different, even invisible role outside the family unit.[7] In contrast, although women in the U.S. are usually the experts in the sphere of domestic life as well as in China, women do not have much power for the following two reasons. First, the sphere of domestic life is not as highly valued as work-related outside-the-home sphere in the U.S. as in China. Second, because the U.S. culture places great value on individualism and independence of individuals, the self is defined as a consistent being independent of other beings and social domains. That is, the individual has a more constant identity, and therefore interactive style, across all social domains. Therefore, people in the U.S. do not readily change their individual interactive styles from one social domain to another, be it work place vs. home, or same-sex interactions vs. mixed-sex interactions.

How this plays out in terms of **Separate Worlds** for men and women (and boys and girls) in the two cultures is as follows. Boys and girls in China may grow up in quite separate worlds in terms of a peer culture made up of same-sex peers. Boys may be quite rough and engage in competitive and naughtiness-display activities with their same-sex peers.[8] Girls may learn to be quite **invisible** and unobtrusive in practicing adult female roles with their same-sex peers. However, what distinguishes the Chinese children is that they may have learned to be **bilingual**, shifting readily between two social

---

[7] Dubisch (1986) has made a similar argument for the power of women in rural Greek village society.

[8] The interactions between C21 and C22 in examples (1) and (2) suggest this; moreover, this was the consensus we obtained when we queried native Chinese speakers about boy-boy relations in China.

spheres, the **domestic** sphere, where women officiate and men are scolded and ordered about and the **nondomestic** sphere, where men officiate and women are silent. Like men, who can be both competitive (outside-the-home) and compliant (inside-the-home), women can be both domineering (inside-the-home) and not domineering (outside-the-home), depending on the sphere of influence instantiated. What differentiates the Chinese from the U.S. speakers is the **bilingualism** of their genderlects and the ability to shift interactive styles between different social domains. Shifting to the domestic theme is not avoided by boys and men — partly because the domestic sphere is not devalued, and partly because one's worth is locally defined by the current social group. The children in this study revealed this in their play.

In conclusion, the concept of gender, in terms of gender separateness, gender hierarchy, and display of gendered styles of interacton, is constructed differently in the U.S. and China. In order to understand the cross-cultural differences, we had to consider gender construction in the larger context of cultural meanings — the different values placed on the family and the different construals of the individual's self identity in the two cultures. With this conclusion, we have come around to two important messages carried in the work of Susan Ervin-Tripp. The first is that gender is a functional social construction deeply rooted in a rich system of cultural meanings. We must understand these functions and meanings in order to see why gendered pattern arises in particular contexts and hence be in a better position to promote gender equity. The second is that in order to understand the meaning of microanalytic discourse-analytic factors, one must consider them in the broader cultural context.

REFERENCES

Bond, M. (Ed.). 1986. *The psychology of the Chinese people.* Hong Kong: Oxford University Press.

Dubisch, J. (1986). Introduction. In J. Dubisch (Ed.), *Gender and power in rural Greece*, (pp. 3-41). Princeton, NJ: Princeton University Press.

Duncan, S. Jr., & Fiske, D. W. (1977). *Face-to-face interaction: Research, methods, and theory.* Hillsdale, NJ: Lawrence Erlbaum Associates.

Ervin-Tripp, S. M., & Lampert, M. D. (1992). Gender differences in the construction of humorous talk. In *Locating Power: Proceedings of the Second Berkeley Women and Language Conference* (pp. 108-117). Berkeley, CA: Berkeley Women and Language Group.

Ervin-Tripp, S. M., O'Connor, M. C., & Rosenberg, J. (1984). Language and power in the family. In C. Kramerae, M. Schultz, & W. M. O'Barr (Eds.), *Language and Power* (pp. 116-135). New York: Sage.

Goodwin, M. J. (1980). Directive-response speech sequences in girls' and boys' task activities. In S. McConnell-Ginet, R. Borker, & N. Furman (Eds.), *Women and language in literature and society* (pp. 157-173). New York: Praeger.

Goodwin, M. J. (1990). *He-said-she-said: Talk as social organization among Black children.* Bloomington: Indiana University Press.

Goodwin, M. J. (1995). "Ay! Chirriona!": Stance-taking in Latina girls' games. *Cultural performances: Proceedings of the Third Berkeley Women and Language Conference* (pp. 232-241). Berkeley, CA: Berkeley Women and Language Group.

Gumperz, J. J., & Berenz, N. (1993). Transcribing conversational exchanges. In J. A. Edwards & M. D. Lampert, *Talking data: Transcription and coding in discourse research* (pp. 91-121). Hillsdale, NJ: Lawrence Erlbaum Associates.

Guo, J. (1994). *Social interaction, meaning, and grammatical form: Children's development and use of modal auxiliaries in Mandarin Chinese.* Unpublished doctoral dissertation, University of California, Berkeley.

Hsu, F. (1970). *Americans and Chinese: Purpose and fulfillment in great civilizations.* Garden City, NY: The Natural History Press.

James, D. & Clarke, S. (1993). Women, men, and interruptions: A criticial review. In D. Tannen, (Ed.), *Gender and conversational interaction* (pp. 231-280). New York: Oxford University Press.

Kyratzis, A. (1992). Gender differences in the use of persuasive justification in children's pretend play. In *Locating Power: Proceedings of the Second Berkeley Women and Languge Conference* (pp. 326-337). Berkeley: Berkeley Women and Language Group.

Lakoff, R. T. (1975). *Language and woman's place.* New York: Harper & Row.

Maccoby, E. E. (1990). Gender and relationships: A developmental account. *American Psychologist,* **45,** 513-520.

Maltz, D. N. & Borker, R. A. (1982). A cultural approach to male-female miscommunication. In J. A. Gumperz (Ed.), *Language and social identity* (pp. 195-216). New York: Cambridge University Press.

Markus, H. R. & Kitayama, S. (1991). Culture and the Self: Implications for cognition, emotion, and motivation. *Psychological Review,* **98,** 224-253.

Paley, V. G. (1984). *Boys and girls: Superheroes in the doll corner.* Chicago: Universoty of Chicago Press.

Sheldon, A. (1990). Pickle fights: Gendered talk in preschool disputes. *Discourse Processes* **13,** 5-31.

Sheldon, A. (1992). Conflict talk: Sociolinguistic challenges to self-assertion and how young girls meet them. *Merrill-Palmer Quarterly* **38,** 25-117.

Tannen, D. (1990). *You just don't understand: Women and men in conversation.* New York: Ballentine.

Thorne, B. (1993). *Gender play: Girls and boys in school.* Rutgers, NJ: Rutgers University Press.

APPENDIX

CODING SCHEME FOR EXAMINING GENDER DIFFERENCES IN PEER TALK

CONFLICT EXCHANGES

Conflict An exchange consisting of at least one challenging move (e.g., a refusal, or a move to take something away from partner) that is responded to. The response does not have to be a challenge or refusal.

Extended Conflict An exchange consisting of at least three moves: an initiating challenge, followed by a response challenge, followed by another move (which can be either a challenge or a capitulation/giving in).

Conflict Resolution Give-in, compromise, abandonment. (Count each give-in and compromise for each partner.)

Challenge Disagreeing with another person on ideas or agenda, such as rejection, refusal, scolding, etc., defined here as the "opening move of a conflict." (Count the number of times each child makes a challenge.)

Refusal Count the number of refusals (disagreeing to go along with what partner wants) within a conflict, omitting the challenge (opening move of the conflict).

CONTROL MOVES

Control moves are attempts to change the behavior of another. This can be a command, refusal, or request.

Direct Commands Moves that directly specify what the speaker wants the addressee to do (e.g., "Wash the dishes"). Also included in this category are need- and want-statements with the intended actor explicitly specified ("I want you to wash the dishes"; "I need you to give that to me").

Interrogatives Question forms of requests. These are open forms that give the addressee an out in terms of complying (e.g., "Could you wash the dishes?" "Wash the dishes, okay?"). This category also includes forms that request the addressee's opinion. ("Should this go here?").

Hints Moves that attempt to elicit an action from the addressee but this action is not explicitly mentioned (e.g., "My coffee is getting cold"; "The book is too far away for me to reach").

Descriptions   During pretend play, these are moves that refer to an action as though it is going to occur without having to be negotiated. But they are also requests for the play partner to go along with the move ("We are going to wash the dishes now"; "He will finish baking the cake").

Prohibitions   Moves intended to stop another person from performing an act (e.g., "Don't touch it").

Refusals   In these moves, the speaker refuses to do something previously requested by an addressee (e.g., Addressee: "Put this here." Speaker: "No, there's no room").

Scoldings   Moves that, with some moral authority, accuse the other person of wrong doings (e.g., "You are so naughty in doing this").

Insults   Negative expressions inflicting personal attacks (e.g., "Stop doing that, **you fool**").

Naughty Moves   These moves threaten a particular object, person, or scenario (e.g., "I'm going to take off the head of the doll").

Justifications   These are reasons that accompany requests. The speaker is telling the addressee why she or he should comply (e.g., "Take the gloves off **because they'll get dirty**").

Agreement   Moves indicating compliance with the addressee's previous control moves (e.g., "Sure, I'd love to work with you").

34 STUDYING GENDER DIFFERENCES IN THE CONVERSATIONAL HUMOR OF ADULTS AND CHILDREN

Martin D. Lampert
Holy Names College
Oakland, California

Over the past twenty-five years, social scientists have shown a growing interest in the study of humor. Much of the research done to date, however, has focused largely on the use and appreciation of jokes and joke routines to the exclusion of other humor-related behaviors, such as teasing, impersonation, and put-ons. Experimental and correlational studies of humor appreciation, for example, have typically investigated subjects' responses to jokes, cartoons, and riddles (e.g., Derks, 1992; Levine, 1969; Masten, 1986; McGhee, 1976a; Ruch, 1992; Shultz, 1972, 1974). Naturalistic studies of humor have likewise focused their attention primarily on jokes and joke telling (McDowell, 1979; Norrick, 1993; Sacks, 1974). Not surprisingly, then, many of the psychological and linguistic theories of humor tend to emphasize phenomena that are important for the performance and understanding of jokes, but may not be necessary nor sufficient for the appreciation of humor in general (see Koestler, 1964; Raskin, 1985; Suls, 1983; Wyer & Collins, 1992).

Recently, investigators have begun to turn their attention away from joke telling *per se* and more toward the study of humor-related attitudes and behaviors, styles of interaction, and coping mechanisms (Crawford & Gressley, 1991; Graham, Papa, & Brooks, 1992; Lefcourt & Martin, 1986; McGhee, 1980). Greater emphasis has also begun to be placed on other domains of humorous behavior such as clowning and teasing (Alberts, 1992; Eder, 1993; Sanford & Eder, 1984; Shapiro, Baumeister, & Kessler, 1991). Along these lines, Susan Ervin-Tripp and I began to investigate the range of humor-related activities in the natural conversations of friends and family members. One of the most striking things that we observed early on was that although humorous remarks occurred with great frequency in the natural conversations of peers (ranging from 1 remark per 8 to 11 turns), very few attempts at humor involved the telling of a joke, pun, or riddle (Lampert & Ervin-Tripp, 1989). In the transcripts of peer interaction that we have analyzed to date, we have in fact observed that most humor tends to center primarily around personal anecdotes, clever commentaries, and good-natured teasing — not joke telling. Interestingly, this trend in natural conversation also seems to find a parallel in the routines of professional comics, who today rely less on prefabricated jokes and more on humorous observations about shared life experiences (Carter, 1989; Stebbins, 1990). The content of stand-up comedy may in fact stem from the comic's desire to recreate the type of humor found in a natural conversation and to generate the kind of rapport with an audience that is typically found among close friends.

The goal of this chapter is to provide an overview of a research program developed by Susan Ervin-Tripp and me to investigate conversational humor, in particular, the differences in conversational humor between men and women as well as boys and girls. As part of this exposition, I describe four seminal studies designed to look specifically at gender, age, and cultural differences in the humorous behavior of adults and children.

STUDYING ADULT HUMOR

Background

When we began our study of humor, we were primarily interested in how context and social roles affected humor use, particularly the humor of men and women in conversation. We had observed that within social interactions, participants' humorous behavior could be keyed, among other things, to their social status within the group and expectations of role appropriate behavior. As Apte (1985), Coser (1960), Howell (1973) and others have noted, high status individuals tend to engage more freely in joking and teasing — especially the teasing of individuals of lower status — in social interactions. In contrast, individuals of comparatively lower group status tend to direct their humor either toward equals or those with even lower status, and rarely toward those of higher standing.

We further recognized that an individual's role within an interaction could restrict the kind and even amount of joking in which he or she might engage. For instance, nurses typically refrain from cracking jokes about illness and physical disability in the presence of their patients and their patients' families; however, when in the company of only nurses, they often make joking remarks about patients' conditions (Coser, 1960; Gordon, 1983).

Given the historical roles of men and women in U.S. society, we expected that status and situational expectations would play a large part in the humorous behavior of the two sexes. We noted that in the 1960s and 1970s researchers had in fact observed that in public or mixed company, men were more likely to joke, tease, and kid, while women were more likely to play the audience (see Coser, 1959, 1960; McGhee, 1979, chapter 8). If women did make humorous remarks or observations, these remarks often tended to be self-directed. Investigators ascribed these gender differences to (1) the traditionally lower status of women and (2) the inappropriateness of women to engage in what may be seen as an aggressive, rather masculine activity, while in the company of men. More recent studies have indicated in fact that when in the company of other women, where no status distinctions based on gender exist, women readily joke about life and other people, in particular, men (Apte, 1985; Jenkins, 1985). In a sense, the social processes that influence when nurses may joke about patients seem to find a parallel in women's jokes about men.

However, with the changing roles of women in society over the last 25 years, we expected that women adopting less traditional sex roles for themselves would use humor more freely in public settings and mixed groups. In experimental research, investigators have in fact found notable differences in the humor appreciation of women and girls with more versus less traditional sex-role orientations. A few studies, for example, have shown that women and girls with less traditional views tend to have a reduced appreciation for female-disparaging humor (Chapman & Gadfield, 1976; Grote & Cvetkovitch, 1972; LaFave, 1972; McGhee & Duffey, 1983; Moore, Griffiths, & Payne, 1987).

With all other things held equal then, we hypothesized that those women least likely to have adopted a traditional sex-role orientation would be the ones most likely to engage in joking and teasing behavior in the company of men. For study, we decided to compare the humorous talk of men and women from cultural backgrounds where pressures to maintain traditional male-female roles are relatively low with the talk of men and women from backgrounds where these pressures are relatively higher. Taking a lead from earlier humor studies (McGhee & Duffey, 1983) and interethnic gender research (Chow, 1987; True, 1990; Vazquez-Nuttall, Romero-Garcia, & De Leon, 1987), we chose individuals from Euro-American (White) families to represent the former group and individuals primarily from Asian-American and Latino backgrounds to represent the latter.

Early Research

For our initial investigation (Lampert & Ervin-Tripp, 1989), we selected 40 transcripts of men only, women only, and mixed men and women conversations involving from two to four individuals from the UC Berkeley Cognitive Science database of natural language, known as *Disclab*. To minimize the possibility of status distinctions other than gender, we selected only transcripts of same-age individuals in peer interactions. To ensure that we would be looking at those individuals who were the most likely to have been influenced by the social changes of the seventies and eighties during a period of identity formation, we further looked only at those individuals who would have been teenagers between the years 1968 and 1988. Overall, we derived a sample of 114 individuals between the ages of 18 and 35. These individuals were then divided into one of eight groups based on (1) their gender (male or female), (2) the composition of the group in which they interacted (same-gender or mixed-gender), and (3) their ethnic background (Euro-American or Asian/Latino).

To evaluate differences in humor use, we identified all narratives, remarks, and behaviors that were either contextually marked by the accompaniment of laughter or accompanied by a statement that what was said was intended to be funny. We included only these items as instances of humor and excluded remarks and stories that an outside observer might consider funny, so as to keep the identification of humor as objective as possible, and to minimize the effects of researcher bias for certain kinds of humor.

After we had identified all humor-related instances across the 40 transcripts, we then subdivided them into four categories: (1) self-directed humor, which included remarks that make light of one's own problems and inadequacies; (2) ingroup-directed humor, which captured all attempts to tease or ridicule a participant within a current social interaction; (3) outgroup-directed humor, which included attempts to joke about individuals not in the social interaction, and (4) socially neutral humor, humor which did not overtly poke fun at anyone. Examples of these four social categories of humor are as follows (in multiple turn excerpts, greater than signs precede the illustrative remarks).

Self-Directed Humor

(1) P: Though I have to say to be honest I've been so busy lately that the only read-
          ing I've done in the last six to eight months or so is those little placards on
          the Muni buses. Y'know the little poetry. It's how you get educated by
          ridin' a lotta different buses.

                              (UCB Disclab transcript CDIN1, lines 431-434)

(2) D: [Referring to cross country trip]
          Look I don't even want a stupid atlas. I don't know where Virginia
          is and I like it that way. I'm just, I'm just going to follow the road signs.

     M: [laughing]
          They don't start in California saying Virginia this way.

>   D: See I've never driven cross country.

     M: [Laughs]

>   D: I just assumed they had like uh...forty nine separate signs with corresponding
          arrows.

                              (UCB Disclab transcript LDIN1, lines 258-269)

Outgroup-Directed Humor

(3) M: Oh by the way, T and I have seen him.

     B: Oh what's the verdict guys?

     M: Well...

>   T: Definite potato shrub.

>   M: Definite potato shrub. [laughs]

>   S: He's from Idaho?

                              (UCB Disclab transcript REHEA, lines 77-84)

(4) M: He had shin splints. We went running on heels, and he thought he was a real
          cool dude and he was running hard and I stopped. We were on this one hill
          and I stopped ... and he goes, "Oh, come on man don't wimp out now." I
          said, "Buddy, don't do it, man!" And now he's all [laugh] hurting.

                              (UCB Disclab transcript LCON3, lines 278-284)

Ingroup-Directed Humor

(5) G: If you cook like this every night Amanda, I'll come down and eat
          with you.

>   V: That's why she doesn't. [laughs]

     G: What?

>   V: I said that's why she doesn't.

     A: [Exaggerated tone] Ooooh, Victor.

     V: I'm just kidding. He knows I'm just kidding.

                              (UCB Disclab transcript CCON5, lines 138-143)

(6) S: Or when you're talking to her on the phone with a problem and the
          only time you know what's going on is when K goes "rrrrg."

K: [Laughs]

B: [Laughs]

S: Cracks me up.

(UCB Disclab transcript FDIN5, lines 446-453)

Socially Neutral Humor

(7) R: I can't wait until McDonald's gets espressos and cappuccinos. They will be McSpresso and [laughs] McPuccino.

(UCB Disclab transcript CCON2, lines 184-186)

(8) B: [Kitchen timer goes off] What's that?

> C: Umm, that's our kitchen timer. You now have twenty minutes before our kitchen blows [laughs]. Oh my god. AAAAH.

(UCB Disclab transcript FDIN2, lines 192-196)

For analysis, each individual's self-, ingroup-, and outgroup-directed, and neutral remarks were tallied, and weighted by the total number of turns the individual took within a group interaction. This procedure was used to control for the possibility that some individuals could have produced more humorous remarks simply because they talked more.

We had anticipated that in mixed groups Euro-American women would be more likely than Asian-American and Latino women to engage in ingroup- and outgroup-directed humor, but less likely to engage in self-directed humor. Median tests revealed that in mixed-gender groups, Euro-American women were in fact the most likely to produce a humorous remark or narrative (Mdn = 10.77 humorous remarks/narratives per 100 turns). The Euro-American and Asian/Latino men in mixed groups followed (Mdn = 8.99 and 8.39, respectively), and the Asian/Latino women had the lowest average (Mdn = 7.09) among the mixed group samples. These results suggested to us that the Euro-American women were indeed less restricted by traditional gender-roles in their use of humor in mixed company than were the Asian and Latino women.

As a further investigation, we looked at the four types of social humor separately. We found no significant differences across groups in the use of socially neutral or ingroup-directed humor. However, we did find some important and notable differences in the uses of outgroup-directed humor. The Euro-American women in mixed groups, followed by the Euro-American men in mixed groups were the most likely to joke about nongroup members (Mdn = 5.36 and 3.37 humorous remarks/stories per 100 turns, respectively). In contrast, the Asian/Latino women and men rarely joked about outsiders in mixed-gender groups (Mdn = 1.58 and 0.00, respectively). In fact, Scheffé-type comparisons (Marascuilo & McSweeney, 1977) revealed that Euro-Americans were significantly more likely than Asian-Americans and Latinos to engage in outgroup humor ($p < .05$).

We also found a surprising, yet telling pattern for self-directed humor. We had expected that Euro-American women would be less likely than Asian-American and Latino women to engage in self-directed, specifically self-deprecating humor in mixed groups. In fact, this expectation was confirmed: In mixed-gender groups, the Euro-American women had a median of 0.00 self-directed remarks per 100 turns compared with 1.44 for their Asian/Latino counterparts.

What we did not anticipate, however, was that the Euro-American men would produce more self-directed remarks in the company of women than the women with whom they interacted did. Euro-American women averaged more self-directed remarks per 100 turns in all female groups (Mdn = 1.80) than in mixed-gender groups (Mdn = 0.00). In contrast, the Euro-American men averaged significantly fewer self-directed remarks in all male groups (Mdn = 0.00) than in mixed groups (Mdn = 2.13). Post-hoc comparisons with Scheffé-type correction in fact revealed that Euro-American men in gender-mixed groups were significantly more likely to engage in self-directed humor than Euro-American men in all male groups, Euro-American women in mixed groups, and Asian/Latino men in mixed groups ($p < .05$).

In short, these earliest findings suggested that both Euro-American men and women felt free enough in mixed company to tell humorous stories and make wisecracks about other people. In contrast, Asian-Americans and Latinos were unlikely to engage in this type of humor in gender-mixed groups. Our initial interpretation of these data was that in mixed-groups Euro-American friends tended to use outgroup humor as means for talking about sensitive issues, but in a nonthreatening and entertaining manner (e.g., male-female relationships, physical appearance, etc.), and as such, joking about others served to build solidarity in these groups.

The patterns for self-directed humor were a bit more difficult to explain. In mixed-gender groups, Euro-American women may have avoided self-directed stories and wisecracks so as to maintain a status of social equality with the men in these interactions. In our all-female groups, self-directed humor tended to focus on intimate experiences and personal problems, which, if told to men, could in fact leave a woman socially vulnerable. Consequently, we would expect women, wanting to maintain an equal footing with men, to avoid these "humorous" stories in their conversations with men.

Likewise, we might have expected men to avoid self-directed remarks for the same reason — that is, so as not to appear vulnerable in the eyes of women. However, this was not the case: Euro-American males actively made jokes about themselves in mixed groups. One interpretation that we offered for this behavior was that White college-age men, self-conscious of appearing egotistical in the eyes of women, may attempt to downplay the cocky "male" image through self-parody. Another interpretation is that these men may try to offset criticism from women — criticism which could place them in lower social standing — by joking about their offending remarks and behavior. In short, self-directed wisecracks may have been used by Euro-American men to minimize their vulnerability to negative reactions from others. A final explanation may simply be that men as well as women are inclined toward greater self-disclosure in the company of women (see Hill & Stull, 1987), thereby leading to more self-directed humor among women in same-gender and men in mixed-gender groups. In our current research on adult humor we have begun to addressed these three possible interpretations for self-directed humor.

Current Directions and Research

From our early work, we were able to see a clear and definite shift among White middle-class college students away from the traditional mixed group pattern with male humorists and female audiences, toward more collaborative groups with both men and women using humor, possibly to build group solidarity and to equalize the status distinctions between them. However, this early work left unclear whether the two sexes used all forms of humor in exactly the same way. In particular we could not fully explain the appearance of self-directed humor in different contexts for men and women.

Recently, however, we have explored the nature of men's and women's self-directed stories and remarks, and have noted some remarkable qualitative differences (Ervin-Tripp & Lampert, 1992; Lampert & Ervin-Tripp, 1992, 1994). In these studies, we found that when Euro-American men spoke with women, self-directed humor tended to appear in the form of a humorous exaggeration of some personal experience (see Example 1) or a wisecrack relating to some socially unacceptable attitudes, remarks, and behaviors (see Example 2). On the other hand, when Euro-American women spoke with other women, self-directed humor tended to come in the form of a reflection on some personal experience that, in retrospect, appeared silly, crazy, or laughable as in the following exchange between two sisters.

(9) E: bu:t the thing is also is that I think I don't buy like mommy 'cause I wear
          what I buy. Occasionally I b- I'll buy things an' then end up not wearing it
          'cause I'll make a stupid decision like I wanted a pair of pants that look like
          this an' I'll buy it even though they're too big or their too small because
          when I looked in the mirror I think like oh I can breathe in [giggle] these.
     L: Right .. right.

                                   (UCB Disclab transcript GCON1, lines 759-770)

The evidence from our more recent work supported the hypothesis that men used self-directed humor to minimize socially unacceptable acts, such as bragging immodestly, or to redirect the conversation away from remarks or behavior open to criticism as in Example 2. They did not necessarily use this type of humor to disclose personal experiences or feeling. Women's self-directed humor, on the other hand, was more likely to emerge as part of a self-disclosing narrative. In short, self-directed humor for Euro-American men functioned more in a self-protective manner to reduce social vulnerability, whereas for women, it worked more to increase social vulnerability and to promote intimacy.

We suspect that this gender difference in self-directed humor is most likely a reflection of broader differences in the organizational styles of men's and women's conversations (see Aries, 1976; Tannen, 1990a, 1990b). For example, Aries (1976) observed that in same-sex groups, college-age women were more likely to talk about their personal experiences and relationships, whereas men are more likely to compete by comparing abilities, exploits, knowledge and so forth. The greater likelihood of women to share personal stories would increase their opportunities to make joking remarks about themselves. Similarly, the greater competitiveness of men would increase their likelihood to want to use humor to trivialize personal behavior that could potentially cast them in a negative light. Our current findings do suggest these possible links between conversational style and humor at least for Euro-American groups.

Whether the patterns of humorous talk that we have noted, however, can be generalized beyond Euro-American groups is unclear, in part, because of our current inability to study a group's ethnic as well as gender composition in a systematic fashion. Although, we have studied to date the conversations of Latino and Asian American students, the number of ethnically homogeneous same- and mixed-gender groups (other than White) were not large enough for us to conclude whether gender differences among Latino and Asian samples reflected (1) actual differences between the sexes or (2) other social phenomenon, in particular, a reluctance to reveal experiences and motives through humor which might not be understood nor appreciated by members of other ethnic backgrounds. As part of our future goals, we plan to address the role played by a group's ethnic mix on humor more fully.

STUDYING CHILDREN'S HUMOR

Background

Considering the early findings from our adult samples, we began in 1990 also to investigate developmental trends in conversational humor in particular to uncover whether pre- and grade school children exhibited the kinds of the gender differences that we observed among college students. We expected that children's use of humor would be affected, in part, by their developing cognitive, verbal, and social skills. McGhee (1979), for example, has suggested that age changes in humor appreciation follow a four stage progression closely linked to Jean Piaget's stages of cognitive development (see Piaget, 1983). According to McGhee, children's first real attempts at humor emerge near the end of the second year with the onset of representational thought and the ability to treat real world objects in imagined ways through pretend play (e.g., to use a stick as a toothbrush). Humor during this period is characterized by the incongruous use of familiar objects. Stage 2 accompanies the learning of language and is characterized by the mislabeling of familiar objects and events (e.g., calling a cat, a "dog"). Stage 3 predominates during the preschool years when children begin to show great delight over the creation of conceptual incongruities through fantasy (e.g., flying pickles, turtles with pink polka dots, etc.), and stage 4 emerges around age 7 when reversible thought and the ability to consider two related ideas simultaneously allow children to appreciate the jokes and riddles built on errors in logic and double word meanings (e.g., *Why are fish so smart? Because they live in schools.*). The last skill, which essentially involves the ability to see overlapping and interconnected themes, is often cited as the cornerstone of adult humor (see Koestler, 1964; Raskin, 1985).

   This general developmental pattern has experimental support (e.g., McGhee, 1971, 1976a). Some naturalistic studies have likewise shown that although preschoolers seem to enjoy jokes and riddles, they do not fully understand their complexities nor possess all the verbal and interactional skills needed to engage successfully in humorous story telling, joke exchanges, and more elaborate joking routines, such as verbal dueling (see Abrahams, 1962; Gossen, 1976; McDowell, 1979; Sanches & Kirschenblatt-Gimblett, 1976). Preschoolers' spontaneous riddles, for example, typically do not contain the word play, the prosodic contours, nor the well-orchestrated banter found in the riddling behavior of older children.

These studies would suggest, then, that the types of stories and wisecracking that Susan Ervin-Tripp and I observed in our adult samples would make a rather late appearance in the humor of children. However, we were careful to note that these earlier studies tended to focus mostly on the telling and appreciation of relatively standard forms of humor with preestablished criteria of adequacy in a limited range of contexts. In natural conversation, however, kidding and teasing remarks do not always conform to the structure of a riddle. We further recognized that because humor, like so many other language activities, is socially constructed, young children could in fact display a higher level of humor competence depending on the people and activities with which they were involved.

Rogoff (1990, pp. 83-85), for example, provides a wonderful illustration of a visual joke successfully executed by a ten-month-old infant and an adult playmate. In a rather simple game, the adult taps down a ring on a ring tower each time the infant tries to bat it up and off. Each time the adult pushes the ring down, the infant smiles and pushes it up again in recognition of the game script until with one confident sweep and broad smile, she knocks the ring off the tower.

This example reveals that even at one year children are able to attend to social cues and engage in the kinds of adult–child interactions suggestive of humorous banter and which may eventually serve as the behavioral base for the latter. In our own observations, we found very young children were quite adept at picking up on the joking cues of adults, older children and siblings, especially if the humor focused on familiar situations or activities. In the following exchange, for example, 4-year-old Adam (A) hands his 2-year-old sister Ella (E) cookie dough and invites her to make Batman and Robin cookies with him. Adam playfully warns Ella not to eat the cookie dough (lines 82-85), and Ella follows by warning Adam not to do the same (lines 92-98). Adam then teasingly violates his own prohibition by pretending to eat the dough (lines 95-105), and Ella in turn imitates Adams "naughty" behavior as they playfully lick and eat the dough together (lines 106-107).

(10) 82 A: [A puts some dough on E's highchair.]
83 A: [looks at E] Here's some good dough. [A steps away from E.]
84 A: There's the dough. You can't eat it, OK?
85 A: Wait until we make the batman, OK? OK Elly? [A is close up to E.]
        [Lines 86-89 omitted]
90 A: [sits at table and takes a piece of dough, handing it to E]
91 A: OK Elly, you need some more?
92 E: Yeah. Don't eat it Adam. Don't eat it.
93 A: I know, it's yucchy. [turns to E] But's it's cookies.
94 E: Cookies.
95 A: Dee-de Dee-de Kh [biting motion]
96 E: And don't eat it.
97 A: Yeah.
98 E: Don't eat it Adam.

99 A: Mn-hm. [begins to eat cookie dough.]
          Yeah it's goo:d. This is good dough.
100 A: Don't eat it. [slamming dough with his hand and laughing]
101 A: Don't worry. [laughs]
102 A: [A stands up on chair and puts mouth to dough.]
103 A: [Looks at E] Mn-yum. Is it good?
104 E: Yeah. [A bites or licks the dough and turns to E] I wanna taste.
105 A: Mm. [A licks dough several times and so does E]
106 E: Mm. Good.
107 A: Mm. That was good. Sure good. [E tastes dough again.]

          (UCB Disclab transcript NI04A, lines 82-107)

As example 10 illustrates, through imitation, very young children have at least one skill at their disposal that allows them to enter into and to maintain a joking relationship with an older child or adult, especially in the context of a familiar activity.

We also noted that when preschoolers were involved in familiar tasks, they were further able to develop activity based jokes that played upon dual and interrelated scripts. In other words, they revealed something of a precursor to the ability believed to serve as the basis for comprehending double-meaning jokes and riddles — that is, the ability to mentally play with multiple themes and definitions at the same time. As an example, consider excerpt 11. In this illustration, 4-year-old Janie (J) and 5-year-old Katie (K) have become soiled while cleaning up the milk that they spilled onto the patio of Janie's house. Sandy (S) is Janie's mother.

(11) 680 S: That's right. What do you think that is?
      681 K: Milk
      682 S: Just milk?
      683 J: Yeah.
      684 S: Anything else but the milk?
      685 J: Di-
      686 K: Dirty.
      687 S: Oh. You just about have it now.
      688 J: Oh. You gonna have to throw me in the garbage can.
      689 S: You just about have it clean.
      690 J: You have to throw me in the garbage.
      691 S: Oh I wouldn't want to do that.
      692 J: Yeah (throw) me in the washing machine.
      693 J: [walking over to do some more sponging with paper towels]
      694 K: You throw me in the washing machine.
      695 J: Munching. Munching it munch the dirt off.
      696 K: Yeah. [gets a paper towel and begins to wipe up milk]
      697 J: I'm a munching machine. A munching a washing.
              [still mopping]

          (UCB Disclab transcript BO02B, lines 680-697)

What is interesting about Janie's statements, *You gonna have to throw me in the garbage can* (line 688) and *Yeah throw me in the washing machine* (line 692) is that they are not just simply jokes that play off of conceptual distortion, as might be expected at this age, but rather are related to the ongoing activity (i.e., becoming dirty while cleaning up) and play off of a related script (i.e., what you do with clothes — not people — when they get dirty). In other words, while she has one situation represented directly in front of her, Janie is able to entertain a second playful possibility and juxtapose the two together in a manner similar to that required to recognize that school means "a group of fish" and "a place of learning" when interpreting the riddling question, *Why are fish so smart?* Although Janie may not fully comprehend double-meaning riddles, she clearly is able to produce remarks that may represent an intermediary step toward the understanding of such jokes.

Example 11 further illustrates a certain level of proficiency among preschoolers to initiate a teasing relationship with others. Note that Janie's remarks are not simply produced to be a source of entertainment for herself, but rather serve to engage her mother in a bit of playful banter which is not lost on her friend Katie who follows Janie's lead and also requests to be thrown into the washing machine (line 694).

In sum, when we began to study children, we expected that preschoolers would reveal certain limitations in their humor, but that they would also possess evolving social and interpersonal skills (e.g., imitation) that would allow them initially to engage in simple humorous exchanges and later more elaborate ones. We also expected, in line with research on storytelling and narratives that older children's conversational humor would depend less and less on ongoing activities to guide it (as in the cases of examples 10 and 11) and would arise solely through talk. Accordingly, we set as our first research goal to look systematically at the organization of children's humorous talk beginning with preschoolers and moving through the elementary and high school years.

Because of our interest in gender differences, we also set out to uncover when boys and girls begin to initiate in- and out-group humor, and in particular, when they begin to use self-directed humor to achieve the social goals that we observed among adults. We recognized that the functions of self-directed humor would be tied in part to the different social experiences of the two sexes, but also to cognitive changes in perspective-taking ability related to personal identity. Considering that social pressures placed on girls to be more collaborative and on boys not to display vulnerability, we expected that as narrative skills improved with age, girls would be more likely than boys to share personal stories, in particular, humorous ones. We also anticipated that as toward later childhood and adolescence children become more socially aware of and sensitive to the social judgments made about them by others (see Damon & Hart, 1988, for a discussion of this trend), they would become increasingly more likely to fend off negative evaluations especially through humor. Again, considering the greater pressures placed on them not to show vulnerability, we expected older boys to be more likely than girls to monitor their talk and to engage in self-directed humor in a self-protective fashion.

Early and Current Research

To date, we have conducted two investigations on children's humor. Our first study (Ervin-Tripp, Lampert, Scales, & Sprott, 1990) examined gender differences in the talk of preschool children and involved an analysis of 46 transcripts collected by Catherine Garvey and her associates (Garvey, 1975; Kramer, Bukowski, & Garvey, 1989) and obtained by us through the CHILDES database (MacWhinney, 1991; MacWhinney & Snow, 1990). What is unusual about the Garvey transcripts is that as part of her research design she began with 16 playmate triads, each containing either two boys and one girl or two girls and one boy, and systematically created one same-sex and two mixed-sex pairings of the children within each triad. Each pair was then brought into a playroom filled with toys and observed through a two-way mirror. Garvey's design allowed her to collect talk from 48 children, each in interaction with two different speaking partners, and allowed us to examine changes in humor-related behavior across 5 male-male, 11 female-female, and 30, male-female dyads (two male-female transcripts were not available).

For analysis, we identified within each dyad all attempts at humor using the criteria that we had established for our first adult study. We then coded each attempt for whether it initiated humorous play or talk or built on or was an imitation of the other child's humorous behavior. In line with earlier characterizations of male and female humor, we were interested here in whether boys were more likely to initiate humor and girls were more likely to follow their male playmates' lead in mixed groups. We also coded attempts at humor for their general type (behavioral, verbal, or narrated behavior), specific nature (e.g., buffoonery, fantasy play, mock threats, story telling, silly songs, word play, joke telling, etc.), social aspect (e.g., self-, other-, or third-party directed), and theme (e.g., morbid, scatological, gender-related, etc.).

In an earlier study, McGhee (1976b) noted that preschool boys were more likely than girls to initiate behavioral forms of humor, but that the two sexes did not differ significantly in their use of verbal humor nor in their frequency of laughter. However, between the ages of 6 and 11 the pattern was quite different with boys more likely to initiate behavioral and verbal forms of humor and to laugh more often.

In our own investigation of preschool humor, we observed a somewhat different pattern, owing in part to our consideration of not only the sex of the child, but also the make-up of the child's play group. Like McGhee, we found that pairs of boys were more likely than pairs of girl to engage in behavioral forms of humor involving buffoonery, clowning, rough-housing and naughty acts. However, unlike McGhee, we observed that verbal forms of humor, in particular, silly songs and word play, were significantly more frequent in female than male dyads. Girls were also more likely to joke about such things as dress-up and pictures and to provide a humorous story to go along with an activity. However, when girls were paired with boys, they engaged in significantly more behavioral humor.

This last finding seems to point to the readiness among preschoolers to accommodate to different playmates and quite possibly the different kinds of activities that boys and girls choose for themselves. In same-gender groups, girls may lean more toward verbal and boys more toward behavioral activities in general. In mixed dyads, preschoolers may oscillate between male- and female-preferred play, leading to preschool girls' greater involvement in behavioral humor when in the company of boys. These findings seem to support the importance of activity structure on a preschooler's use of humor.

The differences in preferred activities and humor that we observed among preschoolers also seemed to foreshadow the differences that we observed among adults. Although we did not find marked differences in the use of self- or other-directed humor among preschoolers, our findings did suggest a greater preference among girls in female dyads for talk around familiar activities and experiences, setting the stage for the greater self-talk and sharing of humorous experiences that we observed in similar groups in the early adult years.

To follow-up our preschool study with the Garvey texts, we began to collect our own data to look for developmental changes during the elementary school years. We were particularly interested in finding evidence for the different interpersonal functions of humor that we had observed among young adults, which we expected to emerge toward middle to late childhood.

In the Fall of 1992, we received the cooperation of an elementary school located in Alameda, CA to record the conversations of second and fifth graders. To organize groups for study, we asked the second- and fifth-grade children to nominate the friends with whom they would like to do a science project. Based on their nominations, we then assigned the children to groups of two and three children each, and on selected days, we invited a different group to eat lunch in an activity room located at their school, and afterwards to participate in a brief chemistry experiment that involved the manufacture of calcium carbonate (chalk) from the combination of calcium chloride and baking soda in water.

On their assigned day, groups brought their lunches to the activity room where a research assistant met and invited them to eat their lunch at a table with microphones attached to a ceiling lamp overhead. The researcher assistant then left the room under the pretext of having to prepare for the science experiment and returned 20 minutes later to conduct the experiment with the children. We recorded the children's talk while they ate their lunch and while they participated in the science experiment; however, for analysis, we focused only on the former, nondirected conversations of the children with their friends.

We gathered and transcribed a total of two second-grade and ten fifth-grade conversations from friends of the same sex (the children rarely nominated friends of the opposite sex, making it impossible for us to systematically construct mixed-gender groups). We ended up with relatively few second grade transcripts, in part, because of a lack of parental consent and, in part, because the second graders themselves spoke little during lunch and focused more on eating and playing with their food. The fifth graders, on the other hand, talked freely, providing us with five male and five female conversations which we explored for gender differences in humor (Ervin-Tripp & Lampert, 1993).

Performing a qualitative analysis, we found evidence for the kinds of humorous talk that we had seen with college students. We noted that the girls tended to construct longer narratives that focused on a single theme than the boys, a finding similar to one reported by Tannen (1990a, 1990b). Also, although all fifth graders showed a growing concern over interpersonal relationships and evaluation by others as anticipated, the girls, like their adult counterparts, were more likely than the boys to talk with bemused reflection about their past behaviors and personal experiences. Examples 12 and 13 provide illustrations of the humorous narratives that we observed among the fifth grade girls. In

Example 12, Olive relates to Chloe and Anita how she once could not stop stuttering, and in Example 13, Lara explains to Erin how she always loses to her sister in volleyball and gives her narrative a humorous twist by exaggerating the point spread of their games (asterisks indicated exaggerated intonation).

(12) 305 O: One time my sister said something, my mom said something to
     306   me, an' I said, but- but- but- *maa. I said, but- but- but- but-
     307   but- I was stuttering. I was tryin'a say, but ma- I said,
     308   but- but- but- but- but-. My sister said, **but **nothin'.
     309 C: [giggle]
     310 A: [giggle]
     311 O: {[laughing] and my *mother *loved it.}
                              (UCB Disclab transcript GFIVE7, lines 305-311)

(13) 196 L: I play volleyball with my sister all the time.
     197   Every night in the house we always play
     198   until my dad says, {[imitating father] stop playing,
     199   I'm tryin' to watch the t.v. now.} [laugh]
     200   ... and .. um.. my sister .. she always have- ..
     201   me and her always have to go to (our) room and play.
     202 E: big one or little? [referring to big or little sister]
     203 L: Big. You know .. she get ten points ..
     204   I get- I get like-two points only. [laughs]
     205 E: Do you win?
     206 L: uh uh. Barely.
                              (UCB Disclab transcript GFIVE6, lines 196-206)

In contrast, when the boys made joking remarks about themselves, they seemed more intent on steering the conversation away from rather than toward a personal matter or point of concern. In Example 14, for instance, Jerrod (J) tries to get Simon (S) to reveal which girl he likes in their class; however, Simon tries to circumvent Jerrod's probing though a series of wisecracking responses (lines 229-234).

(14) 223 J: That's Gina. For you that's Gina.
     224 S: Hell no.
     225 J: You said you liked her. You said you liked her.
     226 S: (   )
     227 J: Who is it for me?
     228 S: Hm?
     229 J: Who is it.
     230 S: This is Cindy Crawford for me.
            [referring to the well-known fashion model]
     231 J: In the class who is it.
     232 S: Nobody.
     233 J: If you would've got shot in the head.
     234 S: I'd get shot in the head.
                              (UCB Disclab transcript GFIVE3, lines 223-234)

In a similar vein, when the boys revealed something personal about themselves, they were also quick to turn it into a joke as in the following excerpt in which Gabe reveals his fear of public speaking, but after a short pause quickly downplays this self-revelation with a humorous tag line.

(15) 48   G: I don't like gettin' in front of people and talkin' ...
     49   'less it's about somebody. [laughs]
                                    (UCB Disclab transcript GFIVE1, lines 48-49)

It would appear then that at least for self-directed humor, the kinds of gender differences that we observed among college students regarding narratives and wisecracking may be in place by age 11.

CONCLUSION

When Susan Ervin-Tripp and I began our work together on humor, we recognized that a number of social, cognitive, and linguistic factors would play a role in the unfolding of humor in conversation. In the four studies outlined in this chapter, we in fact observed how closely conversational humor was tied to social roles and cognitive abilities as well as ongoing linguistic events (e.g., personal narrative) and social activities.

Among adults we anticipated that the changing roles of American women along crosscultural differences would underscore a greater use of humor among women, in particular, Euro-American women, than earlier reported. We also anticipated that White women would be less inclined to engage in self- or female-directed humor in mixed-gender groups than their Asian-American or Latino counterparts. Our findings so far have supported this view as well have given us insight into the different social functions of humor, in particular, self-directed humor among women and men. In all female groups, for example, we observed that women frequently used self-directed humor as part of a narrative to express their feelings about a personal experience and to seek a shared response. In mixed groups, on the other hand, men often used self-directed humor to offset potential criticism or to downplay an unacceptable behavior on their part.

We also attempted to track developmentally the gender differences that we observed among adults. We began by outlining some of the cognitive changes and social experiences likely to influence a child's choice of humorous remarks and focused specifically on how preferred activities, gender roles, and changes in interpersonal awareness were likely to affect the humor of young children and teenagers.

We looked at preschoolers in same- and mixed-sex dyads and found that their humor appeared to be closely tied to the preferred and ongoing activities of their playmates, with girls, for instance, engaged in relatively more physical activities and behavioral humor when in the company of a boy and more verbal activities and humorous stories and songs when in the company of a girl.

We also looked at the humor of fifth-grade boys and girls and observed that although their talk was less tied to the nonverbal activities of their friends, they nonetheless displayed notable gender differences in line with expected preferences for types of talk and developmental changes in social sensitivity. Like college-age women, fifth-grade girls were more likely to use self-directed humor to facilitate discussion of personal experiences, whereas fifth-grade boys, like college-age men, were more likely to use it to minimize the importance of a self-revelation or to divert attention away from an uncomfortable topic. In short, we found older girls and women to use self-directed humor to increase, and conversely, older boys and men to use self-directed humor to decrease interpersonal vulnerability.

To date, we have by no means completed our work on gender differences in conversational humor, and there are still a number of issues involving ethnicity and development that we set out to explore, but as of yet have not been able to address fully. However, what we have accomplished so far is to set an agenda for the study of a wide range of phenomena involving conversational humor, which we hope to address further and invite others to follow.

REFERENCES

Abrahams, R. (1962). Playing the dozens. *Journal of American Folklore, 75*, 209-220.

Alberts, J. K. (1992). An inferential/strategic explanation for the social organization of teases. *Journal of Language and Social Psychology, 11*, 153-177.

Apte, M. (1985). *Humor and Laughter: An anthropological approach.* Ithaca, NY: Cornell University Press.

Aries, E. (1976). Interaction patterns and themes of male, female, and mixed groups. *Small Group Behavior, 7*, 7-18.

Carter, J. (1989). *Stand-up comedy: The book.* New York: Dell.

Chapman, A. J., & Gadfield, N. J. (1976). Is sexual humor sexist? *Journal of Communication, 26*, 141-153.

Chow, E. (1987). The development of feminist consciousness among Asian American women. *Gender & Society, 1*, 284-299.

Coser, R. (1959). Some social functions of laughter. *Human Relations, 12*, 171-182.

Coser, R. (1960). Laughter among colleagues. *Psychiatry, 23*, 81-95.

Crawford, M., & Gressley, D. (1991). Creativity, caring, and context: Women's and men's accounts of humor preferences and practices. *Psychology of Women Quarterly, 15*, 217-231.

Damon, W., & Hart, D. (1988). *Self-understanding in childhood and adolescence.* Cambridge, England: Cambridge University Press.

Derks, P. (1992). Category and ratio scaling of sexual and innocent cartoons. *Humor International Journal of Humor Research, 5*, 319-329

Eder, D. (1993) "Go get ya a French!": Romantic and sexual teasing among adolescent girls. In D. Tannen (Ed.), *Gender and conversational interaction* (pp. 17-31). New York: Oxford University Press.

Ervin-Tripp, S. M., & Lampert, M. (1992). Gender differences in the construction of humorous talk. In K. Hall, M. Buchholtz, & B. Moonwoman (Eds.), *Locating power: Proceedings of the Second Berkeley Women and Language Conference* (pp. 108-117). Berkeley: Berkeley Women and Language Group, University of California.

Ervin-Tripp, S. M., & Lampert, M. D. (1993, March). *Laughter through the ages: Developmental trends in children's conversational humor.* Paper presented at the 1993 biennial meeting of the Society for Research in Child Development, New Orleans, LA.

Ervin-Tripp, S. M., Lampert, M. D., Scales, B., & Sprott, R. (1990, April). The humor of preschool boys and girls in naturalistic settings. In M. D. Lampert (Chair), *Developmental Perspectives on*

Humor Production and Appreciation. Symposium conducted at the 1990 meeting of the Western Psychological Association, Los Angeles, CA.

Garvey, C. (1975). Requests and responses in children's speech. *Journal of Child Language, 2*, 41-63.

Gordon, D. P. (1983). Hospital slang for patients: Crocks, gomers, gorks, and others. *Language in Society, 12*, 173-186.

Gossen, G. H. (1976). Verbal dueling in Chamula. In B. Kirshenblatt-Gimblett (Ed.), *Speech play* (pp. 121-146). Philadelphia: University of Philadelphia Press.

Graham, E. E., Papa, M. J., & Brooks, G. P. (1992) Functions of humor in conversation: Conceptualization and measurement. *Western Journal of Communication, 56*, 161-183.

Grote, B., & Cvetkovitch, G. (1972). Humor appreciation and issue involvement. *Psychonomic Science, 27*, 199-200.

Howell, R. W. (1973). *Teasing relationships.* Reading, MA: Addison-Wesley.

Hill, C. T., & Stull, D. E. (1987). Gender and self-disclosure: Strategies for exploring the issues. In V. J. Derlega & J. H. Berg (Eds.), *Self-disclosure: Theory, research, and therapy* (pp. 81-100). New York: Plenum.

Jenkins, M. M. (1985). What's so funny?: Joking among women. In S. Bremner, N. Caskey, & B. Moonwoman, *Proceedings of the First Berkeley Women and Language Conference.* Berkeley, CA: Berkeley Women and Language Group.

Koestler, A. (1964). *The act of creation.* New York: Macmillan.

Kramer, T. L., Bukowski, W. M., Garvey, C. (1989). The influence of the dyadic context on the conversational and linguistic behavior of its members. *Merrill-Palmer Quarterly, 35*, 327-341.

LaFave, L. (1972). Humor judgments as a function of reference groups and identification classes. In J. H. Goldstein & P. E. McGhee (Eds.), *The psychology of humor* (pp. 195-210). New York: Academic Press.

Lampert, M. D., & Ervin-Tripp, S. M. (1989, August). The interaction of gender and culture on humor production. In M. Hester (Chair), *What are women telling us about humor?* Symposium conducted at the 97th Annual Convention of the American Psychological Association, New Orleans, LA.

Lampert, M. D., & Ervin-Tripp, S. M. (1992, July). *Laughing at yourself: The self-directed humor of college-age men and women.* Paper presented at the 1992 Conference of the International Society for the Study of Humor, Paris, France.

Lampert, M. D., & Ervin-Tripp, S. M. (1994). *Getting a laugh: The humor of college-age men and women in conversation.* Manuscript in preparation.

Lefcourt, H. M., & Martin, R. A. (1986). *Humor and life stress: Antidote to adversity.* New York: Springer-Verlag.

Levine, J. (Ed.). (1969). *Motivation in humor.* New York: Atherton Press.

MacWhinney, B. (1991). *The CHILDES Project: Computational tools for analyzing talk.* Hillsdale, NJ: Lawrence Erlbaum Associates.

MacWhinney, B., & Snow, C. E. (1990). The Child Language Exchange System. *ICAME Journal, 14*, 3-25.

Marascuilo, L. A., & McSweeney, M. (1977). *Nonparametric and distribution free methods for the social sciences.* Monterey, CA: Brooks/Cole.

Masten, A. S. (1986). Humor and competence in school-aged children. *Child Development, 57*, 461-473.

McDowell, J. H. (1979). *Children's riddling.* Bloomington, IN: Indiana University Press.

McGhee, P. E. (1971). The role of operational thinking in children's comprehension and appreciation of humor. *Child Development, 42*, 733-744.

McGhee, P. E. (1976a). Children's appreciation of humor: A test of the cognitive congruency principle. *Child Development, 47*, 420-426.

McGhee, P. E. (1976b). Sex differences in children's humor. *Journal of Communication, 26*, 176-189.

McGhee, P. E. (1979). *Humor: Its origin and development.* San Francisco: Freeman.

McGhee, P. E. (1980). Development of the sense of humour in childhood: A longitudinal study. In P. E. McGhee & A. J. Chapman (Eds.), *Children's humour* (pp. 213-236). Chichester, England: John Wiley.

McGhee, P. E., & Duffey, N. S. (1983). The role of identity of the victim in the development of disparagement humor. *Journal of General Psychology, 108*, 257-270.

Moore, T. E., Griffiths, K., & Payne, B. (1987). Gender, attitudes toward women, and the appreciation of sexist humor. *Sex Roles, 16*, 521-531.

Norrick, N. R. (1993). *Conversational joking.* Bloomington, IN: Indiana University Press.

Piaget, J. (1983). Piaget's theory. In P. H. Mussen (Series Ed.) & W. Kessen (Vol. Ed.), *Handbook of child psychology: Vol. 1. History, theory, and methods* (4th ed., pp. 103-128). New York: Plenum.

Raskin, V. (1985). *Semantic mechanisms of humor.* Dordrecht: D. Reidel.

Rogoff, B. (1990). *Apprenticeship in thinking: Cognitive development in social context.* New York: Oxford University Press.

Ruch, W. (1992). Assessment of appreciation of humor: Studies with the 3WD humor test. In C. D. Spielberger & J. N. Butcher (Eds.), *Advances in personality assessment, Vol. 9* (pp. 27-75). Hillsdale, NJ: Lawrence Erlbaum Associates.

Sacks, H. (1974). An analysis of the course of a joke's telling in conversation. In R. Bauman & J. Sherzer (Eds.), *Explorations in the ethnography of speaking* (pp. 337-353). New York: Cambridge University Press.

Sanches, M., & Kirshenblatt-Gimblett, B. (1976). In B. Kirshenblatt-Gimblett (Ed.), *Speech play* (pp. 65-110). Philadelphia: University of Philadelphia Press.

Sanford, S., & Eder, D. (1984). Adolescent humor during peer interaction. *Social Psychology Quarterly, 47*, 235-243.

Shapiro, J. P., Baumeister, R. F., & Kessler, J. W. (1991). A three-component model of children's teasing: Aggression, humor, and ambiguity. *Journal of Social and Clinical Psychology, 10*, 459-472.

Shultz, T. R. (1972). Role of incongruity and resolution in children's appreciation of cartoon humor. *Journal of Experimental Child Psychology, 13*, 456-477.

Shultz, T. R. (1974). Development of the appreciation of riddles. *Child Development, 45*, 100-105.

Stebbins, R. A. (1990). *The laugh makers: Stand-up comedy as art, business, and life-style.* Montreal: McGill-Queen's University Press.

Suls, J. (1983). Cognitive processes in humor appreciation. In P. E. McGhee & J. H. Goldstein (Eds.), *Handbook of humor research: Vol. 1. Basic Issues* (pp. 39-57). New York: Springer-Verlag.

Tannen, D. (1990a). Gender differences in conversational coherence: Physical alignment and topical cohesion. In B. Dorval (Ed.), *Conversational organization and its development* (pp. 167-206). Norwood, NJ: Ablex.

Tannen, D. (1990b). Gender differences in topical coherence: Creating involvement in best friends' talk. *Discourse Processes, 13*, 73-90.

True, R. H. (1990). Psychotherapeutic issues with Asian American women. *Sex Roles, 22*, 477-486.

Vazquez-Nuttall, E., Romero-Garcia, I., & De Leon, B. (1987). Sex roles and perceptions of femininity and masculinity of Hispanic women: A review of the literature. *Psychology of Women Quarterly, 11*, 409-425.

Wyer, R. S., Jr., & Collins, J. E., II. (1992). A theory of humor elicitation. *Psychological Review, 99*, 663-688.

35 GENDER DIFFERENCES IN INTERRUPTIONS[1]

Gisela Redeker
Vrije Universiteit Amsterdam

Anny Maes
Eindhovens Psychologisch Instituut

INTRODUCTION

The by now classic finding that men interrupt women more often than women interrupt men (West & Zimmerman, 1983; Zimmerman & West, 1975) has never been uncontroversial (for recent reviews, see Aries, 1987, and James & Clarke, 1993). Many studies have failed to find significant differences between men's and women's interruptive behavior in mixed-gender groups (e.g., Beattie, 1981; Woods, 1989), mixed-gender dyads (e.g., Bilous & Krauss, 1988; Leet-Pellegrini, 1980; Marche & Peterson, 1993), or same-gender interactions (e.g., Smith-Lovin & Brody, 1989; Marche & Peterson, 1993). Others report more interruptions by women than by men (e.g., Kennedy & Camden, 1983; Murray & Covelli, 1988; for same-gender interactions also Bilous & Krauss, 1988).

As James and Clarke (1993) and others before them have pointed out, there are many possible reasons for the divergence of these results: differences in the definitions of interruptions, the types of interaction studied, the individual characteristics of the participants such as age, social status, and institutional role, and, finally, differences in the size and composition of the groups studied. There are also methodological problems, for instance, inadequate quantitative comparisons. Most of the studies reviewed by James and Clarke (1993) compared raw counts of interruptions without taking speaking time into account. But raw counts can obviously be misleading unless men and women contribute equally to the interaction. The nine studies in the review that did use a measure that corrected for speaking time did not find any gender differences in mixed-gender dyads or groups.

---

[1] This research was conducted at Tilburg University with support from a senior research fellowship from the Royal Netherlands Academy of Sciences to Redeker, and a grant from Stichting Diogenes, Tilburg, to Maes. We are grateful to the editors of this volume and to various colleagues for their helpful comments on earlier versions of this chapter.

597

With this paper we want to contribute to the theoretical and methodological discussion in this field with a small experimental study of same- and mixed-gender interactions of well-acquainted adult professionals. The gap between observational and experimental studies can, in our view, only be bridged by having nonstudent speakers participate in our experiments and observing the same kinds of speakers in genuine interactions.

Simultaneous speech, interruptions, and dominance

Interruptions occur when one speaker begins to talk while another is speaking. As straightforward as this common-sense definition of interruptions may sound, it does not cover all and only such behavior that we would intuitively classify as interruptive. An interrupter may cut in while the current speaker is pausing and thus not, strictly speaking, talking. Vice versa, listener feedback like *mhm, uhuh,* or *yes* is often produced while the speaker is still talking; yet it is obviously not interruptive. These examples suggest that a useful definition of interruptions should include functional criteria relating to the interactional effect of interruptive behavior.

Many recent studies of interruption behavior implicitly or explicitly apply such functional criteria. Listeners' back-channel contributions that do not, and clearly are not intended to, disrupt the speech flow, are usually excluded from the category of interruptions. Far less consensus exists about accidental turn-final overlaps (MISTIMINGS) and FALSE STARTS, where two or more speakers simultaneously seize the floor after a speaker has relinquished it. The probably strongest arguments in favor of a functional approach come from studies describing cooperative overlaps, which abound in certain kinds of informal interaction (see Edelsky, 1981; Tannen, 1984, 1989, 1990). Cooperative overlaps, that is, finishing another's utterance, adding a supportive comment, and so forth, can hardly be considered disruptive or domineering behavior. Yet, they would have to be classified as interruptions by any purely formal criterion (e.g., one speaker starts talking during another speaker's turn, causing that turn to be discontinued before syntactic and/or intonational closure is reached).

We define interruptions then as attempts by one speaker to disrupt another's utterance in order to gain the floor for a competing turn. To make this definition operational and allow a reliable categorization, we distinguish a number of subcategories, using an adapted version of the Interruption Coding System (ICS) proposed by Roger, Bull, and Smith (1988). This system enables us to distinguish dominance-related interruptive behavior from accidental and cooperative simultaneous speech.

Determinants of interruptive behavior

Like most aspects of interactional behavior, the use of interruptions is strongly influenced by contextual factors, specifically the rules and conventions of the interactional activity and the social status and expertise of the participants (Ervin-Tripp, 1987). Interruptions in a formal discussion, for instance, are clear violations of the expected orderly exchange of opinions, but in informal talk, overlaps and interruptions can be interpreted as signs of involvement and need not be perceived as violations of conversational conventions. Register variation induced by differences in the interactional settings studied may thus be one cause of apparently incompatible results.   Edelsky (1981), for example, found systematic differences in rate of interrupting, rate of speaking, turn lengths, and so forth, between what she identified as two types of conversational floor, a formal, information- and task-oriented FLOOR 1, usually dominated by men, and an informal, interpersonally-oriented FLOOR 2 with more active participation of women.   In order to incorporate this useful distinction into the present study, we collected data from formal and informal discussions, assuming that the former would contain almost exclusively FLOOR 1 interaction and the latter a mixture of FLOOR 1 and FLOOR 2.   Any gender differences we might find, then, should interact with this register variation, showing more (if any) male dominance in the formal than in the informal discussions.

Another aspect of the interactional setting that deserves attention is the size and composition of the group.   Kennedy and Camden (1983) suggest that interruption may be more legitimate in groups than in dyads, due to the greater competition for the floor. Various studies have shown different results for same-gender than for mixed-gender groups or dyads (e.g.   Bilous & Krauss, 1988; Smith-Lovin & Brody, 1989).   In the present study, we have kept group size constant (four participants) and varied the gender composition (all-female, all-male, mixed-gender).

Even stronger and more difficult to control for than the interactional setting are the participants' individual characteristics.   Interactional dominance and thus also interruptive behavior can obviously be expected to increase with higher status and more expertise.   To control for these factors it does not suffice to assess status and expertise objectively. What matters are the participants' perceptions, which in groups of unacquainted men and women are likely to be biased towards attributing lower status and less expertise to women (see Wood & Karten, 1986).   With large samples of speakers a questionnaire can be useful to assess their perceptions, but for small samples only large differences in such ratings are likely to be detected.   For the present study, we have therefore chosen to investigate interactions of a group of befriended men and women with very similar background, age, occupations, and socio-economic status.   Individual differences in speech behavior were controlled for by observing the same persons in formal and informal discussions of mixed- and same-gender groups.

METHOD

Participants

Five men and five women (all native speakers of Dutch) participated in this study, two of them as chairpersons in formal discussions, the others in groups of four as participants in formal and informal discussions.   The participants were 44 to 50 years of age, had academic training and were holding management or advisory positions in business or educational institutions.   All of them had at least some professional experience in the area of education.   They were well acquainted with each other and with the experimenter (the second author), in whose home the recordings were made.

Procedure

Two weeks before the experiment, the participants were informed of the topic for the formal discussions. The chosen topic was one in which all participants had some expertise, namely the highly controversial issue of redefining "basic education," which had just been treated extensively in the media. The participants and chairpersons were given several statements of opinion to facilitate preparation and initiation of the discussions. The chairpersons for the formal discussions were instructed not to actively influence the course of the discussion. After a brief introduction of the topic they were to restrict themselves to keeping order and assigning turns.

The experimental session began with two parallel formal discussions: The four women and the female discussion chair were talking in one room, the four men and the male chair in another. During a short break, the experimenter checked and reset the cassette-recorders. Then she asked two men and two women to go into the first room, and the others into the second, to have another formal discussion. After an informal joint dinner of the whole group, the same pattern (first same-gender, then mixed-gender groups) was repeated for the informal discussions. There were no chairpersons, and no topics were assigned for the informal discussions. The participants discussed the role of creativity in basic research, women's career opportunities, women in a male-dominated society, and other social issues.

The eight discussions were recorded on audiotape. Videotaping was not considered necessary, as the coding system used in this study does not explicitly include nonverbal cues. Moreover, the presence of videocameras would have been much more intrusive than simple audiotaping, especially in the informal discussions. The participants showed occasional awareness of the taperecorder but reported having ignored it most of the time.

The introductory phase of each discussion was excluded from the analyses. The interaction in this phase is obviously different from the main body of the discussions. Moreover, the structure and purpose of the introductions differed between the formal and informal situations, consisting in one case of the chairperson's introductory remarks and in the other of the group's deliberations about suitable topics.

The interruption coding system

Our simultaneous speech coding system (summarized in Fig. 35.1) is based on a proposal by Roger, Bull, and Smith (1988). It specifies a sequential decision procedure to distinguish thirteen types of simultaneous speech, nine of which are considered to be interruptions. The sequential procedure does involve the coders' intuitive judgment of disruptiveness, but this judgment is followed by various structural distinctions specifying the kind of disruption, thus forcing the coders to justify their decision. Roger et al. (1988) report interrater agreements ranging from 75 through 97 percent for their categories, showing that the sequential decision procedure provides sufficiently specific criteria for a reliable classification. We have used the same kind of coding procedure in the present study. The agreement of independent coders was 91 percent for a sample of 227 instances of simultaneous talk (that is, 9.6 percent of all 2373 instances in this study).[2] The validity of the interpretations was enhanced by the second author's acquaintance with the participants.

As Fig. 35.1 shows, an interruption is considered successful if the interrupter seizes the turn and prevents the first speaker from finishing.   An immediately successful interruption attempt is coded as a SUCCESSFUL SINGLE INTERRUPTION.   Success after more than one attempt yields a SUCCESSFUL COMPLEX INTERRUPTION.   Sequences of repeated unsuccessful attempts are coded as UNSUCCESSFUL COMPLEX INTERRUPTIONS.[3]

(1) Successful single interruption

> T: ... *maar tegenwoordig is de afstemming beroep //* {*arbeid*}
> M: *//* {*maar*} *dat ligt bij de beroepsopleiding* ...
> T: ... but nowadays the tuning [between] profession // {[and] work} is
> M: // {but} that's a matter of the professional training

(2) Unsuccessful single interruption

> T: ... *dat het eigenlijk niet doorgezet is, daar windt hij zich voor* [sic!] *op //* {*en dat kon ik*} *goed invoelen* ...
> M: *//* {*van wat er op papier eigenlijk*} -
> T: ... that it wasn't really enforced, that's what he gets upset for [presumable target: about] // {and with that I could} well empathize ...
> M: // {of what['s] there on paper really} -

Extended simultaneous speech where two speakers start talking at the same time and keep competing for the floor, is called PARALLEL TALK.   Unlike FALSE STARTS, where one speaker stops right away, parallel talk is competitive, dominant behavior. These categories are coded separately because there is no interrupted speaker and the criterion for success (the interrupted speaker stops and the interrupter finishes) does not apply. Success in parallel-talk episodes is defined by the effect on the subsequent talk: an utterance that is not acknowledged or reacted to is considered unsuccessful.

(3) Parallel Talk

> N: *// We hebben het over het gymnasium zoals het nú is en zal blijven bestaan.*
> T: *// We hebben het over een combinatie (...) en daar gaat het om.*
> N: // We are talking about high school as it is nów and shall continue to exist.
> T: // We are talking about a combination (...) and that's what it's all about.

---

[2] We are very grateful to Sandra Timan for the thorough coding of the sample material (one of the eight discussions) for this reliability test.

[3] A double slash // is used to mark the beginning of overlapping talk. Curly brackets { } enclose uncertain transcriptions. The translations are essentially word-by-word, except where maintaining the Dutch word order would have distorted the meaning of the utterance. Additions and commentary, marked with square brackets [ ], are used for clarification where necessary.

FIG. 35.1. Simultaneous speech coding system (adapted from Roger et al., 1988)

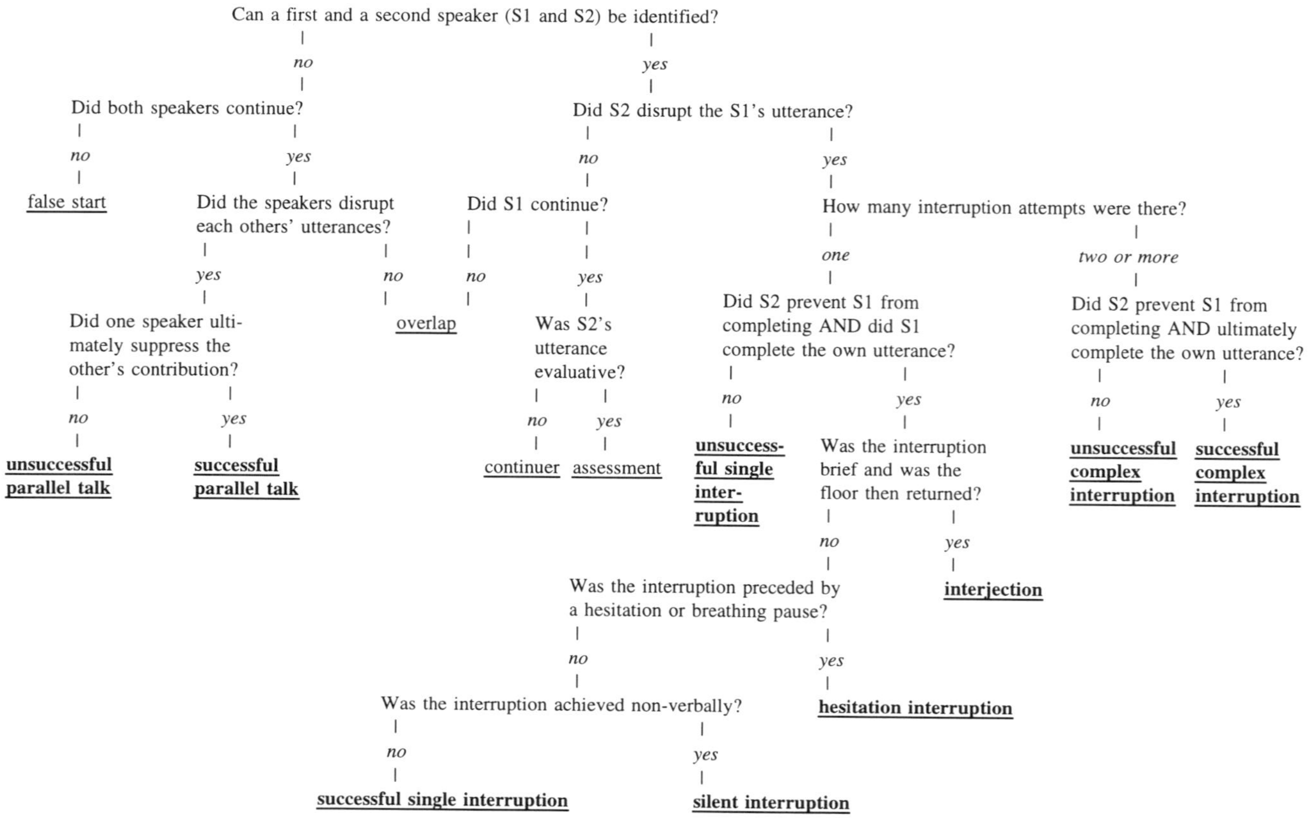

Can a first and a second speaker (S1 and S2) be identified?

no — yes

Did both speakers continue?

no — yes

false start

Did the speakers disrupt each others' utterances?

yes — no

Did one speaker ultimately suppress the other's contribution?

no — yes

unsuccessful parallel talk

successful parallel talk

Did S2 disrupt the S1's utterance?

no — yes

Did S1 continue?

no — yes

overlap

Was S2's utterance evaluative?

no — yes

continuer — assessment

How many interruption attempts were there?

one — two or more

Did S2 prevent S1 from completing AND did S1 complete the own utterance?

no — yes

unsuccessful single interruption

Was the interruption brief and was the floor then returned?

no — yes

interjection

Was the interruption preceded by a hesitation or breathing pause?

no — yes

hesitation interruption

Was the interruption achieved non-verbally?

no — yes

successful single interruption

silent interruption

Did S2 prevent S1 from completing AND ultimately complete the own utterance?

no — yes

unsuccessful complex interruption

successful complex interruption

Note: Coding categories are underlined, **boldface** marks interruptions.

Disruptive turn claims without overlapping talk are coded as SILENT INTERRUPTIONS, following Ferguson (1977). The interruption begins at a point where the first speaker is not pausing or hesitating, but is also not actually vocalizing.

(4) Silent interruption

    T: ... *met het verschil dat je toch mensen //*

    N: *// Daar was ik het niet mee eens omdat .....*

    T: ... with the difference that you still people // [syntactically correct in Dutch]

    N: // This I did not agree with because .....

Closely related to silent interruptions, but functionally distinct, are HESITATION INTERRUP-TIONS, where the interrupter uses a hesitation or breathing pause of the first speaker, who then yields the floor. They are occasioned by a dysfluency of the first speaker, and thus differ from silent interruptions in that they need not be dominance-related. The interruption in (5), for instance, is probably intended as a cooperative contribution by N. But since he does gain the floor and continues, that may well have been one of his reasons for finishing H's utterance. This functional ambiguity is typical for hesitation interruptions.

(5) Hesitation interruption

    H: .... *als je zegt dat eh dat //*

    N: *// Dat zijn allemaal mensen die het proces niet vertrouwen ....*

    H: .... if you say that uh that //

    N: // Those [Dutch: That] are all people who do not trust the process ....

Even more problematic is the interpretation of interjections, that is, short successful interruptions that are followed by an immediate return of the floor to the interrupted speaker. They do not result in the interrupted speaker being prevented from finishing or continuing, but they can still be used or perceived as disruptions and thus as domineering behavior. We consider interjections and hesitation interruptions as weakly dominance-related.

(6) Interjection

    H: ... *maar als je aan het eind van de schaal staat //*

    N: *// je kunt een bonus krijgen.*

    H: *eenmalig elk jaar opnieuw kun je 5% krijgen ...*

    H: ... but if you're at the end of the scale //

    N: // you can get a bonus. [syntactically not a continuation of H's utterance in Dutch]

    H: Once every year again can you get 5% ...

Interjections as (short) turns taken by the listener can be very similar to extended forms of "back channel behavior" (Yngve, 1970), that is, supportive, cooperative contributions within or latched onto the other speaker's turn (see Clark & Schaefer, 1989, pp. 280-283). Most back channel contributions are CONTINUERS, that is, displays of attention and/or acceptance like *mhm, yes,* or *I see,* that encourage the speaker to continue. Less frequent are *assessments* such as *oh really?, right!,* and so forth (in distinguishing between continuers and assessments we follow Schegloff, 1982).

Some instances of simultaneous speech, finally, are simply accidental misalignments of the speakers' turn taking. FALSE STARTS were already mentioned above. Episodes of non-disruptive joint talk, for instance, two speakers making the same point or one speaker finishing the other's utterance, are classified as OVERLAPS.

RESULTS

The frequencies of all categories of simultaneous speech were converted to rates per 10 minutes partner speaking time. It could be argued that the number of turns would be a better reference measure, as interruptions are a turn-change phenomenon. But a rate based on turns would not be adequate for some categories of noninterruptive simultaneous talk, that is, continuers and assessments. Moreover, in multiparty discourse, stories or arguments are often developed jointly by two or more participants. Disrupting such a multi-turn construction would then count as less severe than interrupting the same material produced by just one speaker. This strikes us as counter-intuitive.

Wilcoxon's nonparametric test was used to assess differences between formal and informal and between same-gender and mixed-gender discussions. Gender differences were tested by Mann-Whitney U-tests. All group averages reported are medians.[4] Note that the unit of analysis in the statistical tests was the speaker and not the individual incident of simultaneous talk. For the purposes of these analyses, the data from the four participants of each discussion had to be considered as statistically independent observations. This assumption is a notorious problem in research on dyadic interactions (see, e.g., Kraemer & Jacklin, 1979). We feel justified to assume independence because (i) any pairwise dependencies of the speakers will be obscured by the influence of the other two speakers, and (ii) asymmetries in the distribution of speaking time, which could cause negative correlations in our simultaneous speech measures, were corrected for by our use of rates instead of raw counts.

Speaking time and turns

A description of interactional characteristics like turn lengths and listener feedback can provide important convergent evidence for the interpretation of quantitative differences in interruption behavior. In this study, it also serves to establish the effectiveness of the experimental manipulation that aimed at distinguishing a rather formal, FLOOR 1 situation from one that would allow some FLOOR 2 types of behavior.

The eight discussions differed somewhat in total length. The total speaking time of all four speakers in a discussion group varied between a minimum of 19 minutes and 10 sec and a maximum of 30 minutes 50 seconds. There was no systematic difference in men's and women's speaking times in the mixed-gender discussions (see Table 35.1).

---

[4] Due to the small number of speakers and the skewed distribution of the variable "rate of interruption" (a few very high values), the mean, which is very sensitive to outliers, would not adequately reflect the data. The same arguments apply for our choice of nonparametric statistical tests.

TABLE 35.1.

Total speaking time, number of turns taken, and average turn lengths

Speakers:	Women				Men			
Setting:	Formal		Informal		Formal		Informal	
Group:	Female	Mixed	Female	Mixed	Male	Mixed	Male	Mixed
Speaking time (min;sec)	30;50	26;50	30;35	19;50	23;20	21;15	16;20	19;10
Total number of turns	40	60	52	56	57	62	62	63
Turn length (average)	41s	28s	30s	19s	24s	21s	17s	18s

Men and women alike produced longer turns in the formal than in the informal discussions (overall averages: 28 sec versus 21 sec; $z = 2.5$, $p = .01$). This holds for all-female, all-male, and mixed discussions (see Table 35.1). This significant difference is a first indication that the formal and informal settings succeeded in inducing a difference in interactional style.

In the same-gender discussions, the women produced much longer turns than the men (41 sec versus 24 sec in the formal discussion, $z = 2.0$, $p = .04$, and 30 versus 17 in the informal discussions, $z = 2.3$, $p = .02$). There is no comparable gender difference in the mixed-gender discussions (28 sec versus 21 sec in the formal discussions and 19 sec versus 18 sec in the informal discussions). This is mainly due to a substantial decrease in the length of women's turns. For all four women and for two of the men, the average turn length was greater in the same-gender discussions than in the mixed-gender discussions ($z = 2.1$, $p < .04$; note that the men's turn lengths in the informal discussions do not follow that pattern).

Noninterruptive simultaneous talk

The rate of non-interruptive simultaneous talk was higher in the informal than in the formal discussions for every one of the eight speakers (medians for the women: 28.9 versus 20.7 instances per 10 minutes partner speaking time; for the men: 60.8 versus 29.1; $z = 2.5$, $p = .01$; see Table 35.2). This provides strong evidence that the formal discussions were indeed closer to an exclusively FLOOR 1 interactional style than the informal discussions (the gender difference will be discussed below). False starts occurred only three times, twice among women and once between a woman and a man (in the latter case the median rate for the four men in Table 35.2 is of course still 0.0).

In the same-gender discussions, the women's rate of assessments was much lower than the men's (4.6 in the formal and 4.8 in the informal discussions, versus 11.1 and 18.4 for the men; $z = 2.3$, $p = .02$). For the informal discussions, continuers, assessments, and overlaps were each less frequent in the all-female than in the all-male group. The difference was statistically significant for assessments ($z = 2.3$, $p = .02$) and for overlaps ($z = 2.3$, $p = .02$). For the continuers the difference was not statistically reliable due to large inter-individual variation. The overall rates of noninterruptive simultaneous talk were 19.6 and 22.9 for the formal and informal all-female discussions, and 29.8 and 56.1 for the formal and informal all-male discussions (in the informal same-gender discussions, the gender difference was highly significant: 22.9 versus 56.1, $z = 2.31$, $p = .02$).

TABLE 35.2.
Rate of non-interruptive simultaneous talk per 10 min partner speaking time

Speakers:	Women				Men			
Setting:	Formal		Informal		Formal		Informal	
Group:	Female	Mixed	Female	Mixed	Male	Mixed	Male	Mixed
continuers	12.3	14.9	17.0	21.7	12.5	17.3	34.4	35.1
assessments	4.6	7.2	4.8	12.2	11.1	6.7	18.4	13.1
overlaps	2.6	2.6	1.6	7.5	2.9	2.4	5.7	3.6
false starts	0.2	0.0	0.0	0.7	0.0	0.0	0.0	60.0
Total number of instances	181	192	211	248	197	181	294	308

Note. To avoid differential weighing of the four speakers that contribute to each column, the rates of noninterruptive simultaneous talk were calculated for each speaker separately. The figures reported here are the medians of those rates.

The mixed-gender group, by contrast, showed no significant gender differences in any or all of these categories (the median total rates of non-interruptive simultaneous talk were 22.2 for the women versus 26.3 for the men in the formal, and 37.2 versus 51.6 in the informal mixed-gender discussions). The overall pattern of results suggests that women and men have both adjusted their behavior in the mixed-gender groups: Every one of the four women produced noninterruptive simultaneous talk at a higher rate in the mixed-gender than in the all-female discussions, and three of the four men showed a lower rate in the mixed-gender than in the all-male discussions.

Interruptions

Nine categories of the adapted simultaneous-speech coding system involve a disruption of a speaker's utterance, and can thus be considered dominance-related interruptive behavior. There were 561 such instances of interruptions in the corpus. Table 35.3 gives the rates per 10 minutes partner speaking time for each category. Overall, that is, considering same- and mixed-gender discussions together, the rate of interruptions was higher in the informal than in the formal discussions for seven of the eight speakers (medians: 11.3 versus 9.0 interruptions per 10 minutes partner speaking time; $z = 1.96$, $p = .05$). This is in accordance with the speakers' more involved style in the informal discussions, which was already shown above by the shorter turns and the higher rate of noninterruptive simultaneous talk.

TABLE 35.3.
Successful and unsuccessful interruptions per 10 min partner speaking time

Speakers:	Women				Men			
Setting:	Formal		Informal		Formal		Informal	
Group:	Female	Mixed	Female	Mixed	Male	Mixed	Male	Mixed
	Successful interruptions							
parallel talk	0.2	1.8	0.4	1.0	2.0	2.0	3.1	1.1
complex int.	0.0	0.9	0.5	0.3	1.1	0.0	2.5	1.5
single int.	1.9	2.0	1.0	2.7	1.4	1.9	1.5	2.2
silent int.	0.0	0.3	0.4	0.7	0.5	0.8	0.0	1.4
hesitation int.	0.9	2.1	0.5	1.8	1.3	0.9	2.1	2.6
interjections	1.0	2.1	1.7	3.0	1.3	2.5	5.8	2.4
	Unsuccessful interruptions							
parallel talk	0.0	0.0	0.0	0.0	0.3	0.6	0.0	0.0
complex int.	1.2	1.8	0.7	1.4	1.8	2.3	1.6	1.8
single int.	1.0	1.3	0.6	1.4	1.2	1.3	0.6	1.5
Total rate of interrupting	5.1	12.3	4.4	12.9	9.0	8.8	20.2	12.5
Number of interruptions	47	80	47	73	81	83	73	7.7

Note: To avoid differential weighing of the four speakers that contribute to each column, the rates of each category and the total rate of interrupting (all categories added up) were calculated for each speaker separately. The figures reported here are the medians of those rates. The category rates therefore do not and need not add up to the total rates.

In the mixed-gender discussions, men and women did not differ in the number of interruptions per 10 minutes of their partners' speaking time, even when both the interrupter and the interruptee's gender were taken into account: interruptions of men by men (8.1 per 10 minutes partner speaking time), men by women (14.6), women by men (11.5), and women by women (12.1) all occurred about equally often (none of the pairwise or overall tests comes even close to significance; note, however, that these figures are based on very few observations per speaker).

In the all-female group's discussions, the rate of interruption was significantly lower than in the all-male group (medians: 4.6 versus 14.3 interruptions per 10 minutes partner speaking time; $z = 2.0$, $p = .04$; see Table 35.4). Each of the four women produced fewer interruptions in the all-female than in the mixed-gender discussions. The men tended to interrupt slightly more in the all-male than in the mixed-gender discussions, but the difference was not statistically significant.

TABLE 35.4.   Percentages of each interruption type

Speakers:	Women		Men	
Group:	All-Female	Mixed	All-Male	Mixed
successful parallel talk	6	13	18	15
succ. complex interruptions	5	7	13	6
succ. single interruptions	29	21	13	17
silent interruptions	6	4	3	7
hesitation interruptions	15	16	15	15
interjections	23	23	27	21
unsuccessful parallel talk	2	4	4	4
unsucc. complex interruptions	0	1	1	4
unsucc. single interruptions	13	11	7	14
Total rate of interrupting	4.6	12.6	14.3	10.3
Total number of interruptions	94	153	154	160

The most intriguing result of the above analyses is the interaction between gender and group composition. The overall rates of interruptions suggest a convergence of women's and men's behavior in the mixed groups, paralleling the results for non-interruptive simultaneous talk (again with the women showing greater differences than the men). A closer look at the kinds of interruptions produced reveals that both women and men also showed qualitative differences in interruptive behavior between the mixed-gender and the same-gender situations (see Table 35.4). In the mixed-gender discussions, the distribution across the nine categories was almost identical for women and for men. There was only a slight tendency for single and complex interruptions to be more often successful for female than for male speakers. The same-gender discussions showed much larger differences. For the all-female discussions, the pattern suggests a more orderly and polite interaction with very little parallel talk, few complex interruption episodes, and a high percentage of successful single interruptions. In the all-male discussions, by contrast, the percentages of complex interruptions and interjections were much higher than in the mixed-gender discussions, while the use of silent interruptions and single interruptions, especially unsuccessful ones, decreased. Keeping in mind that repeated unsuccessful interruption attempts were coded as a complex interruption, this pattern of differences can be interpreted as indicating greater competitiveness in the all-male group. This interpretation of the differences between the same-gender groups is supported by the observation reported above that the average turn length in the all-male group discussions was significantly shorter than in the all-female discussions.

DISCUSSION AND CONCLUSIONS

The often-heard stereotype that men tend to use interruptions more often than women, and thus dominate and control discussions, was not confirmed in this study. In mixed-gender discussions, men and women of equal social status, age, and expertise were shown not to differ in interruptive speech behavior. Neither the interrupters' nor the interruptees' gender made a difference. This was true both in formal (FLOOR 1) and in informal (FLOOR 1 and FLOOR 2) mixed-gender discussions. In same-gender discussions, by contrast, women were found to interrupt each other less than men, suggesting that there exist separate female and male registers in this type of talk.

It must be noted, of course, that our results may be specific to well-acquainted white-collar academic professionals talking about political and professional issues. Moreover, we cannot exclude the possibility that the absence of gender differences in the mixed-gender situation may be specific to the rather nonconsequential simulated discussions investigated here (and in most other studies comparing same-gender and mixed-gender dyads or groups). In fact, an earlier study involving political discussions on Dutch radio and television (Linssen-Maes & Redeker, 1992) suggests that these findings may not be generalizable to public discussions where the speakers' reputations are at stake. In that study, men took considerably more and longer turns and interrupted at a higher rate than women (women and men, however, both interrupted male speakers more often than female speakers). The speakers were quite similar to the participants in the present study, but they were not well acquainted. The gender differences thus may have been caused by the kind of perceptual stereotyping discussed at the beginning of this paper. Clearly, more research with naturally occurring (public and private) discussions is needed to determine the role of familiarity and the generalizability of findings from experimental simulations.

A potentially problematic aspect of the repeated measures design used in the present study is the participants' awareness of the experimental manipulation. This might have induced the men to avoid domineering the women in the mixed-gender discussions, and the women to be extra assertive towards the men. But if this were true, then both genders should have interrupted men more often than women in the mixed groups. This was not the case: Women and men were interrupted equally often in the mixed-gender discussions; this was true both for male and female interrupters. Yet, what about the finding that the men were more competitive in the all-male than in the mixed-gender discussions? We do not think that this can be interpreted as polite restraint on the part of the men. The interruption categories they used less in the mixed-gender discussions were the successful complex interruptions and interjections, while the percentage of successful and unsuccessful single interruptions and silent interruptions increased. This suggests that they not only gave up more easily than in the all-male discussions and reduced their interrupting comments, but also succeeded more easily in interrupting their (male and female) partners in the mixed-gender discussions. We are reminded here that we are dealing with an inherently interactive phenomenon: It takes two to produce an interruption, especially a successful one.

We can conclude, then, that the observed convergence of the female and male registers in the mixed-gender discussions was in all likelihood not an artifact of our experimental design. In fact, the pattern of men being more competitive than women in the same-gender situation and no gender difference in the mixed-gender situation corresponds to results reported by Aries (1976), Carli (1989), and others. Some of those studies (e.g., Bilous & Krauss, 1988, and Carli, 1989) also agree with the present study in observing that it is mainly the women who show a reduction in gender-specific interactional behavior when talking in a mixed-gender group (note, however, that Bilous and Krauss found **more** interruptions in all-female than in all-male discussions). The convergence pattern also parallels the findings of Ervin-Tripp and Lampert (1992) on the use of humor by women and by men. They found both women and men to shift their strategies towards a more equal balance in mixed-gender interactions.

There is an intriguing difference, however, between our results and those from other studies: The interactional style in the all-female group does not fully reflect what is assumed to be the typical female register, that is, an involved, collaborative style with frequent simultaneous talk and short turns (Edelsky, 1981; Coates, 1989; Tannen, 1990). The women did use fewer interruptions in the all-female discussions, but they also produced less (instead of more) noninterruptive simultaneous talk and relatively long turns (for a similarly mixed pattern in Dutch women's talk see De Boer, 1987). We can only speculate about the causes of this discrepancy. First of all, neither the formal nor the informal discussions were truly informal with substantial FLOOR 2 interaction, whereas female register in the studies cited has been described for casual conversations or for casual episodes in task-oriented interactions. Our experience with Dutch and (West-Coast) American culture suggests that humor and small talk are more strictly separated from "shop talk" for the Dutch than they are for Americans (compare Ervin-Tripp & Lampert's observation that Americans are sometimes reproached for laughing too much and addressing serious problems with humor). The absence of an involved, collaborative female register in our data thus might be specific to the task-oriented talk we have been looking at, which in Dutch admits some, but not all of Edelsky's FLOOR 2 characteristics and thus only some of the register characteristics associated with FLOOR 2 interaction.

REFERENCES

Aries, E. (1976). Interaction patterns and themes of male, female, and mixed groups. *Small Group Behavior, 7,* 7-18.

Aries, E. (1987). Gender and communication. In P. Shaver & C. Hendrick (Eds.), *Sex and gender* (pp. 149-176). Newbury Park, CA: Sage.

Beattie, G. W. (1981). Interruption in conversational interaction and its relation to the sex and status of the interactants. *Linguistics, 19,* 15-35.

Bilous, F. R., & Krauss, R. M. (1988). Dominance and accommodation in the conversational behaviours of same- and mixed-gender dyads. *Language and Communication*, **8**, 183-194.

Carli, L. L. (1989). Gender differences in interaction style and influence. *Journal of Personality and Social Psychology*, **56**, 565-576.

Clark, H. H., & Schaefer, E. F. (1989). Contributing to discourse. *Cognitive Science*, **13**, 259-294.

Coates, J. (1989). Gossip revisited: Language in all-female groups. In J. Coates & D. Cameron (Eds.), *Women in their speech communities* (pp. 94-122). London: Longman.

De Boer, M. (1987). Sex differences in language: Observations of dyadic conversations between members of the same sex. In D. Brouwer & D. de Haan (Eds.), *Women's language, socialization and self-image* (pp. 148-163). Dordrecht: Foris.

Edelsky, C. (1981). Who's got the floor? *Language in Society*, **10**, 383-421.

Ervin-Tripp, S. (1987). Cross-cultural and developmental sources of pragmatic generalizations. In J. Verschueren & M. B. Papi (Eds.), *The pragmatic perspective* (pp. 47-60). Amsterdam: Benjamins.

Ervin-Tripp, S. M., & Lampert, M. (1992). Gender differences in the construction of humorous talk. In K. Hall, M. Buchholtz, & B. Moonwoman (Eds.), *Locating power: Proceedings of the Second Berkeley Women and Language Conference* (pp. 108-117). Berkeley: Berkeley Women and Language Group, University of California.

Ferguson, N. (1977). Simultaneous speech, interruptions and dominance. *British Journal of Social and Clinical Psychology*, **16**, 295-302.

Holmes, J. (1992). Women's talk in public contexts. *Discourse in Society*, **3**, 131-150.

James, D., & Clarke, S. (1993). Women, men and interruptions: a critical review. In D. Tannen (Ed.), *Gender and Conversational Interaction* (pp. 231-280). New York: Oxford University Press.

Kennedy, C. W., & Camden, C. (1983). A new look at interruptions. *Western Journal of Speech Communication*, **47**, 45-58.

Kraemer, H. C., & Jacklin, C. N. (1979). Statistical analysis of dyadic social behavior. *Psychological Bulletin*, **86**, 217-224.

Leet-Pellegrini, H. M. (1980). Conversational dominance as a function of gender and expertise. In H. Giles, W. P. Robinson, & P. M. Smith (Eds.), *Language: Social psychological perspectives* (pp. 97-104). New York: Pergamon.

Linssen-Maes, A., & Redeker, G. (1992). Interruptiegedrag van vrouwen en mannen in radio- en televisiediscussies [Interruption behavior of women and men in radio and television discussions]. *Gramma/TTT, tijdschrift voor taalkunde*, **1**, 133-148.

Marche, T. A., & Peterson, C. (1993). The developmental and sex-related use of interruption behavior. *Human Communication Research*, **19**, 388-408.

Murray, S. O., & Covelli, L. H. (1988). Women and men speaking at the same time. *Journal of Pragmatics*, **12**, 103-111.

Roger, D. B., Bull, P. E., & Smith, S. (1988). The development of a comprehensive system for classifying interruptions. *Journal of Language and Social Psychology*, **7**, 27-34.

Schegloff, E. A. (1982). Discourse as an interactional achievement: Some uses of "uh huh" and other things that come between sentences. In D. Tannen (Ed.), *Analyzing discourse: Text and talk. 32nd Georgetown Roundtable on Language and Linguistics 1981* (pp. 71-93). Washington, DC: Georgetown University Press.

Smith-Lovin, L., & Brody, C. (1989). Interruptions in group discussions: The effects of gender and group composition. *American Sociological Review*, **54**, 424-435.

Tannen, D. (1984). *Conversational style: Analyzing talk among friends.* Norwood, NJ: Ablex.

Tannen, D. (1989). Interpreting interruption in conversation. *Papers from the 25th Annual Meeting of the Chicago Linguistics Society. Part 2: Parasession on Language and context* (pp. 266-287). Chicago: University of Chicago.

Tannen, D. (1990). *You just don't understand: Women and men in conversation.* New York: Morrow.

West, C., & Zimmerman, D. H. (1983). Small insults: A study of interruptions in cross-sex conversations between unacquainted persons. In B. Thorn, C. Kramarae, & N. Henley (Eds.), *Language, gender and society* (pp. 102-117). Rowley, MA: Newbury House.

Woods, N. (1989). Talking shop: Sex status and status as determiners of floor appointment in a work setting. In J. Coates & D. Cameron (Eds.), *Women in their speech communities* (pp. 141-157). New York: Longman.

Wood, W., & Karten, S. J. (1986). Sex differences in interaction style as a product of perceived sex differences in competence. *Journal of Personality and Social Psychology, 50*, 341-347.

Yngve, V. H. (1970). On getting a word in edgewise. *Papers from the Sixth Regional Meeting of the Chicago Linguistic Society* (pp. 567-578). Chicago: University of Chicago.

Zimmerman, D. H., & West, C. (1975). Sex roles, interruptions and silences in conversation. In B. Thorn & N. Henley (Eds.), *Language and sex: Difference and dominance* (pp. 105-129). Rowley, MA: Newbury House.

36 SHARING THE SAME WORLD, TELLING DIFFERENT STORIES: GENDER DIFFERENCES IN CO-CONSTRUCTED PRETEND NARRATIVES[1]

Amy Sheldon
Lisa Rohleder
University of Minnesota

It is difficult to separate reality from fiction in the playground. The two are in a happy state of confusion; like dinner-party hilarity, when nonsense rises on bubbles of champagne...

Iona Opie. *The People in the Playground.*

This chapter is concerned with the question of how linguistic processes connect individual minds and bodies in and to a larger social order. We will consider how language is socially situated in experience and how that experience shapes us. We will show that children's talk with friends is an important medium for acquiring and displaying explicit and implicit knowledge of the world and of communal sociocultural norms.

Considering that girls and boys spend significant time in childhood with same-sex companions,[2] we can ask if there are differences in these same-sex experiences which socialize children into gender-influenced, normative social practices? Social interaction often depends on shared knowledge and interests in order to be successful and satisfying. Are there differences in girls' and boys' shared knowledge or interests that are relevant to their interactions?

[1] This study was funded by a University of Minnesota Graduate School Grant-in-Aid to Amy Sheldon. Support was also provided by the Center for Research in Learning, Perception and Cognition and grants from the University of Minnesota Undergraduate Research Opportunity Program. We are grateful to the children and parents at the University of Minnesota Child Care Center and to the teachers and staff for their cooperation and assistance. We thank Kathleen Kremer, John Ogawa, Jeff Ringwelski, and Mike Young for their research assistance, and Aron Pilhofer and Jennifer Wesson for research assistance at an earlier stage.

[2] Whiting and Edwards (1988, p. 81) say that the "emergence of same-sex preferences in childhood is a cross-culturally universal and robust phenomenon." Leaper (1994) also discusses childhood gender segregation.

The degree of shared knowledge might be especially relevant for the interaction of young children because they have limited knowledge to begin with. That is, when children's talk with one another is "scripted," i.e., based on events that are familiar to them and valued by the group, their conversations and activities might reach greater levels of attunement. Consequently, their discourse might be longer and more elaborate than when the topic of conversation is not scripted, familiar, or similarly valued. The extension to gender is that young children would choose same-sex partners to play with since they would readily learn that gender is a cue for finding someone whose interests and knowledge they share, someone who is more attuned to them. We would expect, then, that developing shared scripts with one's companions would make social life easier and more fun. A more global implication is that sex-segregation in play groups at early ages results from, but then contributes to, the development of distinct ways of interacting in girls' and boys' groups. Girls and boys would share the same material world, but act on it differently.

Dramatic play is a frequent activity among preschool children. Extensive oral texts are jointly constructed which embody their social interaction and their symbolic worlds. As Bretherton (1984, p. 32) notes, "The simulated territory of symbolic play is not necessarily a straight reproduction of real-world maps." Still, however counterfactual, paradoxical or distorted children's dramatic play may become, it is also based on their knowledge of event schemata, and conventionalized scripting of events, actions, objects, and roles.

Peer culture and language are important socializing influences on young children. This research examines how one aspect of peer culture, sex/gender,[3] organizes the co-construction of stories during pretend play in a Midwestern community of preschoolers. We were interested in knowing the extent to which preschool children incorporate sociocultural prescriptions or cultural stereotypes about gender into the form and content of stories that they weave together in play. We noted that while there has been progress in studying children's monologic narratives, we were interested in extending the research on **collaboratively** developed dramatic play episodes, what we will here call "stories" or "co-constructed narratives." We were interested in how children's gender knowledge can constrain the **communal** working of their socially **shared** symbolic imagination with same-sex friends.

This work is part of a growing body of research which demonstrates the ways in which gender prescriptions influence multiple aspects of children's linguistic and socio-cognitive activity (Leaper, 1994; Maccoby, 1990; Whiting & Edwards, 1988). Previous work has shown that gender organizes children's language and thinking in some of the following ways: dispute talk (Goodwin, 1980; Kyratzis, 1992; Miller, Danaher, & Forbes, 1986; Sheldon, 1990, 1992a, 1992b, 1996; Sheldon & Johnson, 1994), talk during social

---

[3] The terms "sex" and "gender" are often used interchangeably, which results in confusion. By "sex" we mean the biological self which has reproductive potential. By "gender" we refer to the meanings and values that a community or culture gives to physical, sexual differences. These culturally constructed meanings, which constitute a gender order or system, are learned. Sex and gender are often interconnected, however. We have used "sex/gender" to indicate such overlap.

and pretend play (Leaper, 1991; Sachs, 1987), monologic stories (Libby & Aries, 1989; Nicolopoulou, Scales, & Weintraub, 1994; Tarullo, 1994), topic coherence and physical alignment (Tannen, 1990), MLU (Duveen & Lloyd, 1988), reactions to stories with feminist themes (Davies, 1989), and event knowledge (see review in Levy & Fivush, 1993).

HYPOTHESES

The following hypotheses were tested:

1. *Gender-typed Story Preference.*

We hypothesized that co-constructed stories would be organized by and would reflect gender stereotypes and gender preferences.   Based on above-mentioned studies of children's monologic narratives and toy preferences, we expected that girls would prefer domestic story elements and themes which foregrounded kinship relationships and domestic activities.   Boys would prefer stories which featured themes and elements of non-domestic fantasy and adventure, possibly including intense action, danger and threat. We hypothesized that story preferences would be **independent** of the resources available in the setting.   Children would transform the material resources to fit their imaginary world and its co-constructed characters, roles, and events.

2. *Object Transformation.*

We hypothesized that object resources would be transformed to fit gender-typed story preferences.   Since girls were predicted to prefer domestic or culturally-appropriate "feminine" stories, scripted with activities such as preparing dinner and creating family relationships, they were expected to do little if any transformation of the domestic resources in the Housekeeping center.   On the other hand, since it was expected that boys would prefer culturally appropriate "masculine" stories with elements of nondomestic fantasy adventure, we predicted that in the Housekeeping center boys would more frequently transform objects to fit such stories.

METHOD

Participants

Three-, 4- and 5-year-old female and male preschoolers from the Minneapolis-St. Paul area were videotaped in unsupervised play at their day care center.[4]   The majority of participants were White.   The children and the day care center were well known to the first author.   The children were grouped into same-sex triads on the basis of their friend-

---

[4] The discourse practices of this community of children have been discussed in Sheldon (1990, 1992a, 1992b, 1996) and Sheldon and Johnson (1994). In those studies the focus was on the gendered nature of their conflict talk. But conflict often took place during dramatic play, and many of the examples discussed there also reveal the gendered story elements in their dramatic play.

ships, using information provided by their teachers and from this author's previous observations. The children in the study were members of one of the two larger preschool groups in the center; they played everyday with others in their group.

Procedure and resources available

Each of six girl triads ($N = 18$) and six boy triads ($N = 18$) was brought into a familiar play room in their day care center on different occasions by the first author and a graduate assistant. They were introduced to the resources and played for approximately 25 minutes each time. Their play was unsupervised although the author and the assistant observed and took notes from an unobtrusive perch atop the loft at one end of the room.

On two of the occasions that the triads played in the room it was set up with different gender-typed resources for dramatic play: either a Housekeeping center or a Trucks & Dinosaurs center (e.g., see Almqvist, 1989; Caldera, Huston, & O'Brien, 1989; Eisenberg, Wolchik, Hernandez, & Pasternak, 1985; Lloyd, Duveen, & Smith, 1988; Parten, 1933). The total of twelve sessions (six girls' and six boys' sessions) in the Housekeeping center amounted to about five hours of play. In this chapter we will only compare the stories that emerged in the Housekeeping center, which each triad played in for one 25 minute session.

The resources in the Housekeeping center included a toy stove and sink, a basket of plastic replicas of food items, cooking pots, eating utensils, plates and cups, a child-size dining table and three chairs, a doll's high chair, a doll's bed with dolls and blankets in it, a telephone next to a child-size foam chair, dress up clothes, a mirror, and a doctor's kit. A sheet hung over the side of the bottom half of the loft to hide a storage area.

Coding transformations

Phase one: Defining transformations

Two broad classes of transformations were identified: 1) a concrete object is given a new identity and, 2) a function or quality is attributed to the object which it does not ordinarily possess (examples in Table 36.1). In the first category, the child makes the transformation explicit by renaming an existing object and thereby giving it a new identity.

In the second category, the transformation often was more subtle. In some cases an object retained its actual identity while some new quality or function was attributed to it (example 2c in Table 36.1). In other cases the transformation involved attributing a unique function for the object without reference to the identity of the object, per se (example 2a).[5]

---

[5] It was not necessary that the transformation be explicitly stated by a child; in some cases a combination of speech and nonverbal activity was sufficient to identify a transformation of an object. For example, a child puts a toy banana to his ear and says "hi." In this case, one can infer that the banana is being used as a telephone and the transformation was coded accordingly. Transformations could involve multiple objects. In a few instances a set of objects was given a new identity: In one example a child arranged a table and chairs in a specific configuration and announced that this was "the baby

The two classes of transformations we identified can be distinguished from other criteria for transformations which have appeared in the pretend play literature. Matthews (1977) includes among transformations all behaviors in which a toy replica of an object is used as if it were the real object. We did not include such transformations in our criteria. The act of a child pretending to eat plastic food, or cook plastic food in a pot on a wooden play stove, for example, was not considered to entail transformations of the toy food, the toy pot, or the toy stove in our definition of transformations.

We also did not include transformations in the absence of any concrete object to represent the created object or situation, e.g., 1) transformations that involved creating objects (e.g., "I'm cutting the ropes," where the child invents "ropes" on an object being used as a spaceship), or 2) creating situations (e.g., "Let's say it's Christmas"), or 3) creating locations (e.g., "Let's say this is space," where the child refers generally to the play area). Our primary reason for constraining the coding was that the sheer volume of such transformations made coding impractical, since the children were engaged in pretend play for extensive periods during each session.

TABLE 36.1. Two Types of Transformations Identified

1)	*Giving a new identity to a familiar object*
a.	"Here's our space shuttle" (child lies down in the crib). the crib = a space shuttle
b.	"...this is the baby store." (describes a table and chair arrangement). the table and chairs = a store
2)	*Using an object in a nonconventional way; ascribing functions or qualities to an object that the object doesn't ordinarily possess*
a.	"Me going." (child grasps legs of overturned table and makes motor noises). the table = a vehicle
b.	"That's to show where bad guys are coming." (referring to blood pressure cuff). b.p. cuff = shows bad guys
c.	"Our bed is magic." (magical quality attributed to bed).
d.	"I'm going to shoot you. 'Shht'." (child uses his own hand as a gun). a hand = a gun

A second reason for focusing on transformations which changed the identity or function of objects had to do with our particular research question. We wanted a measure that would reveal the extent to which girls' and boys' imaginative constructions during play were consistent or inconsistent with the resources available to them in the Housekeeping setting. Both the boy and girl groups made use of the objects as represen-

---

store" while a second child confirmed this and added that this was where you could get baby food. Although multiple objects were used, such cases were regarded as single transformations (i.e., were only counted once in the total number of transformations for a group).

tations of the real thing. While this provides a measure of how consistent their play was with the Housekeeping setting, it does not provide a measure of inconsistency. The definition of transformation that we used identified transformations that could be either consistent or inconsistent, making it possible to compare and contrast the girls' and boys' transformations on these dimensions. Therefore, we focused on transformations which changed the identity or function of a given object, as these strongly suggest the priority of imagination in directing play — over and above the influence of the obvious stimulus properties of the resources available.

As stated previously, we did not include as transformations speech events or actions that created objects in the absence of any material resource to represent that object. For example, if a child pretended to have a sword in hand when she or he did not in fact have anything in hand, this was not coded as a transformation. This kind of transformation is in many ways complementary to the types of transformations that we did code. Creating objects which reside in the shared imagination of the group — rather than in the physical surroundings — suggests how the content of play is directed by imagination rather than being elicited by the physical properties of the environment. Thus, an examination of these imaginary objects (along with the creation of imaginary locations and events) would be a useful direction for future work. Although we have yet to examine these, our sense of the data is that these transformations operate in much the same way as transformations of the material objects which we did analyze.

Phase two: Coding data

Using the criteria of transformation of identity or function of an existing object, one of the researchers (Rohleder) identified all instances of transformations occurring in each of six girl and six boy Housekeeping sessions, using the videotapes and transcripts. Although we identified two kinds of transformations (Table 36.1) we did not differentiate these for the current analyses. The differentiation was made primarily as a guideline to the coder for the kinds of transformations to include. In each session, the entire session was examined and the first instance of each transformation was identified.

Phase three: Distinguishing transformations as domestic or non-domestic

Each transformation which had been identified was then coded as to whether it was consistent, or not consistent, with the Housekeeping setting, i.e., whether it was a "domestic" or "nondomestic" transformation. Most of the objects available for play in the Housekeeping center were consistent with a domestic theme (having to do with kinship and activities occurring in the home). However, there were some which we did not consider distinctly or primarily domestic. As a result, we developed a coding scheme which took into account the domestic/nondomestic status of the object before it was transformed and as a result of its transformation. The following examples show how objects were coded and give a flavor of the gendered stories, especially the nondomestic ones that the boys developed.

0.   NONDOMESTIC → DOMESTIC (ND→D). An object (or part of an object) that is

not domestic is transformed into a domestic object. *Examples:*[6] a hand becomes a telephone receiver (B1); the floor becomes a baby's bed (B3) and a child's bed (G4); the syringe warms up food (B4) and shoots out sugar (B4).

1. DOMESTIC → DOMESTIC (D→D). A domestic object (or part of the object) is transformed into another kind of domestic object. *Examples:* a banana becomes a phone (B1); cauliflower becomes a marshmallow cake (B1); a piece of food becomes a strawberry "Ho-Ho"[7] (B4); an oven becomes a freezer (B5); a scarf becomes a blanket or a quilt (G2), (G3), (G4); a door on the stove becomes a door to the basement (G3); a toy pear becomes a jar of baby food (G3); a table and chair become a baby food store (G3); a food item becomes baby food (G4); an oven becomes a cupboard for utensils (G5); a kitchen table becomes a bakery (G5).

2. NONDOMESTIC → NONDOMESTIC (ND→ND). An object (or part of the object) that is not "domestic" is transformed into some other object that also is not domestic. *Examples:* the stethoscope is used as a microphone (B3); the microphone on the lapel of their research vest and the button on a back pocket are used as a walkie-talkie (B3); the button on their vests controls which way the robots go, makes the robots fly, makes them explode, and makes them invisible (B3); a hand is used as a walkie-talkie (B3); a syringe becomes a weapon to shoot bean-bullets (B4); a syringe gets the space ship to turn on (B4); some "red stuff" is a child's blood (B5); a syringe is a gun (B5) or a weapon (B6); a hand is a gun (B5); spots on a sheet are bear marks, or tigers, or frogs, or leopards (B6); the ear scope is a camera (B6); a gauge becomes a clock (G1).

3. DOMESTIC → NONDOMESTIC (D→ND). An object (or part of an object) that is domestic is transformed into an object that is not domestic. *Examples:* a corn cob, a pan, two plastic knives, toast and a knife, are competitively offered by the boys as a camera to take a picture of a polar bear (B6); a plastic knife becomes a magic wand used to turn a threatening bear into a piece of gum. (B6); a spoon is a flashlight for an "explore" (B6); a spoon is stolen jewels (B6), eating utensils are tools for the "explore" (B6); beans become bullets (B4); eggplant becomes a sword, (B3); banana becomes a gun (B3); toast is used as a transmitter for robots (B3); a knob on the stove makes the robots go (B3); the crib arm fires lasers (B3); crib, stove, foam chair, table become part of a spaceship (B3); the oven becomes a machine to give a sick baby medicine and to make the baby hot (the baby is placed in the oven) (B1); the foam chair becomes a chair in an airplane (B2); the funnel is used to check a child's mouth (G1); a strainer is used to look at rabbits (G2).

Phase four: coding for domesticity

After the transformations were identified by Rohleder (Coder 1), a graduate student in child development, another graduate student in child development (Coder 2), who was

---

[6] In parenthesis are abbreviations for the boys' (B) and girls' (G) groups described in the tables.

[7] A "Ho-Ho" is a commercial brand name for an individual cake.

naive to the hypotheses of the research and to any identifying information about the subjects, also served in the next phase of coding. This naive coder was given a description of the resources and set-up in the room for the Housekeeping sessions, was advised that some of the objects were considered "domestic" and others "nondomestic," and that a transformation of an object could involve either domestic or non-domestic objects.

Coder 2 was then provided with the four categories and definitions (ND→D, D→D, ND→ND, D→ND) for classifying each of the transformations and was asked to classify the transformations found by Coder 1. Both Coder 1 and 2 independently classified the transformations as either domestic or non-domestic.

Reliability

Reliability was assessed between the naive Coder 2 and the researcher (Coder 1). The reliability (Cohen's Kappa) between the researcher and Coder 2 was .83. Out of 104 transformations identified, there were 12 disagreements, which were resolved through discussion. An example of a disagreement was the boys' transformation of a spoon into a flashlight which was coded as D→ND by Coder 1 and D→D by Coder 2. It was resolved after discussion as D→ND.

TABLE 36.2. Total number of transformations identified per group stories in the constructed in Housekeeping

Girls' triads (N = 18)		Boys' triads (N = 18)	
G1	2	B1	11
G2	2	B2	3
G3	5	B3	34
G4	3	B4	13
G5	2	B5	7
G6	0	B6	22
Subtotals	14		90
% of total trans-formations	13.5		86.5

RESULTS

Table 36.2 shows that the boys' groups produced more than six times as many object transformations (90) compared to the girls' groups (14).[8]

---

[8] The one boy's group (B2) with a low rate of object transformations (3) comparable to the girls' rate contained younger, 3-year-old, boys.

This difference in the proportion of transformations produced by boys compared to girls is consistent with Matthews' (1977) finding that 4-year-old boys produced more transformations of features of tangible objects in dramatic play than girls did.[9]

TABLE 36.3.   Frequency of the four types of transformations in stories constructed per group in Housekeeping

	Transformations whose end-results were:			
	to Domestic:		to Nondomestic:	
	ND → D	D→D	ND→ND	D→ND
Girls' groups				
G1	0	0	1	1
G2	0	1	0	1
G3	0	5	0	0
G4	1	2	0	0
G5	0	2	0	0
G6	0	0	0	0
Column totals	1	10	1	2
Overall totals	11 (78.6%)		3 (21.4%)	
Boys' groups				
B1	0	6	0	5
B2	0	2	0	1
B3	1	1	21	11
B4	2	1	5	5
B5	0	3	4	0
B6	0	0	8	14
Column totals	3	13	38	36
Overall totals	16 (17.77%)		74 (82.22%)	

A comparison of the end result of transformations to a domestic or nondomestic mode is presented in Table 36.3. Here again there is a dramatic difference. In the same

---

[9] Matthews' study was set in a laboratory playroom that contained a variety of play materials, including "dolls, trucks, pounding boards, blocks, puzzles, pots and pans, etc." This setting contains a composite of gender-typed play materials, compared to the Housekeeping center in our study, which was designed with materials that would create a girl-preferred play space.

setting with the same resources, the majority of the girls' object transformations kept the object in a domestic mode. The comparatively low rate of transforming objects to a domestic mode in the girls' groups (two of the girls' groups did not have any transformations to a domestic mode) indexes the fact that girls' play in the Housekeeping center was primarily domestic.

Only three out of a total of 14 transformations made by the girls (21%) changed an object to a non-domestic mode and these three transformations were produced by just two of the six girls' groups. The other four girls' groups did not produce any non-domestic transformations. However, eighty-two percent of the boys' transformations converted an object to a non-domestic mode. Transformations whose end results were non-domestic occurred to objects classified as "non-domestic" about as often as to those classified as "domestic."

These results support the **Gender-typed Story Preference Hypothesis** and the **Object Transformation Hypothesis**. These hypotheses predict girls' preference for domestic stories which foreground kinship relationships and domestic activities, and boys' preference for stories which feature elements of nondomestic fantasy and adventure which might include intense action, danger and threat.

DISCUSSION

The gendered difference in girls' and boys' stories can be more fully appreciated by examining some in which the transformations figured. Although the volume of transformations may be relatively low in some groups, a transformation could have important effects on the direction that the story development took, its length, and the other children's coparticipation in its development. Transformations could create a focus of interest and excitement in the group and draw the other children in as codevelopers of the story elements.

Gender-typed stories and degree of elaboration

The gender-typed stories seemed to result in longer and more complex dramatic play. Thus, girls' play in which domestic themes were scripted developed very complex and detailed story elements and activities. There were either no danger themes (nondomestic or domestic), or ones which were minimally developed and not necessarily set outside of the home, such as the mention of a scary ghost, or a sick child emergency at home, or a fire in the house.

Boys' groups **did** enact domestic themes, but those did not seem to reach the same level of complexity and they differed in some other interesting ways from the girls'. For example, boys' play either did not contain certain domestic elements that girls' play did, such as cleaning up after dinner, or did not go into the same degree of detail, e.g., no boys' group enacted scripts for preparing baby for bed, whereas five girls' groups did. Only two boys' groups did anything related to baby's bedtime, and it was the simple act of lying down with the baby. One boy said it was to "guard" the baby. On the other hand, boys' play in which adventure and fantasy themes were developed had very detailed story elements and activities, more than girls' play did for such themes.

These preliminary results suggest an extension of the **Gender-typed Story Hypothesis** to account for our observation that gender-typed co-constructed narratives seem to have deeper and more extensive story development, with more complex construction, and more detail. A fuller comparison of differences in the story elements in the girls' and boys' domestic play is an important topic for future analysis, posing its own analytical challenges, but it is beyond the scope of this chapter.

Examples of boys' gender-typed stories

All of the boys' Housekeeping sessions contained transformations of an object to a non-domestic mode, which then had a function in developing their stories further. Often at the beginning of the session, the boys did interact with the resources in some domestic mode, but they also slipped into a nondomestic scenario. Some of these nondomestic story threads were especially well-developed and complex, and transformed the setting from the domestic sphere to another world. The following are examples from some of the boys' groups:

(B3): spun a story in which they were police and then robots, they hunted robbers who were getting other people's money, they flew on an airplane to San Francisco where some people were getting hurt, they went in a space ship and fired on the bad guys' ship;

(B4): developed a narrative which involved getting the "bad guys at the 69 turret," shooting lasers, getting in a space shuttle and blasting off;

(B6): went on an "explore," inventing a swamp, a cave, and dangerous animals and characters.

These three groups produced the most object transformations per group and the most complex gender-typed stories. (The **B5** group threw the dishes off the table and turned it over, using the overturned table as a house; needless to say, none of the girls' groups disrupted the Housekeeping setting).

A summary of a story that was co-constructed in the **B6** group gives a flavor of how complex the non-domestic story line could get and the role of some object transformations in the story.

Example: Transforming domestic objects and setting into non-domestic ones

(B6): "There's the bear in our house!"

In this example, the boys made **multiple** and different **types** of transformations in their imaginative play. The complexity of the resulting story isn't fully captured by counting object transformations alone. Not only did they transform objects, they also transformed their play space, creating an alternative non-domestic world to the Housekeeping center. They moved the setting out-of-doors to a less hospitable and safe place, populated it with exciting wild animals (bears, tigers, leopards, a panther, alligators, a lion, frogs, a bat), scary fictional and nonfictional characters and things (a demon, a dragon, witches, goblins, ghosts, "bad people," the Queen of Mystical, lumpy things), and created different settings (a hideout in the kitchen area, a cave, a swamp). Not only do they slip back and forth between the out-of-home and the in-home spheres, the home setting itself also shifts from a tranquil place to a chaotic one and back again.

The session starts out with the boys engaging in a similar but less well-developed domestic script compared to what is found in the girls' sessions (e.g., they prepare food, they eat at the table with their doll-babies). They shift out of the domestic mode when Connor stages an event that takes them out of the home, represented by the Housekeeping center.

He announces that they are leaving the house, "We're going out for a walk, right? . . . there's a bear around here somewhere," which he reframes a few minutes later as, "We're tiptoeing in the woods, remember?," and then recasts as, "Hey, we're going out for another explore, right, Mark?" Mark agrees, "Yeah, but this time we're hunting for alligators." Each reannouncement of leaving the house becomes more adventurous because of the wild animals which are also described to be nearby. The boys create a mood of excitement and anticipation of danger.

The boys see a bear on their "explore." It is a sleeping polar bear. They want to photograph it. Robert, using the doctor kit thermometer, observes, "The bears are not awake yet. See how cold it is, the bears are- can't get awake."[10] The following excerpt illustrates how the boys compete with each other to manufacture a "camera" to photograph the sleeping bear.

(Overlapping talk is printed on the same line in another column. Speaker names are abbreviated: Ma = Mark, Co = Connor, Ro = Robert)

001 Ma:	I got to get a picture of the polar bear.	
002	Hey, where's the camera?	
003	Where's the camera?	
004 Co:	Hey, it's light! It's- the polar bear's	Ro: What? What
005	beginning to break our house in pieces!	did you- what did
006		did you say?
007 Ma:	But where- where- where's the camera?	
008 Co:	There's the bear! There's the bear in our house!	
009 Ma:	Where's the camera?	
010 Ro:	I got a camera. ((picks up cooking pan from	
011	stove top))	
012 Ma:	No, I got a camera.	
013 Co:	Oh, it's light still. It's still light! I'm gonna shot	
014	that bear!	
015 Ma:	No, don't shoot him! Let me- let me take a	
016	picture of him.	
017 Co:	One shot. He's dead. ((Pushes ear scope	

---

[10] The temperature surfaces as a topic a few times in this group. For example, the boys change it from hot to cold and cold to hot as a way of controlling the polar bear, whom they acknowledge likes the cold and not the heat.

018   through space))
019 Ma: No you didn't shoot him.
020 Co: He's too quick for me.
021 Ma: You gotta have a camera.
022 Ro: I got the camera.
023   Click! ((scrapes two plastic knives
024   together in a flourish)) Got him.   Co: There. I got
025 Ma: I got the camera. Where's the camera?   the oh-oh, I-
026   ((rummages around among food and utensils
027   on the kitchen table))
028 Ro: I got the camera. ((holding his two knives))
029 Ma: No, that's the camera.
030 Ro: Nah-ah, I have-
031 Ma: The corn's the camera.
032 Ro: ((*in teasing sing-song*)) I got the camera.
033 Ma: I got the camera. ((scrapes knife
034   across a piece of plastic toast))
035 Co: There's the bear!
036 Ma: Quick! I'm ma- I'm - I'm putting together
037   our camera.
038 Ro: And I'm makin' a- you don't have- you don't
039   have a camera.
040 Ma: Robert, I need that. I need this, 'cuz-.
041   ((tries to grab ear scope from him))
042 Ro: No, I have it.
043 Ma: No, but we- you're- you-.
044 Ro: Click, click, click. ((holds ear scope up to his eye
045   as if taking a picture and taps knife on ear scope))
046 Ma: You're breakin' our camera! You're
047   breakin' our camera!
048 Co: I've got-.
049 Ma: You- you missed him.
050 Co: I got the bear without his feet!   Ro: No, I found- I
051   had it first.
052 Co: Shot.
053 Ma: Robert, you can't- you using-
054   you're not using the camera.
055 Ro: Yes I am.
056 Ma: No you're not.   Ro: Got him! I
057   got him!
058 Ma: No, you didn't. You never got him.
059   Now if- if you don't give that,
060   we'll never make a camera.
061 Ro: Have it.

062 Ma: Robert, you're not making a camera.
063   Now that's a thing, that's for sure.
064 Ro: Get this, I gotta get this in.
065 Ma: ((demonstrating his toast/knife-camera to
066   Robert)) You- if you put this ((knife)) on   Co: Come on.
067   top ((of toast)) and then- ah- and- it- and-
068   and then- and I can put my knife in there,
069   and I can put my knife on, then we get his picture.
070 Ro: Yeah, I got - NO, you can't have that back.
Shortly later, at the hideout in the house:
071 Ro: ((talking to others)) No, we needa make a
072   hideout. Make a hideout.
073   Make a hideout, ok? Make a hideout.
074   ((they all crouch down in a "hideout" behind
075   the stove))
076 Ma: Let's go- let's wait for the pictures to dry out.
077   ((goes over to kitchen table and puts his
078   toast/knife-camera on it))
079 Co: The polar bear's around here somewhere.
080 Ro: But- but how can we- but then- but then we-
081   but then- but lookit- then this stuff.   Co: I took a quick
082   picture of him.
083 Ro: But then they can get IN here.
084 Co: ((loud whisper)) They- but they KNOW
085   that we're IN here, right? We must hide.
086 Ro: I'll lock the door up. ((turns a kitchen chair
087   on its side to make the door on one empty
088   side of their hideout)) Let's say they can't
089   break anything, right? Of this, right?
090 Ma: But he can jump over.
091 Ro: No, but let's say he couldn't.
092 Ma: Yes he can. Put another chair on top.
093 Co: ((loud fearful whisper)) But what if- but what if
094   the bear knocks down our gate?
095 Ro: ((reassuringly)) He won't. ((turns another kitchen
096   chair on its side and places it on top of the other one))
097 Co: If we make a high wall maybe he won't.
098 Ma: ((Gasps)) I- I know just what to do. ((Climbs out)).
099 Ro: This is what to do- I got it. Got a strong door.
100   ((he has finished making the side of the hideout out
101   of piled up chairs, which are now their "strong door"))

The bear comes after them. His "knocking on the door" of their house turns into "breaking the walls." The Housekeeping center comes under siege (008 Co: "There's a bear in our house!"). The polar bear breaks down their home's imaginary door and gets into the imaginary refrigerator. They counter this danger by making the refrigerator hotter (as measured by the thermometer in the doctor kit), because as Mark says, "Polar bears like the cold." The bear escapes to the imaginary freezer and they make the freezer hot too. That's not sufficient so they make a fire, and finally they transform a plastic butter knife into a magic wand, say an incantation, and turn the polar bear into a piece of gum . . . but not before it lays an egg and . . . a **baby** polar bear emerges. The image of a baby polar bear defuses the out-of-home danger and reintroduces the element of domesticity.

Examples of girls' gender-typed stories

The girls produced fewer object transformations overall compared to the boys, and the end result of most of their transformations was domestic. Their play had a quality describable as "life as usual." They produced well-developed and complex domestic scripts, as the following examples show:

(**G3**): having a meal, feeding baby, constructing a dinner party;
(**G5**): having a meal, feeding baby, taking care of a sick baby, cleaning the house, creating a birthday party, going shopping;
(**G6**): having a meal, pretending to be at a restaurant, creating sick child emergencies.

The girls' scripts featured a larger range of domestic activities and roles which were developed in greater detail, a composite picture of these activities collected from the girls' groups reveals multiple activities around food preparation that were enacted or planned, e.g., setting the table, eating, feeding the baby, cleaning up after dinner, shopping for groceries, going on a picnic, going to a restaurant, having a birthday party. There were also a variety of activities connected to taking care of the baby when it was well and when sick, and other home-centered activities, e.g., getting and making phone calls, going to bed, etc.

The degree of detail connected to food preparation in the girls' sessions, and an illustration of one kind of activity connected to taking care of baby, are shown in the following excerpt from the **G2** group.

Example: Life as usual in girls' domestic play

G2: "Sit down at the table and put your chair up while I'm making jam."

Sue is in the kitchen area preparing food while Mary and Lisa are playing with the dolls at the doll bed. There is cross-talk between the two play areas as Sue includes Mary and Lisa in her food preparations. The two domestic scripts play out side by side. They are represented in separate columns below.

(Su = Sue, Li = Lisa, Ma = Mary)

001 Su: ((preparing food)) Lisa,
002   do you want eggs?
003 Li: I want eggs, yeah,   Ma: ((at doll bed)) I want eggs.
004   eggs are really good.   Su: Ok.
005 Ma: I want eggs.
006 Ma: Let's cut it in half, so we um-

007 Su: I'll cut it in half.
008 Ma: I'll cut it in half. One for Lisa, one for
009   me, 'kay?
010 Su: Now I'll cut this in half, I'll cut sandwich
011   in half. One for Lisa, one for you, and one for me.
012 Ma: ((at the doll bed)) No. Well, I gotta
013   put the quilt on while I'm waiting, Lisa.
014 Li: Quilt?
015 Su: I got a peanut butter sandwich.
016 Ma: ((sings)) Holding the quilt.
017   The quilt on here.   Li: The quilt on
018   here? The quilt?
019 Li: I'm not- I'm- I'm- I'm- I'm not on
020   there so you can put it right on   Ma: Here's the knife.
021   there.
022 Li: ((to Mary who is standing near))
023   Are you waiting for me to move?
024 Su: I'm putting jam on yours.
025 Ma: I don't need jam.
026 Li: I don't want jam.
027 Ma: I don't want jam.
028 Su: But you- I'm gonna have jam.
029   Do you want butter?
030 Ma: Yeah, I want butter.   Li: Yeah, I want butter.
031 Ma: I want butter
032 Su: Ok, you guys can have butter
033   and I'll have jam.
034 Li: ((at the doll bed)) Mary, are you   Ma: I had to call the fire.
035   playing- are you playing with
036   this doll?
037 Ma: Yes
038 Li: Ok, then, I won't get it. I'll just- I'll
039   just put-.
040 Ma: Let's put these- um, put this-.
041 Su: I'm gonna have peanut butter on my jam.
042 Li: Peanut butter on your jam? Oh.
043 Su: Do you want peanut butter?
044 Li: Yeah, I want peanut butter on my jam.
045 Su: Do you want peanut butter, Mary?
046 Ma: No, I want butter, I want   Su: Ok, I'll do it.
047   just butter.
048 Su: Want just butter, ok?
049 Li: I want peanut butter.
050 Ma: ((To Lisa who is attending to the doll))

051		I'm waiting.	
052	Li:	((attending to baby in doll bed)) You	
053		waiting, waiting.	
054	Su:	I'm making jam for you, jam for you.	
055		Sit down at the table and put your chair	
056		up while I'm making jam. Will you do that?	
057		((To Mary)) You're waiting for the jam?	
058	Ma:	No, I'm waiting to put this blanket on.	
059	Su:	Oh, I could give you a jam.	
060	Ma:	I'm waiting, Lisa.	Su: We're gonna have it
061			outside
062	Li:	Well- well you- well you- well-	
063		well you can't put it ((the quilt)) on	
064		now.	
065	Ma:	No, no, um- this is- um- my baby's	
066		nightgown, so don't change-	Su: Yeah. This is the
067		her nightgown ((sings under her	coffee.
068		breath)).	
069	Li:	I won't change her nightgown.	Su: Everybody needs to
070			have a spoon of coffee.
071	Ma:	((Sings to self)).	
072	Li:	Baby can't wear this outfit, it's too big	
073		for her.	
074	Su:	Lisa, want this spoon? I get some spoons.	

This excerpt gives a flavor of some of the extensive conversational detail in the two frequent story elements in the girls' groups: food preparation and putting baby to bed.

CONCLUSION

Co-constructing stories in dramatic play with friends is a mundane activity for preschoolers in this community. This study underscores the importance of talk as a medium through which children's knowledge of sociocultural prescriptions about gender is coordinated. Planning and enacting co-constructed narrative play with same-sex peers provides daily opportunities to observe, learn about, transmit and practice gender-stereotyped knowledge as well as other sorts of knowledge about the world. Co-constructing stories requires children to coordinate their **individual** knowledge states. Furthermore, children are implicitly attaching value to that knowledge and to the satisfying, and often exciting, interpersonal experiences which they create with it.

The power that gender-related knowledge has to shape the stories that emerge in group play is seen in how a room which is set up with the same material resources can be transformed into various symbolic worlds with quite different meanings. The House-keeping center is a setting in which groups of girls and groups of boys coordinate their imaginations to create narrated symbolic worlds with different events, actions, contexts, conversations, and affect. The same objects are reinterpreted to fit gender-typed themes and to play pivotal roles in how the story unfolds. These object transformations (or nontransformations) reflect the way that gender-typed knowledge shapes preschoolers' symbolic imaginations and frames their narrative play. Such cultural understanding can facilitate (or resist) the construction of gender-typed scripts.

The bias in these groups toward composing gender-typed stories seemed to result in better developed domestic scripts by girls and more developed non-domestic scripts by boys. This selectivity toward the content of dramatic play with same-sex friends, which appears to result in more in-depth enactment and sharing of gender-typed knowledge, creates a divergence in the socially shared story-making experiences of girls and boys.[11] It suggests that girls' and boys' accumulated dramatic play histories — subjective experiences of the world — are different in crucial ways. Displaying gender-typed knowledge in co-constructed play narratives may further encourage sex-segregated play, reflecting the fundamental roles that language and cognition play in sociocultural development.

The asymmetry in girls' and boys' story preferences seen here may be an artifact of some aspect of the **context** in which the stories were composed, for example, the Housekeeping setting, or the sex/gender of their playmates. We might wonder if the bias toward gendered stories continues when girls and boys play together in a housekeeping center or if they play in same-sex of mixed-sex groups in other settings? What form and content do stories in those contexts take? Do girls and boys continue the same sort of thematically asymmetrical narrative play in mixed-groups? Can they? Do they arrive at a division of roles and "imagination-labor" in mixed-sex play which reflects the division of labor in "real world" gender arrangements? A story constructed in mixed-sex play might have elements of both the feminine and masculine narratives, with gender-typed roles given to or predictably claimed by the girls and boys. On the other hand, it is possible that the sort of thematically asymmetrical narrative play found here might be reduced to some degree in mixed-sex peer play. These are important questions which should be pursued in the future.

We opened this chapter wondering about how experience shapes us. Given the results of this study, it is apparent that besides the important adults in a child's life and other obvious sources of information about gender-appropriateness (books, television, movies, songs, toys, clothes, etc.), children's own companions are powerful agents of socialization as well. Implicit in this statement, and often overlooked, is the fact that the child herself or himself is a major participant in their own experience of gender. She or he **does** gender by acquiring knowledge and attitudes, and by behaving in gender-consistent ways, which usually entail language. Maintaining and perpetuating the

---

[11] While we must be cautious in hypothesizing the degree of complexity in the children's **underlying knowledge representations**, i.e., the cognitive basis for what gets told or not told in these stories, our finding of an asymmetry in story preferences should be of interest in light of speculation that girls' mental representations of scripts for "masculine events" would be equally developed and complex as their representations of "feminine events," whereas boys' representations of masculine scripts would be better represented than feminine scripts (Levy & Fivush, 1993, p. 141).

gender beliefs, attitudes and linguistic style of one's peer and/or adult communities is essential to the process of taking gender on, accepting it (more or less), and "getting it right." We do not assume, however, that gender socialization is achieved, or even desired, to the same degree by every child. One direction for future research raised by this work is to study the extent to which, and the reasons why, individual children do or do not join in or lead their peer culture in its behavioral displays of gender-appropriateness, and the extent to which children actively resist such displays.

A major goal of this study of object transformations has been to look at the relation between stories these children construct during play and the material resources available for creating stories. The results show that object transformations are one feature of their stories which reflect preferences for gender-stereotyped themes in social play in the Housekeeping center.[12] The results of this study indicate that young children's co-constructed stories can be a major vehicle for learning about and perpetuating gender knowledge and the community's gender arrangements. Children's imagination, knowledge, social and linguistic skills combine in stories to gender their world. Girls and boys might live in the same physical world, but to some as yet unknown degree they act on it differently, creating different symbolic, narrative, and subjective worlds.

REFERENCES

Almqvist, B. (1989). Age and gender differences in children's Christmas requests. *Play and Culture*, 2, 2-19.

Bretherton, I. (Ed.). (1984). *Symbolic play*. Orlando, FL: Academic.

Caldera, Y., Huston, A., & O'Brien, M. (1989). Social interactions and actions and play patterns of parents of toddlers with feminine, masculine and neutral toys. *Child Development*, 60, 70-76.

Davies, B. (1989). *Frogs and snails and feminist tales*. Sydney: Allen & Unwin.

Duveen, G., & Lloyd, B. (1988). Gender as an influence in the development of scripted pretend play. *British Journal of Developmental Psychology*, 6, 89-95.

Eisenberg, N., Wolchik, S. A., Hernandez, R., & Pasternak, J. F. (1985). Parental socialization of young children's play. *Child Development*, 56, 1506-1513.

Goodwin, M. H. (1980). Directive/response speech sequences in girls' and boys' task activities. In S. McConnell-Ginet, R. Borker, & N. Furman (Eds.), *Women and language in literature and society* (pp. 157-173). New York: Praeger.

Kyratzis, A. (1992). Gender differences in the use of persuasive justification in children's pretend play. In R. Hall, M. Bucholtz, & B. Moonwomon (Eds.), *Locating power. Proceedings of the Second Berkeley Women and Language Conference* (pp. 326-337). Berkeley: University of California.

Leaper, C. (1991). Influence and involvement in children's discourse: Age, gender, and partner effects. *Child Development*, 62, 797-811.

Leaper, C. (Ed.). (1994). Childhood gender segregation: Causes and consequences, *New directions for child development*, 65. San Francisco: Jossey-Bass Publishers.

---

[12] There are other types of transformations which we are studying, as well as thematic differences.

Levy, G. D., & Fivush, R. (1993). Scripts and gender: A new approach for examining gender role development. *Developmental Review*, **13**, 126-146.

Libby, M. N., & Aries, E. (1989). Gender differences in preschool children's narrative fantasy. *Psychology of Women Quarterly*, **13**, 296-306.

Lloyd, B., Duveen, G., & Smith, C. (1988). Social representations of gender and young children's play: A replication. *British Journal of Developmental Psychology*, **6**, 83-88.

Maccoby, E. (1990). Gender and relationships. A developmental account. *American Psychologist*, **45**, 513-520.

Matthews, W. S. (1977). Modes of transformation in the initiation of fantasy play. *Developmental Psychology*, **13**, 212-216.

Miller, P., Danaher, D., & Forbes, D. (1986). Sex-related strategies for coping with interpersonal conflict in children aged five and seven. *Developmental Psychology*, **22**, 543-548.

Nicolopoulou, A., Scales, B., & Weintraub, J. (1994). Gender differences and symbolic imagination in the stories of four-year-olds. In A. H. Dyson, & C. Genishi (Eds.), *The need for story: Cultural diversity in classroom and community* (pp. 102-123). Urbana, IL: National Council of Teachers of English.

Opie, I. (1993). *The People in the Playground*. Oxford: Oxford University Press.

Parten, M. (1933). Social play among preschool children. *Journal of Abnormal and Social Psychology*, **28**, 136-147.

Sachs, J. (1987). Preschool boys' and girls' language use in pretend play. In S. U. Philips, S. Steele, & C. Tanz (Eds.), *Language, gender and sex in comparative perspective* (pp. 178-188). New York: Cambridge University Press.

Sheldon, A. (1990). Pickle fights: Gendered talk in preschool disputes. *Discourse Processes*, **13**, 5-31.

Sheldon, A. (1992a). Conflict talk: Sociolinguistic challenges to self-assertion and how young girls meet them. *Merrill-Palmer Quarterly*, **38**, 95-117.

Sheldon, A. (1992b). Preschool girls' discourse competence: managing conflict. In K. Hall, M. Bucholtz, & B. Moonwomon (Eds.), *Locating power. Proceedings of the Second Berkeley Women and Language Conference* (pp. 529-539). Berkeley: University of California.

Sheldon, A. (1996). You can be the baby brother but you aren't born yet: Preschool girls' negotiation for power and access in pretend play. In A. Sheldon (Ed.), *Constituting gender through talk in early childhood: Conversations in parent-child, sibling, and peer relationships*, special issue of *Research on Language and Social Interaction*, **29**, 1-25. Hillsdale, NJ: Lawrence Erlbaum Associates.

Sheldon, A., & Johnson, D. (1994). Preschool negotiators: Gender differences in double-voice discourse as a conflict talk style in early childhood. B. Sheppard, R. Lewicki, & R. Bies (Eds.), *Research on negotiation in organizations, Vol. 4* (pp. 27-57). Greenwich, CT: JAI Press.

Tannen, D. (1990). Gender differences in conversational coherence: Physical alignment and topical cohesion. In B. Dorval (Ed.), *Conversational coherence and its development* (pp. 167-206). Norwood, NJ: Ablex.

Tarullo, L. B. (1994). Windows on social worlds: Gender differences in children's play narratives. In A. Slade & D. P. Wolf (Eds.), *Children at play* (pp. 169-187). New York: Oxford University Press.

Whiting, B. B., & Edwards, C. P. (1988). *Children of different worlds*. Cambridge, MA: Harvard University Press.

Author Index

S

Sachs, J., 127, 142, 253, 615, 632
Sacks, H., 72, 82, 259, 262, 395, 413, 483, 493, 579, 596
Sampson, E. E., 39, 51
Sanches, M., 586, 596
Sandhu, H. S., 421, 434
Sanford, S., 579, 596
Sankoff, D., 132, 142
Sass, L. A., 489, 493
Savasir, I., 31, 36, 345, 366
Scales, B., 326, 327, 369, 381, 382, 384, 389, 515, 519, 526, 527, 557, 562, 574, 589, 594, 615, 632
Scalise, S., 61, 69
Schaefer, E. F., 603, 610
Schafer, R., 451, 456, 465
Schegloff, E. A., 72, 82, 105, 111, 253, 259, 262, 395, 413, 452, 465, 483, 493, 603, 611
Schieffelin, B. B., 125, 142, 152, 155, 176, 189, 221, 234, 251, 252, 253, 254, 255, 256, 257, 258, 259, 261, 262, 265, 286
Schiffrin, D., 132, 142, 288, 304, 457, 458, 465
Schrage, M., 546, 553
Schwartzman, H., 519
Scollon, R., 474, 480
Scollon, S., 252, 262, 474, 480
Scott, C., 356, 366
Scribner, S., 309, 327
Searle, J. R., 483, 493
Sebeok, T. A., 7
Seiter, W., 177, 189
Selfe, C. L., 548, 553
Shapiro, J. P., 579, 596
Shapiro, L. R., 379, 389
Shatz, M., 127, 142, 153, 155
Shaw, L. K., 272, 285
Shea, S., 330, 337, 340, 341
Sheldon, A., 514, 527, 555, 556, 561, 575, 615, 632
Shen, Y., 360, 366
Shenker, S., 547, 553
Shore, B., 126, 142
Shriberg, E., 372, 389
Shultz, J. J., 73, 82

Shultz, T. R., 579, 596
Shweder, R. A., 39, 51
Sibata, T., 247, 250
Silver, S., 113, 121
Silverstein, M., 343, 367
Sinclair, H., 372, 389
Sinclair, J. M., 132, 142
Skinner, D., 513, 527
Slobin, D. I., 9, 125, 126, 142, 143, 145, 153, 154, 155, 157, 175, 189, 265, 266, 268, 269, 275, 282, 285, 286, 310, 327, 343, 344, 345, 346, 351, 352, 360, 362, 364, 365, 366
Slomkowski, C., 192, 194, 199, 200, 204
Smith, C., 616, 631
Smith, P. K., 193, 204
Smith, R., 221, 231, 234
Smith, S., 598, 600, 602, 611
Smith-Hefner, N. J., 45
Smith-Lovin, L., 597, 599, 611
Snow, C. E., 125, 142, 205, 207, 209, 216, 217, 347, 372, 389, 393, 414, 366, 590, 595
So, C. S., 26, 36
Song, K. S., 25, 36,
Spence, D. P., 451, 454, 465
Sperber, D., 279, 286
Sperry, L., 351
Spradley, J. P., 80, 82
Sprott, R. A., 125, 133, 140, 142, 298, 300, 304, 589, 594
Stambak, M., 372, 389
Starn, R., 489, 493
Stebbins, R. A., 579, 596
Stein, N. L., 200, 201, 204, 310, 314, 327, 379, 389
Sterba, R., 454, 465
Stevenson, M., 197, 204
Steward, J., 113, 121
Stinson, C., 451, 457, 459, 464, 465, 466
Stone, C. A., 376, 389, 496, 499, 509
Stotsky, S., 99, 110
Strage, A., 32, 36, 158, 173
Stull, D. E., 584, 595
Sue, S., 423, 424, 432, 434
Suls, J., 579, 596
Sulzby, E., 372, 389
Sunar, D., 311, 327

Subject Index

Y

yes-no questions
    acquisition of, 283-284
    and negation, 60-62, 63, 66

Z

zone of proximal development, Vygotsky's,
    373, 404, 407, 410, 411, 412